EVERY DAY A NIGHTMARE

Number 131

WILLIAMS-FORD TEXAS A&M UNIVERSITY

MILITARY HISTORY SERIES

WILLIAM H. BARTSCH

EVERY DAY A
NIGHTMARE

American Pursuit Pilots in the
Defense of Java, 1941–1942

TEXAS A&M UNIVERSITY PRESS

College Station

This paper meets the requirements of ANSI/NISO Z39.48-1992 (Permanence of Paper).
Binding materials have been chosen for durability.

Unless otherwise indicated, maps are by Rick Britten.

Library of Congress Cataloging-in-Publication Data

Bartsch, William H., 1933–
Every day a nightmare : American pursuit pilots in the defense of Java, 1941–1942 /
William H. Bartsch. — 1st ed.
p. cm. — (Number 131: Williams-Ford Texas A&M University military history series)
Includes bibliographical references and index.
ISBN-13: 978-1-60344-176-6 (cloth : alk. paper)
ISBN-10: 1-60344-176-X (cloth : alk. paper) 1. World War, 1939–1945—Aerial operations,
American. 2. World War, 1939–1945—Campaigns—Indonesia—Java. 3. World War, 1939–
1945—Regimental histories—United States. 4. United States. Army—History—World War,
1939–1945. 5. United States. Army. Air Corps—History. 6. Fighter pilots—United States—
History—20th century. I. Title. II. Series: Williams-Ford Texas A&M University military
history series ; no. 131.
D767.7.B376 2010
940.54'25982—dc22
2009051151

This book is dedicated to the memory of

GEORGE A. WELLER

(July 13, 1907–December 12, 2002)

CONTENTS

ILLUSTRATIONS

MAPS

FOREWORD

MY FATHER, THE AMERICAN war correspondent George Weller—who would soon win a Pulitzer Prize in foreign reporting for the *Chicago Daily News*—spent most of February 1942 on Java. He had arrived, through great luck, from besieged Singapore on a freighter under attack by the Japanese. Through an even greater stroke of luck he would leave Java on March 3 from the southern port of Tjilatjap aboard an island steamer, the final boat to make it safely out to Australia despite heavy strafing and bombardment.

During the intervening weeks, as the heart of the Netherlands East Indies gradually collapsed to the relentless enemy onslaught, Weller crossed Java's vastness four times and, as he put it, was "bombed in Batavia, bombed in Soerabaya and bombed in Bandoeng." By the end of March he'd written thirty articles for his paper on the fall of the NEI, and for the next six decades the many complex dramas of that loss stayed with him. None, I feel it safe to say, meant as much to him as the one you are about to read, explored in full for the first time.

The saga that so captured my father's attention on Java is still little known today: the courageous efforts, across only a few weeks, of a small band of young American fighter pilots to defend the doomed island. Within the bounds of military secrecy Weller was able to write several dispatches that revealed their gallant deeds without revealing the location of their secret airfield. He happened on the story by chance, running into several of the squadron at the crammed Hôtel des Indes in Batavia and swapping around fellow reporters and guests until the flyers had somewhere to sleep. They told him of their exploits, which he was able to pursue in detail, and report on, over the coming month.

Later in the war, in Australia and New Guinea, he followed the careers of surviving pilots of the squadron and learned as much as he could. The saga wouldn't let him go, and by early 1943 he had turned it into a short book, *"Luck to the Fighters!"* Unlike his two other wartime histories, it never found a hardback publisher but was serialized in three issues of a military quarterly in 1944–45. (A version I abridged recently appeared in a collection of his reportage, *Weller's War.*) He inevitably got some important facts wrong, and there were gaps in the saga, but at least he preserved the young men's heroism and was able to gather many eyewitness accounts before war scattered the pilots far afield and before peace "sickled over the memories."

And there—along with brief mentions in air histories of the Pacific war—might the matter have rested forever were it not for the present remarkable and authoritative volume.

Human memory and written history are often rivals, especially in wartime. For the foreign correspondent, the documentary record is useless; it usually comes years too late. He must rely on eyewitness accounts and on his own stamina and luck in cross-checking them. Sometimes the only reliable observers are dead, or beyond reach in enemy hands, and all he has to go on is secondhand or worse.

Warfare is reported and recorded much differently today than it was in the first half of the twentieth century. The all-consuming camera and microphone, which carry an incontrovertible allure of truth, are seemingly everywhere—and whatever they miss cannot, surely, be very important, can it? A serious war correspondent knows better, but it is rarely in the media's interests to admit shortcomings. Likewise, the historian knows better, but it remains to be seen how determined tomorrow's chroniclers of today's wars will be at ferreting out facts.

Bill Bartsch has written, after two decades of exhaustive research across eyewitness and documentary sources, both Allied and Japanese, the work that my father dreamed of: the complete story of the U.S. Army pilots who opposed the Japanese aerial onslaught against the Netherlands East Indies. (To every admiring reader I recommend Bartsch's earlier books, *December 8, 1941: MacArthur's Pearl Harbor* and *Doomed at the Start: American Pursuit Pilots in the Philippines, 1941–1942.*)

This invaluable volume of history, unique in the much explored terrain of World War II, also covers the experiences of the pilots in Australia before they even reached Java. Among the book's secondary achievements are its recounting of the devastating Japanese attack on Darwin (February 19, 1942) in fresher detail than ever before, and likewise the sinking of the USS *Lang-*

ley days later. Finally, and for me of equal importance, this book tells what happened to these remarkable young pilots in the months and years to come.

It is all too rare when a fine historian and a fine narrator occupy the same mind. The research Bartsch has done for this book is daunting, and unlike a surprising number of professional colleagues, he knows the physical terrain he writes about intimately as well. No one has ever gone as deeply into the subject, and I suspect that the superb quality of his achievement will have repercussions far beyond its immediate boundaries. For anyone fascinated by aerial combat or the Pacific War—or by the psychology of what brave men held together in a selfless cause are capable of—this powerful book will be unforgettable.

Anthony Weller

WHEN I WROTE *DOOMED AT THE START* almost twenty years ago, I left the story untold of the seventeen Philippines pursuit veterans who in late December 1941 and the beginning of January 1942 were flown out of the beleaguered islands, for they never returned to the Philippines as planned by MacArthur. They had been sent to Australia to ferry back P-40s that had just arrived there, intended by the War Department to reinforce MacArthur's depleted Far East Air Force. In this book I relate the circumstances that prevented them from reuniting with their comrades on Bataan. Instead, they were now being ordered to the Dutch East Indies to try to stem the unrelenting Japanese movement southwards that was ultimately aimed at seizing the rich oil reserves of the Dutch colony and its "jewel in the crown," the island of Java.

But of course they alone were not meant to defend the skies over the Indies. Joining them would be two groups of very recent flying school graduates who had originally been ordered to the Philippines from their California bases and had arrived in Brisbane, Australia, in late December 1941 and mid-January 1942. Few of their total of 101 had any prior combat training or anywhere near sufficient hours in their P-40s to stand a chance against seasoned Japanese veterans in their almost invincible Zeros.

Back in the 1970s—before I started research on *Doomed at the Start*— I became captivated by the 1944 account I had found in a military history journal of the experiences of American pursuit pilots in the Java campaign. The author of the three-part article—"Luck to the Fighters"—was George A. Weller, a war correspondent for the *Chicago Daily News* who I found out in 1994 was still alive at age eighty-seven and living in a small town outside Rome, Italy. I determined to contact him to let him know I was planning to fulfill his wish that "someone speak for them" and complete the story of his unsung pilots. In his reply to my letter, Weller expressed his enthusiasm that I was taking up his wartime account and willingness to write a foreword for my planned book.

During the course of my sixteen-year research for the story Weller wanted to see more fully developed, I was able to locate all the surviving pilots and several of the enlisted men, as well as the families of many of the deceased. In the process I was given access to the diaries of fifteen of the pilots and two of the enlisted men that—along with several memoirs—gave me real insight into the feelings as well as the experiences of the pilots and men in the doomed Java campaign. This primary source material also was instrumental in enabling me to back up and cover their pre-Java experiences in Australia that Weller had not included in his story. Checking with detailed Japanese combat records that friends translated for me also allowed me to come up with a more accurate tally of Japanese aircraft shot down than that the American pilots related to Weller during wartime, which was based on their impressions.

And now with the publication of this book Weller's wish is fulfilled. My only regret is that he did not live to see the (I hope) complete story in which he was so emotionally involved. His son has kindly substituted for him in writing the foreword.

ACKNOWLEDGMENTS

BASED AS THIS STORY IS on the personal experiences of those who participated in the events chronicled, my major debt of gratitude is to those individuals who provided me the pieces of the puzzle that allowed me to reconstruct these events of over sixty-five years ago. They include American and Dutch participants themselves, the families of the deceased, and unrelated persons who had collected information on them.

Sadly, so many of the participants who had survived their wartime experiences have died during the sixteen years it has taken me to complete this project. In this category are several of my most persevering supporters, including Walt Coss, Tommy Hayes, Nathaniel (Cy) Blanton, Bryce Wilhite, Vern Head, and Ken Glassburn, whose contributions make up a significant portion of this book. But others who were equally supportive live on, including Bob McMahon, whose near photographic memory provided me a vivid picture of the February 1942 attack on Darwin as well as of life in Australia at the beginning of the war as he experienced it. Paul Gambonini shared with me his invaluable Java diary, and his fellow Californian Jim Morehead regaled me with colorful accounts of his experiences. Other participants— some now deceased—should also be acknowledged for relating their personal experiences, including pilots Bob McWherter, Bryan Brown, Marion Fuchs, Walter Haines, Jim Naylor, Dick Suehr, B. J. Oliver, Dave Coleman, Harold Lund, Ralph Martin, Gene Wahl, Ray Melikian, Elwin Jackson, and Larry Selman. I would like to thank former enlisted men Bernie Badura, Bud Boise, Dave Burnside, Murray Nichols, Dale Holt, Real Bujold, Julian Guerrero, Bill Hardgrove, Cecil Ingram, and Richard Rufener for relating their experiences as crew chiefs, armorers, and radiomen. Only Holt and Rufener survive at the time I am writing this.

Of the four Dutch participants who helped with the NEIAF side of the story, I owe a special debt to Arie Geurtz, now ninety-four years old and living in Ohio, for his ardent support and unstinting help in trying to re-create events he experienced as the Dutch liaison officer for the American pursuit squadron at Ngoro. The three others—pilots Gerard Bruggink, Jan Bruinier, and Alex van der Vossen—responded to my questions about their operations during the last days at Ngoro Field.

The assistance of the families of the deceased was critical in my reconstructing this story. Particularly helpful were those relatives who unearthed diaries that covered day-by-day experiences in Australia and the Dutch East Indies: Martha Gies (daughter), Peg Hague Baum (sister), Roger A. Dutton (son), Michael Hennon Raudenbush (son), Mary J. (Lolly) Cooper (sister of Spence Johnson), Michael G. Parker (son), Eleanor Johnsen (widow), Trudi A. Katz (daughter of Robert Oestreicher), and Margaret Borckardt (sister of J. Calvin Smith).

Other relatives who provided helpful information include Barbara Adkins Matthews (sister), Arvon Staats (nephew of Sgt. Samuel Foster), Jim Crane (son), Reid Wiecks (son), John Egenes (brother), David Latane (son), Inez Buzzard (sister of Quanah Fields), Katherine Landry Hansen (sister), Lewis Baum (nephew of Jesse Hague), Louise Hayes (widow of Tommy Hayes), Richard P. Hoskyn (brother), Kenneth H. Loving (brother-in-law of Spence Johnson), Mildred Daggett (widow of John Lewis), William H. Martin (brother of Joe Martin), Flora R. Lamborn (sister of John Rex), Philip A. Schott (son), Charles M. Sprague (son), Foster L. Thompson (brother), Robert B. Gallienne (son), Jane Pingree (sister-in-law), Virginia Bound (widow), Betty Coleman (widow), and Michele Bujold Hansen (daughter).

A great number of individuals of no family relationship with the participants helped me with useful information, including documentation. In the United States they include the late Patty Groves, Don Kehn, Dwight Messimer, Charlie Pehl, Maj. Robert Gladman, Carlos Dannacher, Rick Markley, Rear Adm. Kemp Tolley, Bruce Yoran, Bob Cutler, and Ron Smithfield. In this category my greatest debt is to Edward Rogers, whose passion for digging for materials lost to history—particularly by contacting families of the deceased in connection with his own research on early air operations of the Pacific War—is matched only by my own.

Outside the United States I have received remarkable help over the years from several Australians I now consider good friends. Gordon Birkett is at the top of this list. My files bulge with the e-mails and regular mailed documentation Gordy has sent me during the past six years that he gleaned from his searches through the National Archives of Australia and other institutions as well as from fellow enthusiasts. Another Australian enthusiast and provider of information is Shane Johnston, indefatigable searcher for the remains of the American P-40s shot down in the Darwin raid and passionate believer in keeping alive the memory of the sacrifices of their ill-fated pilots. Bob Alford, Peter Dunn, and C. (Bus) Busby have also weighed in with information, as well as David Vincent on rare photos he has collected and copied for me for this book.

In the Netherlands the reigning expert on Dutch air operations in the Netherlands East Indies campaign, Peter Boer, has unfailingly responded to my frequent requests for detailed information on the Dutch side that intersected with the operations of the Americans on Java. Earlier, Max Schep provided me with information gleaned from his many interviews with Dutch pilots and ground personnel who survived their Java experiences. The memoir of his father that Adriaan Kik provided me expanded my knowledge of the voyage of his freighter, the *Abbekerk,* while fellow Hollander Gerben Tornij helped me with rare photos.

Of course this book is not derived exclusively from the personal experiences of the participants. At the outset of my research I located and made copies of the voluminous records in the National Archives' Record Group 338 (U.S. Army Forces in Australia section) and to a lesser extent in Record Group 407 (also USAFIA section), which provided documentation on the movements and orders in radiogram and memorandum form of the higher-ups in the USAFIA and American-British-Dutch-Australian Command (ABDA-COM) that provided the skeleton of the story. Note that since the time of my research for this book, the USAFIA records in Record Group 338 have been transferred to Record Group 495.2.

Also useful were the records at the Air Force Historical Research Agency, whose Marcie Green kindly responded to frequent requests for documentation. I also benefited greatly from relevant records held at the National Archives of Australia, all identified and transmitted to me by Gordy Birkett. The Australian War Memorial and the Aviation Heritage Museum of Western Australia provided copies of photos for my use. In Kew, England, the Public Records Office (now National Archives) proved to be a useful source on the ABDACOM cable traffic to and from London, Melbourne, and Washington, located and copied for me by my consultant Bob O'Hara.

Extremely important for the analysis included in this book has been access to Japanese Naval Air Force operations reports, required to match up with American accounts of aerial attacks of each side. In this connection I am once again deeply indebted to Osamu Tagaya, who faithfully responded to my requests for details on particular operations of land-based Betty and Zero units, which he translated from Japanese for me from his collection of such reports. Similarly, Jim Sawruk provided me translations he made of the operations reports of the Japanese navy's carriers whose air crews participated in the Darwin attack.

I would be remiss if I failed to thank two other supporters. The aviation artist—and B-17 copilot in the Indies campaign—Paul Eckley has kindly allowed me to use his painting of a lost P-40 following a B-17 into its Java base as the cover for my book. I am grateful to Anthony Weller for writing the foreword to this book, as well as for sharing with me the results of his sifting through the moldering dispatches of his late father's trunks held in his home outside Rome for any items that could add to my Java story. He has saved all his father's mostly unpublished work from historical oblivion by including it in his recently released book, *Weller's War* (see the picture of George Weller, Anthony's father, in part four).

One final acknowledgment: I would like to thank my copyeditor, Noel Parsons, for his meticulous efforts in weeding out all my slip-ups and introducing improvements to produce as fine a text as I could ever hope for.

ABBREVIATIONS AND ACRONYMS

AAF	Army Air Forces
ABDACOM	American-British-Dutch-Australian Command
ABDAFLOAT	Navy Command, ABDACOM
ABDAIR	Air Command, ABDACOM
AFHRA	Air Force Historical Research Agency, Maxwell AFB, Alabama
AG	Adjutant General
AGWAR	Adjutant General, War Department
CCS	Combined Chiefs of Staff
CO	Commanding Officer
C/S	Chief of Staff
CSF	Combined Striking Force
EASGROUP	East Group, Java Air Command
FEAF	Far East Air Force
GHQ	General Headquarters
Hq	Headquarters
JAC	Java Air Command
KM	Koninklikje Marine (Royal Netherlands Navy)
KNIL	Koninklikje Nederlands-Indisch Leger (Royal Netherlands Indies Army)
KNIL-ML	Koninklikje Nederlands-Indisch Leger–Militaire Luchtvaart (Royal Netherlands Indies Army Air Force)
KNILM	Koninklikje Nederlands-Indisch Luchtvaart Maatschappij (Royal Netherlands Indies Airways)

Kokutai	Naval Air Group
LOC	Library of Congress
MMA	MacArthur Memorial Archives, Norfolk, Virginia
NAA	National Archives of Australia
NARA C.P.	National Archives and Records Administration, College Park, Maryland
NARA D.C.	National Archives and Records Administration, Washington, D.C.
NEIAF	Netherlands East Indies Army Air Force
NHC	Naval Historical Center
RAAF	Royal Australian Air Force
RG	Record Group
S.O.	Special Orders
TD	Technische Dienst (Technical Service of the KNIL)
USAFA	U.S. Air Force Academy, Colorado Springs, Colorado
USAFFE	U.S. Army Forces Far East
USAFIA	U.S. Army Forces in Australia
USSBS	U.S. Strategic Bombing Survey
Vl.G.	Vliegtuiggroep (flying group of the KNIL-ML)
WD	War Department
WPD	War Plans Division

EVERY DAY A NIGHTMARE

"Never in Our History Has There Been a Time Like the Present"

IT WAS 1000 ON THE MORNING of Saturday, July 27, 1940, in Tokyo when Prime Minister Fumimaro Konoe and eleven other formally attired men faced the emperor's empty chair, bowed deeply, and took their assigned seats in Room One-East of Japan's Imperial Palace. In their full uniforms, eight of the participants represented the military, including the war and navy ministers and the army and navy chiefs of staff of Imperial General Headquarters. Appointed as prime minister for a second time only five days earlier, Konoe with his cabinet members was meeting with the military supreme command in this imperial headquarters–government liaison conference to seek formal agreement on a matter of momentous importance: the future direction of Japan's foreign policy.[1]

But the meeting was really just a formality. Both sides were familiar with the subject matter of the proposed policy change and had agreed to it earlier. Imperial General Headquarters—following agreement between its army and navy sections—had prepared a paper indicating what it wanted the Konoe government to do "to cope with the changing world situation." Germany had occupied France and the Netherlands, and it looked like Great Britain would fall soon. Japan needed to take action to ensure the availability for its own needs of the rich natural resources in the Dutch and British colonies in Southeast Asia. "Never in our history has there been a time like the present," the army had argued. Germany's victories were affording Japan the opportunity to break its economic dependence on the United States, Great Britain, and the Netherlands East Indies by incorporating all the southern area east of India and north of Australia and New Zealand into a "Greater East Asia Co-Prosperity Sphere"[2]

In the ensuing discussions, the group reached agreement on the new policy and the means by which to carry it out: diplomacy first, but if that failed, force. The participants recognized that such a policy would run the risk of war with the United States and Great Britain, but even the prime minister—an opponent of war with those powers—offered no objections to the military-driven proposal. At 1130 they filed out of the room, having approved a "general prescription for a southern advance." The Dutch East Indies, British Malaya, and other "resources-rich" areas of Southeast Asia were to be incorporated into the "New Order," and formal military ties were to be developed with Germany and Italy to gain support for Japan's new position.

The new direction of Japan's foreign policy only formalized what had been the navy's long-standing objective. As early as 1936, navy planners had initiated planning for Southern Operations. In particular, they had included occupation of the Dutch East Indies in their plans. They coveted the oil of the Indies, the life blood of the navy's ships. Now the army was also aboard, currently occupied with planning for the first step in Southern Operations: the acquisition of bases in French Indochina. To that purpose, in early September, intimidated by visiting Japanese army officers, the governor general and the Vichy French regime acceded to their demand to station troops and use air bases in northern Indochina. "Diplomacy" was working.[3]

On September 26, 1940, Japanese troops landed on the coast of French Indochina and began taking up positions at their new stations in the north. The following day, Japan secured the support of its new allies for its changed foreign policy direction when Konoe's government signed the Tripartite Pact with Germany and Italy. In his imperial rescript following approval of the military agreement, Emperor Hirohito cited Japan's new partners as "nations which share the same intentions as ourselves"—securing "the eight corners of the world under one roof" (*hakko ichiu*).

In Washington, Secretary of State Cordell Hull registered the U.S. government's "disapproval" of Japan's incursion as upsetting the status quo in Indochina. Three days later, President Roosevelt ordered a complete embargo on export of scrap iron and steel except to Great Britain and Latin America, a move clearly aimed against Japan, which was almost completely dependent on imports of such materials for its war machine. Suspecting Japanese plans for a move southwards, the United States declared it would not allow Japan to take control of the Dutch East Indies and Singapore. It was opting for political and economic pressure to serve as a deterrent.[4]

But the Roosevelt administration declined to support Great Britain and the Dutch East Indies in a military pact, refusing to take responsibility for the defense of Southeast Asia and its British and Dutch possessions. Continuing long-standing War Department policy, even America's own Philippines commonwealth would not be defended strongly through military reinforcement, and its loss would be accepted in any Japanese southern advance. This stance was confirmed with the approval by the Joint Army and Navy Board in November 1940 of Plan Dog. In the event of war, the United States would focus on operations against Germany and stand on the defensive in the Pacific and Far East.[5]

In Japan, planning for a southward movement now was relying more on military than diplomatic means. In October both army and navy staff planners were making preparations for Southern Operations, despite the risk such an aggressive movement would have for war with the United States. Though he was not privy to such secret deliberations, Japanese intentions were clear to Adm. Thomas Hart, commander-in-chief of the Manila-based U.S. Asiatic Fleet. "There seems no doubt Japan is resolved on a southward movement, employing force if necessary," he wrote the chief of naval operations in November. "Her most important early objective is the oil supplied from the East Indies."[6]

By April the following year, the army and navy sections of Imperial General Headquarters formally approved plans for the establishment of the Greater East Asia Co-Prosperity Sphere and agreed that if diplomatic means failed, force would be applied if Japan's "existence" were threatened by an American-British-Dutch embargo or if American-British-Dutch "encirclement" of Japan were tightened. The Japanese had gotten wind of the highly secret talks held in Singapore in April among the United States, Great Britain, China, British India, Australia, and the Dutch East Indies aimed at a military pact to strengthen their defenses and oppose a Japanese movement south.[7]

Emboldened by the unexpected German invasion of the USSR on June 22, Japan's navy minister the following day decided to establish bases and airfields in southern Indochina, a decision approved days later by the Konoe government and the emperor. Diplomatic "negotiations" with Vichy France once again proved successful, and on July 25 more than forty thousand Japanese troops began entering and occupying southern French Indochina without meeting resistance. Three weeks following formal endorsement by the government and the emperor of a southward advance, Japan had taken a major step in its Southern Operations, regardless of the distinct risk of provoking the United States into war.[8]

In Washington the reaction to Japan's sudden aggressive move was immediate. On July 26 Roosevelt issued an executive order freezing all Japanese assets in the United States, thus halting all trade with Japan and resulting in a de facto oil embargo. The president took this dramatic move against the advice of his top military commanders—Chief of Staff Marshall and Chief of Naval Operations Stark—who felt the move would most likely force the Japanese to meet their oil needs by seizing the Dutch East Indies and thus risk precipitating war. Following the president's lead, the British and the Dutch immediately imposed oil embargos too.[9]

The Japanese fully grasped the impact of the embargo proclamation. Fully ninety percent of Japan's total oil supplies were imported and would now be cut off. They estimated that their navy's operations would be entirely closed down in two years. The Konoe government saw its options limited: either "capitulate" under the economic pressure of the embargo or "take some other course to end, neutralize, or escape the pressure." But the first option was not acceptable. Too much effort and prestige had been invested for the government to accede to U.S. demands to evacuate the Asian mainland.[10]

In the end, Roosevelt's drastic new economic deterrent had the opposite effect from that desired. Instead of halting Japan's southward movement, it was speeding it up. On September 6 the emperor accepted the Konoe government's position proposed three days earlier: if there were no prospect of diplomatic resolution of the impasse by early October, "we shall immediately decide to initiate war with the U.S., Great Britain, and the Netherlands." Japan and the United States were now on a collision course.[11]

Although unaware of the secret decision of Japan not to give in to the oil embargo move, the War Department now added a military deterrent to its arsenal of pressures on the Japanese government. Reversing its long-standing policy of no military reinforcement of the Philippines, it now decided not only to build up the defensive capabilities of the islands but also to add an offensive dimension to serve as a threat to the Japanese mainland itself. Chief of Staff Marshall and Secretary of War Stimson, enamored of the potential of the new B-17 and B-24 bombers entering Army Air Forces service, had convinced themselves that the threat posed by a buildup of a large force of the long-range heavy bombers on the northernmost island of the Philippines would deter Japan's military-dominated government from further moves south. Presiding over the massive buildup of air and land forces in the Philippines would be the former U.S. Army chief of staff and current military advisor to the Philippine commonwealth, Gen. Douglas MacArthur, recalled from retirement in late July and picked to head the newly established command, U.S. Army Forces in the Far East (USAFFE).[12]

But Marshall and Stimson recognized that it would take time before the full force of heavy bombers envisaged would be in place in the Philippines. The first contingent of B-17s had already arrived in mid-September, but they estimated that it would not be before March 1942 before all 272 bombers were at their Philippines bases. In the meantime, the United States should keep the Washington negotiations with the Japanese going to buy time while at the same time developing plans for military cooperation with Great Britain and the Dutch East Indies for the defense of the Far East.[13]

On October 3 Marshall instructed MacArthur to initiate discussions with the British in Singapore "at once," with a view to reaching an agreement for use of airfields in Singapore, Darwin, Rabaul, and Port Moresby for his B-17s. Arrangements should also be made with the Dutch for use of their airfields in the Indies. The United States was now willing to support the air defense of Australia, the Dutch East Indies, and Singapore—as well as its Philippine commonwealth—in the event of war with Japan. Indeed, the revised (in October) Rainbow Five war plan called for MacArthur's USAFFE to cooperate with the British and Dutch in defense of their territories.

The earlier reluctance of the Roosevelt administration to become involved in the defense of the colonial possessions of Britain and the Netherlands had now given way under the threat of a Japanese thrust to the south that would precipitate war. And should the basing of a force of heavy bombers within striking range of Japan's mainland be perceived in Japan more as an incentive for it to strike early instead of a deterrent to their plans to move south, hostilities would begin earlier than expected by the War Department and the president.

PART ONE

"Plans for Reaching You Quickly with Pursuit Are Jeopardized"

WITH THE ARMY AND NAVY high commands now wielding the effective power in his government, and having apparently lost the support of Emperor Hirohito, who believed that war was now unavoidable, Premier Fumimaro Konoe submitted his resignation on October 16, 1941. He was replaced the following day by his cabinet's most ardent advocate for war, Army Minister Hideki Tojo.[1]

By the end of October the army's General Staff and the staff officers of the assigned field armies reached agreement on a plan for the proposed invasions under Southern Operations. The navy's operations plan, which now included the attack on Pearl Harbor, had been approved on October 20. The Combined Fleet set December 8 as the target date for starting the war—December 7 on the other side of the international date line.[2]

At the imperial conference held on November 5, Emperor Hirohito sanctioned the December 1 deadline set four days earlier for terminating negotiations with the United States and the same day approved the Pearl Harbor operations of the navy's plan. He was now committed to war and was playing for time until his military commanders were ready to start operations. The following day, the army chief of staff activated the Southern Army and ordered it to make immediate preparations for the invasion of the southern area. The attack orders were given a week later. The Combined Fleet was also ordered to make final preparations for war and to advance its forces to the designated assembly points.[3]

The army-navy strategy for the Pacific War involved three phases, detailed agreements on which had been worked out between the involved army and navy commanders. In a first phase, Japanese forces would eliminate Allied forces in Hong Kong, Guam, Wake Island, and the Gilbert Islands in the central Pacific and immobilize the Pacific Fleet at Pearl Harbor, after which they would occupy Thailand, northern Malaya, and British Borneo and invade the Philippines as the beginning stage of Southern Operations. In the second phase they would seize the rest of Malaya and Singapore as well as southern Burma and the northern islands of the Dutch East Indies—Dutch Borneo and the Celebes—and the Bismarcks to the east. Finally, in the third phase they would take Sumatra, Burma, and the main objective of Southern Operations: Java. Only five months were allocated for the occupation of this vast area— an objective on a scale unprecedented in history. The core Southern Operations component alone extended over two thousand miles east to west and two thousand miles north to south.[4]

For the Philippines operation, the strategy called for destruction of U.S. air forces on Luzon first, then the occupation of their airfields. The main invasion force would land at Lingayen in western Luzon fifteen days after the opening attack, and a smaller force at Lamon Bay in southeastern Luzon. Manila was to be seized in fifty days.

In Washington at this time both Army Chief of Staff Gen. George C. Marshall and Chief of Naval Operations Adm. Harold R. Stark were arguing for a strategy to avoid war with Japan until completion of the Philippine airpower buildup, which was expected by February or March 1942. By then, if Japan had not yet commenced hostilities, the Philippines force might deter Japan from initiating operations south and west of the Philippines. In the meantime, the United States should remain on the defensive in the Pacific, only going to war if Japan attacked or threatened U.S., British, or Dutch possessions and some parts of Thailand. President Roosevelt agreed with this scenario.[5]

In the Philippines, General MacArthur had succeeded in gaining Washington's approval of his proposal to extend his defense responsibilities to cover all the Philippines, not just Manila Bay. He was also developing close military cooperation with the Australians, British, and Dutch, including use of his B-17 force to provide defense of their territories. By early November he had already received twenty-six additional B-17s flown across the Pacific from California and fifty modern P-40E pursuit ships. An eight-ship convoy had left San Francisco for Manila on November 20 with eighteen additional P-40s and fifty-two A-24 dive bombers, plus five thousand troops.

But in late November President Roosevelt was worried that the Japanese timetable in the current crisis was not in line with his own. He sensed the Japanese were dissatisfied with the ongoing negotiations in Washington and "will soon cut loose." However, Marshall doubted an early move on the part of the Japanese, believing the deterrent strategy would hold.[6]

On the diplomatic front, a frustrated Secretary of State Cordell Hull—without consulting either Secretary of War Stimson or Marshall—prepared a note that stipulated the conditions the United States wanted met to end the crisis with Japan and delivered it to the Japanese negotiating team on November 26. The note required Japan to withdraw its military forces from Indochina and China in exchange for an unfreezing of Japanese assets in the United States and the signing of a liberal trade agreement. But he felt certain that the terms would be rejected.[7]

On receipt of Hull's note the following day, Premier Tojo (incorrectly) maintained that it represented an "ultimatum" to Japan and that the "hard-line" U.S. position would force Japan to "opt for war in self-defense." At the imperial conference of December 1, Privy Council president Yoshimichi Hara argued that caving in to the U.S. demands would mean "giving up the fruits of the Sino-Japanese war." Hirohito agreed and supported those participants who called for war. The December 1 deadline had been reached. Now five days out of Hitokappu Bay, the six-carrier Pearl Harbor strike force had received no message to return.

Immediately following the December 1 conference, Hirohito began finalizing the text of his imperial rescript declaring war on the United States and the British Empire. He made no references to international law or to the Greater East Asia Co-Prosperity Sphere; the Japanese Empire was simply going to fight "for its existence and self-defense." On the following day, December 8 was officially confirmed as the date for opening hostilities.

On the afternoon of December 4, troops of Lt. Gen. Tomayuki Yamashita's 25th Army left China's southern coast escorted by twenty-four cruisers and destroyers. They were headed south for their scheduled landings in southern Thailand and northern Malaya.[8]

The following morning, Vice Adm. Tom Phillips, commander-in-chief of the Singapore-based British Far Eastern Fleet, flew into Manila to meet with Adm. Thomas Hart to begin planning for joint British-American naval operations in the Far Eastern theater. Invited to participate in the discussions that day, General MacArthur expressed his confidence in his air force's defensive capabilities. But on the second day of the meetings between Phillips and Hart they received startling news: a Japanese convoy of twenty-five transports escorted by warships had been spotted heading for Thailand and Malaya. Phillips broke off the discussions and immediately flew back to Singapore.[9]

In Washington the news of the movement of the Japanese expeditionary force confirmed Roosevelt's forebodings about Japanese intentions and marked the failure of Stimson's and Marshall's deterrent strategy. If the troops landed on British territory, Roosevelt intended to come to Britain's aid, even if such an action exceeded his constitutional prerogatives. There was another indication that diplomacy had come to an end. The War Department had learned from an intercepted radio message that the Japanese negotiating team in Washington would be presenting a note on the morning of December 7 stating that Japan was breaking off negotiations.

Across the date line it was already December 7. That evening Japanese transports were off the Kra Isthmus, while others were approaching the northern tip of Malaya. To the northeast that same evening, twelve transports were heading south from the Pescadores with troops scheduled to land on northern Luzon on December 10, their mission to seize small airfields. On Formosa, just north of the Pescadores, 43 Japanese army bombers were preparing for takeoff to attack targets on northern Luzon, while 108 navy attack bombers and 90 Zero fighters were scheduled to head for Luzon at dawn for attacks on Clark and Iba Fields. For the Malaya operation the navy was providing 99 attack bombers and 27 Zeros from Indochina bases.[10]

The Japanese navy's 11th Air Fleet headquarters on Formosa was exuding confidence, believing its Zeros could easily outperform what they (incorrectly) believed were mainly "old type" American fighters on Luzon's fields. Quickly knocking out American air power in the Philippines—especially the B-17s at Clark Field that threatened Japanese southward sea and air movements to Malaya, Singapore, and the Dutch East Indies—was critical for the success of Southern Operations.[11] British air power on Malaya and at Singapore—obsolete Buffalo fighters and Blenheim and Hudson bombers—was considered a minor threat to Malaya operations, outnumbered as it was three to one by Japanese army and navy fighters and bombers.

"MY GOD, THIS CAN'T BE TRUE, this must mean the Philippines," Secretary of the Navy Frank Knox in Washington exclaimed after being handed a dispatch just after 1400 on Sunday, December 7, 1941. The short message reported that Pearl Harbor was under attack: "this is no drill." It *was* true—the dispatch originated in the office of the commander-in-chief, Pacific Fleet.[12]

At 0753 Hawaiian time—1323 in Washington—183 Japanese Navy torpedo bombers, dive bombers, and fighters flying off six carriers caught Pearl Harbor's defenses unaware and began a systematic destruction of the Pacific Fleet and army and navy airfields on Oahu. Two hours earlier, the spearhead group of Yamashita's 25th Army landed at Kota Bharu at the northern tip of Malaya and at Singora and Pattani in south Thailand and quickly moved forward against feeble opposition at Kota Bharu and none at Singora and Pattani.[13] In the Philippines, Japanese army bombers struck northern Luzon in the morning, three hours after navy carrier bombers and fighters had attacked Davao on Mindanao to the south, but the big blow was in central Luzon, where Zeros and twin-engine bombers of the 11th Air Fleet demolished Clark and Iba Fields during attacks beginning at 1235. Caught on the ground, twelve of the nineteen B-17s at Clark and thirty-four of the ninety Luzon-based P-40s were destroyed, eliminating two of the five pursuit squadrons as fighting units.[14] It was the blackest day in American military history.

For the Japanese, the Southern Operations plan was off to a flying start. In the days to follow, Japanese troops pushed south on Malaya against ineffective resistance and after coming ashore secured airfields at Vigan and Aparri on the northern tip of the Philippines, followed on December 12 by another landing at Legaspi in southern Luzon. Invaded on December 8, Hong Kong would fall on Christmas Day. On December 15, troops landed on British North Borneo, gateway to the Dutch East Indies. In the air, land-based Japanese navy torpedo bombers shocked the world by sinking the British battleship *Prince of Wales* and battle cruiser *Repulse* off the coast of Malaya on December 10.

Immediately following the Pearl Harbor attack, the War Department cabled MacArthur to "cooperate with the British and Dutch to the utmost," though "without jeopardizing accomplishment of your primary mission of defense of the Philippines."[15] But with the near destruction of the Far East Air Force (FEAF), which had been counted on to defend British and Dutch possessions, the War Department's focus would be on boosting the defense of its own Philippine commonwealth. Reinforcements were to be rushed to MacArthur, who on advice of his air chief, Lewis Brereton, asked Marshall for ten squadrons of pursuit planes in particular, to be delivered by navy aircraft carrier.[16] This priority of air and other reinforcements to MacArthur was agreed to at U.S.-British-Dutch-Chinese conferences at Chungking and Singapore in mid-December aimed at coordinating American, British, Dutch, and Australian operations.[17]

In view of the deteriorating situation on Luzon, the reinforcements would have to reach the Philippines via Australia. On December 13 a convoy of eight ships, the so-called *Pensacola* convoy—carrying twenty-six hundred Army Air Forces personnel (including forty-eight pursuit pilots) and two thousand other troops (including field artillery) to the Philippines, which had left San Francisco on November 20, was ordered in mid-Pacific to divert to Brisbane, Australia. On board two of the cargo vessels were eighteen P-40Es and fifty-two A-24 dive bombers. Five days later, fifty-five more P-40Es, along with a pilot, crew chief, and armorer for each, left San Francisco for Manila via Brisbane on the *President Polk*. Chief of the Army Air Forces Hap Arnold was also preparing to send eighty heavy bombers via Cairo for ferry to the Philippines.[18]

On December 17, while on a special mission in China, Army Air Forces Maj. Gen. George Brett was ordered to Australia to take command of all U.S. forces expected to arrive there, assuming command on his scheduled arrival of December 31 from Brig. Gen. Julian Barnes, who was to come in with the *Pensacola* convoy on December 23. Brett's command—the U.S. Army Forces in Australia (USAFIA)—would be under MacArthur's USAFFE and charged with setting up a supply line for transfer of aircraft and other supplies and men to the Philippines as quickly as possible.

Six weeks before war's outbreak, the War Department had anticipated the need for a ferry route from Australia to the Philippines via the Netherlands East Indies in the event of war, and MacArthur had accordingly begun sending FEAF officers to Australia to develop it in cooperation with the Royal Australian Air Force (RAAF). In mid-November he had sent Brereton himself on a ten-day mission, but with the focus more on establishment of bases in northern Australia and the NEI from which B-17s and B-24s could operate if it became necessary to withdraw them from the Philippines.[19] However, MacArthur's emphasis was now on his need for pursuit and how to get them up to Luzon fields. The December 18–20 Singapore conference gave priority to development of a ferry route, extending twenty-four hundred miles from Darwin, over which short-range pursuit and single-engine dive bombers would hop to Koepang on Dutch Timor and on to Makassar (Celebes) and then to Tarakan (Borneo) via Balikpapan before heading for Del Monte on Mindanao.[20]

The Philippines campaign was going badly for MacArthur. On December 22 the main Japanese invasion force—forty-three thousand troops of General Homma's 14th Army in eighty-five transports—landed virtually unopposed at Lingayen Bay on western Luzon and broke through feeble defenses to begin moving down central Luzon. Another smaller force of seven thousand men landed on southeastern Luzon at Lamon Bay on December 24 and began moving north to link up with Homma and encircle MacArthur's troops.[21] MacArthur reluctantly reverted to the prewar War Plan Orange-3 strategy for defense of the Philippines and ordered his troops into Bataan Peninsula. He agreed to Brereton's proposal to shift his FEAF headquarters to Australia with his remaining B-17s, which had begun evacuating a week earlier. Col. Harold George was left behind to operate the remnants of his pursuit force.

Brereton was ordered to organize advanced operating bases from which to support defense of the Philippines.[22]

But with the fall of Luzon MacArthur also lost his airfields there, the final intended destination of aerial reinforcements to be flown over the ferry route. To the War Department this meant that "plans for reaching you quickly with pursuit are jeopardized."[23] Accordingly, "We will push for strong U.S. air power in Australia," he was informed. But the War Department had overlooked the airfields on northern Mindanao, still in American hands, an oversight not lost on MacArthur, who argued that he was building up air base facilities on Mindanao for receiving pursuit ships over the ferry route "or by carrier," a delivery method he was still considering possible despite (unknown to him) the navy's veto.[24]

Anticipating that pursuit and dive bomber reinforcements that began arriving in Brisbane on December 23 would be ferried (after their assembly) through the Dutch East Indies to Mindanao, MacArthur began sending many of the most experienced of his P-40 and A-24 pilots to Australia in mid-December to fly the single-engine aircraft over the ferry route to the Philippines The remaining pursuit aircraft and dive bombers would be flown north by pilots newly arrived in Australia after they received additional training there. In the meantime, Brereton was organizing B-17 strikes from Australia on Japanese transports assembling in the Davao area of Mindanao. On December 27 he offered his B-17s to repel any Japanese landings in the Dutch East Indies, leaving his 5th Bomber Command chief behind on Java to direct such heavy bomber operations from Singosari in eastern Java.[25]

On the arrival of the *Pensacola* convoy on December 23, the USAFIA was set up under Brig. Gen. Julian Barnes with the primary mission of sending supplies to the Philippines but within the framework of a broader defensive strategy for Southeast Asia. Following his arrival in Australia on December 31, fifty-five-year-old Major General Brett took over command of USAFIA on January 1, with Barnes designated his chief of staff. In addition to pursuit and dive bomber reinforcements and ammunition he was receiving for MacArthur, Brett was being sent fifty-five B-17s and B-24s via the African and Pacific routes to assist in defense of the Far East under so-called Project X.[26]

IN WASHINGTON, TOP ARMY and navy staff officers from December 24 were occupied with the Arcadia Conference, at which they and their British counterparts were shaping a grand military strategy for prosecuting World War II. The main conclusion of the meetings, extending over three weeks, was to give Europe first priority and remain on the defensive in the Far East and Pacific. The two allies intended to try to hold the "Malay barrier"—stretching seventeen hundred miles from peninsular Malaya to Sumatra, Java, and the lesser Sunda Islands—as well as Burma and Australia—and to reestablish communications through the Dutch East Indies with Luzon and support the Philippine garrison. For President Roosevelt the overriding concern in this theater was the maintenance of the security of Australia as a base from which any counteroffensive would begin, a commitment in the Southwest Pacific that had not previously been considered.[27]

At the Arcadia Conference, Marshall proposed to set up a unified command in the Far East that would extend from Burma to the west to Dutch Amboina to the east, three hundred miles further west than the Malay barrier. Although the new command would be called ABDACOM—for American, British, Dutch, Australian Command—the Dutch and the Australians were left out of the talks, a source of resentment for the Australians and disappointment for the Dutch. Northern Australia was not even included as part of the ABDA area, despite its importance as a jumping-off point for operations north. The British maintained that they spoke on behalf of Australia, a member of the British Commonwealth, while the Dutch were excluded from the negotiations because of their military weakness. They were presented with a fait accompli and would have to "bow to U.S. and British wishes."[28]

Lt. Gen. Sir Archibald Wavell, commander-in-chief, India, was appointed ABDACOM commander on December 30 to operate from headquarters in Bandoeng, Java. He was to report to a new British-U.S. military committee to be established in Washington, the Combined Chiefs of Staff, made up of the senior U.S. and British officers participating in the Arcadia Conference. In carrying out the strategy assigned to him, Wavell was to maintain as many key positions as possible in the ABDA area and take the offensive at the earliest opportunity. In that connection his first priority would be to gain general air superiority as soon as possible and minimize piecemeal employment of his air forces.[29]

But the highly respected British officer was faced with many limitations on his authority, which reflected Marshall's concerns. Wavell would not be allowed to move ground forces from one territory to another within the ABDA area, could shift only those air forces that the governments decided to provide him, and would have no power to relieve national commanders or their subordinates or to intervene in decisions on organization or deployment of their forces.[30] Furthermore, despite Marshall's argument that the whole ABDA area represented "a single natural theater," Prime Minister Churchill felt that it would not be possible for a single commander to control the scattered operations in such a large area. In the view of the British, it was not a natural theater of operations but was "artificial nonsense."[31]

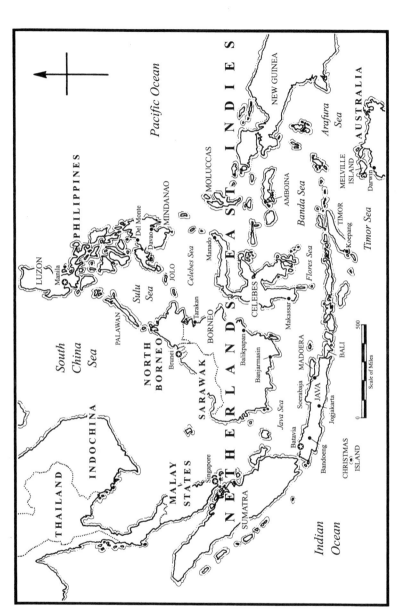

Central ABDA Area and the Philippines, 1941–42.

Wavell left India on January 5 to take up his new command on Java, where he was expected to arrive five days later after a stopover at Singapore.[32] He would face a rapidly deteriorating military situation. Japanese troops were progressing at a fast clip down the Malay peninsula, British North Borneo was under their occupation, and MacArthur was isolated on Corregidor, with his troops bottled up on Bataan, Manila having been ceded to Homma on January 1. Japan's Southern Operations plan was proving unstoppable, its land, sea, and air forces crushing all resistance in their path.

WITH ALL THE PREREQUISITES SECURED, Japanese military commanders were now ready to launch the next phase in Southern Operations: the seizure of the Netherlands Indies and the ultimate objective, Java. They planned to lead off with the capture of the outlying islands of Borneo and Celebes and their airfields, followed, after the expected surrender of Singapore, by a double envelopment from east to west through synchronized sea and land operations spearheaded by air strikes from their newly acquired Borneo and Celebes bases.[33] Already, on January 7 sixteen transports began sailing from Davao with troops to seize the first outer island base, Tarakan on northeastern Borneo.[34]

The Dutch had little with which to oppose the Japanese juggernaut. The Dutch navy included only three light cruisers, eight destroyers, fifteen submarines, and a number of small auxiliaries as well as an air service of thirty-seven Dornier and twenty-five PBY Catalina flying boats.[35] The thirty-eight-thousand-man Dutch army was intended more for policing the Indies than for countering external aggression and lacked the necessary training, equipment, and command organization to take on the Japanese effectively.[36] The army's air force consisted of fifty-eight Dutch export-version Martin B-10 bombers of mid-1930s vintage, eighty-three Brewster Buffalos, eighteen Curtiss-Wright CW-21Bs, twenty-seven Koolhoven FK-51 biplanes, ten Lockheed Lodestars, and nine Lockheed 12s, none of which stood a chance in the air against Japanese Zero fighters.[37]

The Dutch would need British and, particularly, American military support to oppose Japanese naval forays into their waters, troop landings on their soil, and penetration of their skies with Zero fighters and twin-engine Type 96 "Nell" and Type 1 "Betty" attack bombers. American assistance would be in the form of aerial forces. Marshall in Washington was planning to establish nine Army Air Forces groups in the Southwest Pacific for the defense of the Dutch East Indies, including two of heavy bombers, two of medium bombers, one of light bombers, and two of pursuit. This force would represent the largest concentration of air power outside the Western Hemisphere.[38] Brereton on January 4 had told the Australians that he was going to send the P-40s currently being completed in Australia to protect bases in the Indies.[39]

But the Australians had their own worries, with the Japanese approaching their doorstep. Brereton found himself under political pressure to adjust allocation of American air reinforcements to ABDACOM to provide for the aerial defense of Australia, too.[40] Under current arrangements, however, it was not possible: Australia was not included in ABDACOM's theater of operations.

CHAPTER ONE

"We Are Virtually a Floating Ammunition Dump"

IN THE WOODEN BACHELOR OFFICERS' barracks of the 35th Pursuit Group at Hamilton Field, California, 2nd Lt. Bryan Brown was meeting with six of his 41-E flying school classmates in early October 1941. All but one were fellow Texans assigned from Stockton Field, California, in July 1941 following their graduation. They were going to cut cards to determine which two among them would gain overseas assignments to a location code-named PLUM with their 34th Pursuit Squadron, to depart on November 1 on the USAT *President Coolidge*. All seven were keen on the change, for it offered excitement in the future. None of them knew where PLUM was but suspected it was the Philippines.[1]

Brown drew a low card, as did Wade Holman, George Hynes, Ray Thompson, and Bill Stauter. Charlie Gaskell and Jim Henry held the two high cards. Brown and the other four were disappointed to miss the November 1 sailing but had been told by Squadron Commander Sam Marett that the *Coolidge* could carry only half of the 34th Squadron because of space limitations, and that they would be going out on a second transport with the rest of the squadron later in November.[2]

The oldest of the low-card drawers, twenty-seven-year-old Stauter, from Hammond, Indiana, was hoping for a more exciting career in the Army Air Forces than he had experienced with the Marine Corps, in which he had served as a corporal from August 1937 to October 1940 before being accepted for army flying school. The youngest, Hynes, had just turned twenty-three. He was of strong Catholic upbringing, from San Antonio, Texas, and he had obtained his wings at Stockton relatively easily, having gained a civilian pilot's license while in college.

Elsewhere in the 35th Group barracks, four other 41-E Stockton classmates assigned to the sister 21st Pursuit Squadron were also cutting cards for the two places open to them on the November 1 sailing. The squadron's commanding officer, 1st Lt. Ed Dyess, would be taking only twelve of his pilots with him to PLUM, and all but two places were going to the more senior pilots in his squadron, mainly 41-C and 41-D flying school graduates. Oregonian Dave Coleman was "pretty upset" when he and Chester Trout drew low cards, losing to Gus Williams from Globe, Arizona, and Johnny McCown from Grandview, Texas.[3]

Another 21st Pursuiter was also upset about missing the November 1 sailing, but for another reason than a cut of the cards. Jim Morehead was one of the squadron's more experienced 41-C flying school graduates and was earmarked for the transfer, but a midair collision had put him in the hospital. Known as "Wild Man Morehead" for his daredevil antics, the twenty-five-year-old Oklahoman had collided in midair over San Pablo Bay on October 16 in his P-40C.[4] With Morehead now unavailable for the transfer, Dyess picked a low-ranking 41-F pilot, I. B. Jack Donalson, to go in his stead. But Donalson was the exception for assignment of his classmates. The other 41-Fs assigned to the 35th Pursuit Group from Kelly Field in August 15, 1941, following their graduation, would need to await the second sailing to join their squadron mates in PLUM.

One of the 41-Fs assigned to the 34th Pursuit, twenty-seven-year-old Quanah P. Fields, was a Cherokee Indian anxious to see the world. He had signed up for army flying school with the intention of not ending up as a farmer, like most of his fellow Cherokees. Squadron mate Hal Lund considered himself lucky even to be flying pursuit ships. At 6 feet 4 inches he was way over the Army Air Forces' limit of 5 feet 10 inches for pursuit pilots and had been assigned to Hamilton Field to fly twin-engine B-25 bombers, but since there were none based there, he had managed to get the 35th Group's commander, Lt. Col. George P. Tourtellot, to keep him.[5]

Although twenty-two-year-old Bryce Wilhite had arrived to take up his assignment to the 34th Pursuit Squadron only on October 3 after graduation from Kelly Field on September 26, he and most of the 35th Group's other twenty 41-G pilot graduates were hoping for an assignment to PLUM too, at least on the second sailing. However, when the Cullman, Alabama, native and the others were called into a meeting with Tourtellot and told about PLUM, they were also informed that, with the little experience they had in the P-40 at Hamilton Field, they would not be going. Disappointed not to be going on "the great adventure," they saluted and asked to be excused.[6]

But in the hall, they caucused. Wilhite and most of the other 41-Gs decided to ask for another meeting with the group commander to ask him to reconsider. Tourtellot acquiesced and the following day called them back. He told them they could go on the second sailing provided they could fire fifty rounds of .30-caliber ammunition from one gun on the P-40. Elated, they thanked him for the opportunity. All nine of those assigned to the 21st Pursuit and all four assigned to the 34th Pursuit were selected after they met the gunnery requirement. The eight classmates assigned to the 70th Pursuit would not be going, as the 70th was not being assigned to PLUM at that time. In making his decision, Tourtellot recognized that even his 41-Es and 41-Fs had little flying time in P-40s since their assignment to Hamilton—most five to ten hours only. They were thus not much better qualified than the lowly Gs for the overseas assignment.

But assignment where? Bob McMahon in the 21st Pursuit didn't think it was to Panama, despite the Spanish lessons he and the others had been required to take. The young South Dakotan thought it was clear, after noting the crates of P-40s stenciled "PLUM" that were being readied for shipment, that they were being assigned to the Philippines. One of the 41-Gs even came up with a nickname for the Philippines—"the Plum of the Orient." By the end of October, McMahon had completed some seven hours in the P-40, and just before they were scheduled to sail, on November 20, he got in another six hours and also fulfilled Tourtellot's gunnery requirements. With immunization shots and other administrative details completed, McMahon and the others were now set to embark on the great adventure.[7]

SEVEN THOUSAND MILES AWAY—at Darwin on the northern tip of Australia—spectators on Monday, November 17, watched as an Army Air Forces B-18 bomber approached the Royal Australian Air Force (RAAF) field and then touched down at 1229. Four American Air Forces officers—a major, a captain, and two lieutenants—climbed out of the old twin-engine aircraft. RAAF officers warmly greeted them but then asked the purpose of their visit. The Australians had been informed only that a B-18 would be arriving at Darwin from Manila that day via the Netherlands East Indies, with Major Caldwell, Captain Pell, and Lieutenants McCallum and Carroll as the passengers.[8]

Capt. Floyd Pell was puzzled. Had the Australians so soon forgotten his visit the previous month and his informing the RAAF on his return to the Philippines of his intention to visit Australia again via Darwin for a follow-up mission? He had discussed the results of that mission—to collect information on all Australian aerodromes—with the newly arrived U.S. military attaché, Col. Van S. Merle-Smith, during meetings with him from October 24 to 27. The mission had been on the orders of Gen. Douglas MacArthur himself.

There was a distinct possibility that fighter reinforcements to the Philippines from the United States might have to go through Australia and be ferried up from there in the event of an outbreak of war with Japan and resultant disruption of the direct route to the Philippines. Highly regarded by MacArthur's Far East Air Force headquarters, the twenty-nine-year-old Pell—a Mormon from Ogden, Utah, and 1937 graduate of West Point—had been selected for this important mission.[9]

For twenty-seven-year-old Gerald "Bo" McCallum, from Ruston, Louisiana, the secret mission was a welcome change from his Philippine duties, a plum assignment, he felt. Like his buddy, Grant Mahony, a 40-A graduate from Kelly Field, McCallum had been regarded by the FEAF brass as a "problem child" for his unmilitary behavior, and like Mahony he had volunteered out of his pursuit squadron to air base positions months after arriving in the Philippines in December 1940. In their new jobs both had the opportunity to fly bombers and other nonpursuit aircraft in addition to their pursuit ships, and because of their experience they had been approached by Pell—commanding officer of Headquarters and Headquarters Squadron, 20th Air Base Group—for one of them to join him on his follow-up mission to Australia. When McCallum drew a jack of spades and Mahony a "doggoned six of Diamonds," McCallum got the assignment. For "Lucky Bo"—as Mahony and his other mates now called him—it would be a "six months or more affair," after which he would get to return to the States, according to Pell.[10]

The foursome had flown out of Manila at 0700 on November 14 and had spent their first night at Tarakan, Borneo, continuing on to Balikpapan, Borneo, and Koepang, Timor, the following day, where they spent their second night out and the following day. Second Lt. Frank Carroll of the 28th Bomb Squadron was doing the navigating, while Maj. Charles Caldwell—the forty-one-year-old G-3 (operations officer) of FEAF—was sharing the flying duties with Pell and McCallum. Caldwell was to link up with the FEAF's chief, Maj. Gen. Lewis Brereton, during Brereton's exploratory mission to Australia days later.[11]

After a night at Darwin, Pell, at the controls, was off in the B-18 the next morning at 0725 for Townsville, on the east coast, with the others as passengers. They were to discuss with the RAAF the suitability of Townsville as the headquarters field for American air operations in Australia in the event of war.[12]

LATE IN THE AFTERNOON OF FRIDAY, November 21, 1941, the U.S. Army transport *Republic* shuddered as it was pulled out of Pier 47 in San Francisco Bay by tugboats, one day behind its original departure date. Among the twenty-seven hundred troops jammed on board the former World War I transport were forty-eight pilots of the 21st and 34th Pursuit Squadrons, 35th Pursuit Group. They were listed as "casuals."[13] The pursuiters had been assigned four to a stateroom, all in the same immediate area of the transport. McMahon grumbled that "our cruise quarters were slightly larger than a shoebox," with two double-deck bunks on either side. At least he had his closest buddy, fellow 41-G graduate Wally MacLean, with him to share the voyage.[14]

Gazing at the Golden Gate bridge overhead as the *Republic* headed for open sea, Bryce Wilhite and other pilots on deck began having second thoughts about the wisdom of choosing to leave the United States for parts unknown and at a time of international tension. Then they overheard one of the senior noncoms standing nearby bellow out what he felt about the situation: "All right you guys. This is what I call carrying a rumor too fuckin' far!"[15]

Not long after clearing the Golden Gate, the *Republic* began rolling heavily in the open sea, huge waves crashing over the bow. Few of the troops had ever been on a ship before, and soon they were vomiting all over the ship. And the ship was going very slowly, only fifteen miles an hour, 2nd Lt. Hubert Egenes estimated. He also noticed that it was sailing without an escort despite the tense international situation.[16]

That night, with the ship blacked out, Egenes and others on the deck groped around in the pitch dark, grabbing each other and stumbling over chairs. The twenty-three-year-old Norwegian-American from Story City, Iowa, was also hopping mad to find out that his trunk marked "cabin," which contained all his toilet articles and clothing except what he was wearing, had instead been put in the hold. About half the other pilots were complaining about the same carelessness. It meant that they would have to wait until docking in Honolulu to get access to clean clothing and toilet articles. Egenes—as a 40-F flying school graduate the most senior of the 21st Pursuiters on board—didn't relish going around unshaven for a week.[17]

Fortunately for Bob McMahon, he would not be without his essentials for the long voyage; they were carried at his request to his stateroom by a soldier on the pier. Carefully wrapped inside the small trunk were three bottles of bourbon, three scotch, two gin, two vodka, two rum, and one small vermouth, all purchased just before boarding. The "bon vivant" of the 35th Group knew it was against army regulations to take liquor on board an army transport, but he was Army *Air Corps,* he told himself.[18]

Soon McMahon was having little nightly "jam sessions" in his cramped stateroom with his roomie MacLean and a naval officer he had befriended, also a jazz enthusiast like McMahon. And MacLean had gotten his trumpet out of his cabin baggage. But as they conducted their liquid-induced bull sessions into the night, they had sentries on alert for army brass, "or their spies," that might approach. The main nemesis was an old cavalry officer who seemed to have assumed command over all the 35th Group pilots, Lt. Col. Geoffrey Galwey. He strutted around the transport "like a bantam rooster" in his riding pants and boots, wielding a riding crop, demonstrating his authority to a group of young officers he clearly did not like.[19]

As light was breaking on the morning of Friday, November 28, Wilhite joined fellow officers and went on deck to peer through the gray morning fog. Molokai came into view, then Oahu and Diamond Head. A few planes buzzed them. Than at 1100 the *Republic* docked in Honolulu harbor, and all troops were given shore leave until 2300. McMahon enjoyed himself fully, mixing with naval officers and others (mainly ladies), but after "doing the town," flying school classmate Cal Smith—a slightly built twenty-one-year-old farm boy from Troy, Ohio—was happy to leave the "dirty, squalid-looking city."[20]

The following morning the *Republic* pulled out at 0700 as AAF planes buzzed an aloha. Towards noon the old transport joined a six-ship convoy, guarded by the old cruiser *Pensacola*. Egenes heard that one of the freighters in the convoy was carrying aircraft.[21] Egenes also was informed that the *Republic* had now slowed to nine knots so that the freighters could keep up, and the ship was now headed south instead of west. "Why south?" he wondered. With such a roundabout route it would take thirty-nine days from Hawaii to reach Manila, he figured. To Smith also it looked like their destination was indeed the Philippines; he'd heard a rumor that they were headed there via Fiji and Melbourne.[22]

IN THE LATE AFTERNOON of Saturday, December 6, 1941, 2nd Lt. George Parker boarded the USAT *President Garfield* in San Francisco Bay with other pilots of his 70th Pursuit Squadron, 35th Pursuit Group, as well as eight hundred troops and one hundred officers of other army units. As the last load of baggage and supplies went down the hatch at 1745, the *Garfield*'s horn "thundered and bellowed" to signal that the transport was about to depart for Honolulu. On the dock family members of the departing troops cheered and waved goodbye.[23]

At exactly 1800 the *Garfield* turned and headed out of the bay to the stirring strains of "Columbia, the Gem of the Ocean." Chills ran up and down Parker's spine. Then, as the national anthem boomed over the loudspeakers, every man on board stood at attention when the ship slid silently under the Golden Gate Bridge. Parker—a twenty-four-year-old native of Riverside, California, who had received his wings in the class of 41-F—wondered what fate had in store for him. All he knew was that they were being sent to PLUM, first stop Honolulu.

That night, after turning in after watching the lights of San Francisco disappear beyond the horizon, Parker found he could not sleep because of the rolling and pitching of the ship. In the dining room the next morning there were many empty chairs; many on board were too ill to come to breakfast.[24] At 1115 Parker was sitting in a deck chair on the port side reading the introductory paragraphs of *The Sun Is My Undoing* when the peaceful morning was shaken by an announcement over someone's portable radio. The Japanese had attacked Honolulu and Manila. "At last it has come," was Parker's reaction—"The little yellow men are in for it!" Looking into the ocean, Parker noticed a curve in the wake and realized that the *Garfield* had changed course and turned about. Then he heard that a transport—a lumber boat—ahead of them had been torpedoed. Next, he was put in charge of a provisional company of sixty of the troops on board, all of whom were given lifebelts. Parker passed the word to them that they were headed back to San Francisco.

At 2300 Parker took a walk on the deck in a blackout. With the *Garfield* traveling at a fast clip, he figured they should see the lights of San Francisco about 0100. He wondered whether the *Tasker H. Bliss* and the *President Johnson* had turned around too. He was particularly worried about the *Johnson,* which had left the same day as the *Garfield.* His squadron commander as well as all of the squadron's enlisted men and supplies were aboard her.[25] At 0145 Parker spotted the lights of San Francisco, and at 0300 the *Garfield* passed under the Golden Gate, with the *Bliss* following behind. "But where is the *Johnson?*" Parker wondered. It would be another twenty-four hours before he learned that the *Johnson* had arrived safely.[26]

Back in port, Parker also found out that the rest of his 70th Squadron's pilots had been scheduled to leave on the gleaming white Matson liner SS *Monterey* on the morning of December 8. Their baggage was already on board at 0800, and sailing was set for 0900 when they received orders to disembark and report back to Hamilton Field.[27]

SHORTLY AFTER 1100 ON THE MORNING of Sunday, December 7, Bryce Wilhite was sitting in the salon of the *Republic* after religious service, reading a book. Suddenly a bell rang, immediately followed by a loud whistle, then "Now hear this!" blared out over the loudspeakers as a general call to quarters. Wilhite and the others rushed to designated locations, thinking it was just another of the many drills they had been put through.[28] Another loud, shrill whistle came over the speaker system, this time in a very high tone for attention. The captain began to speak in a soft but clear voice. "The Japanese

Imperial Army [sic] has bombed Pearl Harbor," he announced. "Now a state of war exists between the United States and the Japanese Empire. As you know, we are not well armed. However, with our inadequate arms we will try to defend ourselves as best we can. May God be with us!"[29]

Wilhite was not completely surprised. It was the news that some of them had been fearing when the *Republic*'s course had been altered after leaving Honolulu. But still he had a strange weak feeling in the pit of his stomach. While others shouted and struck or clutched each other, Wilhite said a prayer. Here they were, midway between Hawaii and Fiji "with only one brave little cruiser for protection." It was not so much that he was anxious for himself, but rather for his family back home. They did not know where he was. Immediately, arrangements for the defensive preparation of the *Republic* began. Rifles and pistols were issued, though Wilhite knew they were useless except to ward off sharks, should they be torpedoed and sunk. The ship's crew began painting the ship in grey war paint, a "fast and furious job" they had almost completed by nightfall.[30]

All during the rest of the day and until late that night the young pilots sat anxiously by the radio and tried to piece together the confused accounts of what had happened. The Japanese had apparently bombed Pearl Harbor, Wake, Guam, and Midway. They believed they would have been on a fatal collision course with the Pearl Harbor attack force if they had not altered course to go south after leaving Honolulu.

As the following days slipped by with no encounters with the Japanese, speculation ran high about their actual destination. Near nightfall on December 13 their intermediate stop became clear when the Fiji Islands came into view and the convoy entered the harbor of Suva. Confined to the *Republic* during the one-day layover, Wilhite and the others were struck with the beauty of the place as they took in the view from the deck. He had never seen "such loveliness spread over one little spot."[31]

That afternoon a message had been received by General Barnes from George C. Marshall. The chief of staff informed him he was being made commander of U.S. Forces in Australia. Word soon spread among the troops, ending weeks of speculation.[32]

ABOUT MIDNIGHT OF DECEMBER 14 the seven pilots assigned to the 26th Pursuit Squadron, 51st Pursuit Group, were asleep in the barracks at Mines Field, Inglewood, California, when their commanding officer—1st Lt. Francis E. Brenner—came in and rousted them out of bed. Brenner wanted three volunteers to join a fighter team that was being formed to go to PLUM. His request was greeted with dead silence; they suspected PLUM was the Philippines, and they knew what was going on there.[33] The drowsy pilots decided to draw cards. Those who drew the three lowest cards would have to go. Jesse Dore ended up with the lowest card, with Bob Oestreicher holding the next lowest and Gene Wahl the third lowest.[34] The same selection process was going on with the 51st Group's other two tactical squadrons, the 16th and 25th. They were to produce the other five pilots being requested to reach the group's quota of eight. At the 16th Pursuit, Frank Adkins and Morris Caldwell—both 41-E graduates of Kelly Field—"volunteered" also.[35]

In addition to the eight pilots, the 51st Group was to provide a crew chief and an armorer for each of them. The enlisted men of the group had only been back at Mines Field for a day or two when at about 2400 that same night someone entered their barracks, announcing, "We want volunteers to go to PLUM." Almost in unison, they bellowed, "You're crazy!" No one volunteered. But later a basket was brought in with all the names of the crew chiefs and armorers on slips of paper. Sgt. Dale Holt—from Lebanon, Missouri—grimaced when his name was one of those drawn in the crew chief selection.[36]

Back at the 26th Squadron's quarters, Oestreicher, Wahl, and Dore packed their duffel bags and climbed into an army staff car for the drive eastward to Riverside and March Field, the 51st's home base. Early the next morning the threesome and the other five pilot selectees of the group repacked at March Field for the truck ride to the railroad terminal in Los Angeles and the train trip to San Francisco, where they would be picked up for the short ride to Hamilton Field. In the enlisted men's barracks, Dale Holt and the other fifteen enlisted men assigned to PLUM packed their tool kits and clothing and set out for the train, too.[37]

During the long train ride the eight young pilots must have reflected on their lack of experience in pursuit ships. The twenty-four-year-old Oestreicher, a 1940 graduate of Miami University, Ohio, had accumulated only fourteen hours in P-40s immediately after his graduation in the class of 41-E from Brooks Field and assignment to the group. His year older classmate Gene Wahl—from Indianapolis, Indiana, and a 1939 graduate of Wabash College—had only twelve hours' flying time in the pursuit ships. The whole 51st Group had only twelve P-40s, not enough to give its pilots more flying time.[38]

At March Field at Riverside, east of Los Angeles, seven pilots of the 14th Pursuit Group based there were selected, too, but in the last minute two were dropped and three others added to reach the group's revised quota of eight for the PLUM assignment. Of the eight, five were 41-H flying school graduates of Mather Field who had been assigned to March Field only six weeks earlier after receiving their wings on October 31, 1941. Max Wiecks, from Ponca City, Oklahoma, was the oldest at twenty-six. After receiving a BA in

1936 and an LLB in 1939, both from the University of Oklahoma, Wiecks had practiced law for public utilities in Dallas before deciding to drop his legal career and fulfill his passion to join the Air Corps and sign up for flight training. He had now logged a total of twelve hours in the P-40.[39]

George Parker was not surprised when the sixteen pilots of the 14th and 51st Groups showed up at Hamilton Field on the afternoon of December 16. Four days earlier he had heard that the COs of his 35th Group and of the sister 20th Group were down at March Field "working on our fate" with the brass of the 4th Interceptor Command based there. Evidently Hamilton Field was short on the number of pilots required for a renewed PLUM assignment. Days later, Parker got confirmation that a fifty-five-pilot pursuit combat team was being formed to go with the fifty-five P-40Es that the brass had managed to scrape up for shipping to PLUM. The 35th Group's headquarters and 70th Pursuit Squadron were providing twenty-seven pilots, the 20th Group was sending twelve and the 14th and 51st Groups eight each. The 35th Group was now cleaned out of flying officers, all being assigned to the combat team except for the group and squadron commanding officers.[40]

For the 35th Group's pilots, the news was not unexpected, for many had earlier been assigned to PLUM and had even departed on the aborted *Garfield* and *Johnson* sailings a week before. Now their numbers had been augmented with the pilots of the other three groups. To 2nd Lt. Jesse Hague of the 35th Group's 70th Squadron, however, the team being formed was "a conglomeration of Group jealousies." The short but muscular native of Adel, Iowa, a former member of Iowa State University's wrestling team, had just turned twenty-four. "Butch" Hague was known among his 41-F flying school classmates for his independence of mind and outspokenness.[41]

Over at the 20th Pursuit Group, 2nd Lt. Larry Landry had been wondering for over a week when he and the other pilots selected from the group's three tactical squadrons would be going to their new overseas location, generally believed to be the Philippines. Originally six had been chosen from each of the 55th, 77th, and 79th squadrons, but now the quota had been scaled back to four from each squadron. Landry, a twenty-four-year-old native of Baton Rouge, Louisiana, had served two years in the army as an enlisted man before being accepted for flight training and graduating in the class of 41-E at Kelly Field.[42] He had accumulated about two hundred hours' flying time in the P-40 since arriving at Hamilton Field in mid-July 1941. Ten of the twelve pilots selected for the combat team were 41-E graduates, and the other two were from 41-C and 41-D, all with considerable P-40 time. It upset Landry to learn that most of the pilots from the other groups "had just gotten out of flying school" and "didn't have more than 10–12 hours in the P-40," yet "have to go over and fight for their lives."[43] Fellow 41-E graduate Les Johnsen in the 79th Squadron, from South Bend, Washington, had about 150 hours himself in the P-40. Short and a college athlete like Hague, the twenty-six-year-old of Norwegian parents had been a track champion at Stanford University, where he graduated in 1940 with a major in history.[44]

AT 0530 ON THURSDAY, DECEMBER 18, 1941, 2nd Lt. George Parker was rousted out of his bed in the barracks of the 35th Pursuit Group at Hamilton Field and told to report at 0730 after breakfast for a final preparatory meeting of all officers assigned to the Pursuit Combat Team. Some of the pilots were late to the meeting, not having been notified in time. At 0830, following the meeting, they all piled into army recon cars and headed down Route 101 for the San Francisco docks, twenty-two miles due south.[45]

At Pier 45, a steady drizzle stung their faces. It was another cold, dreary, foggy day in San Francisco. But it wasn't only the weather that was different than on December 5 when Parker and others of the rump 35th Group had boarded the *Garfield*. "The atmosphere vibrates War! War!" Parker noted in his diary that night. Instead of a "gay white," the transport that would be taking them overseas this time—the *President Polk*—"wears the dingy gray cloak of war," Parker observed. After much "confusion and milling around," an army colonel began handing out boarding tickets to each of the 55 pilots and 110 enlisted men as they reached the gangplank. The tickets indicated which stateroom they would be occupying. "Once you get on, you can't get off, and you've got to get on now," the colonel barked as they began boarding at 1130.[46]

In passing through the warehouses at the pier to reach the gangplank, Jesse Hague had been impressed with the quantity of munitions laid out on the floor for loading. He noted all sizes of bombs and shells, "2,000 pounds to .22 caliber." But that was nothing compared to what he found when he reached the deck and saw what had already been loaded. "We are virtually a floating ammunition dump!" he recorded in his diary that night.

As they headed for their designated cabins, the pilots had no idea what kind of accommodations they were to have. When he found his stateroom, 2nd Lt. Paul Gambonini was quite pleased to find he had been assigned a first-class room, not what he would have expected for a troopship. Just pressed into army service on this, its maiden voyage, the *Polk* had not been reconfigured to hold the maximum number of troops. Fellow 70th Pursuiter Tommy Hayes had learned that the *Polk* was a combined cargo/passenger liner and was carrying only 340 passengers, including the crew. The Pursuit Combat Team's 165 officers and enlisted men accounted for almost half the total.[47]

Officer assignment of rooms had been by group. Jesse Hague reached his

Stateroom No. 1 ahead of the other three assigned to it and staked his claim to the upper bunk of the two in the room. Fellow squadron mate Vern Head took the other upper bunk, and Jim Hamilton the lower bunk, leaving the last bunk in the room to John Glover, one of the 41-Gs assigned from the 35th Group to the team.[48] Bob Oestreicher of the 51st Group found himself sharing with Bill Ackerman, Harry Pressfield, and Jesse Dore. Next door, the other four from the 51st—Gene Wahl, Frank Adkins, Charlie McNutt, and Morris Caldwell— were settling in too. The twelve pilots of the 20th Group were assigned by squadron, with B. J. Oliver, Jim Ryan, Bill Turner, and Les Johnsen of the 79th Pursuit sharing accommodations. In another room, Larry Landry and his best friend, squadron mate Connie Reagan, shared with Larry Selman and Jim Handley. The third stateroom accommodated the remaining four of the group: Andy Reynolds, Bob McWherter, Elwin Jackson, and Wally Hoskyn.[49]

SSgt. Murray Nichols, a thirty-year-old armorer from Lubbock, Texas, assigned to Headquarters and Headquarters Squadron, 35th Group, and the other fourteen staff sergeants of the 35th Group, plus four from the 20th Group and one from the 51st, were pleased to find that they rated first-class accommodations too. They were also being allowed to eat with the officers. First Lt. William "Shady" Lane, commanding officer of the 35th Group's Headquarters and Headquarters Squadron and now commander of the Pursuit Combat Team as its ranking officer, had told Nichols that he would be the ranking noncommissioned officer on the trip.[50]

All that afternoon the pilots were on deck, watching the ship's crew and longshoremen loading the transport with bombs, torpedo heads, and ammunition, then finally crates of what were rumored to be fifty-five brand-new P-40Es. In late afternoon the ship's crew closed the hatches, but they were still loading cargo on the deck, including three Douglas C-53 transport planes from a barge that pulled up alongside.[51] It was not until almost 2200 that loading was completed, but at midnight the *Polk* was still in port. George Parker took a farewell look at San Francisco in the distance and turned in. "God be with us," he prayed.[52]

Early the next morning Parker was up on the deck observing the direction the *Polk* was taking. He noted that it was traveling due south, about a hundred miles off the California coast. Parker figured that Hawaii was not going to be its first destination after all. "Could we be going to New Zealand or Australia?" he wondered.[53] The rolling of the ship did not particularly bother him, but many of the others were not faring well. Vern Head had become seasick even before daylight, and Paul Gambonini had passed out at the rail. Marion Fuchs "heaved and gagged until he was green" in the face. Jesse Hague figured that "about half the boys lost their cookies" this day, though he himself was getting by, though barely. As he watched his comrades retch, he wondered why they should be seasick after all the hours they'd spent in the air.[54]

But a more important problem than seasickness preoccupied them. They had found out that they would not be convoyed by any warship on their long voyage. Larry Landry thought, "This means that we are taking a big chance—we are just sitting out here on thousands of pounds of dynamite." George Parker mused that there would be no need for lifeboats: "If we are hit we'll be blown to bits. Comforting thought!" Anyway, Tommy Hayes figured there was no point in worrying, because "if anything happens, it would be instantaneous." It depended on the will of God for them to get through or not, he rationalized.[55]

The following day, tension increased when the *Polk* received a wireless message in the morning that two transports had been torpedoed and probably sunk, one off the coast of Santa Cruz and the other off of Blunt's Reef. Shocked, Parker remarked that "we passed right by those waters." Hague had also heard that the *Polk* was the first ship to try to make it all the way to its Pacific destination since war had opened. "I like firsts in lots of things, but not this one," he recorded in his diary that night.[56]

Very disturbing news was disseminated in the ship's newspaper on the fourth day of the trip. It was reported that one hundred thousand Japanese troops had landed in the Philippines at Lingayen Gulf, Luzon. "We all feel like the 600 who rode into the Valley of Hell," Larry Landry wrote his parents that day in reaction to the news. Like the others, he was sure they were heading for the Philippines—but would they get through?

That evening, Paul Gambonini, Jim Hamilton, Verne Augustine, and Jesse Hague sat at one side of the deck while some of the more carefree among them were playing instruments. Hague later that evening noted that they had "cursed the ignorance of the guiding powers for not having better planes than the P-40, having such a lack of power in the needed places, and most of all having us sitting on this floating arsenal without escort."[57]

AT BRISBANE AIRFIELD IN AUSTRALIA, Floyd Pell was awaiting arrival of a civilian Royal Netherlands Indies Airways (KNILM) DC-3, expected in on a regular flight from Batavia, Dutch East Indies, after an overnight stop at Darwin. Pell was scheduled to meet this day, December 21, with its pilot, Capt. Gerson "Fiets" van Messel, to discuss conditions in the Indies for a ferry route from Australia to the Philippines.[58]

With the imminent expected arrival of the first group of American pursuit pilots on the *Republic*, Pell was making final arrangements for the establishment of a ferry service to the Philippines via the Dutch East Indies. Thirty-nine-years old, the veteran Van Messel knew conditions in the NEI better than anyone else from years of flying through the islands. He had been selected by Dutch army headquarters at Bandoeng, Java, to meet with Pell, as arranged by Col. Van Merle-Smith, U.S. military attaché in Brisbane.[59]

Earlier, following his return to Australia on November 17, Pell had been busy coordinating with the RAAF on arrangements for setting up headquarters for the Army Air Forces in Australia at Townsville, seven hundred miles to the north, in accordance with General MacArthur's instructions. On December 11 Pell had informed Washington that Townsville was now prepared to handle all USAAF operations and Air Corps personnel matters, as coordinated with the RAAF.[60]

AFTER THE LONG SEA VOYAGE from San Francisco, Spence Johnson and the other forty-seven army pursuit pilots on board the *Republic* were elated to see "sweet land" as the transport entered Moreton Bay at the mouth of Brisbane River on the afternoon of Monday, December 22. But then it unexpectedly halted and anchored, much to the dismay of the passengers. They were informed that it was low tide, and the muddy river was too shallow for a ship the size of the *Republic* to continue in. All that night a British tanker pumped fuel oil from the *Republic*'s tanks to lighten the load.[61]

Early next morning, all the troops on board were ordered to the bow to balance the ship so that the *Republic*'s propellers could clear the mud as the tide came in. The transport now began moving slowly up the river as Wilhite and the others gazed at the scenery on each side. Much of it reminded them of places in the United States.[62] It was about noon when the *Republic* finally docked at the Brisbane pier and the men began going down the gangplank. They were now wearing their summer khakis. It seemed the entire population of Brisbane was out to welcome their American "saviors," happy and relieved to have them on their soil.[63]

As the young men were being transported through Brisbane city, they wondered where they were going to be quartered. Much to their surprise the vehicles entered a racetrack on the outskirts of the city. Inside it they saw tents that had been set up to accommodate them and other troops from the *Republic*. The Australians had converted the Ascot Race Track into a temporary army camp.[64] Most of the young pilots began settling into their new quarters, but a few others were more interested in exploring Brisbane immediately. Wilhite found that his buddy Mel Price had arranged for a taxi to pick him up at the gate. Price was asking Wilhite and a few other 41-G flying school classmates to join him and share the taxi ride. It was a strange experience for them: the taxi burned coke instead of scarce gasoline, generating

Spence Johnson strikes a "tough guy" pose for fellow 34th Pursuiter John Lewis in their stateroom on board the USAT *Republic*, November 1941. *Courtesy Mildred Daggett, from John Lewis Collection.*

a bad smell and obliging the driver to stop frequently to stoke the burner. "After much puffing and shifting of gears," the taxi reached Lennon's Hotel, a cream-colored four-story neo-deco structure and Brisbane's only modern hotel. After paying the taxi driver, the excited young men bounded into the hotel, where they were pleasantly surprised by its large rooms, ballroom, dining room, and bar. What's more, the room rates were ridiculously low in U.S.

dollars. On the spot, they all decided to stay there instead of in their tents at the racetrack. There were no senior army officers around to order them otherwise, anyway.[65]

Classmates Bob MacMahon and Wally MacLean had not even bothered to go with the others to the racetrack in the first place. Dressed to kill in their pinks and greens and Sam Browne belts instead of the more mundane summer khakis of the others, they had decided to play big shots to impress the Australian dignitaries and had gotten permission to take the *Republic*'s troop roster directly to Australian army headquarters personally. After going down the gangplank, they had spotted a 1941 Plymouth in Australian markings at the pier and impressed the driver to take them there. But after careening through downtown Brisbane on what to him was the wrong side of the street, McMahon asked to be dropped off at a decent first-class hotel while MacLean would go on to Aussie headquarters with the roster.[66]

The taxi stopped in front of Lennon's. Impressed with the hotel, as Wilhite and the others would be later, McMahon signed up for a double room and asked the lady manager to hold more rooms for other pilots he would encourage to stay there instead of the racetrack. Later in the afternoon MacLean showed up, bringing McMahon's overnight bag; the rest of his baggage had been sent out to the racetrack, where he and the others were supposed to be quartered. After MacLean got settled in too, the two buddies decided to check out a pub around the corner, hoping to find some girls, but they were informed that women were not permitted in the "saloon." Returning to the hotel, they found several of their 35th Group comrades checking into the hotel. After freshening up with a shower, McMahon and MacLean proceeded to the hotel lounge and positioned themselves to check out the females walking in and sitting down. It was not long before McMahon had succeeded in having two of the most attractive ones join them at their table for a drink.

But for those fellow pilots who remained in their pup tents at the racetrack, in the heat of Australia's summer, life at the new base country was proving less rewarding. The Australian Home Guard had prepared a mutton roast dinner for them that first afternoon as a "special treat," but only a few were hungry enough to eat it. Undiplomatically, they complained about it to the "very unhappy" hosts.[67]

ON THE DAY AFTER THE *Republic* and the other ships of the *Pensacola* convoy docked in the Brisbane River, a huge Royal Australian Air Force Short Empire flying boat circled and came in for a landing at Hamilton Reach in the river, putting down near the *Pensacola* convoy ships. When the doors of the aircraft opened, twenty-one American dive bomber pilots and three pursuit pilots, all veterans of the disastrous three-week air war in the Philippines, piled out. They had left Nichols Field outside Manila in the small hours of December 17 in a C-39 transport with orders for Australia, from where they were to ferry A-24 dive bombers and P-40 pursuit ships back to the Philippines. After hopping to Del Monte on Mindanao, Tarakan and Balikpapan on Borneo, Makassar in the Celebes, and Timor, the C-39 had finally struggled in to Darwin at 1545 on December 20. There the pilots had been picked up by the flying boat—marked *Centaurus*—and flown to Brisbane via Groote Eylandt, Townsville, and Rockhampton.[68]

"Looking like tramps" after having sat on the floor of the flying boat for two days, the Philippines veterans were taken to Lennon's Hotel on arrival in Brisbane. After the rough living conditions the past weeks in the Philippines, it was "wonderful to walk on a deep rug and see modern furnishings and furniture," 27th Bomb Group pilot Harry Mangan felt. But the purpose of their mission was not far from their thoughts.[69]

The three pursuit pilots were particularly concerned about the welfare of their buddies left behind on Luzon as the campaign there continued to go badly. Grant Mahony, Gerry Keenan, and Allison Strauss were flying school 40-A classmates of Kelly Field days and had been in the Philippines since December 1940. They were among the most experienced P-40 pilots in the Philippines and were being counted on by MacArthur's air force commander to ferry back P-40s of the *Pensacola* convoy as soon as they could be assembled.[70]

Already, Australian longshoremen were offloading the crated aircraft from the freighters *Admiral Halstead* and *Meigs*. The eighteen P-40Es on the *Halstead* were to be loaded on trucks and hauled for assembly to Amberley RAAF Base, thirty-five miles away over a hilly and winding road, while the fifty-two A-24s from the *Meigs* would be assembled at Archerfield, Brisbane's civil airfield, as well as at Amberley Field.[71]

CHAPTER TWO

"We Came 4,700 Miles and Are Pigeon-holed!"

IT WAS CHRISTMAS DAY IN BRISBANE, and Bryce Wilhite and his buddy Mel Price had an invitation to dinner from an American businessman and his wife they had met the day before. The pilots' taxi chugged to the front gate of Mr. and Mrs. Cleveland's house, arriving at "the earliest polite hour" by Australian standards. During the course of the day Wilhite and Price enjoyed the meal—not mutton—the drinks, and the conversation. Then they excused themselves to return to Lennon's Hotel—but not before Mrs. Cleveland had promised to introduce Wilhite to a young Australian lady the following day.[1]

Fellow flying school classmate Bob McMahon also had an invitation for Christmas Day, but in his case it was of a more exciting nature. He had made the acquaintance of a very attractive Australian girl in the hotel lounge, and she had invited him to spend the holidays with her and her parents at their beach house at Surfers Paradise, some forty miles south of Brisbane. Arriving in Surfers Paradise by train in the afternoon of Christmas Eve, McMahon found Mickey to be without inhibitions, and he managed to get himself seduced on the beach before dinner, then again afterwards. Christmas day proved equally eventful, with beers at noon with the family and a near run-in with three huge sharks sweeping by as he was swimming a bit too far out. And there were more adventures with his lady friend, who turned out to be married to an Australian officer serving in the Middle East.[2]

But for the other 35th Group pilots living "in the stables" at Ascot Race Track, Christmas was "rather dull," at least in the view of Cal Smith. The Ohio farm boy thought it was "strange to be going around with sleeves rolled up and wearing a pith helmet in the hot sun on Christmas."[3]

Boxing Day, December 26, continued uneventful for the Race Track inmates, but not so for those still staying at Lennon's. Bryce Wilhite had arranged a date with the girl introduced to him over the phone by Mrs. Cleveland. He was somewhat smitten on meeting her in the early evening at the entrance to the hotel—"a small girl with golden blonde hair and skin to match." After a drink at the hotel bar, Wilhite and Mel Price with their dates repaired to a movie theater down the street, then after the show they returned to the hotel. The girls surprised them by suggesting they go to the airmen's rooms, but the young men soon found out it was not for the reason they thought. The evening ended with a "smoky and smelly" taxi ride to drop the girls off at their homes.[4]

At Surfers Paradise that day, Bob McMahon was joined by buddy Mac MacLean and several other pilots for a day at the beach. Afterwards they all got together for a tea dance at Surfers Paradise Hotel and met some RAAF flight officers, with whom they became chummy. Ever the social animals, McMahon and MacLean decided on the spot to throw a big New Year's Eve party at Lennon's. MacLean took the train back to Brisbane and traded their room for a large suite, spreading the word about the party. McMahon himself decided to spend a few more days at Surfers Paradise with his lady love.[5]

WHILE THE YOUNG SECOND LIEUTENANTS of the 35th Group staying at Lennon's Hotel were living it up over the Christmas holidays, matters of a more serious nature were being taken up by higher-ranked AAF officers and the RAAF leadership. In a conference held between the two groups on December 28, they agreed to a plan that called for the assembly of the eighteen P-40s off the *Admiral Halstead* and the fifty-two A-24 dive bombers from the *Meigs* as rapidly as possible. As soon as assembled, the first ten of the P-40s and first fifteen of the A-24s should be flown to the Philippines immediately.[6]

But who would be the pilots to ferry them to the Philippines? The meeting identified three possible sources: (1) pilots brought in from the Philippines, (2) after sufficient training, the pilots off the *Pensacola* convoy, and (3) Australian pilots. As regarded option 1, at least some of the pilots flown in from the Philippines four days earlier would be needed to provide instruction for the newly arrived pilots. Option 2 would not be a quick solution: the *Pensacola* convoy pilots reportedly had never fired their guns and were deemed "not ready for combat." Certainly the thirty-nine unassigned pilots who had arrived on the USAT *Holbrook* with the other ships of the *Pensacola* convoy were not; they were novices just weeks out of flying school class 41-H before boarding their transport. Still, the emphasis would have to be on training the *Pensacola* pilots, given the inadequate numbers of Philippines veterans. In the meeting Maj. John Davies, CO of the dive bomber pilots from the Philippines, was designated by Brig. Gen. Henry Clagett to be the senior U.S. officer in charge of all training.[7]

On the following day the conference continued, this time devoted to detailed plans and arrangement of training for the *Pensacola* pilots. Major Davies set forth his program of training. That for pursuit pilots would be held at Amberley Field, and that for the dive bomber pilots at Archerfield.[8] Davies identified Capt. Herman Lowery, a squadron commander of his 27th Group attending the meeting, as being in charge of the A-24 training and similarly pointed out 1st Lt. Gerry Keenan as the officer to supervise P-40 instruction. To Keenan, who had arrived just five days earlier, it was beginning to look like he would not be heading back to the Philippines soon after all.[9]

For the training on the P-40s the syllabus that Davies approved provided for fourteen hours of instruction, beginning with a minimum of one hour in the cockpit for familiarization with all controls. Two hours would be devoted to handling and flying characteristics of the P-40E, with a further two hours to combat technique and formation flying. To develop air-to-air gunnery skills, two hours would be spent on operation of the ship's six .50s and four hours on practice firing attacks on a sleeve target, with each pilot firing one hundred rounds using only one gun. Night flying ability would be developed through two periods of one hour each, including landing. Not included in the fourteen hours' instruction were four periods of practicing acrobatics, including two-ship work.[10] Major Davies requested Keenan to arrange for the assembly at Amberley Field of the pilots who were to receive training in the P-40 and Captain Lowery of those at Archerfield for the A-24 training. If there were more planes than pilots scheduled for the training, the shortfall in pilots should be reported to the RAAF so that RAAF candidates could be selected.[11]

Three days later, Major Davies informed General Clagett that flight training would start on January 2 at Amberley and Archerfield. He reported that forty-five pilots were scheduled for P-40 training and fifty-six for A-24 instruction. There was indeed no shortage of trainee pilots.[12]

ON THE AFTERNOON OF DECEMBER 31, Bob McMahon returned to Brisbane after his long holiday stay at Surfers Paradise and headed straight for Lennon's Hotel, arriving just in time to contribute his booze supply to the party that was getting underway in his suite. He found that the private party he and MacLean had arranged was in competition with a dinner dance being held in the hotel's ballroom, but he didn't mind, as people were coming and leaving his party from 1700 onward.[13] But classmate Bryce Wilhite, who had taken his lady friend of the past week to the hotel dance, remained there. He found the ballroom crowded with USAAF and RAAF officers, each with his date for the evening. His American friends, the Clevelands, were there, too, but Wilhite was embarrassed when the couple got drunk and started fighting.[14]

To entice people to come up to the party he and McMahon were throwing, Wally MacLean was going through the hallways dressed in a kilt, "knobby knees and all," and leading two real Scotsmen—who had exchanged their dress for MacLean's uniform pants and cap—playing bagpipes as he blew his trumpet. When hotel guests would open their door to see what was going on, MacLean would invite them to their party.[15] Things were becoming wild as the booze flowed freely. Somehow, McMahon and Mickey ended up in bed, and when they awoke they found MacLean passed out under a large coffee table, flat on his back, snoring loudly. Empty bottles were strewn everywhere. Some of their squadron mates were just now leaving, and Mickey told McMahon she had to get back home. He staggered downstairs to get her a cab, then returned to the suite to crash.

On New Year's Day, McMahon and MacLean checked out of the suite and moved back to their old room. Word was out that the *Republic* pilots had been ordered to Amberley Field. Evidently those who had been staying at the Ascot Race Track had already moved to Amberley. They were all to be billeted in the bachelor officers' quarters with the RAAF officers at the base. Bryce Wilhite had been invited by his girlfriend's mother to go down for the day with them to the beach at Southport, just north of Surfers Paradise. They played in the surf, had lunch on the beach, then "high tea" (dinner) back in Brisbane at the family house. Returning to his room that evening, Wilhite found orders to move to Amberley Field the next day awaiting him. It looked like the good life was coming to an end for them.[16]

WHILE MCMAHON, MACLEAN, WILHITE, and other *Republic* pilots staying at Lennon's were celebrating New Year's Eve in Brisbane, a group of seven bedraggled pursuit pilots 3,700 miles to the north was spending the waning hours of the year at the Del Monte pineapple plantation club on Mindanao Island in the southern Philippines. On orders from their commander, Brig. Gen. Harold George, to proceed to Australia to fly P-40s there back to Bataan, they had left Bataan Field at 1500 that day in a civilian Beechcraft 18 twin-engine aircraft. At the controls was Capt. Louis J. Connelly, a former Philippine Air Lines pilot, who was using only a page torn from an atlas as a guide for the long and hazardous trip. He had hedge-hopped over the 450 miles of the first leg to Mindanao, never more than thirty feet off the water or ground, to avoid detection by marauding Japanese aircraft and had gotten them safely to Del Monte at 1830.[17]

At the club the seven combat veterans of the Philippines air war were finally able to unwind, away from the grim conditions on Luzon. Walt Coss, from Brighton, Pennsylvania, was the most senior of the group, a class 40-A flying school graduate. Frank Neri, of Rochester, New York, was the next most senior, a 40-D graduate. Joe Kruzel (Wilkes-Barre, Pennsylvania), Nathaniel "Cy" Blanton (Shawnee, Oklahoma), Jack Dale (Willoughby, Ohio), and Ed Gilmore (Highland Park, Michigan) were all 40-H graduates. Carl Parker Gies was the most junior, a 41-B from Salem, Oregon.[18]

After tucking into the first real meal they'd had since war started three weeks earlier—chicken, potatoes, gravy, peas, and bread—they shifted to the club's bar and proceeded to drown out bad memories. They were planning to stay up the rest of the night, since they were to get up at 0215 for the next leg of the flight, but Gies among others had too much to drink "and went to bed drunk" at 0100 instead.[19] Rising on schedule an hour later, the bleary-eyed pursuiters headed for the grass field after breakfast and reboarded the Beechcraft. Connelly took off into the pitch dark at 0330, with Gilmore by his side, the copilot for this leg to Tarakan, North Borneo. At about 0730 Manila time, they arrived over the Dutch field, wheels down, but were forced to keep circling; there were barricades on the concrete runways. Almost out of gas, Connelly finally decided to put the ship down to the right of the barricades on a grassy strip that turned out to be in deep mud. As the Beech rolled down the strip, Cy Blanton noticed everyone on the field were in green uniforms, which looked like Japanese to him. Had the Japanese seized Tarakan too?[20]

Climbing out of the Beech, Blanton and the others drew their .45s as they approached the "Japanese," who had their pistols drawn, too. Then Blanton noticed one of them was a "blond-headed guy." They realized that the "Japanese" were actually dark-skinned native soldiers in their Dutch East Indies Army uniforms, along with white-skinned Dutch officers. Ironically, the soldiers thought the unexpected and unrecognized Beechcraft was bringing in Japanese troops. Blanton and the others spent a nervous two hours on the field as their transport was being refueled for the next leg of the trip. Then they reboarded and at 0950, "with full flaps," barely got off the muddy strip and cleared the fence at the end of the field, Balikpapan to the south their next stop.

Back on Bataan later that morning, a second contingent of senior pursuit pilots being sent out on orders of General George was getting ready to board another Beechcraft 18 at Orani Field. As they lugged five-gallon cans of gasoline into the cabin for *ad hoc* in-flight refueling, they wondered what their chances were to make it to Australia in one piece. The old transport had more than 130 bullet holes in it, the result of being strafed earlier in the campaign. The entire leading edge of the left wing had been replaced with a piece of sheet metal.[21]

And who would pilot the Beech on the dangerous journey? None of the pursuiters—Capt. Charles "Bud" Sprague, 1st Lts. Boyd "Buzz" Wagner and William "Red" Sheppard, and 2nd Lts. Bill Hennon, George "Ed" Kiser, Ben Irvin, and Jim Rowland—had ever flown a Beech 18. The only officer flying out with them who was not a pursuit pilot—Capt. Cecil S. McFarland—appeared to be the best candidate and was agreed upon by the group. At 1350 the overloaded eight-passenger transport cleared the dirt strip and headed for Del Monte, the first stop on its southward journey.[22]

AT 0845 ON JANUARY 2, a meeting of USAAF officers was just starting in Lennon's Hotel, but it was not for the purpose of arranging a party. These were higher-ranked officers assembled in the temporary headquarters of the newly designated U.S. Army Forces in Australia, or USAFIA. Maj. Gen. Lewis H. Brereton, commanding general, Far East Air Force, had called the meeting. He had arrived three days earlier in Australia, via the Dutch East Indies, to take over operations in Australia, with direct orders from General MacArthur in the Philippines, and wanted to have a briefing from his staff on the situation.[23] Capt. Floyd Pell was attending the conference, too. He was still staying at Lennon's, although the junior officers from the *Republic* were now clearing out of the hotel to move to Amberley Field. Pell was not involved in the training program being organized at Amberley for them; he was still occupied in coordinating matters with the RAAF and with making arrangements for the ferry route to the Philippines.[24]

In the meeting Brereton particularly wanted information about the status of the training program for the *Pensacola* convoy pilots. Major Davies informed him that the organization for the program had been set up, and the pilots were scheduled to start training that morning.[25] There was a limiting factor, however. The flying component of the training syllabus would depend on the speed of assembly of the aircraft off the *Pensacola* convoy. As of noon the day before, only one P-40 had been assembled and was ready to fly, and another was ready for flight testing before being turned over for flight training. Another nine had wings on their fuselages, and eleven had tail assemblies installed. But there was only enough Prestone coolant to operate two of the ships; none had been sent with the convoy.[26]

Many more A-24s were assembled and flight-tested than P-40s, but they were not of any use for bombing and gunnery training. Neither front nor rear guns would fire; no solenoids or guns sights had been sent with them. Also, bombs would not fit their racks without the addition of another lug. Davies had written Clagett the day before that "the parties responsible for providing armament supplies and equipment for the A-24s" should be "charged with criminal negligence."[27]

Wanting to see first-hand what the situation was with the A-24s, Brereton drove over to nearby Archerfield at 1015 after the conference wound up. The visit confirmed Davies's complaint that the A-24s had been "loaded carelessly." Some of the assembled ships still had mud on their undercarriages and fuselages. None had any machine gun mounts for the rear .30s or trigger motors for the forward-firing guns.[28]

At the 0845 meeting Pell had not been asked by Brereton about the status of the ferry route for the P-40s and A-24s from Australia to the Philippines. It had been agreed earlier that the ferry route would run from Brisbane to Townsville to the north, then west to Cloncurry and north up to Darwin, the jumping-off point for the Dutch East Indies. From Darwin the route was to go through Koepang on Timor, Makassar in the southern Celebes, Balikpapan on southeast Borneo, Tarakan on northeast Borneo, and then to Del Monte. From Del Monte the P-40 and A-24 pilots would make intermediate stops on Panay, Negros, or Cebu in the central Philippines before proceeding on to their final destination, Bataan.[29]

Pell had been busy arranging for gasoline supplies for all these fields over the nearly five thousand mile route. But he and others were increasingly concerned about the likelihood that the inexorable Japanese advance southwards would cut the ferry route soon at key junctures. It was possible that Del Monte might fall, or at least lose its usefulness, as the Japanese had occupied Davao, 150 miles to the southeast on Mindanao, since December 20. Even more ominous, on Christmas day the enemy had seized Jolo Island in the Sulu Archipelago, lying astride the critical Tarakan–Del Monte ferry flight segment, and from there they could operate their invincible Zero fighters against the ferried P-40s and A-24s passing over the area. Unknown to Pell and the FEAF staff, the crack Tainan Kokutai had begun moving its forty-seven Zeros into Jolo on December 26, and by January 7 they had transferred all of them. On December 30 they had attacked Tarakan for the first time.[30]

ON THE MORNING OF JANUARY 2 Bob McMahon and several other fellow pilots off the *Republic* were making their way with their baggage on the narrow, two-lane road to Amberley Field in a big command car that they had "finagled" from one of the army units. Driving erratically on the unfamiliar left-hand side of the road, they intimidated drivers coming in the other direc-

Wallace MacLean (*left*) and Bob McMahon outside their tent at Amberley Field, early January 1942. *Courtesy Mildred Daggett, from John Lewis Collection.*

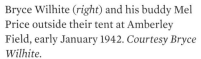

Bryce Wilhite (*right*) and his buddy Mel Price outside their tent at Amberley Field, early January 1942. *Courtesy Bryce Wilhite.*

tion, who gave them a wide berth.[31] On arrival at the RAAF field, McMahon and his friends found that more senior *Pensacola* convoy officers had beaten them to the bachelor officers' barracks. He and three of his companions from his old 21st Pursuit Squadron nevertheless were content to claim a "pretty solid" tent with a wooden floor that was intended for eight men, but as officers they only had to share it among themselves. Flying school classmate Bryce Wilhite and his buddy Mel Price arrived too late to get into the barracks or one of the big pyramidal tents like the one McMahon had claimed. The floor of the two-man tent they ended up with was "the best grade of Queensland sand," very dirty and red, but at least it had the advantage that it dried quickly after a rain and was thus never muddy. They hung their clothes on the crossarm of the center pole, which also served to hold up their mosquito net.[32]

The *Republic* pilots had been informed that the purpose of their transfer to Amberley Field was to gain further instruction in the P-40, but they found themselves assigned instead to assembling the ships. But where were the crated P-40s? They heard that most were still on the docks in Brisbane, although they had arrived in Australia ten days earlier. Wilhite and the others observed the flatbed trucks arriving at Amberley Field day and night with the crates of P-40 sections. It seemed a very slow process. Despite his meager skills in driving large trucks, Wilhite volunteered to assist the drivers. During the next days he managed to make several round trips, "uncomfortable" driving on the left side of the narrow, hilly, and crooked road between Brisbane and Amberley.[33]

One of the FEAF officers from the Philippines who had arrived on December 24 in the Australian flying boat—1st Lt. Fred Hoffman—had been trying to cut through the red tape and speed up the movement of the unassembled P-40s to Amberley and A-24s to Archerfield. With previous experience at the Philippine Air Depot, Hoffman had been appointed engineering officer in charge of assembly of all American aircraft coming into Australia. Transportation of the crates to Amberley and Archerfield was his first task, and he was now making progress.[34] Hoffman still faced the problem of who would actually assemble the aircraft. In the case of the P-40s, no mechanics with experience in putting them together had been sent with the *Pensacola* convoy. On the other hand, seventy-five enlisted men recruited for the American Volunteer Group (Flying Tigers) who had been on their way to Burma on the Dutch transport SS *Blomfontein,* which had joined the *Pensacola* convoy, were available. Although their commanding officer, 1st Lt. Richard Taylor, protested, they were ordered by USAFIA to Amberley Field to help erect the P-40s, along with 7th Bomb Group mechanics of the *Pensacola* convoy who were unfamiliar with the P-40. The pursuit pilots from the *Republic* would supervise them.[35]

It seemed to McMahon and the others that the main work of assembling the P-40s fell to them, despite their lack of any appropriate training. Only a few of the *Republic* pilots had engineering backgrounds. Nevertheless, McMahon found himself assigned to a four-hour shift, then eight hours off, on a twenty-four-hour, round-the-clock operation. He was supervising the work of some eight or nine mechanics, most of whom—except for a few AVG men—had never worked on a P-40 before. The assemblers were using "hit or miss" methods because they lacked assembly instructions. He sometimes found that propellers were hooked up incorrectly, gear and flap valves confused, ailerons reversed, trim tabs on elevator controls off, and cables reversed, among other mistakes. Correcting them was slowing down the assembly process.[36]

Bryce Wilhite did find army technical orders, but he felt they were "gobbledygook" of no value to any of the assemblers under him. However, he was benefiting from his education and experience as a draftsman to explain

Australian and American personnel check the engine of the first P-40E off the cargo ship *Admiral Halstead* and assembled at Amberley Field, January 2, 1942. *Photograph P. 00264.005 © Australian War Memorial.*

the schematic drawings of the hydraulic and electrical systems of the P-40 and helping the other pilots in deciding "where the pipes and wires went." But when assembly was finished and the ships were turned over for testing, another problem faced them· no Prestone. Without the coolant, the liquid-cooled Allison engines would burn out in a few minutes.[37]

By 1800 on January 4 the boxes of all eighteen P-40Es off the *Admiral Halstead* had reached Amberley and had been uncrated, and eighty-five percent of the assembly work had been completed, Major Davies reported to General Brereton. Lack of Prestone was slowing up testing of the ships, but the first four had been flight-tested and another two were ready for testing, using the available supply of coolant, including that procured locally. Davies informed Brereton that he expected two to three of the P-40s would be turned out each day from then on, but he was overoptimistic. Three days later only seven of the eighteen had been assembled.[38]

Davies also reported that thirty-four of the forty-eight *Republic* pilots were attending the pursuit training school at Amberley as of January 4. They were receiving ground instruction in the operation of the P-40E and employing it in combat operations. However, actual flying instruction was being held up until adequate Prestone was made available, which Davies expected the next day. Bob McMahon and Bryce Wilhite were not among the thirty-four trainees. As the lowest-ranked pilots of the *Republic* group, they and their 41-G classmates apparently were being given the lowest priority for training provided during the first week at Amberley.

ON BOARD THE *Polk,* proceeding slowly southwest out in the vast Pacific, the long and boring voyage was getting on everyone's nerves. As Butch Hague put it, there was "little to do and too much time to do it in." Vernon Head was even tired of eating the fine meals that were served. And they were also tired of each other's company, resulting in all sorts of arguments. Hague continued to be involved in "bitch sessions" in which they railed against the "decadence" of the army.[39] But finally, at 1215 on Tuesday, January 6, 1942—eighteen days into the trip—they caught sight of land, the islands of New Zealand. George Parker and Tommy Hayes went up to the deck after finishing their lunch and from the bow observed the scenery as the *Polk* headed south down the west coast of New Zealand then turned into Wellington Harbor at the north tip of South Island. They were in a squall, with heavy winds blowing and some rain falling. A pilot boat pulled alongside and slowly guided the *Polk* to the dock, a long process that didn't end until 1900.[40]

Hague and the others were now up on the deck, too, pacing around, anxious to get off the ship. Finally, word was spread at about 2200 that they could go into Wellington and remain until noon the next day. The pilots and enlisted men rushed down the gangplank. It was very cold, and Wellington looked deserted and dark.[41] As they all headed down the streets of the half-blacked-out city, they were struck by the absence of all but a few autos, with trams and trolleys seeming to be about the only transportation means. Then they spotted a nightclub and went in. The entrance said "The Majestic," but to Head it looked "rather shabby." The club was packed with locals singing and dancing jitterbug to old music. Greeting the new arrivals warmly, the New Zealanders expressed surprise that American servicemen had arrived in their country; there had been no mention of it in the media. They told Head that the Americans' presence gave them a feeling of security. Parker and Hayes sat down at a table and ordered tea and crumpets, ice cream, and fruit salad. Their bill came to half a New Zealand crown, or only about forty cents U.S. But there were no drinks available—the Americans were told that no drinks could be served after 1800.

The Majestic was supposed to close at midnight, but the exuberant Americans kept things going, the pilots dancing and the enlisted men singing. Hague was dancing with a girl whose escort "became so displeased that he stomped out." Finally, at 0200 the club closed down for the night, and the men reluctantly left to return to the *Polk.* But not Head and some others, who managed to find a club that was still open. However, they didn't stay long; it was "the worst place I've seen," Head recorded in his diary.

After being woken up at 0700 the next morning, Hague and Head decided to go into town and have breakfast there rather than on the boat. It was a bad experience—the ham was all right, but the eggs were greasy, the French fries and bread soggy. They were also disappointed in their shopping attempt: no stores opened before 0900. As they walked the streets, the locals stared at them. Many stopped them and asked questions. To Hague their attitude seemed to be, "Can we do *anything* for you?" He couldn't believe how far out of their way they went to be nice to them.[42] A couple of girls came up to Head as he walked with Marion Fuchs and Elwin Jackson and asked them for their autographs. Then they asked them to follow them to the office where they worked so they could meet the rest of their colleagues. The three young men enjoyed being the center of attention in the office as everyone stopped working and bombarded them "with a million questions" until noon.[43]

In the afternoon, the girls took Head, Fuchs, and Jackson on a sightseeing tour of the city, showing them the university and places of historical interest. Four of the others—Al Dutton, Paul Gambonini, Tommy Hayes, and George Parker—were the recipients of New Zealand hospitality too, spending two hours at the home of an elderly lady who approached them on a tram and invited them for tea.[44] Butch Hague and his CO, 1st Lt. William Lane, were also riding a tram in the early afternoon, but they had decided to pay a visit on the Royal New Zealand Air Force Station at Rongotai, five miles southeast of downtown Wellington. At the gate to the base they were greeted with salutes from the enlisted men and taken to the station commander, who arranged for a tour of the very small field. Hague and Lane noted that they had only "a few relics" in the way of aircraft but were impressed by the earnestness of the trainees they visited in flight training class. Tea followed in the office of the station commander, who then drove them back to the docks to reboard the *Polk*. But they need not have come back so early; they were all now being allowed off the boat until 0800 the following morning.[45]

When Hague entered his stateroom at 0230 that night, after having attended a dance party in town for the pilots put on by a USO-type organization, he noticed a big burlap sack in the corner. John Glover had lugged it on board, and it was filled with thirteen quarts of beer and wine that he'd bought in town. Evidently Hague's roommate was planning on extending the Wellington good times in their cabin.[46]

Pooped out from their late evening exertions, the pilots were suddenly awakened at 0830 the next morning by the shuddering of the *Polk* as it left port. They were all sad to leave New Zealand. Hague felt the people were "the most hospitable, unselfish, and brave I have ever known." He was hoping to come back some day. Parker liked the girls; they were *not* shy and retiring, as he had expected. Vern Head, however, felt the people weren't very good looking, with "very poor and discolored teeth." In his view, they all resembled each other. The ship's doctor told him that it was due to too much inbreeding.[47]

At 1500 Lieutenant Lane called a meeting of all the pilots and enlisted men. They were scolded for lack of the discipline that Lane expected of all of them. He cited unfavorable incidents during the two-day visit.[48] Next morning, many of the pilots called their crew chiefs and armorers into their staterooms to discuss deportment and relationships. In the afternoon they attended a lecture for two and one-half hours on tactics of pursuit combat and to study the characteristics of Japanese aircraft and warships, using silhouettes. Head felt that such a meeting was long overdue. Some "hot arguments" ensued on the question of whether they should shoot any Japanese pilots who bailed out. Gene Bound felt that "if we don't do it, maybe they won't." Hague, "not an idealist," disagreed; that was "wishful thinking," he argued, hoping to convert those among his comrades he considered naïve on the issue.[49] They still didn't know their destination. Tommy Hayes's guess was that it was "Darwin or some place on the northern coast of Australia." Only the captain knew, and he wasn't saying.[50]

AT 1600 ON TUESDAY, JANUARY 6, 1942, a four-engined B-24 in USAAF markings landed at Brisbane with a group of seven former Philippines pursuit pilots in dirty uniforms. The most junior of them, 2nd Lt. Parker Gies, was pooped after the eight-and-one-half-hour flight from Darwin. Jammed in the bomb bay of the Liberator during most of the flight, he had tried to get some sleep, but to no avail.[51] Gies and his comrades had spent the past four days at Darwin after arriving there in the Beechcraft 18 that Capt. Louis Connelly had zigzagged through the Dutch East Indies to their Australian destination. His vision obscured in the sudden rainstorm that hit the area, Connelly had taxied the Beech into a hole on landing at Darwin's civilian field, but with no damage to the aircraft. The Philippines veterans reported to Col. Francis Brady, Major General Brereton's chief of staff, on January 3 and were ordered to proceed to Brisbane, where they were to "help organize squadrons" and "fight our way north—slowly." But the RAAF Sunderland flying boat they had boarded in the early afternoon of January 4 developed engine trouble an hour and a half into the flight and had returned to Darwin. When it was not repaired by the end of the following day, the pilots were reassigned to one of the two B-24s on the field for a morning takeoff on January 6.[52]

After disembarking from the B-24 at Brisbane, the group of seven headed into town and checked in at the "swanky" Lennon's Hotel. That evening they indulged themselves at dinner for the first real meal they'd had since New Year's Eve at Del Monte. Later in the evening, Grant Mahony, Al Strauss, and Gerry Keenan came into the hotel for a joyous reunion over drinks with their old comrades from the Philippines. Mahony informed them that only eight of the P-40s they were supposed to ferry back to the Philippines had been assembled and were flyable. Mahony and Strauss then excused themselves when Keenan, Jack Dale, Ed Gilmore, and Gies turned their attention to three Aussie airline hostesses in the bar. "Dale took the best-looking one home," a disappointed Gies recorded in his diary.[53]

The next morning at breakfast they were interrupted when a U.S. Army colonel came over and reprimanded them for their "shabby appearance"— no tie and wearing nonissue Australian shorts and short-sleeved shirts they had been given at Darwin by the RAAF. The colonel identified himself as Alexander L. P. Johnson, the American Army base commander in Brisbane. The pilots' explanation that they'd just come out of the Philippines fell on deaf dears. When Johnson told them he didn't want them "cluttering up the hotel," they got mad. Johnson then ordered them to report to Amberley Field the following morning.[54]

But that was for tomorrow. Jack Dale, Cy Blanton, and Joe Kruzel decided to make the most of their short stay at Lennon's. They lined up four Aussie girls—one for Gies, too—and partied with them most of the night. But a disgusted Gies felt the girls were "playing American officers for suckers" and dropped out of the arrangement. He felt bad about "everybody partying, living in luxury while the boys were on Bataan." Lennon's was "just one big playhouse," he felt.[55]

The next morning the Philippines veterans really got mad with Colonel Johnson. Their orders were changed; they were now to report to Ascot Race Track, where a camp had evidently been set up, and stand by for further instructions. What for? There were no planes there. "We came 4,700 miles and are pigeon-holed," Gies complained in his diary. To add insult to injury, the base adjutant told them he couldn't get transportation for them to go to Ascot, although they could see six army command cars parked in front of the hotel.[56] After piling into two taxis, the seven were taken to the racetrack and reported to a Captain Hicks. In no uncertain terms they told Hicks that "we aren't going to be treated as cadets." They would "do what we want." They had come down to get their aircraft for combat. No ground officer was going to tell them what to do.[57] In a foul mood, the combat veterans checked into the tents assigned to them. Dale, Kruzel, and Blanton—40-H flying school classmates and former 17th Pursuit Squadron buddies in the Philippines—wondered what the hell they were doing, "sitting in a tent in a civilized country." They decided to leave and eluded a guard at the gate by going through a hole in the fence around the camp. Gies, Neri, and Gilmore also opted out of the Ascot arrangement. Only Walt Coss—the most senior of the group—decided to remain.[58] The six contrarians hailed a taxi outside the race track and headed back to Lennon's. Their plan was to return to Ascot in the morning and remain during the day there, but they would spend nights in Brisbane, "to eat, drink, and party again." This time they stayed up all night, with "a lot more girls" in their party.[59] The next morning—January 9—Gies revived himself with a shower, dressed, and got out to Ascot at about 0930. He had a good time entertaining the fledgling 41-H flying school graduates off the USAT *Holbrook* and still at Ascot with stories of his wartime experiences in the Philippines. They told Gies in what a disorganized way the Ascot operation was being run and complained that they hadn't flown since graduating on October 31 from flying school.[60]

There was some good news for the Philippines veterans. Walt Coss told Gies that Maj. Erickson S. Nichols—the S-1 on Brett's USAFIA air staff—had informed him that the seven would be assigned to Amberley Field after all. Evidently their bitching had paid off. Mollified, Gies decided to forego Lennon's for the evening and slept in his tent at Ascot instead.

On Saturday, January 10, Gies and the others reported in at Amberley. Gies was surprised to find fellow Philippines veterans Bud Sprague, Buzz Wagner, Bill Hennon, Ed Kiser, Jim Rowland, and Ben Irvin at the field. In vivid terms, Sprague and Wagner described their odyssey from the Philippines that had started out from Bataan on New Year's Day in the Beechcraft 18 and ended with their arrival in Amberley the previous afternoon in a B-18 bomber. They had to give up on the worn-out Beech at Bandjermasin in southern Borneo when the right engine wouldn't start and took a Navy PBY to Soerabaja, where they had to leave Red Sheppard in a hospital, down with an illness diagnosed as diphtheria. The remaining six arrived in Darwin on the afternoon of January 7 in a B-24 and the next morning boarded the B-18 for Amberley but stopped in Cloncurry for the night before continuing on to Brisbane and Amberley the next day.[61]

Sprague and Wagner told Gies that they were going to form a new pursuit group, on the orders received by Colonel Johnson from Brigadier General Barnes at USAFIA headquarters.[62] Sprague would serve as the CO of the group, and the three squadrons would be led by Wagner, Strauss, and Mahony. The Philippines veterans would be split up, and the group would be filled in with new pilots. There would be "plenty of planes and pilots" for the group.

Capt. Charles A. "Bud" Sprague as a second lieutenant at Kelly Field Advanced Flying School in 1938. *Courtesy National Archives and Records Administration.*

"This is a good set-up and is gonna be lots of fun," Bill Hennon thought.[63] But that morning Hennon, Kiser, and Rowland wanted to sort out a more practical matter. Although they liked the meals they were being given and the quarters assigned them on their arrival at the field, they didn't have any spending money. After "swiping" a jeep at the field, they headed into Brisbane. Parking outside Lennon's Hotel, they went up to the USAFIA headquarters in the building and entered its finance office to collect per diem owed them. It took all morning to cut through the red tape, but they finally were paid fifty-four dollars each. Hennon finally was now able to buy some shoes and send a cable home. The three now also could afford a room at the hotel for the evening and to spend money on their Aussie dates for the night.[64]

Late that afternoon, at the end of their duty day, Parker Gies and the others of Coss's group also left Amberley to return to their rooms in Lennon's. Gies, Neri, and Gilmore were going to spend one last night at the hotel before moving to the Amberley base. But Cy Blanton, Jack Dale, and Joe Kruzel had decided to keep their rooms at Lennon's. They would spend their nights in Brisbane and report in for duty at Amberley during the day. Their old Philippines buddy, Fred Hoffman, had agreed to send a jeep to the hotel from Amberley to pick them up each morning and drop them back at the hotel in the evening.[65]

On Sunday morning, January 11, Gies checked out of the hotel. After borrowing money and paying the bill, he climbed into the jeep that Hennon, Kiser, and Rowland had parked outside, and all four headed back to Amberley Field. They were looking forward to Monday and the start-up of the new group's operations. Already yesterday, Jack Dale and Frank Neri had flown in a six-plane review with newly assembled P-40Es, giving Archerfield and Brisbane "a good buzzing."[66]

PART TWO

"The News from Wavell Is All Bad"

SHORTLY AFTER 1000 ON SATURDAY, January 10, 1942, a Dutch army twin-engine Lockheed Lodestar touched down at Batavia's Kemajoran Airport and disembarked three high-ranking British officers. There to greet them at the capital of the Netherlands East Indies were U.S. Army Lt. Gen. George H. Brett, Maj. Gen. Lewis H. Brereton, and Adm. Thomas C. Hart, along with RAAF Air Chf. Mshl. Sir Charles Burnett, who had flown in the afternoon before from Soerabaja. Promoted just three days before, Brett was relinquishing his post as commanding general of U.S. Army Forces in Australia to report to ABDACOM Supreme Commander Sir Archibald Wavell as the deputy commander of ABDACOM, with Brereton to be introduced as the commanding general of the American Far East Air Force. Admiral Hart was being designated commander of ABDACOM's naval forces (ABDAFLOAT).[1]

Wavell had sent advance notice that he and his staff—Lt. Gen. Sir Henry Pownall (his chief of staff) and Maj. Gen. Ian Playfair—were traveling informally to take up their new assignments, but the Dutch governor general had made their arrival a very formal affair. As Brett, Brereton, and Adm. Thomas Hart and his chief of staff, Rear Adm. William R. Purnell, stood at attention, a Dutch battalion guard of honor presented arms and played "God Save the King." Waiting to hear the American national anthem, the Americans were miffed when Wavell immediately proceeded to inspect the battalion.[2] Also there to greet Wavell was Lt. Gen. Hein ter Poorten, commander in chief of the Netherlands East Indies Army.

That afternoon as the British, American, Australian, and Dutch officers met at Dutch navy headquarters to discuss organizational arrangements of their new ABDA command, Brereton was surprised to find that he was being

Gen. Sir Archibald Wavell (*second from left*) arrives at Kemajoran Airport, Batavia, on January 10, 1942, to take up his ABDA command and is greeted by Adm. Thomas Hart (*far left*), chief of his naval staff; Lt. Gen. George Brett, designated deputy commander, ABDACOM (*far right*); and Lieutenant Colonel Lanzing, representing the Dutch governor general of the Netherlands East Indies.
Photograph No. 011603 © Australian War Memorial.

designated deputy commander of the air arm of the command, to be known as ABDAIR. He would be acting chief until the commander, Air Mshl. Sir Richard Peirse, arrived from England to take over. He had earlier insisted that he have no staff duties interfering with his command of the FEAF, but he was assured he would be retaining that command.[3]

But more disturbing to the other conference participants was the report they had just received that a Japanese landing force had been spotted ten miles off the island of Tarakan, northeast Dutch Borneo, by a Dutch Dornier flying boat.[4] Lumbering Netherlands East Indies Air Force Martin bombers were ordered to attack the Japanese transports, but in the face of heavy anti-aircraft fire they were unsuccessful in carrying out their mission. At 1600 the Dutch commander at Tarakan ordered the destruction of the island's oil wells and facilities, the seizure of which was a main objective of the Japanese landing.[5] Before dawn on the eleventh, Japanese troops from sixteen transports came ashore on the smoke- and fire-shrouded island, defended by a garrison of only thirteen hundred men who the following morning would surrender.[6]

Also in the early hours of the eleventh, a second force of Japanese that had also set sail from Davao disembarked from eleven transports and landed on the northeast tip of the Celebes, at Manado. Unlike Tarakan, Manado had no oil wealth, but it was important for Japanese plans for its airfield. Its fifteen hundred defenders were easily overwhelmed the same day by the invaders, but still the Japanese decided to drop 334 paratroopers over the northern part of the peninsula, an operation of no importance for their occupation.[7]

On a mission to strike the transports lying off Tarakan, seven of Brereton's Java-based B-17Ds had taken off from Singosari on January 11, but because of bad weather only three made it to the target, and their bombing runs were inconsequential. The Dutch tried two days later with their antique Martins, but with disastrous results: six were shot down by Zeros. With such a heavy loss of aircrews, it was decided to halt air operations against Tarakan on January 14.[8]

Wavell's headquarters was now ready, and on January 15 he departed Batavia with his staff for Bandoeng and then on up to the resort town of Lembang eight miles further north, a location regarded safe from Japanese air raids. There he moved into the Grand Hotel Lembang with key staff, with personnel of the other divisions of his command occupying nearby buildings in the small town. Each of his five divisions—General Staff, Naval Staff, Air Staff, Intelligence, and Signal Office—would be manned by Australian, British, Dutch, and American representatives.[9]

Brereton, however, found that his command responsibilities were not over yet. The same day he arrived in Lembang, the War Department in Washington directed him to assume command of all American forces in Australia and the Dutch East Indies, ground as well as air.[10] Brereton realized that he could not take this command and at the same time remain on Wavell's ABDACOM staff. He immediately took up the matter with his superiors, Wavell and Brett, both of whom agreed to leave the decision to Brereton.[11] He asked Wavell to notify the War Department that he wished to remain on Wavell's staff and in command of the American Air Force.[12]

After three days of conferences, Brereton took his leave of Wavell and departed Batavia on the early morning of January 18 for Australia, not having received a response to his request from the War Department. There were "many unsatisfactory conditions" in Australia that he as commander of USAFIA needed to resolve. Arriving in Darwin, he closed his FEAF headquarters there and sent his staff to ABDACOM. That morning of January 19 he also assembled the pursuit pilots of the newly established 17th Pursuit Squadron (Provisional) waiting at Darwin for orders to fly north and briefed them on the situation. With the airfield in Tarakan in Japanese hands, the ferry route to the Philippines had been broken. The pilots would be based on Java in defense of the Dutch East Indies instead.[13]

In Brisbane on January 20 Brereton was dissatisfied with the rate at which aircraft arriving from the United States were being unloaded. Their congestion at the dock area posed a risk of disaster should the Japanese attack.[14] The USAT *Polk* had arrived with fifty-five P-40Es and pilots on January 13, and the *Mormacsun* on January 20 with sixty-seven P-40Es, augmenting those eighteen that had been brought in on the *Pensacola* convoy. Until the week before, the P-40s were being assembled haphazardly by 7th Group mechanics off the *Republic* who had no familiarity with pursuit planes. There were also problems with the assembly of the A-24 dive bombers because of missing parts.

Brereton's 5th Bomber Command at Singosari, under Col. Eugene Eubank, was having its own problems, mainly with the weather experienced during the long missions and little results when they did get through. On a strike against the Japanese airfield at Sungei Patani in northwestern Malaya on January 15, two of the seven B-17Ds had to abort.[15] The new-model B-17Es, a great improvement over the D models, which lacked a tail gun, had begun arriving on January 14. By January 19 ten of the 7th and 19th Groups' B-17Es had arrived, plus four 7th Group LB-30s, British export models of the B-24A taken over by the Army Air Forces.[16]

On January 16, the newly arrived B-17Es of the 7th Group went into operation, two flying along with three LB-30s of the group on a strike mission on Langoan Field, south of Manado, and transport shipping in Manado Bay, with a stop at Kendari to refuel. Three days later, with a planned stop at Del Monte, eight B-17Es of the 7th and 19th Groups took off to bomb the airfield at Jolo, southern Philippines, where the Japanese were building up air strength, but the target was socked in by the weather and the mission was aborted.[17]

New targets were rapidly developing for Eubanks's bombers. On the afternoon of January 23 an invasion force of sixteen transports that had departed Tarakan anchored off the port of Balikpapan. The NEIAF's Martins attacked the transports, escorting cruiser, and ten destroyers, reporting two transports sunk, while a Dutch submarine sank another. But the biggest Japanese losses occurred during a bold late-night attack by four American destroyers, which torpedoed and sank three more transports silhouetted against burning oil fields. It was the U.S. Navy's first surface action since the Spanish-American War.[18]

The transport losses did not deter the Japanese from landing before dawn the next day. The outmatched Dutch garrison of two hundred men put up a brief resistance before retreating to the interior of Borneo. Anticipating the landing, the Dutch commander had ordered the oil fields and refineries around Balikpapan set afire as soon as the Japanese invasion fleet should appear and in defiance of earlier Japanese threats of reprisal.[19]

With Balikpapan in Japanese hands, the B-17s went into action. Eight of the Flying Fortresses from the 7th and 19th Groups bombed ships off Balikpapan on January 24, followed by eight more the next day, an attack that ended badly when six had to make forced landings on their way back to Singosari. On the twenty-sixth, five more were sent out, and the following day six more. Dutch Martins also raided the Japanese transports on the twenty-fourth and twenty-fifth, but the American and Dutch air attacks resulted in only one Japanese ship sunk or damaged: the converted seaplane tender *Sanuki Maru*, sunk on the twenty-sixth by the B-17s.[20]

In Staring Bay, 450 miles southeast of Balikpapan in the Celebes, another Japanese landing force in six transports appeared at 0200 on the early morning of January 24, escorted by eight destroyers. At Kendari, the target of the invasion, the defending force of only four hundred men—many of the native component had already deserted—could put up little resistance as the Japanese came ashore, although it managed to destroy most of the airfield installations and fuel supplies. By that evening the airfield—regarded as the best in the Dutch East Indies—was in Japanese hands at a price of only two wounded. No B-17 attacks had been mounted against the landing, nor did the Dutch use their Martin bombers—they were unavailable, all needing repair and the crews rest.[21] Within twenty-four hours the Kendari airfield was operational again, ready for occupancy by the 21st Koku Sentai's Betty bombers and Zero fighters on January 25. Three days later, the sister 23rd Koku Sentai could begin operations from the Balikpapan field.[22] Japanese bomber and fighter pilots were now within range of all targets on Java, including the key naval base and airfield at Soerabaja.

While the Japanese continued their step-by-step conquest of the outer islands of the Indies aimed at isolating Java, Brereton was in Melbourne, Australia, occupied in conferences with his USAFIA staff that had moved there from Brisbane in early January and with Australian officials. On January 24, approval had been given to include the Darwin area of Australia as the southern perimeter of the ABDACOM defense arena. But the Australian government wanted fighter defense of its increasingly threatened northern area. Air Chief Marshal Burnett was pressuring Brereton to reallocate a squadron of his P-40s from ABDACOM to Australian defense on a "temporary" basis, a request Brereton passed to Wavell for decision. Assuming that the request would be granted, Brereton on January 24 ordered the newly formed 20th Pursuit Squadron (Provisional) at Brisbane to prepare to leave with its twenty-five newly assembled P-40Es for Port Moresby, New Guinea, according to Burnett's wishes. But Brett, acting on behalf of Wavell, rejected the request, arguing that the pursuit ships were needed for Java defense.[23]

With conditions deteriorating in the Indies, Brett and Wavell were pressing USAFIA to speed up dispatch of the newly formed pursuit squadrons to Java. But the time-consuming process of assembling the ships to form new provisional squadrons and having the short-ranged ships flown by inexperienced pilots over the vast inhospitable interior of Australia to Darwin were proving to be a piecemeal activity, exactly what Wavell and Brett had wanted to avoid. The urgent need for more pursuit ships was militating against their original directive.[24]

On January 27 Brereton's unwanted tenure as commanding general of USAFIA came to an end with an order from the War Department—in response to Wavell's earlier request—relieving him of the command and turning it over to his deputy, now Major General Barnes. Brereton would now revert to his former position as commander of the Far East Air Force and Wavell's deputy commander of ABDAIR under Air Marshal Peirse, who arrived from England that day. Also that day Brereton departed Melbourne for Darwin and on the following day left for Soerabaja and his bomber base at Singosari. Accompanying him from Melbourne was Lt. Col. William H. Murphy, a Signal Corps communications expert whom FEAF headquarters in Bandoeng wanted to overhaul the primitive Dutch-operated air warning system in Soerabaja.[25]

Responsible exclusively for air operations again, Brereton plunged into meetings at Singosari with his 5th Bomber Command chief, Gene Eubank, and his staff on January 29. Eubank's striking force had expanded greatly with the steady daily arrival of more and more B-17Es of the 7th and 19th Groups over the past two weeks, now totaling seventeen through that day, but four had been lost in crashes or strafing attacks. He also had received seven LB-30s flown in by the 7th Group's 11th Bomb Squadron, but three of them had been destroyed. However, with Singosari now within striking range of the Japanese at Kendari, Brereton wanted to minimize damage from attacks the Singosari field could expect soon. He ordered Eubank to move his command post away from the airdrome and decentralize his command as much as possible to group and squadron commanding officers. He should also keep his bombers out of the hangars to allow for quicker takeoff in the event of an impending attack. Brereton also wanted better and more detailed information on Japanese air strength for predicting likely intentions.[26]

The following day Brereton was back at his ABDAIR headquarters at Lembang, involved in continuous conferences with Brett and others at ABDACOM and with his own FEAF staff. Concerned about the deteriorating situation northeast of Australia, Air Chief Marshal Burnett was pressing Brett again for P-40s, proposing in a cable to the ABDACOM deputy chief on January 28 that eighteen of those now being assembled at Brisbane be loaned to the RAAF at once. When Brett, miffed, failed to reply, Burnett sent a follow-up cable on January 31.[27]

Wavell and Brett were preoccupied with the more pressing matter of continued steady encroachment of the Japanese. There were reports that Japanese forces on January 27 were moving by barge down the coast of Borneo from Balikpapan, evidently heading for Bandjermasin. That evening a convoy arrived off the coast of Amboina to the east and in a triple envelopment begin occupying the island the following day.[28]

In Washington, Brig. Gen. Dwight D. Eisenhower, on a special assignment for Marshall in the War Department, was keeping abreast of the deteriorating situation in the ABDA area through dispatches sent from Wavell to the Combined Chiefs of Staff. On January 30 the report that the Commonwealth troops in Malaya were "giving up and going back to Singapore tonight" particularly upset him. "The news from Wavell is all bad," he recorded in his diary that evening.[29]

CHAPTER THREE

"There Goes Our Ferry Route"

WHEN PARKER GIES REPORTED IN at Amberley Field on Monday, January 12, he found that he was being assigned to the first of the three squadrons planned for Sprague's new group, the squadron to be led by Allison Strauss and designated the 17th Pursuit Squadron (Provisional). It would be flying seventeen P-40Es of the *Pensacola* convoy that were now assembled and flight-tested. One other P-40E of the convoy's shipment had been sent from the States minus a rudder and left wingtip and could not be made operational.[1]

But Gies was now wondering whether the planned ferry operation to the Philippines was really feasible anymore. Word was out at Amberley that the Japanese had landed at Tarakan on Borneo two days earlier and at Manado in the northern Celebes the day before. Tarakan was one of the stops on the ferry route north, and another one—Makassar in the southern Celebes—would be threatened now, too. "There goes our ferry route," Gies thought. He figured they would now probably be going to Java instead.[2] Gies was also wondering if it was a wise decision to rush a single squadron northward with only seventeen planes. Wouldn't it be better to wait until the whole group had been formed? He feared that with only seventeen P-40s, this quick movement would end up in a repetition of what he had already gone through in the Philippines. Gies's worries this day carried over into questioning his own flying capabilities after slow-timing one of the fifteen new P-40Es now assembled and operational. He had not flown a P-40 since December 22, three weeks earlier. The air today over Amberley was "very rough," and he had made a "terrible landing" coming back to the field.[3]

The following day, Al Strauss called the first operations meeting of the new squadron. Strauss designated Walt Coss to lead B flight of six ships and Bo McCallum C flight of five only, while he would lead A flight's six P-40Es. Besides Coss, only Ben Irvin, Gies, Rowland, and Hennon of the two Bataan Beechcraft groups would be flying with the squadron, each as an element leader. Ten of the *Republic* pilots would fill in the squadron, each as a wingman, except for the more senior Hubert Egenes, who was also assigned as an element leader.[4]

Sprague had picked whom he regarded as the most experienced of the *Republic* lot for Strauss's squadron. George Hynes, Bill Stauter, Wade Holman, Ray Thompson, Bryan Brown, Chester Trout, and Dave Coleman were 41-E flying school graduates, and Spence Johnson and Phil Metsker were 41-Fs. Gies had heard that each of them had 75–90 hours' flying time in the P-40 before coming to Australia. Along with more experienced Egenes and Dwight Muckley, they were listed by USAFIA as those *Republic* pilots "qualified to fly P-40s."[5]

The next morning Gies was up at 0530 to swing the compass in the P-40E assigned to him. He noticed an oil leak in his engine and came back in for another bad landing. After going over the ship with a mechanic, he took it up again. The oil leak was fixed, but he made yet a third bad landing. That afternoon, Gies took his plane up once more, this time for some formation flying practice as an element leader in B flight. He was not happy with his performance, blaming it on his unfamiliarity with the type of formation flying flight leader Coss and the others in the old 17th Pursuit did in the Philippines. To top it off, he made another "terrible landing," almost spinning in.[6]

When Gies landed, he met Bud Sprague and Buzz Wagner, who had returned to Amberley after being absent for two days. Sprague apparently had been in meetings to make arrangements for the departure of the squadron north. But now Gies was informed that the "old deal" was off. Sprague himself would lead the squadron north and take with him all the Bataan Beechcraft veterans plus Bo McCallum, who had arrived in Australia almost two months earlier. They totaled thirteen of the seventeen pilots needed. Four of the "newies" were retained to fill the remaining positions, all 41-Es: Brown, Trout, Stauter, and Thompson. The newly designated 17th Pursuit Squadron (Provisional) was being ordered to Darwin, there to "await further orders."[7]

Al Strauss was being held back to lead one of the next squadrons formed, as was Grant Mahony. But Buzz Wagner would remain behind. He and Sprague had flipped a coin to see who would stay in Australia and give the pilots who had arrived on the *Polk* two days earlier further essentially needed training and who would lead the 17th Provisional to the Philippines. Wagner lost the toss and would remain. The chance result was also logical: Sprague was the group commander, and he was also slightly senior to Wagner.[8]

With Friday, January 16, set as the day for takeoff, Gies and Ed Kiser—put in charge of all personnel equipment—were scouring Brisbane the day before for "guns, belts, ammunition, canteens, headsets, flashlights, tin hats, gas masks, mosquito netting, and life vests" the pilots needed to take along on the flight. It was only with the authorization of Lieutenant General Brett that they succeeded in cutting the red tape to get everything they needed.[9]

Sprague called them all together that day to make assignments of the seventeen P-40Es, numbered 1 to 17. When the pilots were all lined up, he announced that he was taking No. 1, then looked at Walt Coss, second to Sprague in seniority, for him to make his selection. Coss opted for No. 15. Gies decided to take No. 6. Cy Blanton was at the end of the line and ended up with the remaining ship, No. 17.[10] Later that afternoon each pilot took his assigned P-40E up to familiarize himself with the machine that would have to take him thousands of miles north. Blanton found that the brake was not working on the left side of his No. 17 and reported it to the mechanic.[11]

To provide maintenance support for the seventeen ships, an armorer and a crew chief were assigned to each plane, and a radio maintenance man served the whole squadron. The thirty-five enlisted men were to be flown to Darwin in two transports, commercial ones if no military aircraft were available. The USAFIA had no military transports available, but it was found that the RAAF had ten DC-2s, formerly with Eastern Air Lines.[12] Except for the radioman, all the selected men were just off the *Polk*, the first P-40 mechanics and armorers to arrive in Australia. The *Polk* carried no radiomen, however, so the only one who had arrived in the *Pensacola* convoy, Sgt. Louis A. "Bud" Boise of the 7th Bomb Group, was selected to go with the squadron to head up its radio section.[13]

BEFORE DAYBREAK ON MONDAY, January 12, Vern Head, George Parker, and many of the others of the fifty-five-pilot Pursuit Combat Team were on the deck of the *President Polk*, watching as light signals from several different points slowly directed the way for the transport into Moreton Bay. After twenty-five days at sea they had finally reached Australia. But at noon, while still in the bay at the mouth of the Brisbane River, the *Polk* unexpectedly dropped anchor. Australian authorities came on board, along with a U.S. Army captain and two enlisted men. When it was announced that they would have to stay overnight in the bay, everyone got "pretty angry." They were counting on shore leave. Disgruntled, Head decided to pack his things that evening so he could leave the ship as quickly as possible the next day.[14]

Early the following morning the *Polk* was already several miles up the Brisbane River when Head went on deck to watch the sights. There were masses of jellyfish in the channel. The land was flat on each side of the river, dotted with factories. Finally, at 1000 the *Polk* docked at an old warehouse marked "Bretts."[15] After lunch—their final meal on the *Polk*—Jesse Hague and many of the others went around shaking hands and exchanging well-wishes with the naval officers they had befriended on the long voyage, then they began disembarking at 1430. From the dock they were marched in the Australian summer heat to Brisbane to board trucks that were waiting to take them to their new accommodations: Ascot Race Track, or Camp Ascot, as it was now called by the U.S. Army. It was very windy and dusty as they entered the three-man tents set up for them. After first-class staterooms on the *Polk,* they were not very pleased with their new lodgings.[16]

After settling in, all but eight of the fifty-five pilots were allowed to go into Brisbane. To Head, the people seemed "not nearly as friendly" as the New Zealanders, probably because they were now used to American soldiers, he figured. He went to see a movie, then returned to the camp at 2300 and lay down in his tent on a "hard bed with a straw-filled mattress."[17] Hague had picked up some scuttlebutt about the command situation in Australia. Evidently the higher-ranking U.S. Army officers in Brisbane were leaving for Melbourne to the south "as soon as the next rank above them is gone." Rumor had it that USAFIA headquarters was there now, too, "the farthest comfortable place from the theater of war." Hague was not surprised; it fit his view of army leadership.[18]

After breakfast on Wednesday morning the *Polk* pilots and enlisted men were ordered to fall in and march up the road from the camp to hear a talk by a U.S. Army colonel. Thinking they were not going far, Hague came out of his tent with moccasins and no socks for what turned out to be about a mile-long walk in very dusty sand. When they were assembled before the cavalry colonel, they were given a lecture about the dangers of the "spy system" set up in Australia concerning movements of U.S. troops into Australia. The colonel informed them that the coast guard had found a packet on the beach of all the messages from the *Republic* back and forth to other ships of the *Pensacola* convoy while it was at sea. He also told them that a few nights earlier a Tokyo broadcast had given the number of men, name of their outfits, and other pertinent information on all the men in Australia and the theater of war at the time. In conclusion, the colonel warned them "to keep our mouths shut."[19] George Parker was displeased that they were having to take orders from a cavalry colonel. To him there seemed to be "no definite Air Corps organization" there. Parker and the others were angry about the "inefficient" setup.

They were hoping that a ranking Air Corps officer would show up soon to take command of them.[20]

Later that day the crew chiefs and armorers of the combat team left Camp Ascot for Amberley Field in order to begin assembling their fifty-five P-40Es. It was beginning to look like the pilots would soon be taking to the air again. "We all want to see some action," George Parker wrote in his diary that evening. Rumor had it that they would only be remaining at Ascot a few more days. Head had met some of the fellows evacuated from the Philippines who had come down to the camp. He also talked to an old friend from Hamilton Field days, Robert "Blackie" Buel, who was paying a visit from Amberley Field. He and the other *Republic* pilots were only doing "odd jobs" at Amberley, Buel complained. But the P-40s of the *Polk* team were already being "rapidly assembled" at Amberley, he told his buddy.[21]

The following afternoon, the monotony at the Ascot camp—a result of nothing to do—was broken for George Parker when three of the 35th Group Hamilton Field contingent off the *Republic* showed up from Amberley. Parker was glad to see fellow 41-F flying school classmates Phil Metsker, Ralph Martin, and Hal Lund. Metsker told Parker that contrary to the original plan, he would not be going north with the newly formed 17th Pursuit (Provisional) after all. That night the close friends went into town for a lively get-together party and didn't get back to Ascot until the early morning hours. Vern Head was in Brisbane that evening, too. He had arranged to go to the movies with his 41-E classmate off the *Republic,* Bill Stauter. He told Head that he and their flying school classmates Bryan Brown and Ray Thompson would be leaving Amberley tomorrow with the newly formed 17th Pursuit on the ferry route north.[22]

Early on Friday morning, January 16, the *Polk* pilots were wakened in their tents and given the news they had all been waiting for: they were being transferred to Amberley Field. After packing their possessions and loading them on the trucks waiting for them, they climbed on board and sat on their baggage for the thirty-five-mile ride west to their new post. As the trucks entered Amberley Field, they saw a large group of P-40s taking off. "They must be the ones going north," George Parker surmised. But he figured that he and the others without much P-40 time probably wouldn't be going out with the next group for some time. Head felt the same, that only those with the most experience would be sent to Darwin soon.[23] After settling into their new quarters—open barracks and not nearly as dusty conditions as at Ascot—the new arrivals were informed that they were now assigned to the 24th Pursuit Group (Provisional). They hadn't even realized that earlier they had been attached to the 7th Bomb Group, never having been informed by the higher-ups.[24]

WHEN THE 110 CREW CHIEFS and armorers of the Pursuit Combat Team arrived at Amberley Field on the afternoon of Wednesday, January 14, they were immediately put to work assembling the P-40Es that had come with them on the *Polk*. They were replacing the AVG civilians and 7th Bomb Group mechanics who until now had been assembling the pursuit ships off the *Pensacola* convoy, the latter despite their unfamiliarity with P-40s. With other enlisted men—totaling some twelve hundred—of the 7th Group and affiliated units still at Ascot, the 7th Group men at Amberley had been ordered to board the *Polk* for transfer to Soerabaja in the Dutch East Indies.[25]

The crated P-40s were now beginning to arrive at Amberley. It had been quite a job for the combat team's enlisted men to unload them at the Brisbane dock. For Sgt. Julian Guerrero, a crew chief from Des Moines, Iowa, this work was certainly not in his job description. He had been assigned to one of the six-man groups that took turns operating the winch to pull the crates out of the hold and set them on trucks headed to Amberley.[26]

Equipped with the proper tools for assembling the P-40s in the Amberley hangars, the *Polk* mechanics threw themselves into their work, breaking open the crates and extracting the fuselages and wings. They were working from 0700 in the morning to 1700 or 1800 in the late afternoon. For the armorers it was a "hard, dirty, greasy job" to take the six .50-caliber guns out of the wings, where they had been installed in a half inch of Cosmoline, then strip the guns and boil them to remove the grease, and finally put them back together, cleaned and oiled just as the plane came out of the basic assembly hangar.[27] The Curtiss electrically operated propellers were causing difficulties. They would go into low pitch and stay there when tested after installation. Dale Holt, one of the crew chiefs assigned to propeller work, figured out the problem was because of a bad contact in the hub of the prop and was able to fix it.[28]

For thirty-four of the men, the assembly job would be only for a few days. They had been selected to go north as the crew chiefs and armorers with the newly formed 17th Pursuit Squadron (Provisional) and were awaiting air transportation to Darwin. The bonds they had forged on the *Polk* with the combat team pilots to whom they had been assigned were now being broken. Vern Head lost both his crew chief, Vic Cunningham, and his armorer, Glen Harkins; George Parker his crew chief, Lyman Goltry; and Larry Landry his crew chief, Lyle Smith, and armorer, Ben Culpepper.[29]

Life at Amberley for the *Republic* pilots—at the field since January 2—had become boring. Their assembly work had come to a virtual halt after most of the seventeen P-40Es had been assembled by the end of their first week there. Ten of the most senior of the group had gotten in some hours of flying time after they had been assigned to the 17th Pursuit, but six of them had been dropped in favor of Philippines veterans and were now back with the others. The 41-G pilots were the least favored of the lot. At the end of his second week at Amberley, Bryce Wilhite complained that he hadn't been in an airplane since he'd arrived in Australia. Classmate Bob McMahon felt that he should at least be allowed to test fly the two ships he'd helped assemble, arguing that the pilots who put them together should test them, too, but instead the more senior men of 41-E and 41-F maintained that they had the rank and took them up.[30]

With the seventeen P-40Es now taken over by Bud Sprague and his 17th Pursuit, there were no ships to provide flight training. What little instruction the *Republic* pilots were receiving was in the form of classroom lectures that the famed Buzz Wagner and other Philippines veterans were providing, mainly on combat flying based on their experiences against the Zero. Wagner and the others were trying to build up the confidence of the *Republic* pilots, maintaining that "experienced pilots" were "more than a match" for the Japanese fighter. "But where were the experienced pilots?" Wilhite wondered. Like him, most of them were just "kids just out of flying school." "It sort of gives us an empty feeling in our guts," Wilhite recorded in his diary that night.[31]

On a visit to Amberley, Maj. Erickson S. Nichols of USAFIA's air staff in Melbourne put Wagner in charge of training the fifty-five newly arrived *Polk* pilots as soon as their P-40Es were put together. Wagner was to inform Nichols when sufficient planes had been erected and pilots trained to form a second squadron to go north.[32] While Wagner's capabilities were recognized by Nichols, they attracted less attention from the army brass running Amberley than the state of his dress. Shortly after his arrival in Australia on January 9 in the clothes he'd worn on the long trip from the Philippines, Wagner had been bawled out by Colonel Galwey for his shabby appearance when they bumped into each other in Lennon's. Later, Bob McMahon, when talking with Wagner days later in Lennon's, had warned him about the commanding officer of Base Section 3 in charge of Amberley. McMahon had informed Wagner—a black patch over his eye that was damaged in the Philippines—that wearing his open khaki shirt without a tie around the base would incur the sanction of Colonel Johnson, who would consider him out of uniform. "Bull shit," Wagner retorted. No desk-pounding infantry colonel was going to tell him how to dress.[33]

Johnson was in bad odor with the *Republic* pilots, too. To Wilhite it seemed that Johnson's headquarters staff was "always riding me for something." Now Johnson had also put Brisbane off limits to him and the others unless they were on official business. Undeterred, McMahon was coming up with ploys to get into Brisbane in the afternoons, including visits to his girlfriend, Mickey, during his "official" trips. More defiantly, Wilhite was sneaking out some nights without any authorization, determined to see "the bright lights of Brisbane" and visit his girlfriend, Winsome.[34]

ON FRIDAY, JANUARY 16, Gies was up at 0630 and joined the breakfast meeting at Amberley Field that Bud Sprague had called for the pilots of the 17th. This morning they were to start out on their long ferry flight to Darwin, two thousand miles to the northwest. Sprague would lead the first echelon of nine ships. As the ranking officer in the squadron behind Sprague, Walt Coss had been selected by Sprague to lead the second flight of eight.[35]

They would need navigation help, especially to cross the great Australian outback, with its lack of landmarks. Philippines veteran Paul "Pappy" Gunn would guide Sprague's group in one of the old Beechcrafts that had flown them out of the Philippines, while the RAAF had provided two of its obsolete Fairey Battles—now used as trainers—to lead Coss's flight. Sprague's flight would take off first, followed shortly afterwards by Coss's pilots.[36] After the meeting, Sprague and his men carried their little duffel bags packed with all their worldly possessions to their ships and crammed them into the fuselage behind the on-board gasoline tank. A mosquito net was put under their parachute seats, with two others in their duffel bags. Each also had a new leather jacket.[37]

Sprague started the Allison engine on his P-40E No. 1 and commenced taxiing out on the field for the takeoff, with Ed "Kay" Kiser, Bill Hennon, Jim Rowland, Parker Gies, Ed Gilmore, Frank Neri, Bill Stauter, and Chester Trout trailing behind him. Each aircraft had a belly tank attached. It was 0730. But when they assembled over the field and circled after takeoff, they could not find Gunn in his Beechcraft. To add to the problem, Kiser called to report a leak in his fuselage gasoline tank. Sprague decided to return to Amberley. Finally, at 0915, they were off again, but doing their own navigation to their first stop, the commercial airport at Rockhampton, 320 miles up the east coast of Australia.[38]

At 1015 another problem hit the flight. The entire electrical system on Gies's No. 6 suddenly went out. Struggling to get to Rockhampton, he spotted the field, but although he manually pumped down the wheels, he was too slow in getting the flaps down. Landing downwind with no brakes, he overshot the field but had no power to take off again. The P-40E went into a ground loop, wrecking his left wing, left landing gear, belly tank, and aileron rod. The fuselage was broken behind the left wing. But Gies managed to climb

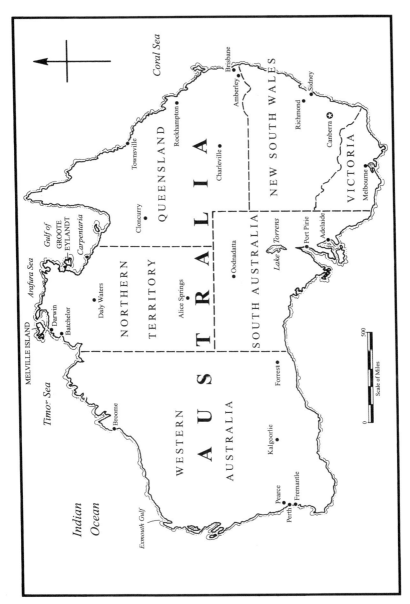

Australia.

out of his ship, uninjured.[39] Sprague and the others commiserated with Gies at lunch (Australian dinner) in Rockhampton, then climbed into their ships for the next leg of their journey, to Townsville, 360 miles north. Gies was left to send a wire to Amberley Field for instructions.[40]

In coming in to land at Townsville's Garbutt Field, Ed Kiser in No. 2 somehow "lost his wingtip on a small house," Bill Hennon noted in his diary that evening. Sprague and his remaining seven pilots, along with Pappy Gunn, who was back as their guide, checked into the Queens Hotel for the evening. To Hennon Townsville was "quite a place."[41]

Back at Amberley, Walt Coss had led his seven pilots—Jack Dale, Joe Kruzel, Cy Blanton, Ben Irvin. Bo McCallum, Bryan Brown, and Ray Thompson—off the field half an hour after Sprague's group had lifted off the second time. Before takeoff, Coss had checked with the pilots of the two Fairey Battles on the course to be followed, cruising speed, altitude, radio frequency, and possible instrument flying. They had no trouble linking up with the Battles to guide them to Townsville, but they were now down to six ships. In taxiing his No. 17 out for takeoff, Cy Blanton found he couldn't even get to the end of the runway because his left brake had gone out completely. He pulled off to the side to await a tow truck to pull his ship back in. Anxious not to be left behind the others in his flight, Blanton urged 2nd Lt. Dwight Muckley—the assistant engineering officer at the field—to fix the brake quickly and once and for all.[42]

Behind the Battles, Coss led his remaining pilots in for a safe landing at Rockhampton. There they talked to Gies about his predicament, then flew on to Townsville, their designated overnight stop. The landing was uneventful, but as Bryan Brown was turning off the runway his right main landing gear collapsed, dropping his ship to the ground. He wouldn't be continuing on with the others.[43]

At Townsville the two groups of the 17th linked up again. Sprague told Coss of Kiser's mishap, and they arranged to send one of the Battles back to Rockhampton to take off the right wingtip of Gies's wrecked ship and bring it to Townsville to replace Kiser's.[44] That evening as the reunited pilots prepared to go to dinner, they were surprised to find Cy Blanton at the hotel, too. He had managed to get his brakes repaired at Amberley then had stopped at an intermediary field to have his ship refueled—but with only the low-octane gas available—and then proceeded on to Townsville on his own navigating skills.[45] But they were still without Parker Gies, left behind at Rockhampton. The Battle had come in to collect the right wingtip of his wrecked ship, then Gies hired a wrecking company to haul his ship over by the field's hangar. He was still awaiting a response to his wire to Amberley. But the situation was not all bad. He had met an RAAF officer whose girlfriend fixed him up with a date for a dance. He had a good time; to the Aussies he was "a big novelty."[46]

THE 17TH PROVISIONAL HAD MADE IT to Townsville, but now it faced its greatest challenge on the ferry flight so far—420 miles due west over the bleak Australian outback to the tiny town of Cloncurry, in the middle of nowhere. As before, they would make the trip in two echelons, now with seven pilots led by Sprague and six under Coss. On the morning of January 17, Sprague lifted his P-40E off Townsville's Garbutt Field, followed by his brood, and at altitude formed behind Gunn's Beechcraft. The old Philippine Air Lines pilot kept them low as they followed a ribbon of railroad track west over the vast, featureless, sandy brown plain. Buffeted by turbulence, they fought the controls all the way. Flying up the eastern Queensland coastline to Townsville was a picnic compared to this.[47] After about two and a half hours, Gunn led them down to Cloncurry and its airfield. The place looked to them like something out of the old American Wild West. After refueling their ships, they went into the town's only hotel and had lunch. Ahead of them lay a 540-mile stretch to Daly Waters.[48]

When they took off in the early afternoon for Daly Waters, they were down to six ships. Ed Gilmore and Frank Neri were not able to get off and would remain behind. The haul to Daly Waters was particularly tiring, with nothing recognizable below but desert and tableland. There were only two checkpoints, and both were sheep stations almost impossible to make out below.[49] At Daly Waters, Sprague decided to continue on the 290 miles to Darwin after they had refueled quickly. No one wanted to remain at Daly Waters any longer than necessary; the flies were driving them crazy. Finally, after flying seven and one-half hours between stops on the way, Sprague's first echelon reached the RAAF field just south of Darwin before sunset.[50]

Back at Cloncurry, Coss had brought his second echelon in from Townsville a few hours after Sprague's group had landed and were still refueling. By the time his own pilots had completed their refueling after Sprague's men had finished their own—a slow process, one plane at a time—Coss decided not to fly on to Daly Waters. He figured they would not be able to make their next stop before nightfall.[51] They would wait until next morning. To Coss, Cloncurry was the hottest place he'd ever been anywhere. Joe Kruzel estimated the temperature at 110–15 degrees. It was so hot that he was able to wash his sweaty shirt and have it dried in ten minutes.[52] It was with relief that they checked into the hotel at Cloncurry for the night. It was a two-story, wooden building in which all the doors and windows were louvered openings, with no screens anywhere. Ed Gilmore and Frank Neri were with them now, left behind when Sprague's group took off.[53] Early the next morning they experienced a real Australian breakfast. "Choose your own medicine," Blanton termed it. They could even have "stayk n iggs," their own favorite. But as they left the dining room to go outside, they felt the heat building up again, and there was no breeze to deter the mosquitoes.

The next leg to Daly Waters seemed particularly long to Blanton because of the monotony of the landscape. He was thankful to have the two Battles up ahead of them to navigate over the difficult country. Even though the pursuiters were flying as high as seventeen thousand feet, they were buffeted by turbulence generated by the terrific heat at ground level.[54] Finally, after about three hours of flying that left them exhausted, they touched down at Daly Waters. But in climbing out of their cockpits they were assailed by flies—"big, black, lazy, slow-flying, blood sucking, biting things by the millions." As they refueled their ships, they found it difficult to breathe without inhaling them. They were everywhere, "trying to get into your mouth, eyes, nostrils, and ears." The Australians advised them to keep their canopies closed the next time until they were ready to leave the aircraft.[55] Coss found that the field was short on the 100-octane gasoline their ships required. He arranged to have the Battles fill up on the available lower-octane Australian gas. The Americans would use it just for their belly tanks.[56]

After takeoff behind the Battles and heading almost due north, Blanton and the others were relieved to find that there was a sort of road that they could follow up to Darwin. At least they now could feel that they were "flying over places where man had been before." It was getting on towards dusk when they spotted the RAAF field just outside Darwin and came in to land. The flight of over eight hundred miles from Cloncurry had taken a lot out of them. But now they could relax and enjoy the luxury of the RAAF officers' club, to which they repaired for the evening after leaving their ships on the field next to those of Sprague's echelon that had arrived the day before.[57]

BACK AT AMBERLEY FIELD it was almost like Old Home Week with the arrival of the *Polk* pilots on January 16. Most of the former 35th Group contingent of the Pursuit Combat Team off the *Polk* previously assigned to Headquarters Squadron and 70th Pursuit Squadron at Hamilton Field were friends of the group's former 21st and 34th Squadron pilots who had gone out on the *Republic* and were now assigned to Amberley. The *Polk*'s 20th Group pilots previously based at Hamilton Field knew many of their 35th Group counterparts at the same field, too. There were also fraternal linkages between the Kelly Field 41-E and F flying school graduates of the *Republic* group and their classmates of the *Polk*'s March Field contingent.[58] However, some of the *Republic* group at Amberley were not so enthusiastic about the arrival of the *Polk*'s pilots. In their view, many of them—such as George Parker—were expressing too much enthusiasm about going into combat and hoping—as did Parker—that the additional training they needed in the P-40 would not take too long, "for we want to fight." "When they've been over here for a month, they won't be so anxious," Bryce Wilhite opined. "Some of the stories from the Philippines will take some of that out of them," he thought.[59]

The fifty-five new arrivals were to be divided up into groups according to hours of experience flying the P-40. Those with the most P-40 time would be getting first call to move north to the combat zone. Butch Hague and Vern Head figured they would be in that group. Even Parker was beginning to think that he might be included, too. But according to Hague's information, fourteen of the fifty-five had less than fifteen hours in the P-40, including his *Polk* cabin mate John Glover, who had twelve hours only. Hague figured they would be at the bottom of the list for assignment to the next provisional squadrons to be formed.[60]

At 0800 on January 17, a meeting was held to brief the new arrivals on the work plan envisaged for them. Vern Head listened intently as "an officer named Wagner" gave them the setup. Head was not impressed with Wagner: "a very mild-mannered fellow" who "doesn't look like a good pursuit pilot."[61] Head learned that Wagner was running a combat flying school at Amberley with the assistance of other Philippine veterans. It was strictly classroom instruction, however; no P-40Es were yet available for flight training.[62] According to the work plan, the main activity of the new arrivals was to help assemble the P-40Es that had been hauled to Amberley from the *Polk*. They would join the *Republic* pilots in this task and be working "hand-in-hand" with the crew chiefs and armorers from the *Polk* already busy in such work, using the RAAF facilities and equipment at Amberley. Four of the *Polk* pilots—Bill Farrior, Larry Selman, Paul May, and Jim Handley—would be responsible for flight testing the ships after assembly.[63]

Following the meeting, the newly arrived pilots were split up into four sections, each to work four-hour shifts on a round-the-clock basis and alternate between assembly and armament work on the ships. Parker, Head, and Hague were assigned to the same section and began work the same day on the 1600–2000 shift, to be followed the next day on the 0800–1200 noon shift. Hague figured this meant that they would only be working eight hours of every thirty-two. He felt they should be putting in more hours.[64]

Ever positive in his attitude, George Parker threw himself into his new job. He welcomed the opportunity to "learn as much as possible" about their P-40Es, for "soon we may have to do lots of this work ourselves." But by the third day Head detected a lack of enthusiasm among his comrades. He noticed that several were not showing up on their shifts. "It sure is disheartening to see the poor cooperation of everyone . . . all down the line, everyone relying on someone else," he recorded in his diary that night. And "the higher officers are all down south and doing nothing," he noted. In Head's observation, "everyone is sure angry at the way things are being run."[65] In Head's estimation, the quality of the work being done was poor. "The planes are more or less slung together" and "might not turn out so good," he felt. He'd heard that one had collapsed on January 17 while being ferried to Darwin. Part of the problem seemed to Head to be the need for P-40 tools. He'd heard from the mechanics that the supply officers at Hamilton Field wouldn't let them take their P-40 tools on the *Polk*.[66]

On the morning of January 19, twenty-one of the *Polk*'s mechanics and armorers plus the radioman Bud Boise boarded two RAAF DC-2 transports for a flight north. They were assigned to the 17th Pursuit Squadron (Provisional) already at Darwin, where they would join SSgts. Jack Evans, Jim Weidman, and Bill O'Rear, who had flown out ahead of them in Pappy Gunn's Beechcraft. The two DC-2s—former Eastern Air Lines transports being used for training purposes—had been flown in to Amberley from Parkes Field by RAAF Flight Officers Noel Webster and John Bonnington, who were surprised to find themselves ordered from the flying school west of Sydney to transport the American enlisted men to Darwin.[67] But shortly after takeoff the two DC-2s ran into bad weather as they headed for Townsville on the first leg of their flight. The two Australian pilots decided to land at Maryborough Airport, just 130 miles north of Amberley, and remain until the weather cleared up. Another transport—a patched up Philippines-veteran B-17C—was supposed to take another ten of the mechanics and armorers to Darwin that morning but was being held on the ground because of the bad weather.[68]

That evening, word was out at Amberley that about twenty of the new pilots would be leaving soon for the front. Some ten of the *Polk*'s P-40Es had been assembled and were now operational, and ten others were nearing completion. George Parker was told informally that he would be one of the twenty to go. It was welcome news; it had been about three months since he'd strapped himself into a P-40.[69] But where would they be sent? Butch Hague had heard that the men in the Philippines were waiting for the *Polk*'s planes, but then the newspapers were reporting that planes would have to be hurried to Singapore if it were to be saved. "It seems a lot of people are depending on the planes we have here," he recorded in his diary that night.[70]

AT THE RAAF FIELD just outside Darwin, fifteen pilots of the 17th Pursuit were assembled on the line at 0820 on Monday, January 19, 1942. Standing before them was Maj. Gen. Lewis H. Brereton, who had flown in the evening before. It was the first time they had seen their old Far East Air Force commanding general since Philippine days months earlier.[71] "I'm so glad to see so many volunteers," Brereton announced at the beginning of his talk to them. "Volunteers"? Cy Blanton and the others politely chuckled at such a remark.[72] Then Brereton in his usual blunt, challenging way immediately got into the gist of his talk. The situation was bleak. With the fall of the stepping stones on the ferry route to the Philippines, they would not be going there to bolster MacArthur's increasingly feeble air defenses after all. Instead they would probably be sent to Kendari on the Celebes, Amboina in the Moluccas, or Balikpapan on Borneo, where they were to slow the Japanese advance southward from northern Borneo and the Celebes. They might be split into two flights and go to different locations.[73] Brereton told them they would be heavily outnumbered from the beginning and could not count on much air support from the British on Singapore, in view of the situation there. But when the time came when they could do no more and the Dutch East Indies were lost, he would see to it that they were evacuated. He himself would be returning to Java as soon as he straightened out some things in Australia during his visit.[74]

His brief talk concluded, Brereton left the group and headed for the four-engined aircraft waiting to take him to his next stop in Australia. As they watched the B-24A lift off at 0840, the pursuiters mulled over the meaning of their commander's talk. Despite his reassurances, many wondered whether they would really be coming back if the Indies fell.[75]

Later that day the 17th Pursuit was down another plane. Ben Irvin's ship had blown a tire. Bud Sprague decided to turn Ray Thompson's ship over to him. If a pilot had to be left behind, it was better that it was the combat-inexperienced 41-E Thompson than Irvin, the 40-G Philippines veteran from Washington, Georgia.[76] The following morning, Sprague put his pilots through some dogfighting practice. "Lots of fun," Bill Hennon thought. But in the afternoon they lost yet another of the ships when one of the wheels on Joe Kruzel's P-40E collapsed as he landed following a practice flight. They decided to take Kruzel's good wheel and put it on Irvin's original ship. Kruzel switched to Thompson's ship now freed up by Irvin. Thompson was still the loser in the two switches.[77]

All day Thursday, January 21, the restless pilots waited for news, but still no orders came through. Then, as darkness was about to fall on the field, two DC-2 transports with RAAF markings touched down just outside the hangar and twenty-two enlisted men emerged. They were the 17th Pursuit's newly assigned mechanics and armorers, plus the radioman for the squadron, arriving from Amberley Field.[78]

As Bud Boise left Flying Officer Bonnington's transport with ten other enlisted men, Sprague approached him and asked if he was the squadron's radioman. Boise acknowledged that he was. Sprague then informed him that there was a junked P-40 in the hangar that had crashed. "What I want you to do is go in there with your tools and take the radio command set out of it and keep it to take with you when we leave for the Indies," Sprague told him. Reluctantly, Boise did as he was ordered, although he hadn't eaten since morning. He was joined by other mechanics who with Boise worked into the night stripping the wreck—Kruzel's ship—of other parts to take to their new base.[79]

That evening, squadron engineering officer Bill Hennon assigned the men to the pilots of the squadron. He himself picked SSgt. John Rex as his crew chief and Pvt. Dick Sheetz as his armorer. Walt Coss got Pvts. Woodie Myers as his crew chief and Bernie Badura as his armorer. Cy Blanton was happy to have SSgt. Mel Donoho—a fellow Oklahoman—as his armorer. The newly assigned men were keen to know how the P-40Es had performed on the long trip from Brisbane. For the 17th Pursuit's pilots it was good to have properly schooled and trained enlisted men to look after their aircraft.[80] Earlier, Sprague had called his pilots together to discuss the relationships he wished to see established in his squadron. He informed them that military protocol would be relaxed so that they could better accomplish their mission. They should get acquainted with the crew chiefs and armorers assigned them. He reminded them that the enlisted men had not been paid. They should share what little money they had with their crew chiefs and armorers. The recommendation was readily accepted.[81]

Meanwhile, the Australian pilots and copilots of the two DC-2s were wondering when they would be returning to their training duties at Parkes Field. In a meeting with the Australian commanding officer of the RAAF Darwin field, Group Capt. Frederick Scherger "suggested" to Flying Officers Webster and Bonnington that they continue to transport the American enlisted men, this time to the squadron's destination in the Indies. Both officers "volunteered" for the duty. A departure date of January 24 was tentatively scheduled.[82]

The next day was Thursday, January 22, and still there was no news for Sprague on a departure date and destination for his pilots. The question of availability of escort airplanes was also holding up matters. For the pilots

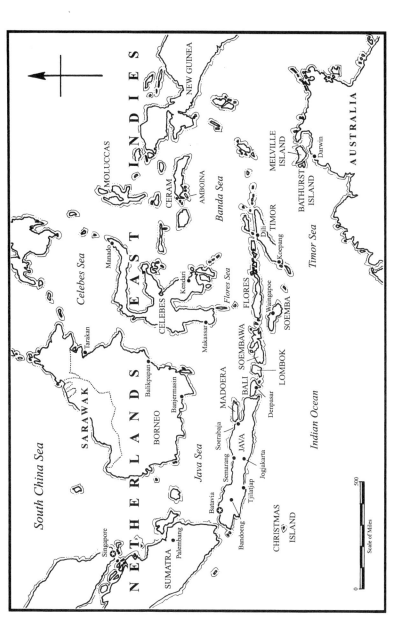

Netherlands Indies, 1942.

it was "awful tiresome waiting." However, Bill Hennon had a feeling that they would be leaving on Friday. And Ray Thompson would be going out with them after all. Another of the "newies," Chester Trout, had come down with dengue fever and would be left behind in the hospital at Darwin. Now Thompson had a plane again—Trout's.[83] Hennon's guess proved correct. An order now came from ABDACOM headquarters on Java for Sprague's squadron to move to Soerabaja, eastern Java, via Koepang on Timor and Waingapoe on Soemba Island. They were to depart Darwin on January 23. They were *not* to proceed to Kendari, ABDACOM emphasized, although that location was originally intended as their new base. A Japanese invasion force had evidently been sighted heading south from Manado in the Peleng Straits, its destination clearly Kendari.[84]

Early on the morning of Friday, January 23, Sprague and his thirteen remaining pilots walked over to the flight line and climbed into their P-40Es for the long flight to their first stop, Koepang. They would go in two flights of seven ships each, with Sprague leading off with Kiser, Hennon, Rowland, Gilmore, Neri, and Stauter, and with Coss following behind with Dale, Kruzel, Blanton, Irvin, McCallum, and Thompson.[85] Pappy Gunn was there on the field, too, in his old Beech 18, prepared to lead the group to its destination. Flying with him were three of the 17th's crew chiefs—with their toolkits—who had been with Gunn since leaving Amberley, taken along to take care of any maintenance needs of the squadron's P-40s. The original plan had been for Gunn to navigate for Sprague's flight only, with a B-17 to lead Coss's flight, but there was no B-17 available at Darwin for Coss's group. Gunn would now need to lead both flights.[86]

Sprague's pilots were anxious about flying 540 miles nonstop over waters known to them to be among the most shark infested in the world. To increase their range in case of difficulty, each ship was carrying a fifty-two-gallon external belly tank under its fuselage. But they knew that there were no provisions for air/sea rescue should they go down in the Timor Sea.[87]

It was about 0800 when Sprague led off his flight into the calm sky, followed shortly afterwards by Coss and his six pilots. As prearranged, they had taken off using the fuel of their internal fuselage tank first and would switch to the belly tank until it was emptied, when they would switch back to the internal fuselage tank and the two wing tanks. At the agreed altitude they formed a circle while getting into a rather wide spread-eagle formation to allow for easy flying over the long haul. Pointing his Beech in the direction of Timor, Gunn was up ahead of Sprague's group, with Coss's echelon following behind. As Cy Blanton looked around to see all the planes with him in formation, he had a good feeling, one of security.[88]

CHAPTER FOUR

"Second Lieutenants Are Expendable"

AT AMBERLEY FIELD, GEORGE PARKER and fourteen fellow pilots of the *Polk* group received some welcome news on the morning of Tuesday, January 20. They were being ordered to Lowood Field, some fifteen miles northwest of Amberley, for a few days of extensive combat and tactical training. After-wards they would be going north to the combat zone.[1] That afternoon Parker took up one of the newly assembled P-40s for an hour, the first time he'd been in one in almost two months. To Parker, "it felt really good to sit in that old cockpit again and feel that powerful engine pull you into the sky."

Some of the others, including Butch Hague—also selected for the Lowood detail—were up also and flying P-40s for the first time that day. Even Bryce Wilhite finally got to go up in a plane, albeit not a P-40. Lt. Bob Ruegg of the 27th Bomb Group offered him a ride in one of the newly assembled A-24s that Ruegg was test flying. With Wilhite in the back seat, Ruegg took the dive bomber around the nearby city of Ipswich for half an hour and then went out near Amberley Field for a practice dive, a frightening experience for the nov-ice pursuiter.[2]

But for the others at Amberley not picked to go to Lowood or offered A-24 rides, the routine at the field continued, mainly involving uncrat-ing and assembling P-40s in the heat of the Australian summer. Vern Head was ordered to report to headquarters building for duty as personnel officer, despite knowing nothing about personnel administration.[3]

That evening eight newly arrived pursuiters, along with eight crew chiefs and eight armorers, reported in at Amberley. They had left San Francisco on December 27 on the transport *Mormacsun* for the Philippines but had been diverted to Sydney, Australia. When they reached Sydney on January 18, however, the ship could not be unloaded of its sixty-seven P-40Es and one C-53 because of a dock strike. It then moved up the coast to Brisbane, arriving on January 20. The pilots and their crews spent that night in Brisbane before moving out to Amberley the next day.[4] One of the eight, David Latane, had been assigned to Selfridge Field after graduating in 41-G at Maxwell Field, Alabama, and had gotten in six and one-half hours in P-40s before being transferred on December 17 to Moffett Field, California. A week later he was ordered to sail for the Philippines. Another of the group, Dick Suehr, along with the six others, had been ordered to the Philippines from the 8th Pursuit Group at Mitchel Field, New York, where they had been assigned following graduation on October 31 in the class of 41-H at Craig Field, Selma, Alabama.[5]

The next day Wilhite was up again, once more in an A-24. This time Gus Kitchen—one of the 41-H casual pilots off the *Holbrook* selected for A-24 training—was the pilot. Kitchen flew on the right wing of a three-ship element. It was the roughest ride Wilhite had ever experienced. After climbing to ten thousand feet in the bumpy air, and with difficulty keeping in formation, Kitchen cruised out over the ocean and dived on a target picked by the element leader. When Kitchen pulled out of the dive after passing over the target, blood poured from Wilhite's nose; his head felt as if "a small charge of explosives has been set loose in it." After several more dives, Kitchen was obliged to take Wilhite back. "The hospital says I'll be all right, but that I wasn't built for a dive bomber," he recorded in his diary that day.[6]

As one of the fortunate ones selected for the Lowood training, George Parker was not reduced to accepting offers to fly back seat in an A-24 for flying experience. Up at 0400 and following a preflight check of his P-40E, he joined several others for two and one-half hours of practicing "scooting through clouds" and maneuvers. On landing, he and the other Lowood bunch were ordered to pack in preparation for leaving at 1300. They rushed to pack their foot lockers and supply boxes to leave behind for storage; only necessities were allowed for the trip. It was 1500 before they climbed into their ships for the short hop to Lowood.[7]

"Powdered dust six inches deep all over the place and a hot wind" greeted them as they climbed out of their ships at the RAAF primary flight training school field. They found that it was still under construction. To Hague it was "a hell of a place." Nor were their accommodations ideal. The floor was "powdered dirt," and the roof was a tent, with cots as beds. To Al Dutton it was "the worst place yet," but "at least we have plenty of cold beer." And Hague felt the dinner in the officer's mess that night was "surprisingly good—mutton and pumpkin."[8]

· Old Philippines hand Gerry Keenan was running the three-day practice for the fifteen pilots. They would be flying the eleven P-40s brought over from Amberley, but with more on the way. Keenan explained to Hague and the others that he wanted to give them "a minimum of 2,000 rounds of shooting" before they left. But Hague felt that was a "lot of hooey . . . the barrels of the .50 caliber guns are only good for 2,000 rounds and there are no spare ones."[9]

The next day—Thursday, January 22—the training program began in earnest. The morning was devoted to discussing combat missions and techniques. A flight schedule was also drawn up.[10] After the ground instruction, the Lowood selectees went up for their first formation flying practice, "a rat race that was just a little upsetting," in Hague's view. They went into slow rolls, loops, 100 mph climbs, and dives over Lowood Field.[11]

Just after coming out of a dive, Hague was doing a slow roll over the field with the others—his first ever in a P-40E. Barely avoiding a crash, he scared the daylights out of the others watching on the field, who were running all over. Managing to get back on the field in one piece, he found the fire truck and ambulance waiting for him. A terrified Pete Childress rushed up to him and begged him not to do it again. Others around him watching Hague's performance had heard their CO, 1st Lt. William Lane, exclaim, "He isn't going to pull out!" For his performance, Hague was given the lowest score for the dive. "I can see that things are going to be exciting whether we get into fighting or not," Hague confided to his diary.[12]

Jim "Hambone" Hamilton didn't get off as easily this first day. While taxiing his ship, the 41-E graduate "got stuck in a dirt pile." Pushing the throttle a bit too far, he nosed his No. 88 over into the ground, ruining the propeller and putting the ship out of commission until a new prop could be installed.[13] Then later in the afternoon, Parker's ship was put out of service. While helping him gas his plane—"old 91"—Roger Williams accidentally dropped a nozzle cap into the fuselage tank. Parker would have to fly the ship back to Amberley to have the cap removed from his tank.[14] After arriving back at Amberley, Parker reported in to Buzz Wagner and told him the bad news. Wagner didn't like it one bit. "We have no time for carelessness," he barked at Parker. That night, a subdued Parker slept on an extra bunk in Paul Gambonini's room. He was happy to see his friends at Amberley again.[15]

The following day—his twenty-sixth birthday—Gambonini tested a newly assembled P-40E and put some slow time on the engine to run it in, then went back to the shop to help assemble some others. His buddy Parker waited around at the field until the cap had been removed from his gas tank, then took off at 1530 for Lowood, arriving back at 1700.[16]

Parker missed the tragic event that occurred at Amberley an hour and a half after he left. At 1700, after two hours of formation flying, Lieutenant Lane was leading a six-ship flight from Lowood in for a landing at Amberley. He informed his young pilots on the radio that he wanted them all on the ground in fifty-foot intervals, landing in train. This would be the "rapid landing" part of the practice of rapid takeoff and landing that Lane was putting the inexperienced young pilots through this day to prepare them for combat conditions. On Lane's wing was Hamilton, with Jim Morehead behind in the second element, Roger Williams on his wing. Butch Hague was leading the third element, and Pete Childress was his wingman.[17]

Hague watched ahead as Lane came in for a normal landing. Behind Lane, on his last leg, Jim Hamilton made an ess turn, obliging Morehead to follow, bringing him even closer—up to fifty feet—to Hamilton. Hague watched as Hamilton landed, then nosed over his ship for some reason Hague didn't understand. Then he saw Morehead land and run into Hamilton "prop first."[18] In Morehead's own recollection, he landed and rolled a few yards when suddenly he saw the wingtips of Hamilton's P-40E out both sides of his cockpit. Morehead jammed full rudder as hard as he could, and his ship veered hard left. But Hamilton was exiting his ship from the left side of his cockpit. Morehead's right wing slashed through the tail of Hamilton's P-40, and his propeller caught Hambone. "In a terrible tangle of wings, tails, and engines, flying parts, sparks, and grinding metal, the skidding planes finally stopped," he recalled. Morehead released his safety belt and leapt out to dash to Hamilton, only to find his body "in pieces, spurting blood and jerking convulsively."[19]

On the field, Vern Head and Bryce Wilhite witnessed what transpired closer up than had Hague. To them it seemed that the first P-40's landing gear had collapsed after the pilot touched down. They saw him standing on the wing after climbing out of the cockpit, evidently to examine the damage to his ship, when the P-40 behind him came in on a low approach and slammed into him, knocking him a big distance from his plane. Wilhite speculated that the pilot had been so absorbed in his own activity that he had forgotten about the other plane coming in behind him. After the collision, the pilot who had hit him got out of his own ship and appeared to Head to be trying to lift his own plane, evidently thinking the pilot who took the blow was caught under it.[20]

Overhead, seeing that the runway was now blocked by the two wrecked P-40s, Hague circled for a while, then led his wingman, Childress, in on another runway for a normal landing. As he climbed out of his ship, Hague was sure that no one had been hurt in the collision he'd witnessed from a distance. But then Paul May ran up to him and held out his hand. "This is what is left of Ham," he exclaimed, showing Hague a handful of brains. Outraged over May's lack of sensitivity, Hague yelled at him to "get the hell out of my way" and headed over to see how Morehead's wingman was reacting to the accident. He found that Williams was taking it "much better than I expected."[21]

In a state of acute shock, Morehead was taken to the base hospital and given morphine to sedate him. He explained that he had been unable to see straight ahead on coming in to land because of the high attitude of the nose of the P-40E on the low approach. Only just before ramming Hamilton's ship did he see it and try to avoid a collision.[22] Later in the day, Hague and others in his flight visited Morehead in the hospital. He was despondent. Yet another accident after those in California, including one in which the other pilot had been killed, too. He was sure the next time it would be he himself who was killed. "They'd better get me to the front before I kill myself," he blurted out to his mates.[23]

To Head, Hamilton's fatal accident was yet another example of the consequences of assembling the P-40s too fast. The Lowood fellows had told him that their planes were "coming apart." In particular, the landing gear of the ships was still causing problems.[24]

"Trouble seems to be dogging us," Parker felt the next day. Larry Landry—one of the most experienced pilots—had ground-looped his P-40E that morning and damaged a wingtip. Then Al Dutton's plane had caught fire in flight near Lowood when a booster coil had short-sparked some splashing oil. Dutton made a forced landing and told everyone he "needed a drink." Jack Peres also made a forced landing at Fort Lytton, Brisbane, damaging his ship's undercarriage, wingtip, fuselage, and aileron.[25]

In the afternoon "everyone who wanted to" was given permission to go to Hamilton's funeral in Brisbane. Parker and the other Lowood detachment pilots wanted to go but had "no way of making it into Brisbane"—that is, except for the unstoppable Hague.[26] To Bryce Wilhite "such losses are hard to take." He thought of what Colonel Johnson—the CO of Base Section 3—had said in his presence a day or two before: "Second Lieutenants are expendable." Angered, Wilhite responded sharply, looking the old infantry colonel in the eye: "Everything is expendable in time of war, Colonel." Johnson didn't appreciate the quick retort.[27]

OUT OVER THE VAST TIMOR SEA at thirteen thousand feet on the morning of Friday, January 23, Capt. Bud Sprague was leading his two-flight formation of fourteen P-40Es west from Darwin in the direction of Timor, flying on the wing of Pappy Gunn, who was navigating for them in his Beech 18. Each pilot was listening carefully to his P-40's droning Allison engine, attentive to any little noise that might not be normal. They were also estimating the time left before their external belly tanks would become empty of the fifty-two gallons of aviation gas they carried. There was no fuel gauge for the external tank, so timing was the only way to know how much fuel was left. And now was about the time for the tank to be running dry and to switch to the fuselage tank.[28]

Suddenly Cy Blanton heard his buddy Joe Kruzel calling excitedly on the radio to Sprague. He was telling his CO that his engine had quit, and although he realized his belly tank had run dry and he had switched to the internal tank, it hadn't restarted. Already he'd lost a thousand feet of altitude. Then abruptly, while still talking to Sprague, his engine caught again. "A little embarrassed," but relieved, he told Sprague he was okay. His eyes fixed on Kruzel's descending ship, Blanton was also relieved to see it stop dropping and fly normally again.[29]

Towards noon Gunn and Sprague led the flights down to Penfui Airdrome at Koepang for an uneventful landing, and their apprehension about flying 540 miles over water ended. However, one of the fourteen—Ben Irvin in Coss's flight—was not feeling well. It appeared he was coming down with dengue fever. On top of it, his ship was out.[30] After discussing the situation, Sprague decided that Irvin should remain behind. Sprague's own flight would continue on towards Java that afternoon, but Coss's group would remain at Koepang overnight and leave the following morning. Coss would arrange to have Irvin hospitalized. Cpl. Angelo Prioreschi—one of the crew chiefs flying in Gunn's Beech—would also remain behind to work on Irvin's plane.[31]

After refueling, Sprague led his seven-plane flight off, Pappy Gunn again navigating for them as they continued to head west. The hop to Waingapoe on Soemba Island was a short one, only 240 miles over the Savu Sea. On landing at the rough field, they were met by two Dutch officers, who offered them "excellent hospitality." They met a local native king, and the natives sang songs as they ate by candlelight. But unfortunately the swarms of mosquitoes were less kindly—Gilly Gilmore was hit with dengue fever, as Irvin had been.[32]

The next morning, although feeling woozy, Gilmore wanted to continue on with the rest of Sprague's flight to Soerabaja. But on takeoff his P-40E blew a tire. He would remain behind as his comrades took off for the final 530-mile leg of the Koepang–Soerabaja flight. Pappy Gunn would fly back to Koepang to send a message to Darwin to send up a new tire.[33]

Later in the day, back at Koepang, in response to Gunn's radio call to Darwin, Capt. Louis Connelly arrived with a new tire for Gilmore's ship. After loading the tire in his Beech, Gunn took off at the head of Coss's flight—minus Irvin—for Waingapoe. Out over the water they were all keeping a sharp eye out for Japanese. Gunn had told them he'd seen a four-engine flying boat over Soemba Island on the way back to Koepang that morning.[34] Landing at Waingapoe Field in late afternoon, Gunn dropped off the tire, which was then put on Gilmore's ship. Despite his dengue fever, Gilmore would be going out with Coss's flight the next morning for Soerabaja. He refused to remain in that isolated place longer than necessary.[35]

Early the next morning—Sunday, January 25—the sun and heat began beating down on the pursuiters' shack. It was time to be on their way to Java. Gilmore and his No. 5 were now ready for the long flight. Leaving Waingapoe behind, Coss's men flew along the northern coast of Soemba Island, then climbed to a higher altitude for the flight over the beautiful, crystal blue waters. Approaching Soembawa Island to the northwest, they descended to get a better look at the mountainous countryside. Then the island of Lombok loomed ahead as they continued at low altitude, not only to take in the sights but also to avoid being spotted by any patrolling Japanese airplanes. Next was Bali and its rice paddies, shrines, and temples built high up in the mountains. Looking out from his cockpit, Blanton thought he'd better take in the beautiful scenery now; God only knew if he would ever see it again.

As he crossed with the others over eastern Java and approached the big city of Soerabaja, Blanton was struck by the distinctive red tile roofs everywhere he looked. Then they saw the big airfield ahead of them and came in for a normal landing. Disembarking after having taxied their ships to the parking area pointed out to them, they were met by Sprague and the others in his flight, who had arrived early the afternoon before from Waingapoe.[36] Sprague and the others showed Coss's group where they would take their lunch each day that they were in Soerabaja and where the sleeping quarters— "proper bunks"—were located. But they were hoping that they wouldn't be there very long. The schedule was for them to move to their "own real base" this day, but there would be a delay, they found out.[37]

Together with Maj. Dick Legg, a fellow West Pointer who had flown in to Soerabaja on January 23 from FEAF headquarters outside Bandoeng, West Java, and Marine Corps Capt. Willard Reed, detached to the 17th Pursuit that same day, Sprague had surveyed possible fields for his squadron's operations on the day of his arrival in Soerabaja, January 24. Of the two candidates, the threesome agreed to pick the one just outside the small East Java town of Ngoro, forty miles to the southwest of Soerabaja. But the field was "not ready for them yet," Sprague told his squadron mates on his return to Soerabaja the same day.[38]

The thirty-two-year-old Legg had arrived in Java on January 19 in a B-17E on orders to report to General MacArthur in the Philippines. However, FEAF headquarters had other ideas for his services: to start up an operational pursuit school in Brisbane. Legg was an experienced pursuit pilot, a 1935 graduate of flying school. But first the FEAF's newly appointed operations officer, Lt. Col. Emmett "Rosie" O'Donnell, recently arrived himself from the Philippines, wanted Legg to go to Soerabaja to help Sprague identify a location for his 17th Pursuit.[39]

Also thirty-two years old and a pilot, Reed—nicknamed "Jess" after boxer Jess Willard—had been sent to Sprague to help with the 17th's operations. He was very familiar with Java conditions, having helped train Dutch navy pilots in Soerabaja on Ryan STMs bought from the United States until war's outbreak, when the flying school was closed. Now free for other assignments, the Harvard-educated Reed was considered ideal to assist Sprague in his Java aerial defense assignment.[40]

ON SUNDAY, JANUARY 25, George Parker and others of the Lowood detail were worrying about not being paid and lack of news on their assignment to go north after the Lowood training. Five of them—Al Dutton, Winfred Gallienne, Larry Landry, Roger Williams, and Parker—decided to hop over to Amberley Field to sort out their situation.[41]

Their decision bore instant fruit. First Lt. William Lane informed them that a flight of twenty-five would be leaving for Port Moresby in the next two days. Lane had picked the twenty-five, and they included Parker and the other four, much to their satisfaction. Parker would be flying in Paul Gambonini's six-ship flight along with Gene Bound, Tommy Hayes, Marion Fuchs, and Connie Reagan, "a bunch of good boys," in Parker's estimation.[42]

Lane had received his orders the day before from Brereton. He was to form immediately a unit designated the 20th Pursuit Squadron (Provisional) and prepare it for immediate movement north to Port Moresby via Townsville and Cairns. The first movement would be of eighteen P-40Es, with the second of the remaining seven ships when they were off the assembly lines, expected momentarily. Lane was authorized to draw on all personnel in the Brisbane area to meet the requirements of twenty-five pilots, twenty-five crew chiefs, twenty-five armorers, three radiomen, and a line chief, with all the enlisted men to be those off the *Polk*. Two C-53 transports would be at his disposal to carry the enlisted men, supplies, and equipment, thirty days' rations, and six hundred thousand rounds of .50-caliber ammunition. The C-53s would also serve as navigation aids the five hundred miles over the Coral Sea between Cairns and Port Moresby.[43]

"Port Moresby?" Lane wondered. This meant that he would not be joining Sprague's 17th Pursuit (Provisional) on Java, but instead would be helping defend the Australian field on the south coast of Papua New Guinea. His orders were to "lend the maximum defense of Port Moresby area against enemy attacks from the air, land, and sea." While he was to coordinate all operations with the commanding officer of the RAAF station there, he would "maintain tactical and operational control of the squadron and order missions accordingly."[44]

With a free hand in selecting the pilots for his squadron, Lane opted to choose all but four from Hamilton Field's 20th and 35th Pursuit Groups that went out on the *Polk* with him, including ten from his own 35th Group. The other four he selected were also former 35th Group pilots, the two most senior pilots off the *Republic*—Hubert Egenes and Dwight Muckley—and two of the relatively more experienced 41-E *Republic* pilots originally assigned to the 17th: George Hynes and Dave Coleman.[45] The day before, Lane had picked Parker Gies for his squadron, too. The Philippines veteran had returned to Amberley on January 23 from Rockhampton following his accident there on January 16 that removed him from the 17th Pursuit's flight to Darwin. But now he learned that he would not be going with Lane after all—"no reason given." A disgruntled Gies couldn't figure out why. None of those Lane had selected—nor Lane himself—had combat experience against the Japanese or flown under tropical weather conditions as Gies had.[46]

The following day Lane received an additional order from Brereton. Because of limited servicing facilities at the refueling points of his flight, as well as poor weather conditions in the New Guinea vicinity, movement of his aircraft from Brisbane to Port Moresby would be in flights of nine aircraft each. He was also to use the two C-53s accompanying his squadron to the best advantage in escorting the P-40s from Cairns to Port Moresby. Lane now figured that since he had only eighteen P-40s at his disposal at this time, and these were the ones to be sent out as soon as possible per his earlier orders, this new instruction meant he would be leaving in two flights of nine ships each.[47]

During the day the newly assigned pilots of the 20th Pursuit Provisional attended meetings and discussions about tactical matters. Twenty-four-year-old RAAF ace Flt. Lt. Peter St. George Turnbull passed on "many valuable hints and suggestions" to the highly receptive Americans based on his recent experience flying Gladiator biplanes, Hurricanes, and P-40Bs in the North African campaign until he was sent home after an accident. Pending his next squadron assignment, Turnbull had been designated chief test pilot at Amberley, and Gies would be serving under him.[48]

The pilots of the 20th spent the rest of January 26 checking out their newly assigned ships for the imminent trip north, now scheduled for the next day. Parker was given No. 72 and spent all his spare time checking it over with his crew chief: "loading guns, checking gauges, fittings and engine operation."

Bob McWherter did the same for his No. 96. He would be flying wing to Winfred "Bill" Gallienne in fourth position in the four-ship flight. He found that only two of his six .50-caliber guns were operative, but "what the hell, two ought to be enough," he figured. Al Dutton in No. 79 would be flying wing to Andy Reynolds. He had a heart and dagger painted on his ship's tail. B. J. Oliver had spent twenty minutes flight testing his No. 89 after getting his last tetanus shot.[49]

At 0500 on Tuesday, January 27, thirteen pilots with Lane at the head were down at the field, ready to start out. However, looking skyward, they were worried. The weather was overcast with a low ceiling of six hundred feet only. Lane was hesitant to take off. But finally at 0800, despite the weather conditions, he taxied onto the field and lifted off, his men following behind.[50] The flight headed inland first, but even there they found the ceiling was barely over a thousand feet. The formation then turned and headed east for the coast. At that point Paul Gambonini peeled off; his engine had conked out. Anxious for his flight leader, Parker broke off and followed Gambonini down, "praying he would make it back to Amberley."[51] Parker then rejoined the formation. When Lane's squadron reached the coast, the weather was really closing in. To Hague it seemed that Lane "became pretty frightened." Coming down through the overcast, flying on Lane's wing, Hague had to "peel up suddenly" when Lane ran into the same cloud with him. At that point Lane decided to abort the flight and made a 180-degree turn to lead the formation back to Amberley.[52]

On the field the rest of the squadron's pilots and other unassigned pilots were surprised to see twelve of the ships coming back only thirty minutes after takeoff, followed later by Gambonini alone. To Gies, also watching, "the return and formation was horrible." He was "dubious about the success of this outfit."[53] The disheartened 20th Pursuiters spent the rest of the day waiting for the weather to clear. Unassigned Vern Head felt that the "late and poor" weather forecasts were largely to blame for Lane's decision to take off, although he felt also that Lane was proving very indecisive as a commander, unsure what to do next. Lane finally cancelled the flight and told his men they would try again the following day.[54]

When Lane rousted his pilots out of bed early the next morning and told them to get breakfast and report to operations, the pilots saw that it was pouring rain. To Parker it seemed the weather was even worse than the day before, and reportedly it extended all the way up the coast to Townsville. Not wanting to repeat the fiasco of the day before, Lane told his "restless" pilots that they would not be flying that morning.[55] Conditions improved somewhat that afternoon, however, and the advance echelon took off again. But the weather over the mountains proved too bad to continue, and they returned to the field to spend the rest of the day on the ground. They would try again the next day.[56]

Later that day, Lane was surprised to receive new orders, forwarded to him from USAFIA headquarters in Melbourne. The deputy commander of ABDACOM on Java, Lt. Gen. George Brett, was ordering the 20th Pursuit (Provisional) to Java immediately. Port Moresby was out. Following up on this order, Brigadier General Barnes in Melbourne provided Lane with the details. His squadron would proceed immediately to Darwin, en route to Java, to await further instructions from Brett. Capt. Paul Davis in a B-24 would escort the flight to Darwin and also carry part of the squadron's supplies. The two C-53 supply and ground personnel transports that had flown to Townsville on January 26, to vainly await the arrival of the pilots, would now fly directly to Darwin—along with a B-18 similarly loaded.[57] So the 20th would be linking up with the 17th after all. And the two-day weather delay at Amberley was proving a blessing in disguise. What if they had been out over the Coral Sea on their way to Port Moresby instead?

AT 0830 ON MONDAY, JANUARY 26, Cpl. Angelo Prioreschi was in the hangar at Penfui airdrome, Koepang, trying to repair the P-40E that had been left behind by Ben Irvin in Walt Coss's flight. Since the afternoon of January 23 he'd been trying to fix the ship's hydraulic leak while Irvin was in the hospital in Koepang with dengue fever.[58] Suddenly, machine gun bullets fired by strafing aircraft began tearing into the hangar. Irvin's terrified crew chief "ran around that hangar like a chicken, trying to dodge those bullets," he later related. During the fifteen minutes of the attack, Prioreschi managed to avoid being hit himself, but Irvin's P-40E was perforated beyond repair.[59]

Earlier that morning two RAAF DC-2s carrying twenty-two of Prioreschi's comrades—crew chiefs and armorers of the 17th Pursuit—had taken off from the field ahead of the arrival of the strafers. They had arrived from Darwin on January 24, but bad weather held them on the field for two days. After a stop at Bali, where they had a Hershey bar lunch, Australian Flight Officers Noel Webster and John Bonnington finally touched down that afternoon at Perak Field, Soerabaja. After they disembarked, Dutch women gave them little sandwiches and coffee.[60]

Bud Sprague and the other 17th Pursuiters were relieved to see their enlisted men safely arrived after their long flight. Sprague had learned of the strafing attack on Penfui Field after they had left in a radiogram he received that afternoon from Irvin: "From Irvin. My fighter on ground [sic] by machine gun fire. Ask leave to go to Darwin to get a new plane. Ask transport as soon as possible to Soerabaya for my crew chief. Answer immediately." Sprague did reply immediately: "To Irvin [Koepang, Timor]. Utilize RAAF transportation to return to Darwin. Bring crew chief and salvageable parts. Wait at Darwin for transportation to Soerabaya."[61]

Since arriving in Soerabaja, Sprague had been busy coordinating his new activities with two liaison officers with whom he would be working closely. His old friend Capt. Frank Kurtz of Philippine days had met him on arrival and informed him of his liaison job at Soerabaja for Col. Eugene Eubank, commander of the 5th Bomber Command and ranking USAAF tactical officer on Java. Kurtz was impressed with Sprague's "can do" attitude—"jumping, like a greyhound on a leash or a welterweight waiting for the bell." An important part of Kurtz's liaison work would be to help get Sprague's pilots settled in their intended new base at Ngoro.[62]

In practical matters related to his new Dutch hosts, however, the main assistance Sprague would receive would be provided by a twenty-six-year-old Dutch army reserve infantry officer assigned to the KNILM who at war's outbreak had asked for an assignment to an active base. Posted to the flight school at Tasikmalaja, Lt. Arie Geurtz, in response to his request, was sent to the No. 2 Squadron, Air Group IV (2-Vl.G.-IV), at Tandjoeg Perak Airfield as general duty officer. Responsible for hosting Sprague's personnel arriving there, the acting squadron commander, 1st Lt. Willem Bedet, then assigned Geurtz—married to an American and fluent in Dutch, English, and the Javanese language—as liaison officer to the 17th Pursuit. He would arrange for the Americans' housing, meals, transport, and other housekeeping requirements at their new base.[63]

Sprague's executive officer, Walt Coss, was in a similar situation related to practical needs for flying operations in order to allow Sprague to be free to take care of his pressing command and liaison responsibilities. Now Sprague was asking him to fly down to Ngoro to see what progress the Dutch were making in final preparations for the 17th's occupancy of the field. Lt. Bedet, with another Dutch pilot in a two-seat civilian biplane, would guide Coss in his P-40E to the highly camouflaged, hidden field. Bedet had borrowed from a local flying club a DeHaviland Tiger Moth painted in bright red, making it easy for Coss to follow it.[64]

After takeoff from Perak Field, Coss easily followed the highly visible Dutch biplane in a southwesterly direction forty miles towards the town of Djombang, then turned due south some twelve miles to Ngoro. But over the stated location of the field he couldn't make out any field below. Still, the Tiger Moth was descending lower and lower over the area, then it touched down and rolled forward. As Bedet taxied his ship back and parked off to the side, Coss realized that this was a marker for him. The biplane was very visible to him as he lined himself up for his landing approach. Still, he was having a hard time convincing himself that he should land into the solid-looking bushes that evidently served as camouflage for the field. But he bit the bullet and came in for a perfect landing on the bushes, which folded down as he passed over them, then snapped right back up behind him.[65]

As he looked around the field after climbing out of his ship, Coss was amazed at the "masterpiece of camouflage" the Dutch had created. The T-shaped field with north/south and east/west runways about two thousand feet long each had been made in an old sugar cane field, he was informed. Javanese laborers had made it look as much like the surrounding rice paddies as possible by digging very small ditches crisscross over the field and placing small lines of bushes about three to four feet high in the ditches. Several dummy roads—coats of tar about the width of a road—were made across the field. From the air, the field looked like a group of rice paddies with a small road running through them.[66]

With his two Dutch associates Coss walked over the area, examining the maintenance and parking areas the Dutch had prepared. He also checked out the surface condition of the field, the possibility of enlarging the runways, the arrangements for dispersing the P-40s, possibilities for ground defense, and the cover and storage for fuel dumps. He also looked at the condition of the road leading from the field to the village of Blimbing a few miles away where the officers and the men would be staying. The decision had been made not to house them at the field, but rather at the village, because any large structures at Ngoro Field would have drawn the attention of Japanese aircraft to the existence of the secret field.[67] After something over an hour, Coss climbed back into his No. 15 and headed down the runway. He felt the strip was somewhat short for takeoff, but he managed without difficulty. Now he would report back to Sprague that in his view the field was about ready for their ships.[68]

Following his assignment as liaison officer for the 17th Pursuit, Arie Geurtz had been very busy driving the jeep assigned to him back and forth between Soerabaja and the site that had been selected for the living quarters of the squadron's personnel. Blimbing was a logical choice because of its nearness and availability of housing. Its inhabitants were mainly employees—Dutch and Javanese—of the sugar mill located ten miles away in the small town of Modjokerto who had been evacuated earlier from their houses to make room for the Americans. Geurtz now had to ensure that the houses were ready for occupancy. He also had to arrange for meals to be prepared for them, including a lunch to be taken to the field. But there were other time-consuming

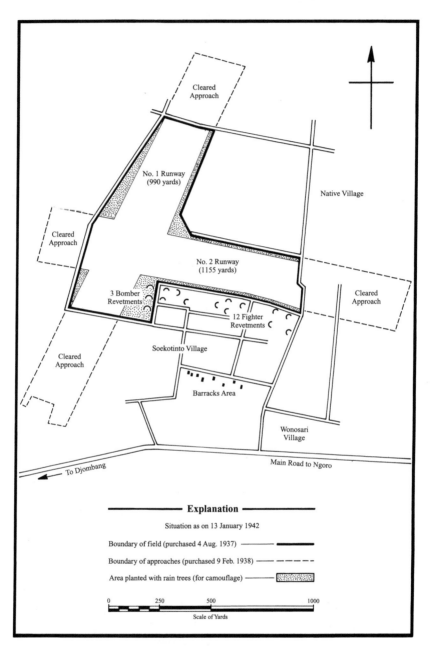

Ngoro (Djombang South) Airfield, Java, January 1942. *Redrawn from "History of the 5th Air Force," Vol. 2, Documents, AFHRA.*

tasks to take care of, too, such as arranging for laundry services, mail delivery, and provision of supplies.[69]

With arrangements at Ngoro and Blimbing now almost completed, Sprague informed his pilots and enlisted men on Tuesday, January 27, that they probably could move to their new base in three days, on Friday. In the meantime, the pilots would continue remaining on alert at Perak and flying occasional missions to investigate unidentified planes as ordered by the Dutch air defense control in Soerabaja.[70]

This day Sprague was presented with an unusual request from Frank Kurtz. On a visit to the nearby Dutch navy headquarters, Commander Van der Straaten had come running up to Kurtz with a plea for help. One of his submarines—K XVIII—had been crippled by depth charges after its attack on a Japanese warship off Borneo and left unable to dive. It was making its way slowly back to Soerabaja, but the two Dutch PBYs that had been protecting it had come under attack by two Zeros. Could Sprague's P-40s keep the Zeros at bay and escort the submarine in?[71] True to form, Sprague accepted the mission and led a six-ship flight toward the area indicated by Van der Straaten. But the weather proved very bad, and the flight had trouble locating the submarine. Then Sprague received a message that the submarine was no longer in danger and that he could return to Perak.[72]

The request from the Dutch navy was the exception to the rule. The 17th Pursuit was subordinate to the Dutch Air Defense Command (ADC) at Soerabaja. It was the ADC that was authorized to order it out on missions, which tended to be to check out unidentified aircraft flying in East Java airspace. On one such mission flown while the squadron was on its daily alert, the intruding aircraft turned out to be one of the American B-17s based at Singosari, near the city of Malang to the south.[73]

On a visit to the bomb-proof building of ADC headquarters on January 25, Sprague and Maj. Dick Legg—still then in Soerabaja on his FEAF headquarters assignment—were shown the operations, headed up by Col. H. J. Ente van Gils, an artillery officer, that covered East Java. The Dutch explained to them that they had a large number of ground observation stations connected by telephone to the filter room, where information received was filtered before being placed on a large gridded map in the operations room. The spotters reported sightings and gave the number of aircraft, approximate altitude, direction of flight, and general type of aircraft. With such information the ADC would order interceptors sent straight to the approaching intruders, citing a coordinate rather than a map reference. Once Sprague's squadron was established at Ngoro Field, the ADC would communicate its interception orders by telephone on the special military ABDAIR line, which was considered secure.[74]

Sprague was unimpressed. In his estimation it was a very primitive operation inferior to that which had been in operation in the Philippines at the beginning of the war. That one used warnings by SCR-270B radar instead of native spotters. As operations officer of the 5th Interceptor Command, he had been intimately familiar with its operations. Sprague preferred to work closely with Bedet's squadron, also at the receiving end of the ADC's questionable orders. Sprague and his fellow pursuiters were all impressed with the enthusiasm of the Dutch pilots, unchecked despite their knowledge that the Japanese were steadily moving step by step towards Java. A spirit of good will and friendship had sprung up between Sprague's and Bedet's men.[75]

One day Sprague had asked Bedet if his squadron's pilots could take his twelve pilots up on a familiarization tour of the geography of East Java. The Dutchman readily agreed. It was arranged that each of the twelve Dutch CW-21B pilots would take off with one of Sprague's men on his wing and would hold his climbing speed down to that of the struggling P-40E's. Looking down from on high, the 17th Pursuiters were impressed with the landscape below, so mountainous in many places and flat and green elsewhere, mainly comprised of rice paddies. To the east of Malang and the Singosari base of the 19th Group's B-17s they saw a huge mountain—Mount Semeru, they were told—that reached up to some twelve thousand feet.[76]

In the evenings the Americans enjoyed the hospitality of a Dutch restaurant owner who spoke good English. He seemed thrilled to have them eat at his restaurant each night. The pilots particularly loved his steaks and fresh tomatoes. Then, after dinner, they would go out to night clubs for drinks. One night Jack Dale, Cy Blanton, and Joe Kruzel were with Ed Gilmore, and all got a bit drunk. The place this evening had an orchestra, and his accomplices had gotten Gilmore, a drummer in an orchestra before joining the Air Corps, to go up and ask to play the drums. Gilmore impressed the patrons with his alcohol-inspired performance.[77]

On Wednesday, January 28, Sprague met for the first time with the commander of 2-Vl.G.-IV, 1st Lt. Ricardo Anemaet, who was now rejoining his squadron and taking over from Bedet. It was clear to Sprague that the slender Anemaet was partly of Javanese ethnicity, a racial characteristic of many of the Dutch pilots. Sprague was impressed with his good command of the English language and his intelligence and took an instant liking to him.[78]

Apparently for the benefit of the American personnel, including the ground echelon of the 7th Bomb Group, arriving at Soerabaja port that day from Australia on the USAT *President Polk,* the 2-Vl.G.-IV pilots put on a

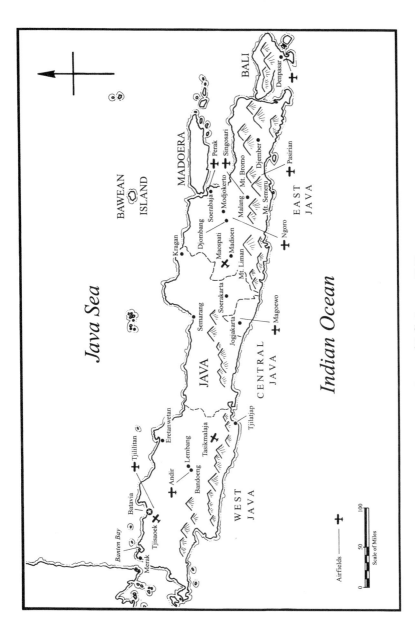

Java and Bali, January 1942.

spectacular aerial show with their Curtiss-Wright CW-21B interceptors. As the 17th Pursuiters at Tanjung Perak Field and the troops on the *President Polk* watched in awe, the brown and green–camouflaged Dutch ships with their big Wright Cyclone engine at the head of their narrow fuselage took off individually toward the center of the field from dispersed locations and "climbed like hell," straight up into the sky. After forming up, they dove onto the field in an attack string and, just before they should hit the ground, turned almost straight up in the air again. Then, a few thousand feet up, the string opened up in all directions, "like petals in a rose." Cy Blanton for one was "amazed" that they could get into formation so quickly from field positions. It was hard to avoid comparisons with their own heavy, slow-climbing P-40Es.[79]

The next day Sprague and Jess Reed paid a visit to Blimbing to check the status of living arrangements for the squadron. Four of his enlisted men were already staying there: crew chiefs Bernie Badura and Jim Collett and armorers Woody Myers and Ben Culpepper. Sprague had sent them ahead the day before by taxi as an advance detail. That evening Sprague and Reed were guests for dinner at the house of the manager of the sugar mill, a Mr. Smit. The four enlisted men were invited, too; they were staying in Smit's house. Smit had made the arrangements for his staff's houses to be taken over by the 17th's personnel.[80]

But one of Sprague's pilots would not be going with the squadron to their new home. Frank Neri was lying in the Dutch general hospital in Soerabaja following a bizarre accident that morning. Returning in a four-ship flight, aborted by bad weather, that Sprague had led on yet another ADC-ordered mission to check out unidentified aircraft, the Philippines veteran pulled his turn too tight coming in from the base leg to the approach leg and at that slow speed stalled enough to flip his ship at the end of the Perak runway. In the crash he hit his head against the P-40E's gunsight and suffered cuts on his face and head, but also had his right ear sliced off.[81]

As soon as Neri was removed from the cockpit and on the way to the hospital, it occurred to Cy Blanton, who was standing nearby, that here was his opportunity to obtain a clock to replace his own, which no longer was running. He figured that Neri's wrecked ship would never be put back in commission, and he might as well help himself to a spare part. Blanton climbed into the cockpit, screwdriver in hand, and succeeded in removing the clock. Then he noticed something out of the ordinary on the floorboard far towards the front of the cockpit. When he picked it up, he realized that it was Neri's severed ear.[82] With the clock in one hand and Neri's ear in the other, Blanton climbed out of the cockpit and headed for the 17th's operations shack to join the others having lunch. Smiling, he flipped the ear on the table with a word

CW-21Bs of the Netherlands East Indies Air Force 2-Vl.G.-IV Squadron lined up at Maospati Airfield, Madioen, in April 1941 before shifting to Perak Airfield, Soerabaja, in December 1941. *Courtesy Royal Netherlands Air Force, Historical Section.*

of explanation, an action that raised loud objections from his squadron mates. His little grotesque prank played out, Blanton picked up the offending item and proceeded to the toilet to flush it down. He hadn't given a thought to the possibility that it could possibly have been reattached to Neri's head.[83]

Blanton was correct in his assessment that Neri's ship would never be put back in commission. That afternoon the 17th's engineering officer, Bill Hennon, looked at the wreck and judged the P-40E to be "completely demolished." He ordered it stripped for usable parts. The 17th was now down to twelve P-40Es of its original seventeen.[84]

Two days later, on Saturday, January 31, Hennon took his own ship west to Maospati Field, near the large Dutch city of Madioen, where the KNIL-ML had its depot. It had been agreed five days earlier that the 17th would use the facilities there for repairing its own ships, too. On landing, the brakes on his P-40E went out, but Hennon managed to get them partially fixed. On return to Perak, however, they acted up again, and Hennon took his aircraft out of commission. On top of that, Joe Kruzel's ship had caught fire on the ground and was a total loss. Hennon had it stripped for spare parts, too.[85]

At Blimbing that day Bernie Badura and the other three of the 17th's advanced detail of crew chiefs and armorers welcomed the rest of their comrades as they were driven in at noon. They brought "lots of supplies" with them that the 17th would require at their isolated location.[86] The pilots were now scheduled to shift to the new base the next day. But with the loss of Kruzel's ship, they would be flying only eleven of their ships into Ngoro. The squadron's original aircraft strength had been depleted by more than a third through accidents and enemy action.[87]

PART THREE

"You Are Not Forgotten Men"

IN EARLY FEBRUARY 1942 the news coming out of ABDACOM at Lembang was still all bad. To Eisenhower in Washington, it appeared that "ABDA is desperate." Wavell was having to deal with five separate Japanese lines of attack: three against the Dutch East Indies (Amboina/Timor, Kendari/Makassar, and Balikpapan/Bandjermasin) plus Johore/Singapore in Malaya and Moulmein/Rangoon in Burma. In each thrust the Japanese were methodically and inexorably advancing behind overwhelming air support. The withdrawal into Singapore from Johore on mainland Malaya at the end of January, with no real possibility of reinforcing British Lt. Gen. Arthur Percival's troops, was particularly distressing to the ABDACOM commander.[1]

In the Dutch East Indies that was his immediate preoccupation, Wavell's naval striking force was proving too small to take on the Japanese invasion forces, and at any rate it was too risky for it to operate even a short distance from Java in the absence of air cover to protect it from Japanese bombers and fighters operating from nearby recently seized airfields. This point was brought home on February 4 when an attempt by Dutch Rear Adm. Karel Doorman's Combined Fleet to stop a Japanese invasion force heading for Makassar ended in disaster: the American cruisers *Marblehead* and *Houston* were badly damaged by Japanese land-based bombers. The ABDACOM commander was pinning his hopes on a buildup of his air power, with U.S. air reinforcements scheduled to arrive during the next few months, but he feared that the new Japanese threat to the key ferry stop for P-40s at Koepang might cut off his supply of American pursuit ships.[2]

Wavell's deputy air commander, Maj. Gen. Lewis Brereton—replaced as acting ABDAIR commander at the end of January on the arrival of British

Air Vice-Mshl. Sir Richard Peirse—was particularly concerned about the air situation on Java, where the Allied position was becoming "increasingly precarious," in his estimation. On February 3 a huge force of Japanese bombers and fighters flying out of bases at Balikpapan and Kendari had staged large-scale and devastating attacks on Soerabaja, Singosari, and Madioen in eastern Java in their first incursion into Java, then followed up two days later with a fighter sweep that finished off the Dutch interceptor force there.[3] His newly arrived provisional pursuit squadron at Ngoro had attempted interception both times, but too late to stop the attacks. A reinforcing pursuit squadron—the 20th Provisional—had been shot up badly on Bali by Zeros on its way to Ngoro from Australia. His bomber command at Singosari was in not much better shape, "battling against every conceivable obstacle," including bad weather, enemy attacks that destroyed its B-17s on the ground, inadequate equipment and personnel, and inferiority in numbers against those of the Japanese naval air force opposing it. To add to his woes, there was too much interference from other ABDACOM commands at Lembang, obliging him to shift his Far East Air Force (redesignated 5th Air Force on February 5) headquarters to the recently vacated Dutch military academy building in Bandoeng.[4]

WITH THE STEADY DETERIORATION in the situation to its north and northwest, the Australian government was becoming increasingly worried about the vulnerability of its Darwin base and other airfields on the northeast coast, a concern only heightened by the report on February 2 of Japanese carriers in the waters to the immediate east (that fortunately turned out to be false). But Wavell appeared more concerned about the weak defenses at Koepang than those of northern Australia, which had been added to his ABDA theater of operations on January 24. He had asked the Australian government to send an Australian Pioneer battalion at Darwin to Koepang (to accompany an American artillery battalion and antiaircraft guns). The Australian prime minister felt that would weaken Darwin's defenses further. However, apparently in exchange for Curtin's concurrence, the Combined Chiefs of Staff (CCS) in Washington agreed on February 4 to divert from ABDACOM to Australia's defense of its northeastern approaches a fighter group of eighty P-40s originally scheduled for the defense of Java but now to operate under command of the RAAF, albeit on a temporary basis only. Eisenhower, who had acceded to the Australian request, was hoping that the transfer "does some good."[5]

The USAFIA commander in Melbourne, Brig. Gen. Julian Barnes, immediately designated the 49th Pursuit Group as the unit to serve under the RAAF at Darwin. It had arrived at Melbourne on February 1 on the liner *Mariposa,* along with the 51st Pursuit Group on the USAT *Coolidge.* Barnes ordered the 51st Group, with its fifty-one crated P-40s from the two transports, to proceed to the NEI, with twenty-nine additional P-40s to be ferried to complete its complement of eighty aircraft. Twelve more P-40s were also to be ferried to the NEI as additional aircraft for the 17th Pursuit (Provisional) at Ngoro.[6]

On February 8 Barnes informed Brett that the February 4 CCS arrangement on diversion of a group to Australia had been revised the following day. The new directive established a rationing schedule for assignment of the P-40 squadrons between ABDACOM and Australia. Under this arrangement the first six squadrons organized were to go to ABDACOM, the seventh to Australia, the eighth and ninth to ABDACOM, the tenth and eleventh to Australia, and the twelfth to ABDACOM. This schedule thus still met the promise of a group (of three squadrons) for the defense of Australia.[7] Indeed, the seventh, tenth, and eleventh squadrons of the timetable, assigned to the 49th Pursuit Group, were already earmarked by Barnes for Darwin. The sixth, eighth, and ninth were squadrons of the 51st Group, selected to go to the Dutch East Indies. The first five squadrons of the timetable were the 17th and 20th, already in Java; the 3rd, which was on its way; and the 33rd and 13th, which were being formed for transfer to Java.

Evincing skepticism about ferrying P-40s by air to Java, Brett had asked Barnes on February 2 to indicate the earliest date the fifty-one crated P-40s off the *Coolidge* and *Mariposa* could reach Tjilatjap on southern Java for assembly in the NEI. Brett also mentioned the possible need to ship assembled P-40s on the seaplane tender USS *Langley* "and another carrier" and wanted to know where they could be loaded besides at Darwin.[8] When informed that crated P-40s could reach Java by February 25 and assembled P-40s could be loaded at Brisbane or Melbourne, Brett on February 7 ordered the fifty-one crated P-40s shipped by sea and assembled P-40s loaded instead at Perth in Western Australia.[9] Brett had given up on flying P-40s—and A-24s—from Darwin to Koepang because of the perceived inability of the antiaircraft defenses of the key Timor ferrying stop to permit entry by the Java-bound pursuit and dive bombers "at any time of day" and decided to suspend all such ferry flights.[10]

In ordering assembled P-40s to be transferred to Java on the *Langley,* Brett had not indicated if they were to be considered part of the 51st Group's totals or as reinforcements for the 17th Pursuit. Barnes assumed the latter and on February 6 had ordered the newly formed 33rd Pursuit (Provisional) to transfer its twenty-five P-40s on February 12 from Brisbane to "the combat zone" by the "first available transport." Its CO, Maj. Floyd Pell, understood those

USS *Langley* at Darwin about February 11, 1942, ordered south to Fremantle to take on board thirty-two P-40Es and their pilots for Java. *Courtesy David Vincent.*

orders to mean he was to fly his squadron's ships to Perth for boarding the *Langley* and to take sea transport to Java.[11] Earmarked also for Java under the CCS arrangement of February 4, the 13th Pursuit Squadron (Provisional), formed on February 10 under Capt. Boyd Wagner, was expected to join the 33rd Pursuit on the *Langley*'s voyage.[12]

On February 12 Brett, in a radiogram to Barnes in Melbourne, indicated the number of P-40s to be loaded on the *Langley* after it arrived in Fremantle from Darwin—"a full complement of P-40s" (or "32")—with "sufficient pilots and mechanics to fly the aircraft from the unloading location in the NEI." Two days later Brett followed up with an order to Barnes to have the thirty-two P-40s ready for loading on February 18, the date the *Langley* was expected to arrive in Fremantle.[13]

Although Barnes had presumed that the *Langley*'s P-40s were being sent to reinforce the 17th Pursuit at Ngoro, Brett had not actually indicated in his radiograms where in Java they were being sent, simply indicating they were "for the NEI." He had kept Barnes (and the COs of the 33rd and 13th Squadrons) in the dark because it was a highly secret matter. As deputy commander of ABDACOM, Brett had sent his February 12 radiogram following a meeting of ABDAIR staff at Bandoeng headquarters, where a new plan for the aerial defense of Java was discussed and approved. An important component was the assignment of two USAAF pursuit squadrons and their thirty-two P-40s to a new, hidden field at Tjisaoek, West Java, to the southwest of the capital of Batavia, that was being prepared for operations by the two squadrons.[14] Brett intended for the 33rd and 13th Pursuit Squadrons and their aircraft slated to board the *Langley* on February 18 to meet the ABDAIR requirement.

But in his February 12 radiogram Brett had also ordered Barnes to send two pursuit squadrons to Darwin, one for local protection and the other to provide escort for a convoy to Koepang and to provide cover for its unloading, then to remain at Koepang. (The convoy was to carry Australian and American troops ordered by Wavell to strengthen Koepang's defenses). With no other P-40 squadrons available to him at the time and the Darwin assignment indicated by Brett as top priority, Barnes had decided to designate the 33rd for the assignment, but with only fifteen of its ships. The 13th would make up the shortfall for the *Langley* transfer. To Barnes the new order seemed to contradict Brett's cable to him of the day before, in which he ordered no more P-40s or A-24s to depart Darwin for the NEI (though "until further orders").[15]

In accordance with Brett's orders, Barnes radioed Pell on the latter's arrival with his squadron's pilots at Melbourne on February 12. Halfway to its Perth destination, the 33rd was to be split up, with fifteen of its pilots to fly their P-40s due north to Darwin on February 14 from Port Pirie, their next refueling stop on the way to Perth.[16]

In the meantime, the officers and men of the 51st Pursuit Group had sailed from Melbourne for the Indies on February 12, first stop Fremantle, where they were expected to arrive on February 18 to coincide with the *Langley*'s arrival. The group's three tactical squadrons and its headquarters squadron were on board the transport *Willard Holbrook* and the Australian coastal liner *Duntroon,* together with the other Australian transport in the convoy, *Katoomba,* designated MS-5, which was carrying 10 of their crated P-40s. The American freighter *Sea Witch* was scheduled to leave Melbourne the following day with 27 other crated P-40s of the group. Of the 51 originally assigned P-40s that had arrived on the *Coolidge* and *Mariposa,* 14 had to be left behind for repairs, having arrived in damaged condition. Additional crated P-40s for the 51st to bring it up to its full complement of 80 were to be picked up in Melbourne by the British aircraft transport ship *Athene,* evidently from those to be unloaded there from the *Hammondsport,* which had been ordered to Melbourne from Brisbane by Barnes to discharge half its crated 111 P-40s that had arrived on February 4.[17]

But at ABDACOM headquarters Brereton was skeptical about the aircraft supply situation. In a meeting on February 8 with ABDACOM commanders, he took a pessimistic view about the chances for reinforcing his pursuit force.

He also opined that his bomber command would be ineffective by the end of March as a result of the losses it was suffering. Since the Malay Barrier could not be defended without a long-range striking force of heavy bombers, he was prepared to recommend to the War Department that the remnants of his air force be withdrawn from Java and sent to Burma or kept in Australia. According to Brereton, both Wavell and Brett criticized him afterwards for what they regarded as an "unwarranted and pessimistic attitude" on his part. Nevertheless, Wavell asked him to prepare and present an estimate of the situation.[18]

MAJ. GEN. HAP ARNOLD, chief of the Army Air Forces in Washington, was also worried about the Java situation and its effect on the morale of his officers and men there. On February 13 Brett received a cable from Arnold requesting Brett to distribute a message to each Air Force officer in the ABDA area. Arnold wanted to assure each one of them "that every effort is being made here to get you the tools you must have. You can be certain that you are not forgotten men, but are . . . a symbol driving each and every one on to higher speed."[19]

His pilots took the message with a degree of cynicism. They knew that the situation in the ABDA area was deteriorating rapidly. Two days later they heard that Singapore—the Far East bastion of the British Empire—had surrendered to the Japanese less than a week after the Japanese had crossed over from Johore after completing their seizure of the Malay peninsula. Even closer to home, they also learned that a Japanese invasion force had landed on south Sumatra and occupied its coveted oil refineries on the same day Singapore fell. It was obvious to Arnold's men—as well as to all the other ABDA personnel on Java—that they were next on the Japanese timetable of conquest.[20]

CHAPTER FIVE

"A Collection of the Worst Landings
I Have Ever Seen"

AT 0600 ON THURSDAY, JANUARY 29, a drowsy Jim Morehead climbed into
his P-40E at Amberley Field. There had been a big party the night before, and
Morehead and the others of the 20th Pursuit (Provisional) had gone to bed
late. Soon afterward, Morehead and his squadron mates took off, destination
Charleville, and lined up behind a B-24A mother ship. Soon they ran into a
heavy overcast with no openings, followed by heavy rain. That was enough
for Lt. Lane; once again the 20th Pursuit's CO decided to abort the flight and
bring it back to Amberley.[1]

In the early afternoon Lane decided to try again. The B-24A and a B-17
that had taken off to check the weather ahead were now back, circling over
the field to signal that the weather was okay. At 1330 Lane led off his flight
of thirteen and formed up behind the B-24A that would navigate for them,
then Lieutenant Muckley followed, leading off his flight of twelve to link up
behind the B-17 that would guide his group.[2]

Morehead, leading a group of four, droned on due west over miles of desolate, monotonous country in the direction of Charleville. The sun beating
down on his cockpit made him even drowsier than in the morning. He fell
asleep. Immediately, his ship "peeled off into a screaming dive," and the three
others followed him down. Going straight down, Morehead suddenly woke
up, grabbed the stick, and pulled out, as did the others behind him, wondering what was going on. Frequent thunderstorms kept Morehead alert the rest
of the way.[3]

It was 1630 when the two flights approached Charleville for landing. They
could see the field was nothing but a narrow dirt strip. Morehead landed early

B-24A serial no. 40-2370 at Amberley Field, January 29, 1942, just before leading P-40Es of the 20th Pursuit Squadron (Provisional) to Charleville on the first leg of their transfer to Java. *Courtesy Tom Wood via David Vincent.*

on and watched as the squadron's novice pilots were having difficulty getting their high-wing-loaded P-40Es down through the very hot, thin air over the field, many of them "slamming down hard." Also watching, Butch Hague felt it was "a collection of the worst landings I have ever seen."[4]

As B. J. Oliver was about to touch down, a crosswind blowing over the field caught his ship and tipped it to the side. Although his wing scraped the ground, he did not ground-loop. Another accident was avoided when Elwin Jackson managed to lower his landing gear manually. His generator had given out after takeoff from Amberley, forcing him to go over to manual controls in the absence of an electrical system.[5]

After the pursuiters parked their ships, they climbed out and headed for the gas dump. They would have to roll the fifty-five-gallon gas drums over to their ships themselves and fill their tanks by hand. It was a slow operation. Dave Coleman and others, feeling like "barnstormers," also took off their cowlings with a screwdriver to check for leaking oil, the only maintenance operation they knew how to do themselves. Les Johnsen, for one, wondered why there were no servicing arrangements and why there was indeed a general lack of organization for operations, despite the field's being under the control of the Army Air Forces.[6]

Butch Hague walked over to the old B-17C that was guiding them to talk to the crew. Its sides and belly were pitted with antiaircraft, machine gun, and cannon shell holes, over one hundred in all, Hague was told. The Philippines veteran—serial number 40-2072—had been shot up on a mission over Davao on December 25 and was now being used exclusively as a transport.[7]

It was not until about 2300 before the refueling of their twenty-four ships was completed and they headed into town to the small hotel where they would get something to eat and spend the night. Hague and Parker were surprised to find that they had been given the bridal suite, including a double bed with a mosquito net over it. They opted instead for beds on the veranda circling the building, on which the hotel's other guests—male and female alike—were stretched out. Hague noted some girls running around in their bras. Bob McWherter and a few of the others decided to check out the bars in the town and in one of them succeeded in latching on to a "barmaid to visit with" for the evening, an action for which they were reprimanded by Lieutenant Lane.[8]

Early the next morning the 20th Pursuiters were back to the field, giving their ships a preflight check. Al Strauss had flown in from Amberley with a new P-40E for Oliver, who turned his slightly damaged ship over to him. At about 1030, Lane gave the order, and the two flights took off for the next stop, Cloncurry, with the B-17C and B-24A navigating for them again. This time it seemed to them that they were flying over "even rougher country" than the day before. Check points were "at a premium," Parker noted.[9]

At about 1330 the two flights reached Cloncurry, but getting their ships safely down proved time-consuming because of the unorganized state of the formation, in Johnsen's view. George Parker had trouble getting his landing gear down, as a result of loss of hydraulic pressure, and crashed on hitting the field. He climbed out uninjured, but fire engulfed his ship, and its .50 caliber ammunition exploded from the heat. Undeterred by the danger, Hague took photos with the camera he had stashed in his plane. The airport manager who witnessed the failed landing told Parker—disheartened over losing his ship—that his left wheel had not been all the way down.[10]

Servicing their planes by hand was again taking a long time. When Bob McWherter and B. J. Oliver had finished, they decided on sightseeing in the strange, barren land despite the 110-degree temperature. They finally spotted four kangaroolike animals they were told were wallabies.[11] By the time all twenty-four P-40Es were gassed up and ready to go, Lane decided it was too late to continue on to their next stop, Daly Waters. The pursuiters all headed into town to the local hotel and checked in. They noticed all the beds on the veranda, many already occupied by men and women, just like the situation at the hotel in Charleville. In the lobby they bumped into Maj. Dick Legg, who was on his way to USAFIA headquarters in Melbourne and then on to Brisbane "to start an operational Pursuit school," he was led to understand. Legg took the opportunity to arrange for a meeting with the pursuiters in the lobby.

It was a question-and-answer session, with Legg providing his attentive audience with information about the Zero and advising on tactics against it. Legg was struck by their enthusiasm for going into action against the Japanese.[12]

The next morning Parker climbed into the old B-17C for the last leg of the trip to Daly Waters and Darwin. He was happy that he'd been ordered to proceed on with the 20th despite having no plane. Captain Gunn would be piloting, navigating alone for them this time.[13] After takeoff at 0900, the loose formation "wandered around for a while," skirting some very bad tropical storms. On the way, they fired their .50s into jungle below, testing them to make sure they were working. It was about noon when they found Daly Waters and its field. They touched down without incident except for George Hynes, who landed long and crashed through a fence, but without much damage to his ship. His generator was out and he had no brakes.[14]

Aborigines helped the pursuiters roll out gas drums to the planes and refuel them. It was the first time they had seen the dark-skinned, rough-hewn Australian native people. After their ships were gassed, Morehead and Bill Turner decided to make the most of their long refueling stop and go hunting. Taking his .22 rifle out of his ship's baggage compartment, the Oklahoma farm boy struck out with his sidekick Turner for the eucalyptus trees and underbrush. When a large animal leapt out of the cover and bounded away, Morehead felled it with a single shot. He recognized the dead creature as a wallaby. With no way to cook it, they dragged the fifty-pound animal back to the field and presented it to the delighted aborigines.[15]

A severe tropical storm delayed the takeoff for Darwin for about an hour, but finally they were off again in the late afternoon in four-ship groups that Lane had ordered. First off, Lane and his three stirred up a huge cloud of red dust that blocked the view of Morehead and those following him in the takeoff sequence. Morehead and the others were "caught in a blur of confusion, unable to see in any direction." Veering right or left risked a crash, while slowing or stopping would put them in danger of being rammed from the rear. The terrified pilots just kept boring ahead at a steady speed, hoping for the best. Fortunately, all managed to clear the field without an accident.[16]

As they approached Darwin at about 1900, they became anxious again: there was a big, black bank of clouds heading towards their destination. It didn't help when Gunn kept leading them—in V echelon, wheels down— through the opaque clouds as they circled, prepared to land. "The bastard!" Hague muttered. He would have liked to shoot him down. "They'll be thinking a Jap got him," he thought.[17] The tropical storm hit with a fury as they taxied their ships back on the field and parked after the incident-free landing. Torrents of rain "with drops as big as plums" struck the field as the pilots climbed out and raced for cover. Their Australian hosts rushed out to meet the drenched Americans and took them to their officers' club to dry out, then invited them to dinner. Afterwards, pooped but relieved after the day's exertions, they spread out and slept on the floor. They had finally reached their jumping-off point for Java and the combat they were all eager for.[18]

BACK AT AMBERLEY FIELD, Buzz Wagner—formally placed in command of all P-40 training in the Brisbane area on January 29—was becoming frustrated. Along with fellow Philippines veterans Grant Mahony and Allison Strauss, he was trying to upgrade the capabilities of the novice pursuit pilots, most of whom had not been flying for several months since leaving the States. When three of the inexperienced pilots cracked up their P-40Es on the first day of his official assignment, Wagner fired off a radiogram to USAFIA headquarters in Melbourne about the situation he faced. "It is absolutely imperative that initial transition of P-40 pilots be in slower type aircraft," he argued. Wagner requested that A-24 dive bombers of the 27th Group be made available to him for such transition training of the pursuit pilots in his charge.[19]

The following day, the air officer on behalf of USAFIA headquarters, Melbourne—Col. Ross G. Hoyt—radioed Major General Brett to ask his authorization to use A-24s for pursuit training. Assuming the proposal would be accepted, USAFIA radioed Brisbane with its approval of Wagner's request. But the A-24s were not made available to Wagner; Brett wanted them for combat in Java.[20]

A day later—February 1—Wagner, Mahony, and Strauss came up with a more radical proposal. They had estimated that it would take three months and fifteen wrecked planes to fully train the seventy "so-called pursuit pilots assigned to us," whose pursuit time was "approximately 15 hours." In view of the pressing need for qualified pursuit pilots in Java, they requested permission to take the C-53 transports to the Philippines to bring back Colonel George and "two squadrons of his experienced pilots" from Bataan. "Consider ourselves very qualified for this mission," which would enjoy "excellent [chance] of success," they maintained. But if this solution were not acceptable—which apparently was not to be taken seriously—they requested that they be allowed to proceed north with a squadron of fully qualified pilots taken mainly from the 27th Bomb Group.[21]

This latter proposal had been submitted to Brett the day before by Colonel Hoyt, evidently after consultation with Wagner. The 27th Group would be given P-40s and trained as a pursuit unit. Their A-24s were not ready for combat, lacking leakproof tanks and adaptors for the non–U.S. Navy bombs they would need. Furthermore, even if fully equipped, the A-24s would be obsolescent, Hoyt pointed out.[22] Hoyt received a stinging rebuke of his proposal the following day from Brett. Why, after a month in Australia, are the A-24s now being considered obsolescent? Why wasn't conversion of the 27th Bomb Group to a pursuit outfit considered earlier? U.S. Navy bombs were available in the NEI, contrary to Hoyt's assumption, and leakproof tanks are "not considered essential in the present emergency." It was "absolutely essential that the A-24s be sent to the NEI immediately" he concluded. [23]

The grim training situation concerned Mahony directly, for on January 27 he had been ordered to form a new pursuit squadron for Java, to be designated the 3rd Pursuit Squadron (Provisional), and was very concerned about the pilot material available to equip it. He picked fellow Philippine veterans Al Strauss, Ben Irvin (now returned from Koepang), and Parker Gies to go with him, but the other twenty-one pilots would have to be selected from those novice pilots undergoing training, now that the possibility of drawing experienced pilots from the 27th Bomb Group was out.[24] Some of the trainee pilots suspected they were being considered for a move north. Vern Head and eleven others found their names posted on January 29 to go to Lowood. He figured the move was to give them the opportunity "to get a few hours flying together." The next day Head took a P-40E up for the first time since leaving the States, and on January 31 he got in more flying, having "a lot of fun . . . buzzing the whole area" with flying school classmate Lloyd Carlos.[25]

On Sunday, February 1, Dick Legg was surprised to find that he would be taking over this day as air officer of Base Section 3 from Floyd Pell, rather than be setting up a pursuit school, a job that had fallen to Buzz Wagner three days earlier. USAFIA's air officer, Colonel Hoyt, had overruled FEAF headquarters' assignment for him. "Why, I'll never know," was his reaction on being informed of his new job, but he was now under USAFIA's orders.[26] The same day, Legg was instructed through Colonel Johnson to order Mahony and his 3rd Pursuit to depart on February 5 with twenty-five P-40s for Darwin. At Base Section 3 headquarters in Brisbane, Mahony was given the details of the movement of his squadron as ordered from USAFIA headquarters in Melbourne. For his enlisted requirements, twelve crew chiefs remaining from the *Polk* group and eight who had arrived on the *Mormacsun* would be assigned him, as well as twenty-one armorers left from those who had arrived on those transports. Five additional crew chiefs, four additional armorers, one line chief, and three radio operators would be supplied later from the *President Coolidge*, expected in on February 1. All these enlisted men would be transported—along with supplies and ammunition—in C-53s provided by the newly formed Air Transport Command at Amberley.[27]

After Mahony returned to Amberley Field following the meeting, Vern

Head was informed that he was one of the twenty-five being picked to leave "as soon as possible" for the north. The young Texan was concerned that "some of the fellows haven't flown since leaving the States." He thus shared his new commander's worries, Mahony having been rebuffed in his earlier efforts to avoid taking inexperienced pilots for his squadron. Going for seniority, Mahony virtually cleaned out the remaining supply of 41-E pilots—Head, Lloyd Carlos, and five others—and was obliged to dip into the 41-F group, taking thirteen from the *Republic* and two from the *Polk*.[28]

The following day, it was raining again. Head and the other new 3rd Pursuiters were assigned their own newly assembled P-40Es, though some had not been checked out yet. They were told to see that their new ships— "scattered over the field"—were cared for properly. Already Head noticed that the guns "are rusting very rapidly."[29]

With the posting of the names of the 3rd Pursuit selectees, Bob McMahon, Bryce Wilhite, and the other twelve 41-Gs off the *Republic* and four from the *Polk* were wondering when their turn would come to join a squadron going north to the combat zone. It was already almost six weeks since the *Republic* group had arrived in Australia. But the news that Pell had been relieved of his air officer duties in order to form a new squadron encouraged them. His successor, Dick Legg, had been ordered to arrange for the forming of additional pursuit squadrons for the remaining P-40s following the assignment of twenty-five to Mahony's squadron and to prepare for their departure at the rate of one a week. The first was to be ready to leave on February 12.[30]

AT NGORO ON SUNDAY, FEBRUARY 1, the crew chiefs and armorers of the 17th Pursuit Squadron (Provisional) spotted a flight of aircraft overhead approaching their secret field. As the planes descended, they could make the lead plane out as one of the Dutch CW-21Bs they had become familiar with at Perak Field, and trailing behind it were their own P-40s. The men ran out to the field to welcome their pilots.[31] But only ten P-40s had come in. What had happened to the squadron's other two ships? Bud Sprague explained that Kruzel's ship had caught fire and burned the day before, a total loss, and his own P-40E had been flown to Maospati Field at Madioen by Bill Hennon to have a brake problem fixed at the NEIAF depot there. Sprague had flown in with Hennon's ship.[32]

Except for Sprague and Coss, it was the first time the pilots had seen their new field. They were amazed at the ingenuity of the Dutch in camouflaging it. Even from fifteen hundred feet it didn't look like an airfield, but instead just a group of rice paddies. As their crew chiefs and armorers checked out their ships, the pilots looked around the field. At the intersection of the two runways was a small open-air, thatched-roof structure, standing under a clump of trees, that was to serve as their operations shack. Four readiness huts had been set up, two at the ends of the longer runway and two at the ends of the shorter one. Along the longer runway they saw U-shaped dirt revetments, reinforced with bamboo stakes, under a grove of coconut palms that were to provide shelter for their ships.[33]

But now it was time to leave the field for the day and head for their new living quarters, where their thirty-five enlisted men had settled in the day before. Two jeeps were available to transport the pilots over the narrow road to the sugar mill village where they would be staying. The enlisted men would pile into the truck for the five-mile trip.[34]

As they entered the village of Blimbing, they could see that it was a one-block affair, with solidly built houses on each side. The enlisted men headed for the row of houses on one side of the street that had been allocated to them, and the pilots entered those on the other side intended for their use. The tile-floored houses were completely empty—evacuated by the Dutch mill personnel—except for a canvas-covered steel cot with a flannel blanket for cover and a mosquito bar in each of the four rooms. Walt Coss and flying school classmate Bo McCallum claimed one of the houses and took in another 17th pilot. Behind the house they found a crude toilet and a shower setup: a large concrete well from which they were to dip a bucket of cold water to pour over themselves. And a Javanese houseboy was assigned to each of the houses to do the cleaning and the laundry.[35]

For their first evening meal Sprague and his pilots and enlisted men proceeded over to the sugar mill, where they found a kitchen and a dining hall in separate buildings. Dutch ladies served them a tureen of soup, followed by water buffalo meat and cabbage with rice, then mangos. To Blanton it was a good meal, though not very appetizing for his Oklahoma taste. Their meal finished, the tired pilots and men headed back to their quarters for an early night.[36]

It was long before dawn—about 0300—the next day when the pursuiters awoke, climbed out of their cots, washed up, and went over to the old sugar mill for coffee served by the Dutch women, then were off to Ngoro in the two jeeps and the truck for their first full day's work at the field, beginning at 0400. With their crew chiefs and armorers, who were on the same schedule, they inspected their P-40Es, then taxied those that were in service out onto the ends of the two runways, where they parked them wingtip to wingtip, ready for takeoff. Those ships that were out of commission were being kept hidden in revetments under the trees, awaiting maintenance.[37]

At about 0730, as the 17th Pursuiters stood alert in the readiness huts near their ships, the squadron truck showed up, and the Dutch women handed out two sandwiches to each of the officers and enlisted men. Blanton was curious about the contents of the sandwiches: a couple of slices of fried meat and cold fried eggs between slices of bread.[38] It was about noon when the squadron truck was back again, circling the field to drop off lunch at the alert huts and the operations shack. The Dutch ladies this time handed out three-tiered mess kits: soup in the top tier, then a cooked mix of vegetables, rice, and chopped meat plus fresh fruit in the other two. To Coss and the others it seemed like a six-course dinner, eaten one layer at a time.[39]

A lone P-40E spotted overhead came in to land on the field. The pilot was Bill Hennon, bringing Sprague's repaired ship to Ngoro. He had spent the night at Madioen at the home of the commanding officer of 1-Vl.G.-IV, based at Maospati—Capt. Max van der Poel—and his wife. Sprague was pleased to have his ship back. He now had eleven P-40Es in commission at the field.[40]

The squadron's personnel remained on alert until late afternoon, when the sky turned dark and the rains came. The pilots at each alert shack had spent the day waiting by the telephone for a possible call from the operations shack to scramble, but none had been made. The Dutch Air Defense Command in Soerabaja had not called the operations shack for any interception this day.[41] But Sprague had warned his men that they could expect a Japanese attack at any time. Their job was to intercept any Japanese incursion over East Java, most likely a direct attack on Soerabaja or the American B-17 base at Singosari. He knew that the Japanese had established air bases 600 miles to the north at Balikpapan, Borneo, and 750 miles to the northeast at Kendari, Celebes.[42]

BACK IN BRISBANE, 2nd Lt. Claude Dean, a 41-H dive bomber pilot staying overnight in Lennon's Hotel, was in the hotel lobby at 0115 on the night of February 2–3 when he was stopped by Major Legg, the newly assigned USAFIA air officer. Legg told Dean that he had just received a message from G-2 in Washington that a Japanese aircraft carrier was on its way to eastern Australia to attack their airfields there. He ordered Dean to spread the word to all the P-40 and A-24 pilots staying at Lennon's that night and tell them to get out to Amberley and Archerfield immediately. Dean and the others took all the taxis and cars they could find at that hour and headed out, the group with Dean arriving back at Amberley Field at 0230.[43]

Bryce Wilhite had just gotten in bed after a tough day at Amberley and was close to falling asleep in the wee hours when an officer came over to his tent, calling all the pilots. Wilhite managed to wake up enough to find out what was happening, "but not long enough to care." As soon as the officer left, he went back to sleep, or at least tried to. The sound of running P-40 engines up and down the flight line and cars and trucks racing about, as well as men running here and there shouting at each other, was keeping him half awake. He decided to remain in bed, figuring there was nothing he could do at that time of night, so "why be foolish and get up before the bombs started falling?"[44]

But 41-G flying school classmate Bob McMahon decided to respond to the call. After "stumbling" into his underwear and flight suit he reported to Base Operations with other pilots at Amberley. It was about 0300 in the morning. "What was up?"[45] When they had all assembled in the room, Buzz Wagner—promoted to captain just four days earlier and the ranking officer there—took charge of the meeting. "A Japanese carrier is entering Brisbane's Moreton Bay, according to Australian intelligence," he reported to the dumbfounded pilots. If the report were accurate, it was likely the Japanese intended to strike the aircraft there at Amberley Field. This would have to be handled as a full emergency alert. All aircraft would have to be dispersed to other fields if a disaster such as he had personally experienced in the Philippines was to be avoided. He told them to go to the flight line to get their ships in flying condition by daybreak for the dispersal operation. He himself would lead a patrol off the coast to look for the carrier, and a second patrol would follow if he didn't find it.[46]

When Vern Head left the operations shack and headed for his ship, he found that it was stuck in the mud following two days of rain in the area. Other P-40Es dispersed around the field were similarly immobilized. Head and the other pilots "pushed and pulled" most of them up to the runway in the darkness into takeoff position. He was upset to find that his own No. 27 had no gun trigger nor life vest, radio mike, or oxygen. It was still dark as he and the others took off and flew their ships over to Lowood Field.[47]

Wagner led off his flight—which included Bob McMahon—into the pre-dawn darkness and headed east out over the water. Shortly after sunrise they climbed above the overcast, then descended in their search mission, flying back and forth for almost an hour. Then they spotted two vessels below, but closer inspection revealed they were just fishing trawlers. After two hours without spotting a carrier, they flew back to Amberley and landed through an opening in the overcast. [48] As Wagner's relief flight took off to continue the patrol, the telephone rang in the operations shack. Wagner was informed that the alert was over. Later, he found out that it was because of an erroneous decoding of a radio message by an RAAF cipher clerk.[49]

Wagner and the others were seething. Two of the P-40Es that had been sent out for dispersion had cracked up in the anxiety of the pilots to get them off Amberley Field. And how much sleep was lost by the pilots and mechanics because of this false report? Wilhite did the smart thing by staying in bed, McMahon mused.[50] The Amberley pilots' disposition did not improve when the commanding officer of Base Section 3 in Brisbane, Colonel Johnson, showed up at 0930 for an inspection of the field after the flap. Evidently clueless, he noted that the P-40s were "mostly engaged in training flights along the coastline." Then he laid into his undisciplined charges. "An undue number of young pilots were occupying hotel rooms in Brisbane without authority," despite being assigned to quarters at Amberley Field, he complained. Evidently apprised that some of the Amberley pilots were not at hand when the alert had been called, he ordered that all personnel were to be in camp and prepared for an emergency at all times: "No one should absent himself from his camp without authority." He then instructed his air officer, Major Legg, to have his command alerted before daybreak daily and to make reconnaissance flights out to sea part of the routine training flights "every day hereafter." Irritated by the infantry colonel's direct intervention in an operational matter of his responsibility—and seemingly holding Johnson responsible for the false alarm—Legg felt that the line officers "better learn something about Air Force if they *must* run it."[51]

AT NGORO FIELD THAT MORNING, Walt Coss and Ed Gilmore were sitting in one of the alert huts, ready for any possible interception order. Lying down on the ground opposite the hut, naked except for his underwear boxer shorts, Jim Rowland was trying to further his tan while on alert duty. Although regulations called for a fighter pilot to be completely covered while flying to afford maximum protection against a possible flash fire in the cockpit, Bud Sprague left his pilots free to wear whatever they wanted in view of the heat and humidity on Java. Rowland was pushing his freedom of choice to the extreme.[52]

Suddenly there was a ring on the phone in the alert shack. Coss answered. Operations was calling with an interception order from the Air Defense Command in Soerabaja. The Dutch officer had just received a report that a Japanese bomber formation was heading towards Soerabaja from the northeast. The coordinates given by the ADC were plotted on the 17th's map in the operations shack.[53]

The news electrified Coss, Gilmore, and Rowland. They would have from twenty to twenty-five minutes to reach Soerabaja to intercept the Japanese at the time the intruders were expected over the city. Bud Sprague was not at the field to lead the interception—he had flown to Air Force headquarters in Bandoeng on administrative matters—so Coss, as most senior officer of the 17th, would be in command. Before taking off he phoned two of the other alert shacks with the interception order. At one, fellow Philippines veterans Ed Kiser and Jack Dale were informed they would lead two two-ship elements, with Bill Hennon and Bill Stauter as their wingmen. At the third alert shack, Bo McCallum, Cy Blanton, and Ray Thompson were told to remain at the field to stand alert, ready to protect the two interception flights on their return.[54]

Coss now hurried to his waiting P-40E No. 15, trailed by Gilmore, heading for his No. 5, and Rowland, still in his undershorts as he reached his ship. Climbing into their aircraft, they put their life vests over their shoulders, strapped on their parachutes, and ran up their engines. At 1020 they thundered down the field, followed minutes later by Kiser, Dale, Hennon, and Stauter. All seven pursuiters applied maximum engine speed to climb as fast as they could in their heavy ships, then headed in the direction of Soerabaja, forty miles to the northeast.[55]

At about 1045, Dale, Kiser, Hennon, and Stauter encountered two V-shaped formations of seventeen twin-engine Mitsubishi G4M Type 1 "Betty" bombers as they were heading north after having bombed Soerabaja port and Perak Airfield. The Dutch Air Defense Command hadn't given the pursuiters enough warning. The bombers—nine in one V formation and eight in the other—were four thousand feet above the P-40s and somewhat ahead of them. They were flying without any escort from Zeros.[56]

As the four P-40s tried to reach the Japanese, the bomber pilots performed a defensive maneuver that Dale, Kiser, and Hennon had not seen while flying combat in the Philippines in December. They broke their two Vs into an in-line echelon, stacked down on the side of the approaching P-40s, one *chutai* (air division) lower than the other. In this way they could bring to bear "a ladder of fire" from their 7.7-mm machine guns and 20-mm cannons against attackers from any level.[57]

Opening up with their .50s at 1050 when they came within firing range, the Americans gave chase out over the Java Sea, but then Kiser and Stauter broke off; they were worried they were getting too low on gas to get back to Ngoro. Dale pressed ahead and made one pass from the rear, firing at extreme range, but his .50s failed to hit his quarry. Now alone, Hennon approached his target at a closer range from the rear and got in one final burst. It was "effective enough to stop him," he felt, but he couldn't judge if it was "a sure victory," as he broke off the attack and headed back to Ngoro at 1100 behind Dale.[58]

In the meantime, Coss, Gilmore, and Rowland had spotted nineteen Mitsubishi G3M Type 96 "Nell" bombers about ten miles south of Soerabaja and heading north from the direction of Malang. Gilmore was weaving above

Mitsubishi G4M1 "Bettys" of Kanoya Kokutai that attacked eastern Java on
February 3, 1942, seen here in early 1942 on a mission during Southern Operations.
Courtesy Robert C. Mikesh.

Coss and Rowland, who had reached seventeen thousand feet, with the Japanese a good four thousand to five thousand feet above them. The three pursuiters figured that the bombers were returning from an attack on the B-17 base at Singosari six miles north of the city. The ADC hadn't given them adequate warning notice. Gilmore signaled to Coss that the Japanese were coming from the right. Coss and Rowland began climbing towards the bombers.[59]

As they followed below and behind the twin-engine bombers, they spotted trouble: six Zeros about four thousand feet directly above them. The Japanese fighters split into two Vs of three ships each and broke away from the bombers they appeared to be escorting, diving down on the Americans. One of the three-ship elements turned head-on into Coss and Rowland, while the other took up a position to attack Gilmore from the rear. Coss and Rowland pulled into the three-ship *shotai* (air section) attacking them and fired head-on at them with their six .50s, then dove away. When Gilmore saw tracers going by his tail, he put his ship into a tight left-hand spiral and also dove away.[60]

Leveling out after their dive, Coss and Rowland began to climb back up, as did Gilmore outside their view. After reaching twenty thousand feet, Gilmore looked around but could not find any Japanese aircraft. But Coss and

Mitsubishi A6M2 Zeros of the 3rd Kokutai on the airfield at Kendari, Celebes, late January 1942, before their attack on Soerabaja on February 3. *Courtesy Tamotsu Yokoyama.*

Rowland at sixteen thousand spotted six more Zeros several thousand feet above them and in the sun. Two of the Zeros dove down on them in a string formation. Coss pulled up and fired at the lead Japanese head-on. The Zero pilot passed by him and turned, continuing to dive but now trailing a slight streamer of smoke. Then Coss spotted another Zero, also diving on him from out of the sun. He fired a burst from his .50s at the Japanese head-on, but with no apparent effect.

Coss had lost contact with Rowland after firing at the first Zero, but now as he tried to maneuver with the second Japanese, he caught a glimpse of Rowland going straight down, trailing white smoke and a Zero directly behind him. When his own opponent managed to get on his tail, Coss eluded him by diving into the clouds.[61] Now running low on gas, Coss decided to head back to Ngoro. As he turned in a southwesterly direction at about ten thousand feet just before 1130, he sighted a formation of six Zeros below him, heading north in the direction of Soerabaja. Diving on them from out of the sun, he fired on the last plane in the group. Immediately it exploded in midair. Overshooting the second Zero in the formation, Coss found himself under attack from the lead Zero, which had turned sharply into him. Again, Coss managed to elude the Japanese by diving into the clouds, then he continued on his return flight to Ngoro.[62]

FAR BELOW ON THE GROUND at Soerabaja, Capt. Frank Kurtz was at NEIAF Operations at Perak Field about 1030 when Dutch officers excitedly announced that a Japanese bomber force was heading south towards them. Colonel Eubanks's liaison officer was "panic-stricken" that the Japanese might branch off and catch his 19th Group B-17s on the ground at their base at Singosari to the south.[63] Twenty minutes later Kurtz could hear the bombers hitting Soerabaja city to the south of Perak Field. He knew they would be next. Kurtz and his Dutch friends ran for their slit trench shelters as they heard the second wave coming in over the harbor next to Perak Airdrome, then the sound of bombs crashing into the oil storage facilities and the naval base at Morokrembangan. Looking up, they spotted the third wave headed straight for their airdrome. Terrified, they hunkered down on the concrete floor of the ditch, their heads reverberating from the explosions on the field. Finally, the bombers completed their attack, and Kurtz and the Dutchmen climbed out of their trench. But then they spotted Zeros swooping low over the field and jumped back in.[64]

Caught out on the field, ten enlisted men of the 20th Pursuit who had come ahead of their pilots, still delayed at Darwin, were too far from the air raid shelters when the air raid siren had gone off. They had not expected a raid today; they figured it was too cloudy that morning for an attack. Now Cpl. Ken Perry and a group of his buddies raced to a nearby machine gun emplacement—minus its gun—and jumped in. They had seen the Dutch CW-21Bs taking off and shooting up into the sky to intercept the Japanese bombers and fighters. They could see the Dutchmen in violent dogfights overhead with the Zeros, but now at least some of the Zeros were down at ground level shooting up Perak Field, passing back and forth across the runway without facing any opposition. One circled so low by the machine gun emplacement—a bare one hundred feet overhead—that Perry wished he had a gun to fire on him.[65]

The 20th Pursuit enlisted men watched transfixed as a crippled CW-21B approached to land on the field, three Zeros on its tail. Suddenly the Dutch ship burst into flames before it was able to touch down. The pilot didn't have a chance, they figured.[66]

Minutes later, it seemed to Perry and his comrades that the Zeros had gone, so they climbed out of the emplacement and headed for the runway to see what they could do to help. Pvt. Herman Langjahr found a jeep with the key still in it and started it up, beckoning for the others to get in. When one of the group asked where they would be going, Langjahr—who seemed to be somewhat inebriated—yelled that he was going over to a hangar to pull out a burning Dutch plane. Expecting the bombers to return, his buddies declined the offer. But when Langjahr accused them of being "yellow," Perry and Cpl. Fred Deyo jumped in. Driving past their "bewildered" squadron mates, they raced across the runway and entered the hangar. But after futile efforts to put out the fire that now engulfed the plane, they drove back and jumped into an air raid shelter: the bombers were back.[67]

Relieved to be in a better shelter this time, Perry and his group listened to the "terrific explosions" as the bombers unloaded. Finally the raid was over, and they peered out. Across from the runway the naval base was a "mass of black smoke and ruins." They climbed up on top of the shelter and waited for something else to happen. When it remained quiet, Perry called to his more cautious buddies inside to come out. But just as a frightened SSgt. Dave Griffith poked his head out and asked, "Is it okay?" a "monstrous rumbling and a curtain of flame shot into the air 200 feet high"; the magazines in the naval base had apparently gone off. His faith in the judgment of Perry lost, Griffith withdrew his head back into the shelter.

AT NGORO FIELD THE TWO FLIGHTS of P-40s came in to land without incident. The pursuiters shared their experiences of first combat in Java with McCallum, Blanton, and Thompson, who had remained behind to cover their return. But there were two Dutch pilots there now, too. They had opted to land at the secret field rather than at their own airdromes.

Lt. Willem Boxman found that the Americans were not in a cheerful mood after the loss of Jim Rowland. Boxman told them of his own harrowing experience intercepting the Zeros as they approached his base at Maospati Field, outside Madioen. They had chased the Zeros all the way to Soerabaja as the Japanese were about to head out over the Java Sea, but Boxman was now the only pilot still pursuing the Japanese of his squadron's seven intercepting Curtiss Hawks. At that point Boxman decided to break off and head back, but to nearer Ngoro instead—he was low on fuel. He had no trouble finding the field; he was the officer who had arranged for its elaborate camouflage in pre-war days. As he approached, he spotted the nearly invisible P-40s of the 17th hidden at the edge of the jungle.[68]

Sgt. H. M. Haye of 2-Vl.G.-IV was at Ngoro too. When his CW-21B was badly shot up by Zeros near Soerabaja, he decided to fly to Ngoro for his safety rather than to bombed out Perak. His squadron mate, Sgt. F. Beerling, had landed at Ngoro not long after and asked Haye for .30-caliber ammunition for his ship. After Haye had given him his last rounds from his CW-21B, Beerling took off for Soerabaja.[69]

The Americans realized that they had been much luckier than their Dutch friends in this first combat over Java for all of them. Flying a P-40 against a Zero was a risky business, but at least it was preferable to taking an outmoded Curtiss Hawk 75 or a Curtiss CW-21B—with its light armament and lack of self-sealing gas tanks—up against them. It didn't help when they were outnumbered by the skillful Japanese pilots, too.

TWO DAYS EARLIER, on February 1, after an uncomfortable night on the floor of the RAAF officers' club at Darwin, the pilots of the 20th Pursuit (Provisional) were up at 0600 for an early morning meeting with their CO. Lieutenant Lane had received their destination orders. They were to proceed immediately to Soerabaja, Java, by way of Koepang, with proper escort.[70] But first they would need to spend this Sunday morning working on their P-40Es to get them ready for the long overwater flight to Koepang, Lane told them. Furthermore, Lane had no intention of taking off before 1530 or so in the afternoon in order to time their arrival close to nightfall. He did not want to risk being attacked by Japanese bombers and strafers on the field at Koepang while their ships were being refueled for the next leg of their flight west, to Denpasar, Bali.[71]

During the "frantic" morning getting their planes in condition for the flight, the pilots reflected on their situation. They were already jittery from listening to the "wild tales" of evacuees from the Philippines and outer islands of the Dutch East Indies that the Japanese had captured. Most of the officers at the RAAF base were sure that there would be an attack on Darwin in less than a week. For Butch Hague it was the constant strafing attacks on Koepang that unnerved him the most. They had no other choice but to use it as a refueling stop on their way to Soerabaja. P-40s should be assigned to it for protection, he felt.[72]

Getting their ships ready was not proving an easy matter. Elwin Jackson had tried to get his generator repaired but found no one at the field who could do it. He would need to continue using manual controls, including those for propeller pitch. For many of the other pilots, their guns were the problem; the gun charging mechanism on their ships was not working properly. Only one of Hague's six .50s would charge, though by afternoon he managed to have them all working.[73]

It was 1700 before they managed to get off. In the B-24A mother ship piloted by Capt. Paul Davis, George Parker looked out to see the bomber surrounded by the twenty-four P-40Es of his squadron that it was leading to Koepang. But the weather was very bad; they were headed into a severe tropical front. After only half an hour into the flight. Lane decided to abort and lead them back to Darwin. It was one "disappointed bunch" who landed in the rain at the RAAF field. However, at least one of the pilots was relieved; Al Dutton "didn't like flying over those sharky waters."[74]

The heavy rain continued all through the next day. Parker doubted if he had ever seen it rain so hard and persistently. High winds, too, buffeted their ships. Gambonini and some of his squadron mates got soaked twice during the day while working on their planes and tying them down in the strong wind.[75] And when the pilots woke up on the morning of their third day at Darwin, it was still rainy and windy. Six inches of rain had fallen the day before, and this day was expected to produce as much, they were told. The frustrated pursuiters began to wonder if they would ever be able to leave. But Parker, always looking at the bright side, regarded their confinement as an opportunity to check their planes thoroughly, a responsibility he'd been given by Lane.[76]

They were still having trouble with their guns. Despite his efforts, Gambonini couldn't get all his guns to fire. But the rain was causing a greater problem. The mud was now getting so thick that they were unable to taxi their ships out. Two had their wheels so deep that the wingtip on one side touched the ground. They struggled to get their ships out on the runway "in case we were attacked," but Hague for one was skeptical they would get off "if we were paid a visit."[77] And now there was a real fear that they would be attacked. A Japanese carrier had been reported about five hundred miles from Darwin. From 1200 to 1700 the pilots stood alert in their ships on the runway. A few flew patrols over Darwin despite the weather conditions. But as the day wore on, it was clear that no attack was forthcoming.[78]

The following morning, the weather seemed to be breaking. After breakfast, Lieutenant Lane was enjoying a good game of snooker when he was given a message from USAFIA headquarters in Melbourne, radioed the day before to Darwin U.S. headquarters, ordering him to take his squadron to the Dutch East Indies at "the earliest practical moment." The radiogram stipulated, "immediate action imperative." It seemed clear to Lane that Brett at ABDACOM on Java and Barnes at USAFIA headquarters were getting angry at him over the delayed departure of his squadron.[79]

Lane now ordered his pilots to perform a final check on their ships and service them in preparation for the flight. But as the morning progressed, the weather began to deteriorate. Several showers brought more rainfall to the drenched airfield. Nevertheless, Lane scheduled the takeoff time for 1625. He didn't want to get further in the bad books of Brett and Barnes by once again delaying their departure.[80]

At the scheduled hour Captain Davis took off in his B-24A mother ship that would again be guiding the squadron to Koepang on this second try. But now a squall hit the field, making visibility difficult for the pursuiters. By the time the fourteenth P-40E, piloted by Bill Turner on instruments, cleared the field, the rain became so heavy that Les Johnsen and the other remaining pilots "could not see halfway down the field." They halted their takeoff. [81]

It was almost 1700 before Lane and his contingent, "cruising about" in the bumpy weather, finally formed around the B-24A and headed out to sea for Koepang to the northwest. For the first two hours into the flight, Davis in the B-24A fought the rain and clouds, sometimes flying only two hundred feet above the turbulent sea. For the pursuit pilots it was even worse. Jim Morehead and the others were in "constant terror," flying with rain-blurred canopies in the violent turbulence, often just fifty feet above the waves, constantly in danger of colliding with one another. It was a "struggle to survive." They kept losing sight of the B-24A as it dropped from view from time to time. They struggled with mushy controls to hang on to the wing of their flight leaders, bouncing up and down and lurching through the heavy rain. A worried Parker was surprised to see from the window of the B-24A that despite the elements his squadron mates were keeping good formation.[82]

Finally, the storm eased off. About 1915 Captain Davis approached the island of Timor and ordered his gunners into position in the B-24A. But just as the big four-engined bomber "skimmed across the thatched roofs" to Penfui Airdrome, bad weather returned. At 2000 Davis touched down without incident on the jungle field. Behind him, "soaking in sweat" from mental and physical exhaustion, Jim Morehead and the other pursuiters descended and came in to land just as it was turning dark. Morehead had only five to ten gallons of gas left in his ship. Gambonini had eight gallons remaining. Their gauges were all on empty. Some of the pilots had been calling "mayday" on their radios, expecting to have to ditch. For Morehead, it had been "the worst flight of my life." He was angry with Lane for continuing on in the impossible weather and not turning the flight back instead, as he would have done if he had been the commanding officer. Never again would he trust Lane's judgment.[83]

As they dispersed their ships and refueled them, they were watched by the curious, ever-present, dark-skinned natives. Looking around, the pursuiters saw the effects of the Japanese strafing raids on the airdrome. Hague noticed a burned up Lockheed Hudson on the field and examined the remains of Irvin's shot up P-40 in the hangar. They were told that the Zeros were showing up every day between 0900 and 1000 in the morning for their unchallenged strafing runs.[84]

After finishing a meal of buffalo stew served by native boys in the thatch-roofed mess hall, the exhausted pilots stretched out fully clothed on hard benches at the sides of the mess hall, a blanket under each. Larry Landry and Hague managed to "steal" pillows for their heads. As they listened to the continuous rain splattering off the thatched roof all night, their thoughts turned to the next leg of their trip, to Denpasar, Bali. Lane had scheduled their takeoff for just before sunrise. He didn't want to run the risk of their being caught on the ground by the Zeros on the next early morning strafing raid by the Japanese. After refueling at Bali, they were to proceed to Soerabaja, but without a guide ship, according to the instructions Lane had just received from the Dutch ADC commander in Soerabaja, Col. Ente van Gils.[85]

CHAPTER SIX

"I'm All Shot to Hell!"

ALTHOUGH IT HAD BEEN NOISILY raining all night, the 20th Pursuit pilots at Koepang woke up refreshed at 0430 on February 5 after their Timor Sea ordeal of the day before. Following breakfast at 0530 and a short briefing from Lieutenant Lane, they went down to the field and preflighted their ships, then were off for their next stop, Denpasar, Bali, at 0600. Again they were following Captain Davis' B-24A that had guided them from Darwin. Taking off ahead of the bomber was a C-53 transport that had overnighted at Koepang too and was now headed for Soerabaja with a second contingent of the 20th Pursuit's enlisted men.[1] But the pursuiters were down to thirteen ships for this leg of their trip. Bob McWherter couldn't get his P-40E started. As Butch Hague and the others bade goodbye to McWherter, Hague figured that McWherter's ship probably would be strafed by Zeros that morning or the next. If not, McWherter would follow with the remaining pilots due in from Darwin.[2]

For once the air was calm, allowing smooth formation flying, as the pilots began passing over the string of islands beneath their path leading them to Bali, six hundred miles to the west. As it was for the others, it was a relief for Jim Morehead not to be flying over open ocean as they had done during the traumatic trip the day before. He was enjoying the view below: the "lush green islands with their coconut palms, banana plantations, terraced rice fields, and white beaches."[3] But their reverie was broken early in the flight when the B-24A reported that it had spotted four planes, which had ducked into a cloud. Lieutenant Muckley radioed that the unidentified aircraft had been following their ships. There was no question of chasing; they had just enough gas to make it to Bali.[4]

At 0830 Bali came into view, and at 0845 the pursuiters passed over the adjacent island of Lombok. They now broke away from their B-24A mother ship, which descended to five hundred feet for the remainder of its flight to Soerabaja. Unlike the P-40s, it did not need to refuel at Bali.[5] At about 09:00 the pursuiters touched down at Denpasar, a sod field lined with coconut palms. Everywhere they looked, they saw people. Some of the native women in their topless dress and regal bearing struck Morehead, for one, as beautiful.[6]

But they needed to concentrate on refueling their ships for the hop to Soerabaja, two hundred miles further west. Fifty-five-gallon drums of aviation gas had been stacked up nearby for their use, but there was only a single hand pump. One by one the pilots—starting with Lieutenant Lane—taxied their P-40Es up to the drums from their dispersed positions on the field. As a native cranked the pump, each pilot would hold the nozzle in the gas tank of his ship.[7] This was going to be a time-consuming operation, Hague and Larry Landry felt, so why not look around a bit in the meantime? After they had refueled their ships, they strolled down to the beach and picked up pieces of coral. Then they had some of the very sweet coffee that the Dutch served.[8]

As Hague and Landry headed back to the field, Jim Morehead—waiting in last position to refuel his ship—looked up and noticed a plane in the sky, turning away from the airfield. It was just before 1000. He yelled to Lieutenant Lane about it, then joined by his two squadron mates continued drinking juice out of a coconut that natives had cut for them. But now Lane called out that enemy planes were approaching and ordered off all those pilots whose planes had been refueled.[9] Lane hurriedly climbed into his ship, fastened up, and led off, with Gene Bound behind him as his wingman. Bill Gallienne and Hague followed, although Hague had not gotten oil for his plane yet. Just below them were Dwight Muckley and his wingman, Bill Turner. Landry and his buddy and wingman Connie Reagan trailed them. On the ground, Paul Gambonini was in the middle of refueling his ship, with Tommy Hayes, Marion Fuchs, George Hynes, and Morehead waiting their turns.[10]

When Lane and Bound reached five thousand feet, still climbing, they were bounced from above by three Zeros. All eight P-40Es immediately scattered in trying to avoid the Zeros that swarmed around them. Below, Gambonini was witnessing the uneven struggle and decided to abort his refueling, taking off with tanks only partly refilled to join his squadron mates in the melee.[11]

When one of the Zeros came down between Lane and Bound, Bound had him clearly in his sights and fired all six of his ship's .50-caliber machine guns at the Japanese. The Zero "went off in a violent turn," but Bound didn't see whether it crashed. He had now lost sight of Lane after his CO had flown into a cloud bank. Looking around for any of his squadron mates, Bound noticed two planes below him at some distance; the lead one he identified as a P-40E. Bound dropped down to join them but immediately realized that the trailing ship was a Zero, not another P-40. Closing in behind the Japanese, Bound fired a single burst and thought he saw the Zero "go to pieces and plunge, nose-first, into the water below."[12]

A few moments later, Bound was shocked to see fire coming out of his engine—he'd been hit by a Zero he hadn't seen. The Japanese continued to pour fire into his ship as it began losing speed. Bound realized his ship was a goner and headed for a small cloud in which to bail out. At three thousand feet he jumped, but he refrained from pulling the ripcord until he was at about one thousand feet; he feared the Japanese would strafe him in his chute. As the chute blossomed out at eight hundred feet, the harness split, dislocating his shoulder severely. Bound crashed into a tree, where he would hang twenty feet off the ground for about forty-five minutes before natives showed up to rescue him. Initially, they thought Bound was a Japanese and were "most unfriendly." Their attitude changed when Bound exclaimed that "President Roosevelt is going to be awfully sore at you guys about this!" The natives released him from the tree and took him to a nearby medical station, where it was found he had dislocated his shoulder so badly that the bone had splintered and nerves and muscles were snapped.[13]

As Hague was climbing in fourth position, he saw Bound being attacked by the Zero, its 20 mm cannon fire "eating away his windscreen and dashboard" and setting his engine on fire before Bound headed for the cloud to bail out. But now Hague had troubles of his own. Two Zeros were coming straight down at him. Hague peeled off as tracers from one of the ships passed just over his right wing. He went into a dive that shook off his pursuer, but as he climbed back up another Zero got on his tail from above. At that point he remembered to drop his belly tank. A few seconds later, his engine "coughed and sputtered"; he'd forgotten to switch to the main tank. Correcting his error, Hague dove down again, and the engine caught. "Gunning it up to about 60 inches" of manifold pressure, he raced along the beach below.[14]

Hague spotted another P-40 and heard someone ask "Who is that?" over the radio. Thinking the pilot was referring to him, Hague answered, but then a Zero took after him. Reacting immediately, he turned inland and "started up a cut," but every time he looked back, the Japanese was still on his tail, firing on him, but no shells were hitting his ship. Trying to shake the Zero, Hague poured on the coals, running his indicated air speed up to 310 miles an hour as he flew up one canyon then branched on every Y he came to and ducked behind every hill. "This was the fastest, wildest ride I have ever taken," he later recorded in his diary. After Hague made a very steep turn near the edge of a cliff, he looked back and saw that his pursuer was about five hundred feet higher, still following him but now about a mile back. Hague figured that the Japanese had run out of ammunition and was going to give up the chase. He turned his P-40 to head west, out over the water to Java. But exactly where was he? He "wandered about" over the Java mainland, then climbed to twelve thousand feet to get a better perspective, "all the while watching his tail and the sun." A deep volcanic mountain came into view. He checked with his map and identified it. Now able to orient himself, he set course north to Soerabaja.[15]

Earlier, Dwight Muckley, climbing behind Hague, had spotted a P-40 being attacked by several Zeros. With his wingman Bill Turner he dove down to drive off the Japanese. But in descending, Muckley became separated from Turner, then saw that Turner was under attack from eight other Zeros above him. Then three of the diving Zeros came after Muckley, too. He put his P-40 into a steep dive at full throttle, watching his speed climb from 300 finally to 630 miles an hour before he leveled off above the Balinese jungle and streaked for Soerabaja. The Zeros were still on his tail but were falling behind and finally broke off their chase. Turner's ship was "shot up a bit," but he escaped the Zeros and opted to get back to Denpasar Field. He landed with a flat tire.[16]

Larry Landry, leading the fourth two-ship element to get off, saw his wingman and close friend Connie Reagan in serious trouble from attacking Zeros and went to his rescue. Landry managed to get fire into one of Reagan's pursuers but did not see the two Zeros coming up from his rear. Shells from the Japanese sent his ship into the sea. Landry did not get out. Reagan—his rudder shot up, engine cutting out, and hydraulic system shot out—landed back at Denpasar, wheels up, wiping out his ship.[17]

On the ground, Tommy Hayes had finished refueling his P-40 and was helping Marion Fuchs gas up his ship when suddenly they saw someone coming in with his wheels up and then touching down off the runway. (It was Reagan's ship, they found out later.) Then another P-40 came in to land, this one on the runway. They later found it was Bill Turner.[18]

But Fuchs was preoccupied with something else now. "Look up there," he yelled to Hayes. High in the sky, at some eighteen thousand to twenty thousand feet, they estimated—was a "beautiful" V-shaped formation of twenty-seven twin-engine bombers, the sun glinting off them. Now they appeared to be lining up for a run over the field.[19]

Just before, Paul Gambonini had come in and landed on the field, out of gas. The last 20th Pursuiter to get off during the attack by the Zeros, Gambonini had interceded to help a squadron mate being chased by a Zero but in the process was himself set upon by one of the Japanese. His ship damaged and fuel exhausted after an hour and a half in the air, he had no choice of landing site other than Denpasar.[20]

As he climbed out of his ship, a Dutch officer came alongside on a motorcycle and picked him up. They raced to an air raid shelter and jumped in just as the first salvo of the bombs detonated on the field. Immediately after the Japanese finished their run, Gambonini and his Dutch friend climbed out of the shelter; it was full and they had piled on top of everybody. Running, they were only halfway to a preferred shelter—a nearby coconut grove—when they heard the second wave of bombers approaching. As the first bombs hit, they dived into a ditch. Stunned by the concussion, they frantically clawed the earth to get as low as possible. Shrapnel was tearing the leaves off the coconut palms around them, and the natives were running in all directions. After the bombers passed by, Gambonini and the Dutchman got up again and continued their run to the coconut palm grove, where they hunkered down as the third wave of bombers began unloading on the field.[21]

Meanwhile, Hayes and Fuchs—now joined by Jim Morehead, his P-40 not yet refueled, and terrified natives—raced for the jungle as the first wave dropped its bombs. Running across an old rock basin, they all jumped in and hunkered down. After the first pass, they got up and headed back to the field, but that was a mistake: the Japanese were beginning another run. This time they took shelter in a palm grove. Bomb fragments tore into the palms and knocked down coconuts on them.[22] But now, after the third bomb run, Morehead decided to leave his companions and go back to the field. He wanted to save his P-40, if possible. As avgas drums exploded nearby, Morehead climbed into his ship and started it up. Kicking up dust and grass, he taxied his apparently undamaged ship off the runway to a meadow some three hundred feet away. Jumping out, he headed back to the field again for any other serviceable P-40s he could disperse. But now he realized he wouldn't make it; bombs were falling again. He jumped into a shallow ditch as explosions straddled him only feet away. After the bombers passed, he got up and looked around the field but could identify only one more intact P-40. In another ship that was on fire, .22-caliber ammunition was cooking off. Morehead realized it was Fuchs's plane. Fuchs had been carrying a carton of five hundred rounds for Morehead's .22 rifle in his baggage compartment.[23]

Morehead approached the other P-40. He could see that it had a gaping hole in the propeller hub. Then Bill Turner came up to him and told Morehead it was his ship. The propeller had been perforated by a bomb fragment during the attack after he had landed it. Morehead and Turner pushed the plane into the brush and covered it with palm fronds. Then joined by Fuchs, Morehead and Turner headed over to Morehead's plane, pushed it under some trees, and covered it as well.[24] Nearby, George Hynes was also trying to move his P-40 to safety. It had not been damaged in the bombing, so he was in the cockpit, taxiing it toward trees. But he didn't see the bomb crater in front of him, and his ship fell into the hole, bending the propeller.[25]

Gambonini and his Dutch officer friend were also back on the field again after the bombing attack, surveying the damage. Gambonini found his own ship still burning after having been blown up. Only the wingtips and tail section were still intact. Fuchs's P-40 also was burning.[26] Nearby, Tommy Hayes was pleasantly surprised to find that his P-40, like that of Hynes, had apparently survived the bombing. However, when he got in and tried to start it up, the prop went around a few times only and then stopped. Climbing out on his ship's nose, he saw a big fragment hole behind the propeller. Further examination resulted in discovery of another one, this one in the gearbox.[27]

As Turner and Morehead were putting fronds on Turner's P-40E, a Dutch officer drove up in a jeep. Morehead asked him if he could arrange to have the bomb craters filled in on a strip wide enough for a P-40 to take off. Soon dozens of natives were hard at work with shovels and shoulder baskets. While they repaired the strip, Turner and Morehead took a good propeller from a burned-out P-40 and installed it on Turner's damaged ship.[28]

Hayes and Hynes decided on a similar solution for Hynes's ship. Joined by two others, they took the propeller off of Hayes's damaged P-40 and put it on Hynes's ship after it had been extricated from the bomb crater. They now had two P-40Es in flying condition, though Morehead's was not in mint condition; it had holes in the canopy.[29]

TWO HUNDRED MILES WEST, at Perak Field, Soerabaja, Cpl. Ken Perry and his buddies in the 20th Pursuit were witnessing another strafing attack over the harbor in late morning when they noticed two planes—one big and one small—coming in from the opposite direction. Moments later, someone identified them as American ships—a twin-engine transport and a P-40. The pilot of the pursuit plane made a bad landing, almost nosing over, then "flopped back on its tail wheel" and came to a stop. The engine continued running for several seconds, "then sputtered and died." The pilot climbed out very slowly and walked to the rear of his plane, examining the tail. In the meantime, the C-53 transport had also landed and pulled up in front of the hangar. Perry and his comrades yelled that there was a raid on and the all clear had not been sounded. The terrified passengers—other 20th Pursuit enlisted men—hurriedly disembarked, over the objections of the pilot, who wanted to take off and get out of there.[30]

The P-40 pilot now walked up to Perry's group. Someone asked him how he was. In a hysterical voice, he blurted, "I'm all shot to hell!" It turned out that he was Dwight Muckley, one of the pilots assigned to their squadron. Perry and the others ran out to take a look at his ship. Indeed, it had been "shot to hell." The right wing looked like "someone had punched holes every inch with a screwdriver." The left wing was in no better condition, "pulverized with cannon shot." The aileron cables "were severed, dangling down, swinging in the breeze." The rudders and elevator were locked due to machine gun fire. In the side of the fuselage was a hole "a foot square." The radio was "all shot up." The propeller had several holes in it. A rear view mirror "had been clipped neatly off" just two inches from the pilot's head. And Muckley had landed with two flat tires, "no mean feat for a P-40," in Perry's estimation.

Muckley now spotted a B-24 coming in to land and recognized it as Captain Davis's bomber that had guided them to Bali that morning from Koepang. He jumped into a car and headed towards the B-24, waving his arms. Still shaken from his experience, Muckley was greeted by his squadron mate George Parker as Parker disembarked. In an agitated voice he related his terrifying experience to Parker and Captain Davis.[31] Parker noticed two other P-40s on the ground near Muckley's shot-up ship. He found that Bill Gallienne and Butch Hague were there, too, having escaped their Zero pursuers under circumstances similar to Muckley's. But they were not traumatized, as was their squadron mate. Gallienne had come all the way with his belly tank still attached—"a lucky bastard," in Hague's view. Hague himself had only about fifteen minutes of gas left in his ship when he touched down.[32] But where was the squadron commander, Lieutenant Lane? The mystery was solved when a telephone call came in shortly afterwards; Lane was calling with the message that he was safe "at a P-40 field" sixty miles from Soerabaja.[33]

When Bud Sprague at Ngoro Field was informed that three P-40s had come in to Perak Field and that Lane was at Singosari, he assigned Cy Blanton to fly to Singosari and guide Lane in, while he would lead in the other three pilots. But on arriving at Perak Field Sprague found that Muckley's ship would need to remain at Perak for repairs. That left Hague and Gallienne. But it was arranged that Gallienne board the C-53 and the more senior Muckley fly in Gallienne's ship instead. Parker also now switched to the C-53, as Davis was not scheduled to go beyond Soerabaja in his B-24A.[34]

When Blanton landed at Singosari at about 1500, he found a very distraught Lane waiting for him. Lane's nervous condition didn't improve as Blanton led him around thunderstorms all the way to Ngoro. It was not only the weather that made him jittery; he was afraid they might be intercepted by Zeros on the way to the field.[35] On arrival at Ngoro, Lane met with the 17th Pursuit's pilots. They could easily see that he was traumatized from his Bali experience. Muckley appeared to be in the same shape. Bill Hennon felt that "there is something wrong with Lane and Muckley—they've been scared." Among the pilots as well as the enlisted men, Lane was now referred to—out of earshot—as "Shaky" Lane, rather than "Shady" Lane.[36]

Back at Denpasar Field, the seven grounded pursuiters of the 20th were taken to the town and checked into the Bali Hotel for the night. They were still "badly shaken up" after the day's events. "What a day!" Tommy Hayes wrote in his diary that evening.[37]

FOR BUD SPRAGUE—NOW A MAJOR after his promotion the day before—it had been a busy time since his return to Ngoro from Bandoeng at 1000 on February 4. Only forty minutes after he had landed, the Dutch ADC radioed and asked for a four-ship flight to fly out to protect the U.S. light cruiser *Marblehead*. The ship was under attack from Japanese twin-engine bombers off the southern coast of Madoera Island and was trying to reach Tjilatjap on the southern coast of Java. But 150 miles out from Ngoro, heading northeast, Sprague and the three others he was leading—Ed Kiser, Ed Gilmore, and Bill Hennon—were called back: the weather was too bad. Coming back in to land at Ngoro in "mucky weather" gave them a "tough time," but Capt. Willard Reed, the Marine Corps officer posted to them who was running operations from the field, directed them in safely from the south.[38] There was some bad news waiting for Sprague and the others when they landed. The Dutch had found Big Jim Rowland's body. It appeared he had been killed in his plane when shot down the day before.[39]

The next day, the ADC radioed again at about 0945. It had just received two reports of enemy bombers. One had them low over the B-17 base at Malang, and the other over their own field at Ngoro, heading north. Responding immediately, Sprague took off at the head of A flight with Kiser, Gilmore, and Thompson. Hennon with four others followed in B flight. The heavy P-40Es struggled to gain altitude as they headed towards Soerabaja to the northeast. Sprague intended to catch the Japanese as they passed over the city on their return route. As the two flights neared Soerabaja, they finally had reached twenty-two thousand feet. But where were the Japanese bombers? Hennon figured they must have hit Singosari and headed back before he and the others could reach them. Once again, they hadn't been given sufficient warning to get to Soerabaja in time for an interception. It was also taking too long to get high up enough to attack. "We need height and can't get it," he complained in his diary.[40]

After landing back at Ngoro Field at 1130, the frustrated pursuiters were informed that both ADC reports were based on erroneous information. The "Japanese bombers over Malang" were actually American B-17Es that had taken off from their field at Singosari, six miles north of Malang, and were heading north on a bombing mission.[41] Sprague and his pilots were seething over the ADC's incompetence in sending them on such a misinformed interception of their own bombers. It was bad enough that the pursuiters could barely understand the heavily accented English of the Dutch radio and telephone calls from the ADC or that the information provided, including that on altitude, was so meager and that not enough warning was being given for a successful interception, but now the ADC was reacting to a completely erroneous identification of aircraft. To "straighten out" the Dutch operation control and "improve its effectiveness," Sprague ordered Jack Dale to fly to Soerabaja and confer with the ADC officers.[42] In the meantime, the four new 20th Pursuit pilots settled in at their new base. It was decided that they and their aircraft should be incorporated into the 17th and Lieutenant Lane assigned as Bud Sprague's executive officer. The 20th no longer existed as a separate entity.[43]

At a more practical level, Butch Hague was satisfied with the housing arrangements at Blimbing for him and the three other new arrivals: "better than the floor at Darwin and Koepang." Their new quarters were a large, high-ceilinged house of five rooms. Beds and benches were the only furniture, however. Each bed had only a canvas stretched across it, with mosquito netting over the top and a "mat to cover up with."[44]

The twenty-six new enlisted men who arrived with the C-53 carrying Parker and Gallienne were also absorbed into the 17th. Ken Perry's group of ten had also come into Blimbing from Soerabaja on February 5, but by truck rather than by air. The "Unholy Ten," as they called themselves, were assigned a warehouse as their quarters.[45]

Two other unexpected guests would also be staying at Blimbing for an indefinite period. Lts. A. Doug Moore and John Crandell had cracked up the C-53 they were piloting on landing at Ngoro and would be remaining until the transport was repaired. While making their final approach, they had come in too low. The transport's tail hit a barricade, ripping open the fuselage aft of the door. The barracks bags of the enlisted men tumbled out onto the landing strip, and the passenger cabin filled with dust, but no one was hurt in the mishap.[46]

JUST BEFORE DARK ON FEBRUARY 5, Capt. Louis Connelly in his twin-engine Beech 18 approached Penfui Field, Koepang, at the head of a group of ten P-40s. The second contingent of the pilots of the 20th Pursuit was arriving at their destination almost twenty-four hours after the first group had landed the day before. Like his squadron mates, Les Johnsen breathed a sigh of relief as he touched down; he had done "some fancy sweating" in his single-engine ship flying over the 540 miles of water that separated Darwin from Koepang.[47] As the pursuiters climbed out of their ships, they were surprised to find Bob McWherter there to greet them. Their squadron mate told them about his inability to get his engine started for the onward leg of the trip to Bali with the first group. He would be joining them for their flight the next morning.

While they refueled their ships, Johnsen worried about the nature of the runway. It was well made, but of coral, which he figured was hard on their ships' tires. Many burned hulks of Lockheed Hudsons and other aircraft littered the field, which served to remind him that they were in a war zone now. The Japanese had been raiding Koepang "for a week or so," he was told.[48] After a meal of water buffalo prepared by Timorese natives, Johnsen and the others were taken to their quarters for the night. To Johnsen it seemed to be a barn. After turning in, he noticed rats scurrying around them.

At dawn the next morning the pursuiters climbed into their ships and began to fire up their engines for the six-hundred-mile trip to Denpasar, Bali. Johnsen with the others was taxiing out for takeoff position when suddenly his tail wheel tire blew out. Now, on top of having "no brakes, no generator, and both tires ready to blow out due to large blisters," he had no tail wheel tire. Everyone yelled at him to remain behind until his tail wheel could be fixed, but as the others went into their takeoff rolls, Johnsen decided to go with them anyway; the burned-out P-40 he passed reminded him of the risk of being caught on the ground in a Zero strafing attack.[49]

But after a difficult takeoff without an inflated tail wheel, Johnsen now faced the problem of locating the ten who had preceded him as well as Connelly's Beech, which was again leading the flight. He knew they were heading for Bali, but without a map he feared becoming lost in the "maze of tropical islands" below. Soon his anxiety gave way to relief when he spotted "three specks" in the sky. As he sped towards the group, he could see it was the Beech with two other P-40s. He felt lucky; the slow Beech had been holding down the speed of the others, allowing Johnsen to catch up.[50]

It was a bright, sunny day as Connelly and his brood were flying west out over the Savu Sea at about twelve thousand feet. Then, at about 0630—almost halfway to the next island, Soemba—Connelly noticed a "strange-looking" twin-engine plane at lower altitude that appeared to be altering its course and was now heading for him. As it came closer, from its twin vertical stabilizers he identified it as Japanese—perhaps a Messerschmitt 110? Apparently its pilot was intending to attack his Beech.[51] Unarmed and with no radio in his transport, Connelly began "going up and down frantically" to signal his predicament to the ten P-40s, then dove for the water. The pursuiters sized up the situation immediately. With flight leader Hubert Egenes in the lead and four others following, they peeled off and headed down at maximum speed. Although only two of his .50s were working, Bob McWherter managed to flame the Japanese ship's left engine at once, drawing pieces from it. Then Andy Reynolds in a dive from above knocked out the starboard motor. Egenes followed and "sawed off" a wing. Right behind Egenes were Dave Coleman and Al Dutton, but before they could attack, the enemy plane was heading down in flames into the sea below. Dutton looked at his watch. It was 0640.[52]

When an excited McWherter had climbed back to altitude, he looked around and spotted Reynolds, Dutton, and Coleman, but flight leader Egenes and the Beech were nowhere to be seen. He noticed that Coleman and Dutton had dropped their belly tanks—correct procedure before entering into combat—but he and Reynolds had neglected to do so.[53] Without the Beech to navigate for them, and with no maps in their cockpits, the four realized they were lost. McWherter thought they were south of the island string leading to Bali, but Reynolds disagreed, thinking that the islands lay to the south of them. They decided to split, with Reynolds and Coleman turning to the south to look for land, while McWherter and Dutton turned north. But shortly afterwards, McWherter noticed that Reynolds and Coleman were heading back north to join them. Then they spotted an island below, along the intended flight path. McWherter figured it might be Flores.

As all four were following along together, Coleman and Dutton radioed McWherter and Reynolds with an ominous message: they were running low on fuel and would not have enough left to make it the remaining one and one-half hours to Bali. They had mistakenly been flying on their main tank instead of the belly tank, as was the procedure for the first leg of a long flight. When they had dropped their belly tanks, along went fifty-two gallons of precious avgas needed to make it to their destination. They would need to ditch somewhere.[54]

Later, as the four approached Lombok Island, just to the east of Bali, they spotted what looked like a sandy beach on its east coast. Virtually out of gas,

Coleman and Dutton decided that was their best hope for a crash-landing. But as Coleman descended in the lead and the beach came better into view, he didn't like its looks and opted for a nearby cow pasture instead. Since the spot was so short, with palm trees at each end, he decided to land wheels up, figuring he would not be able to stop before reaching the end of the pasture if he used his wheels. His ship made a "helluva racket" as it slid through rocks that he hadn't noticed coming in, almost flipping over.[55] Uninjured, Coleman climbed out and watched as Dutton made his approach. On the first try, Dutton overshot the landing spot and went around again. His gas gauge now read empty. Touching down, like Coleman he slid his ship on its belly through the rock-strewn field. He realized that he had injured his hip when he had a difficult time getting out of his plane.[56]

Overhead, McWherter and Reynolds observed the belly landings of their squadron mates. It appeared they were all right. They themselves were also now getting low on fuel as they set course for Bali, some one hundred miles straight ahead. As they approached Denpasar Field and began descending, they could see that it was pock-marked with bomb craters. Dodging the holes on a straight-in approach, the two landed between the craters without mishap, their tanks drained.[57]

Greeting them as they climbed out of their ships were Egenes and the other six of their flight—Roger Williams, Les Johnsen, Wally Hoskyn, Elwin Jackson, Jim Ryan, and B. J. Oliver. They were elated to see McWherter and Reynolds again, not knowing what had happened to them after they made the attack on the twin-engine Japanese plane and became separated from Egenes, who alone had rejoined the others. But what of Coleman and Dutton? McWherter and Reynolds told them that they had belly-landed on Lombok but were all right.[58] Egenes's group of seven had succeeded in landing on the cratered Denpasar Field at about 0945 without incident, except for Johnsen. With no brakes and no tail wheel tire, and trying to avoid the craters, he had ground-looped his ship, but with no real damage. It was being repaired.[59]

The nine now met up with the seven of the first echelon that had preceded them from Darwin and were grounded at Bali after the devastating attack of the day before. The damaged P-40Es of Turner and Hynes were almost flyable again after new propellers had been put on them. Morehead's ship was already in flying condition, with just a few holes in the canopy. But Hayes, Fuchs, Reagan, and Gambonini were planeless, their ships destroyed or damaged beyond repair.

Morehead was keen to fly his ship out right away. When he found out that Connelly would be continuing on to Soerabaja, leading the nine who had just come in, he volunteered to fly as top cover for the Beech. Mindful of the close call that morning with the twin-engine Japanese plane, Connelly accepted Morehead's offer. It was also agreed that Gambonini and Fuchs would go to Soerabaja as passengers in the Beech. Hayes and Reagan would remain behind for the time being.[60]

As he sped down the damaged field to link up with the Beech, Morehead apprehensively strained to look over the long nose of his P-40 in order to maneuver past any holes on the runway. So did the others, including Johnsen, who had the added handicap of no tail wheel tire. However, all got off safely and soon were grouped up behind the Beech, Morehead above them. After an uneventful flight of two hours, they descended over Soerabaja and landed at Perak Field.[61]

There to meet them was Bud Sprague, who had flown in from Ngoro to guide them to the secret field. Les Johnsen was pleased when Sprague picked him to fly on his wing. Seeking to impress his new CO, Johnsen "stuck close and steady" to Sprague, and when Sprague began "gesturing frantically"—there was no radio contact—Johnsen moved in closer, but Sprague only increased his arm-waving, to Johnsen's puzzlement. But the incident became secondary in importance when Sprague signaled for them all as they neared Ngoro to turn around; they were running into a thunderstorm, and Sprague didn't want to risk landing accidents among his novice pursuiters. One hour after their take-off from Perak, they were back on the field again. Sprague informed Johnsen and the others that when flying in a combat zone they were to loosen the formation, not fly closely to each other, in order to cover each other's tail. After the lecture, Sprague headed back to Ngoro, and the others went into Soerabaja for their "first good meal in many days" and a night's sleep at a local hotel.[62]

IN THE MEANTIME, ON LOMBOK ISLAND to the east, Coleman and Dutton had climbed out of their ships and were looking around that morning. They had no idea where they were. There was nobody around at first, but then they saw natives approaching, "all with big knives, wearing bright loin cloths." They came up to the two worried pursuiters and kneeled before them. Dutton and Coleman gave them cigarettes, and they all sat around together smoking while the Americans wondered what they should do next.[63] After a while the natives in sign language indicated to Coleman and Dutton that they should follow them. After entering a clearing, they climbed up and down a hill, then ran into four or five other natives carrying rifles who, they found out, were native Dutch police. Shortly afterwards a Dutchman arrived in an open Ford and indicated they should get in. Dutton climbed in the front seat, and Coleman got in the back. The Dutchman drove to what turned out to be the house

Abandoned P-40Es of the 20th Pursuit Squadron (Provisional) that were damaged on February 5, 1942, in the Japanese bombing attack on Denpasar Field, Bali, and later captured. *Author's collection.*

of the mayor. Much to their surprise, Coleman and Dutton were offered Johnny Walker and given clean clothes. After taking a bath, native style, they were served a rice dinner "with chicken, eggs, soybeans, vegetables, and livers . . . a million things," Dutton thought.

After dinner the Dutch resident governor came for them and drove them across the island to his palace at Mataram, facing Bali across the Lombok Strait. There they were given another dinner before being taken at 2330 to the coast to board a thirty-foot sailing boat, the *Patricia*. All that night the two worked-up Americans tried to catch some sleep as the *Patricia* slowly plied its way the fifty miles towards Bali and then down the coast to Denpasar.

EARLY THE NEXT MORNING, sometime after 0730, a P-40E came in to land at Perak. Only Hubert Egenes recognized the pilot as he climbed out: Philippine veteran Walt Coss. Egenes alone of his flight of nine had been at Amberley when Coss was still there before leaving on January 16 for Darwin and Java. Egenes picked Andy Reynolds, Roger Williams, Les Johnsen, and Wally Hoskyn to fly with him in the group Coss would lead to their new home field at Ngoro. Jack Dale, due in shortly, would lead Elwin Jackson, Jim Ryan, B. J. Oliver, and Bob McWherter to the field. But three of the 20th Pursuiters at the field would be left behind. Jim Morehead opted to spend another night at Soerabaja with his ship rather than follow the others to Ngoro. Planeless, Paul Gambonini and Marion Fuchs had no choice but to remain behind, too. They would "wait for the fellows from the field to come after us," Gambonini recorded in his diary that night.[64]

As the nine rookie pilots followed behind their flight leaders—Coss's group twenty minutes ahead of Dale's—they scanned the Javanese terrain below, wondering where this secret new field was located. After about half an hour, Coss began descending after having made several ninety-degree turns at checkpoints, his charges following behind. They were obviously approaching the field, but where was it? It was 0930 when Coss touched down on ground covered with bushes, with a disbelieving Egenes, Williams, Reynolds, and Hoskyn behind him. At 0950 Dale came in and landed ahead of Jackson, Ryan, Oliver, and McWherter. Climbing out, the new arrivals were amazed at the camouflaging job on the field; they knew they could never have found it on their own.[65]

As they were introduced around to the 17th Pursuiters on the field, the nine new pilots sensed a somberness that pervaded the base. They were told that the day before, Jess Reed—the popular Marine pilot on detail to the 17th Pursuit—had been killed in an accident while trying to land back on the field. The blow hit hard; Reed was regarded as a "kind of foster father"—the "guardian angel"—of the 17th.[66]

Reed had taken Walt Coss's No. 15 up, soloing in the P-40E, after having checked out the controls with Sprague's approval. But he was unfamiliar with the characteristics of the pursuit ship, having flown only Ryan STMs as an instructor to the Dutch Naval Air Force at Soerabaja since arriving in the Dutch East Indies. As Reed was coming back, the eyes of most of the 17th's officers and men were fixed on him. They wondered if the inexperienced pilot would handle the landing all right. Suddenly they heard Reed's engine cut out. Butch Hague thought that Reed had inadvertently pulled back on his mixture control rather than the throttle to the right. Apparently trying to go around again, Reed turned ninety degrees, close to the ground, then his engine coughed. His ship came down in a rice paddy at the end of the runway and flipped over on its back.[67]

When Reed crashed, Cy Blanton and Bill Hennon were down at the end of the runway and saw that the P-40 had come completely around and was facing the other way, away from the runway. They crossed a river to reach the paddy where the plane lay partially submerged in water. There was "gas everywhere" from the ruptured tanks. Blanton and Hennon tried to raise the tail, but it was too heavy. Blanton got down under the cockpit and managed to release Reed's safety belt, freeing his body from the cockpit. But he could see that Reed had suffered a grievous blow to his forehead from the P-40s gunsight and was dead, more likely from drowning than from the blow. Soon they were surrounded by natives, whom Blanton and Hennon beseeched in sign language to lift the plane, but in vain. Only when a Dutch sergeant arrived and told the natives in their own language what he wanted them to do did they understand and lift the plane up from the muck sufficiently for Blanton and Hennon to extricate Reed's body. The operation had taken several hours. Later in the day, Reed was buried nearby.[68]

But now on this morning of February 7 it was back to business. A message had come in at 1110 from the ADC: there was a Japanese bomber reported over the city. Minutes later the ADC radioed them that an enemy pursuit formation, an estimated six planes, was approaching Soerabaja from the north. The 17th was ready to respond to any such warning. Four P-40Es were on alert status at each of four ready posts off the two runways, prepared for immediate takeoff.[69]

In response to the first warning Bud Sprague immediately took off at the head of A flight: Ed Gilmore, Ed Kiser, and Dwight Muckley. To intercept the Japanese fighter formation, Walt Coss led off his B flight, with Bill Stauter, Hubert Egenes, and Bill Hennon behind him. But then, at 1125 ADC ordered off C and D flights to aid in the interception. Lieutenant Lane headed C flight, with Bill Gallienne, Joe Kruzel, and Ray Thompson, while D flight was led by Bo McCallum, with Cy Blanton, Jack Dale, and Butch Hague following him.[70] All four flights patrolled over the Soerabaja area at between 20,000 and 24,000 feet for two hours, but the pursuiters made no contact with the reported bomber or Zero fighters. They grumbled that once again they had been misdirected by the ADC. This time the bad order "kept us chasing ourselves." Hague was one of those affected. His engine had conked out at 16,500 feet, obliging him to drop out of D flight, and when he climbed back to 18,500 after his engine caught again, he was attacked by six of his own squadron mates, forcing him to dive for a cloud.[71]

Below, grounded pilots Jim Morehead, Paul Gambonini, and Marion Fuchs were experiencing the air raid on Soerabaja that the ADC had anticipated in its warnings sent to Ngoro. As they were eating a late breakfast in their hotel, the air raid alarm went off, and they crawled under their table for safety. But it appeared the Zeros were after the Dutch flying boat base nearby rather than the city. They were meeting no aerial opposition, unseen by the high-flying P-40s that expected the Japanese at their altitude.[72]

After the fruitless patrol, Sprague led his pilots back to Ngoro for landings spaced at ten-minute intervals, beginning at 1230. By 1400 they were all on the ground again, except for Muckley and Gallienne. Flying in Wally Hoskyn's ship, the still jittery Muckley called in to inform Sprague that he had made a forced landing at Perak "due to failure of the propeller pitch control," but he was uninjured and his ship undamaged. Gallienne also called in; he had crash-landed on a beach after engine failure. He was not hurt, but his P-40 was a wreck.[73]

But even before Sprague's four flights had completed landing at Ngoro, another flight was ordered off, this one to patrol between Ngoro and Soerabaja. At 1330 McCallum, Dale, and Hague took off again, joined by Cy Blanton. They patrolled at eighteen thousand feet for two hours, but once more sighted no enemy planes. When they aired their frustrations later to George Parker, who had not yet been assigned by Sprague on an interception mission, the normally uncritical 20th Pursuiter concluded that "[communications between] Dutch Air Defense and us must improve."[74] Then, just after 1400, the ADC ordered the 17th Pursuit off once more. They were to patrol north of Malang to provide protection for B-17s returning from the north to Singosari, with landing expected at 1600. Having refueled after their morning patrols, Sprague, followed by Hennon, Kiser, Stauter, Coss, and Kruzel, lifted off at 1415 and headed southeast to Malang, reaching eighteen thousand feet over the area. Soon, six B-17Es passed below them and came in to land at Singosari at 1500. The pursuiters sighted no enemy planes in the area to threaten the bombers. Five of the flight then headed back to the field at Ngoro. The sixth, Ed Kiser, broke off from the others and headed due north instead, detached to fly to Perak Field to guide Jim Morehead to Ngoro.[75]

Back on the ground that afternoon after his second interception effort of the day, Butch Hague was not surprised to learn of Gallienne's engine failure and crash landing. He knew that the planes were "past the inspection hour" and that some of them were "in need of work," but the 17th "kept flying them" anyway. Now they had one less to send up.[76] But late that afternoon they received a replacement for Gallienne's written-off ship, when Ed Kiser guided Jim Morehead in. Morehead's ship had not been hit during the attack on Soerabaja that morning.[77] And Wally Hoskyn's P-40E that Muckley had force-landed at Perak was back, too, flown in by Elwin Jackson after a couple of mechanics that Bill Hennon had sent to Perak in the squadron truck had finished their work on the ship's propeller. Jackson had driven to the field to fly the ship back the afternoon of his arrival at Ngoro that morning behind Dale.[78]

Earlier that day the squadron had received several trucks, two jeeps, and a couple of staff cars to accommodate the transportation needs of its growing numbers. "Mighty useful," Hennon felt.[79] Some of the vehicles were put to use to transport the ten new arrivals of the 20th Pursuit to their new quarters at Blimbing late that afternoon. They had been assigned houses with thatched roofs. As Bob McWherter and some of the others lay on their cots early that evening, to amuse themselves they took potshots with their Colt .45s at the lizards scrambling about on the ceiling. Later they went into Ngoro town and walked up and down the main street, a very short journey. Street salesmen accosted them, trying to get the young men to buy the products they were selling. But the pursuiters weren't interested in the wares of either the hawkers or the local merchants, except for some of the food items, particularly roasted peanuts.[80]

The next morning—Sunday, February 8—four flights of four pilots each were on alert duty again. At one of the alert areas, George Parker—assigned as wingman to Bud Sprague, who was leading A flight—was suffering from anxiety. It would be his first combat interception since arriving at Ngoro three days earlier. It would also be the first for Bob McWherter, slated to fly wing to second element leader Bill Hennon in Sprague's flight. Nearby, at another alert area, Jack Dale's B flight was also awaiting a possible takeoff order. His wingman was a newcomer too: Wally Hoskyn. Dale's second element was headed by Dwight Muckley, with Les Johnsen as his wingman. Even though McWherter, Hoskyn, and Johnsen had just arrived, Sprague was already pressing them into duty.[81]

Suddenly the phones connected in boxes hung on trees rang at A and B flight areas. The operations shack informed Sprague and Dale that the ADC was ordering them off to intercept a reported formation of nine Japanese bombers coming in from the north. Sprague and Dale passed the word, and all eight pilots rushed to their waiting ships for a 1000 takeoff. Parker repressed a pang of fear as he thundered down the field behind Sprague. In B flight, Bob McWherter was also worrying; he felt he was off to a bad start with the 17th when he barely cleared the trees at the end of the runway on his takeoff.[82]

The eight pursuiters climbed northward to about twenty thousand feet, looking around for enemy bombers. Half an hour into their patrol, they were joined by another four P-40s: Ed Kiser had led off his C flight at 1035 to aid in the interception. But as the three flights milled around, they saw no Japanese bombers in the vicinity. Then they spotted B-17s though cloud cover below them, individually heading south for Singosari. ADC again had erroneously given them reports of their own formations.[83]

As the three flights approached Ngoro on their return at about 1230 after yet another frustrating experience, they found that four P-40s were over the field, providing landing protection for them. Bo McCallum's D flight had been ordered off at 1120 for that purpose. But no Japanese were sighted in the immediate area, and all twelve P-40s returned safely. The four rookies of A and B flights had acquitted themselves satisfactorily, including Parker, who was pleased to find that his initial fear had given way to calm and alertness once he started his patrol.[84]

After only an hour back on the field, Bill Hennon took off again, at 1345, for a familiarization flight for McWherter, Hubert Egenes, and Ray Thompson. To McWherter, flying as Hennon's wing man again, Hennon was a "fast and tricky leader," and he found he could "just barely keep up" with him as they flew around East Java at ten thousand feet.[85] Soon the weather began to deteriorate. With Ngoro Field closed in, Hennon led the flight to the Mount Semeru area east of Malang, where he circled the twelve-thousand-foot mountain while waiting for the weather to clear so that they could come into Ngoro from the south. But Hennon and McWherter had become separated from Egenes and Thompson, and now Hennon had lost McWherter, too.[86]

Unable to locate his flight members, Hennon headed down to the south coast, then swung inland to come into Ngoro at 1520. McWherter had a more difficult time finding his way back but finally located the field and came in with "only enough gasoline to coast down the runway." Meanwhile, Egenes and Thompson had wandered to the east and were caught in a rainstorm some 150 miles from Ngoro. Egenes decided to try a forced landing on a grassy field he'd spotted below. The two managed to get their P-40s down without damage to either ship or to themselves, then climbed out and started walking along a path. Suddenly, about two hundred "hostile natives" came towards them. When they were about fifty feet away, Egenes reached for his pistol, and the natives "scattered in all directions." Egenes and Thompson ran back to their planes, but moments later the natives "came at us again." Egenes "waved his arms, shouted, and smiled" at them, but they didn't understand. Finally, three natives in sarongs came up and squatted besides Egenes's plane, a sign that Egenes knew meant they were friendly.[87]

After much effort, Egenes got the three locals to understand that he wanted to see the Dutch officials in the town of Djember that he knew was about three miles away. When they took the American pilots there, Egenes used a telephone in the police station and called Ngoro Field to let Sprague know that they were safe and to give their location. It was agreed that Sprague would send Hennon down the following morning in a staff car to fly off Thompson's plane and lead Egenes in his own ship back to the field. Thompson could return in the car. But they would need to clear an area for them to take off.[88]

Egenes had the Dutch officials tell the natives that they wanted trees cut down along the road near where they had landed so that they would be able to fly the P-40s off. Egenes and Thompson were amazed that "within an hour" the natives had managed to cut down "a mile of trees, about six inches in diameter" with only "small knives." They were also pleasantly surprised when the natives brought them bananas and coconuts—and much against their expectations, "hard-boiled eggs"—that the Americans had requested.[89]

ON BALI, DAVE COLEMAN and Al Dutton were experiencing another form of local hospitality. After arriving on the island from Lombok, the "pure-blooded" Dutch governor made arrangements for the two planeless 20th Pursuiters to stay cost-free at the Bali Hotel. That afternoon they checked in, wearing the khaki clothing they'd been flying in; all their other possessions had been left behind in their wrecked planes on Lombok. They were being "treated like royalty," with free drinks at the "open bar" and lots of food."[90] But they were the only guests in the hotel. Their squadron mates Bill Turner, George Hynes, Connie Reagan, and Tommy Hayes had left for Soerabaja earlier in the day, before Coleman and Dutton had checked in. They called Ngoro to let Sprague know where they were. With no one to report to at Denpasar Field, they were to remain where they were until someone came for them.[91]

At Soerabaja that afternoon, Paul Gambonini and Marion Fuchs welcomed the arrival of Turner and Hynes, who had flown from Bali in their repaired P-40s, each with a replacement propeller installed. Later in the afternoon Hayes and Reagan also came in from Bali, but as passengers in the Beech 18. Their own ships were wrecks on Denpasar Field. However, their stop was only temporary; the Beech took off for Ngoro shortly afterwards with them.[92] Turner and Hynes would not be going on to Ngoro by themselves that afternoon, because they didn't know how to find the secret field. When they called Sprague to inform him of their arrival at Soerabaja, they were told that Cy Blanton would fly from Ngoro early the next morning to lead them in. But planeless Gambonini and Fuchs would not be traveling by air to Ngoro. A truck from Ngoro that was to pick up supplies for the squadron in Soerabaja the next day would collect them for the trip to the field. Except for Coleman and Dutton, enjoying life as tourists on Bali, Gambonini and Fuchs would be the last of the 20th Pursuit's pilots to arrive at their Java destination.[93]

CHAPTER SEVEN

"These Guys Are Really Inexperienced"

AT AMBERLEY FIELD ON THE MORNING of Wednesday, February 4, 2nd Lt. Vern Head and twenty-three other pilots assigned to the 3rd Pursuit Squadron (Provisional) were assigned P-40Es and told to get ready for the flight north. Their CO, 1st Lt. Grant Mahony, had just received his orders to lead his newly formed squadron to Darwin "by first available transport" for onward transfer to Java. With the help of Air Officer Dick Legg, he was preparing to leave the following morning.[1]

At nearby Archerfield the commanding officer of the 27th Bomb Group's 91st Bomb Squadron had received his movement orders, too. The group's CO, John "Big Jim" Davies, had ordered Capt. Ed Backus to take his squadron's fifteen A-24 dive bombers to Darwin as soon as possible and from there to proceed to Java. He was not to leave Darwin without the escort of Mahony's squadron, however.[2]

Both Mahony and Davies were under pressure from USAFIA in Melbourne to get their P-40s and A-24s to East Java over the ferry route at the "earliest practicable moment." "Immediate action imperative," Brigadier General Barnes had emphasized. The USAFIA's commanding general was under fire from his boss, Major General Brett, who had been shaken by the sudden Japanese aerial attack on Soerabaja on February 3 and had ordered Barnes the same day to "forward all airplanes immediately."[3]

But there were problems with the aircraft. Head felt that his No. 27 was in "pretty good shape" for the long haul to Darwin, but "everything was wrong" with most of the others. Several had "cracked up" the day before as a result of having been "defectively put together," in Head's assessment. It was taking all day to get them in flying condition. Head was also worried that "the fellows have little total time and haven't flown in several months."[4] And now it looked like one of the few experienced pilots Mahony had assigned to his squadron might be dropped. Philippines veteran Parker Gies was in the hospital with "fever all over." Assigned by Mahony to lead one of the flights going north, he was "anxious to get out" before the squadron should take off for Darwin the next morning.[5]

Ed Backus had his troubles, too. The 91st's A-24s now had trigger motors and solenoids to operate the guns, but other armament equipment was improvised. As in the case of the other A-24s of the group, Backus's ships still did not have self-sealing gas tanks or armor for the rear gunner.[6]

But a small group of other men who had arrived at Amberley from Melbourne that afternoon was much more contented with their own situation. SSgt. Cecil Ingram, from Longview, Texas, and twelve other enlisted men who had been transferred from Headquarters Squadron, 35th Pursuit Group, and the Air Corps team on the *Coolidge* to the 3rd Pursuit were all glad to be leaving their old squadron, "because none of us liked it." At Amberley they were happy to meet some of the others they knew from Hamilton Field and enjoyed a good supper at the field that evening. Ingram and his comrades comprised the vanguard of the 3rd Pursuit's mechanics and armorers who were being transferred to Java and scheduled to go out the next morning.[7]

At 0830 the next morning Mahony led off half his new squadron mates, and Al Strauss took off at the lead of the rest. Their destination was Charleville, their first refueling stop. Gies was not with them; he had gotten out of the hospital too late, and another pilot had taken his place. Leaving with them were the thirteen enlisted men of the squadron in a C-53 transport. With a greater range than that of the P-40s, the twin-engine Douglas transport would be skipping Charleville and making its first refueling stop further along the route, at Cloncurry. From Archerfield Backus took off in the rain with the first group of seven A-24s, also bound for Charleville. The second group of eight under 1st Lt. Harry Galusha would be going out the following day.[8]

After two hours the 3rd Pursuiters approached Charleville and reduced altitude for landing. When Mahony's group had touched down on the crude field without incident, Strauss began leading his pilots in. One of them, 41-F Ralph Martin from Detroit, Michigan, who had turned twenty-six nine days earlier, was preparing to land when his wingman radioed him that he had engine trouble. Martin gave the wingman permission to land ahead of him. But as Martin himself was about to touch down behind his wingman, his ship, No. 13, was suddenly picked up by a whirlwind and dumped upside down on the runway. His canopy open preparatory to landing, Martin was knocked unconscious when his head struck the hard surface of the runway. The pilots of the squadron who had landed ahead of him rushed to Martin's plane to pull him out from under his ship. He was soaked in battery acid and gasoline.[9] Mahony rushed Martin to the local hospital. His injuries were severe but not fatal. Meanwhile, the pursuiters were trying to have their ships refueled. They were not impressed with operations at the field; it had "no servicing facilities to speak of." Head and the others had to roll barrels of gasoline to their ships and hand-pump fuel into them themselves.[10]

Their refueling chore completed, Mahony and Strauss took off with the remaining twenty-two pilots from Charleville at 1300, and except for one of them they reached Cloncurry about 1600. Head's 41-E flying school classmate Wade Holman had left the formation and headed back to Amberley for reasons unknown to Head or the others. The landing at Cloncurry was uneventful, although Robert Oestreicher had to hand-pump his wheels and flaps down to land; he was having trouble with his hydraulic system.[11]

Waiting to service their ships were the thirteen enlisted men of the squadron; they had landed in the C-53 two hours earlier. The field's refueling crew was ill with dengue fever, so "almost roasting" in the heat, the 3rd Pursuit men hand-pumped gas into the P-40Es, then turned their attention to the six A-24s of Backus's group that had landed at Cloncurry too on their way to Darwin; one had been left behind at Charleville with a "bum engine." But that was not all for the tired men; they had their own transport to refuel, plus a B-17 that had come in to guide the pursuiters to their next stop, Daly Waters, the following morning.[12]

It was late at night before Ingram and his comrades finished their time-consuming work. They had missed the dance that the people of Cloncurry had put on for them. But when they checked into the town's hotel, the owner invited them to go kangaroo hunting with him. Driving around in the bush, using the car's headlights to sight the 'roos, was exciting. They spotted only one, and Ingram fired his .45 at it but missed; it jumped up and "was on its way to parts unknown." Back at the hotel very late, the owner insisted on bringing them tea and cookies before they finally got to bed. Already sound asleep elsewhere in the "poor hotel" were Head and his squadron mates.[13]

At 0845 the next morning, February 6, the pursuiters were off again, following the B-17 guiding them over "very desolate country" to their next stop, Daly Waters. They themselves were escorting the C-53 transport until it veered off and headed directly for Darwin, not requiring a stop at Daly Waters for refueling.[14] The flight of three and one-half hours over 540 miles of featureless country was very boring. Spence Johnson broke the monotony by amusing himself testing his guns on wallabies and kangaroos he spotted below. Finally, Daly Waters came into view. The landing strip looked to Head as if it had been "cleared out of open country." As Oestreicher prepared to land, once again he had to hand-pump his wheels and flaps down.[15]

It was shortly after 1130 when Mahony, leading the first group of twelve circling the field, descended to make a perfect landing. The next pilot bounced as he touched down and apparently damaged his ship, though he retained control of it.[16] In third position, Bryan Brown was less fortunate. Coming in too low and short of the field, he didn't notice the barbed wire fence at the near end and smacked into it, damaging his left wing. After climbing out of his P-40E, Brown waved his arms to alert Ray Melikian coming in behind him, also too low and short of the field, but it was too late—Melikian couldn't avoid the fence in time and went through it too, sustaining similar damage to his ship, now half turned over.[17]

Observing the tribulations of the pursuiters was Cecil Brown, a CBS war correspondent on his way from Darwin to Amberley, and 2nd Lt. Henry J. Rose, who was providing him transport in a twin-engine B-18. Refueling their ships with Rose were the pilots of the six A-24s Ed Backus had led in without incident minutes earlier. Rose, an A-24 pilot detached from the 16th Bomb Squadron, was particularly exercised as he watched the crackups. "What the hell's the matter with them?" he screamed. "They've got all the field in the world here to land on and they are coming down in the grass and weeds." From his position Rose hadn't noticed the fence at the far end of the field and thought the pursuiters had hit a ditch.[18]

It was with some relief that the war correspondent and Rose watched the next seven pursuiters manage to get down without damage to their aircraft. But the twelfth pilot was having problems. In five attempts to land, each time when he was four or five feet off the ground he opted to go around and try again.[19] "You can imagine what that poor kid in there is going through," Rose said to Brown and the A-24 crews standing around watching the ordeal. A sergeant mechanic from the B-18 blurted, "The only way we'll get him down is shoot him down!" War correspondent Brown shared his opinion with the others: "If a pilot couldn't make a simple landing in a strange and good field, how could he fight in combat with the enemy on his tail?" The tremulous pilot finally touched down on the field without incident. Brown chalked up the performance of the pursuiters to insufficient experience. They were "youngsters just out of flying school," he reasoned. But what could be done? Even untrained men were "desperately needed if Java were to be saved," Brown concluded.

Brown and Melikian's ships were beyond repair at the isolated field and would have to be left behind. With the squadron's mechanics unavailable, the third pilot who had also damaged his P-40E on landing "pounded his ship back into some sort of shape with a 2x4 and a hammer" as his squadron mate Oestreicher watched. Oestreicher himself was occupied with charging his ship's battery, "a helluva job."[20]

That afternoon "quick showers of rain" started coming in as the squadron's P-40s were being refueled. Finally, at 1740 the remaining twenty-one P-40s took off for the last leg of their trip, to Darwin 360 miles north-northwest of Daly Waters. One flight of ten ships followed the B-17, while the other eleven "more or less" followed a railroad track leading to Darwin. Flying with Mahony and Wahl, Oestreicher had more trouble with his ship: his engine was "cutting out and missing." Running into several rain squalls, they all flew "rather close and low."[21]

It was about 1940 when they approached the RAAF field at Darwin. In coming in to land, 41-F pilot Oscar Handy cracked up, reducing Mahony's strength to twenty ships. But "nearly all the others need working on," Head surmised after bringing his own plane in without problem.[22] Waiting to greet them on their arrival were Ed Backus and the pilots of the other five remaining A-24s who had landed at 1520 that afternoon. The thirteen enlisted men of the squadron were there, too. They had arrived in the early afternoon in the C-53. Their pilot had managed to land on a clear runway. As they looked out the windows on the C-53's approach, the men saw that another runway was covered with empty gasoline drums, which they figured were meant to prevent a surprise landing by Japanese aircraft.[23]

That evening Head and the other officers of the 3rd Pursuit and the 91st Bomb spent an uncomfortable night sleeping on the floor of the officers lounge. Ingram and the other enlisted men of the 3rd stretched out on the floor of the NCOs mess, where they had eaten their dinner earlier that evening.[24] "Well, we are getting closer to real action now," Head wrote in his diary that night. Second Lt. J. Allen Anderson of the 7th Bomb Group who was at Darwin, too, was also thinking about what the future held for the 3rd Pursuiters after having witnessed Handy's crash earlier. "It is a shame to send boys like that into combat when we do have trained personnel. Many will die for lack of training," he wrote in his own diary that evening.[25]

The next day, Saturday, February 7, was very windy. Vern Head was upset that the dust being blown up was "just ruining our guns." The pursuiters were working on their planes most of the day. Except for the few enlisted men of their squadron, there was little help at Darwin to give their ships the attention they should have, Head complained. In his estimation there was "something wrong with nearly all of them." Bob Buel's ship "kept burning out generators," while Oestreicher's had engine trouble. With the help of two of the squadron's privates, Oestreicher tore the engine apart on his *Miss Nadine* and put it back together, installing a rebuilt carburetor from a cracked up P-40.[26]

The squadron's thirteen enlisted men were on standby in case their C-53 pilot got the order to go north that he was expecting. To Ingram and the others he seemed "plenty worried," since the transport did not carry any guns, and he knew that the previous transport that went north, piloted by John Crandell and Doug Moore, had not come back from Java. He wanted the enlisted men to catch a ride to Java in a bomber, instead. It was all the same to Ingram and his buddies: "We aren't scared much."[27]

Just before 1630 they noticed eight single-engine aircraft approaching the field, which they soon made out as A-24 dive bombers. After touching down, 1st Lt. Harry Galusha and seven other pilots in his flight climbed out of their ships with their rear seat gunners and were greeted by their CO, Ed Backus, and the other pilots who had arrived the day before. Two of Galusha's A-24s were in bad shape, one with excessive oil use and the other with three bad cylinders. They would need to remain at Darwin for repairs.[28]

The following morning the 3rd Pursuiters continued working on their planes. Several in flying condition were taken up for test hops, including flights by some officers who were not pursuit pilots. Four former 19th Bomb Group pilots Mahony knew well from his Philippine days had arrived on February 5 on two LB-30 Liberator bombers evacuating 19th Group personnel from Mindanao, and Mahony let them take four of his P-40s up on familiarization flights. Thirty-year-old Maj. Bill Fisher—former commander of the group's 28th Bomb Squadron—was under orders to report to Major General Brereton at ABDACOM Headquarters, Bandoeng, Java, for possible assignment to the Air Defense Command at Soerabaja. Three of his pilots, 1st Lts. Jim Bruce, Tom "Speed" Hubbard, and Tom Christian, were highly experienced flying school graduates from 1939 and 1940 but like Fisher had never flown a P-40 before. Just as one of the four was coming in to land an abrupt rain squall caught his ship, but he succeeded in landing safely.[29]

Mahony was not surprised to find that the former bomber pilots could also handle pursuit ships. Although Bruce, Hubbard, and Christian were not assigned to his squadron, he needed more experienced pilots than the ones he'd been given to take to Java. It was agreed that one—Tom Christian (class 40-C)—would replace one of his less experienced pilots, while Fisher would take the ship of another to get to Java for his new assignment. Mahony

P-40E of the 3rd Pursuit Squadron (Provisional) at the RAAF field, Darwin, February 7–9, 1942, awaiting their ferry flight to Java. *Courtesy Eugene A. Wahl.*

couldn't pick Bruce (39-A) and Hubbard (39-B) to join him, because they would outrank him (40-A) as commanding officer of the squadron. Second Lts. Benny Johnson and Bob Kaiser—both 41-F flying school graduates—were selected by Mahony to return to Amberley and bring back planes in the next transfer of P-40s to Darwin and Java.[30]

Late that afternoon the air raid siren went off at the field. Forty Japanese bombers were reported on their way to Darwin. Mahony ordered off the eighteen pilots whose ships were now airworthy. Oestreicher's and Buel's were still out of commission. Head and the seventeen others climbed to high altitude and patrolled north of Darwin for three hours but saw nothing. It was evidently a false report, the pilots supposed.[31] Below, SSgt. Cecil Ingram and Sgt. Gene Chapman, a fellow Texan, had taken over an unmanned .50-caliber machine gun and were waiting in the pit for the Japanese. When the bombers did not show up, they figured that "somebody must have warned them" that the P-40s "were waiting for them, because they turned tail and headed home."[32]

That evening, all the Java-assigned A-24 and P-40 pilots as well as the 3rd

Pursuit's enlisted men were still waiting for their takeoff orders. Evidently the delay was a result of the nonavailability of a navigating aircraft to guide them to Koepang.[33]

AT AMBERLEY FIELD ON THE MORNING of February 4 those pursuit pilots who were not getting ready to go north with Mahony's 3rd Pursuit Squadron (Provisional) the following day were assembled in the hangar classroom. Maj. Floyd Pell (promoted on January 30), relieved from his duties as air officer under Colonel Johnson of Brisbane's Base Section 3, had called them together. He was going to select pilots for his newly designated 33rd Pursuit Squadron (Provisional), per orders received on February 1 from USAFIA headquarters in Melbourne.[34] One by one Pell called out the names of the twenty-four he was selecting. The pickings were very thin; the stock of pursuit pilots available off the *Republic, Polk,* and *Mormacsun* had greatly dwindled following the assignment of pilots to the 17th, 20th, and 3rd Squadrons during the past three weeks. In addition, four had been assigned to the Brisbane assembly depot, and three had elected to join the recently created Air Transport Command, which was in need of pilots for its transport ships. For the first time it would be necessary to tap into the most junior group: the flying school graduates of 41-G and 41-H classes.[35]

The selection process was not without a humorous incident. When Pell called out the name of one of the six 41-H pilots he was picking for his squadron, there was no reply from the pilots assembled. After several more times calling his name, Pell was becoming agitated and menacingly inquired, "Where the hell is he?" At that point a short, dark-complexioned, barrel-chested man stood up and boomed out, "The name is pronounced *Seer,* sir, not *Sewer!*" Everyone broke out in laughter, and even Pell cracked a smile, then replied, "Okay, Stinky, sit down." From then on, Dick Suehr would be known as Stinky.[36]

By the end of the meeting Pell had picked five 41-E and six 41-F pilots to go along with the six 41-Gs and six 41-Hs, in addition to 40-A Philippines veteran and flying instructor Gerry Keenan, who would be second in command in the squadron. Philippines veteran Parker Gies was not at the meeting; he was still ill with fever. Dropped from the 3rd Pursuit for its takeoff the next morning, he was not being selected by Pell for the 33rd Pursuit, either. He would remain assigned to the Brisbane assembly depot. Gies was not impressed with the qualifications of those Slugger Pell had selected for the 33rd. "These guys are really inexperienced," he wrote in his diary.[37] Their new twenty-eight-year-old commanding officer made a strong impression on his charges, however. In physical appearance the West Pointer was "tall and

Floyd Pell, later commanding officer of the 33rd Pursuit Squadron (Provisional), as a second lieutenant in advanced flying training at Kelly Field in 1938. *Courtesy National Archives and Records Administration.*

heavy, with a thatch of close-cropped blond hair." In personality he seemed "explosive" to them. David Latane, a 41-G off the *Mormacsun,* felt he was a "tough guy."[38]

During the following days, the 33rd Pursuit's new pilots took their newly assigned ships up to gain flying time in the P-40Es. Pell had them practicing formation flying, simulated combat tactics, and three-point spot landings, but they got no gunnery practice at all, much to Bob McMahon's disappointment. Within a few days, impressed with his flying ability, Pell orally designated McMahon as one of his four flight leaders, the only 41-G picked for such a responsibility. Pell himself would head up A flight, with 41-F Jack Peres leading B flight and Gerry Keenan in charge of C flight.[39]

Bryce Wilhite was pleased to find himself finally assigned to a combat squadron going north after two and one-half months since arriving on the *Republic,* though he was perhaps a bit intimidated to be picked as one of the 41-Gs for Pell's own flight. The morning he was selected for the 33rd, he had lost his No. 13 to one of the 3rd Pursuiters going out the next day—Ralph Martin—but now had been given a replacement aircraft in which to participate in the 33rd's flying practices. Like a mother hen, Pell had filled his own flight with the most junior of those he had selected for the squadron: two 41-Hs and three 41-Gs, to go along with Bob Kerstetter, a 41-F.[40]

On February 8 Pell formally announced his flight composition selections by posting them on the hangar bulletin board, the first written orders the new 33rd Pursuiters had seen. There were a few personnel changes indicated in the flight compositions. Ken Glassburn, a 41-F selectee, had been dropped on the orders of USAFIA headquarters; he should not have been chosen because he was permanently assigned to the Brisbane assembly depot. In his place Pell picked another 41-G, Jim Naylor. He also dropped 41-H pilot Clarence Simpson and substituted another 41-G, Gerry Dix. Both changes involved pilots in his own A flight.[41]

The following day, Pell sent Wilhite up in his new aircraft to practice dogfighting with another new 33rd Pursuiter. Wilhite was to fly wingman in formation until the pair reached twelve thousand feet, then they were to separate, fly in a circle until they passed each other head-on, and at that point commence the dogfight. To Wilhite it seemed like a useless exercise, as they had been told many times earlier to avoid dogfighting a Zero in a P-40.[42] Wilhite also was rather apprehensive about the exercise, as the compass on his ship had not yet been swung for magnetic deviation, he had no maps, and his radio had not been tuned to a frequency over which he could talk to his leader. He knew he would need to keep his attention focused on the other pilot's ship and on his own instruments.

After taking off in formation and climbing through the clouds to the designated altitude, the two started the dogfight. Immediately, Wilhite erred in turning too quickly and tightly, and his ship reacted by trying to go into a high-speed stall. When Wilhite relaxed his turn, the other pilot easily got on to his tail; Wilhite was dead meat. On a second try, Wilhite's engine, running at high RPM and manifold pressure, started overheating. He signaled by hand to the other pilot that they should go down, but instead of waiting for Wilhite to latch onto his wing, the leader dove past and disappeared through the overcast.

With no map, no radio, and no reliable compass, Wilhite decided to head east towards the ocean as the safest place over which to descend through the cloud cover. However, before he reached the ocean, he began descending and barely missed a small mountain. He found himself in a valley surrounded by small mountains and rain storms. Climbing back up, the fuselage tank ran dry, so he switched to the main wing tank and again headed out towards the ocean. But the fuel in the wing tank was quickly depleted, obliging Wilhite to switch to his last gas source, the reserve wing tank.

Flying above the clouds for what seemed like a long time trying in vain to find a hole in the clouds, Wilhite decided to descend again anyway. It was a mistake; he realized he was flying between peaks of the mountain, though he had come down on a small valley. Circling it without finding a field long enough to land a P-40 wheels down, he then spotted a small depression on another field long enough for a landing. He figured the depression would wreck his ship if he came in wheels down, so he opted to try coming in wheels up instead. As he approached the depression at low speed, he passed over a fence, cut the magneto and main switch, and hit the ground. His ship skidded through the length of the depression and came to a halt. After climbing out of the cockpit, he found he was not injured, but what about damage to the plane? A quick inspection indicated that the propeller was ruined, but there was only slight damage to the flaps, undercarriage, and oil and glycol coolers.[43]

Wilhite spotted a farmer, his wife, and children running across the field towards him. After being taken to the house of the flabbergasted farmer, Wilhite called Amberley Field. Handed the phone, the farmer told the sergeant who replied where Wilhite had bellied in: Harrisville, some twenty miles south of Amberley Field. Within an hour a jeep arrived from the field to pick Wilhite up and take him back to Amberley.[44] Buzz Wagner, furious, tore into Wilhite for crash-landing the P-40 he had assigned to him. Did Wilhite realize how much each P-40 was needed in the combat zone? After keeping quiet to allow Wagner to finish his tirade, Wilhite explained that the ship was not badly damaged and that if he had opted to bail out rather than crash-land, there would be no ship to repair. Wagner then cooled off and accepted Wilhite's argument. He then assigned another P-40 to him to take to the combat zone. It was No. 25, which Wagner himself had tested and slow-timed. Relieved, Wilhite promptly named his new ship *Winsome* after his Australian girlfriend.[45]

The next day—Monday, February 10—Squadron Commander Pell informed Wilhite and the others that they would be leaving the next morning for Perth in Western Australia to board the aircraft carrier *Langley* there. Pell's original orders of February 1 had instructed him to take his squadron to Darwin for a February 12 departure for Java, but under his new orders of February 6 he was now to leave "on or about" February 12 from Brisbane to the "combat zone" and "by the first available transport." It looked like they would be leaving Australia by sea rather than by air in their own ships.[46] Pell explained that once the *Langley* reached Java, they would not be flying their ships off the carrier. The *Langley* had only half of its flight deck, and no airplane could take off from it. Their P-40s would be loaded on what remained of the flight deck for unloading in Java.[47]

Along with the rest of his pilots, Pell was now making last-minute preparations for the move. He had asked Lt. Mel Price—recently assigned as assistant air officer to Dick Legg at Base Section 3 headquarters—to type up his last will and testament for him. In the suite of rooms at Lennon's Hotel that Price had arranged as his office, Pell showed up while Price's close friend Wilhite was visiting him. Price handed the typed document to Pell, who read it then asked Wilhite to sign it as one of the required witnesses.[48]

AT THE RAAF FIELD IN DARWIN, Al Strauss was preparing to lead a flight of nine P-40Es to Koepang in midafternoon of February 9. Six of the pilots under him were fellow 3rd Pursuiters who had flown into Darwin with him on February 6 from Amberley Field: 41-Es Vern Head and Lloyd Carlos and 41-Fs Bruce Erwin, Pete Childress, John Lewis, and Phil Metsker. In addition, 3rd Pursuit CO Grant Mahony had picked his old Philippines comrade, Tom Christian, to fly with them, though Christian had not been formally assigned to his squadron. Maj. Bill Fisher would exceptionally be flying with them, too, but just as the means to get to Bandoeng for orders to his new assignment with the Air Defense Command in Soerabaja.

They finally now had a mother ship to navigate for them over the 540 miles of the Timor Sea to their destination. First Lt. Clyde Kelsay of the 7th Bomb Group had flown in to Darwin in his LB-30 the day before to take up the assignment. He anticipated no problems during the briefing for the mission; the weather appeared good. They would be taking off late in order to arrive in Koepang towards dusk to avoid the possibility of Zeros strafing the field.[49] Kelsay's ship would also be navigating for Capt. Ed Backus and two very junior (41-H) A-24 pilots of his 91st Bomb Squadron—Charlie Able and J. R. Criswell—who would also be making the trip that afternoon. The 91st's other nine A-24s in commission at Darwin would follow the next day. But Kelsay would not be providing transport to Java for the thirteen enlisted men of the 3rd Pursuit; another Liberator bomber had come in and had been assigned the task, much to the relief of the C-53 pilot who had now been let off the hook for that duty.[50]

At 1540 Kelsay took off, followed by Strauss's nine P-40s and Backus's three A-24s. After assembling behind the LB-30, the group began heading out over the Timor Sea. But only half an hour into the flight, Fisher broke radio silence and called Strauss; his P-40 had developed engine trouble, and he wanted to return to Darwin. After Strauss approved the request, Fisher turned and headed back, his magneto out. He arrived safely at Darwin at 1630.[51] The remaining P-40s continued on in good weather, but Backus and his 91st Bomb Squadron charges had fallen behind and lost sight of the LB-30 from their slow A-24s. This situation did not bother the 91st's CO, however; he was a veteran of seven years of flying in commercial airlines and was confident he could find Koepang by following his own course.[52]

But now as Kelsay and the pursuiters approached the southern shoreline of Timor, the weather took a turn for the worse. They were heading into a huge tropical rainstorm, with clouds up to thirty thousand to forty thousand feet, by Head's estimation. As Kelsay entered the storm, Head and the other pursuiters closed the gap with the LB-30 and got right under it, "like a bunch of little chicks." Hugging close to each other, they were coming in and out of the blinding rain as Kelsay, unable to spot Koepang below, kept circling and circling, all flying very low. Finally, Kelsay gave up and started heading up the west coast of Timor in search of an alternate place for the P-40s, trailing behind him, to land. Head figured Kelsay was looking for the auxiliary field he'd heard was at Atambua, a bit inland of their position. Pete Childress, among others, was getting worried; his gas supply was down to a half hour of flying time.[53]

As they began flying up the coast, Childress "was wondering what the other fellows are thinking and what the next half hour held for us." It seemed that "nothing was in sight but a narrow, rocky beach, jungle, and hills." Then, with only about five minutes of gas left, the pursuiters found what looked like a good field to land on: "large, level, and with grass." Strauss descended and buzzed the field, then came in for a landing, wheels and flaps down, with his wingman, Bruce Erwin, right behind him. Overhead, Kelsay had noticed the field, too, and climbed higher to be clear of the P-40s and watch the P-40 flight leader and his wingman prepare to land.[54] Also observing the touchdown, Childress, in third position to land, was shocked to see Strauss's ship nose over as it hit the field and do a complete somersault, then Erwin's P-40 do a repeat. Childress immediately aborted his landing and climbed to two thousand feet; he was going to bail out rather than face the fate of Strauss and Erwin, whom he assumed had been killed. Thinking of home and "uttering a little prayer," Childress rolled his ship over on its back and jumped. Floating down in his chute seemed "like a dream," but when he fell flat on his face in mud, "grim reality" took over. Childress unhooked his harness and headed over to the site of the two crashed P-40s. He found them both broken in half, right behind the cockpit, lying in "muck and mud" and covered with about eight inches of water. What they thought was a field was actually a swamp. He was relieved to find both Strauss and Erwin alive. Strauss had a badly injured nose, while Erwin had a cut on his forehead from banging it against the gunsight.[55] Childress found that two of the other fellows were with Strauss and Erwin: Lloyd Carlos and John Lewis. They had realized that Strauss and Erwin had landed in a swamp, but with virtually no gas left they had opted to come down in the same swamp for a wheels-up landing. They succeed in getting down "without a scratch," their intact ships skidding across the muck and water.

Overhead at a high altitude, Kelsay thought that all four had landed successfully on a field. His crew threw out all survival gear that might be useful, then turned around to head back to Darwin. Unable to locate Koepang in the storm, Kelsay felt that he had no other option but to return.[56] As the five pursuiters were trying to decide what to do next, they heard aircraft engines overhead and saw three Lockheed Hudsons flying over their area. They waved at the twin-engine ships, glad to know that their crash location would be reported and rescue efforts organized for them.[57]

Meanwhile, Vern Head—flying with Tom Christian and Phil Metsker—had witnessed the crash landings below and decided not to duplicate his squadron mates' experience but instead to continue to follow the LB-30 as it turned inland towards Atambua. With five minutes of gas left, he was going to give himself two minutes to find the auxiliary field there, or, failing that, turn back for the coast. Not succeeding in sighting any field, and back to the west coast shoreline, he noticed a sandy stretch of beach that looked good to him. Darkness was falling as he lowered his wheels and flaps then touched down, rolling along at about sixty mph. Suddenly he was confronted by a tree. He used his rudder to try to get around the obstacle, but the wheels of the P-40 dug into the sand as it turned, flipping the ship over onto its back. Thrown forward, his head hit the ship's gunsight, and he cut his lip badly. The tail of the upside-down P-40 was held by the tree, which his plane had split. Head fell to the ground from his cockpit and crawled out from under his ship. In addition to the pain from his forehead and lip injuries, he was stinging all over from ants whose nest he'd demolished in the crash.[58] As he straightened up, he was surprised to find a little native boy standing near him, shaking his head and saying what sounded like "soo, soo, soo" in Timorese. Head walked back to his wrecked ship and took out his parachute, mosquito net, and musette bag, then followed the boy a few hundred yards to a shack underneath the coconut palms at the end of the approach to the beach. Lying down on his mosquito net, he tried to put bandages on his bleeding lip, later adding iodine from a bottle the native boy brought him. As night began to fall, Head stretched out on straw mats in the hut, the rain pounding down on his temporary shelter.

Overhead, Tom Christian had followed Head to the beach site and observed Head's crash landing. "That's not for me," he thought. He continued to fly around a few minutes longer, then decided to bail out. He floated down for a good landing near a native village.[59] In the meantime, Strauss's group of five had left the swamp area of their crashes and struck out for the beach, as it was getting very dark. As the rain poured down, they took refuge for the night under a tree, sitting on a log, trying to keep dry and beating off swarms of mosquitoes. It was so wet that John Lewis had a hard time even smoking.[60]

That evening the eighth pilot in the flight, Phil Metsker, was lying lifeless on the ground near his crashed plane. After running out of gas he had bailed out, but he broke his neck when his head struck the tailplane. His parachute unopened, he plummeted to the ground below.[61]

AT PENFUI AIRDROME, KOEPANG, Ed Backus had succeeded in finding the field in late afternoon, despite the storm. As he led his two neophyte squadron mates in for a landing, he was stunned to find antiaircraft fire heading in his direction. His gas tank was hit, and the stabilizer on his right elevator was shot off. The other two A-24s were also damaged from the fire. After landing, Backus stormed over to the Australian operations officer and tore into him for the unwelcome reception by his men. The browbeaten Australian feebly explained that they thought the three A-24s were Zeros. They had not been informed that the dive bombers were expected at Koepang that afternoon.[62]

Cecil Ingram and his twelve comrades of the 3rd Pursuit also had a close call that afternoon during their flight from Darwin to Java, albeit not because of friendly fire. About one hour and two hundred miles out of Darwin in the B-24A that was taking them on their transfer to Java, they were startled to find that three Zeros were coming up fast on their tail. But before the Japanese were able to get within firing range, Capt. Paul Davis nosed the big bomber down into a forty-five-degree dive, clocking over four hundred miles per hour on the airspeed indicator. Before the Zeros could reach them, Davis entered a cloud bank in his dive and then exited it. He then pulled out of the dive at what Ingram estimated was one hundred feet above the water, straightened out, and continued on the flight, but just above the sea. There were no Zeros in sight.[63]

After reaching East Java Davis could not locate the well-camouflaged

Ngoro Airfield to drop off his passengers, so he turned the B-24A around and headed northeast to Soerabaja, landing at Perak Field. As the 3rd Pursuit enlisted men disembarked, Ingram was surprised to find Lieutenant Gallienne there. The 3rd Pursuiter explained that he was waiting to catch a ride to Blimbing after having lost his P-40 in a forced landing in a rice field. Ingram and the others had "good chow" at the mess hall at the Dutch naval base, despite the fact that the day before a Japanese bomb "had blown heck out of it." Returning to Soerabaja, they were assigned bunks in some evacuated houses. After taking showers following a false air raid alarm, they turned in. Trying to sleep, Ingram was assailed by "about 10 million mosquitoes" that had managed to get in under his mosquito net.[64]

LATE ON THE MORNING OF FEBRUARY 9, sixteen pilots of the 17th Provisional were on alert at Ngoro Field, anticipating the usual interception mission. Each of the four flights was headed by a senior Philippines veteran, with other such veterans as element leaders except in the case of Bill Stauter. Recently arrived former 20th Pursuit pilots, none with any combat experience, filled the eight wingmen positions.[65]

The expected daily call from the Air Defense Command in Soerabaja came in shortly after 1035. A formation of Japanese bombers had been reported heading for Malang, near the 19th Bomb Group's base at Singosari. However, the Japanese were now too close to Malang for the slow-climbing P-40s to reach them before they would have unloaded on the base. The ADC wanted the pursuiters to cut them off north of Soerabaja on their return flight.[66]

At 1050 Bo McCallum, at the head of A flight; Walt Coss, leading B flight; Jack Dale at the front of C flight; and Ed "Kay" Kiser leading D flight thundered down the two strips for the interception, each followed by three other pursuiters, their adrenalin pumping. Dale's flight was using the north-south field, "too short and too soft" to suit Butch Hague, causing him to "stagger off" the runway. Airborne, the sixteen P-40s began their climb towards the northeast, slowly moving up to their assigned altitude of twenty-three thousand feet. But by the time they had reached that great height, they were strung out over a wide area, the four flights separated from each other. The Allison-powered ships were behaving sluggishly in the rarefied air as the pilots searched for the expected Japanese bombers.[67] Unseen by the pursuiters, two formations of Betty bombers—one of eight ships, the other of nine—were beginning to head north towards them after having bombed, at 1128 and again at 1139, the barracks area of the 131st Field Artillery just off Singosari Field, some fifty miles due south of the pursuiters' patrolling area. The

Japanese had been spotted at 1107 by the base approaching the field at fifteen thousand feet from the west, fifteen minutes after the air raid alarm had sounded at Singosari.[68]

Suddenly, Roger Williams, flying as wingman to Joe Kruzel in Dale's C flight, spotted the bombers. He radioed the sighting to the others, but his agitated warning was not understood by those who picked it up. The incoherent call did not come as a surprise to them; the excitable, talkative Williams was once referred to as "that guy [who] jumps around like spit on a hot stove."[69]

Butch Hague had sighted the bombers, too. He was alone, having lost his element leader, Ed Gilmore, when the Philippines veteran broke off from him as they were climbing for altitude after the takeoff. Hague had followed him down and became separated from the rest of B flight before realizing that Gilmore was headed back to Ngoro Field. (Gilmore's guns were not working).[70] Climbing back to altitude, Hague looked around and could find no P-40s anywhere in the sky. Then he spotted eight bombers toward the south. Switching on his radio, Hague excitedly called out, "Send some help! I've got eight Nips surrounded!" But he got no response from his squadron mates, who were scattered all over the vast area.[71]

Hague flew across the formation of bombers and began a climb to 25,500 feet, again calling out, but still he could get no one on the radio. As the Japanese continued flying north, Hague followed them but stayed above them and just out of range of their gunfire. He was taking "quite a while" to decide whether to attack by himself or not. Finally, as the Betty bombers started to pass out of Java and over the Strait of Madoera, he decided to take them on alone. He was very worked up. It would be the first time he had ever fired at a target. When almost directly behind the Japanese, Hague brought his gunsight to bear, then fired his six .50s, but his bullets were falling short. Too excited, he had "wobbled his fire all over the sky." The bomber pilots began dropping down in formation on the side he was attacking, allowing all their guns to bear on him. As he made further passes on the Japanese, Hague could see that he was scoring hits and didn't seem to be taking any hits himself. But then his guns stopped firing after about four hundred rounds, much to his frustration. He broke off his attack and headed back to Ngoro.[72]

Earlier, B flight leader Walt Coss and his wingman, Bob McWherter, had continued climbing after losing Gilmore and Hague of their second element. Still in their climb, they spotted twin-engined bombers and single-engined planes far away. As Coss and McWherter came closer, they could make them out as seventeen Betty bombers and nine escorting Zero fighters, heading towards Malang. Moments later, the Zeros went into a high-speed dive towards them. Trying to elude them, Coss and McWherter pointed their ships down and went into a steep dive. After pulling out and turning away from the direction of the Japanese, McWherter began climbing again, then leveled out. Minutes later he spotted a nine-ship formation of bombers heading north from Malang, evidently returning after having bombed the base. There were no Zeros in sight, so McWherter assumed they had left the bombers to strafe the field after the bombing. His leader, Coss, was not around after having become separated from him in the dive and evasive action.[73]

McWherter now began climbing up to the altitude of the nine Bettys. They appeared to him to be flying at maximum speed in an effort to escape him. With his P-40 flying only slightly faster than the Japanese, it took McWherter fifteen minutes to catch up with them. Finally, at about twenty-five thousand feet he approached them from the rear. He "brightened his gun sight" and ambitiously "prepared to shoot down all nine of them." After checking his rear to make sure there were no Zeros behind him, he drew a bead on the bomber on the extreme left side of the V formation and began firing his six .50s, causing smoke from its left engine. But to his great surprise he had noticed "twinkling fire" from the tail guns of all nine bombers. He didn't know that the Betty carried a 20 mm cannon in its tail; no picture he'd ever seen of it showed it.

On his second and third passes McWherter directed fire at the rear of all nine bombers in order to knock out their tail gunners. But now all his ammunition was expended, and he dived away to return to his base. He was elated — the Betty with the smoking engine would surely crash. He had seen another P-40 make a pass at the bombers, too, but it was rather far back to have scored any hits, he figured.[74]

Back on the ground at Ngoro Field, the pursuiters excitedly compared experiences. In addition to Hague and McWherter, their leader Coss told them he had attacked the bombers, too, claims that Williams and Elwin Jackson in Dale's C flight made as well. As for McCallum's A flight, the pilots said that they had seen nothing while patrolling for one hour and forty-five minutes north-northeast and southwest of Soerabaja. Kiser's D flight did not report any action either.[75]

In his interception of the bombers, Coss was impressed with the speed of the Betty; at twenty-five thousand feet the P-40 "only had 8–10 miles [per hour] on it," he reported. And they all agreed that at that altitude their P-40s performed sluggishly. Still, Hague felt that if the four flights had stayed together instead of splintering, "we'd have gotten at least eight of them." Instead, it appeared that they had one victory only, a Betty that the ADC reported as going down northeast of Soerabaja on Madoera Island. They figured it must have been the one hit in the engine by McWherter. But in general, Hague felt that he and the other new pilots "had learned a lot today" and gained "more confidence" in their abilities.[76]

BACK AT DARWIN, SPENCE JOHNSON and his buddy "Chief" Quanah Fields were playing phonograph records all morning Tuesday, February 10, as they waited for the hours to tick by before they would be taking off for Koepang. "Indian Summer" was the one they played most of the time. "Damn, but we are homesick," Johnson recorded in his diary. Finally, at about 1630 their squadron commander, Grant Mahony, climbed into his P-40E and led his flight of nine off the field. They were the last 3rd Pursuit (Provisional) pilots to be transferred to Java. Two more were being left behind: Oestreicher and Buel still had engine troubles. Of Mahony's flight, Ben Irvin (40-G) was the most senior next to the 3rd Pursuit CO; he was making his second try to reach Java after losing his original ship to strafers at Koepang two weeks earlier. The remaining seven were 41-Es (Morris "Moe" Caldwell, Gene Wahl, and Frank Adkins) and 41-Fs (Johnson, Fields, Bob Dockstader, and Hal Lund).[77] No Liberator bomber or any other mother ship would be leading the flight to Koepang. Mahony was a veteran of flying all over the Philippines in 1940–41 and was sure he could find Koepang by dead reckoning on his own. The independent Irishman did not lack in self-confidence.[78]

After taking off, they formed up, then headed west out over the Timor Sea. Johnson was flying behind Fields, keeping an eye on his Indian friend. Fields was making the "long and treacherous hop" with a bad propeller. Johnson himself was anxious; he felt it was likely that the Japanese would be waiting for them on the other end, considering all the reports they had seen on Japanese attacks on Koepang.[79] It was with a sigh of relief that the pursuiters reached Penfui Field at Koepang just before nightfall after a three-hour flight in decent weather and without being attacked. But the Japanese had certainly "shot hell out of everything" at the place. As he had approached the town, Johnson thought all the rooftops looked like they were "full of woodpecker holes." The runway itself was pockmarked with craters. It did not help Johnson's spirits to learn after landing that the other half of the squadron had lost all their planes the day before because of bad weather and that his flying school classmate Phil Metsker had been killed in his parachute jump.[80]

Early the next morning—at 0500—Mahony led his pilots off from Penfui Airdrome for their next stop, Waingapoe, on the north coast of Soemba Island. He had decided to refuel there rather than at Bali, the usual stop. At the hour of departure it was still dark, and none of the 3rd Pursuiters had ever made a night takeoff before. There was only the light from a lantern at the

P-40Es of the 3rd Pursuit Squadron (Provisional) being refueled at Waingapoe Field, Soemba Island, on the way to Java, February 11, 1942. *Courtesy Eugene A. Wahl.*

end of the field to guide them. When Gene Wahl reached the light, he pulled the stick back and could see that he had barely cleared the palm trees at the end of the field.[81] Wahl and the others climbed and looked for Mahony's ship circling high over the field. They knew that if they missed their demanding leader on his first or second circle, they would be left behind. But all managed to link up and follow Mahony westward over the 250-mile flight above the Savu Sea, although Johnson got a sore neck looking all around for Japanese Zeros. As they approached Waingapoe to land, they noticed natives scurrying around, removing barricades on the field to allow them to come in.

After refueling their ships by hand pump, they were off again for Soerabaja. In bypassing Bali, Mahony would be covering 570 miles nonstop to Soerabaja, stretching the range of the P-40 to the maximum. But in any event, as they passed Bali and reached the southern coast of Java they ran into a heavy rainstorm. Mahony opted to bring them down at the little auxiliary field at Pasirian, sixty-five miles southeast of Soerabaja. In coming in to land in the rain on the muddy strip, Adkins nosed his ship over and Fields belly-landed, putting both P-40s out of commission.[82] While waiting for the tropical storm to blow over, Mahony managed to get in a call to Ngoro to inform Bud Sprague of their whereabouts. The 17th Pursuit CO then took Bo McCallum and Jack Dale with him and flew down to Pasirian in order to lead the new arrivals to the secret Ngoro Field, only a seventy-mile hop for them. After exchanging greetings with his old Philippine buddies, and leaving Fields and Adkins behind, Mahony took off with the remaining six and, following the 17th Pursuit trio, landed at 1530 at Ngoro. It was the end of a long day's flying for Mahony's novices, elated to be reunited with their buddies in the old 20th Pursuit Squadron "and vice versa."[83]

FEBRUARY 11 HAD BEEN THE FIRST full day of work at Ngoro Field for SSgt. Cecil Ingram and the other twelve enlisted men of the 3rd Pursuit, now united with their squadron pilots. But they would be responsible to Sprague now instead of Mahony, since the rump 3rd Pursuit was being absorbed into the 17th and losing its identity. That was no problem to Ingram and the others, for they had taken an immediate shine to Sprague; they regarded him as "a good squadron commander [who] seems to look after his men." The morning of the day before, the thirteen had gotten into a Dutch truck at Soerabaja for the sixty-five-mile road trip to their new base. But after trying for twenty minutes to get the native driver started, SSgt. Edgar English—sent down to guide the driver to Ngoro—got out his Malay language dictionary and looked up the word "go." It elicited an immediate response from the driver. As they drove "through the jungle . . . thickly populated and [with] a thousand smells—most of them bad," Ingram felt the experience was "like something out of a story book." The driver, showing "complete disregard" for their lives, blew his horn at hundreds of natives on bicycles, oxcarts, or walking. They were relieved finally to reach Ngoro about noon without having run over anyone.[84]

Two days before, Paul Gambonini also had been subjected to a traumatic truck ride on the Soerabaja–Ngoro run. The native driver had come in to Soerabaja to pick up supplies for the 17th. Stuck in the city after having lost their aircraft four days earlier, Gambonini and Marion Fuchs took advantage of the opportunity and got on board for the return trip to Ngoro. There was no room inside the cab, so Gambonini climbed on top of the load of supplies. As the driver began leaving, he passed under an overhanging shed, which caught Gambonini in the back and threw him half-way across the load. The blow "damned near broke my back and hurt my knee," Gambonini wrote in his diary that night.[85]

Still, Gambonini was happy to be reunited with his comrades in the 20th Pursuit who had preceded him to their new base. Old Hamilton Field friends Bob Dockstader and Hal Lund were now there, too, and with Moe Caldwell would be moving in with him in the house he was sharing with Marion Fuchs at Blimbing. At supper the newcomers were amused with the cooking style of the Javanese responsible for preparing the 17th's evening meals. The day before, while cooking a chicken dinner, the chef was standing on the stove in his bare feet, walking back and forth while turning the chicken.[86]

One of Gambonini's 20th Pursuit squadron mates, Bob McWherter, was still making nightly forays into the town of Ngoro with his buddies. Eager Javanese hawkers as usual accosted them, but now they were offering another item they thought would appeal to the young, virile men: the services of their sisters. The young native men would whisper to them, "mak mak," which the Americans soon found out was the local word for sex. Some of the pilots "responded with enthusiasm," but McWherter and others held off. The previous evening the squadron surgeon had given the pilots a lecture on the incidence of syphilis among the Javanese; he maintained that the prevalence rate was eighty to ninety percent.[87]

Amateur poet and squadron wag Spence Johnson later composed an ode to one of the 17th Pursuit's Philippines veterans who was a frequent customer of the services of the Javanese girls:

O'er Soerabaya the air was full of thundering planes
The earth quivered from bursting ack-ack
But Captain––, fond of his tail
Was back in Blimbing getting mak mak."[88]

But except for occasional sexual relations and purchases of peanuts and beer, there was little personal contact between the pilots and the Javanese. A history major at Stanford University, Les Johnsen, among others, regretted not being able to speak their language. Johnsen wanted to communicate with them and find out more about them. They seemed to him to be "a very warm, busy people."[89] Cpl. Ken Perry and many other enlisted men of the squadron also wished to know more about the natives. Whenever they traveled on their days off, when they could borrow a jeep or truck, between Blimbing and Soerabaja, they saw the Javanese everywhere, "washing clothes in the river, dressed in their 'Sunday best' on a day off in the town, squatting along the streets and crowding around to sell you something. . . . We liked being able to see half-primitive modes of living, of hearing strange words spoken and guessing at their meaning," he wrote in his diary.[90] But mostly life was long hours of work for the mechanics and armorers of the squadron. They were responsible for keeping the P-40s in top flying condition, despite the lack of spare parts and overused Allison engines. Squadron Engineering Officer Bill Hennon would also send details of them to outlying areas to repair or strip crashed ships.

Hennon was now at Ngoro Field again after flying Ray Thompson's ship back from Djember on February 10 with Hubert Egenes trailing him in his own P-40. The afternoon of the eleventh he sent several men down to Pasirian to work on the two P-40s that Adkins and Fields had cracked up there that day. One was to be repaired and the other stripped for parts.[91]

Earlier on the eleventh, at 1030, Hennon had taken off as an element leader in Sprague's A flight, along with B flight under Lane and C flight led by Dale. It was the second time up that day for these twelve of the sixteen pilots on alert duty. At 0840 ADC had reported enemy planes coming from the north and headed west, but after taking off at 0900 and climbing to intercept, the four flights had found nothing and returned after patrolling for half an hour.[92] For the 1030 takeoff mission the three flights were airborne even before receiving the air raid signal from the ADC, alerted of the impending raid by natives beating on the hollow log near the field. "We really had the jump on them," George Parker, flying as wingman to Dale, felt. The twelve pursuiters reached their altitude of twenty-five thousand feet and patrolled over the Soerabaja area, "just waiting for them." But when no enemy planes were sighted, they headed back to Ngoro, "buzzing up the countryside on the way," and began landing at 1130 at five-minute intervals between flights. Lane couldn't find the field and asked his wingman, Paul Gambonini, to lead B flight in.[93]

It was a repeat of the day before. On February 10 all four flights of sixteen P-40s, led by Sprague, Coss, McCallum, and Kiser, had taken off at 1050 "in anticipation of Japanese raids," but no bombers were seen. At about 1145 Sprague ordered C flight back to the field, followed at intervals by A, B, and D flights.[94]

AT DAYBREAK ON FEBRUARY 10 Vern Head woke up "stiff and sore" in the native hut on East Timor where he had spent the night. Several of the natives from the village near where he had crash-landed had now returned after fleeing the scene the day before. After eating the chocolate bar in his survival kit, Head decided to strike out for Koepang to the south and was joined by the native boy who had helped him the day before and was now carrying Head's parachute for him. One of the newly returned village men was coming along, too, at the boy's insistence; he was supposed to speak English.[95]

After crossing a swollen river, in which he failed to notice the crocodiles, Head and the natives came within sight of the four crashed P-40s and two of his squadron mates near the planes. One of them drew his .45 and shot in the air, for reasons unknown to Head, who reciprocated by pulling out his own gun, too, and shooting in the air to let them know he was approaching. On the beach Head found five of his comrades: Pete Childress, Bruce Erwin, Lloyd Carlos, John Lewis, and Al Strauss. They told Head that a Lockheed Hudson

Pilots of the 3rd Pursuit Squadron (Provisional) on Timor with natives, February 10, 1942, after crash-landing the day before. *Left to right:* Bruce Erwin, Lloyd Carlos, Al Strauss, and Pete Childress. *Courtesy Mildred Daggett, from John Lewis Collection.*

bomber had found them and had dropped some biscuits and a note to them, indicating that they would be picked up around noon by a boat. They should remain where they were.

Later, a native handed the pursuiters another note he had found on the beach. This one stated that a rescue party was being sent overland for them and, again, they should stay where they were. But by late afternoon no rescue party—whether by land or sea—had shown up.[96]

That afternoon the whole village turned out to "look us over." "They are a horrible-looking bunch," Head felt, and "they apparently have nothing to eat but coconuts." Not much better off, all Head and the others had to consume that day was "coconut milk, chocolate, biscuits, and water—dirty water." The natives "talk some sort of gibberish." When they asked them in sign language how far it was to Koepang, they shook their heads. To Atambua? They would point in the other direction. All the so-called English-speaking native could say in English was "Sydney good, Melbourne good." That night they slept fitfully in a little hut. The mosquitoes were terrible. Head and one of the others slept under Head's mosquito net, but the other four "were almost eaten." One was bitten on the bottom lip so badly that it looked worse than Head's crash-inflicted cut.

The next morning things were looking more promising. The native boy they now called "Friday" was using sign language to indicate that they could reach the large village of Atambua to the east by 1700, or, as he put the time, "sun three fourths down." Two other Timorese arrived with bananas and syrup for them to eat for breakfast. Afterwards, they packed and set out for Atambua, several of the natives carrying their belongings.[97]

CHAPTER EIGHT

"Someone Is Crazy—This Is Murder"

AT AMBERLEY FIELD THE TWENTY-FOUR pilots assigned to the 33rd Pursuit Squadron (Provisional) had just finished lunch on Wednesday, February 11, when they were called together by their commanding officer, Maj. Floyd Pell. He told them to get ready to leave for Port Pirie, South Australia, in two hours on the first leg of their transfer trip to Java. Their first stop would be Sydney, a 450-mile hop, where they would spend the night. The RAAF would be providing them with maps over the full fourteen-hundred-mile route.[1]

As instructed by Pell, Bob McMahon left all his belongs in his tent except for his musette bag, his camera, his .45-caliber pistol, and a .22-caliber pistol he wanted to bring along too. As he stowed his bag and other items in his P-40E, whose fuselage he had decorated as *Bahootee the Cootee,* his buddy Wally MacLean came up to him, "down in the face," to say goodbye. MacLean was assigned to the assembly depot at Amberley and would not be going out with McMahon's outfit. "Well, we gotta go some time," McMahon told him, then, thinking of the recent war news, added, "The way things are going we are all damn well going to get killed." But only eleven of the squadron's pilots would be leaving that afternoon, Pell had decided: those in his A flight and in McMahon's D flight, plus Jack Peres, the leader of B flight, and John Glover with him. Gerry Keenan, the C flight leader and deputy to Pell, would lead the others out the following day.[2]

The takeoff signal was relayed down the line of the partially dispersed P-40Es at 1530. At the far end McMahon taxied out past his wingman and his element leader, giving them the "follow me" wave. After Pell cleared the field, his wingman and other A flight members followed at ten-second intervals, then Peres and Glover, and finally McMahon's three.[3] As Pell came back over the field at only one thousand feet, McMahon and the others were barely able to slide under him and form up, in stacked-down position, as instructed before takeoff by their CO. It was nerve-wracking to form up with only a couple hundred feet clearance above the ground. But by the time Pell headed the formation for Brisbane, all eleven were in a "reasonable facsimile of formation." However, McMahon, among others, felt that their leader was "a little new at leading a pursuit formation."[4]

In Pell's flight Jim Naylor was having serious trouble with his ship. On takeoff his prop had "run away," and he was unable to correct the problem either manually or electrically after joining up with the formation, his engine revolutions on or near three thousand. About twenty minutes out of Amberley, he decided to abort. Flying ahead to Pell's wing, he signaled his CO that he had a problem and wanted to return to Amberley. Pell signaled his okay, and Naylor reversed his direction and flew away from the flight.[5] On the return flight Naylor was becoming increasingly desperate. His Allison engine was "running extremely hot," and he was losing power. To get his oil and engine temperatures down, he was throttling back. Figuring he had no chance to get back to Amberley in time, Naylor decided to look for some place for an emergency landing. He spotted a rather large clearing in trees ahead and to the left and descended to about five hundred feet before seeing that the clearing was full of tree stumps after a recent cutting.

Naylor felt trapped; now he could not gain any altitude. About one or two miles out of Amberley, limping on towards the field, he noticed his oil pressure gauge had dropped to zero, then saw smoke and a burst of flame from his engine. "This is it," he realized. He pulled the throttle and mixture back, cut all switches, dropped his belly tank, and opened his canopy for the crash landing. But then he saw a long row of Avro Ansons directly in front of him, parked wingtip to wingtip at the edge of the field. Reacting immediately, he glanced to the right and spotted a small clearing in the trees. Cocking his plane on its right wingtip, he pushed his nose down and hit the ground some three hundred yards short of the field. With his P-40 with one wing torn off and the rest of it burning from nose to tail in a farmer's garden, Naylor was dragged away from the plane in the mud and taken to Amberley infirmary. Although he had hit his head on the gunsight and "ripped the left side of my head open" from rattling around in the cockpit, he had still managed to climb out of the plane.

In the meantime, the others were approaching Coffs Harbor, 180 miles south of Amberley and about halfway to their Sydney destination, when Bob Kerstetter broke radio silence and called out, "Engine trouble." His flight leader, Pell, swiftly responded with a compass heading for a landing at a field near Coffs Harbor. As he started to descend, his wingman, Bryce Wilhite, followed him down, ignorant of what the problem was. Noticing Wilhite following him, Kerstetter waved to him to break off and return to the formation. Moments later, Kerstetter crash-landed, but without injury.[6]

After rejoining the formation, Wilhite flew on without an element leader. No longer flying as wingman, he was now able to take in the sights of the southern coast of New South Wales. The afternoon sun was shining brightly as they approached Sydney harbor, ferry boats trailing long white wakes.[7] As they flew over the red tile roofs of houses on the northern side of the bay and began to descend, McMahon slid back his canopy. Suddenly, out flew his felt garrison hat, tumbling earthward. Dismayed at the loss of his expensive possession, McMahon continued on down and with the others hit the ground at Mascot Field on the western side of the city.[8]

After spending the night at Mascot Field, the remaining pilots of Pell's formation began their takeoff runs in their refueled ships at 0600, the city still gray in the dawn. Their vision obscured by dust clouds stirred up by the P-40s up front, Wilhite and the others in the back of the flight had to go over to instruments. They were going to make a stop in Canberra on the way to their destination, Laverton Field at Melbourne. Pell referred to it as a refueling stop, but McMahon suspected that it was more "to show the flag" in Australia's capital city.[9] Pell kept the flight south-southwest to Canberra so low that they were "almost scraping the trees at times," in Wilhite's estimation. Evidently their CO was trying to stay under the heavy clouds over the mountains on the 150-mile inland hop. Wilhite thought Pell was also probably giving his fledgling pilots "some practice in making a sneak attack."[10]

After a brief refueling and a "spot of tea," Pell made a phone call, and they were back to their ships for the remaining part of the flight to Melbourne. From his cockpit the CO gave the startup signal, and McMahon relayed it down the line. At that moment, an Australian mechanic was checking the coolant on McMahon's engine, but when McMahon told him to hurry it up, he dropped his wrench into the bowels of the Allison. As the others took off, McMahon remained on the ground as he and the mechanic removed the engine side panel to get the wrench out, with success. Hurriedly, McMahon cleared the field and raced to catch up with the others. When he finally did, he was halfway to Melbourne and now "tail-end Charlie" instead of in position as D flight leader.[11]

At the end of the three-hundred-mile stretch southwest to Melbourne, Pell led his pilots into a descent for the landing at Laverton Field on the western outskirts of the big city. They could see that there was no dedicated runway, just a large, grass-covered landing area. When McMahon climbed out of his ship, he noticed Pell standing at the other end of the line, chatting with several of the others, evidently critiquing the flight. When McMahon approached him, Pell began telling him off in front of the other pilots. "How come you can't keep up with your flight?" Pell wanted to know. McMahon tried to explain, but Pell was already heading into the operations building at the field, his pilots in tow. The 33rd's CO spent about fifteen minutes in operations, then was out, "barking orders, jobs, and assignments" to his pilots. Glover and Bill Walker were told to collect two dozen watches in town, Bob Vaught to collect maps, and Jack Peres to check on Gerry Keenan's situation and give a report to Pell at the Menzies Hotel, where they would be spending the night. As for McMahon, he was being assigned as squadron adjutant, "since you screwed up." Pell ignored McMahon's point that Wilhite was already the adjutant.

Staff cars were waiting for them, and they all climbed in for the ride into the center of Melbourne to the Menzies Hotel. To Wilhite the reddish-brown sandstone building appeared old, but they were told it was the best hotel in Melbourne. Pell was impatient for news from Keenan, scheduled to bring in the rest of the 33rd's pilots from Amberley in the afternoon. When newly appointed adjutant McMahon checked at the desk for messages, he was handed one from Keenan to Pell that Peres had obtained: "Arriving Melbourne with thirteen planes plus McMahon's hat." When McMahon handed his CO the welcome message, Pell's demeanor had changed, and he now accepted McMahon's explanation for what had happened to him at Canberra. Shortly afterwards, McMahon was preoccupied with unofficial matters; in the lounge he had picked up a striking lady who would prove not averse to spending the evening with him.[12]

The next morning, February 13, at 0800, Pell called McMahon to come down for breakfast with him. His CO had a list of things to be done, including collecting the maps and other things for the onward trip to Port Pirie. Keenan's group, which had landed the afternoon before, would need them, too. McMahon had missed its arrival.[13] Riding out to the field with McMahon later that morning when all arrangements had been taken care of, Pell surprised his new adjutant by informing him that he and several others were "volunteers" to fly north with him to Darwin. That was the first he had heard of the change in orders. McMahon was both flattered and disappointed. He had hoped he would be continuing to Perth to board the carrier for Java. He thought he would be able to fly off the carrier, which would be a first for an army pilot.[14] Pell had already discussed the change of orders with Keenan, who had left Amberley the morning before at 0810 with thirteen other pilots. After losing two of his flight—Bill Borden and Gerry Dix—because of engine troubles, Keenan told Pell that he had overshot the navigation leg to Laverton with ten of the remaining eleven of his flight and landed by mistake at 1745 at the RAAF field at Point Cook, four miles to the west of Laverton. Forty-five minutes later, Charles Hughes in his No. 94, separated from the others and almost out of gas, also set down at the Point Cook base.[15]

Pell told Keenan that he had received orders from USAFIA to depart Port Pirie at dawn "on or about February 14" with fifteen P-40s, to arrive in Darwin by late afternoon February 15. From Keenan's reunited group of fourteen—Dix and Borden had now joined up after being delayed at Sydney, and Hughes had flown in during the morning from Point Cook—six would be picked to join Pell and his remaining eight pilots for the northern trip.[16]

At the field to prepare for takeoff to Port Pirie—a 490-mile flight west to South Australia—McMahon was pleasantly surprised to find his garrison hat on his chute seat. He had missed his benefactor Keenan in trips back and forth from Laverton to Melbourne that morning. Keenan later explained that a lady in Sydney had found the hat on her property and had brought it to Mascot Field, where Keenan had picked it up during his stopover there.[17]

The pursuiters were ready for takeoff, but there were RAAF officers and enlisted men climbing all over their P-40Es. These were the first "Kittyhawks" they had ever seen, and the Aussies bombarded the Americans with questions about the ship's performance. Wilhite and the others were "not too happy" with their clambering over their planes; their antics were delaying their departure.[18] Wilhite had checked out his No. 25 just before getting it in line for takeoff. It seemed in fine condition then, but when Pell gave the startup signal and Wilhite pushed the throttle forward for takeoff and began his roll, he sensed that something was not right with his ship. He quickly throttled back to abort his takeoff. Too close to the end of the field to continue forward, and wanting to clear the way for the pilot behind him, he slowly applied brakes and steered his ship in a wide arc towards the corner of the field, where it stopped without mishap. After taxiing back to the ramp, he "felt stupid" because he could not tell the RAAF crews what was wrong with his plane.

Now down to eight P-40s, Pell led his flight out over Melbourne harbor, then struck out westward for Port Pirie. Keenan followed with his fourteen ships. Three and a half hours later, all came down safely at the tiny field in South Australia.[19] After climbing out of their ships, Pell called all twenty-one of the pilots for a meeting to discuss reorganization for the Darwin and Perth flights. Although he had been ordered to bring fifteen P-40s to Darwin, he figured he could get by with fewer, but abided by his orders. When he asked for hands, most of Keenan's fourteen held them up, and Pell picked seven to go with his eight: Jesse Dore, Elton Perry, Max Wiecks, Dick Pingree, Borden, Hughes, and Suehr. His own group consisted of Burt Rice, Bill Walker, Jack Peres, John Glover, Dave Latane, Vaught, and McMahon besides himself. The fact that Darwin was fifteen hundred miles away, and the route over some of the most inhospitable desert in the world, didn't seem to faze Pell. Keenan himself wouldn't be joining them; he was needed to get the six remaining pilots of his group plus himself, as well as twenty-five additional pilots at Amberley, to Perth to board the *Langley*.[20]

The next few hours were spent in scouring Port Pirie for maps to delineate a course north to Darwin. The pilots ended up with "a mélange of the damndest variety of charts and maps that were ever assembled," in McMahon's view. McMahon himself, as well as Pell and the other flight leader, Peres, obtained maps for the full route, although McMahon's was just a copy from an issue of *National Geographic*. There were no unique landmarks or radio facilities to guide them. An old bush pilot Pell located wasn't really much help. His final comment on "landmarks" was to mention that if they spotted a "bloody big red rock that sticks up 300 to 400 feet" near Alice Springs, "you're too far to the left—wheel around to the right and head southeast, then you can't miss Alice Springs."[21] McMahon for one was taken aback at the old Aussie's navigation methods. He feared the flight could prove a disaster.

BACK AT AMBERLEY FIELD, BUZZ WAGNER days before had just formed a fifth provisional pursuit squadron, designated the 13th, by scouring the base for pursuit pilots who were still at the field. He picked three assigned earlier to the 3rd—Wade Holman, Oscar Handy, and Benny Johnson—who had returned following accidents or had been sent back by Mahony to bring more P-40s to Darwin. USAFIA headquarters had also ordered three former 28th Bomb Squadron pilots who had been evacuated to Darwin February 5 to report to Wagner for assignment to his squadron, but Tom Christian had already left Darwin for Koepang on February 9, so just Jim Bruce and Speed Hubbard were assigned; they would add some seniority to the newly formed unit. Wagner was so short of candidates that even two who were assigned to the assembly depot and previously ineligible to join tactical units—Ken Glassburn and Wally MacLean—were being pulled out to meet the demand.[22]

All the pilots selected for Wagner's squadron—except Wagner himself and the two Philippines veterans Bruce and Hubbard—were needed by USAFIA to meet the shortfall of pilots for the *Langley* assignment occasioned by the Darwin diversion of fifteen of the 33rd's pilots. Still assigned to the assembly depot after losing Glassburn and MacLean, Parker Gies was appalled at the way the brass were cleaning out Amberley and sending inexperienced pilots

An unhappy Carl Parker Gies, still assigned to assembly depot duties, Amberley Field, February–March 1942. *Courtesy Ken Glassburn.*

all the way across Australia to Perth, twenty-six hundred miles away. Nine of the pilots assigned had graduated only three months earlier, in the class of 41-H at Craig Field, Alabama; eight had arrived on the *Mormacsun* on January 20 and one on the *Coolidge* on February 1.[23] Gies was wondering why hadn't they picked him, at least, a Philippines veteran who had been passed over before and who was ready and willing to go. As he watched thirteen of them taking off on February 13 for the first leg of the trip, to Mascot Field, outside of Sydney—"Pilots who haven't even checked out in P-40s"—he felt that "someone is crazy. This is murder." Shortly afterwards, at 0915, the second flight of eleven P-40Es departed for Sydney, too, but had been ordered to land at Sydney's Richmond Field instead.[24]

P-40Es of the 13th Pursuit Squadron (Provisional) at Richmond Field, Sydney, Febrary 13, 1942, for refueling before continuing their flight to Perth to board the USS *Langley*. *Courtesy Gordon Birkett.*

Philippines veteran Jim Bruce, leading the flight of thirteen to Mascot, soon became lost after takeoff and began descending near Newcastle, ninety-five miles short of his Sydney destination. As the six ships in Ken Glassburn's group were preparing to land at Newcastle's Williamtown Field, two hours out of Amberley, Glassburn's engine began throwing oil all over his windshield, impairing his vision. He had to "slip it in" at a higher speed, and when his ship hit the ground at the intersection where the two runways crossed, it flipped over. His P-40E was a wreck, and he had suffered a broken arm, putting him in the hospital. Former 3rd Pursuiter Wade Holman also cracked up on landing, damaging his undercarriage, wing, and propeller.[25]

AT 1630 THE DAY BEFORE, another group of inexperienced pursuit pilots— these of the 51st Pursuit Group—was departing Melbourne on the USAT *Willard Holbrook,* heading for Fremantle port in a convoy with four other vessels and the cruiser *Phoenix* as escort. Its commander, thirty-seven-year-old Maj. Homer Sanders, had been unofficially told at USAFIA headquarters in Melbourne ten days earlier by his old friend Ross Hoyt, air officer of USAFIA headquarters, that his 51st Pursuit Group was being sent to the Dutch East Indies, but Sanders still had received no formal destination orders. He was worried. "I wonder if our men know what we are sailing into," he wrote in his diary that evening. "Some are offering 2–1 that we don't make it," he added. Sanders himself subscribed to those odds. Colonel Hoyt had told him his 51st Group "wouldn't be coming back" from Java.[26]

EARLY ON WEDNESDAY MORNING, February 12, Maj. Edwin Broadhurst, executive officer of the 5th Bomber Command at Singosari, was on the phone to Bud Sprague at Ngoro. He was worried about the likelihood of another strafing attack on the B-17s at the 19th Bomb Group's base there that morning. Could Sprague send up P-40s over the Malang-Singosari area for protection? On his side he was holding his B-17s on the ground ready for immediate takeoff should the base's air raid alarm be sounded and was sending three of them to Pasirian for the day for dispersion.[27]

At 0800, Sprague ordered a flight of six of his P-40s to patrol over the Malang-Singosari area in response to Broadhurst's request. When it returned following an uneventful patrol, Sprague sent six other flights of four ships each at 1115 to take over patrolling in anticipation of a bombing attack. Sprague himself led A flight, with Hoskyn, Hennon, and Ryan, while B flight was headed up by McCallum, with Hayes, Gilmore, and Reynolds; C flight by Kiser, with Jackson, Kruzel, and Reagan; D flight by Coss, with Stauter, Egenes, and Hynes; E flight by Mahony, with Hague, Irvin and Johnson; and F flight by Dale, with McWherter, Muckley, and Turner. It was the first time that the 17th Pursuit was able to send up twenty-four P-40s on a mission—all that were in commission—thanks to the recent additions with the arrival of Mahony's group the day before.[28] After two hours of flying around the area on the lookout for Zeros and bombers threatening their "big brothers" at Singosari Field, the pursuiters returned to Ngoro. The protective mission had been flown on orders from Sprague; there had been no warning that day from the Dutch ADC of any impending Japanese attack. The inactivity of the Japanese appeared suspicious to George Parker, for one. "The Japs must be planning something," he figured.[29]

When McCallum and Gilmore landed, Sprague called them over for another assignment. He wanted the two Philippines veterans to fly over to Pasirian and lead back seven P-40s that were reported to have landed there on their transfer from Australia to his squadron. The two took off at 1400 on the short hop eastward, but on arrival at the field found that the "P-40s" were actually A-24 dive bombers, and there were ten of them, not seven. Lt. Harry Galusha of the 91st Bomb Squadron had led them in from Darwin via Koepang.[30]

Cy Blanton had not been up on the protective mission this day, but now

Sprague had an assignment for him, too. At 1420 he flew up to Perak Field to lead back Winfred Gallienne. The former 20th Pursuit pilot had crash-landed in the outskirts of Soerabaja on February 7 but was now finally able to fly back to Ngoro in P-40E No. 18, which had been repaired.[31] Sprague hoped to have another P-40 in commission when he sent Ray Thompson over to the Dutch air depot at Maospati Field, Madioen, some sixty miles west of Ngoro, to have the ship's hydraulic system repaired. However, the field there was wet from flooding. When Thompson touched down, his plane skidded into a native's truck, killing the Javanese. His P-40 was washed out in the accident, but Thompson suffered no injury. The Dutch and Javanese depot workers immediately set to stripping the plane, but they agreed to send the works back to Ngoro to 17th Pursuit engineering officer Bill Hennon. Thompson remained overnight at the base.[32]

Hennon would be getting additional mechanics and armorers to help with the repair and maintenance of his increased stock of P-40s at Ngoro. That evening a truck pulled up in Blimbing and discharged twelve enlisted men of the 3rd Pursuit, pooped out after a fifty-mile trip west to Blimbing from the B-17 base at Singosari, the journey interrupted several times at checkpoints by Javanese under Dutch officers. It had been a long day for the six crew chiefs and six armorers, beginning with their departure from Darwin late that morning as passengers in Clyde Kelsay's LB-30 No. 515. SSgt. Murray Nichols (Lubbock, Texas) and Sgt. Dave Burnside (Spokane, Washington)—both armorers—had alternated as tail gunners during the flight. Kelsay had a "helluva time" figuring out where to land at Singosari because of the shot-up condition of the runways, but he finally touched down at 1538 and disembarked his passengers before continuing on to Jogjakarta.[33]

In Blimbing the twelve were taken to one of the remaining Dutch houses and each given two blankets and a burlap bag filled with straw as a mattress. The group split up among the three bedrooms and threw their mattresses on the floor for the night. They were told they would be wakened at 0230 the next morning to go out to the field and help get the P-40s ready for the regular morning alert.[34]

The 17th Pursuit now also had three additional officers to help run field operations. At 2300 on February 11, 1st Lts. Jim McAfee and Pete Bender and 2nd Lt. Bob Stafford had arrived in Blimbing in a staff car after a five-hour trip from Soerabaja. Fueled by "much [Heineken] beer," they had "rather loudly wended their way" to their new post, the driver getting lost twice in the darkness. The three 27th Bomb Group officers had arrived in Soerabaja on February 9 as passengers in the submarine USS *Seawolf,* which had evacuated them and others from the Philippines. In Soerabaja for two days' enjoyment at the Oranje Hotel, they had been met by Sprague and informed they were being attached to his 17th Pursuit, but in nonflying duties, a cause for much puzzlement on their part.[35]

The next morning the threesome reported to Ngoro Field and discussed their new duties with Sprague. Bender was being assigned as supply officer for the 17th, and McAfee as an acting administrative/finance officer responsible for, among other things, camouflage and gas, while Stafford was also given administrative tasks. McAfee, a West Pointer, felt he was going to be doing things that "anyone could do" and sensed that Sprague "was not anxious to have us flying." All three discontented officers assumed their new duties in a "rather lackadaisical manner," hoping to get checked out eventually in the P-40s and fly with the 17th. After all, they were flying officers and senior to almost all the others.

At 0630 the following morning—February 13—Joe Kruzel took off with B. J. Oliver to make radio and weather checks and try to intercept an expected Japanese reconnaissance bomber that had been spotted flying in the area early each morning. After patrolling for an hour and fifteen minutes without seeing any enemy planes, they returned to Ngoro. The ADC hadn't reported any intruders, either.[36]

However, Fifth Bomber Command at Singosari believed there would be a big attack on the B-17 base that day and once again asked Sprague to mount a patrol over the Singosari-Malang area. The 17th's CO decided to send up sixteen P-40s in four flights of four ships each to provide protection for the base for three hours. From 1200 to 1345, A flight (Sprague, Johnsen, Gilmore, and Lund) and B flight (Coss, Hoskyn, Egenes, and Hynes) patrolled over the area, being joined at 1315 by C flight (Mahony, Hague, Irvin, and Reagan) and D flight (Lane, Reynolds, Gambonini, and Fuchs), which also covered the area at an altitude of twenty-two thousand feet until returning to land at 1515. Remaining on alert on the ground were E flight (McCallum, Johnson, Blanton, and Caldwell) and F flight (Dale, Wahl, Kruzel, and Oliver). The 5th Bomber Command's fears proved unfounded: no Japanese aircraft made an appearance.[37]

Casualties caused by the 17th Pursuit the past few days were not Japanese. In clearing their guns following takeoff and climb to altitude, the pursuiters had inadvertently killed several Javanese natives on the ground, an unfortunate result of their operations on the densely populated island. Disturbed by the incident, B. J. Oliver recorded it in his diary that night.[38]

The absence of any Japanese air attacks continued the following day. During the calm period Sprague allowed several of his pilots to take some time off and visit the nearby larger towns. Bill Hennon and Kay Kiser had driven over

A flight of P-40Es ready for takeoff near the alert shack at Ngoro Field, February 1942. *Courtesy Joseph Kruzel.*

to Soerabaja the day before "to visit various places and houses," returning the following morning to Ngoro. On their return, former 20th Pursuiters Gambonini, Fuchs, Hayes, Reynolds, and Hoskyn left on a drive of five and one-half hours to Jogjakarta to bring back four U.S. Army staff cars being provided the squadron. Following a "nice dinner," they went to a show, then turned in at the Grand Hotel de Djokjakarta for the night.[39]

Many of the other pursuiters were still standing alert for possible ADC warnings on this rainy day, while others were flying brief patrols. George Parker considered his "more of a training flight" than a patrol. Cy Blanton took "Chief" Quanah Fields up for 30–45 minutes of close formation flying and acrobatics and was impressed by how well Fields handled the P-40.[40] On the ground the mechanics had put two more P-40s into commission that day, bringing the total available for operations to twenty-six, with five still out. Butch Hague was particularly pleased with how well his "damn good crew," Cpl. Bob Reeves, his crew chief from Alvia, Iowa, and Pfc. Jack Crawford, armorer from Henderson, Texas, was looking after his ship. In addition to his

Joe Kruzel, flanked by his crew chief and armorer, poses in mid-February 1942 in front of his P40E, its nose painted with a fire-breathing dragon. *Courtesy Joseph Kruzel.*

maintenance capabilities, Joe Kruzel's crew chief had also displayed artistic abilities. As others had stood around kibitzing, he had painted a large, detailed dragon on Kruzel's P-40E that extended from the prop spinner back past the engine compartment, a multicolor job. Kruzel's No. 14 was the only one of the 17th's ships with any decoration on it.[41]

ON TIMOR, AFTER HAVING ABORTED their trek to Atambua and spending the night in a native house on the advice of a Dutch captain they had met, Vern Head and his five squadron mates prepared to resume walking early on the morning of February 12. The Dutch officer guiding them explained that they would need to cover about sixteen miles of jungle and mountains before they reached the nearest road. He suggested using horses that were available to them, but the pursuiters said that they preferred to walk. The little Timorese laughing boy, "Friday," would carry Head's possessions for him.[42] About five hours into the hike, shortly after noon, the party reached the road. There they found two trucks waiting for them that drove them to Atambua. The Dutch and Timorese personnel at the base bandaged their cuts, washed their clothes, gave them a good dinner at the rest house, and put them up in "nice, clean beds."

Head and the others were relieved to find Tom Christian at the base. He told them that he had bailed out near a native village and had been brought in to Atambua the day before. But there was some bad news, too. The Dutch captain informed them that he had received a report that Phil Metsker had been found dead near his plane. It wasn't clear whether his chute had failed to open or whether he had been thrown out of the plane when it crashed.[43]

The next morning—Friday, February 13—the pursuiters climbed into two Chevrolet pickups with all their equipment, joined by a Dutch doctor. The truck drivers were Australians who had a regular run over the island. At about 0830 they set out over a "narrow, crooked, and rugged" road for the trip to Koepang. After stops at a Dutch settlement for coffee at about 1000 and at another one for lunch, they arrived at Tjamplong, twenty-five miles short of Koepang, about 1700. There an Australian doctor looked at their wounds. He decided that Head should stay behind a few days to have stitches put in his lip. The injuries to the others were deemed not serious and didn't require his services. They would continue on to Koepang that afternoon.

WHEN BOB MCMAHON REPORTED IN at the field at Port Pirie at daybreak, 06:48, on Saturday, February 14, 1942, for the takeoff for Darwin, he was surprised to see an altar covered with a sheet over a few crates on a little green lawn in front of operations. A local priest was giving a sunrise mass for the thirteen pilots of the 33rd set to make the north-south cross-Australia flight to Darwin. McMahon noticed that Dick Suehr, on both knees on the grass, was leading off those receiving holy communion. Joining the rear of the group, McMahon decided not to come forward for communion. He was feeling guilty after having spent the night before with a Tasmanian girl.[44]

The mass was completed in only about fifteen minutes. McMahon and the others headed for a hurried breakfast, then said goodbye to their Australian hosts before climbing into their P-40s for the first leg of their flight, to Alice Springs. They would be flying without Dick Pingree and Bill Borden, both of whom had engine trouble and were to be left behind at Port Pirie.[45] After climbing to cruising altitude, six thousand feet, the flight formed up in three loose, irregular formations, with their CO Pell on the right, Jack Peres in the center, and McMahon on the extreme left. Pell had them unusually spread out, stretching over five miles to allow them to do their own navigating. As they spotted any significant features below that could be landmarks for their flight, they called out on their radios, but Pell finally ordered them to restrict such calls to emergencies.

Some one hundred miles into their northward flight, the pursuiters looked around for their first checkpoint, which was supposed to be a large blue lake—Lake Torrens—with some mountains off to the right: the Flinders Range. Although it was supposed to be a large lake, about half the size of one of their Great Lakes, what they made out below seemed to be just a dry, grey flat of desert, with only an alkaline line to delineate it from the rest of the desert around it. They were beginning to think that their compass headings would be a better navigation aid than such landmarks. Once they had passed over the lake, they dropped down to about two thousand feet to try to pick up details harder to see from higher up: single telegraph lines, trails, old fence lines, an old single-track railway line. They needed to find Oodnadatta, a small RAAF field three hundred miles north-northwest of Lake Torrens where they would refuel for the onward flight to Alice Springs. Finally, after having left Port Pirie three hours earlier, they spotted the field out in the middle of nowhere and came in to land without incident.[46]

No fuel truck came out to meet them. They would have to refuel their ships by hand from rows of fifty-five-gallon drums. Under vicious attack by swarms of flies, they rolled the drums out to their planes. As one pilot operated one of the few rotary hand pumps, the other fed the hose or fueled the gas tanks, while all the others were swatting flies. Each P-40 took about three barrels of gas. Since they couldn't refuel more than a few planes at a time because of the shortage of hand pumps, the waiting pilots went to the mess shack for an early lunch. Getting down the mutton stew, white bread, and warm beer proved difficult even within the shack's screened enclosure; the persistent flies got into their noses, ears, and mouths and couldn't be shooed off.[47]

After lunch the pursuiters resumed their flight north, this time looking for Alice Springs. But after flying the estimated two and one-half hours to reach the field, McMahon and the others still hadn't spotted the big red rock that was supposed to be the landmark for Alice Springs to the right and were getting nervous. Then Peres saw it and called out to the others, and soon Pell confirmed it. A few minutes later they noticed a "small dark smudge" on the grey-brown horizon that soon became a dull green, and they realized they had found their destination.[48] Pell, McMahon, and nine of the others of the thirteen touched down without incident at the field, but Dave Latane and Jess Dore blew their tail wheel tires on landing, Latane having run a thorn through his. They would not be able to continue north with the others the following morning.[49]

That afternoon, at 1630, a radiogram came in for Pell from USAFIA headquarters in response to his report on the accidents. He was ordered to continue on to Darwin with the eleven P-40s still flyable. Two C-53s would arrive at Alice Springs the following day with two tail wheels for Dore's and Latane's P-40s, along with mechanics for the 33rd's operations at Darwin. McMahon felt Pell's flight was "snakebit"; if the transport had accompanied them in the first place with mechanics and spare parts, the two ships could have been repaired on the spot and ready to continue on with the others to Darwin.[50]

The next morning, February 15, Pell led off the remaining eleven ships for Daly Waters, 510 miles due north. The 33rd's CO had rearranged the three flights after leaving Dore and Latane behind. Peres and McMahon were now leading three-ship flights, while Pell retained his five. Peres was navigating for both his and McMahon's flights behind Pell's. This leg of the trip was proving easier than that of the day before; there were railroad and telegraph lines as well as a road to guide them to their destination.[51]

After a little over three hours, Daly Waters appeared below them. To McMahon the field looked oddly shaped—basically rectangular—and very large. It had a single rutted corrugated metal hangar at one side and a white wood fence to delineate part of one of the field's perimeters. Despite heavy dust stirred up by Pell's five in landing, Peres's flight of three succeeded in getting down all right, and now it was McMahon's flight's turn. As McMahon descended, he noted that the others had now taxied to the service area of the field. He opted to bring his ship in on a different part of the huge field and at an angle. McMahon touched down without mishap, as did the pilots behind him.[52]

After the servicing of their ships was completed, Pell led off with his flight. By the time those five ships were aloft, the center of the field was enveloped in dust. Peres followed with his two flight members, taking off to the right of Pell's flight and slightly upwind, virtually in a line abreast. The dust was building up so much now that visibility was down to a few hundred feet.[53] Under such conditions McMahon decided to wait for the dust to settle before leading off his flight. After a few minutes, with Pell's flight circling overhead, the CO's voice boomed out over McMahon's radio: "OK, where the hell is C Flight?" Without explaining why he was delaying his take-off, McMahon radioed back, "We'll be rolling in about ten seconds."

Nodding for the roll, McMahon led Bill Walker and Dick Suehr down the field in a line abreast. Each one was holding his space and heading as they hit takeoff speed. Checking over to Walker for his drift, then shifting his eyes back to his gyro, McMahon noticed something out of the corner of his left eye; it looked like someone was jumping off some sort of vehicle. As he automatically pulled back on the stick, he heard a "whomp," and his ship bounced into the air. McMahon added power and climbed straight out in the direction taken by Pell, wondering what had happened. Glancing back down at the field to the left, McMahon saw someone running away from what appeared to be a large yellow tractor, then noticed a strip of torn aluminum flapping back almost under his fuselage. He called Walker on the radio and asked him to slide over under him to check what damage his ship had sustained. "Jesus Christ!" is all McMahon heard when Walker inspected. "Y'all got a real mess. If I were you, I'd take it back and bail out or belly in," the Jacksonville, Texas, native drawled back after his short inspection of McMahon's ship.[54]

Deciding to take Walker's advice, a shocked McMahon made a slow turn back toward the field. Really "pissed off" at the "stupid jackass" who would drive a tractor through the dust in front of airplanes taking off, he thought of using his .45 on him when he got his ship down. But then as he looked at the desolate little hangar as he approached the field, McMahon concluded that it would be futile to expect the Aussies there to fix his badly damaged ship. He recalled hearing that the RAAF field at Darwin was large and modern. Certainly it would have a metal shop. McMahon went into a slow turn and headed back on a north-northwesterly course for Darwin, three hundred miles away. He added extra power to compensate for his ship's drag and opened his canopy another notch. He wanted to keep a sharp eye on the upper surface of his wing. If he should see even a wrinkle or bulge on it, he was going to go over the side, even if it meant landing in the bush of the outback.

After a little more than an hour in the air at high throttle, McMahon noticed several specks on the horizon slightly above him. As he came closer, he made them out to be the other ten P-40s of his flight. But one of the tail end members was slowly dropping behind the others. McMahon figured the pilot had seen him and was dropping back to link up with him and accompany him in to Darwin. Then McMahon realized that the "kind soul" had a problem of his own; his prop was rotating slower and slower. When the ship was about three hundred yards in front of McMahon, the propeller slowly milled to a stop and the P-40 dropped below McMahon's level, heading for a "large green billabong" (pond) off to the left. As McMahon watched, the pilot made a perfect three-point landing on the green, rolled straight ahead for about one hundred yards, then abruptly went up on his nose. McMahon throttled back and descended to within a few hundred feet of the scene. As he made a pass over the upturned P-40, the pilot crawled out of the cockpit and was close enough for McMahon to identify him. It was Dick Suehr of his

C flight; there was no mistaking the "ear to ear grin on that olive face." Suehr waved at McMahon, who in response rocked his wing gently in acknowledgment after reversing course in a slow climb, then headed back on course for Darwin. But by the time he marked the forced landing spot on his map—some sixty miles south of Darwin—and got back to his flight's altitude, the others were no longer in sight.[55]

Soon McMahon made out the hazy coastline of northern Australia and prepared to come in at the big RAAF field at Darwin. He wasn't sure if he could land his damaged ship or would have to belly in. After several near-stall tries over the longest runway, he figured he could make it gear down. Barely above landing speed, he touched down, applying the brake intermittently. His *Bahootee the Cootee* swung left across the two main runway intersections and back down and across the other runway, stopping on the grass between the runways. With a gasp of relief, McMahon climbed out and looked at the damaged wing. He nearly threw up. It looked like a madman with an ax had opened up the bottom. The main spar was broken and the others mangled, with only its aluminum skin to support the wing.[56]

McMahon walked across the runway and ramp to the closest hangar, where an Aussie informed him that "your chaps are working out of that other hangar." He headed for what they called Squadron 12 hangar. There he was informed that Pell had already gassed up after coming in and with two other P-40s—evidently including Peres—had headed out over the Timor Sea to try and intercept some Nip flying boat shadowing a convoy. McMahon figured that the three P-40s he had noticed headed west from the field as he had come in for his landing must have been those of Pell's patrol.[57]

While looking around the hangar, McMahon noticed an A-24 dive bomber near the door and recognized the pilot near it as one of the 27th Bomb Group bunch from Amberley, 2nd Lt. J. W. Jacobs. When he informed McMahon that his ship was indeed flyable, McMahon told him that one of his squadron mates was down sixty miles south of Darwin and needed a supply drop if he couldn't be picked up. McMahon then checked by phone with RAAF operations, which confirmed that the RAAF had no light planes that could land near the billabong to pick up Suehr. In the meantime, an Aussie NCO who had overheard McMahon describing Suehr's dilemma had obtained an empty practice bomb and showed it to McMahon. The two loaded it with some tinned supplies and rigged up a drogue chute for it. It was agreed that McMahon would fly in the back seat with Jacobs piloting the A-24, and McMahon would drop the supply canister to Suehr. As they were about to depart, McMahon was surprised to see an American Army infantry officer enter the hangar whom he knew from the *Republic* voyage, 2nd. Lt. Aubrey

Tobias. Assigned to headquarters, FEAF detachment, Darwin, Tobias was bored with his work and begged McMahon to allow him to take McMahon's place in the A-24; he had never been up in a plane. McMahon accepted the request and briefed Tobias on Suehr's location. In the late afternoon the A-24 was off on its special mission.[58]

Returning to his wrecked ship, McMahon stripped it of all transferable parts, then took his personal possessions to the bachelor officers' quarters on the second floor of the RAAF officers' quarters complex. After claiming a bed, he returned to the flight line and entered Hangar 12 again. There he looked over two "hangar queen" P-40s that had been left behind by other provisional squadrons transiting Darwin and were awaiting major parts or maintenance. He picked one with a bent propeller from a noseover as the best candidate for a replacement aircraft for himself. An A-24 mechanic in the hangar was willing to help him replace the propeller.[59]

HIGH IN THE SKY OVER THE TIMOR SEA—about 130 miles northwest of Darwin—in mid-afternoon that February 15, 2nd Lt. Robert "Blackie" Buel in his P-40E was searching the watery expanse below for a convoy of eight ships, led by the cruiser *Houston,* that was headed for Koepang, Timor, with troop reinforcements for ABDACOM. The Army Air Forces' operations officer at Darwin, 1st Lt. Hewitt "Shorty" Wheless, after consulting with Wing Cmdr. Stuart Griffith, the CO of the RAAF field, had ordered Buel at about 1400 to search for a four-engine Japanese flying boat that was attacking the convoy. A radio message from the *Houston* that Griffith had received at 1145 reported that the convoy was being shadowed by the flying boat northwest of Darwin and gave its exact location. Then about two hours later—just before Buel took off—another radio message was received: the convoy was being bombed by the Kawanishi flying boat about 130 miles northwest of Darwin.[60] Wheless had attempted to contact the pilot of the only other operational P-40 at Darwin at the time, 2nd Lt. Robert Oestreicher, but could not get him on his radio as he patrolled over the Darwin area. Wheless wanted Oestreicher to accompany Buel in the search, but with no response from Oestreicher reluctantly sent Buel out alone on the hazardous overwater mission.[61]

It was now just before 1500 when Buel spotted the convoy below and flew over it, but he did not see any flying boat in the area. After radioing RAAF Darwin with his sighting, he continued in his search for the flying boat, identified by the convoy as a Kawanishi H6K, code-named "Mavis." Then he spotted it, flying at about thirteen thousand feet on a northerly course.[62]

The Mavis dipped into a cloud, and Buel entered it from the opposite direction, commencing a cat- and- mouse chase that would extend over fif-

Robert J. "Blackie" Buel at Ascot Race Track, Brisbane, shortly after his arrival on the USAT *Republic*, December 22, 1941. *Courtesy Mildred Daggett, from John Lewis Collection.*.

teen to twenty minutes. Then, when the P-40 was momentarily out of sight, the Japanese plane made a pass over the *Houston* at ten thousand feet but was forced higher by antiaircraft fire from the cruiser before dropping bombs that fell off the mark.[63] But now Buel was approaching the Japanese from the rear, unaware that the H6K4 flying boat carried a 20 mm cannon in its tail. As Buel poured fire from his six .50-caliber wing guns into the fuselage of the huge target, its tail gunner fired back with his cannon, scoring hits on the P-40. Soon white smoke was coming from Buel's tail, and his plane went into a dive as the Japanese continued firing at it. But flames were now issuing from the Mavis's fuselage tank where Buel had struck it, and the flying boat began losing altitude rapidly. It leveled off a bit in its dive, then plunged into the sea.[64]

In the meantime, Oestreicher had come in to land at Darwin at about 1445 after his patrol. While he was refueling his P-40, he was informed by RAAF operations that his 3rd Pursuit squadron mate Buel had been sent on a mission to search for the convoy and the Japanese flying boat but had not been heard from since his call, received shortly before, indicating that he had found the convoy but not the Mavis. Oestreicher was given a course by RAAF intelligence and ordered to take off again and search for Buel.[65] His refueling completed, Oestreicher took off and headed in a northwesterly direction out over the Timor Sea. When he reached the location given him, he swung his P-40 around to cover about twenty miles on each side of his course but saw no trace of Buel, nor did he spot the convoy. The weather was beginning to deteriorate, with scattered rain. Figuring it was pointless to continue his search, Oestreicher decided to return to Darwin, where he landed two and one-half hours after his takeoff.

It was about 1830—forty-five minutes before sunset—when Pell touched down at the RAAF field with Peres and the third pilot of his patrol. He also had flown out to the position reported to Darwin about an hour after Oestreicher had been sent out. At 1720 he had found the convoy, then 150 miles west of Darwin on its westerly course, and had flown over it. Pell and his two squadron mates searched the area up to six thousand feet but found no enemy aircraft that he had been informed was attacking the convoy.[66]

On the field, Oestreicher was asked by Pell to give an account of his earlier search mission for Buel, now presumed to be lost. After Pell had received Oestreicher's oral report, Bob McMahon entered operations to report in to his CO with his report on what had happened to him on the Daly Waters–Darwin flight that had separated him from Pell's group. Pell was not happy to learn that McMahon had damaged his P-40 beyond repair—though managing to bring it in to Darwin—and that a second of the eleven ships he led out of Daly Waters—Suehr's—had force-landed in the outback. With six of the nine remaining to him needing work, he was now left with just three operational P-40s of the fifteen that he was expected to have on hand for Darwin operations. And to top it off, his patrol had been ineffective in finding either Buel or the Japanese flying boat.[67]

McMahon tried valiantly to put a better face on the P-40 situation. He told Pell that he believed they could repair the two P-40s left behind in the hangar with the help of the 33rd's mechanics expected the following day. Pell himself acknowledged that the other ships of his group that were out of commission could be brought into flying condition within three days. And there was Oestreicher's unassigned P-40 that was available to him, too. As for pilots, McMahon felt that they would get Suehr back from the bush in time for future operations.[68]

Pell asked McMahon if he knew the two pilots ordered to fly the convoy search mission before his group arrived, mentioning Oestreicher and Buel by name. McMahon said he knew both from Amberley days. Buel was a good friend; they had both flown with the old 21st Pursuit Squadron, 35th Group, at Hamilton Field and had come over together on the *Republic*. Pell then informed McMahon that Buel was missing and Oestreicher had told him he didn't know the circumstances. The account he had received from Oestreicher about his patrol conflicted with other information he had received. It was not clear if he had flown over the convoy with Buel or had flown out alone and not found the convoy or Buel.[69]

After the long and trying day, Pell and his squadron mates felt beat. They ate "a sort of a meal," then turned in by 2100. McMahon was too wound up to fall off to sleep immediately. As he was about to doze off, he detected the intermittent drone of an A-24's radial engine. It seemed to last for about ten minutes, then there was a "wide open roar" and silence.[70]

STILL AT THE RAAF LAVERTON FIELD at Melbourne after aborting his takeoff with his 33rd Squadron the day before, Bryce Wilhite was surprised to see a huge puddle of Prestone coolant completely surrounding his P-40E when he went down to the flight line on the morning of Saturday, February 14. "My intuition not to take off yesterday was right," he thought. He figured if he had left with the others to Port Pirie, he would have lost all the coolant during the flight and would have had to make a forced landing with a dead engine and stick. He would not have had a chance to keep flying for a while until he found a suitable field for putting his ship down.[71]

While he was waiting at the field for his coolant leak to be repaired, a large group of P-40s came in to land. The lead pilot was someone he did not recognize, Capt. Jim Bruce, he found out later. Wilhite did not know the pilots of the squadron, either—they were assigned to the 13th Pursuit (Provisional), he was informed. He also wondered where the P-40s they were flying came from, as he thought his 33rd had cleaned out all the remaining P-40s at Amberley.[72] Later that day, Wilhite found out that Captain Bruce had sent one of his pilots into Melbourne and had cleaned out a jewelry store of all its Longines watches. On his return to the field, the watches were given out to each of the pilots. Wilhite grabbed one for himself. These stainless steel watches were considered very suitable for time-distance navigation, such as for measuring the time to checkpoints, and were protected from magnetic fields. All the pilots were now wearing two watches—their own personal one and the new addition.[73]

The next morning, his P-40E No. 25 now repaired, Wilhite joined the fifteen pilots of the 13th Pursuit at the field for the flight to Port Pirie, their next stop on the way to Fremantle. Captain Bruce led the group off the field. After Wilhite landed with the others following an uneventful flight, he was informed that Pell had taken thirteen of his 33rd Provisional to Darwin the day before, while Keenan had flown on to Fremantle with the rest of the squadron. However, two of his 33rd Squadron mates were still there at Port Pirie—Dick Pingree and Bill Borden. Pingree told Wilhite he had an engine problem, but Wilhite did not know why Borden had remained behind.[74]

The newly arrived pursuiters had picked up the rumor being spread by the RAAF that they were being transferred to Fremantle to board the carrier *Langley* and that they would meet Pell in Java. Wilhite knew from Pell that the story was true but would not confirm or deny it when asked by the others not in the know. He felt they were talking too freely about the plan without knowing who might be listening.[75]

That night they slept in the RAAF officers' quarters. Wilhite talked to Borden about what they should do, since their commanding officer, Pell, was not there to give them orders. With Borden's ship now in commission again, they decided on their own to follow Bruce's group to Fremantle. Squadron mate Pingree would have to remain behind; he still had a problem with his ship's engine.

On the following morning of Monday, February 16, Wilhite and Borden joined the pilots of the 13th at the flight line and prepared to take off for Fremantle, on the west coast. It would be a two-day trip for the inexperienced pursuiters, 1,250 miles due west across the southern rim of Australia, with stops scheduled at Forrest—575 miles out of Port Pirie—and Kalgoorlie.[76]

With his visibility limited by the long nose and wing of his P-40, Wilhite did not notice the tie-down ring support extending above the surface of the grass field as he taxied No. 25 out from the tarmac. His left tire hit the ob-

Kenneth Koebel's No. 196 in front of other P-40Es of the 33rd Pursuit Squadron (Provisional) during a fueling stop at Forrest, Western Australia, on the way to Perth to board the USS *Langley,* February 16, 1942. *Courtesy John Lever via Peter Dunn.*

stacle, but Wilhite assumed it had gone into one of the small depressions on the field as he stopped and waited for the P-40 ahead of him to go into its takeoff roll. Now his turn, Wilhite gunned his engine to pass through the "small depression." Over the engine noise he heard his tire blow out. His ship dropped about a foot toward the left wing. Confused about what had happened, Wilhite cut his engine and climbed out of his stricken ship. Examining the left wheel, he was surprised to find that the fabric of the tire had been torn and the air had forced the inner tube into the outer layer of rubber. Now he realized what had happened. When he was trying to get his ship out of what he thought was a small depression, he was actually pulling it over the bulge in the tire, causing the blowout. Once again, he mused, he was being left behind as the others took off for their destination.

PART FOUR

"I Deeply Regret Failure to Hold ABDA Area"

FOLLOWING THE JAPANESE LANDING on Sumatra on February 14, the Dutch defense forces had counterattacked and appeared in a position to defeat the Japanese paratroops tenuously holding the Palembang No. 1 airstrip. However, additional paratroopers were dropped in the area, and another Japanese force in barges succeeded in moving up the Moesi River to join the fray. Allied air strikes on the Japanese landing forces could not slow the Japanese advance. With the arrival of the main Japanese force off Palembang on February 17, virtually all Allied forces on Sumatra were evacuated across the Sunda Strait to Java under chaotic conditions. West Java now lay open to Japanese invasion.[1]

Japanese strategy for the seizure of the Java prize had now reached the third phase, the isolation of Java from the east. The plan comprised three almost simultaneous operations: the seizure of Bali to serve as a springboard for air operations against East Java, the occupation of Timor to cut off the ferry route to Java from Australia, and a massive aerial attack on Darwin, eliminating it as a threat to the Timor invasion and as the supply point for the Indies.[2]

On February 17 the Bali and Timor invasion forces set out from Makassar and Amboina, respectively, while the carrier force that would strike Darwin arrived in Kendari the same day in preparation for a fast night passage of the Banda Sea to put it in a position to launch on the morning of February 19. Army troops of the Timor force were heading for Koepang in nine transports escorted by a cruiser and eight destroyers, while five additional transports carried troops to occupy Portuguese Dili to the north, where only four hundred Dutch and Australian troops would be opposing them. The Bali invasion force was much smaller, comprised of a single battalion embarked in two transports with destroyer escort.[3]

The Bali force was the first to reach its destination, on the evening of February 18, and landings began early the following morning. The main action occurred at sea, where Dutch cruisers and Dutch and American destroyers engaged the Japanese in the Badoeng Strait in a confused action resulting in the loss of a Dutch destroyer and heavy damage to an American destroyer, a "dismally fought action on the Allied part."[4] An aerial attack on the Japanese landing forces on the morning of February 20 by American P-40s and A-24s cost five of the fighters and two of the dive bombers, with no Japanese ships damaged or sunk. With the failure to stop the Japanese ground force, the Allies lost Denpasar Airfield, leaving nearby Soerabaja and the American B-17 base at Singosari wide open to incessant bombing and strafing attacks.

At Darwin, the arrival at 0940 of 188 aircraft launched from the *Akagi*, *Kaga, Soryu,* and *Hiryu* of Nagumo's 1st Air Fleet over the town's harbor and airfields caught the Australians completely by surprise, despite the early warning they had received. The defenders were totally ill prepared for such a massive aerial attack, without a single Australian fighter to defend the base and only a few antiaircraft guns emplaced. Darwin posed a lucrative target, with more than forty-five ships in the harbor and nine RAAF Hudson bombers on the field, but the Japanese also went after the dockyards, oil depot, and even the town itself.[5]

Also caught unprepared for the attack, the pilots of ten P-40s that were transiting Darwin for Java were overwhelmed by the Zeros and all but one shot down or destroyed on takeoff. Four of the pilots were killed, including the commanding officer of the 33rd Pursuit Squadron (Provisional). An LB-30, six of the Hudsons, and three Beechcraft transports were destroyed on the ground, as well as four PBY flying boats of Patrol Wing 10 near Melville Island, shot up by the Zeros on their way to Darwin. Eight ships in the harbor were sunk, including the U.S. destroyer *Peary;* three others were beached; and ten were damaged. To add to the destruction, fifty-four Japanese land-based Betty and Nell bombers from Kendari followed up at 1158 with further attacks on the RAAF field.[6]

The first-ever attack on Australian territory by a foreign power triggered a panic among military personnel and civilians alike, who streamed out of the Darwin area by foot or whatever other means were available. Some 243 Allied personnel had been killed and an estimated 400 wounded. Its RAAF station and dockyard facilities completely devastated, Darwin would be written off for months to come.[7] The cost for the Japanese was a mere two aircraft: one Zero of the thirty-six in the attack and one Val dive bomber of seventy-one

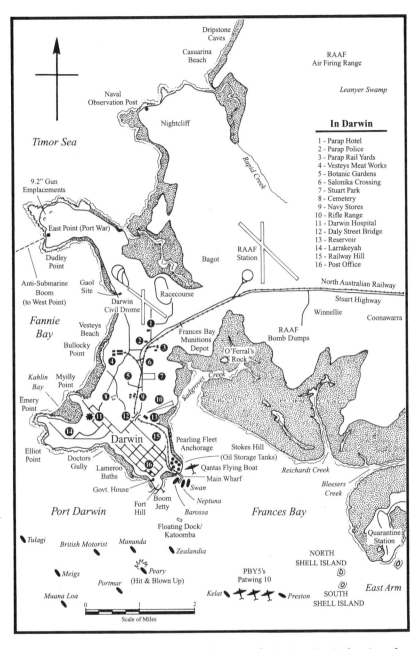

In Darwin

1 - Parap Hotel
2 - Parap Police
3 - Parap Rail Yards
4 - Vesteys Meat Works
5 - Botanic Gardens
6 - Salonika Crossing
7 - Stuart Park
8 - Cemetery
9 - Navy Stores
10 - Rifle Range
11 - Darwin Hospital
12 - Daly Street Bridge
13 - Reservoir
14 - Larrakeyah
15 - Railway Hill
16 - Post Office

Dripstone Caves

Casuarina Beach

RAAF Air Firing Range

Naval Observation Post

Leanyer Swamp

Nightcliff

Timor Sea

9.2" Gun Emplacements

East Point (Port War)

Dudley Point

Anti-Submarine Boom (to West Point)

Gaol Site

Rapid Creek

RAAF Station

Bagot

Fannie Bay

Vesteys Beach

Bullocky Point

Darwin Civil Drome

Racecourse

Frances Bay Munitions Depot

O'Ferral's Rock

RAAF Bomb Dumps

North Australian Railway

Stuart Highway

Winnellie

Coonawarra

Kahlin Bay

Myilly Point

Sadgroves Creek

Emery Point

Darwin

Elliot Point

Doctors Gully

Lameroo Baths

Govt. House

Pearling Fleet Anchorage

Stokes Hill (Oil Storage Tanks)

Qantas Flying Boat

Main Wharf

Swan

Reichardt Creek

Bleesers Creek

Port Darwin

Fort Hill

Boom Jetty

Neptuna

Barossa

Frances Bay

Floating Dock/ Katoomba

Quarantine Station

Tulagi

British Motorist

Manunda

Zealandia

NORTH SHELL ISLAND

Meigs

Portmar

Peary (Hit & Blown Up)

PBY5's Patwing 10

Muana Loa

Kelat

Preston

SOUTH SHELL ISLAND

East Arm

0   1   2

Scale of Miles

Darwin Area, February 1942. *Redrawn from map of Aviation Historical Society of Northern Territory. Used with permission.*

participating, each by antiaircraft fire. None of the eighty-one B5N "Kate" level bombers were lost, nor were any of the fifty-four Betty bombers.

That evening Japanese invasion forces arrived off the coasts of Timor, and by early morning the next day all troops were ashore. Allied forces in Koepang were evacuated, leaving the key airfield in Japanese hands. In three days all the defenders had become prisoners. To the north, Portuguese Dili was also easily captured. Elated with the prospect of completing his conquest of Southeast Asia, Admiral Isoroku Yamamoto on February 20 now made plans for the complete envelopment of Java.[8]

The loss of Bali and Timor, coupled with the fear of a Japanese follow-up invasion of defenseless northern Australia, heightened the state of anxiety of Australia's war cabinet. When Prime Minister Curtin learned of ABDACOM plans to go ahead with the shipment of thirty-two P-40s from Fremantle to seemingly doomed Java, he cabled the Australian minister in Washington on February 21 as a matter of top priority to recommend to the War Department that the aircraft instead be retained for the defense of Australia. After meeting with Marshall and Arnold, the minister informed Curtin that the *Langley* P-40s were not in actuality going to Java: they were being sent to India or Burma, for whose defense it was alleged they were vital.[9]

Unknown to the Australian government, Wavell, on the instigation of his deputy, Major General Brett, days earlier had agreed to the rerouting of the *Langley* and the rest of the MS-5 convoy, originally destined for Java, to Calcutta or Burma instead in order to prepare for "coming operations in the area." Four days later, on February 21, Brett radioed the Adjutant General, War Department (AGWAR), that he had completed plans for the evacuation of Java and was sending his air force chief, Brereton, to India while also recommending that he himself also proceed to India. "The real theater for American forces is through Burma into China," he asserted.[10] In confirmation of Brett's decision, Wavell wrote Curtin the same day, apologizing for failure to maintain positions in the NEI and emphasizing the need to hold bases in Burma and Australia, with Burma "the more pressing problem."[11] As Brett had informed AGWAR, "sufficient personnel now available or due in Australia to handle the problem there." Curtin's argument for retaining the *Langley* (and *Sea Witch*) P-40s for the defense of Australia had been dismissed.

If the Australians were miffed, the Dutch were furious about the change in plans. Under the agreement of February 5 allocating P-40 squadrons between Java and Australia, the 33rd and 13th Pursuit Squadrons (Provisional) were set to go to Java, as were the 16th, 25th, and 26th Squadrons of the 51st Pursuit Group. Now Brett, with Wavell's approval, was diverting the thirty-two P-40s and the pilots of the 33rd and 13th, set to sail for Java on the *Langley*

American cargo vessel *Sea Witch* in August 1941, its large U.S. flag proclaiming its neutrality status at the time. *Photograph 303914* © *Australian War Memorial.*

on February 22, as well as the P-40s and personnel of the three squadrons of the 51st Pursuit Group in the same convoy, to India/Burma instead. The lieutenant governor of the Dutch East Indies, Hubertus van Mook, cabled Marshall on February 22 and beseeched him to keep sending material and men to Java.[12] Marshall evidently acquiesced, not wanting to be seen as letting the Dutch allies down despite the rapidly deteriorating situation. The following day Arnold in Washington radioed General Barnes at USAFIA in Melbourne to take whatever action he could to meet the request of Van Mook to expedite the transfer of aircraft to Java.[13]

When the *Langley, Sea Witch,* and other three ships of Convoy MS-5 got underway from Fremantle on the afternoon of February 22, their orders were for Colombo, Ceylon, with the ultimate destination Bombay, "subject to change."[14] But at 2124 that evening the captain of the cruiser USS *Phoenix* received a dispatch from the Australians directing the *Langley* to break off and proceed to Tjilatjap, Java, "with all dispatch" in accordance with orders received from ABDAFLOAT (Dutch Vice Adm. C. E. L. Helfrich, who had assumed command of ABDA naval forces on February 14) and approved by Wavell.[15] Then at 0819 on February 25, the *Phoenix's* captain relayed an order from ABDACOM to the *Sea Witch* that it detach itself (with its cargo of twenty-seven crated P-40Es) and proceed to Tjilatjap, also "with all dispatch."[16] But the pilots and mechanics of the 51st Group in the three other ships of MS-5 with ten of their P-40s were to continue to India.

The February 12 plan of ABDAIR for the Langley's thirty-two P-40s and their pilots to be assigned to Tjisaoek Field in the defense of West Java was now resurrected. The twenty-seven crated Sea Witch P-40s were to be offloaded and transported by rail to Andir and Tasikmalaja Fields on West Java for assembly and subsequent assignment, twelve to a Dutch squadron and the other twelve to an RAF squadron, to be based at Tasikmalaja and Tjililitan, respectively, with the remaining three aircraft to be sent to Ngoro as reinforcements for the American 17th Pursuit (Provisional).[17]

On February 24 Brereton (in Bandoeng as FEAF commander) had radioed Brett, now in Melbourne, that he had deemed it "necessary"—evidently as deputy commander of ABDAIR at that time—in supporting the Helfrich/ Wavell decision on February 22 to detach the Sea Witch and divert the American freighter to Java for an additional reason: to unload the 400,000 rounds of .50-caliber ammunition it was ferrying to meet the needs of the thirty-two P-40s on the Langley, which were armed with only the 48,000 rounds that they carried for their guns. The 17th Pursuit had less than 150,000 rounds left on Java. Preliminary arrangements had been made to assemble the Sea Witch's twenty-seven P-40Es on its arrival at Tjilatjap.[18]

Brett and Wavell had been obliged to back down in the face of Dutch protests and as a means of placating their ally on a broader issue: the winding up of ABDACOM, as decided by Wavell and Brett on February 20 and recommended to London and the CCS in Washington, "when the fighter defense of Java would be no longer possible."[19] That meant now to Wavell and Brett, for they—and everyone but the Dutch—knew that diverting the P-40s of the Langley and the Sea Witch, and the pilots on the Langley, would not make any difference at this late stage. Already on February 19, with the backing of Brett, Brereton had decided to withdraw his Far East Air Force from Java, and after securing the agreement of Wavell, he received permission to do so from Marshall in Washington on February 22.[20] On that date the CCS had informed Wavell that while "all fighting units for which there are arms must continue to fight," "air forces which can more usefully operate from bases outside Java and their personnel without aircraft" should be withdrawn to Australia from Java.[21] Combat aircraft remaining on Java were now under Maj. Gen. L. H. van Oyen, who was replacing Air Mshl. Sir Richard Peirse as commanding officer of ABDAIR, now to be slimmed down and renamed Java Air Command. The latter would include the American East Group (EASGROUP), operating from Central and East Java.[22] On the evening of February 24 Brereton with

Maj. Gen. Lewis H. Brereton arriving in Colombo, Ceylon, February 25, 1942, after giving up his FEAF command and flying out of Jogjakarta the evening before. *Author's collection.*

staff members was flown out of Jogjakarta for Colombo. The previous night Brett himself had left for Australia to take up command of USAFIA, his India wishes having been turned down.[23]

On February 24, the CCS in Washington formally decided to turn over command of the ABDA area, or what was left of it, to the Dutch and return Wavell as commander-in-chief of India. It merely ratified Wavell's transfer two days earlier of Java air forces to General Van Oyen. Lt. Gen. Hein ter Poorten—who had commanded the Allied army forces—now also was appointed commander-in-chief, ABDA area. At Wavell's request his own new

Chicago Daily News war correspondent George Weller (r.) in a meeting in Bandoeng, Java, with Maj. Gen. L. H. van Oyen, Dutch commander of Java Air Command, late February 1942. *Courtesy Anthony Weller.*

command was now to include operations in Burma, which was being hived off from ABDA's responsibility.[24] When the Australian government asked Wavell for the return of the north Australia area of ABDACOM to its control, Wavell agreed, but the CCS decided it should pass to Dutch headquarters control (now under Ter Poorten) as successor to Wavell's headquarters.[25] But in effect, all that really remained now of the ABDA area was Java, for whose defense the Dutch alone would be in command. The CCS had decided that the ABDA area concept should "fade out gradually and not be suddenly extinguished" as the best way for the Dutch to "hold on."[26]

At noon on February 25 Wavell formally turned over command of a now misnamed ABDACOM to the Dutch, and that evening he left Java on a FEAF LB-30 with his staff for Colombo.[27] "I deeply regret failure to hold ABDA area," he communicated to the CCS in his last telegram from Java. In explaining the loss, he opined, "It was a race against time, and the enemy was too quick for us."[28]

But the winding down of ABDACOM was not to mean that the Allies were no longer supporting the defense of Java, and they continued to send reinforcements.[29] Wavell on his last day had ordered air forces still on Java to "defend Java to the last," and only when further resistance proved impossible were any serviceable aircraft left to be flown to Australia.[30] However, in respect to fighter aircraft viewed as vital for Java's defense, Marshall was leaving the decision whether to transfer additional P-40s—beyond those already on their way on the *Langley* and *Sea Witch*—to Brett in his new role as commanding general of USAFIA. "The extent to which pursuit planes should be transferred to Java must be determined by you in accordance with the desire of the ABDA commander, the availability of shipping, and the practicality of landing these planes in Java and operating them effectively therefrom," Marshall informed Brett on February 25.[31] Marshall was hedging on the promise President Roosevelt would give the Dutch queen the following day to "do everything possible to get more fighter planes into Java."[32] Van Mook's outspoken view that Java could still be held if "men and materials" continued to be sent to defend it had ostensibly gained the support of Roosevelt, who Van Mook declared had assured him of "the greatest possible American help in the fight for the Indies."[33]

However, Brett continued to take a more realistic view of the logic of sending more P-40s to Java. When he had arrived in Melbourne on February 24 to take over command of USAFIA again, he told his staff privately that it was "all over" in Java.[34] Despite being overruled, he was still opposed to sending the *Langley* and *Sea Witch* to Java. On February 26 he instructed Brig. Gen. Earl Naiden—in charge of the FEAF in Java—to divert both the *Langley* and *Sea Witch* to Bombay if there was not a "reasonable possibility" of unloading them at Tjilatjap. He also requested that "all available noncombatant officers and enlisted men and experienced fighter and bombardment crews" be returned to Australia.[35]

CHAPTER NINE

"I Was Thoroughly Enjoying Myself"

EARLY MONDAY MORNING, February 16 the commander of the 33rd Pursuit Squadron (Provisional) called a meeting of his nine pilots plus the 3rd Pursuiter Bob Oestreicher at RAAF operations at Darwin Field. Slugger Pell wanted to assign four of them to fly two two-plane patrols out over the Timor Sea to search for Bob Buel and to check on the convoy's progress to Timor. Pell himself would lead one, and he picked Oestreicher, whom he now attached to his 33rd Squadron, to lead the other.[1] During his patrol Oestreicher and his wingman flew north to Bathurst and Melville Islands but found no trace of Buel during their two-hour, forty-five-minute patrol. Pell and his wingman continued on into the Timor Sea and located the convoy, now some one hundred miles short of its Koepang destination. No enemy aircraft were sighted in the vicinity.[2]

Shortly after the two patrols returned, Pell was informed by the RAAF station that the *Houston* had radioed at 1030 that the convoy was under attack by a large formation of twin-engine Japanese bombers when it was about eighty miles out of Koepang. It wanted fighter help, but it was obvious to Pell and the others that the message was received too late to provide it.[3]

That morning McMahon went back to the hangar to see what progress was being made on getting the hangar queen in flying condition for him. When he walked in, he was surprised to find Lieutenant Tobias waiting for him with bandaged head and arm. Tobias apologized to McMahon for getting blood on McMahon's parachute and thanked him for making his first military airplane ride a possibility, despite the outcome. He explained that he had dropped Dick Suehr's aid package all right after Jacobs had located Suehr's position in the outback, but on returning to Darwin at 2115 Jacobs had landed at the civil, instead of RAAF, airdrome and had cracked up his A-24 when the lights were not turned on for him. He had run through barrels on the side of the field, completely washing out the dive bomber. Jacobs had suffered a concussion and facial cuts, while he himself had a badly cut left arm.[4]

Now McMahon understood the roar of a plane landing that he had heard the night before. As Tobias excused himself to get back to his staff duties, McMahon reasoned that at least his squadron mate Suehr now had a chance to survive in the outback. Tobias had seen Suehr pick up the canister and wave back at him.

That afternoon, McMahon and the others were happy to see a C-53 transport coming in to land on the RAAF field, for they knew it was carrying a load of the 33rd's crew chiefs and armorers. The enlisted men had brought their tools with them and immediately started work on the squadron's out-of-commission P-40s. McMahon succeeded in having two of them assigned to Hangar 12 to change the propeller on his hangar queen and work on the other damaged P-40.[5]

The next morning, February 17, Pell scheduled a four-ship flight to patrol over Bathurst and Melville Islands at ten thousand feet. They saw nothing unusual and came in to land without incident. The afternoon patrol was ordered by Pell to fly out to the convoy. After the bombing attack the day before, the convoy had been ordered by ABDACOM to abort its voyage to Timor and return immediately to Darwin. The four P-40s of the patrol were to provide protection for the eight ships of the convoy as they made their way back to Darwin. It was estimated that they now were nearer to Darwin than to Koepang.[6]

For the mission McMahon was assigned one of the squadron's flyable P-40s and ordered to fly wing to Jack Peres, who would lead the four-ship flight. Oestreicher, who was junior to Peres, was to lead the second element of the flight, with Charles Hughes as his wingman. As the four walked out to their planes, Oestreicher suggested that on the way out they should orbit Bathurst Island so that if they had engine trouble, they could use the strip on the island for an emergency landing.[7]

When they reached Bathurst Island following takeoff, they spotted the strip, which to McMahon looked to be barely long enough for a P-40 to land on. Orbiting over the island for about twenty minutes, they looked around for the convoy but were unable to spot it. Peres called on the radio and suggested they go out further on a southwesterly course to try to locate the ships. After about fifteen minutes Peres and McMahon caught sight of the scattered ships below and identified them as belonging to the convoy. Spread out some distance from Peres in the search, McMahon looked around but could not see Oestreicher or Hughes anywhere. Turning, Peres and McMahon headed back to Darwin via Bathurst Island. There, about five miles off the southern tip, they spotted two orbiting P-40s. Oestreicher had evidently decided to hold his element over Bathurst instead of following Peres and McMahon out to look for the convoy. After the patrol landed back at Darwin, Peres walked over to Oestreicher and asked him why he hadn't followed him out to look for the convoy. Oestreicher replied that it was his understanding that someone should orbit Bathurst in case they should need to make an interception. His response puzzled Peres.[8]

That evening McMahon was pleased to find that the squadron's mechanics had succeeded in replacing the propeller on the hangar queen. He would now have a ship again. He decorated it as *Bahootee the Cootee No. 2* on the left side and had *Mac* painted on the right side of the fuselage. It had earlier carried the number (in black) 22 on the tail.[9]

Early the next morning, February 18, a patrol flight took off to locate and escort the convoy—now only some fifty miles out—safely back into Darwin harbor. Pell decided the flight should orbit over Bathurst Island in order to be in a position to intercept any Japanese bombers that might possibly come in from their known base on Amboina, five hundred miles due north of Bathurst. With this arrangement his pilots would have a chance of recovering or of force-landing their ships in the event of a problem.[10]

After the patrol departed, Bob McMahon walked over to the newly repaired P-40 that had been assigned to him. He was eager to test *Bahootee the Cootee No. 2,* confident that the newly arrived mechanics "had the magic touch" to put it into flying condition. He taxied it out for a "quick run-up" and takeoff for a test flight. But halfway down the runway the engine started to run away with the replacement propeller in high pitch.[11] McMahon knew that he had flying speed but decided not to chance the tall eucalyptus trees off the end of the runway. He began applying brakes for a stop, then dropped full flaps, but then let up on the brakes to let them cool, preferring to ground loop at the end of the runway. Going at only about ten miles per hour, he figured the green grass overrun he noticed would slow him down more, and if he did have to ground-loop, the grass would be easier on the wingtip than a hard surface.

Ten feet into the overrun, McMahon found that the grass indeed did slow him down. "Flump!" went his landing gear, his ship stopping in three feet, but in the sudden halt his head banged the gunsight. Climbing out, McMahon found he had run into a twenty-foot-long log that had been inadvertently left or dragged across the centerline in what appeared to be a taxiway. As McMahon cursed his luck and checked for blood on his forehead, his CO drove up in a jeep. In his usual sarcastic way, Pell implied that McMahon had wrecked yet another ship in his efforts to avoid going to Java. Infuriated, ready to slug anyone, McMahon lost his self-control and told off his CO. Pell "got the message," put his jeep in reverse, and "cleared out." By the time McMahon had taken off the top panel over his ship's carburetor, several of the squadron mechanics appeared. Squadron mate Jack Peres showed up, too, to see what had happened. The enlisted men removed the carburetor, so hot it had to be handled with rags, before the engine had even cooled off.

As McMahon walked back with Peres to the mess hall, the air raid siren went off. They immediately headed for a slit trench adjacent to the perimeter road of the base. They were standing beside the trench, looking up to the sky for possible Japanese aircraft, when their attention shifted to the ground and a staff car with Aussie markings that pulled up next to them. A "spindly-legged," forty-something officer in shorts and bush jacket stepped out of the vehicle. Pointing to the ditch, he barked, "Here, you men, where are your tin hats and why aren't you in the trench?" Peres tried to explain to the "RAAF equivalent of a Col. Blimp": "Sir, we don't have room in our planes to carry a helmet." But an incensed McMahon interrupted his squadron mate. "Commander, we're not your men," he snapped. "We are U.S. Army Air Corps officers, and if there were an air raid, we'd already be in the ditch. I'll be damned if I'm going to get my only uniform all muddy in that ditch so I can play in some stupid air raid drill. Some of us are actually trying to go up to fight a war and don't need any crap slowing us up." The high-ranking RAAF officer—whom they found out later was Wing Cmdr. Stuart de Burg Griffith, the commander of RAAF Station, Darwin—turned without a word, got back in his staff car, and drove off. Resuming their walk to the mess, McMahon for one felt "pretty good" after the verbal exchange. Even the ache from the bump on his forehead seemed to have eased off.[12]

McMahon was delighted to find that the second hangar queen had now been repaired. By afternoon, runup, compass swinging, and bore sighting for the P-40E had been completed and the ship assigned to him. However, the brakes would not hold during the runup, apparently because of a hydraulic leak, a problem that bleeding them did not solve. The radio's transmitter and receiver didn't work, either. McMahon put two radiomen on it, but with little success.

Late that afternoon, Pell held another meeting of his pilots. They now had eleven P-40s in commission after six that were in maintenance twenty-four hours earlier were now made serviceable, including McMahon's second hangar queen. Pell informed his ten squadron mates that while their convoy cover duties were now off, following the safe return of the convoy that morning, their planned transfer to Koepang was still on. He had not received any word from USAFIA or ABDACOM canceling it. Takeoff for Penfui Field, Koepang, would be at dawn the following morning. Pell had discussed at length with Wheless and Connelly at USAAF headquarters, Darwin, whether the flight should go out then, in view of the uncertain weather, but it had finally been agreed among them to proceed.[13]

Pell divided his pilots into two flights for the trip. He himself would lead A flight, which would include Charles Hughes, McMahon, Burt Rice, Bob Vaught, and Jack Glover. Oestreicher was given B flight, with Peres, Elton Perry, Max Wiecks, and Bill Walker. A B-17E would provide navigation for them, while an LB-30 would transport their mechanics. That evening the pursuiters should ensure that their ships were gassed and combat-loaded, that their maps and personal effects were packed, and that their Australian currency was changed into Dutch guilders.[14] As McMahon turned in for the evening, he thought about his buddy Stinky Suehr, who had not made it back to Darwin in time to join them on this flight to Java, as he had originally expected. He figured Suehr was now three days into his trek, and he wondered how he was doing.[15]

ON SUNDAY MORNING, FEBRUARY 15, at 0630, Bud Sprague revved up his P-40E No. 14 and headed down the strip at Ngoro for a long, 350-mile flight westwards to Bandoeng. The day before, Lt. Col. Emmett "Rosie" O'Donnell, operations officer of Brereton's Far East Air Force, had called him from headquarters in Bandoeng to request Sprague to report to him for final instructions for a special mission he wanted Sprague's 17th Pursuit to fly. He had told Sprague earlier that it would be a fighter-bomber attack on the Japanese who had landed in the Palembang, Sumatra, area the day before.[16]

Before Sprague departed, he spoke to nine of his most senior pilots whom he had picked to go on the mission with him. Seven of them were veterans who had served with him in the Philippines: Capts. Walt Coss and Grant Mahony and 1st Lts. Bo McCallum, Ed Kiser, Joe Kruzel, Bill Hennon, and Ed Gilmore. Hubert Egenes and Dwight Muckley were also to fly the mission. The selected group would be flying nine of the original planes the 17th Pursuit had taken to Java: Coss in Bill Stauter's No. 8, Mahony in Sprague's No. 1, McCallum in his original No. 10, Kiser in his original No. 2, Kruzel in Thompson's No. 3, Gilmore in his original No. 5, Hennon in his original No. 11, Muckley in No. 7, and Egenes in Blanton's No. 17.[17] Sprague instructed the nine to fly to the Dutch depot field at Maospati, Madioen, that morning to load four 20 kg (44-pound) bombs on the wing bomb racks of each of their P-40s. From there they were to proceed on to Batavia to join Sprague for final preparations for the attack. For George Parker and the others left behind at Ngoro, this was big news. Sprague had told them that it would be a strafing and bombing attack against an aerodrome the Japanese had taken at Palembang, and that B-17 attacks were to follow. This would be the first attack mission of the 17th after weeks of defensive operations and the first time their P-40s would be used as fighter-bombers.[18]

At 0800 Mahony led them off from Ngoro for the short hop to Madioen. On landing they expected it would be a simple matter to hang bombs on the racks and check the release mechanisms before continuing on to Batavia. Much to their dismay, it turned out the fittings of the bombs were too large for the racks. While they succeeded in getting a few bombs on the racks, the bombs wouldn't release. So it became a tedious process of modifying each bomb to fit the specific rack it was to ride on. This involved filing the bomb fittings by hand, mounting each bomb, and activating the cockpit release. If the bomb didn't release, it was back to the filing.[19]

Walt Coss was also trying to fix the light bulb in his gunsight, which had burned out on the way to Madioen. After obtaining a spare and trying to change the bulb while sitting in the cockpit operating the bomb release mechanism shortly before noon, his work was interrupted when base personnel came running out; a Japanese formation was reported heading for Madioen. Coss and his squadron mates had to get their P-40s off the field as fast as they could. They fired up the ships right where they were parked at the ramp and took off down the nearest runway. Coss had never before made a takeoff in a fighter without having buckled his parachute and fastened his safety belt, but he and the others needed to get airborne fast so as not to be caught in a takeoff situation by Zeros.[20] After gaining some altitude and milling around for thirty or forty minutes, they were radioed that the emergency was over; the Japanese had evidently gone elsewhere. So it was back to the field to continue with the bomb-adapting exercise.

It was midafternoon before they had succeeded in fitting four bombs on the wings of all their P-40s, but Coss and the others were not confident the releases would work in an actual attack. They were also worried that a minor accident might set the bombs off. At any rate, after topping off their tanks again to make up for the gas wasted during the false alarm, they were ready finally for the flight to Batavia—all, that is, except Gilmore, who had to be left behind because of a nonoperational ship.[21]

Minus Gilmore the eight pursuiters reached Tjililitan Field, south of Batavia, just at dusk. Landing on the unfamiliar field, virtually in the dark and with rain showers around limiting visibility, proved difficult, but all managed to get down safely except Muckley, who badly damaged his plane while landing, although he did not sustain any injuries. They were all relieved that their bombs did not go off—not even Muckley's—when they hit the runway.[22]

It took a while for the pursuiters to park their ships on the field and to get guards posted on them. Finally they were driven into "strange and dark" Batavia and taken to the Hôtel des Indes. Having eaten little during the long day, they were starved and headed for the dining room. However, when they tried to order dinner at the late hour, 2100, the headwaiter told them "rather emphatically" that the dining room was closed and could not provide any food. In an effort to get him to change his mind, three of the pursuiters quietly laid their .45-caliber automatic pistols on the table, making sure they were visible. Immediately "a waiter started running for the kitchen," and in a few minutes "a very reasonable dish of rice and chicken" was put on their table.[23]

But now they faced the problem of obtaining rooms for the night. The manager of the hotel told them he could accept no more guests; all the hotels in Batavia were overflowing with refugees from Singapore and Sumatra, British, Dutch, and Americans alike. The airmen would have to look elsewhere. As they sat dejected in the dining room, wondering what to do, an American war correspondent who had overheard their plight came up to them and introduced himself. He was George Weller of the *Chicago Daily News*. To Weller, the young Americans looked very tired. "It looks as though we'll have to go back to the field and sleep under the planes," one of them told Weller. Weller got up and went to the manager but was told that he could do nothing for the Americans, whom he had misidentified as bomber pilots, knowing nothing about American fighter pilots on Java.[24]

While the pursuiters were still eating their dinner, Weller excused himself. He returned shortly afterwards with good news for them. He and two other war correspondents also staying in the hotel—Bill Dunn of Columbia Broadcasting Company and Sydney Albright of NBC—had personally checked out the occupancy situation of all the rooms in the hotel and had found that some were temporarily unoccupied and others had only one guest that night. The three correspondents switched to these rooms and were now offering their own to the eight pilots.[25]

"Dirty and tired"—looking like "a tug-of-war team at the end of a fraternity picnic"—the pilots were ready to head up to their benefactors' rooms, but not before getting the latest news. The correspondents told them that Japanese paratroops had dropped over Palembang the day before. "Oh, oh—so that's it," one of them remarked, now realizing why they were on this mission. They themselves could not provide the correspondents with information on the reason why they had flown to Batavia, of course—that was secret. But Mahony and Coss stayed on after their comrades had left to turn in for the night to respond to queries the writers had about their battle exploits in the Philippines.[26]

Bud Sprague was not with his men that evening. After landing at Andir Field, on the western outskirts of Bandoeng, he was picked up by a waiting staff car for the ride to FEAF headquarters. His arrival at Andir in his P-40 had caused quite a stir. Everyone at the field "swarmed over this brand-new, modern fighter," not having seen one before at Andir Field, a base for obsolete Martin B-10 bombers and Brewster Buffaloes that the Dutch were flying against the Japanese.[27] One of those greeting Sprague was an old family friend, Capt. James E. Crane, a twenty-eight-year-old medical officer of the FEAF who had been assigned by General Brett to set up a medical installation at Lembang. Crane was pleasantly surprised by the visit of Sprague, whose father in Bridgeport, Connecticut, like Crane's father in nearby Stamford, was also a physician. The elder men were close friends. Curiously enough, Crane's first patient at his small Lembang facility was one of Sprague's pilots, Frank Neri, who had been flown to Bandoeng from a Soerabaja hospital for further medical care following his accident of January 29, when he lost his ear. Neri was now chafing to be released, but Crane was holding him, feeling he needed further rest and recuperation.[28]

The staff car wound its way with Sprague through Bandoeng city to the northeastern outskirts and halted in front of a large building in Houtmanstraat, where FEAF headquarters was now located. Entering, Sprague was taken to the G-3 operations office, where he was warmly greeted by his old Philippines friend, Rosie O'Donnell. The two had not seen each other since mid-December, when O'Donnell was CO of the 14th Bomb Squadron and Sprague was operations officer of the 5th Interceptor Command.[29]

Sprague was briefed in detail on the Palembang mission O'Donnell planned for Sprague's P-40s. They would attack the Japanese still landing from boats in the Moesi River and the oil refinery town's two airfields, named Palembang 1 and 2.[30] O'Donnell also called in newly promoted Maj. Ed Backus for meetings this day. O'Donnell wanted Backus to call to Modjokerto and order his 91st Bomb Squadron to Tjililitan, too; the A-24 dive bombers were also in his attack plan. The FEAF operations officer was using Colonel Eubank's heavy bombers for attacks in the Palembang area as well. The day before, their mission had to be aborted because of bad weather, but this morning another one was to be flown by B-17s of the 19th and 7th Bomb Groups and three LB-30s of the 7th.[31]

Back at Batavia the following morning, the weather was continuing unfavorable for operations, with a low mist reducing visibility. Now having returned to his pilots, Sprague decided to delay the attack. "It was no use taking off for a place one had never seen, under weather where the landing parties could not be observed even if one knew where they were," he reasoned. But he knew the delay would give the Japanese an additional day to occupy the airfields in the Palembang area and allow more troops to land.[32] With the mission called off for the day, Sprague's men had time on their hands. Hennon and the others loafed around Batavia. Coss went down to Tjililitan Field at midday, where he spotted a British Hawker Hurricane in RAF markings parked on the other side of the field from their planes. He thought it might have been flown down from Singapore, which had fallen to the Japanese the day before. Never having seen a Hurricane before, he decided to examine it more closely. Climbing up on the wing, he got a good look in the cockpit. The pilot was not around to talk to, much to Coss's disappointment.[33]

Late in the afternoon a flight of eleven A-24s was coming in to land at Tjililitan. But in the poor light one of them taxied into a barrier and another landed short, in a buffalo wallow. Their pilots had been ordered to fly across Java to the unfamiliar field by Backus in a telephone call to Modjokerto the previous day, but they didn't know the purpose of the mission. Greeting them was their commanding officer, back from his Lembang meeting with O'Donnell. That evening Backus took them all into Batavia for dinner, then they went back to Tjililitan to sleep in the abandoned Dutch officers' quarters near the field.[34]

The following morning—Tuesday, February 17—Sprague's pilots noted a slight improvement in the weather, "but not much." The clouds were still there, with occasional rain showers around the Batavia area, but the ceiling was somewhat higher. Sprague decided to go ahead with the mission. Each of the P-40s was carrying a belly tank and, except for Sprague's ship, the four 20 kg bombs under the wings.[35] At about 0900, Sprague led off the eight-ship formation and started climbing on a direct course for Palembang, 250 miles to the northwest. Over the Java Sea for most of the flight in light rain at five hundred feet, the pursuiters then made landfall on the big island of Sumatra. They climbed to eight thousand to ten thousand feet over thick jungle and headed for Palembang 1. But just a few miles short of their destination they spotted a flight of fixed-landing-gear fighters coming directly towards them at their altitude. It looked like there were eight of them, Nakajima Type 97 "Nates," they ascertained. Thick smoke was rising from the Palembang oil refineries below. It was 1020.[36]

Sprague called over the radio to his squadron mates to drop their wing bombs and belly tanks and engage the Japanese interceptors. Of the eight they had spotted, only six appeared to be taking on the Americans. It was the first time the 17th Pursuit had not been outnumbered in aerial combat.[37] Responding to Sprague's order, Coss dropped his belly tank and his bombs, figuring it "didn't seem too good an idea to carry them into a dogfight." McCallum and Kruzel also dropped their belly tanks and bombs, but Egenes, Mahony, Kiser, and Hennon only dropped the gas tanks, retaining their bombs.[38]

Dog-fighting the old, lightly armed Japanese fighters during the three minutes the combat lasted was not as easy as they had expected. The Nates proved to be highly maneuverable, with a very short turning radius. Coss had three firing opportunities. Each time he pulled behind one of the Nates and began firing, the Japanese "would pull up and climb at an angle I could not follow." On the third try a frustrated Coss decided to pull up at the same climb angle anyway, continuing to fire all the while. But in a few moments he found himself out of airspeed, his ship in a whip-stall. In the last moment he broke off the climb. The Nate was almost stalled, too, but then it flipped over and came straight back down.[39]

Still carrying his wing bombs, Hennon managed to score on two of the Type 97s, but then his guns jammed, and he dropped out of the combat. Clearing his guns, he dove down on some troop-laden barges on the Moesi River and released his bombs. After strafing river boats, he tried to find the Palembang 1 airfield but ran into two more Nates, "hitting one of them very hard." Returning to the Moesi, he spotted "dozens of small boats" filled with troops, "paddling furiously." Dropping down to within twenty-five feet of the river, Hennon flew overhead and poured .50-caliber fire into the hapless Japanese. Some of the boats overturned, and troops were jumping overboard from others to avoid his attack. Afterwards, Hennon flew over the town of Palembang at very low altitude; it was in flames, and he noted considerable ground fighting going on.[40]

Earlier, Mahony, Egenes, and Kiser had made bombing runs on the ships and barges alongside the riverbank. In aerial combat with the Type 97s with Kruzel, they believed they had downed several of the Japanese.[41] But now their gas was getting very low. Hennon was reluctant to leave, however: "I was thoroughly enjoying myself," he recorded in his diary that evening. For Coss, the decision was made when he "suddenly found the sky completely unpopulated" after his combat with the Nates. He picked up a heading back to Batavia and went into a shallow dive so that he could maintain a relatively high cruising speed. After crossing the Sumatra coast, he leveled off at about five hundred feet and stayed low so as to be hard to spot against the water.[42] Approaching Batavia, Coss followed the prescribed Dutch flight paths in preparation for landing. But shortly before touching down, using his cockpit controls to lower his landing gear and extend his flaps, he found that neither responded. Realizing he had an electrical problem, he resorted to the emergency method: pumping the gear and flaps down with a hand pump in the cockpit. His efforts were rewarded, and he touched down safely at about noon after the three-hour mission.[43]

Seven of the P-40s were now back, but where was Hennon's? Just when Sprague and the others were about to give up on their comrade as lost, his familiar No. 11 came into view and landed. Hennon climbed out and told them that he had run his tanks dry. His ship also had developed a bad oil leak.[44]

Maj. William "Hoot" Horrigan from O'Donnell's staff in Bandoeng was there to greet them and learn the results of their mission. The excited pilots claimed five of the intercepting six Type 97s shot down—one each by Kiser, Kruzel, Sprague, McCallum, and Egenes. The only damage they had sustained to their own ships—and that inconsequential—was from four hits from the two 7.7 mm guns the Nates mounted on the upper fuselage decking. Most of them felt that their P-40s completely outclassed the Type 97s.[45] After hearing of their success, Horrigan invited them all to fly back to Bandoeng with him for a congratulations party. All accepted the invitation except Muckley, who had not flown the mission, his P-40 still out of commission at Tjililitan, and Hennon, who wanted to stay behind while British mechanics worked on his oil leak. Coss's ship needed work, too, but Coss decided to fly it to Bandoeng instead for the Dutch depot mechanics at Andir Field to fix the problem. When they landed at Andir after a half-hour flight, Coss left his ship with the mechanics and joined the others for the short ride into Bandoeng. That evening O'Donnell threw a very nice party for them: "good dinner and drinks." Coss and the others were now feeling a lot better about the Palembang mission than they had two days earlier at Madioen.[46]

After spending the night at Bandoeng, Sprague and the others were back at Andir Field the following morning. Coss was disappointed to find "several miles of wire" hanging out of his ship's cockpit. As Sprague and the five others took off for the four-hour flight back to Ngoro, Coss asked the mechanics how matters stood with the repair job. It soon became obvious that there was no progress at all in fixing the hydraulics. Miffed, Coss insisted they bundle the wire back into his ship; he was going to take it back to its regular crew chief at Ngoro. About noon he took off and headed on an easterly course for his home field.[47]

At Tjililitan that morning Bill Hennon was also feeling frustrated with the mechanics working on his ship. He had had "a hell of a time getting the damn British to do any work" the day before to repair his oil leak. Lt. Ricardo Anemaet, the 17th Pursuit's old NEIAF friend from Soerabaja days, was there, too, looking sour and "just as pissed off." But finally, after using a line from Muckley's wreck, they were able to fix Hennon's ship. He then took off alone for the nonstop flight all the way to Ngoro Field, 420 miles to the east.[48]

AT NGORO FIELD THINGS HAD BEEN quiet since the Palembang pilots left on February 15. There had been no calls by the ADC in Soerabaja for interceptions, no Japanese bombers having made an appearance over Java since February 9. With no interception requests, the Ngoro pilots had time on their hands. After spending the day before in Jogjakarta, Paul Gambonini, along with Tommy Hayes, Marion Fuchs, Andy Reynolds, and Wally Hoskyn, returned on the afternoon of the fifteenth in olive drab U.S. Army cars they had picked up there for the squadron's use. The following day Butch Hague and Bill Stauter, on their own day off, took one of the cars and set out for Malang, "a beautiful two hour drive" over the mountains. After wandering around the city they had dinner, listened to classical music at the officers' club, and, sleepy, turned in at the Palace Hotel at 2100. They returned to Ngoro the following morning.[49]

But for those who did not go visiting during the uneventful period, life at the remote Java location was becoming monotonous. B. J. Oliver and his housemates were spending their after-duty hours in front of their house in Blimbing, eating lots of peanuts and bananas before leaving for supper and drinking beer at the canteen operated by Sgt. Reecy Wassan. Like Spence Johnson, the Ngoro pilots were feeling homesick and kept talking about the things they used to do in the States. To break the boredom, Johnson made lots of huge firecrackers by filling bamboo shoots with gunpowder from .50-caliber ammunition and "scared the hell out of the nervous part of the personnel" when he exploded them.[50]

On February 16 Frank Adkins and Chief Fields, who had nosed over their P-40s at Pasirian five days earlier on their way in to Ngoro from Australia, flew in. On this rainy day Ed Gilmore also returned to the field after having aborted the Palembang mission with engine trouble at Madioen the day before.[51] The field also had a surprise visitor. Maj. Bill Fisher showed up to discuss details on the new arrangements for operations at the ADC, where he was now taking over as interceptor control officer. After his aborted attempt to reach Java from Darwin in a P-40 in Strauss's flight on February 9, he had spent several days in Melbourne at USAFIA headquarters before leaving on February 14 in a bomber for Bandoeng, where he met with the FEAF command on his new duties. Then, in Soerabaja the ADC commander, Ente van Gils, had handed over operation of the interceptor control to Fisher under amicable circumstances. Now the American liaison team at the ADC responsible for operational contacts with the 17th Pursuit at Ngoro would be working under a fellow American officer.[52]

During his Soerabaja visit Fisher had sized up problems of the interceptor control system operated by the Dutch to date. For starters, the native ground observers were unable to differentiate between enemy and friendly aircraft. Fisher emphasized the importance of knowing the location of all friendly planes and the times of their return from missions in order to avoid situations in which they might be fired on by antiaircraft guns or intercepted by P-40s, as had been happening the past two weeks. Coordination with the B-17 command at Singosari should be improved, he insisted. But that still left the problem of inadequate warning time for the P-40s to intercept. With spotters unable to pick up Japanese flights beyond ninety miles out, ADC could give the pursuiters at Ngoro only about thirty minutes' advance warning, as against the forty minutes they needed from the time the interception order was received to the time they reached altitude and were ready to intercept the high-flying Japanese.[53] In his meeting with the Ngoro pilots Fisher also discussed some other improvements. He wanted, for example, to introduce a radio check with the field to clear up any possible difficulties and to make code and operating arrangements for the following day's operations.

The weather was still bad at Ngoro the following day, February 17, but it was decided to send up patrol flights in the afternoon anyway. Paul Gambonini led his C flight on a two-hour patrol over Soerabaja at 1400, flying at twenty-three thousand to twenty-seven thousand feet. One hour later, D flight took off for its patrol. Hal Lund got separated from the others in the bad flying conditions and did not return with them. Two ships were sent out to look for him, but without success. At 1900 a call came in to the field from Lund. Out of gas, he had made a wheels-up landing in a rice field near Madioen. He reported to his worried comrades that he was not injured and that his ship was not badly damaged: just the radiator had suffered, and his propeller was bent.[54]

At 0900 the following morning Bud Sprague was spotted approaching the field with seven others of the Palembang mission. After they touched down, they were bombarded with questions. But two special visitors had priority on Sprague's attention. Major General Brereton and his superior, Air Chief Marshal Peirse, had arrived at Ngoro by car from Malang earlier in the morning to meet with Sprague and had just completed the inspection of his squadron when Sprague landed. The 17th Pursuit's CO, "in excellent spirit" after his Palembang mission, impressed Peirse immensely with "his calm air of efficiency, confidence, and good humor." Later, Peirse asked Brereton if he would let Sprague join his ABDAIR staff, but Brereton refused the request. Sprague was indispensable to organize and command the Ngoro fighter group, Brereton maintained.[55]

On the line, Butch Hague and Jim Morehead were attaching their ships' belly tanks in anticipation of an order to take off for another mission to Palembang. They had earlier requested and received permission from 1st Lieutenant Lane, in charge of the field in Sprague's absence, to fly on such an anticipated followup mission. Suddenly, at 1045 they saw the P-40s that were on alert from early that morning taking off. The ADC, with Fisher now issuing the orders, had called and requested an interception of three different formations of bombers that had been sighted heading towards Soerabaja. With Sprague and all the other senior 17th Pursuit pilots away at the time, Cy Blanton had been designated to lead the interception.[56]

In addition to the ships of Hague and Morehead, two other of the field's P-40s were not on alert. Wanting to join in the interception, the two eager pilots dropped their activity and raced over to the other aircraft. But they were too late: the irrepressible Mahony, less than two hours back from his long return flight from Bandoeng, and Gilmore, frustrated by having had to abort the Palembang mission, reached the ships ahead of Hague and Morehead. Not one ever to give up, Hague headed over to Lane in the operations shack and asked if he and Morehead could take the belly tanks off their ships and join the others. He was kept waiting for forty-five minutes before Lane finally agreed to let them take their ships up on the interception too.[57]

In the meantime, Blanton was leading the flights—quite spread out—towards Soerabaja and had now climbed to twenty-six thousand feet. Then they spotted the Japanese: nine Betty bombers about four thousand feet below them. They were over Soerabaja, heading north, apparently without escorting Zeros. The pursuiters felt confident; for once they were at an advantage against a Japanese bomber formation.[58] At 1158, Blanton led his own flight of four ships into the attack out of the sun, at about a forty-five-degree angle to the line of flight of the Bettys. Then he realized that he was leading them in a little too fast, cutting down on the time for the first firing pass. Blanton concentrated his .50-caliber fire on the lead Betty, and after seeing his tracers going into the right engine, he switched his fire to the cockpit when the engine started smoking. Finishing his very short firing run, he dove past the Japanese formation and saw his victim heading down. Halting his dive and turning back, Blanton came up underneath the rear end of the group and made a firing pass at the tail-end Charlie. But now he spotted Zeros approaching them and two more groups of bombers heading north on the return flight at very high speed.[59]

Leading the second flight behind Blanton's, Paul Gambonini signaled to his wingman and started his approach at 1210 on the flight of Bettys to the right of the first. Narrowing the distance separating them to get within firing range, Gambonini glanced to his side and noticed a couple of the bombers in the flight to his left falling out of formation and spinning to earth, trailing black smoke. There were fighters buzzing around them; he could not make them out but was sure they were his fellow 17th Pursuiters. Everything seemed to be happening in slow motion, as if in a movie.[60]

Gambonini looked back to check on his wingman but was surprised to find that he was not with him after all. For some reason he was flying straight and level on their old course. And now he realized his approach on the dull grey bombers was terrible; he had not led them enough. Trying to keep a lead on them, Gambonini put his ship in a skid, "scattering his fire all over the sky and doing absolutely no damage." Finishing his unsatisfactory run, he dove down under the Japanese and then came up on the other side, directly under one of the bombers. This time when he fired he could see hits and the right engine smoking.

But just as he began his dive after the firing pass, Gambonini was startled to hear what sounded like hail on a tin roof. The rear of his P-40E was being hit by 7.7 mm bullets. Then he felt the concussion of a 20 mm cannon shell that just barely missed him. Terrified, Gambonini pushed the stick forward and firewalled it, dirt and debris filling the cockpit. Looking up, he saw a Zero right above him, "a big orange meatball on his wing." The Japanese turned left and followed Gambonini down. With the Zero on his tail, firing all the while, Gambonini "stood on the rudder" to keep the P-40 flying straight in its dive. At about ten thousand feet he headed into a cloud bank, and on exiting a few second later he was relieved to find the Zero nowhere to be seen. Where had that guy come from, Gambonini wondered as he set course for Ngoro Field.[61]

Jock Caldwell, called "Little Tarzan" because of his physique, also attacked one of the bomber divisions heading north, but without interference from the Zeros. This group was flying in a stepped down formation so that the tail gunner of each aircraft could protect the belly of the bomber above with his potent 20 mm cannon. Proceeding down the staircase, Caldwell set the top and bottom bombers afire, but at a cost: the massed fire from the tail gunners had hit his ship, and his cockpit was "falling to pieces." His ship clocking 450 miles an hour in its dive, Caldwell opened his cockpit and struggled to get out, but the slipstream kept pushing him back. Finally, after getting his feet up on the seat and giving himself a big shove, he succeeded in bailing out. Unsure of the altitude, he decided to open his chute immediately. Minutes later he hit the ground, uninjured.[62]

Bud Sprague was waiting at the operations shack as the pursuiters came in to land one by one, some two hours after their takeoff. Gambonini showed Sprague the damage his ship had sustained. The rudder tab had been shot off, and there were about forty 7.7 mm holes all over the rear of his fuselage and into his fuselage tank.[63] The worked-up pilots described their combat experiences and put in their victory claims, or at least probables. Ben Irvin was sure he got one, having fired a long burst from the rear into a Betty that was seen crashing into the sea as it was trying to return to base. It was the general consensus that at least four more of the bombers were shot down, with credits going to Frank Adkins, Blanton, Mahony, and Gilmore. Some thought that they got nine of the bombers plus four of the Zeros. Of these, Gambonini, Reagan, Williams, and Fuchs were believed to have shot down one each.[64]

Only one of the P-40s was reported shot down, that of Jock Caldwell, but he was seen bailing out, and the pilots assumed he was all right. Spence Johnson was upset, however, that the plane lost was his old No. 45 that Caldwell took up that morning. Unknown to the pilots, Caldwell was slowly making his way south towards Ngoro, stopping at each village on the way and being obliged each time to have a cup of tea with the locals before proceeding on.[65]

But where was Adkins? He had not returned with the others. They subsequently learned that on this, Adkins's first mission, he had become separated while being chased by Zeros after a diving attack on the Bettys. He managed to elude his pursuers but was now lost, not knowing in which direction to head back to look for his highly camouflaged field. Then he spotted a B-17 below him, with its gear down, apparently heading in for a landing at a big field, which he figured must be its Singosari base. Adkins decided to follow the big ship in. He watched as it landed on a grass field then rolled across what looked like a railroad track. Adkins lowered his gear and touched down, then continued across the track, too. Taxiing up in front of a hangar, he parked his ship, cut the throttle, and started to climb out of the cockpit. Curious 19th Bomb Group personnel were watching the surprise visitor closely. His guns had been knocked out, and he had taken a hit in his gas tank. Suddenly, the trauma at being shot at for the first time hit Adkins, and he threw up all over his cockpit.[66]

AT MAYLANDS CIVIL AIRDROME, located in a suburb three miles northeast of Perth in Western Australia, Capt. Jim Bruce was leading the fourteen novice pilots of his 13th Pursuit Squadron and Bill Borden of the 33rd Pursuit in for a landing on February 17. It was the end of their 1,250-mile trip from Port Pirie. But as Joe Martin came in, the starboard wing of his P-40E hit the fifteen-foot-high windsock pole at the field, and the ship struck the ground heavily on the right main wheel, collapsing the undercarriage. His plane skidded sideways before finally coming to a halt. Martin was uninjured, but the P-40E was wiped out.[67]

Already at Perth to greet the new arrivals was Gerry Keenan of the 33rd and his six squadron mates who had arrived from Port Pirie the day before. Not counting the ship of Bruce, who was being ordered back, and with Martin's ship wrecked, Keenan now had twenty-one P-40s ready to be loaded on the *Langley*. Buzz Wagner and Speed Hubbard were bringing others to ensure that thirty-two were ready at Perth to be hoisted aboard the *Langley*, as per orders.[68] Without his ship, Joe Martin was not expected to board the *Langley* with the thirty-two other pilots, but he asked to go anyway as an extra pilot, and Keenan acquiesced. On the other hand, Bryce Wilhite and Dick Pingree, who had missed joining Bruce's flight to Perth for going aboard the *Langley*, were still at Port Pirie, Wilhite with a torn tire and Pingree with engine trouble. The RAAF was making arrangements for a new tire to be shipped to Port Pirie for Wilhite's P-40, but they estimated it would take a week to arrive. There was nothing for the two 33rd Pursuiters to do but to make the best of the situation as guests of the RAAF officers.[69]

The following day, February 18, the *Langley* failed to show at Fremantle as scheduled. It was running late in its trip from Darwin and was not expected in until the nineteenth or twentieth. Eleven other P-40Es had now been flown in and were ready for the *Langley* when it should arrive. There were actually thirty-five P-40Es at Maylands now, but flight leaders Bruce, Wagner, and Hubbard were under USAFIA orders to bring their three P-40Es back to Laverton, Melbourne's field. The three senior pursuit pilots were not to board the *Langley*, needed as they were in Australia for other duties.[70]

Some of the others who had set out from Amberley—including several pilots off the *Coolidge* and *Mariposa* that had arrived at Melbourne on February 1 with the 49th Pursuit Group—did not make it to Perth. Inducted into the 13th Pursuit (Provisional), 2nd Lts. Earl Kingsley and Bill Levitan had wrecked their ships at Richmond, the field outside Sydney. Two others also had P-40s at Richmond that were out of commission. Of the thirty-three pilots assigned to fly with Wagner, Bruce, and Hubbard in the 13th—including eleven additional to the original twenty-four—eight had not reached their Perth destination.[71]

Gerry Keenan now faced the problem of how to get the thirty-two P-40Es some twenty miles by road southwest from Maylands Airdrome to Fremantle port for hoisting aboard the *Langley*. But that was not his worry. First Lt. Robert L. Morrissey—who had arrived on the *Mariposa* as the CO of the 49th Group's 7th Pursuit Squadron—had been ordered to Perth to arrange for the loading of the P-40s with the help of an RAAF officer.[72] After studying the situation, Morrissey and the RAAF liaison officer concluded that the P-40s would have to be towed backwards from Maylands to Fremantle on their own landing gear. It would not be possible to taxi them under their own power over such a distance; their water-cooled Allison engines would be over-strained and would risk overheating. The decision made, Morrissey arranged with a local machine shop to make a special towing attachment, and thirty-two of them were completed. He and his Australian counterpart also rounded up the required number of trucks and personnel to tow the P-40s and control the route. It was being planned as a midnight operation to avoid traffic problems on the road. Two large concrete pillars that barred the entrance to Fremantle dock were dynamited to open the way.

But they faced another obstacle: eight large trees on private property in an exclusive part of Perth were too close to the road for the wings of the P-40s to pass. Morrissey wanted to get the permission of the owners to fell the trees, but the idea was vetoed by the RAAF officer: he knew the locals would never agree to losing the stately old trees. Instead, he proposed a more direct solution: station a crew of men with the proper tools at each tree the night of the proposed movement, and at midnight, cut the trees down.

STILL IN THE HOSPITAL AT TJAMPLONG, Timor, with a slowly healing lip wound on February 16, Vern Head was becoming increasingly restless. He decided to call the Penfui Airdrome at Koepang to find out whether the other six of those who had crashed with him on Timor a week earlier were now set up to head back to Australia. They were supposed to let their squadron mate know when arrangements had been made, but he had heard nothing from them. But Head was unable to get through to them on the phone. No problem, he figured: the doctor had told him that he could leave the hospital the following day and go into Koepang to find out first-hand what was happening.[73] The next morning, Head got a lift to Penfui in a truck and arrived at the field at about 1000 after a twenty-five-mile trip. He was relieved to find that all the fellows—Strauss, Christian, Carlos, Childress, Erwin, and Lewis— were still there, waiting for transportation to Darwin. About 1145 the air raid alarm at the field went off, but they just sat around at the field for a while because they had been told that most such warnings were false. Then they heard the planes. It appeared there were about fifty to sixty twin-engine bombers unloading over the Koepang harbor area, but they didn't approach Penfui Field—there were no planes there anyway.[74]

Head and the others spent almost all the next day, February 18, playing cards while waiting for news on their evacuation. Late in the afternoon they were told that some bombers were coming in to take them to Darwin. RAAF Wing Cmdr. Frank Headlam, in command of the Penfui base, had received orders to evacuate all RAAF staff and the Americans. It was clear that the Japanese would be invading Timor very soon. To lighten the load, none of the evacuation planes would be carrying bombs.[75] At dusk they watched as six RAAF twin-engine Hudson bombers touched down at Penfui Field. That evening Head and his squadron mates waited around with their possessions, limited to twenty pounds of necessities. All the RAAF officers and men at the base, except for a rear guard of twenty-nine who had volunteered to stay behind, were waiting with them to be evacuated too. At about 0315 that night the seven Americans finally boarded one of the Hudsons along with two Australians and the four Australian crew members and at 0330 the bomber with the five others took off for Darwin. Head was anxious; the overloaded Hudson had to cover 512 miles of water, and none of the evacuees had a parachute.[76]

ON THE EVENING OF FEBRUARY 15 Al Dutton and Dave Coleman were having their usual dinner in the Bali Hotel when two Dutch flying officers approached them and told the stranded American pursuiters that Singapore had fallen and the Dutch were getting ready to evacuate Bali. "What about us?" Dutton and Coleman asked. Unable to answer the query, the Dutch pilots excused themselves to call Soerabaja, then returned to the table. "You're going with us," they told the relieved pilots. They figured that without any P-40s to fly, they were regarded as of no use to the Dutch anymore.[77]

The next morning, Dutton and Coleman climbed aboard one of the two Dutch Lockheed Lodestars at Denpasar Field, along with other evacuees. The Dutch pilots, Lts. A. Reyers and J. Jansen, were under orders to land first in Broome, then continue on the next day to Brisbane, to arrive there on February 18. As the twin-engine Lodestars cleared the field, Dutton and Coleman grasped that their pleasant but enforced Bali sojourn was at an end. The Air Forces brass at Base Section 3 would be putting them back in harness again at Amberley Field.

CHAPTER TEN

"Nothing Will Ever Happen to Me"

IT WAS 0730 ON FEBRUARY 19 when the RAAF Hudsons carrying Vern Head and the other six crashed Timor pilots reached the RAAF field at Darwin after a four-hour night flight from Koepang, uneventful except for the lead Hudson's being fired on by Darwin's antiaircraft guns as it was coming in. Relieved to be back in peaceful Australia, the Americans washed up, shaved, and headed for the officers' mess for breakfast. After eating, they went outside, watching a B-17 and some P-40s taking off.[1]

The objects of their attention were ten pilots of Maj. Floyd Pell's 33rd Pursuit taking off for the flight to Koepang. Their departure had been planned for dawn but was delayed while the squadron's mechanics tried to fix a coolant leak in Pell's ship, No. 3. Giving up waiting for the repair job as it became later and later in the morning, Pell had switched to Bob Vaught's No. 28 and at 0915 was finally leading the flight off. Vaught would remain behind. Pell's A flight was now down to five ships with the loss of Vaught as second element leader, while Bob Oestreicher was following behind with his five-ship flight.[2]

Shortly after takeoff, Bob McMahon in Pell's flight discovered that his radio transmitter and receiver were not working. He decided to drop back in the formation and replace John Glover in the rear. Airborne, the two flights joined up in stacked-down configuration with the B-17 mother ship that would be leading them to Koepang. When McMahon's gunsight stuttered on and off following the linkup, he began to wonder if it wasn't his ship's electrical system that was acting up on him.[3] But more worrisome to McMahon was the buildup of clouds that could be seen lying right across their flight path to Koepang and extending all the way up to some twenty thousand feet. They were typical of the local weather about 1600 or 1700 in the afternoon, but it was just a little past 0900. Without radio contact and a with dubious electrical system, McMahon resolved that if there was no clear way through the bottom of the front when they reached it, he would abort.

While McMahon was checking his fuel consumption gauge, he looked up and was surprised to find Pell crossing over in front of him, signaling for a return to Darwin. Unknown to McMahon, Pell had received a message from Shorty Wheless and Lou Connelly on the field that was relayed to him from the escorting B-17: the weather over Timor was deteriorating, and the ceiling was down to six hundred feet. In their view Pell should return to Darwin, but the decision was his to make. Probably mindful of the loss of the whole flight of eight P-40s of Mahony's 3rd Pursuit in bad weather over Timor ten days earlier, Pell accepted the advice of the two senior AAF officers in charge of Darwin operations. Turning through 180 degrees, he began heading back to the field, his nine inexperienced pursuiters following behind. But the B-17 was not with them. It was continuing on to Java.

It was 0934 when Pell's group arrived over Darwin Harbor. As they continued on and the field came in view, Pell radioed Oestreicher to hold his B flight in a standing patrol to provide top cover while A flight touched down, standard operating procedure when two flights were landing. Pell and his brood spiraled down one by one at 0950 to come in over the black asphalt main runway. By 1000, Pell and his wingman, John Hughes; second element leader Burt Rice and his wingman, John Glover; and McMahon were parked along the near ends of the runway. Their crew chiefs were out to the ships to find out what had happened.[4]

But McMahon's crew chief and armorer weren't there. Usually they would be peering over his shoulder and asking about mechanical problems. Then he spotted them standing on the berm of a trench fifteen or twenty yards away, shading their eyes and looking into the sky to the north. Realizing that McMahon was observing them, one of them hurried over to McMahon, yelling, "Lieutenant, I think it's an air raid!" McMahon lifted the left ear flap of his flight helmet but couldn't hear any air raid siren. "Why do you think there's an air raid?" McMahon asked. The crew chief pointed up to the sky to the north and said that he'd heard a lot of machine-gun fire and saw what looked like a dogfight overhead.[5] Then he pointed to the east and told McMahon that he'd seen a P-40 coming down "in a helluva dive" over there. McMahon couldn't see anything in the sky to the north or east, but he did hear an inertia starter on one of his flight's P-40s winding up to his left. That was enough for him. Hurriedly, he rebuckled his chute and seat belt and ran through his trim tabs. Then he heard another engine starting. Suddenly, a Bren gun carrier pulled up at the mouth of the dispersal bay, and someone jumped out and came rushing towards him. He was surprised to see that it was Jack Peres from Oestreicher's flight, "his chute bobbling off his butt" as he ran. Wordlessly, Peres was pointing up in the sky, then stopped and headed back to the Bren gun carrier in a cloud of dust.

At the other end of the field from McMahon, Slugger Pell was yelling something to his crew chief, but Roy Bopp couldn't make out what it was over the noise of the running Allison engine of his ship. The 33rd's CO had a strange expression on his face and was pointing behind him with a gloved hand. Finally, Bopp could make out one word: "Zeros!" Pell released his belly tank, which hit the runway with a thud. Realizing it was in the path of the tail wheel of Pell's P-40, Bopp half-rolled and half-dragged the heavy gas-loaded tank out of the way, then yelled to Pell to take off.[6] Behind him followed Hughes, then Rice and Glover.

McMahon had already dropped his belly tank and was taxiing out to the runway when he caught sight of Rice and Glover tearing down the field. Just as Glover was retracting his landing gear, the right one struck one of the empty barrels the Australians had put out on the field as obstacles. The barrel went flying, then bouncing, but Glover managed to keep going in his takeoff.[7] McMahon taxied at maximum speed towards the runway to his right, ready to pour on the gas for his takeoff. Turning his attention to the right towards the runway approach end, he caught sight of the banking silhouette of a plane flashing through the breaks in the trees. He stopped his P-40 just short of the runway, the ship's nose swung around and pointed in the direction for takeoff. He could now make out that the incoming plane was another P-40. As it flashed by at a high rate of speed, no flaps down and belly tank still on, McMahon could make it out as Bill Walker's ship. It came to a screeching halt at the far end of the runway. "What's going on?" McMahon wondered. Why had one of the B flight pilots providing top cover for them come in like that and with his tank still on? "They must have run into some Jap bombers or flying boats overhead," McMahon speculated. "Couldn't be Zeros," he reasoned. Zeros wouldn't have the range to reach Darwin from their NEI land bases.

Applying maximum power for takeoff, McMahon headed down the runway at about 1004. Just before becoming airborne he lifted his left wing to avoid hitting the rudder of Walker's P-40. Automatically turning his head to the right rear, he caught a glimpse of three radial-engine aircraft stacked up as if to peel off for a landing. "Why the hell is the control tower letting those A-24s come in to land if there is an air raid on?" he murmured to himself. But as they came closer, the A-24 dive bombers he remembered from Amberley Field looked more like T-6 Texan trainers to him. "Wait a minute," he thought, "there aren't any Texans here in Australia." Then he did a double-take. Those ships had red meatballs on their wings: Zeros!

The three Japanese were about five hundred feet above him and slightly to the right, jockeying into a line abreast formation. Reacting sharply, McMahon slowly banked and skidded under the last one in the formation. He was hoping the leader wouldn't do a barrel roll over his flight to get at him. McMahon had now reached two hundred feet and was thinking that he should perhaps head northeast and try to outrun the Japanese, but then the lead Zero broke into a wide diving turn. Deciding to turn into the Japanese, McMahon rolled into a steep bank, pulled the stick back in a maximum-G turn, then leveled his wings. The Zeros were coming around in a string, "like a row of ducks in a gallery," it seemed to him.[8]

SHORTLY AFTER B FLIGHT HAD taken up position to circle over the field to provide top cover for A flight's landing, the pilots heard a high-pitched, whining static over their radios. Were there Japanese nearby trying to jam their frequency? Then they picked up an unidentified voice ordering all the P-40s overhead to return to the field. It wasn't Pell's voice. Confused about what to do, Jack Peres, leading the first element, decided on his own to head back to the field to get a clarification, and apparently without informing the others he left his wingman, Elton Perry, to lead the element.[9] Bob Oestreicher would continue as the weaver for the flight.[10]

Some fifteen minutes later, at about 1000, Oestreicher was weaving over and above the P-40s of Max Wiecks and his wingman, Bill Walker, unwittingly distracting them from searching the sky for possible intruders. As the B flight leader started to weave back across them, he suddenly rolled to the right and went into a steep dive. Walker thought Oestreicher was in trouble and watched him in his sudden descent, then saw him drop his belly tank about five hundred feet into the dive. A few seconds later, Walker heard Oestreicher yell "Zeros" over the radio. Thinking that Oestreicher was mistakenly diving on an A-24, Walker visually followed him in his dive to about two thousand feet, where Oestreicher began his pullout and then headed south at a high rate of speed.[11] Turning his attention again to the sky overhead, Walker spotted nine radial-engine ships diving on him and his element leader, Wiecks, in front of him. There was no need for closer identification; these were Zeros, he realized immediately. Throwing on his gun switch, Walker pulled around and up into the Japanese and started firing his .50s but couldn't score any hits because of their diving turn. He tried to turn tighter, but then a burst came through his cockpit and tore a lemon-sized hunk out of his left deltoid. Physically unable to operate the hand release to drop his belly tank, he dove for the field.[12]

Wiecks had his head down in the cockpit, trying to get his radio functioning when he glanced up to check his position and saw out of his right periphery a stream of tracers heading towards the lead P-40, that of Elton Perry, now without his element leader, Peres. Turning his head to the right, he spotted the Zero just below his level that was firing at Perry. Wiecks chopped back and tried to get behind the Japanese, but in his turn found himself taking tracer fire from behind. All of a sudden his ship went out of control and into a dive. He tried to pull out, but it was no use—he couldn't get any response from the controls as he fell like a leaf. Now down to four thousand feet or less, he decided to bail out, but after opening the canopy and undoing his safety belt the gyrations of his P-40 and the bulky British-type back pack parachute he had on were impeding his efforts. Finally he was pulled out and managed to get his chute open at a very low altitude. A moment later he heard a "terrific thud" below and saw his ship hit the water right underneath him. Then he hit the water himself. One of the chute straps caught on his canteen so that he was being dragged through the water, "bounding like a porpoise." To free the strap he yanked off his web belt, then immediately collapsed his troublesome chute. Wiecks blew into his mae west to inflate it just as he saw a Zero passing overhead at no higher than two hundred feet. He ducked, and the pilot apparently didn't spot him.[13] Wiecks glanced at his watch. It had stopped at 0955. That must have been the time he hit the water, he figured.[14] Wiecks's efforts to help Perry had been to no avail. His last view of his squadron mate was as his ship was on fire and heading down.[15]

RIGHT BEHIND PELL IN HIS TAKEOFF, Charlie Hughes just barely cleared the field and was heading north when he was jumped just above treetop level by a Zero. He escaped unscathed on the Zero's first pass, but after the Japanese did a complete 360-degree loop and came in behind him again, he was not so fortunate. His ship riddled by fire, Hughes crashed into the brush one to two miles from the north end of the runway.[16]

Having himself evaded the attention of three Zeros on takeoff, Slugger Pell headed north. As he passed over Lee Point and swung around to the right, still at treetop level and about ten miles northeast of the RAAF field, a Zero suddenly dived on him. The Japanese pilot fired continuously into the P-40's tail, then the ship "sort of coughed." Pell opened his canopy and at not over one hundred feet, jumped. His chute did not open before he struck the ground, a hard clay pan in a swamp about three hundred feet from where his ship crashed.[17]

In third position for takeoff, Burt Rice had immediately reacted to Peres's shout and, barely missing the obstacles on the field, cleared the runway heading in a northeast direction. But at about fifteen hundred feet the three Zeros picked him up. Rice went into a shallow dive at maximum engine speed and managed to pull out of the range of their fire. He was able to maintain his lead as he went into a slow climb, but the Zeros were gaining on him. In a fairly tight turn, the Zeros turned inside of him, getting ready to fire again. Rice headed back to the southeast, but the slams and rattles he heard confirmed that the Japanese were hitting his plane with their machine-gun and cannon fire. Trying to evade them, he put his ship into a shallow dive, but he suddenly realized he had no elevator control. That was enough for him. Rice released his seat belt and stood up in his cockpit, then jumped, but his face hit his ship's tail, which knocked him momentarily unconscious. When he came to he was floating down in his chute, picking up the sound of aircraft droning around him and machine-gun fire nearby. Moments later he crashed into large mangrove trees in a swamp some ten miles east of the RAAF field, on the east side of the Howard River in the area of the present-day Shoal Bay Coastal Reserve. He was uninjured except for a severe eye wound from hitting the tail of his P-40 while bailing out.[18]

Next to Rice in the parking bay off the runway, Glover had also reacted immediately to Peres's yell to scramble and was just five seconds behind his element leader Rice in taking off, fortuitously clearing the field despite banging into the barrel on the runway. Unmolested by the three Zeros that attacked Rice shortly after his takeoff, Glover headed out to the northeast and climbed to about three thousand feet at maximum RPM, then turned right to the east, intending to climb higher. As he began his high-speed shallow climb, he noticed a parachute and three radial-engine planes circling it about five hundred feet below him. Glover checked his gunsight and guns and headed for what he now concluded were Zeros. One of the Japanese was leveling out for a straight course for the chute and had started firing at the hapless pilot when Glover closed on the Zero from behind at a twenty-degree angle and poured fire from all six of his .50-caliber guns into the Japanese. To Glover the Zero appeared to explode.[19]

When the other two Japanese climbed away, Glover circled the parachute. He recognized the parachutist as Rice, who seemed inert in the descending chute. Believing that the Japanese had executed his helpless comrade, Glover was enraged and looked around for the killers. But they were coming for him instead, now having climbed to his eight o'clock high position. Glover quickly decided to lead the two Nips back to the field and over some Australian machine-gun pits that he recalled were on the north side. Applying maximum military power, he went into a shallow dive from twenty-eight hundred feet, then eased up to see if the Zeros were still behind him. They appeared to be gone. Slowing down, he headed towards treetops not far in front of him that were only some fifty to one hundred feet lower than he was. He glanced back and was shocked to see the two Zeros he thought he had eluded closing on him and firing at him. Automatically he shoved the throttle to the firewall.

Glover was now over the northeast boundary of the field, which was bordered by a thick forest of tall eucalyptus trees. When he turned his head forward, after having fixed on the Zeros, he was shocked to find himself flying right into the trees. On impact, his propeller chopped a hole through the greenery and flew off the fuselage; simultaneously, a tree trunk ripped off his right wing. What remained of his ship bounced off the ground in an open area before coming to a halt in a huge cloud of dust a hundred yards from the trees. Dazed and bleeding profusely from a deep gash extending from his forehead down to his chest, Glover managed to extricate himself from the cockpit and stagger a few steps, then sat down on his chute pack, his head in his hands.[20]

Glover had crashed his ship within forty yards of one of the sandbagged machine-gun nests off the end of the field. When two of the Australian gunners saw one of the Zeros descending and strafing the helpless pilot, they climbed out of their secure position, ran over to him, and half-carried and dragged the semiconscious American back to their pit, braving the fire of the Japanese. The Aussies gave Glover what first aid they could to stem the heavy bleeding, intending to get him to a hospital at first opportunity.[21]

Meanwhile, Bob McMahon had problems of his own after clearing the field and trying to evade the Zeros that had spotted him. After sliding under the last plane in the Zero formation and hoping the Japanese hadn't seen him, he pointed his nose down and opened the throttle, heading northeast. But the Zero flight leader simultaneously pulled off and down in a shallow, high-speed diving turn. McMahon realized that if he continued on his course the Japanese would end up on his tail within shooting range before he could pull away. He rolled back to the left in a maximum-g-force turn and pulled up into the flight leader for a head-on firing pass. His tracers "laced high and inside," and the Japanese pulled up. Seconds later the flight leader's wingman approached within six hundred yards and was boring in on McMahon. Head on, the two exchanged fire. McMahon saw a small black object fly off the Zero's engine section just before the Japanese flashed past him. The third Zero now sprang up from his flight path "like a rebounding yo-yo," and McMahon pulled up to meet him. But his airspeed was down to the stall point, so he dropped his nose to pick up speed and started a turn to the right.[22]

Glancing down, he spotted a P-40 being chased by two Zeros racing across the periphery of the RAAF field. But his attention was diverted by a sudden rattling sound and a couple of loud bangs, then his P-40 shook. McMahon chopped his throttle and looked over his right shoulder to see a Zero coming up on his right and firing at him. Suddenly he was almost thrown forward by a sudden deceleration of his ship. His wheels had not been locked in position, and his hydraulic lines had apparently been hit. A second Zero dove at him from its eight o'clock position as he dove and skidded under the Zero that had riddled his ship. McMahon saw 7.7 mm bullets hitting his left wingtip as he skidded, then reversed the skid in an attempt to look like his aircraft was falling out of control. Waffling his way eastward and descending, he did his best to imitate a shot-up ship. It looked like the Japanese believed he was about to crash, as none attempted to follow him.

Down to about four hundred feet, McMahon leveled out and "poured the coal" to his ship, now out of firing range of the Zeros, which he noticed looked as if they were reforming. But the Japanese had caught on to McMahon's ruse. Two quickly had caught up to him and were diving on his flanks, while a third headed for his tail. Knowing that with his wheels down there was no way he could outrun the Zeros, McMahon headed off to the right, where he thought Rice and Glover were who could come to his aid. When the Zero on his tail began firing, McMahon pulled his P-40 up and around in a snap roll, then began a turn to take him north and to Darwin Harbor, whose antiaircraft guns he hoped could extricate him from his situation.

After much acrobatic flying to avoid the fire of the pursuing Japanese, McMahon headed west, parallel to the coastline, the three Zeros after him now "jockeying for a real gunnery exercise." The two on his flanks were alternating with the third, which was diving in firing passes from the rear. McMahon could actually see the 20 mm rounds from their wing cannons heading toward his ship. McMahon's coolant warning light now began flashing. He knew that in a few minutes his Allison would freeze up. Pushing the coolant flap on his engine wide open, he headed down. The flap produced more drag, but at least the light stopped blinking.

McMahon looked up and spotted more trouble. Another flight of at least six Zeros was joining the fray, diving down from a high angle and right between his original pursuers. "Like fish in a feeding frenzy," they were all trying to get into the action at the same time against the lone P-40. McMahon concentrated on avoiding a collision as they broke one way or another, missing him and each other by feet. He continued heading west for Darwin's Larrakeyah Barracks, two miles northeast of downtown Darwin, and its protecting antiaircraft guns. He noticed a large formation of single-engine aircraft flying by the far side of the barracks at about eight thousand feet in three-ship formations, evidently heading for the ships in the harbor. Strangely enough, no guns appeared to be firing at them.

Suddenly he sighted what looked like a P-40 heading towards him, but when it began firing at him he wondered if it wasn't a German Messerschmitt Bf 109 instead. Attempting a fancy maneuver he'd learned in flying school, McMahon instead ended up in a dive, one thousand feet above Fannie Bay, and when he eased forward on the power he found himself facing thirty-foot beach cliffs and further inland forty-foot trees. Bringing power for speed to climb the banks and trees, he was startled to see tracer fire from his guns going into the trees above the cliffs: he had inadvertently touched the firing switch. Moments later he found himself now over the far reaches of east Darwin. Over Darwin Hospital he looked down and tried to see what was transpiring in the harbor, but smoke was obscuring his vision, apparently from oil fires.

Given a minute or two of relative quiet, McMahon tried to assess the damage to his ship. It still flew, but the instrument panel and canopy were in shambles, while puffs of oil smoke emanated from the right exhaust stack, although the engine was still responding. But with the fire around the exhaust stack continuing to erupt, hindering his vision to the right and ahead, he figured he would have to bail out soon. But once again he found Zeros closing in on him. Noticing two large tanks of a navy fuel oil farm near the harbor bellowing thick smoke, he dove into the smoke to elude his pursuers and on exiting found himself flying barely above the tin roofs of Darwin. Picking up a Zero again, McMahon broke left and down in the opposite direction, putting him parallel to the Darwin Harbor anchorages. Then he spotted what he was looking for, an old four-stack destroyer that was "firing everything it had" at the Japanese attacking it. But when he approached it, he came under its fire, too. With his landing gear down, he must have looked like one of the Japanese dive bombers harassing it, he figured. Rolling right, McMahon flashed his ship's belly at the destroyer and the antiaircraft fire stopped, but when he banked back left and flew a parallel course at twenty feet off the water, he was shocked when the destroyer opened up on him again, this time with its machine guns. But at least all this fire seemed to cause his Zero pursuers to break off and head to the northeast. Now the crew recognized his ship as a P-40 and was waving at him from the deck.

After flying past a large hospital ship, the AHS *Manunda,* McMahon climbed to about two thousand feet and headed for the northern side of Darwin Harbor. To the east it was all explosions, fire, dust, debris, and smoke. Then he made out PBY flying boats at anchor near a seaplane tender—the USS *William B. Preston*—and figured he should bail out near them. But as he

P-40E, believed to be that of Bob McMahon, climbing above the Australian cargo ship *Zealandia* during the February 19, 1942, attack on Darwin harbor. The hospital ship *Manunda* is to the far right. *Photograph 304956 © Australian War Memorial.*

approached, he was startled to see one of them erupt in a large ball of flames, then moments later a large orange life raft inflating and crew members swimming and diving underwater. From the erupting fountains of water around them, he grasped that they were being strafed by three Zeros he now spotted. "Really pissed off" that they were shooting at men in an unarmed life raft, McMahon decided to go after them. Picking out one of them, he dove straight down and caught the Japanese in his sights, raking the Zero with .50-caliber fire. Breaking his dive, he was so low that he thought he might just glide in towards a mangrove beach he had spotted. The smoke from his engine's exhaust was no longer belching out, and he was afraid the lack of oil meant the engine might seize up on him if he added power. But the Allison responded to the throttle with a burst of power he figured could get him up to one thousand feet. The strafers had left the scene, and he decided to head for land. No luck—he spotted two more Zeros heading for him just hundreds of yards away. Chopping his throttle, McMahon saw one Zero shoot by him. For a moment the Japanese's ship was "as big as a barn door" in McMahon's gunsight, but when McMahon squeezed the trigger, not a single shot was forthcoming.[23]

Opening his canopy, McMahon lifted himself out and jumped, his feet clearing the P-40's tail. Watching his old bird continuing on its westerly heading, he picked up the sound of machine-gun fire to his rear. He figured it was strafers after the PBYs again, then was shocked to see that Zeros were making firing passes at him, trying to kill him in his chute. Recalling a drill for a situation like this, McMahon collapsed his chute by working the risers and assumed a fetal position as the Zeros approached him, the tracers slicing through the shroud lines above him. Seconds later, just above the verdant jungle, he released the risers and then crashed into thick mangroves. He was uninjured in the fall but had a "good size wound" in his lower right leg inflicted during his combat.[24]

McMahon was hanging from one of the trees and was unable to free himself from the chute. Soon he spotted a small whaleboat chugging along in the immediate area—the west arm of Darwin Harbor, twelve miles west of Darwin—heading in his direction and flying Old Glory from her stern. McMahon started yelling, then jumped into the water and, swinging his mae west, which he had taken off, managed to attract the attention of a man in the stern. After being hauled aboard, the crew determined his need for medical treatment for his leg and, after snaking their way along the shoreline during the bombing attack on Darwin, eventually dropped him off on a small spit. Incongruously, while sitting on the sand he retrieved his small notebook and an indelible pencil from a pocket and began recording his recollections of the day's experiences.[25]

SOUTH OF DARWIN, BOB OESTREICHER was flying in cloud cover after having dived away from the other four in his flight. He was wondering if he had not shown poor leadership but rationalized that in alerting them to the attacking Zeros he had tried to save their lives. With so few hours in a P-40 and never having fired its guns, his comrades would have been easy meat for the Japanese, he believed.[26] After flying in and out of the clouds for about half an hour, observing many planes over Darwin, Oestreicher spotted something in the distance. At first it seemed to him no more than a flash of sun off a canopy. Heading in that direction, he was now able to make out two single-engine planes with their landing gear down. He first thought they must be P-40s with gear down heading towards Batchelor Field south of Darwin for a landing, but then he saw the big meatballs on their fuselages and realized they were Japanese fixed-landing-gear dive bombers. They were at about fifteen hundred feet.[27] As soon as Oestreicher began firing his .50s, the two Japanese broke up their formation in the "bursting bomb" type of defense, one heading to the right and the other to the left. Oestreicher believed he saw the one to his right "burst into flames and go down," then went after the other one but lost him as he entered into clouds. The dive bomber appeared to be smoking slightly, but Oestreicher wasn't sure if it was a result of hits from his guns or from the Japanese "ramming his throttle home."[28]

After his combat Oestreicher ducked back into the clouds. About fifteen minutes later he picked up the railroad tracks below and followed them to Darwin and the RAAF aerodrome. As he arrived over the field at about 1145, he rocked his wings so that the Australians "would be damn sure to recognize me" and then came in for a landing. But three-quarters of the way down the runway, Oestreicher stopped his ship, fearing a ground loop. Climbing out, he inspected his ship and found that his left wheel and tire were "shot to hell," which he figured would indeed have caused a ground loop if he had continued.[29]

Despite conditions at the field, Oestreicher wanted his crew chief and armorer to service his ship and search the base for a wheel and tire they could put on the P-40E. The aerodrome had "really taken a beating" and was burning to beat all hell. It appeared to Oestreicher that the dive bombers had hit the bays particularly hard but that the hangars and workshops had also been damaged in the raid. Oestreicher headed for what remained of No. 12 Squadron Hangar and reported in to Shorty Wheless. He told Wheless that he thought he had shot down one plane, and the other could be classed as a "probable." But as he was talking to Wheless, the siren went off. They first thought it was the "all clear," but it wasn't. There were twenty-seven twin-engine bombers overhead. Without further ado they ran as fast as they could to the closest slit trench.[30]

EARLIER THAT MORNING AUSSIE GUNNERS Keith Johns and Clyde Freake were making their way under difficult conditions across a swamp to reach a point where they had seen a P-40 pilot bail out at treetop level some twenty minutes earlier after being chased by a Zero. The two members of the 4th Anti-Tank Regiment had been heading out to relieve two members of their antitank crew dug in at the edge of King Creek on Shoal Bay Peninsula some nine miles northeast of Darwin's RAAF airdrome. When they reached the crash site—a tidal flat known as Cameron's Beach—they found two other soldiers already there, looking over the scene. Near what remained of the P-40—the number 28 painted in black on its tail—they saw the body of a man in overalls sitting in a squat position, hunched over slightly. He had apparently been killed in bailing out at too low an altitude, his parachute not opening.[31]

Sgts. Les Bushby and H. Ridley of the 19th Light Machine Gun Regiment told Freake and Johns that they were only twenty yards away when the P-40 had dived into the mud, the crash shearing off its wings. When Bushby had

All that remained of P-40E No. 28 of the 33rd Pursuit Squadron (Provisional), piloted by the squadron's CO, Maj. Floyd Pell, after he was shot down and killed northeast of Darwin's RAAF airfield. *Courtesy Norman Obst via Shane Johnston.*

run over to the pilot, who was lying only some fifteen feet from the plane, the Zero that had shot him down returned and fired into the wreckage of the P-40, exploding it. Bushby was thrown into the air by the explosion and landed face down in the mud. After having survived being strafed by the Zero without being hit, Bushby returned to the pilot but found him dead. He looked into the pilot's shirt pocket and took out a little paybook that indicated it belonged to Capt. Floyd J. Pell, U.S. Army Air Forces.[32]

Soon two other men showed up after having slogged in water and mud a half mile from where they had left their ambulance. Corpsman Max George and his assistant had been ordered from Winnellie Camp just south of the RAAF field to the site to recover the body. George found the pilot's oak leaf major's insignia lying nearby. As they were carrying Pell's body in a stretcher over the tortuous route, they heard many airplanes overhead and looked up. It was a second raid on Darwin. Taking cover, they put Pell's body down and lay down in the mud and water until the Japanese formation had passed by.[33] When the ambulance reached Darwin's Berrimah Army General Hospital, one mile from the end of the main runway of the RAAF airdrome, the sight of many bodies lying on the front lawn in body bags greeted them. They carried Pell's body inside and departed.

Just a week earlier, Pell had sent his last will and testament to his father in Utah. "Don't show it to mom and don't open it unless notified of a casualty," he enjoined his father in the covering letter. "But then nothing will ever happen to me," he concluded, and signed "Da Slug."[34]

EARLIER THAT MORNING ANOTHER ambulance drew up at Berrimah Hospital. A badly wounded American pilot was taken out on a stretcher and into the recently opened facility of twelve hundred beds. The hospital's matron in the admission office directed the stretcher bearers to a ward where the aviator was placed on a bed and had his bandages removed. A gaping wound, bleeding profusely, extended down the center of his face from the forehead through the nose and chin. The matron tried to arrest the bleeding and cleaned the wound as best she could for inspection by a doctor. The American was restless and only semiconscious. When he revived, he identified himself as Lt. John G. Glover of the U.S. Army Air Forces. Glover wanted to know where he was. He explained the circumstances of his being shot down and crash-landing his P-40. "I got one of those little yellow devils, but one got me," he told the hospital staff.[35]

Just as he was being given an injection of morphine, he heard a great number of airplanes overhead. The Japanese were back for a second raid on the area. Glover became highly agitated. He could see that the roof of the hospital had so many holes in it that it looked like a colander, the result of being machine-gunned in the earlier attack. He felt "exposed and defenseless" without his own fighter plane. To ease his concern, the matron and an orderly lifted Glover on his mattress and slid him under the bed. Glover talked incoherently as she squatted next to him with a steel helmet on. He seemed mainly concerned about the loss of two watches that he had been wearing, one on each wrist. Soon he fell asleep from the effects of the morphine, just as the raid was ending.[36]

NEAR THE HOSPITAL, ONLY ONE MILE from the end of the RAAF airdrome's main landing strip, Oestreicher's French-Canadian armorer, Pvt. Real Bujold, was walking with another armorer, Pvt. Jean Gunter, to Oestreicher's just-landed P-40 on the far end of the runway, quite a distance from the hangars, when the air raid alarm went off at 1158. The two 33rd Pursuit mechanics ran to the nearest slit trench, an L-shaped trench not more than two feet deep.[37] Looking up, they saw what seemed like "100 bombers," the sky covered with them. Then bombs began falling on the airfield. Hunkered down on his stomach, buffeted by the concussions as dirt and rocks flew in all directions, Bujold felt a piece of shrapnel hit his back. Expecting to see blood, he was relieved to find that it was his canteen, twisted around on his back, that had taken the hit.

Nearby, the six pilots just in from Timor, inspecting the damage on the field from the earlier attack, were also caught out in the open when the alarm sounded, and they saw two waves of fifty-four bombers overhead. They scattered in different directions, Vern Head and some others running to the woods. Pete Childress opted instead for a nearby foxhole, jumping in just as the first bombs exploded on the field. One detonated a bare ten yards from his foxhole, but "all I got was a case of jumping nerves" and a lot of dirt thrown on him. The explosion had made a crater twenty feet wide and ten feet deep. The Australian in the foxhole with him was so shaken that he couldn't even hold a match still enough to light his cigarette and had to ask Childress to do it for him.[38]

When the noise from the explosions finally died out and the "all clear" siren sounded at 1240, Bujold and Gunter emerged from their trench and looked around. The place was in complete chaos. Planes were burning, and the hangars were on fire, too. They were undecided what to do under the circumstances. They were expecting planes from their 33rd Pursuit to return and refuel and have their guns reloaded.[39] After a few minutes the two armorers decided to head over to the burning hangar, but on the way there they noticed through the smoke that the runways were full of holes. No planes would be coming back to land here, they figured. Then an Australian sergeant, surprised to see them, told them to evacuate, because Japanese parachutists were expected at any moment. "Where should we go?" Bujold asked. "I don't care, just go!" the sergeant barked back. Bujold and Gunter decided to head down the only road they knew of, one that led south. As they plodded along the road, an Australian military truck pulled up. The driver told them to hop in. He would be taking them to Batchelor Field, forty-eight miles south of Darwin by road.

FAR TO THE SOUTH, AT PORT PIRIE, Bryce Wilhite had received bad news early that morning. The RAAF had informed him that his 33rd squadron mate Richard Pingree had just crashed after having taken his P-40E up on a test hop to determine whether repairs had put his engine back in good order.[40] According to the control tower, Pingree had been turning to the left at low speed for his final approach to the field when his ship apparently stalled, perhaps because the small fuselage access door on the left side had sprung open, as spotted by the tower. His P-40E had gone into a steep dive, and the crash had created a crater some twenty feet deep in marshy terrain about twelve hundred feet west of Port Pirie cemetery.

Burned remains of a P-40E, probably Floyd Pell's No. 3, in the wrecked
RAAF Squadron 12 hangar following the February 19, 1942, attack on Darwin.
Courtesy Ernest McDowell.

When Wilhite arrived at the site shortly afterwards with several RAAF
officers and enlisted men, he found a huge hole filled with water. Shaken
over the tragic death of his squadron mate, Wilhite suggested that Pingree be
buried with his plane and a monument placed over it. But the RAAF officers
demurred and began digging the crumpled wreck from the deep hole as Wilhite watched from a distance. After extracting the remains of the P-40, they
managed to cut Pingree's mutilated body free from the cockpit and lowered it
into a lead-lined coffin for shipment back to the United States.[41]

Later, at the Port Pirie railway station, as he fought back his emotions, Wilhite stood at attention and saluted as "Taps" was played. Then he removed
the U.S. flag from Pingree's coffin and folded it into a triangle, as regulations
required, before placing it again on the coffin lid. Wilhite had known Pingree
only a short time, but the sudden demise of the twenty-one-year-old Mormon from Ogden, Utah—married only a month before his departure from the
States—would haunt him for years.[42]

AT THE 17TH PURSUIT'S SECRET FIELD in East Java, Joe Kruzel and Cy
Blanton in early morning of the nineteenth were preparing with Butch Hague

for a recon mission to the east as far as Lombok Island. They were to look for indications of a Japanese landing in the Bali area that had been reported. However, before they could take off, word reached Ngoro that the Japanese invasion force had already gone ashore on the southeast coast of Bali before dawn.[43] The plan was now for the 17th Pursuit to escort A-24s of the 91st Bomb Squadron for an attack on the ships of the invasion force off the Bali coast. Already from very early morning small groups of B-17s and LB-30s from Singosari and Madioen were mounting missions to bomb the transports and escorting warships, but with little result. It was hoped that the 91st's seven dive bombers that had landed at Singosari between 0705 and 0720 for service and bombs would be more effective against the ships. However, the morning dragged on as personnel at Singosari Field struggled to adapt the one 300 kg and two 50 kg bombs to the racks of the A-24s and as arrangements for the P-40 escort were held up. Finally it was decided to call off the strike mission, which would have been the first for the 91st on Java.[44]

But at about 1130 a mission did materialize for the pursuiters when Major Fisher at the ADC in Soerabaja ordered them to intercept a Japanese force of bombers and fighters heading in its direction. Sixteen P-40s on alert took off immediately from Ngoro in four flights led by Grant Mahony.[45] Approaching the Soerabaja area, the Americans spotted the Betty bombers heading in over the Flores Sea. Mahony detached two of his flights to intercept them, but instead of continuing in, the eighteen bombers were seen to drop their loads on Bawean Island, one hundred miles due north of Soerabaja, and start back. Had the Japanese spotted the P-40s and turned back?[46]

Although the bombers aborted their attack on Java, the eighteen escorting Zeros were seen continuing in. When the other two P-40 flights, one headed by Mahony and the other by Walt Coss, reached the Soerabaja area, they spotted a *chutai* of nine Zeros already there and with altitude advantage on the eight Americans. Joe Kruzel's wingman Butch Hague watched as the Zeros attacked the cover flight below him. He saw the four P-40s pull up into the Zero formation "and then about six planes started spiraling for the ground," evidently all shot down. When a couple of the Zeros got on his tail, Hague immediately pointed his ship straight down and dove for a stratum of clouds. Leveling out, he saw three Zeros at different times in the next few minutes on the tail of P-40s. Going to his comrades' defense, Hague fired at one at long range, forcing the Japanese to break off. Slow-rolling down on a second Zero, Hague fired at closer range this time and saw the Japanese go into a cloud, smoking. Diving on a third Zero and leading him with his six .50s, Hague watched as his bullets sprayed all about and into the ship, but to his great frustration the Zero wouldn't catch fire. When Hague turned 90 degrees to line up his nemesis again, he was shocked to see the Japanese going into a 360-degree turn, and begin chasing Hague instead. Hague dove for the trees and ran "as if my life depended on it." The Zero pilot chased Hague all the way to the south side of Java before he broke off.[47]

In the cover flight Cy Blanton and his wingman, Chief Fields, were at about sixteen thousand to eighteen thousand feet—lower altitude than usual for an interception—when they and the other two in the flight were dived on by the nine Zeros that Hague had witnessed. The Americans turned to face the Zeros head-on, expecting the Japanese as usual to pull up sharply just as they were about to collide and afford them a belly shot.[48] Blanton and the Zero pilot he faced exchanged fire as they approached each other, then both pulled up. Just as the Japanese started his roll to see where Blanton was, he momentarily presented himself as a perfect target. Blanton fired all of his .50s at the Zero, which exploded in a huge ball of fire before the startled Oklahoman. He flew through the fire, smoke, and debris, then realized that he was in trouble himself: heavy smoke was pouring out of his Allison engine on both sides. At first Blanton thought that his P-40 had caught fire from the explosion, but then he realized was it was worse than that; he couldn't get any reaction from his throttle. He feared his throttle linkage may have been shot away. But with his engine burning up rapidly—apparently because his coolant system was shot up—Blanton figured he would be losing his engine completely at any rate.[49]

Blanton looked around and saw that the sky was clear of all aircraft, so he decided now was the time to bail out of his stricken ship. Pulling back his canopy, jerking off his oxygen mask, and undoing his safety belt, he was about to jump when he spotted two Zeros diving on him. He aborted his bailout and rolled his ship over and headed straight down. When he leveled out over the rice paddies below at about two thousand feet, he found that the Zeros were gone. "They probably found other game on the way down or somebody got after them," he figured.

Surprisingly, his P-40 was still flying along, even though the engine was making "achunk, achunk, achunk" noises and losing power. And he had no controls. He knew he would have to do something soon and opted for a belly landing. The water below off the coast of north Java looked better than the ground inland. He went into a ninety-degree turn and braced himself in his seat as his ship began to stall. He could see that the right wing was slightly low when the P-40 went into a full stall, but he was almost parallel with the shoreline. Just as his ship hit the water, he was tossed around in the cockpit; he had forgotten to refasten his safety belt. The P-40 slowed to a stop almost immediately in the water. Blanton stood up in his cockpit and noticed that his wingtips were sticking out of the water. It was very shallow. Then he looked up and saw trouble. Two Zeros were headed down towards him. Painfully, his back aching, he managed to climb out of the cockpit and lay down on one of the wingtips, getting ready to roll over into the water. Just then the two Zeros flew over him in level flight at about one thousand to fifteen hundred feet and continued on. "They must have been out of ammunition," a relieved Blanton thought.

Leaving his plane behind, Blanton stood up and began wading to shore, which looked to be only about one hundred yards away. Back on terra firma again, he spotted a native settlement close by, but strangely enough there was not a soul around. "Perhaps they are as scared as I am," he speculated. He began walking slowly towards the east on a dike that separated rice paddies all around, his back hurting with every step. Soon he spotted a man in western dress standing on the dike ahead of him. Blanton hollered, *"Kawan kompeni, Kawan kompeni,"* native words, meaning "friendly army," he was told by the Dutch liaison officer, Arie Geurtz, to use if he were ever shot down.[50] The Javanese didn't respond or approach Blanton, so Blanton kept walking towards him. When he reached the native and said "Soerabaja," while indicating that he wanted to be taken there, the Javanese seemed to understand and began leading Blanton in a fast-paced walk. Blanton wanted the native to slow down—his back was hurting—but got no response to his motion to slow down. Only when he grabbed the jacket of the Javanese and held on did the pace slow as they continued along the dikes. About thirty minutes later they reached a narrow road and the buildings of what turned out to be a Dutch outpost. Entering one of them, he found an English-speaking Dutch officer on duty inside and explained his situation. Blanton thanked the Javanese for guiding him, and the Dutchman asked him to return to his village and keep an eye on Blanton's aircraft.

Soon Blanton arrived back in Soerabaja in transport provided by the Dutch officer and was dropped off at the Oranje Hotel, as requested. He asked the reception for Lieutenant Kurtz, the Far East Air Force liaison officer, and found him in the dining room. Blanton felt embarrassed in the respectable hotel to confront Kurtz in his half-soaked uniform and mud-caked trousers and shoes. After hearing of Blanton's escapade, Kurtz led Blanton to his room and gave him clean khakis, then made arrangements for transportation back to his Ngoro base for him. He also let Blanton use his phone for a call to the field to let Sprague know that he was all right and would soon be on his way back.[51]

In the meantime, the four flights had come back in to land at Ngoro about two to three hours after their combat with the aggressive Zeros and were

Quanah "Chief" Fields, the first native American killed in World War II, shot down over the Soerabaja area, February 19, 1942. *Courtesy Georgia Fields Hallett.*

pained to find that three of their number were missing. Mission leader Mahony's wingman, Ed "Gilly" Gilmore, was known to have been shot down but was seen to bail out with his P-40 on fire. Blanton was thought to have made a water landing off the Java coast. But Chief Fields was believed to be dead, shot down in an encounter with the Zeros, a loss that hit his close friend Spence Johnson particularly hard.[52]

The five returning pilots from the two flights that had fought the Zeros vividly described their experiences to their squadron mates. B. J. Oliver said that he had fired his guns at the Zeros from whatever angle he could manage, even in a vertical climb. It was not easy to get in a good shot at them, though he felt he got one in. Hague bitterly complained that "the bastards are a thousand percent more maneuverable than us."[53] Still, they claimed four Zeros shot down. Mahony and Kruzel put in a claim for one each, and Hague claimed a probable. They didn't know if Gilmore, Blanton, or Fields had any victories before being shot down.[54]

Remains of Bill Walker's P-40E No. 46 on the tarmac in front of the Squadron 12 hangar at Darwin's RAAF field after being strafed by Zeros on February 19, 1942. *Courtesy Bob Alford.*

Shortly afterwards, a call came in to Ngoro. It was Blanton, telephoning from Soerabaja, explaining that he was okay and expected to arrive back at the field by early evening. Gilmore soon reported in, too, favoring leg wounds from burns he had received when his ship had caught fire and that Dutch doctors had treated. But it was clear to squadron mate Bill Hennon and the others that "Gilly's nerves are shot" after his harrowing experience. "In fact, everybody is getting jumpy," Hennon wrote in his diary that evening in reflecting on the heavy losses they had sustained this day.[55]

BACK IN DARWIN, in Berrimah Hospital, it was 2200 before the hospital's surgical staff finally were able to attend to John Glover's wounds. Bob McMahon was there, too, waiting for the surgeons to treat his leg wound after having been brought in by Australian soldiers. It was about 0200 when the surgical team—all men stripped to the waist—gave him anesthesia and treated the wound during a twenty- to thirty-minute operation.[56] Also brought to the hospital after his emergency landing that morning, Bill Walker required treatment for the bullet wound in his left shoulder. He had managed to taxi his P-40E No. 46 to the tarmac in front of No. 12 hangar and had been helped out of his ship before it was destroyed by strafing Zeros.[57]

More fortunate than the 33rd's pilots this day, Vern Head, Pete Childress, and the other Timor crash survivors of Mahony's 3rd Pursuit had been driven in the evening by truck to Batchelor Field, where a C-53 was waiting to evacuate them back to Amberley. At 0300 they boarded the transport for the flight to the southeast. The most senior of their group, Tom Christian and Al Strauss, were at the controls of the transport. All were relieved to be escaping the nightmare of Darwin.[58]

But Bob Oestreicher was still at the RAAF field. With the help of some remaining 33rd Pursuit mechanics, he was trying to put a new wheel and tire on his P-40 to replace those shredded by a Zero's cannon shell. The job completed, he turned in for a few hours of sleep. He would be taking off at dawn for Daly Waters, beyond the range of the Japanese, as ordered by Captain Connelly.[59]

CHAPTER ELEVEN

"He Was Wholly Unrecognizable"

ON THE ROAD BETWEEN Maylands civil airdrome and Perth's port of Fremantle, 1st Lt. Robert Morrissey was supervising a strange procession during the wee hours of Friday, February 20. Flatbed trucks were slowly towing thirty-two P-40Es by their tail wheels over the twenty miles that separated the airfield from the port. Lt. Gerry Dix and the other intended pilots of the pursuit planes were driving the 6x6 flatbed Aussie trucks, while ground crewmen from the 51st Pursuit Group were riding on the tailgates to ensure that the tie-downs held. There were no obstructions on either side of the road to block their movement. The only possible impediment, large trees in the residential area of Perth, had been furtively chopped down at midnight.[1]

Moored at the Fremantle dock astern of the U.S. cruiser *Phoenix,* where it had arrived on the afternoon of the nineteenth, the old former aircraft carrier USS *Langley*—now a seaplane tender—was ready to take aboard the P-40s and their thirty-three pilots for the trip to Java. Also waiting to go aboard were twelve crew chiefs selected for the voyage from the 51st Pursuit Group's men who had arrived at Fremantle the day before on the USAT *Holbrook* and the Australian troopship SS *Duntroon* as part of the MS-5 convoy from Melbourne.[2]

For the next five and a half hours the *Langley*'s air officer supervised the hoisting aboard of the P-40s, using special slings the *Langley* was carrying for that purpose. To his relief the whole operation went off without a hitch. On the cut-back flight deck, now reduced to fifty-nine percent of its original length, twenty-seven of the P-40s were spread out, while the remaining five were positioned on the quarterdeck, below the flight deck, along with barrels of gasoline.[3]

After the planes had been loaded, the thirty-three pilots—including Joe Martin, whose ship had been wrecked at Maylands but who wanted to go to Java anyway as a spare—boarded the seaplane tender. The twelve enlisted men of the 51st Group boarded as well, but shortly after they settled in they were recalled by the 51st Group's CO, and twelve others—a radio mechanic, a propeller specialist, and ten crew chiefs, drawn mainly from the 35th Group's Headquarters Squadron men on the *Duntroon*—were substituted for them. "See you in Java!" one of the twelve replacements called out to his 35th Group buddies on the *Duntroon* as he prepared to board the *Langley*. The *Duntroon* men were envious, wishing they had been picked to travel to Java on the U.S. Navy ship, with its great meals, rather than on an Australian transport.[4]

When the loading of men and machines was completed, the *Langley*'s skipper, Cdr. Robert P. McConnell, invited Morrissey and Capt. Boyd "Buzz" Wagner, commanding officer of the 13th Pursuit Squadron (Provisional), to join him for breakfast, along with some of the pilots. Morrissey and Wagner were toying with the idea of remaining on the *Langley* for its voyage to Java, but a message arrived ordering them to report back. (Later, when Morrissey returned to his Perth hotel room, he was confronted by the irate owners of the trees he'd ordered chopped down. They rejected his promises to seek compensation for them from USAFIA headquarters and finally left only when he persisted in arguing that there was nothing else he could do.)[5]

BEFORE DAYBREAK ON FRIDAY, February 20, crew chiefs at Ngoro Field were busy hooking drop tanks on the bellies of sixteen of their P-40s on the line. The 17th Pursuit was being ordered to fly down to Singosari to link up with seven A-24 dive bombers and three LB-30s for an attack on the Japanese invasion force that had landed off the southern coast of Bali the day before. Bud Sprague himself at the head of the first flight would be leading the formation, with Grant Mahony, Walt Coss, and Joe Kruzel heading up the other three flights of four ships each. Just the day before, Sprague had been promoted to lieutenant colonel.[6] At the order for takeoff, the sixteen pilots climbed into their P-40s parked at the east end of the main, east-west, runway. Sprague wanted each pilot to take off individually in rapid succession so that the P-40s could be formed up in the air with a minimum of maneuvering. The timing for their rendezvous with the A-24s and LB-30s over Singosari Field would be critical.[7]

Fifteen of the Allison engines started immediately, but that of Walt Coss's ship refused to turn over. Abandoning the balky aircraft, Coss ran and climbed into a spare P-40 on the field. Its engine started right up. Only a few minutes were lost in the timing of the takeoff. Between 0615 and 0630, the sixteen

P-40s thundered down the runway towards the west, formed up on a turn to the southeast, and climbed away on that heading. With Bud Sprague navigating for the formation, all four flights reached the rendezvous right on time, the A-24s below them waiting for their escort, each lugging a full bomb load.[8] The three LB-30s were below, too, circling over Singosari following their departure at 0615 from their field at Jogjakarta, 140 miles to the southwest. Observing from below, the 19th Group's officers and men were impressed with the perfect coordination and timing of the linkup.[9]

On this bright blue morning, Sprague led his brood out to sea past the island of Java on a southeasterly course at between twelve thousand and fourteen thousand feet. As they completed their two-hundred-mile flight to the south of Denpasar, on the southern tip of Bali, they turned north to approach Bali from the sea. There, Sprague formed the four flights in a large box at fifteen thousand feet, a flight of four P-40s in each corner. Coss took the right front corner, Mahony the left rear, and Kruzel the right rear, with Sprague on the left front. They could see Denpasar Airfield off to the left and Japanese ships milling around in the harbor off of Sanur, on the southeast tip of Bali. There were at least six vessels in the Lombok Strait and barges along the shore. Directly below their P-40s they could make out the three LB-30s, and underneath them, the A-24s moving about. It was shortly after 0800.[10]

Suddenly, Ed Gilmore, behind Coss's flight, yelled "Zeros!" over the radio and called for them to break to the right. He was the first to spot the Japanese above in their dive. Responding instantly, Coss led his flight in a hard right turn as the Zeros pounced on them. He was not hit in the diving pass, but Tommy Hayes in his flight was less fortunate.[11] Watching the A-24s going into their dives at 0812, Hayes had heard "Break—Zeros on your tail—break left!" Kicking his P-40 hard left, Hayes looked behind and saw balls of cannon fire from a diving Zero streaking toward him. The 20 mm shells crashed into his fuselage and tail, ripping up his elevator. Hayes headed straight down, desperately trying to evade his pursuer. On leveling out, he was relieved to find the Japanese was nowhere in sight.[12] Now Hayes's main concern was to get home. As he headed west for Java's coast, struggling to hold excessive rudder, he feared his damaged ship would not keep flying or that he wouldn't have enough gas remaining to get back to Ngoro Field. He knew he would have to crash-land rather than bail out: a 20 mm shell had dislodged the canopy off its track, preventing him from cranking it open.

After Joe Kruzel led his flight in a dive away from the Zeros, he spotted one by itself under attack from three P-40s. As the Japanese climbed for a steep turn to evade his pursuers, he presented a perfect target for Kruzel. A long burst from his six .50s sent the Zero crashing into the sea.[13]

In his own corner of the action, B. J. Oliver had been observing the white circles of water below created by the near misses of the dive bombers. He saw no large plumes of smoke indicating a hit. Then he spotted two P-40s heading westward being pursued by a lone Zero.[14] With the advantage of a few thousand feet in altitude, Oliver followed in a slow descent after the Zero. But when he had narrowed the distance between them, he was startled to see the Japanese pilot pull up in a steep climb and for a moment hang before Oliver as if in slow motion. His gunsight centered on the Zero's cowling, Oliver opened up with a medium-length burst. To his surprise the Zero didn't explode. Turning to avoid a collision, Oliver set course for Ngoro, not looking back even once.[15]

While Bill Hennon's wingman, Spence Johnson, was watching the bombs from the A-24s falling, he spotted a lone Zero above him. He started after the Japanese, but suddenly there were now several of them after him instead. In the brief encounter the Zeros "shot hell" out of his P-40. Johnson feared he would crash on Bali in the midst of the newly landed Japanese troops. He decided to set course for the west towards Java, hoping he could make it back to the base.[16]

Ed Kiser and his wingman, Winfred "Bill" Gallienne, were also heading back to Java from Bali, having escaped the attention of the Zeros. Suddenly Kiser heard cannon fire. Looking up, he was shocked to see Gallienne's P-40 heading down in flames, but he couldn't tell whether Bill had bailed out.[17] Gallienne had forgotten to jettison his drop tank upon entering combat with the Zeros, and one of them had put a 20 mm shell through it, exploding the nearly empty, vapor-filled tank and setting the P-40 afire. His face badly burned in the conflagration in the cockpit, Gallienne managed to bail out and landed in fairly shallow water.[18]

In the meantime, Walt Coss had found the sky around him clear of all aircraft after having dived away from the Zeros in their initial pass. Looking down from his altitude of about eight thousand feet, he could clearly make out the airfield at Denpasar to the west. He knew it was now occupied by the Japanese and figured it would make a good target for a strafing attack. Shifting his position to have the sun at his back, Coss went into a dive, heading for the airfield. But as he approached, he could see that the field was empty of aircraft except for a single Zero parked outside the main hangar. Down to fifty feet, Coss gave it a long burst from all six guns.[19]

With no more targets of opportunity around, Coss set course for the return trip to Ngoro. Flying westward at one thousand feet above the Bali Strait, he noticed that another P-40 was joining up with him. As the two ships neared each other, Coss could see that the pilot was Bill Stauter. Using hand signals,

Stauter was trying to indicate that he was worried that he would not have enough fuel to make it back to Ngoro. When the two made landfall on the eastern tip of Java, Coss watched as Stauter headed north, up to the Java coast. It was about 1030 when Coss came within view of Ngoro Field, his fuel tanks nearly empty. As he made his landing approach, he noticed a wrecked P-40 on the east end of the main runway. "Whose ship is that?" he wondered.[20]

Earlier, Butch Hague had witnessed the pilot's crash and had run out to the site, expecting to find the flier dead from such a horrendous crackup. The canopy was closed, and blood all over it "almost made it opaque." Hague and another who had rushed to the wreck clawed at the canopy, trying to slide it open, but it was stuck, evidently from a cannon shell hit. Then Hague threw the emergency release, and his assistant on the other side lifted the canopy off. They recognized the semiconscious pilot as Tommy Hayes and helped him out of the cockpit. He had a bad cut on the left side of his head but otherwise seemed uninjured. He was put in a jeep that was waiting at the site and taken to a Dutch first aid station at the field. Examining the wreck of the P-40, Hague was upset to find that it was his own ship, *Colleen*, with the name painted on the left side of the fuselage.[21]

Back at the operations shack after his uneventful landing, Coss joined those who had returned from the mission before him. It soon became clear as the minutes ticked by—and with fuel supplies certainly exhausted—that only eleven of the sixteen who had taken off had made it back, including Hayes. Two of the missing, Spence Johnson and Bill Stauter, were believed to have made belly landings on Java, and another, Paul Gambonini, had been seen aborting the mission and heading back fifteen minutes before they reached Bali. Gallienne was known to have been shot down, but was he alive? Someone had seen a pilot bail out over sea about a mile off the shore of Bali and believed he was Gallienne. But the biggest concern was for their CO, Bud Sprague, whose fate was unknown. They feared he was lost in combat but hoped he was the parachutist who had been seen bailing out near the Bali coast.[22]

They had lost five of their P-40s. Had they made the Japanese pay for them? Reconstructing their combat experience over Bali, they believed they had definitely shot down three of the Zeros and probably one more. Joe Kruzel was being credited with one certain, and Bill Hennon claimed another. Like the others, Hennon had been jumped by the Zeros on arrival over Bali but had made a heads-on pass at one flying very low. Both ships were shot up in the firing exchange, but Hennon believed the Japanese pilot did not make it back to base. Wally Hoskyn also claimed to have shot down one of the Zeros.[23]

Walt Coss was amused to find that almost everyone, as well as himself, mentioned having fired at the Zero on the field. Only Grant Mahony, however, put in for its destruction. In describing the incident, Mahony told the others that he had almost been shot down from above in his strafing attack on the field. A Zero that he couldn't shake had latched onto his tail, so he had gone right down to the deck and headed north over Bali at maximum throttle. But the Zero pilot was staying right with him. Reaching a cliff at treetop level, Mahony dove down, made a sharp turn, and headed for home. The Japanese apparently missed Mahony's turn momentarily, allowing him to escape.[24]

AT 0910 THAT DAY, A CREWMAN aboard an eighty-three-foot, two-masted interisland schooner anchored in Rajeg Wesi Bay, on the southeast coast of Java, yelled, "Plane coming in!" Lt. Kemp Tolley, the thirty-three-year-old U.S. Navy commander of the schooner—the USS *Lanikai*—turned to watch a fighter plane come down to masthead level and run parallel to the shoreline, wheels up, then belly-land on the sand beach at the north shore of the bay.[25]

"What nationality is that plane? Tolley and his four crew members wondered. "Is the pilot okay?" What possibility is there for salvage?" Tolley ordered the crew to get underway for the crash site, where shortly afterwards he anchored the *Lanikai* about two hundred yards off the beach. Then Tolley, his pharmacist's mate, and two other crewmen carrying salvage equipment climbed in the schooner's dinghy and headed through the surf to the beach. As they neared the shore over waves built up by a stiff breeze, they saw that the pilot had climbed out of the plane, apparently unhurt, and was walking around waving his arms. A stream of English swear words reached their ears. "Boy, he sure cusses beautiful, don't you think, Captain?" Tolley's chief gunnery mate said to him. Nearby, the plane, which they identified as a P-40, was lying intact on its belly, its wings resting flat on the hard-packed sand.

Tolley and his crew disembarked from the dinghy carrying a tackle, wrenches, chisel, and hammers for possible salvage work and approached the pilot. He appeared to be on his guard, apparently believing they thought he was a Japanese and were "coming ashore to finish me off." But his suspicions were immediately allayed, and he introduced himself as Lt. Robert S. Johnson, U.S. Army Air Forces. In just five minutes Johnson vividly described his experience. He also volunteered his views on the Japanese, the performance of P-40s and Zeros, and the way the war was being run, using "adjectives that would have made any out-back Australian sheepman green with envy." There was nothing to stop the Japanese in the east, following their landing on Bali, he asserted. It became evident that when Johnson had been jumped by Zeros over Bali, he dropped his belly tank, as was the standard procedure when entering into combat. The only problem was that he had been flying on gas from his internal tanks instead of the drop tank and soon found his fuel supply rapidly reaching zero. Hoping to get back to base before it ran out, he had put his P-40 in a long glide that carried him across Bali Strait to Rajeg Wesi Bay before his tanks ran dry.[26]

An inspection of the P-40 revealed only a few bullet holes from the combat plus some small dents from the wheels-up landing. Tolley's men, aided by natives who had turned up, tried to move the P-40 off the beach to higher ground, using the tackle secured to a tree, but it proved impossible to budge. Then they worked with hammers and chisels to cut through the wing's tough aluminum alloy skin to get at the guns, which Tolley wanted to mount on the *Lanikai,* but were not meeting with any success. The only items of significance they could salvage were eight hundred rounds of "shiny .50 caliber ammunition." It appeared that Johnson had not fired many rounds in his combat with the Zeros.[27] As the hours passed, they could hear the sounds of heavy explosions to the east, obviously emanating from Bali. But now the tide was rising, threatening to engulf the P-40. Continued efforts to salvage additional equipment were proving impossible.[28]

BACK AT DARWIN IT WAS EARLY morning when Bill Walker, wandering in the hall of Berrimah Army General Hospital, suddenly yelled a loud greeting and exclaimed, "My God, here comes another one!" There, at the entrance to the hospital's hall, stood fellow 33rd Pursuiter Max Wiecks, a dazed, semi-fixed smile on his face. To Bob McMahon he looked "like a skinny, semi-drowned rat." Shivering, smiling, and shaking hands with Walker, McMahon, and Glover, he appeared to be suffering from "hypothermia, shock, or both." His face and hands were burned, evidently from excessive exposure to the sun.[29] The hospital staff took off Wiecks's soaked flying suit and found that he had a cut on his leg that would need treating. They wrapped him in blankets, then put him on a cot near the door. He dozed off, as did his other three 33rd Pursuit comrades.

When they all awoke about 1030, they began exchanging stories of their experiences the day before. Still groggy, Wiecks was the slowest to respond. After describing the circumstances of being shot down, he described his ordeal of over twelve hours in the Timor Sea north of Darwin. He had been so far out and low in the water in his mae west that he couldn't see land, but high-flying twin-engine Japanese bombers overhead that he assumed were heading for Darwin gave him orientation. Soon he saw smoke rising, confirming his supposition, and he began swimming in that direction, but he soon became tired and realized that he wasn't making any progress because of the tide going out against him. He gave up and just floated in his mae west instead, all the while "sweating out sharks."[30]

Some hours later, Wiecks rose up in the water and sighted land in the distance. Encouraged, he began swimming again but found he was making little progress. It was now getting dark, but the moon overhead was shining brightly. Finally, he saw something sticking out of the water: a clump of five little trees. Wiecks swam towards them and caught hold of one—a little mangrove—and climbed up into it. After hooking his legs over two limbs and wrapping the belt of his flying suit around a branch, he dropped off to sleep, totally exhausted. However, painful cramps kept waking him up and interrupting his slumber.

As it began to get light, Wiecks noticed that the tide had gone all the way out, exposing rocks. Figuring he was now only some one hundred yards short of the shore, he began walking along a path made by the rocks and reached the shore, where he collapsed on a rock. After resting, he began walking again over the rocks and coral of the shore but found it "difficult going"; he was barefoot, having earlier pulled off his shoes while trying to swim. After hiking along the shore for a mile or so, Wiecks ran into an Aussie patrol. Thinking he was Japanese, the Australian soldiers were just getting ready to fire on him when they realized they had misidentified him. They lifted him up and carried him to their camp, where he was given some hot food. He was then taken to a nearby hospital and afterwards transported to Berrimah Hospital.

A fifth survivor of their squadron had now showed up at the hospital. Burt Rice's story was somewhat similar to that of Wiecks. After recovering from his parachute landing in mangrove trees about ten miles east of the RAAF airdrome, he had spent the night sleeping in a tree to avoid the crocodiles in the crash area. In the morning, as he was walking along the edge of the mangrove bushes that lined the Howard River, he was spotted from their emplacement by two members of the 19th Light Machine Gun Regiment. As he appeared almost opposite the gun position, one of the Australians yelled "Jap" and was about to fire when Rice yelled back, "No, American!" He was told to walk north along the river for about fifty or a hundred yards to a point where it was shallow enough to wade across and link up with the Australians. They would provide him protection from the crocodiles in the river with their guns. He was taken to the campsite of the Australians, near their machine gun position, and given a cup of tea after informing their commanding officer of his name and serial number. After asking to be returned to his unit, Rice left with the commander and was eventually taken to Berrimah for treatment of his severe eye wound.[31]

But what had happened to the other five of their flight of ten the day before? they wondered. They had heard that Oestreicher had survived without being shot down, but Wiecks and Walker, who had been patrolling with him, did not see Oestreicher again after he had dived away from them and yelled "Zeros" on the radio. Wiecks told them that he had seen what he believed was Peres's P-40 going down when chased by a Zero, but he didn't know what had happened to his wingman, Perry. Neither had been brought in to the hospital, so they assumed both were dead. They had heard that Hughes had been killed in taking off, but his body had not been brought in.[32] But their commanding officer was there, in the rear of the hospital, covered with a sheet. McMahon had made his way on crutches to view the body, lying with about six or seven others who appeared to be RAAF. He identified Pell but didn't want to remove the sheet over him.[33]

The hospital staff asked their five wounded American airmen patients if they wished to be evacuated on the Australian hospital ship *Manunda,* which was set to leave Darwin later in the day. Walker, Rice, Wiecks, and Glover answered in the affirmative and paired up to go. Glover's facial wound had been stitched well enough for him to be in adequate enough condition to go out on the hospital ship. He was in a good mood—both his treasured wristwatches lost in his crash had been recovered and returned to him that morning.[34]

Despite being on crutches, McMahon opted to stay behind. Shorty Wheless had offered to pick him up and take him to the hospital at Bachelor Field to the south. When Wheless arrived at the hospital, McMahon bid goodbye to the others and climbed into the jeep. After McMahon braced himself in the jeep with his crutches, Wheless set out on the south road to Batchelor. Twenty minutes later, McMahon dozed off. It was two and a half hours later before Wheless reached the small hospital at Batchelor, where McMahon checked in. Although his right leg was throbbing, he felt rested. He had had more sleep than during the last two nights.[35]

BACK AT NGORO FIELD that afternoon, the mood was somber. Bill Stauter had reported in by telephone from the hospital in Malang, where he had been taken after crash-landing on a beach in northeast Java. But there was still no word from Spence Johnson, though they believed he was all right. By 1600 there was still no news of Sprague and Gallienne, either. The 17th Pursuiters feared the worst.[36] But their attention returned to the war at hand when shortly before 1600 a call came in from Soerabaja. The Air Defense Command was reporting nine planes high over Malang. The ADC had earlier mistaken them for P-40s, but now they were identified as Japanese. Four flights of sixteen P-40s scrambled for an interception, but when the pilots returned through a rainstorm raging over the area, they reported having failed to find

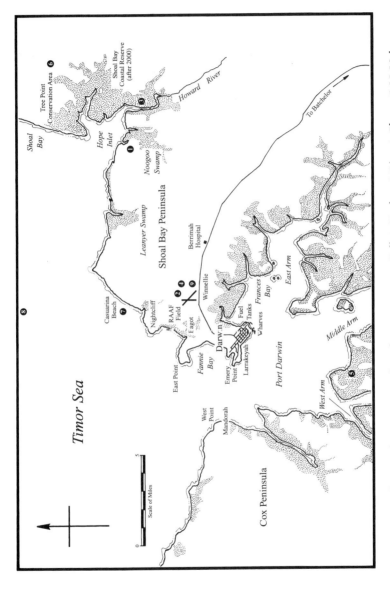

Locations of Downed P-40s at Darwin, February 19, 1942. 1, Pell; 2, Hughes; 3, Rice; 4, Glover; 5, McMahon; 6, Peres; 7, Perry; 8, Wiecks; 9, Walker (strafed on ground). *Locations courtesy Shane Johnston.*

them.[37] When they returned to base, they found Paul Gambonini back from his aborted Bali flight. He had "staggered" in to the bomber field at Singosari with a malfunctioning propeller and had had it fixed there. It turned out that just after he took off from Singosari to return to Ngoro, the Zeros had arrived over the field. The pursuiters heard that about five of the B-17s on the ground had been destroyed.[38]

It now definitely looked like their CO was not going to be coming back. The loss of their twenty-eight-year-old commanding officer hit the 17th Pursuit pilots hard. Butch Hague remembered Sprague, "with his big, boyish grin," as "the most eager man among us, always cussin' because he couldn't contact more Japs." He was held in esteem by his pilots for his leadership qualities, and they recalled his concern for their welfare, so evident in his informal get-togethers with them several times a week. Sprague emphasized that should the Japanese reach Java, "we'll fight as long as we can, but if things get hot, we'll leave with three days' start."[39] With the Japanese occupation of Bali and Koepang that broke the link of landing fields for flights from Darwin to Ngoro, the 17th Pursuit pilots knew they could expect no further replacements of planes and pilots. "Everyone resigned themselves to the fact that we were a token force for the Dutch and that we would probably not get out," Les Johnsen wrote in his diary that evening. With their commander now gone went his assurances of evacuation. There were no arrangements for their escape from Java that they knew of. Now they "would only plan from hour to hour, not knowing if we would be alive to the next hour," Johnsen recorded.[40]

ON THE BEACH OF RAJEG WESI BAY, the tide was going out in early evening, fully exposing Spence Johnson's wrecked P-40. To Lt. Kemp Tolley and his four crewmen it looked useless to continue to try to salvage any other equipment from the ship. Johnson reluctantly gave them permission to pour the remaining gasoline from his fuselage tanks over the cockpit and set the plane afire so as to leave nothing for the Japanese. It was 1910 as flames engulfed his P-40. Tolley asked Johnson if he would like to join them on his schooner for his trip westward to Tjilatjap, south central Java, but Johnson indicated that he preferred to head back to his base by foot. As Tolley and his men reboarded their dinghy with the ammunition and a few salvaged items, they bid goodbye to their friend. Unknown to Johnson as he set out on his trek, Malang base was ninety miles away, and his Ngoro Field an additional thirty.[41]

THAT EVENING, NEAR THE SMALL village of Sampalan on the little island of Nusa Penida, across the Badoeng Strait from Bali, a Dutch navy seaman was resting after having swum ashore in the early hours of the morning from his sinking destroyer, *Piet Hein,* lost to a powerful Japanese naval force supporting the Bali landing. It was about midnight when natives approached him carrying the body of a pilot. Earlier, the seaman, Sgt. Christian Bram, recalled that while swimming to Nusa Penida he had seen three Japanese fighters overhead attacking a lone Allied fighter and shooting it down. "This must be the pilot of the fighter," he thought. To Bram, "he was wholly unrecognizable." The pilot's parachute was "covered with blood." Bram noted that he wore "a pair of green suede shoes with thick rubber soles." Looking in the pocket of the pilot's shirt, he found "a white bone knife with the inscription C. A. Sprague." The Dutch seaman assumed the dead pilot was an Australian, because his parachute, oxygen apparatus, and lifebelt were inscribed "RAAF."

With the help of natives, Bram buried the pilot in the cemetery on the beach near Sampalan village. He put some markings on the grave, indicating that the deceased was an Australian, but figured they would be erased over the years. Nearby, the charred remains of the pilot's plane lay scattered on the beach.[42]

CHAPTER TWELVE

"How Can We Operate against Such Odds?"

FROM 0500 ON SATURDAY, February 21, sixteen pilots were standing alert at Ngoro Field for a possible interception order from the Dutch Air Defense Command. At 0930 the order came through: a Japanese bomber force had been picked up heading for Soerabaja. With their commander lost the day before, Capt. Grant Mahony—the highest ranking of the remaining pursuiters—would be leading them off on the mission at the head of A flight, followed by Jack Dale leading B flight. Shortly afterwards, Walt Coss took off with his C flight, followed by Ed Kiser at the head of D flight.[1]

When A and B flights reached the Soerabaja area, they began patrolling at twenty-one thousand feet. Shortly afterwards, they spotted two formations of Betty bombers about fifty miles out to sea, but to George Parker in B flight they appeared to turn and head back north. With no interception possible, the eight pursuiters started heading back to their base. Suddenly, they were jumped by six Zeros from above that they had not seen earlier. Several of the Americans entered into dogfights with the Zeros but were forced to dive away. All escaped except for Mahony's wingman, George Hynes, who had been hit in the diving pass by the Zeros and was seen to crash on the beach.[2]

In the meantime, C and D flights had spotted the bombers as they were returning from their attack on Soerabaja harbor. In Coss's C flight, B. J. Oliver, Gene Wahl, and Wally Hoskyn went after a lone Betty they spotted heading northeast out over the Java Sea. After about a fifteen-minute chase, the Betty went into a shallow dive in an effort to outrun its pursuers. Oliver was now in the lead, with Wahl and Hoskyn about a half mile behind and a thousand feet higher. Oliver's first burst—a short one at twenty degrees deflection, appeared to be ineffective, so he positioned himself directly astern for

A P-40E coming in to land at Ngoro Field after a combat mission, late February 1942. *Courtesy Peg Baum Hague, from Jesse Hague film.*

a medium burst. Sighting along the top edge of the Betty's fuselage to allow for a slight drop in trajectory, Oliver fired again. He was disappointed to see that his tracers were flying where he had aimed instead of where he had intended.[3] Suddenly, his radio crackled; someone was yelling that his P-40 was smoking. Oliver couldn't see any smoke but feared his ship must have been hit by unseen Zeros that had dived on him. Wally Hoskyn *knew* that his P-40 had been hit; after his one diving pass on the Betty he cried out on the radio that his engine had been hit and that he would try to glide back to the Java coast and bail out.[4] Following the diving attack by the Zeros, C and D flights turned and headed back to Java and their Ngoro base. Fortunately, the Zeros did not give pursuit. As Wahl and Oliver reached the Java coast, they noticed Hoskyn's P-40 on the beach. It appeared to Oliver that he had attempted a wheels-down landing and had nosed over. Or had he bailed out as he said he would?[5]

After landing back at Ngoro between 1115 and 1130, the fourteen returned pilots expressed concern about the fate of their two comrades. No one was sure about Hynes, but they figured that Hoskyn was okay. He was seen to have had plenty of altitude when he began his glide back to land. But no one was prepared to go up immediately on another mission that the 17th had agreed to earlier: four P-40s to provide protection for B-17s expected back at

Singosari at 1200 after a bombing mission to Bali. There would not be enough time to take off and reach high altitude over Singosari Field by noon.[6]

The 17th Pursuit was becoming dispirited from the unrelenting and unequal combat with the Zeros. As Hubert Egenes, flying as element leader in B flight that day, wrote his best friend, "It's no fun when the Jap Zeros come at you. You wish mighty fast that you were thousands of miles away from that spot. And all this propaganda we get in the U.S! The Japs are super pilots, they must have thousands of airplanes, and their planes are the very best."[7] For George Parker it was the numbers they faced. Like the others, he knew they could expect no more planes or pilots with the fall of Bali and Timor, and they were now down to eighteen P-40s. "We are desperate. How can we operate against such odds?" he wrote in his diary that night.[8] Jim McAfee, the detached 27th Bomb Group pilot serving as administrative officer at Ngoro, shared Parker's feelings. "I have an awful feeling about Java," he wrote in his diary that day. "The Japs will certainly take a crack at it, and I know it'll fall flatter than a cake and twice as quick."[9]

ON BOARD THE USAT *Willard A. Holbrook* in Fremantle harbor on Sunday, February 22, Maj. Homer Sanders, commanding officer of the 51st Pursuit Group, was relieved when the *Holbrook*, carrying the officers and men of his Headquarters, 25th, and 26th Squadrons, finally began moving out at noon as part of a convoy designated MS-5. The afternoon before, it had looked as if they were finally off to Java when tugs moved into position, but at 1615 orders had come through to delay sailing until noon the following day. No reason was given to Sanders, but he suspected the 51st Group's transfer to Java was off.[10]

An Australian army band was playing on the dock as the convoy, headed up by the escorting cruiser USS *Phoenix*, proceeded out of the harbor at 1346, the melodies of "Beer Barrel Polka" and "Waltzing Matilda" reverberating in the ears of the passengers. As the *Langley* glided past the *Duntroon*, carrying Headquarters Squadron, 35th Group, and 16th Squadron, 51st Group—the band struck up "The Star Spangled Banner." The U.S. Air Force officers and men on the *Duntroon* emotionally watched as a thin line of the thirty-three U.S. Army pilots and twelve enlisted men on the *Langley* stood at attention on the flight deck while the national anthem was played.[11]

On the *Holbrook*, Major Sanders and his 51st Pursuit Group men were wondering about the significance of the Hawaiian "Farewell to Thee" now being played by the band. They felt in their case it was really meant. "There is no doubt but what we are sailing into most dangerous waters," Sanders wrote in his diary that day.[12]

Not all the men under Major Sanders's command were embarked on the

Holbrook and *Duntroon*. On board the U.S. freighter MS *Sea Witch*, which was carrying twenty-seven crated P-40Es of the 51st Group, were seventeen men of the 692nd Ordnance Company (Aviation Pursuit), attached to the group, under the command of Capt. G. S. Johnson. One of the men, Pfc. Charles W. Bowles, was unimpressed by the freighter's defensive armament: four .303-caliber World War I–era Vickers water-cooled machine guns mounted on swivels welded to the deck and bridge. Bowles noticed the nervousness of the *Sea Witch*'s civilian crew about leaving for Java with such inadequate firepower handled by inexperienced army recruits. As the *Sea Witch* cleared Fremantle harbor with the other ships of the MS-5 convoy, Bowles, like others in the convoy, was sure their trip was for a lost cause; Java surely would be falling to the Japanese, and very soon.[13]

BACK AT NGORO, FOUR P-40S of A flight had taken off at 0724 that morning with orders to cover Singosari Airfield. They were followed by B flight with four more at 0733 for another patrol, and finally C and D flights with eight more on yet another interception call. A flight arrived over Singosari and patrolled above overcast, which prevented the pursuiters from sighting a lone Zero below that was strafing the field and also firing on Hangar No. 3. Fortunately the Japanese did not do any damage.[14]

Not assigned to the interception flights this day, and given a twenty-four-hour leave, Paul Gambonini and his squadron mate George Parker slept in this morning, then took one of the squadron's cars for a trip to Soerabaja and a "pleasant relaxation" break from the dismal war situation in the Indies. During the drive they noticed air raid light alarm signals along the road and heard the familiar drumbeats of the natives. They stopped to watch "the show"; above them "some of the boys were playing around," but in their patrolling they did not seem to have found any Japanese to intercept.[15]

After arriving in Soerabaja and checking in at Hotel Brunet for a shared room, they found Ed Kiser and Bill Hennon there, too, also given twenty-four-hour leaves the day before after having flown the February 21 combat mission. The two Philippines buddies had gone on dates with two Dutch girls to a night club the evening before and now were heading back to Ngoro. For their evening, before turning in for the night, Gambonini and Parker settled for a good steak, ice cream, and other food items they hadn't seen since their arrival in Java.[16] Unknown to Gambonini and Parker, their squadron mate George Hynes was lying in a nearby Dutch hospital, where he had been taken after being removed from his wrecked P-40 on a northern Java beach. Badly wounded, the quiet, religious, twenty-three-year-old native of San Antonio, who usually carried rosary beads in his pocket, died during the day. The day before, during a visit to Soerabaja, Jim McAfee had been asked to identify the body of another of the 17th's pilots who had been shot down and was in the morgue. The pilot "looked horrible." McAfee recognized him as Chief Fields, shot down two days earlier. The 17th's administrative officer felt "real bad" after having identified Fields mainly by an American penny in his pocket.[17]

When Ed Kiser and Bill Hennon arrived back at the field at Ngoro in the afternoon, they were informed that the Japanese were reported to have flown several strafing missions on fields that day. In the morning a single Zero had come down over the auxiliary field at Pasirian to the southeast and had flamed one of the four old B-17Ds dispersed there, then in the afternoon six Zeros finished off the other three B-17Ds there as well as Fields's old P-40, still lying on the field after his crash-landing on February 11.[18] There was other distressing news. Wally Hoskyn's plane and body had been found on the beach where he had come down the day before. It appeared that he had decided to bail out instead of riding the plane in for a wheels-down landing. In the jump he apparently had hit the tail of his ship, since his parachute was not opened. Unlike in Fields's case, his body was not disfigured. Arrangements were made for his burial in a cemetery near Soerabaja.[19]

The day before his fatal February 21 flight, Hoskyn had asked his crew chief, Cpl. Fred Deyo, and his armorer, Cpl. Ken Perry, to paint *Stub and Lou* on his P-40. Unlike on other previous takeoffs, Hoskyn this time had forgotten to give his rounded thumb and forefinger signal to his line chief as he cleared the field. Since Bud Sprague had had a name painted on his P-40 before his fatal February 20 Bali mission, too, the superstitious ground crews of the 17th now were unwilling to paint names on any other of the squadron's ships.[20]

Kiser and Hennon were given a final bit of news. Major General Brereton at FEAF headquarters in Bandoeng had sent a signal to Ngoro Field that he was appointing Grant Mahony as the squadron's new commanding officer. The selection did not come as a surprise. Promoted to captain on February 4, Mahony was the ranking officer among the pilots and was highly admired for his aggressive flying abilities, a reputation gained during his Philippine days.[21]

AT 0940 THE FOLLOWING MONDAY, February 23, the call came in from the ADC for three flights of the 17th's P-40s to intercept Japanese approaching from the east. Bo McCallum led off his A flight, followed by Ed Kiser at the head of B flight, then Cy Blanton leading C flight.[22] As the twelve pilots approached Malang at twenty-two thousand feet, they spotted nine Bettys about two thousand feet below them, apparently heading for the 19th Bomb Group's base at Singosari. The Japanese bombers had an escort of nine Zeros higher up and behind them. Before the Zeros could intercept them, A flight's

McCallum, B. J. Oliver, and Ray Thompson dove down on the bombers in a firing pass, scoring hits.²³ B flight's Ed Kiser, with Bill Hennon and Hal Lund, also dove on the Bettys but were immediately pounced on by the Zeros. But the Japanese had not noticed the fourth member of B flight, Jim Morehead, who was lagging behind and below the others in a "dog of an old P-40." Unmolested, Morehead approached the Bettys at their own altitude. Not wanting to face the deadly 20 mm cannons in the tails of the bombers, he decided to fly ahead of the nine-ship formation and then turn into them at a forty-five-degree angle for a frontal attack. After completing his turn, Morehead fired a burst into the lead Betty of the second three-ship V. He "felt like a fool" when he saw his bullets falling behind the formation; he realized he was out of range and his lead was "in great error." Pulling the nose of his P-40 forward, he fired another burst; this time his tracers hit home. Then he pulled further forward, close to the lead Betty he was targeting, and saw that he was scoring more hits, including some on the left engine of the bomber. Dangerously close to his quarry, Morehead put his ship in a dive to avoid ramming it.²⁴

Morehead now prepared for his next firing pass. He was again planning to fly out in front of the Betty formation and then turn to make a head-on attack. But as he headed out to get into position, he spotted a Zero straight ahead, heading right for him. Reacting immediately, he decided to try to trick the Zero pilot by pretending to dive away, then he would turn back into the bombers before the Japanese pilot realized what he was up to. Morehead was determined to get in another firing pass, Zero or no Zero.²⁵ Doing a split ess that put the Zero pilot on his tail, Morehead then pulled back hard on the stick and brought his ship up under the Betty formation in a loop. He was now directly under a lead bomber in another of the three-ship formations. He fired his .50s into its belly at such short range that he "scared himself." Figuring that the Zeros would really be after him following this brazen attack, Morehead put his P-40 in a steep, screaming, dive, "skidding and yawing and jinking all the way to the ground," Zeros in hot pursuit.

As he broke his dive and leveled out, Morehead found his vision was obscured—his canopy had fogged over. Wondering if the Zeros were still after him, he rolled back the canopy, turned back and forth to clear his tail, and looked all around. There were no Zeros around. Directly below him he saw a large airfield. Since he was obviously nearly out of gas, he decided to land and get his ship refueled. Morehead put his "old dog" into a steep turn, lowered his landing gear, and came in to land without problem. As he taxied off the runway and headed his ship towards a big hangar that he noticed, he was puzzled; he could see no planes or people anywhere. But as he approached to within about thirty yards of the hangar, two soldiers suddenly rose up from foxholes, climbed out, and looked at him. It was then that Morehead realized that the field was under attack.

Morehead shut down his engine. When the prop stopped turning, one of the men yelled, "Can we help you, Lieutenant?" They wondered who the pilot was; he had no shirt on and was wearing only his helmet, goggles, and pants. They were taken aback when, "so mad he was bawling like a kid," he screamed that he wanted gas and ammunition to be able to go back up again.[26] Morehead asked where he was and what outfit the men were with. "Singosari Field, 19th Bomb Group," they replied. "Did you see the fight overhead?" Morehead asked them. Yes, they had. They had seen three P-40s tangling with Zeros, then diving away. Then a lone fighter had attacked the leaders of two of the three groups of three Bettys and one had crashed and the other gone down, trailing smoke. The whole flight of nine had dropped their bombs wide of the airfield in an open area. Morehead was elated to hear that his attacks had been successful and he had apparently caused the Bettys to jettison their bomb loads.[27]

One of the men guided Morehead as he taxied his ship over to an underground gasoline storage tank. After they filled his tanks, the two guided him back to the hangar. One of the men went into the hangar and brought out a belt of .50 caliber ammunition. As he opened Morehead's gun ports and loaded the bullets, he asked Morehead his name. His ship now regassed and rearmed, a calmed-down Morehead thanked his benefactors. He was touched when in turn they thanked him for his efforts that had saved the field from a bombing.[28]

One hour after he had touched down at Singosari Field, Morehead was up again. The Japanese were now long gone, so he headed northwest for Ngoro. Uncertain of his location, he had earlier asked for directions to get back to his base.[29] When Morehead identified the camouflaged field after the thirty-five-mile hop, he came in low. Just above the runway he went into a victory roll, then went around and did another. He knew that such antics had been strictly forbidden by Bud Sprague, but their old CO was no longer there to enforce his rules, and besides, he was very excited. Before his ship had stopped rolling, Morehead threw back the canopy, stood up in the cockpit, grinning, two fingers in the air, and yelled, "Hell, you guys are crazy! Those Japs can't shoot!" A check of his ship revealed he only had a single bullet hole, in his stabilizer.[30]

It was now after 1230. His squadron mates had been worried for Morehead when he failed to return with the others at 1130. After over an hour had gone by they figured he must have run out of gas by then and crashed somewhere.[31] Ed Kiser met with Morehead and the other two in his B flight for

Left to right: Jim Morehead, Roger Williams, Ben Irvin, and Frank Adkins awaiting a takeoff call at the north alert area, Ngoro Field, mid-February 1942. *Courtesy Louis Boise.*

their accounts of what had happened to them during the combat. Who had attacked the bombers? Morehead confirmed that he had, in two passes, and the others said they hadn't. Kiser told them that the Dutch had just reported that a bomber had crashed on Java. Morehead acknowledged that he hadn't seen any of the bombers he attacked actually crash, but he was given credit for the downed Betty based on the evidence.[32] Morehead's squadron mates were impressed with his fearless attack on the bombers. "Nice work for a day," Butch Hague wrote in his diary that night. However, he felt that "one day he'll get shot down playing like that." To Hague and the others who knew him best, Morehead was living up to his nickname of "Wild Man Morehead."[33]

AT NOON ON FEBRUARY 23 the USAT *Willard A. Holbrook* was 298 miles out of Fremantle, but Maj. Homer Sanders, CO of the 51st Pursuit Group, still had "no accurate knowledge as to where we are going." But he felt they were not heading for Java. The "popular rumor" was that their destination was Calcutta, India.[34] Sanders noted that the convoy was now down to five ships: his *Holbrook,* the Australian troopships *Duntroon* and *Katoomba,* the American freighter *Sea Witch,* and the escorting cruiser USS *Phoenix.* He had been informed that the *Langley* had left the convoy the night before. It was headed "to an unknown destination."[35]

On board the *Langley,* Gerry Dix and the other pilots found that they were now heading alone to Java, having hived off from the convoy the night before. Their leader, 1st Lt. Gerry Keenan, had called them together for a briefing by the captain of the *Langley,* Cmdr. Robert P. McConnell, on what he expected of them on their solitary run into Java. The *Langley*'s skipper was particularly concerned about maintaining complete darkness after dusk except in the wardroom and quarters area. Dix and the others felt it was unreasonable for him to forbid smoking on the deck.[36]

They were all looking forward to arriving in Tjilatjap so that they would have the opportunity to fly their aircraft in combat. Dix and the other less experienced pilots were feeling confident of their flying abilities after having successfully ferried their P-40s all the way across southern Australia to Perth despite the few hours' experience they had in the aircraft. However, some were concerned about the possibility of losing their planes on their arrival in Java to the more experienced, combat-tested pilots of the 17th Pursuit there. To improve their chances of keeping their aircraft on disembarking, they had stuffed their personal belongs and extra clothing into the compartments of their P-40s. In the meantime, the 33rd and 13th Pursuit (Provisional) pilots were getting to know each other better. Verne Augustine of the 13th was proving to be a real comedian, keeping them all laughing. Good rapport was also being developed with the ten crew chiefs on board, who were ensuring that the P-40s were in top shape during the voyage.[37]

AT 1700 IN THE AFTERNOON of February 23, with rain pouring down as usual, Grant Mahony called a meeting of his pilots in the operations shack of the 17th Pursuit at Ngoro Field. Orders had come in from Major Fisher in Soerabaja to send ten of the pilots and twenty enlisted men to an undisclosed destination, via Soerabaja. Newly promoted Capt. Walt Coss would be leading the group. Picked by Mahony to leave with Coss were Bill Turner, Jim Ryan, Elwin Jackson, B. J. Oliver, Jesse Hague, Dwight Muckley, George Parker, Cy Blanton, and Hubert Egenes.[38] "Where you guys are going, you're going to get a good deal," Mahony told them. There would be a "better set-up" there, "with more airplanes." "I'd like to go with you," their CO asserted. He told them to return to their quarters in Blimbing, collect their belongings, and be ready to leave for Soerabaja by squadron truck and car.[39]

At about 2000 the ten pilots and twenty crew chiefs and armorers piled into the waiting vehicles for the night trip to Soerabaja, where they were to catch a train very early the next morning for Jogjakarta. Sgt. Cecil Ingram bought some bananas to eat during the fifty-mile trip. Except when the staff car with Coss got separated temporarily from the trucks, the drive was uneventful.[40] As the vehicles slowly made their way through thunderstorms in the darkness of the Java countryside to Soerabaja, the subject of conversation was, "Where are we going?" From what Mahony had told them, Hague thought maybe Rangoon or Darwin. "Or perhaps they were putting planes together on Java somewhere," he wondered. But it seemed most likely to Hague that "we are gracefully evacuating Java," for without more P-40s "we aren't going to scare the Japs," he wrote in his diary.[41]

It was late in the evening before the caravan reached Soerabaja and their quarters for the night, a building for the Dutch military known as Singapore Way. Hungry after the long ride, Ingram and some of the other enlisted men went looking for a restaurant that was still open. They found a Dutch restaurant, but the waiter was very busy and couldn't speak English. A Dutch officer intervened for them, and they managed to get something to eat. Ingram didn't like it very much, but at least it was better than what they used to eating at Blimbing, in his view. When they all retired to their sleeping quarters in the building, they found that they had been given cots with flannel sheets and without mosquito bars. The aggressive flying insects and the high heat and humidity resulted in one of the most miserable nights Hague had ever experienced. Cy Blanton was in even more wretched condition, suffering from seven boils in his right armpit, one of which had broken a few days earlier. Assailed by the mosquitoes, he finally gave up and went out to one of the cars and used his cigarette lighter to rid it of mosquitoes, but after a while he had to lower the window to get fresh air.[42]

At 0400 they were awakened after only a few hours of fitful sleep and once again got in the cars and trucks, this time for the short trip through the city to the railway station, where they boarded the train for Jogjakarta for its 0600 departure. The Americans occupied the first-class section of the train, restricted to Caucasians, but they were jammed eight to a compartment; the other compartments were for just two and four persons. The natives were confined to other wagons. At breakfast, Hague and others sat with a white woman: "What an experience." Although a Dutch officer told Hague he wasn't allowed to take any pictures, he ignored the restriction and used his 8 mm movie camera to film chain-bound native prisoners in the wagon behind theirs. Ingram was glad to leave "the stink of the jungle" for the hills of Central Java, which was "beautiful country," he felt. Hague also enjoyed the view of terraced rice fields all around them. Ingram was amused to see the natives bathing themselves and their water buffalo in the rivers. All along the 180-mile, winding route, adults and children alike waved at them.[43]

After having passed through the East Java towns of Modjokerto, Kertosono, Nganjuk, and Madioen, the train reached Central Java, pulling into Soerakarta, then finally reaching the railway station at Jogjakarta at noon. To Ingram it was "the nicest place" he'd ever seen in Java. He and the enlisted men were taken to "beautiful barracks" in a house up on a high cliff overlooking a swift river, an active volcano in the distance. Coss and the other pilots were transported to officers' barracks in a former school and were given lunch. They spent the afternoon waiting for further orders. Coss went off to 7th Bomb Group headquarters to inform them of their arrival and make sure they knew where the 17th Pursuit personnel were located. He was told they were being administratively attached to the 7th Group for movement out of Java. Now Coss understood why they had been sent to Jogjakarta.[44]

While eating dinner, they were surprised to run into Tommy Hayes, Bill Stauter, and Gene Bound. Their injured comrades had arrived on a train— "a real creeper"—from Malang after being evacuated as invalids from the hospital there. Hayes's head was still wrapped in gauze, while it was evident to Hague that Bound "was not doing so well" with his dislocated shoulder. Stauter had his arm in a sling and one eye bandaged.[45]

By the end of the day, still no orders had come through for the 17th Pursuiters. Hayes, Stauter, and Bound knew that any orders for them would be for evacuation, as they were not on flying status. Hayes figured that all the officers and men, including them, would be going to Rangoon or back to Australia. But whether it was to the north or to the south, the whole group felt they would be leaving by boat rather than by air.[46]

CHAPTER THIRTEEN

"Every Day a Nightmare!"

IT WAS 0430 WHEN Paul Gambonini climbed out of bed in his house at Blimbing and with fifteen other pilots and their mechanics headed out in the dark for the field at Ngoro on this Tuesday, February 24, for yet another day of alert duty. This time he was assigned as an element leader in Jack Dale's C flight. Ed Kiser was to head up B flight, and Joe Kruzel D flight, while their CO, Grant Mahony would be leading A flight.[1] Not surprisingly, an interception order came through from the ADC, this time at 0915. Japanese bombers had been picked up heading west. The ADC was assuming that Soerabaja was the target again.

With Mahony in the lead, the pursuiters thundered down the field and headed northeast in a climb to meet their adversaries. As they approached the Soerabaja area at about 1000, flying at twenty-seven thousand feet, they spotted the Japanese in the distance; they looked like twenty-four Betty bombers in two waves. It appeared they had bombed Soerabaja harbor and were beginning to head home. The Americans took after them, but only the four in Kiser's flight were able to coax their struggling ships at such a high altitude to catch up with the speedy bombers. In firing passes, Kiser and Robert "Dock" Dockstader scored hits on the Bettys in one of the formations. But nine unseen Zeros were now after the Americans. Several of the P-40s were shot up before the four flights headed back to Ngoro.[2]

At about noon, all sixteen P-40s came in to land back at Ngoro Field without incident. Ed Kiser put in a claim for one of the bombers he believed had crashed into the ground, while the ADC reported seeing another fall into the sea, which the pursuiters thought was the one that Dockstader had attacked.

269

The pilots regarded themselves as lucky to have survived the attack by the Zeros. An inspection of their ships revealed that six were too badly damaged to take up again without repairs.[3] With no more P-40s expected as reinforcements, the ground crews were straining to keep their dwindling number of ships in airworthy condition. The Allison engines were wearing out, with too many hours on them, but there were no new motors available to replace them. The brakes were in bad condition, too, and the planes' tachometers gone or broken. The squadron's armorers were struggling with rust in their efforts to keep the .50-caliber wing guns in firing condition, yet often only half of them were working. Ammunition for the guns was running short, too, and they could not expect any additional supplies.[4]

That afternoon, the squadron got the news that they would be losing their new CO after only two days as head of the 17th. FEAF headquarters in Bandoeng had ordered him out to serve in a position directly under Major General Brereton in India. Mahony was going "to prepare the place for us," he told Bill Hennon and the others, but that was just Mahony's assumption. No official word was forthcoming on what their "secret destination" was. In addition, Maj. Bill Fisher in Soerabaja was ordering two more of the squadron pilots, plus twenty-five enlisted men, to depart as well, again to an unknown destination. In his last meeting with his pilots, Mahony picked Gene Wahl and Ray Thompson as the two to leave. Hennon refused to be considered for the evacuation. He had asked Mahony to let him stay to the last.[5]

Later in the afternoon, Mahony left with Wahl, Thompson, and the enlisted men for Soerabaja, where they were to board a train for Jogjakarta. Mahony's 40-A flying school classmate, Bo McCallum, was left in charge as the most senior officer remaining. McCallum had been promoted to captain five days earlier.[6] In charge of the enlisted men in the van taking them to Soerabaja was MSgt. Murray Nichols, the thirty-year-old armorer from Lubbock, Texas, whom Mahony had appointed as the squadron's first sergeant the day before. On arriving at the Soerabaja railway station, Nichols ran into Capt. Frank Kurtz, Colonel Eubank's liaison officer, whom he had known as a cadet at Randolph Field in 1938. At Kurtz's request, Nichols and the men helped some wounded sailors from the USS *Marblehead* get on the train to Jogjakarta.

Afterwards, Nichols's group boarded the wood-burning train. It proved to be quite an experience. Nichols recalled later that each time the underpowered "Toonerville Trolley" reached an incline, it came to a halt and the train crew would run along the corridors and yell something in Javanese. After the third occurrence, Nichols asked what the Javanese were yelling. He was informed they were saying, "First class passengers keep your seats, second

Gerald "Bo" McCallum in a jeep at Ngoro Field, February 1942. *Courtesy Joseph Kruzel via N. H. Blanton.*

class passengers get off, third class passengers get off and push." The Americans were not expected to get off or to push.[7]

BACK AT NGORO, THE MOOD among the remaining officers and men was not good. Like the others, Gambonini felt that "we are left here, holding the bag." They all knew that it was just a matter of a day or two before their secret field would be discovered by some Japanese pilot. In fact, some feared that it had already been spotted. Cpl. Ken Perry and other enlisted men had watched breathlessly one morning some days before as four Zeros came over the field and circled around it before finally heading back toward Soerabaja.[8]

Not only the remaining pilots and men of the 17th Pursuit, but also the three officers of the 27th Bomb Group assigned in administrative duties at the field were increasingly concerned about their fate. They could see that the pursuit pilots were being sent out—albeit piecemeal—but no provision was being made for their own evacuation. That afternoon they decided to take matters into their own hands. Jim McAfee drafted orders for the evacuation of Pete Bender, Bob Stafford, and himself and took them to Bo McCallum for his approval. McCallum signed them; he had no objection to their leaving if they could make it out somehow. Unknown to McCallum, they were pinning their hopes on leaving on the old C-53 transport still lying unrepaired on the field if they could get an elevator bar in Bandoeng to make it flyable.[9]

On the morning of the twenty-fifth, Paul Gambonini found himself again assigned with the alert group, once more under Jack Dale. But this time there were only twelve of them to stand alert. The squadron mechanics had managed to get a few more of their eight out-of-commission P-40s in flying condition early that morning, but only enough to equip three flights. In the event of an interception order, new squadron CO Bo McCallum would be leading A flight, with Ben Irvin as second element leader, while Gambonini again would be element leader in Dale's B flight. Newly returned Spence Johnson would be flying as Dale's wingman. Ed Kiser's C flight again had Bill Hennon assigned as element leader, with Frank Adkins flying Kiser's wing and Andy Reynolds on Hennon's. At 0930 the interception order came through from ADC. For the third day running, Japanese formations were reported heading for the Soerabaja area. In their patched-up P-40Es, the remnants of the 17th Pursuit Squadron (Provisional) roared off and headed east, McCallum in the lead.[10]

As they approached Soerabaja at twenty-six thousand feet, they spotted the bombers, twenty G4M1s in several formations, but they were above them, at twenty-seven thousand feet or higher. At about thirty thousand feet the ever-present escort Zeros—nine of them—were waiting for the Americans. "Much too high for us," Bill Hennon in C flight thought as he observed the bombers. Nevertheless, the pursuiters in the other two flights went after the bombers in a climb. However, as they were trying to reach the Bettys, six of the Zeros pounced on them from on high. Ben Irvin in McCallum's flight had seen them before they dived and dropped back to avoid their expected diving attack. The others in A and B flights tried to elude the Zeros by diving away, but in trying to cover the tail of one of those in his flight, McCallum took hits. His engine smoking, he was seen to bail out. Jack Dale at the head of B flight nearly met a similar fate when he "almost got his ass shot off" as he was jumped by two of the Zeros at fifty feet over treetops after pulling out of his dive. But Ben Irvin, down low with Dale too, managed to get in hits on one of the Zeros and believed he had downed it.[11] When the Zeros went down after the diving P-40s of A and B flights, Ed Kiser's C flight found itself in a position to dive in turn on the Japanese. With Kiser giving the signals, Adkins, Hennon, and Reynolds followed their leader down. Catching the Zero pilots off guard, Hennon and Reynolds each managed to get in firing passes at a Zero.[12]

Two hours after takeoff, the eleven survivors began trickling in to the field. They were all hoping that popular Bo McCallum was all right after bailing out. But the Japanese had paid for their lone victory: Irvin, Hennon, and Reynolds were believed to have downed a Zero each.[13]

The day's work was not over for Kiser and Hennon, however. ADC wanted a recon mission flown out over Bawean Island in the Java Sea, one hundred miles due north of Soerabaja, to investigate a report of a Japanese invasion fleet approaching Java. The two took off at 1600. Over Bawean, they could seen no sign of any ships at all and returned to the base at 1800.[14] Later that afternoon the pilots and men of the squadron watched as three barrellike Brewster Buffaloes came in to land at the field. The ADC had informed them earlier that the Dutch Brewsters would be arriving to work with the 17th, with four more to be expected the following day. Lt. H. H. J. Simons climbed out of his lead ship and introduced himself and the other pilots—Ensign B. Wink and Sgt. G. van Haarlem—to Kiser and the others.[15] But the 17th Pursuit was not encouraged by the additional support. They were feeling too demoralized about their situation. Even the birthday party for Bob McWherter that day was "a little celebrated event." Like the others, McWherter just "gave thanks to God for sparing me this far.[16]

However, God had not spared Bo McCallum. Major Fisher at ADC called Ngoro with the bad news. McCallum's body had been found, machine-gunned in his chute. There were thirty holes in his chute, and he had been hit twice in his heart and twice in the head.[17]

AT JOGJAKARTA ON THE MORNING of February 25, George Parker and the other 17th Pursuit evacuee pilots were surprised to see squadron mates Gene Wahl, Ray Thompson, and Grant Mahony. The three, and the twenty-five enlisted men of the squadron with them, had just arrived on the train from Soerabaja. The new arrivals told Parker and the others that they expected the remaining personnel would be following soon. Mahony explained that he would not be going out with them; he was to leave for India to join Major General Brereton. He'd missed Brereton's flight to Colombo, Ceylon, from Jogjakarta the night before but would be going out on another LB-30 bomber that evening to link up with the general. Mahony's restless squadron mates still didn't know their destination, though. They spent the day in town, "stewing about, wondering what we were about to do." One of the squad-

Capt. Grant Mahony on arrival in Colombo, Ceylon, February 26, 1942, after being relieved as commanding officer of the 17th Pursuit Squadron (Provisional) two days earlier to serve on Major General Brereton's staff in India. *Author's collection.*

ron's armorers evacuated the day before, Sgt. Lewis McNeil, spotted Mahony across the street and yelled a greeting to him. To McNeil and the other men who talked to him that day, the usually vibrant Mahony had "the darkest, tiredest eyes, with deep rings under them."[18]

The town was crawling with Army Air Forces enlisted men waiting for evacuation. To George Parker it seemed that bombardment squadron personnel were coming into Jogjakarta "every hour." Unknown to Parker, the entire ground echelon of the 19th Bomb Group and some of its combat crews had arrived from Malang unexpectedly the afternoon before and were creating a serious housing and messing problem for the resident 7th Group.[19]

Despite being constrained by his dislocated shoulder, Gene Bound paid a visit on his old flying school friend, 2nd Lt. Vic Poncik, one of the pilots of the 7th Group's 11th Bombardment Squadron based in Jogjakarta. To Poncik, Bound "looked a bedraggled, dirty mess" following his rail trip the day before, having sat in the third-class section of the soot-belching train. Bound explained that he had lost all his clothing except for what he was wearing in the evacuation from Malang. Poncik took him to his barracks, where he loaned him a razor and towel and told him to take a bath. Afterwards, Poncik fitted Bound with a clean suntan uniform of his own. Bound now felt ready for his impending evacuation trip.[20]

That evening, Mahony was down at the Jogjakarta airfield, waiting for a lift to India. Brereton's chief of staff, Brig. Gen. Earl Naiden, was there, too, arranging for Mahony to join his new boss. An LB-30 bomber was on the field preparing to take off, and Naiden told Mahony to get on board. Entering the cabin, Mahony was surprised to find a distinguished-looking, white-haired gentleman already seated, along with a British major. The pilot, Capt. Horace Wade of the 11th Bomb Squadron, informed Mahony that the important-looking gentleman was none other than the British commander of just-dissolved ABDACOM, Field Marshal Sir Archibald Wavell, evacuating with the members of his staff and Naiden to India.[21] Following their arrival at Jogjakarta from ABDACOM headquarters in Bandoeng, Wavell and Naiden had commandeered Wade's ship just as he had been preparing to depart on a flight to Australia. *Minnie from Trinidad* was loaded with Wavell's personal effects, which its radio operator–gunner Pfc. John Laurie noticed included two cases of whiskey and golf clubs. Wade had been obliged to lighten the load by leaving his bombardier behind. At 2215 Wade lifted *Minnie* into the night sky and turned to the northwest for the long flight to Ceylon.[22]

George Parker and the other 17th personnel had heard rumors that afternoon that they would be leaving this night, too, for evacuation from the port city of Tjilatjap by ship. However, when official word came down, only the injured Hayes, Stauter, and Bound, plus all but twelve of the squadron's enlisted men who had arrived at Jogjakarta so far, were selected for the sea journey to an undisclosed destination.[23] In the middle of the night, the evacuee group was driven to the Jogjakarta railway station, and at 0300 they joined many bomb group men to board the train for Tjilatjap, the southern Java port city ninety miles to the west. Hayes and Bound were disappointed to find that it was the same kind of soot-discharging train that had brought them to Jogjakarta earlier, and they were again seated in the jammed third-class section. So much for getting a clean uniform from Poncik, Bound lamented.[24]

ONLY TWELVE PILOTS—including the three Dutchmen in the Brewsters—were on alert at Ngoro Field on the early morning of Thursday, February 26. After the loss of McCallum and his ship the day before, the 17th Pursuit was down to seventeen P-40s, and only fourteen were in commission. Ed Kiser was now acting as squadron commander, with fellow 40-H flying school comrades Jack Dale and Joe Kruzel as the other two flight leaders.[25] The alert pilots were not surprised when the call came through from the ADC at 0930 again; once more the Japanese were heading in force for yet another bombing attack on Soerabaja. Within minutes they were airborne, Kiser at the head of the formation. As they approached Soerabaja in overcast skies at twenty-six thousand feet, they found the Betty bombers—twenty-six of them—high up, at between twenty-seven thousand and thirty thousand feet, as the day before. And once again the pursuiters were unable to pull their worn-out ships above twenty-six thousand to reach them, nor could the Dutch in their Brewsters. But the heavy cloud cover proved an effective defense: the Bettys were dropping their bombs from high altitude ineffectively, almost all of them falling into the water, none hitting any of the warships of the Combined Striking Force in Soerabaja harbor.[26]

Suddenly, the Allied pilots were bounced by escorting Zeros flying at twenty-seven thousand feet—eight of them this time—but dived away without suffering any losses. As the Zeros began returning to their base at Denpasar, Hennon spotted two of them flying along to the east at fifteen thousand feet. Ever ready for a fight, Hennon went after them and approached the Japanese unseen from the rear. Coming so close to one that he almost rammed it, Hennon pushed the trigger switch, but his guns "didn't work well." Still he saw the Zero heading down after taking some hits. The other Zero pilot continued speeding away.[27]

After landing back at Ngoro at 1115, the pursuiters shared impressions of the mission before the lunch truck appeared on the field. They were all sure that Hennon had gotten a Zero, his latest victory.[28]

But how long could they keep this up? Spence Johnson was particularly dispirited. "Every day a nightmare!" he inscribed in his diary that day. "More raids, more Japs, never ceasing air raids and the native tom-toms which forecast their arrival. Half our outfit left or killed and no planes coming. We are encircled and terribly outnumbered!" It didn't help the pilots' morale when an order came in from Colonel Eubank that day ordering the remaining 17th Pursuiters to "fight to the last plane"—and that "while he sits downtown in Soerabaja," Johnson bitterly noted in his diary. This was the same Colonel Eubank whose command had called earlier and asked for P-40 protection as it moved its B-17s and headquarters to Jogjakarta. The ADC turned down the request; too few P-40s remained for such a purpose.[29]

In Soerabaja, Frank Kurtz was worrying about his friend Jack Dale and the others of the 17th Pursuit. Colonel Eubank had made no provision for the evacuation of the remaining pilots and enlisted men of the squadron, although he was the ranking U.S. Army Air Force officer on Java following Brereton's departure two days earlier. To the contrary, the day before he had ordered, "Pursuit pilots not to be moved."[30] Eubank was visiting Soerabaja on the twenty-sixth and met with Kurtz to ask his liaison officer to join him immediately in Jogjakarta. Eubank was preoccupied with the question of moving his 5th Bomber Command from Malang to Jogjakarta in the rapidly deteriorating situation. But Kurtz requested that he be allowed to remain "a little longer" in Soerabaja. He told Eubank that he wanted to arrange for the evacuation of the 17th Pursuit, as "no one else was looking after them." Backing down on his position of the day before, Eubank accepted Kurtz's request. He could remain under his own orders as to how and when he himself would be evacuated.[31]

BACK AT NGORO, A MESSAGE came in at lunchtime on the twenty-sixth that stated that the 17th was going to get help after all in its last-ditch efforts to stave off the Japanese—not from the American command in Australia, but rather from Maj. Gen. L. H. van Oyen, the Dutch commander now in charge of all Java air operations. The ADC informed Kiser that four more Dutch Brewsters were going to arrive at Ngoro that day, as well as seven of its Hurricane fighters. At 1400 three Buffaloes touched down at Ngoro Field, piloted by Lt. G. J. de Haas, Ensign C. A. Vonck, and Sgt. Gerard Bruggink. A fourth Brewster had to return to Andir with an engine malfunction.[32]

But now it looked like they might be receiving P-40 reinforcements, too. Major Fisher at ADC had called and ordered six of the 17th's pilots to depart immediately for Soerabaja and on to Tjilatjap to pick up P-40s reportedly coming in on the seaplane tender *Langley*. But were they to lead the *Langley* P-40s to another field instead? Fisher was sending them to a "secret destination" without clarifying the instructions he had received. The Dutch liaison officer at Ngoro, Arie Geurtz, would accompany them to Soerabaja in the squadron's cars. Picked for the special duty were Ben Irvin, Bill Hennon, Jim Morehead, Robert Dockstader, Andy Reynolds, and Roger Williams.[33]

At about 1600, after the six had said goodbye to their comrades and got in the cars for the ride to Soerabaja, six Dutch Hurricanes approached Ngoro Field and came in to land. Ed Kiser, Jack Dale, Joe Kruzel, and Ed Gilmore warmly greeted the flight leader, Lt. Ricardo Anemaet, whom they had known from the 17th Pursuit's stay at Perak Field the last week of January. Anemaet introduced the other five from his 2-Vl.G.-IV squadron: 2nd Lt. A. J. Marinus, Sgt. Maj. P. Boonstoppel, and Sgts. F. J. De Wilde, H. J. Mulder, and A. Kok. Anemaet explained that the seventh Hurricane expected in had developed mechanical trouble and would be flown in as soon as it was repaired.[34] The Americans were surprised to find that these Hurricanes sported a different national insignia on their fuselages than the one they had seen at Perak Field on the Dutch Curtiss Wright CW-21B interceptors. The familiar black-bordered orange triangle had been painted over with a rectangular red, white-, and blue-striped Netherlands flag. The Dutchmen explained that the switch was made because the triangle had often been mistaken for the Japanese red-orange *hinomaru* marking.[35]

Ed Kiser called the new Brewster and Hurricane pilots together for a briefing. Anemaet translated into Dutch for them as Kiser described the situation in English. After the briefing the Dutchmen joined their new American comrades for the ride to Blimbing to settle in and for some socializing. Meeting around the "fish pond" that the sugar mill administrator Mr. Smit had dug for the purpose, they pulled out bottles of chilled Amstel beer and passed them around for a Dutch-American "happy hour."[36]

With the departure of Irvin's group to Tjilatjap, there were now almost as many Dutch pilots (twelve) at Ngoro as American (fourteen), and three more Hurricane pilots would be arriving later by car and train. In addition to the four original 17th Pursuiters—Kiser, Dale, Kruzel, and Gilmore—only Gambonini, Johnsen, Johnson, McWherter, Reagan, Adkins, Caldwell, Fuchs, and Lund remained. Lieutenant Lane was still there, too, but was not on flying duty. But the Hurricanes the Dutchmen flew in would not at present be adding to the air defense capabilities of the squadron's remaining twelve in-commission P-40s: they did not have the right crystals for their radios required for interception work. A supply of the essential components was to be flown in to Ngoro, Anemaet informed Kiser.[37]

ON A TRAIN THAT LEFT BANDOENG that morning at 0800, another 17th Pursuit pilot was heading for Tjilatjap, but not to join Irvin's group to meet the *Langley*. Lt. Frank Neri, along with other wounded airmen, was being sent for evacuation under the care of Capt. James Crane, the USAAF doctor who had been ordered the day before to close his dispensary at Lembang, where he had been treating Neri for his severed ear.[38] Packed in the train's end wagon that had been specially added to accommodate the fleeing Allies, Crane and a bandaged Neri were among a motley array of American officers and enlisted men who had been based at FEAF headquarters. They and all their earthly possessions were now piled high in the wagon. The chaos created as the men boarded the train reminded Crane of scenes in a movie he'd seen of the last hours of Paris before the Nazi occupation.

By the afternoon the train had passed through Tasikmalaja and now was stopping at Banjar on its 140-mile, winding, zigzag journey to the southeast. Here the end wagon was detached and pulled to a siding before finally being reattached, after much confusion, to a freight train that would carry the evacuees further to the southern coast of Java and outside the port city of Tjilatjap. There they were met by several other members of the FEAF staff who had driven there earlier from Bandoeng by car. Immediately, Crane, Neri, and the others were taken from the train with their belongings and transported to the docks of Tjilatjap, where a scene of "complete bedlam" greeted them.

Now it was just a question of finding the ship that was supposed to take them out of Java. Passing by many warehouses and antiaircraft installations, they finally reached their destination, a Dutch freighter named the *Abbekerk,* lined up alongside other ships. As Crane's party walked towards the dilapidated-looking vessel, Crane was "touched with the pitiful signs of anxiety I saw around me." On all sides were vast stores of Air Force supplies, including bales of parachutes and even boxes containing aerial cameras. A bonfire was also burning. There seemed to be no organization at all of the evacuees' movements.

Second Lt. Paul Eckley was also at the docks that afternoon, having arrived from Jogjakarta by train with other 19th and 7th Group pilots and enlisted men to catch the *Abbekerk.* The twenty-two-year-old B-17 copilot was shocked to see trucks dumping loads of material on the docks, then being driven off the wharf into the water. Eckley and other 19th Group personnel pulled tommy guns and ammunition out of one pile for their own personal use. They also had their choice of life vests, bandoliers, machetes, pistols, and tin hats, "all for the taking." One of the men was amusing himself by picking up parachutes, pulling the D ring, and throwing them in the bonfire to watch them explode. When Captain Crane saw the man destroying the parachutes, as well as winter flying equipment, he ordered him to stop; Crane knew they could be used on board the *Abbekerk* for warmth. Many of the men on the dock appeared to be drunk.[39]

On board the *Abbekerk,* the freighter's twenty-two-year-old assistant engineer, Adriaan Kik, was watching as workers were hurriedly unloading the ship's cargo of ammunition and bombs that it taken aboard in Scotland but that had been only partially unloaded at its Singapore destination. But as the time for boarding arrived, the unloading had to stop, with the lower cargo bay still full. To Kik, the passengers coming aboard were the most diverse group of men he had ever seen: "aircraft crew with thick jackets, high-level officers, soldiers, sailors, and civilians, with worried and tired faces."[40]

Getting all the men and their baggage on board the *Abbekerk* was proving a chaotic process. The usual formalities for checking individuals, orders, and authorizations had been dispensed with. Anyone in an army uniform standing in line was allowed to board. Told that he was the only medical officer who would be on the ship, Captain Crane made his way up the gangplank and was taken by the chief mate to his cabin, where to his surprise he found

Far East Air Force evacuees boarding the *Abbekerk* using the single gangplank,
Tjilatjap, February 26, 1942. *Courtesy Paul Eckley.*

several other medical associates who had been scattered around Java. They
split up their responsibilities and set about tending the wounded, vacating
the cabin. Because of the limited quarters on the *Abbekerk,* a freighter, not
a transport, and with some fourteen hundred evacuees—British, Dutch, and
Australians besides American Far East Air Force men—to be accommodated,
only the severely wounded were assigned space in the six cabins available
that could just take nineteen persons. Frank Neri and Crane's other charges
did not qualify and would be staying with Crane at a location he had staked
out on the upper deck.[41] The 17th Pursuit's three other wounded pilots—
Tommy Hayes, Gene Bound, and Bill Stauter—didn't qualify, either. After
boarding the *Abbekerk,* they settled down on the deck. They had brought on
board mae wests that they intended to use as mattresses on the hard and cold
deck.[42]

By 2000 that evening, all the FEAF evacuees were on board the ship. However, it soon became apparent that provisions for safety were vastly inadequate. Officers were sent back ashore to bring back bamboo from the surrounding jungle for making life rafts. Javanese natives on the dock lashed the
wide-diameter bamboo to empty fifty-gallon drums and brought the make-
shift rafts on board. Berthed next to the *Abbekerk* was a large ship, also a

Dutch freighter, the *Kota Gede,* that was being loaded with RAF personnel and their materials. Loading was halted at about 2030 when the air raid siren went off. On the *Abbekerk* men started running in panic to get off until a major went up to the bridge to calm them down and give assurances. The raid never materialized.[43]

Shivering in the cold night air, Sgt. Murray Nichols was looking around on the decks for something to keep him warm. He spotted a large crate of A-2 leather USAAF flying jackets on the third deck. Opening it up, he extracted one jacket for himself and passed out others to his fellow 17th Pursuit enlisted men. Elsewhere on the *Abbekerk,* Captain Crane had obtained one of the jackets for himself, too. At 2330 he wrapped himself in it and, adding a light blanket, lay down on the steel deck in the hope of getting some sleep this night.[44]

Also at Tjilatjap on that evening of February 26 was a Dutch reserve second lieutenant of the Technische Dienst (TD, Technical Service) of the Militaire Luchtvaart (Netherlands Indies Air Force) who had arrived in the afternoon from Andir Field with others of his team on a highly secret mission unrelated to any evacuation arrangements. In civilian life a deputy office chief, J. C. Benschop had been made responsible by Major General Van Oyen's Java Air Command headquarters at Bandoeng for managing the transfer to Andir of the thirty-two USAAF P-40s and their pilots expected in at Tjilatjap on the USS *Langley* the following morning. To facilitate this operation, the written orders he carried specified that he was to coordinate with the American pilots being sent from Ngoro to meet the *Langley* on its arrival as part of the same Dutch plan.[45]

Arrangements for the transfer of the Americans and their aircraft were quite elaborate. The P-40s were to be off-loaded from the *Langley* onto an improvised runway that had been built on the quay with the help of infantrymen of the Dutch army. After takeoff from the strip, the *Langley* pilots would link up with a twin-engine Dutch Lockheed 212 (or 12A) that would be circling overhead for the rendezvous to guide the pilots through one of the mountain passes to Andir Field, some 110 miles to the northwest. Benschop would have to coordinate with Andir to ensure the timely arrival of the Lockheed, of which two were on standby at the field.[46]

But what was to be the role of the six Ngoro pilots that were leaving Soerabaja by train that evening for Tjilatjap? Evidently they were to take over six of the *Langley* P-40s and provide escort behind the Lockheed for small groups of the new arrivals on the flight to Andir. After arrival, the P-40s would undergo a technical check at the TD's facilities, and the following morning the Ngoro pilots would continue with the *Langley* pilots to the their final destination, the new field at Tjisaoek, which was ready to receive them with supplies of 100-octane gasoline and .50-caliber ammunition. The 110-mile flight west from Andir to Tjisaoek would have to be flown in early morning to lessen the risk of encountering marauding Japanese Army Ki-43 Hayabusa pilots, who dominated the airspace over West Java. To provide combat-experienced leadership for the untried *Langley* pilots, the six Ngoro pilots would remain at Tjisaoek. Benschop realized, as did his Dutch comrades in Java Air Command, that this was a risky operation. To them a force of thirty-two new P-40s would represent a kind of last chance to stave off the invasion of West Java, expected any day.[47]

ON THEIR TRAIN TRIP FROM Soerabaja to Tjilatjap, Bill Hennon and his five comrades were trying to get some sleep the night of the twenty-sixth, but without luck. The Soerabaja–Jogjakarta train was chugging along at twenty to thirty miles per hour. They were "packed in like sardines." Jim Morehead for one had no seat and spent most of the time hanging out the side. On arrival at Jogjakarta station the next morning, they would have to get off and wait to board a troop train for the last segment of the trip into Tjilatjap.[48]

BACK AT BLIMBING THE 17th Pursuiters and their new Dutch comrades had returned to their quarters after dinner. The low morale of the Americans evident to Anemaet's group was in sharp contrast to their own high spirits, even though the Dutchmen knew the Americans would be pulling out soon and they would be left to defend their country alone. That evening, as he turned to his diary, Spence Johnson reflected the feelings of himself and his squadron mates. He recorded that "Every night we were thankful that day was over and that we were still living."[49]

★ ★ ★ ★ ★

PART FIVE

"Nothing Less than Desertion"

AFTER BREAKING OFF AT 2315 on February 22 and heading for Java, the *Langley* was only seventy-five nautical miles southeast of its Tjilatjap destination at 1140 on the morning of February 27 when two formations of Mitsubishi G4M1 "Betty" bombers that had taken off from newly occupied Denpasar Field on Bali approached it at fifteen thousand feet. Zigzagging to avoid the bomb runs of the sixteen Bettys, the captain of the *Langley* succeeded in eluding hits on the first pass, but on the second run the old seaplane tender was struck by five high-explosive bombs. Escorting Zeros then strafed the listing ship, setting fire to many of the P-40Es the *Langley* was carrying to Java with their pilots. That afternoon the old ship finally slipped below the water, but not before survivors were picked up by the destroyers *Whipple* and *Edsall* that had left Tjilatjap that morning to rendezvous with the *Langley*.[1]

When Maj. Gen. George Brett, now USAFIA commander in Melbourne, got word the following day that the *Langley* was "badly damaged" in an attack by Japanese bombers, he was furious. Vice Adm. C. L. Helfrich, the Dutch officer now commanding ABDAFLOAT, had personally assured him that he would provide suitable protection for the *Langley* in its solitary dash to Java, but he had let Brett down. The USAFIA commander immediately cabled Marshall in Washington requesting rescindment of the order sending the *Sea Witch* to Java and asking that no further equipment be sent to Java "in view of impossibility of NEI to protect." He would consider any further shipments "unwarranted wastage."[2] In reply, Marshall agreed that no further planes should be shipped to Java "unless there is a change in the situation that promises greater safety in transit." But he did not mention aborting the voyage of *Sea Witch*.[3]

Dutch freighter *Abbekerk* at Fremantle, Western Australia, in 1941. *Photograph 302839* © *Australian War Memorial.*

Pursuant to Brett's request of February 26 to ABDACOM in Bandoeng, evacuation from Java to Australia of remaining FEAF personnel got underway on the evening of February 28, when the first group was flown out of Jogjakarta to Broome.[4] Personnel designated to be evacuated by sea instead left Tjilatjap on the overloaded Dutch freighter *Abbekerk* the afternoon before, bound for Fremantle, as arranged by Col. Eugene Eubank, 5th Bomber Command chief. But, incomprehensibly, the thirty-one pursuit pilots who had survived the *Langley* sinking were being ordered to Java on the destroyer *Edsall* at the same time their comrades were being removed from the island. Apparently, based on a message from the *Whipple* that the pilots had been rescued, Adm. William Glassford, commander of U.S. naval forces on Java under Dutch ABDAFLOAT commander Vice Admiral Helfrich, on the afternoon of February 28 ordered the *Edsall* to return to Tjilatjap with the pilots.[5]

EARLY ON THE MORNING of March 1 the East Java invasion force in forty-one transports anchored off Kragan, precipitating desperate Allied air efforts to oppose it. Two days before, the Japanese armada had been attacked by ABDACOM naval forces as it approached, setting off the famed Battle of the Java Sea, in which the Allies suffered a disastrous defeat that spelled the end of their naval operations in the Indies. During the six-phase battle that ended on the morning of March 1, Dutch Admiral Doorman's Combined Striking Force lost three cruisers and four destroyers in the pitched fighting, the first major encounter between fleets since the Battle of Jutland in 1916.[6] However, Japanese landing operations scheduled for February 28 were delayed by one day. FEAF bombers and fighters that were being held back for one last operation in defense of Java now flew Dutch-ordered bombing sorties and a strafing mission against the invasion forces, but with no appreciable effect.

At the other end of Java, at Banten Bay and Merak on the northwestern tip and at Eretanwetan on the north coast 145 miles to the east, the second and third prongs of the Japanese invasion force began landing on the evening of February 28 from fifty-six transports. The Banten Bay/Merak transports were attacked hours later by the U.S. cruiser *Houston* and the Australian cruiser *Perth*, which had inadvertently run into the force as they were attempting to escape from Java via the Sunda Strait. However, when three cruisers and nine destroyers of a nearby Japanese force came to the rescue of the endangered transports, both outmatched Allied ships were sunk in fierce night action.[7]

At Java Air Command (JAC) headquarters in Bandoeng at about 0700 on March 1, Dutch Maj. Gen. L. H. van Oyen was handed a situation report on the three-pronged Japanese invasion force landings on the north coast of Java. After discussing the matter with the KNIL-ML (Dutch East Indies Army Air Force) commander, Col. E. T. Kengen, and the BRITAIR commander, Air Vice Mshl. Peter C. Maltby, Van Oyen called his EASGROUP commander, Colonel Eubank, in Jogjakarta about the Japanese advances and countermeasures being taken. An hour later, Eubank phoned Van Oyen back with startling news: he was proposing to evacuate his 5th Bomber Command and his B-17s and LB-30s to Australia, along with the remaining P-40 pilots at Ngoro. He would operate in the defense of Java from Broome instead, to ensure security of his dwindling number of heavy bombers. Furious, Van Oyen rejected Eubank's plan out of hand. He probably was thinking that Maltby's BRITAIR with its RAF and RAAF squadrons was remaining on Java to fight on, so why should the Americans evacuate?[8]

To the south of Java, Nagumo's First Air Fleet was positioned in the Indian Ocean, ready to cut off any sea movements between Java and Australia. On the afternoon of March 1, dive bombers from three of its carriers attacked and sank the fleet oiler *Pecos*, which was carrying *Langley* survivors. A few hours after the *Pecos* went down, the Japanese cruiser *Tone* in Nagumo's force spotted the destroyer *Edsall*, which was only some twenty-five to thirty-five nautical miles from the *Pecos*. After Admiral Glassford that morning had issued new orders for his ships to "clear the region" and thus canceled orders for the *Edsall* to proceed north to Tjilatjap with the thirty-one P-40 pilots from the *Langley,* the *Edsall* was headed south and had apparently veered off to come to the assistance of the *Pecos.* Firing at great range, the cruiser *Chikuma* and two battleships, *Hiei* and *Kirishima,* initially failed to strike the destroyer, but finally they scored hits. When the *Edsall* appeared still to be operational, Nagumo's dive bombers were called in to finish the job, and at 1850 they set the hopelessly outmatched destroyer ablaze. As the *Edsall* lay dead in the water, the *Chikuma* moved in and finally sent the valiant ship to the bottom at 1900. The two cruisers picked up survivors, who evidently were taken to POW camp at Makassar.[9]

Back on Java, Eubank was trying to contact Van Oyen in Bandoeng again on the afternoon of March 1. He had been notified about 1400 that orders had been received from Dutch headquarters to destroy the airdromes at Madioen and Jogjakarta and transfer all remaining FEAF aircraft to Singosari Field. But Eubank was not able to get through to Van Oyen; the telephone lines between Jogjakarta and Bandoeng were out. Turning to his Dutch liaison officer, Eubank gave him the message he wanted to be passed on to Van Oyen: he was going to carry out his intention to transfer his aircraft and personnel to Broome and operate from there instead of Singosari.[10]

Already the remaining Ngoro P-40 pilots who had returned from the March 1 strafing attack at Kragan were on their way to Jogjakarta for evacuation, along with the other 17th Pursuit (Provisional) personnel, as authorized by Eubank that morning. Flight crews of the 19th and 7th Bomber Groups who had participated in bombing attacks earlier in the day were preparing to leave Jogjakarta and Madioen, too. During the late afternoon and evening of March 1, B-17s and LB-30s took off from the two airfields before the Dutch destruction of the airdromes with the last of the FEAF personnel on Java—including Eubank and his staff—and headed for Broome.

In Melbourne, Brett had concluded that it was "improbable" that the twenty-seven crated P-40Es on the *Sea Witch* could be assembled on reaching Java in view of the current situation there. Accordingly, he gave orders to have the freighter diverted to Bombay. If it had already arrived at Tjilatjap, it was to be ordered to "immediately sail" for Bombay before being unloaded, unless there were "definite indications" that the P-40s on board could be assembled "and used to advantage in defense of Java."[11] But Brett's message arrived too late. The *Sea Witch* had anchored in Tjilatjap harbor at midday. February 28, and by the following day all the crated P-40Es were unloaded and put on trains for Bandoeng and Tasikmalaja for assembly by Dutch technicians. But when the Dutch fighter pilots who had been ordered from Ngoro to Bandoeng's Andir Field on March 1 arrived at their destination on the afternoon of the following day, they found that the P-40s were just beginning to be assembled. It appeared to them that the effort was going to be too late. They knew it would be days before the P-40s could be made operational, and the Japanese who had landed on West Java were rapidly moving south in the direction of Batavia and Bandoeng.

At Broome on the northwest coast of Australia the coming and going of rising numbers of planes to and from Java was overwhelming the capacity of the small field to service them, causing delays in moving their evacuees from Java south to Perth and Melbourne. At 0930 on the morning of March 3, with the harbor jammed with flying boats loaded with Dutch evacuees and two B-24As and two B-17Es, among other aircraft, on the airfield, nine Zeros flying nonstop from Timor staged a devastating attack, shooting up all the hapless aircraft in Roebuck Bay and on the field.[12] As at Darwin two weeks earlier, panic ensued as the remaining military and civilians tried to get out of Broome before the expected paratroop landings.

IN WASHINGTON ON MARCH 3 Army Chief of Staff George C. Marshall was reading a message from the governor general of the NEI that disturbed him greatly. Lt. Gen. Hein ter Poorten, commander-in-chief, ABDA area, had asked the NEI governor general to relay to Washington a complaint Van Oyen had made to Ter Poorten on March 1 and 2 in which Van Oyen accused Colonel Eubank—in command of all FEAF units on Java—of leaving Java for Broome against orders on the evening of March 1 with all his remaining personnel and heavy bombers.[13]

According to Van Oyen, by previous agreement with Eubank he had approved sending only combat-unfit heavy bombers out of Java and had not agreed to the departure of Eubank himself or to hand over remaining P-40s to Dutch pilots, who he maintained had "no experience" in them. Ter Poorten added that Eubank by his actions had disobeyed Marshall's orders of February 21. Furthermore, according to the statement made by Eubank's two Dutch liaison officers to Van Oyen, the departure had "the appearance of a panicky flight, with Eubank in the first departing machine." In Ter Poorten's (and Van Oyen's) opinion, Eubank's action "is nothing less than desertion" and has "made an extremely bad impression."[14]

In response to the accusation, Marshall radioed Brett at USAFIA headquarters the same day to report at once on the orders under which Eubank was operating on Java and on the "actual facts" regarding Eubank's departure from Java. Brett was also instructed to contact the Dutch commander-in-chief of the ABDA area to determine how to "remedy the damage" caused by Eubank's departure and to "correct the terribly unfortunate impression" it had created.[15]

On March 5 Brett cabled Marshall, stating that he had issued no orders to Eubank concerning his own departure from Java, and whatever orders were issued were "based on orders or instructions" issued by the ABDACOM commander, Wavell. Brett indicated he was "in continual contact" with the current ABDA commander and was trying to provide assistance "even to what might be considered unwarranted wastage of valuable equipment and personnel."[16]

Three days later, Brett forwarded Eubank's response to the accusations. Eubank stated that Brereton had instructed him on February 21 to operate American air units only as long as an effective force remained, with the decision on termination of operations left to him and with Dutch headquarters to be notified. He was to evacuate to Australia all personnel not needed for tactical operations as well as those for whom no aircraft remained suitable for such operations. He had notified Van Oyen on February 28 that he planned to transfer all his bombers to Broome, because of the impossibility of operations any longer from Java airfields, and to operate them out of Broome using the Java fields as advanced fields for night operations. When Van Oyen objected and insisted Eubank continue to operate from Java, using Malang (Singosari) as a base, Eubank had told him that the field there was not suitable, given that he had recently lost five B-17s on it.[17]

Continuing his defense, Eubank stated that he had made a maximum effort on March 1, employing his one LB-30 and five B-17s on ten missions, and that he had been notified on that date by Dutch headquarters that the fields at Madioen and Jogjakarta were to be destroyed, leaving only Malang, which Eubank regarded as totally unsuitable because of enemy attacks. He informed Van Oyen through the Dutch commander's liaison officer that he intended to carry out his plan to transfer remaining planes and personnel to Broome, with any future operations from there. As regards the P-40s, Eubank asserted that after their March 1 strafing attack that left all remaining ships unfit for action, Major Fisher had been informed by the Dutch interceptor commander at Soerabaja that instructions had been received from Bandoeng for American pursuit personnel to report to Jogjakarta for evacuation.

Brett backed up Eubank in his reply to Marshall. In his understanding, Eubank had followed the orders of Brereton and Wavell, the latter as instructed by the CCS in Washington. (Curiously enough, Brett did not mention that he himself, now as commanding general of USAFIA in Melbourne, had ordered Brigadier General Naiden at Bandoeng on February 26 to have all experienced fighter and bomber crews returned to Australia for operations from Broome.)[18] Furthermore, Brett maintained that Van Oyen was incorrect in his accusation related to the P-40s; the Dutch government had requested that they be transferred to the Dutch air force, since according to the request their pilots were competent to fly them. In Brett's view, instead of being chastised Eubank should be "commended for his courage in evacuating at the time he did." Van Oyen's complaint was a "face saving" message or a "failure to appreciate conditions as they were," Brett asserted. Indeed, "every effort" had been made to comply with "oftentimes unreasonable requests" by the Dutch.

In retrospect, it would appear that any "face saving" efforts were being made more for Brett's benefit as Eubank's commander than by Van Oyen, whose dogged insistence on carrying out the air campaign to the last, with the support to his own forces of the British and American air units still available on Java, was within his rights, despite how doomed the campaign appeared to be. With the transfer of ABDAIR command on February 23 to the newly established Java Air Command under Van Oyen, the formal authority to end air operations by American, British, and Dutch units rested with Van Oyen, not with Brereton, whose authority had lapsed on that date. Similarly, Brereton's superior, Brett, now in Australia, had no authority either in unilaterally requesting on February 26 that all ground officers and men as well as flight crews be evacuated to Australia. Any change in Van Oyen's authority would have had to come from the Combined Chiefs of Staff in Washington, whose February 22 instruction to Wavell calling for conditional withdrawal of air forces from Java was now apparently inoperative.[19] It was not just a matter of notifying Dutch headquarters of his intention to evacuate, as Eubank claimed. Indeed, why would he have pointedly indicated in his defense that Dutch headquarters in Bandoeng had authorized evacuation of American (Ngoro) personnel if such Dutch approval were not necessary?[20] Furthermore, Eubank's argument that Singosari Field was not suitable as a base for his remaining heavy bombers is subject to challenge. According to a Dutch authority on the NEI aerial campaign, Singosari Field had a large dispersal area that could have provided adequate protection for the B-17s and LB-30s. Earlier losses of B-17s, he alleges, were a result of failure to disperse the aircraft at the time of the Japanese attacks in February.[21]

Van Oyen was on weaker ground in arguing against the handing over of the Ngoro P-40s to Dutch pilots on the grounds that the pilots had no experience in them. While in fact the 2-Vl.G.-IV pilots earmarked to fly the P-40s indeed hadn't flown the P-40 before, their experience since 1940 in flying its radial-engine predecessor, the Hawk 75—virtually the same aircraft except for the switch to a liquid-cooled engine—would have made transition to the P-40 a matter of a few flying hours only.[22]

While Eubank may be criticized for disobeying his Dutch commander's orders not to evacuate, from the standpoint of American interests his decision was understandable on practical grounds. He undoubtedly felt that by delaying his departure and that of his personnel, he risked that all would fall into Japanese hands and spend the rest of the war as POWs. Indeed, this fate befell his British counterpart, Air Vice Marshal Maltby, and the personnel of his RAF and RAAF squadrons that fought on after March 1.

JUST BEFORE MARSHALL READ the explanations by Brett and Eubank, the aftermath of one Dutch "unreasonable request," as Brett had termed it, was playing out on Java. On the night of March 7–8, Dutch air force personnel at Andir and Tasikmalaja were destroying the half-assembled P-40s of the *Sea Witch* just ahead of Japanese troops moving into the area. Van Oyen had gambled that he would receive P-40 (and Hurricane) reinforcements in time to oppose the Japanese invasion of Java, but he had lost his race against the clock. The dogged air and land campaign that the Dutch had pursued with the aid of the British and Australians during the first week of March in West Java had come to a bitter end.[23]

With total Japanese control of the air, and not wanting to put Bandoeng through the ordeal of Japanese attack, Lieutenant General Ter Poorten accepted Lt. Gen. Hitoshi Imamura's request on March 8 to surrender. This order was broadcast to Dutch forces the following day, and on March 12 American, British, and Australian forces followed suit, albeit reluctantly.[24]

In just two months the campaign in the Dutch East Indies was over. For the Dutch and their allies it was "nothing short of a total, humiliating disaster."[25] Although the Americans would hold out for two more months in the Philippines, Southern Operations had proven a complete success for the Japanese.

CHAPTER FOURTEEN

"Thousands of Men Gone Completely Mad"

UP ON THE SIGNAL BRIDGE of the USS *Langley* in the early morning of Friday, February 27, 2nd Lt. Bill Ackerman was beginning the sixth day of his self-styled "joy ride" on the old seaplane tender since leaving Fremantle for Java. The 13th Pursuit Squadron (Provisional) pilot was standing next to 33rd Pursuiter Gerry Dix, sharing lookout duties on this the Sydney, Nebraska, native's twenty-third birthday. From the bridge Ackerman and Dix had an unobstructed 360-degree view.[1]

Suddenly, at 0810 their spirits took a dive when they spotted a plane very high up. Suspecting it was a Japanese reconnaissance ship, they reported their finding by voice tube to the navigation bridge to Captain McConnell. With no previous experience in such situations, Ackerman felt it was probably only a routine inspection by the Japanese pilot, but the others knew better—Japanese bombers would soon be on their way. This was bad news—the *Langley* still had about one hundred miles to go before it would reach its destination, Tjilatjap harbor.[2]

At 1140 their fears were realized: two formations of what appeared to be twin-engine bombers were approaching the *Langley* and its escorts, the destroyers USS *Edsall* and USS *Whipple*. Captain McConnell sounded general quarters and climbed a ladder to the signal bridge to join Dix, Ackerman, and the other eleven men there: McConnell's talker, his gunnery officer, and nine machine gunners. They all watched as the bombers took up a position dead astern, closing rapidly at about fifteen thousand feet. On each of the four corners of the signal bridge the gunners were ready to fire their .50-caliber machine guns.[3]

Flak from the *Langley* and the two destroyers burst below the seven bombers of the first group as they went into their bomb run on the old seaplane tender. As each bomber released a 250 kg (551-pound) bomb in salvo, McConnell called for hard right rudder over the voice tube, and the *Langley* heeled to the left. All seven bombs exploded in the water, but two close to the ship's side buckled plates, allowing tons of water to pour through the openings.[4]

When the second group of nine bombers approached for its run in three Vs of three ships each, the *Langley* zigzagged while its four three-inch anti-aircraft guns fired at the Japanese. Concentrating on picking the moment of release, McConnell yelled "Hard left rudder!" and the *Langley* turned away from the expected bomb drop. But the Japanese withheld releasing their bombs as they passed over the *Langley*'s original track, then swung around in a wide turn for another try.

This time the Japanese leader came in slowly to avoid overshooting the *Langley*'s turning point in changing course. Just as McConnell called for a turn to the left, the bombers followed the ship, dead astern, then picked up her turn to the right. The formation again turned with the *Langley*, lined up on her, and began releasing a mixture of 250 kg and 60 kg (132-pound) bombs.

The first bomb exploded on the main deck on the starboard side, starting fires and spraying shrapnel in all directions. Shrapnel from the second and third bombs that had landed on the port side of the elevator and set fire to P-40s on the main deck hit Dix and Ackerman, one piece slicing into Dix's left arm and another shattering his jaw. Ackerman took shrapnel in the hand and arm. The fourth bomb also hit on the port side, shattering P-40s on the flight deck. The fifth bomb penetrated the flight deck on the starboard side aft, starting fierce fires.[5]

After the bombers finished their bomb run, Dix and Ackerman were carried from the signal bridge to the sick bay. Dix was given morphine, and the wounds of both pursuiters, as well as the sailors wounded in the attack, were dressed. But it was not yet over for the *Langley*. Suddenly sweeping in, six Zeros began firing their 20 mm cannons into the forecastle, bridge, and flight deck, setting fire to several of the P-40s. After finishing their run, nine more Zeros dived down and repeated the strafing attack on the P-40s and the deck structures, killing a number of Army Air Force and navy personnel.[6]

As the Zeros concluded their attack and formed up on the bombers for the return to their base at about 1230, the *Langley* was left listing ten degrees to port and losing way. McConnell feared that the 104 tons of P-40s would reduce the stability of the *Langley* to a dangerous degree. In order to partially correct the list, five of the ruined P-40s on the port side of the flight deck were ordered jettisoned. But the action didn't make much of a difference, and

Gerry Dix on the deck of the USAT *President Polk* during its transpacific voyage, December 1941–January 1942, ending in Brisbane. *Courtesy of Peg Hague Baum, from Jesse Hague film.*

now the list was about fifteen degrees. Counterflooding failed to correct the list, too. McConnell gave orders to prepare to abandon ship. Boats and life rafts were made ready for lowering. But many misunderstood the command and jumped overboard, joining others who had been blown overboard during the attack. All were picked up by the *Edsall*.[7]

Shortly afterwards, McConnell received word that the engines were stopped because of flooding in the motor pits, and the fire rooms were also flooding. The *Langley*'s skipper decided it was time to abandon ship in order to save the crew and the AAF personnel while the escorts *Whipple* and *Edsall* were still available to take them on board. At 1345 he gave the order "over the side," and nine life rafts, a whaleboat, and a motor launch were lowered into the calm sea. Dix and Ackerman climbed aboard the one remaining boat— the number two whaleboat—but as it was lowered away the ropes holding it caught fire, and it plunged into the sea. Dix grabbed the upper section of the *Langley*'s deck and managed to chin his way back, despite his shattered jaw. On board again he found a life jacket and jumped into the water. Ackerman was left swimming around for some time before being picked up with others by the *Edsall*. Dix was already on board by that time.[8]

Strangely enough, the *Langley* did not seem to be sinking. The *Whipple* fired nine four-inch rounds into its hull, but with little effect, as with the first

Crew members of USS *Whipple* watch as USS *Edsall* (in background) completes the rescue of personnel from the sinking USS *Langley* on February 27, 1942. *Courtesy Capt. Lawrence E. Divoli, USN, via Naval Historical Center.*

torpedo it fired afterwards. However, a second torpedo resulted in a terrific explosion and fire that covered the entire after part of the *Langley*. Still, the old seaplane tender was not settling. McConnell was anxious that the Japanese might return, so at 1446 he ordered the area cleared. The two destroyers sped away on a southwesterly course. No one saw the *Langley* take its final plunge, seventy-four miles south of Tjilatjap.[9]

AT NGORO THE DUTCH PILOTS of the Brewsters were on standby before daylight the morning of the twenty-seventh, ready to fly two-ship protective patrols above the Combined Striking Force (CSF) along the north coast of Java on the lookout for any Japanese reconnaissance planes searching for the allied warships. The Dutch rather than the American pilots were selected for the mission, as their Buffaloes had a greater range than that of the P-40s, which were to join in only if the CSF were within range. At 0515, Lieutenant Simons and Sergeant Van Haarlem took off on the first patrol and flew above the westward bound ships until 0700, when they were relieved by Lieutenant de Haas and Ensign Wink. Half an hour into their patrol, they spotted a fast-moving Betty about three thousand feet above them that had obviously caught sight of the CSF below. Unable to radio the ADC at Soerabaja because of radio failure, they returned to Ngoro at about 0745 and telephoned the ADC with the bad news that the CSF had been discovered by the Japanese.[10]

Not called upon for the protective patrols, the remaining 17th Pursuiters at Ngoro spent their morning without receiving any orders from the ADC to intercept the daily run of Japanese bombers heading for Soerabaja. Unknown to the Americans, the weather had spared them: a force of Bettys and Zeros had taken off on a mission to attack Soerabaja but had to turn back because of poor weather. It was a welcome respite for the overworked pilots and their worn P-40s. But it was not to last. Bill Fisher had arrived at Ngoro from Soerabaja to brief Ed Kiser and Lieutenant de Haas with all the information he'd received from the Java Air Command and its East Group on the Japanese ships that had been sighted near Bawean Island, seventy-five miles north of Soerabaja, and to give orders for a critical mission. Fisher informed Kiser and de Haas that the JAC had ordered all the operational P-40s and Brewsters at Ngoro to provide support to Admiral Doorman's CSF during his planned attack on the Japanese invasion transports. First, the P-40s and Brewsters would provide escort for three A-24 dive bombers that would determine the location of the Japanese and carry out an initial attack on them, then the fighters would clear the sky of any Japanese aircraft in the expected area of action between the two naval forces. Fisher informed Kiser and de Haas that the plan had been discussed with the Dutch naval commander in Soerabaja.[11]

Kiser and de Haas now briefed their pilots, giving them the purpose of the mission, the time of takeoff, and the time of rendezvous with the A-24s that would be flying from Singosari. Kiser would be acting as overall commander of the ten P-40s, and De Haas would lead the Brewsters.[12] At 1515 Kiser, at the head of the four ships in A flight, roared down the field, followed by Jack Dale leading another five in B flight. Behind the P-40s Lt. De Haas headed five Dutch Brewsters. As they climbed to twelve thousand feet on reaching Soerabaja, they spotted the three A-24s that had taken off from Singosari before them and linked up.[13]

It was with mixed feelings that the pursuit–dive bomber group headed north at sixteen thousand feet in fair weather for Bawean Island. Spence Johnson, flying wing to Jack Dale in B flight, felt it was ridiculous to send just three dive bombers on such a mission. Capt. Harry Galusha, at the head of the three A-24s, shared his view, but his 91st Bomb Squadron now had only three flyable ships left, all in poor condition and which "should never have left the ground." Galusha, 1st Lt. Zeke Summers, and 2nd Lt. J. W. Ferguson all had volunteered to fly the mission, wanting to make one last attempt to help "the gallant Dutch warriors." Robert Hambaugh had also volunteered but was forced to abort his takeoff when his hydraulic system went out.[14]

Their orders were to attack the transports, but on reaching the target area in the Java Sea at about 1630, they spotted only a single line of warships, six cruisers and five destroyers, and saw no transports. Galusha headed his flight further out to sea, again passing a line of fighting ships, which appeared to be six cruisers, three destroyers, and three battleships—and which fired anti-aircraft guns at them—but still no transports. Continuing further out, after assuming the first line had been Allied ships and the second Japanese, they spotted a third line of ships. The six ships in this line, all identified as cruisers, were definitely regarded as Japanese, but again, there were no transports among them. Severe antiaircraft fire from the cruisers obliged the A-24s and escorting P-40s and Buffaloes to break up their formations. Proceeding further out to about sixty nautical miles northwest of Bawean Island, they saw two lines of ships below them this time, a ring of fifteen destroyers protecting what they counted as forty-three troop transports. The warships turned broadside to the flight and let loose a barrage of antiaircraft fire so intense Galusha wondered if the A-24s would be able to break through.[15]

Above the dive bombers flying over the massed ships the pilots of the P-40s and Buffaloes encountered no aerial opposition and were reduced to being spectators. To Gambonini the Japanese ships they had passed were "lined up as far as you could see, clear to the horizon," engaged in a furious naval battle with the Allied warships. For Les Johnsen, watching "near misses, longs, and shorts" on both sides as the adversaries exchanged fire, it was "a sight that made my stomach sink." Spence Johnson had similar feelings—"looking down upon thousands of men gone completely mad was chilling to my blood," he wrote in his diary that day.[16] All the while watching the scene below, the Pursuiters soon realized that they were also the object of attention of the warships of both sides. That the allied ships were also firing their antiaircraft guns at them was particularly upsetting. It seemed that "the entire sky was filled with gunsmoke." Some of the explosions were dangerously close to their ships.

Finally, after executing "daring maneuvers" to reach a suitable attack position, each of the 91st pilots selected the largest transport in his sight and plummeted down from ninety-five hundred feet to an altitude of between three thousand and four thousand feet. It was 1647. Releasing their single 300 kg (660-pound) and two 50 kg (110-pound) bombs, they tried to assess the results. It appeared that they had scored six direct hits and three very close misses on the three targeted transports, which were seen to "buck and roll."[17]

Their mission completed, Galusha turned to lead his flight without fighter escort back to their Singosari base at low level and radioed the ADC with what he believed were the results of their attack. Summers and Ferguson lost

Galusha, but all three managed to get back to the field on their own. On landing, they found the base deserted except for two officers of their own 91st Squadron. The pilots received orders to fly their three remaining A-24s to Jogjakarta, while the enlisted men were to get there by car.[18]

Freed of their escort obligation, the P-40 and Brewster pilots continued flying above the warring naval ships to give the CSF the air protection included under their tasks for the mission. Unable to approach the Japanese warships at a lower altitude because of the heavy antiaircraft fire, the Americans and Dutch flew in a rectangular circuit around the two forces at about twenty-five thousand feet. At about 1700 Kiser radioed the ADC with the position of the Japanese transports as they headed west of Bawean and to ask it to inform the Netherlands Navy headquarters (that is, Admiral Helfrich) that they would soon have to leave the area. It was now becoming too difficult for Kiser from his altitude to make out which ships were Allied and which were Japanese.[19]

When Kiser and the others returned to their field, with no losses, they exchanged their grim impressions of what they had experienced. Some reported that they had seen the A-24s score a direct hit on a fourteen-thousand-ton transport, which was reported as having sunk "soon after." However, Paul Gambonini was skeptical of the claim: "our puny force didn't amount to anything," in his view.[20]

AT TJILATJAP THE TROOP TRAIN carrying Ben Irvin's party of six 17th Pursuiters finally pulled into the station the afternoon of the twenty-seventh. After disembarking, they made their way to the port city's docks, where they saw the preparations the Dutch had made for off-loading the Langley's P-40s and facilitating their takeoffs. The quay that ran parallel to the docks had been made suitable as a runway by chopping down bordering trees and moving telephone poles and wires.[21] But where were the Dutch the Ngoro pilots were expecting to meet them and brief them on their mission? There was just a mass of people thronging the docks. In the totally confused situation, they searched for their Dutch contacts.[22] Then Jim Morehead spotted a Caucasian civilian who identified himself as a reporter for a Chicago newspaper and asked what Morehead and his group were doing there. The reporter gave them shocking news: the Langley had been bombed, but he was not sure whether it had been sunk. On the assumption that it might yet get into Tjilatjap, Morehead and the others decided to wait and checked into a local hotel.[23]

Over at the pier where the Abbekerk was berthed, the FEAF troops, as well as other evacuees, were anxiously waiting for the freighter to get underway and take them out of Java to safety. They had passed a very uncomfortable night trying to sleep on the deck. The morning had dragged on with no word on a departure time. Tommy Hayes was told that the delay was because of the need to wait for British troops who had evacuated Singapore and Malaya. No breakfast had been served. Captain Crane opened a can of sardines and put them on some crackers to ease his hunger.[24]

Tommy Hayes and Gene Bound received permission to go into town to do some last-minute shopping. They were mainly interested in getting food. After not having been served breakfast, they were not sure if they would be fed during the voyage. They were told to be back on board by 1500. When they returned to the pier, they had with them a forty-eight-bottle case of Australian beer, cases of Del Monte canned pineapples and Libby peaches, and a couple of mattresses to substitute for the uncomfortable mae wests they had slept on the previous night. After paying the Javanese porters who had carried the cache to the docks, Hayes and Bound hauled it on board.[25]

At about 1700 in the afternoon several tugs came alongside and pulled the *Abbekerk* into the harbor. As it moved out, Captain Crane counted twenty-five freighters waiting to berth and unload war supplies. How ridiculous it seemed to Crane; the material would just fall into the hands of the Japanese, perhaps even before the ships were unloaded. As the *Abbekerk* cleared the harbor, it passed a destroyer at anchor and several other ships waiting to form up in a convoy. Crane figured they were heading for India. Sgt. Murray Nichols saw two Asiatic Fleet gunboats flying Old Glory on aft in the breeze. Stirred by patriotism, Nichols and the other 17th Pursuit men around him came to attention and saluted. A huge roar went up.[26]

The *Abbekerk*'s captain issued instructions that there was to be no smoking on deck after sunset, and no rubbish was to be thrown overboard until nightfall. He didn't want Japanese planes tracking their course. None of the *Abbekerk*'s crew spoke to the evacuees about the ship's lethal cargo of over two thousand tons of munitions, out of sight in the lower cargo bays, feeling it was better to keep the unnerving information secret. However, Captain Crane had heard that the cargo included bombs and .50-caliber ammunition. Sgt. Dave Burnside, another of the enlisted men evacuees of the 17th Pursuit on board, knew first-hand about the cargo. The day before, he had helped stabilize 250-pound bombs in the hold that he believed were British from Singapore.[27]

BACK AT JOGJAKARTA, George Parker and the other eleven pilots and the twelve enlisted men of the 17th Pursuit waiting for evacuation were spending another day of dissatisfaction near their barracks. After four days in the city, they still had received no orders from 5th Bomber Command headquarters, despite the persistent efforts of Walt Coss and Parker in visits to its office. The pursuiters also had heard that six more pilots had left Blimbing but wondered where they were; they hadn't seen them in Jogjakarta and wondered if they hadn't gone straight through to Tjilatjap to board the *Abbekerk* with Hayes, Bound, and Stauter. They had also heard that there were some seventy Japanese ships fifty miles off the Java coast, a bit of information that did not ease their anxiety.[28]

"GOD, WHAT A PLACE!" Dick Legg thought as he stepped out of the B-24A onto the field at Broome, on Australia's northwest coast, on the morning of February 27 after an eleven-hour flight from Melbourne. The desolate area reminded him of the cattle towns of the Wild West as portrayed in movies. Two days before, Legg had been ordered to Broome by the new USAFIA chief, General Brett, to take charge of evacuation of FEAF personnel from Java. He was to get all Air Forces officers and men out of Java and onward to Perth and Melbourne on the B-17s, B-24s, and LB-30s being assigned him. It was seemingly a welcome change from his air officer job at Amberley that had proved to be an administrative headache for him, with "everyone in my hair," including USAFIA headquarters in Melbourne. But now he wondered if this new posting would really be an improvement.[29]

Legg was replacing Col. Edward S. Perrin, who had arrived at Broome on February 22 from Java, where he had served as staff assistant to Brett. Finding "complete disorganization," Perrin, scheduled to continue on to Melbourne to serve under his old chief, had decided to stay on and provide the necessary leadership in organizing evacuation to Broome. When Col. Reginald Vance, the thirty-eight-year-old G-2 to Brereton in Bandoeng, flew in the following day, Perrin asked him to stay on too and help him take over.[30]

Fearing a Japanese attack, already the women and children of the civilian population of about seventeen hundred persons had been ordered evacuated, and now it appeared that the males were going to flee, leaving the base short-handed of help for the vital evacuation operation. At the meeting where Legg and Perrin changed command, discussions were held with a "civic committee" on ways to prevent male civilians from leaving. When Legg suggested declaring martial law and the committee asked what could be done if it were not obeyed, Legg "nonchalantly" tapped each of the two pistols he was wearing on his hips and suggested casually that after a few civilians had been shot, the rest would probably stay. The Australians were "flabbergasted" but agreed that such an approach would probably work.[31]

Vance himself tried such an intimidating approach with Broome's civilian airport manager. While he was at the airfield trying to convert the only defense Broome had—ten .30-caliber water-cooled machine guns that had been flown in on a B-24A on February 21—to shoot up against enemy aircraft, he took the airport manager's truck against the manager's will for transportation back and forth from the welding shop that was converting the guns. When the pistol-packing manager indirectly threatened to shoot Vance if he ever crossed him again, the six-foot, four-inch Vance let the word get around that he was quite a hand with pistols himself and "played the wild west stuff" around Broome, practicing quick draws from his holster for all to see. Afterwards, he had no more trouble from the manager.[32]

But Broome's aborigines proved more difficult for Perrin and Legg to handle. A group of them had been hired to help service the increasing flow of American, Dutch, and Australian aircraft coming in with Java evacuees because the work was too tiring for the exhausted flight crews, most of whom were just in Broome overnight before continuing south or returning to Java. However, the aborigines had evidently become familiar with Australian union laws and were refusing to come to work at the airfield before 0800 in the morning nor to stay and work overtime at night. Given the essential nature of refueling aircraft to get them on their way as quickly as possible, Perrin and now Legg had no alternative but to use aircrews during night refueling operations.[33]

EARLY IN THE MORNING of Saturday, February 28, Bill Ackerman and Gerry Dix on board the *Edsall* had found out that the *Edsall* and the *Whipple* were heading south in the Indian Ocean towards Christmas Island with the survivors of the *Langley*. By 0820, the two destroyers were steaming back and forth off of Flying Fish Cove on the north side of the island awaiting the arrival of a tanker, the *Pecos,* that would take the survivors to Australia. A launch sent out by the island's phosphate company now arrived off the *Whipple* to ferry the *Langley* pilots and the twelve aviation mechanics from the *Whipple* to the *Edsall.* On board the *Edsall,* Dix and Ackerman were joyfully reunited with the other thirty-one *Langley* pilots after they boarded from the launch. But there was only one mechanic with them: Sgt John W. Mabry, also wounded in the attack on the *Langley.* Eleven were missing, not picked up by the *Whipple.*[34]

In the meantime, the *Pecos* had arrived to take on board the *Langley* survivors from the *Whipple* and *Edsall* and proceed to Exmouth Gulf on Australia's west coast.[35] But before the transfer of the *Langley* survivors could be completed, three twin-engine bombers suddenly appeared overhead at 1020 and began dropping bombs on the edge of Flying Fish Cove, evidently intending to hit the phosphate company's dock and radio station. All transfer operations were immediately halted. In a second pass, two of the Japanese bombers flew at high altitude almost directly over the three ships as the vessels entered a rain squall nearby for protection, but the aircraft did not release any bombs; evidently they had exhausted their loads on the ground targets. Half an hour later, the *Pecos, Edsall,* and *Whipple* emerged from the squall to find the Japanese aircraft gone. But on the expectation that the Japanese pilots would alert their base to the presence of the three American ships, the ranking naval commander of the group—Cmdr. Edwin Crouch on the *Whipple,* decided to head south and finish transferring the *Langley* survivors at sea instead.[36]

AT TJILATJAP, BILL HENNON and the other five pursuiters who had arrived from Ngoro the day before got the bad news this morning: the *Langley* was confirmed as sunk. There would be no P-40s for them to pick up after all. All around the pilots, women, children, troops, navy personnel, and newspaper correspondents were crowded together, trying to get on any ship leaving Java. "It's hopeless now," Hennon felt.[37] Hennon and the others wondered how they would be able to get back to Ngoro. Fortunately, they met the commander of a submarine who helped them get a car. As they piled in and decided on the route to follow, they realized it was going to be a long haul to get back to their base over some 280 miles of winding roads.

While Hennon's group was heading back to join the remaining pilots at their base and an uncertain evacuation situation, George Parker and the other eleven at Jogjakarta were beginning their fifth day of waiting for their evacuation orders. Finally, while they were eating breakfast, they received their long-awaited orders from Colonel Eubank to proceed to the airport immediately. Parker and the other pilots plus the twelve enlisted men excitedly rushed back to their quarters to pack their few possessions. An army bus had been provided to take them to the field, but without a driver. One of the 17th Pursuit's crew chiefs happily volunteered for the job. After Walt Coss, in charge of the 17th's evacuees, checked the roster to ensure that everyone was present, they all climbed into the fully loaded bus and started off. At the field Coss reported in to Colonel Eubank and was told where to deliver his charges. Then they were split up into smaller groups and assigned to two B-17Es and a B-24A that would be taking them and other FEAF evacuees out to Australia. But they would have to wait until evening for the takeoff. It was too risky to fly during daylight hours with the marauding Zeros around. Also, one of the Flying Fortresses required engine repairs.[38]

IN THE SUNSHINE OF "a lovely tropical day," Pfc. Charles Bowles watched as the MS *Sea Witch* approached the southern coast of Java. It was just before noon, February 28. All that morning the unescorted freighter had been making its way in the open towards its Tjilatjap destination and miraculously had not been spotted so far by Japanese aircraft. However, there was a graphic reminder of how dangerous these waters were: before Bowles and the others had come in sight of land, they were unnerved by the sight of debris littering the sea around them, obviously from an Allied ship that had been sunk.[39] Just outside the channel leading to Tjilatjap port, the *Sea Witch* now turned in a continuous tight circle with other ships to try to avoid submarine attack while waiting its turn to enter the channel. The circle was so tight that the centrifugal force was creating a problem for Bowles and the others who were trying to eat lunch. They had to hold the plates, cutlery, and cups to keep them from sliding to the end of the dining table. Finally, after about an hour, the *Sea Witch* received clearance from port authorities to come in and dock.

After the *Sea Witch* had been secured at a pier, a Dutch civilian, along with Javanese stevedores, clambered aboard and began the process of transferring the crates of P-40s in the hold to flat-bottomed barges alongside the freighter. To Bowles the Dutch supervisor seemed excessively harsh in his treatment of the natives, ordering them around "like slaves," although he had no whip. But as the work progressed, the Javanese "laughing, jabbering, and stealing constantly," Bowles reflected that perhaps the draconian supervision was necessary to get the job done. Still, Bowles felt the Dutchman was "one of the meanest men" he had ever seen.[40]

BACK AT NGORO FIELD, the 17th Pursuit was being forced to keep all its few remaining P-40s on alert all day, making it impossible to carry out needed maintenance. The evening before, at 1900, the squadron's mechanics still managed to have fourteen of their seventeen P-40s in commission. Now, at 0900 this morning of February 28, the 17th was being ordered to intercept Zeros reportedly heading for Soerabaja. However, the three flights of P-40s and four Dutch Brewsters sent up were unable to locate the Japanese. After landing, they were ordered off again at 1100 but again didn't run into any Japanese planes.[41]

Having flown on both earlier interceptions, Paul Gambonini was tired but found himself ordered on yet another mission at 1410. Japanese bombers escorted by Zeros were reported heading in to attack Soerabaja. With nine squadron mates and four Dutchmen—De Haas, Simons, Wink, and Vonck— Gambonini took off at 1430 and headed northeast. Nearing the target area, he spotted six Betty bombers and twelve Zeros above him, but only the Brewsters could reach them; they were too high for the worn-out P-40s to engage.

As the Dutchmen climbed, they were fired on by diving Zeros. The Brewsters of Vonck and Simons were badly hit, but both pilots managed to continue flying the sturdy ships and headed back after brief combat. On returning to Ngoro, however, Vonck's damaged engine seized up, and he was obliged to bail out. Simon's Brewster held up, and the Dutchman landed at Maospati Field, Madioen, for needed repairs.[42]

Spared from combat, Gambonini and eight other Americans came in to land at Ngoro in late afternoon with the two remaining Dutchmen. One of the 17th's pilots had aborted the mission because of mechanical problems and returned earlier. Shortly after climbing out of their ships and heading to the operations shack, Gambonini and his demoralized squadron mates heard the drone of engines in the distance and looked up. What they saw dispirited them further: a flight of Japanese bombers heading towards the field. But the usual late afternoon thunderstorm was rapidly developing and covered the field just as the Japanese roared overhead. Although relieved to have been spared a bombing attack, Gambonini and the remaining pursuiters of the squadron concluded that the Japanese had now finally found their field. With the Japanese landing forces expected momentarily, they knew it was hopeless now. Java and their little secret field were doomed.[43]

STEAMING SOUTH ALL ALONE on the afternoon of February 28, the *Abbekerk* was now about three hundred miles out of Tjilatjap, traveling "at a good clip" on the deep blue Indian Ocean, but Paul Eckley and the other evacuees jammed on the deck were jittery. A plane had passed overhead earlier in the day. They couldn't make it out, but they worried that it was Japanese.[44] The evacuees' fears accelerated when at about 1700 someone noticed another black speck in the sky and called out. All eyes were focused on the aircraft as it came closer and closer, "as a chicken might watch a hawk," Captain Crane observed. Then someone yelled "Rising Sun! It's the Japs!" Crane thought it looked like a dive bomber, and that would mean it was off a nearby Japanese carrier. General quarters was sounded.[45] Adriaan Kik, relieved from his engine room duties, saw the plane, too. He was regretting that the two Bofors antiaircraft guns that had been installed in Scotland had been removed for Sumatra's defense just before the ship arrived in Tjiltatjap. He knew what one bomb hit could do to the *Abbekerk* with its load of munitions.[46]

Determined to put up a fight, Cpl. Ken Perry and other enlisted men of the 17th Pursuit and the 7th Bomb Group brought up on deck four .50-caliber machine guns that had been salvaged from P-40s, hooked them up on pieces of pipe, and tied them to the ship's railing with rope. As the Japanese pilot circled for a second pass, Perry and others lined up on both sides of the *Abbekerk* with rifles and joined those ready to fire the machine guns. "He'll bomb for sure this time," one of the men exclaimed.[47] As the plane came over the *Abbekerk* again and went into its dive, it was met by intense fire from the men on the deck that apparently forced it to climb away. Perry figured it had been hit. However, the Japanese pilot came around a third time, flying low and slow, just about mast height. Once again the rifles and machine guns opened up on him as the Dutch captain of the *Abbekerk* maneuvered to present as small a target as possible. As before, the Japanese did not return their fire but dropped something—a bomb?—about a hundred feet off the *Abbekerk*'s stern before abandoning his fruitless mission and flying away.[48]

To Captain Crane the whole business "was like a scene in a B-rated movie." In their enthusiasm, the men had shot down the ship's radio tower and put several holes in its funnel. But Paul Eckley took the incident more seriously than did Crane: "I don't like the game of tag when you are 'it,'" he wrote in his diary that evening. Tommy Hayes figured that "our goose is cooked"; he was sure the Japanese pilot would notify his commander, and more planes or subs would be on their way. But darkness was now descending, and they knew they would be safe until the morning. To improve their chances the captain had also made a radical course change.[49]

Also heading south on the afternoon of February 28, the oiler *Pecos* and destroyers *Edsall* and *Whipple* were putting distance between themselves and any Japanese land-based bombers that could attack them when Commander Crouch on the *Whipple* received a message from Adm. William Glassford, Java-based commander of all U.S. Navy ships in the area. After transfer of the *Langley* survivors to the *Pecos* had been completed at sea, the *Whipple* was to proceed to the Cocos Islands to the west, but the *Edsall* was to retain its *Langley* P-40 pilot survivors and return to Tjilatjap.[50]

At 0634 the next morning, under moderate sea conditions, thirty-one *Langley* pilots and one enlisted man watched dejectedly as the *Edsall* began transferring all the remaining *Langley* survivors it had picked up to the *Pecos*—including the wounded Gerry Dix and Bill Ackerman—but not them. After the transfer operation was finished at about 0800, the *Edsall* was preparing to head north as the *Whipple* turned to head west and the *Pecos* to the south. But first the *Edsall*'s commander, Lt. Joshua J. Nix, signaled Crouch at 0815 with a query: "Any further orders for me?" The reply confirmed the order of the afternoon before: "Proceed Tjilatjap . . . to arrive dawn tomorrow." The *Edsall* swung about and began heading northeast.[51]

The confirmation that they were to head for Tjilatjap instead of Australia came as a shock to Gerry Keenan and the pilots and enlisted man under his command. Why were they being ordered to Java? The P-40s they were supposed to fly were lying at the bottom of the Indian Ocean.

AT MAGOEWO AIRFIELD, located in the northeast outskirts of Jogjakarta, the twelve pilots and twelve enlisted men of the 17th Pursuit, split into three groups, had been waiting all afternoon of February 28 to board the two B-17Es and the B-24A that were scheduled to fly them out to Australia that evening. Also waiting to board were other FEAF personnel, including men from the 7th and 19th Bomb Groups.[52] Finally, at 1040 the Flying Fortress of Capt. Al Key was ready for boarding, as was that of his younger brother, Fred Key. George Parker, along with fellow pilots Bill Turner, Jim Ryan, Ray Thompson, Gene Wahl, and Elwin Jackson, climbed into Al Key's ship, joined by Sgts. Dale Holt and Charles Schaffer plus Cpls. Selby Cockcroft, Bland King, and Angelo Prioreschi and Pvt. Carl Warner. Three of the other pilots—Walt Coss, Cy Blanton, and B. J. Oliver—were instructed to board Fred Key's ship along with two more of the twelve enlisted men.[53]

At 1100 the Key brothers—famed for their prewar flying feats—lifted off the field for the long flight to Broome on Australia's northwest coast. In Al Key's Fortress, jammed with twenty-three passengers and crew, Holt was obliged to stand in the catwalk in the bomb bay. B. J. Oliver in Fred Key's ship was pressed into the Plexiglas nose for the trip. But they were all relieved to be getting out of Java ahead of the Japanese. Parker managed to inscribe in his diary, "Goodbye to Java. May God spare them." He was thinking of his squadron mates they had left behind at Ngoro.[54]

Three of the 17th's pilot evacuees were still on the field when the two Fortresses lifted off, as well as four of the enlisted men. But at 1150 they were told to climb aboard the B-24A that Capt. Paul Davis had flown in from Broome. Dwight Muckley, Hubert Egenes, and Butch Hague all took places on board *Arabian Knight,* as did SSgts. Leo Burden, Jim Freeman, Dave Griffith, and Jim Swanson. At fifty minutes past midnight Davis cleared the field and headed south for Broome.[55]

AT 0200 ON MARCH 1, Maj. Bill Fisher was awakened in his quarters at Soerabaja by a phone call. It was Capt. Frank Kurtz Colonel Eubank's liaison officer, on the line. Kurtz had picked up the news that the Japanese in landing barges had been sighted off the Java coast near Kragan, just ninety miles west of Soerabaja.[56] Kurtz and Fisher were worried that the remaining 17th Pursuit Squadron (Provisional) pilots and men would be cut off by the Japanese invasion force, now only eighty-five miles northwest of Ngoro, if arrangements weren't made to get them across Java to Jogjakarta for evacuation.

The day before, Fisher had informed Eubank that the remaining P-40s were in very bad condition and that continued operations would be unwise and would only result in the loss of more valuable pilots. Eubank had agreed that the 17th operate only as long as it could do so effectively. Now, following the news of the approaching Japanese invasion force, he instructed Fisher to go to Ngoro and personally check the condition of the squadron. Major General Van Oyen, Colonel Eubank's Dutch superior at Java Air Command in Bandoeng, wanted the American and Dutch pilots at Ngoro to attack the Japanese as they landed at Kragan at daybreak. Eubank ordered Fisher to perform the mission "if possible," as it was "very important" (to the Dutch).[57] After carrying out the mission, the remaining American pilots and enlisted men at Ngoro should report to Eubank at Jogjakarta for evacuation.[58]

Fisher now called the 17th Pursuit's acting CO, Ed Kiser, and informed him of the Japanese landing and Van Oyen's order for the strafing mission. Kiser told Fisher that he was sending Bill Hennon, who had returned that evening with the five others from the fruitless Tjilatjap trip, to Soerabaja to pick up Kurtz and Fisher and bring them to Ngoro Field.[59] As soon as Hennon arrived, at 0400, Kurtz and Fisher piled into his car, and the three headed out in the pitch darkness over the fifty miles of winding road to Ngoro. They reached the field before dawn. Fisher met with Kiser and the other pilots about mounting the strafing mission. It would be flown by all nine in-commission P-40s, the five Brewsters, and the seven Hurricanes. Pooped out after driving all night to Ngoro and then to Soerabaja and back, Hennon was told he would not be flying the mission himself.[60]

CHAPTER FIFTEEN

"Senseless in All Senses"

JUST BEFORE SUNRISE ON THE morning of Sunday, March 1, Jan Bruinier was arguing with his squadron commander, Lieutenant Anemaet, at the 17th Pursuit's operations shack on the field at Ngoro. Over the opposition of Anemaet, the Dutch RAF veteran was maintaining that he should lead their squadron's seven serviceable Hawker Hurricanes in the Dutch-American strafing mission scheduled by Maj. Bill Fisher against the Japanese landing forces on the northeastern coast of Java. Bruinier complained that he had been allowed to fly only one mission in the squadron's Hurricanes, being too tied down with logistics work as Anemaet's deputy, and that his familiarity with the latest RAF tactics qualified him to lead the 2-Vl.G.-IV's pilots. Finally, Anemaet, who would not be flying himself on the mission, gave in to Bruinier's entreaties and approved his request.[1]

But the Hurricanes would be the last planes in the formation. As ordered by Fisher, ten P-40s—the last serviceable ships of the squadron, all with engines with too much time on them—would lead off, followed by the five remaining flyable Dutch Brewster Buffaloes, led by Lt. G. J. de Haas. With twelve aircraft vs. ten, the Dutch pilots regarded the mission as more Dutch than American.[2]

Standing off the field as the first rays of sunrise lit the area, Paul Gambonini watched as the ten P-40s began taking off at 0530. He was operations officer this day and would not be one of the handful of the remaining who would be flying. He was not enthusiastic about the chances for success—"a suicide mission, almost," he felt. With the invasion force coming ashore northwest of them, the situation looked "really bad here." He couldn't understand why the squadron had not been evacuated from Ngoro by now.[3] Gambonini and the other 17th Pursuiters were not privy to the information that FEAF liaison officer Frank Kurtz and Major Fisher had about evacuation plans. Neither had told them that this would be their last mission in defense of the Indies and that they would be flown out of Jogjakarta to Australia that evening after the return of the pilots. But Kurtz was anxious as he watched the takeoff, particularly for his close friend Jack Dale. "Would those kids come back alive in time to get across Java" for the evacuation flight from Jogjakarta?[4]

Leading the Americans off, squadron commander Ed Kiser had selected Frank Adkins and Spence Johnson to fly with him in A flight as his wingmen. Dale was at the head of B flight, with Mo Caldwell and Marion Fuchs on his wings. Joe Kruzel had Connie Reagan and Bob McWherter as his wingmen in C flight.[5] After the P-40s cleared the field, Lt. De Haas led off the five Brewsters, followed by Bruinier at the head of the seven Hurricanes. But just after the Dutch-American group formed up over the field, De Haas and his Brewsters raced ahead of Kiser's P-40s and took over the lead of the spread-out formation, evidently feeling that the Dutch should be heading this last joint Dutch-American aerial effort to oppose the invaders of their land. The early morning sun now illuminated the terrain below as the twenty-one fighters headed due west in the direction of Madioen, then turned north for the coast of East Java and their destination, the beach at Kragan, where the Japanese invasion force was reported to be going ashore.[6]

After reaching the shoreline east of Kragan, De Haas led the mixed group out to sea in sight of all the Japanese warships supporting the landing, then swung inland to the east to prepare to attack from out of the morning sun. There were their targets: about thirty transports anchored in a line parallel to the coast, with barges in long columns carrying troops and plying between the shore and the transports. It appeared that many of the Japanese had already landed on the narrow, two-mile-long beachhead.[7] Screaming in at just thirty feet above the sea, the Brewsters, followed by the P-40s, then the Hurricanes, began spraying machine-gun fire into the hapless troops on the barges and beach. The American and Dutch pilots were relieved not to have any Zeros diving into them. They assumed that they were flying too low to have been spotted by any covering Japanese fighters. But the strafers ran into a barrage of anti aircraft fire from the barges, shore batteries that had already been set up, and destroyers offshore that caught them in a deadly crossfire.[8]

Bob McWherter in Kruzel's C flight made his own initial pass on one of the destroyers, figuring that its crew wouldn't notice him if he approached them from the seaward side as it fired on the strafers. He met no opposition as he cleared the deck of its gunners then headed in to join the attack on the barges. Kruzel himself was flying down the length of the beachhead, firing at troops running across the beach and inland for the cover of trees. But as he turned inland after a second sweep, hot oil started streaming into the cockpit. The expanding fumes were making his eyes water. Assuming that fresh air would get rid of the fumes and relieve the stinging in his eyes, Kruzel opened the canopy a little. Suddenly he was sprayed all over with oil instead. The suction effect had drawn the sticky mess from the floor of the cockpit and showered his face and bare arms and legs—he was wearing Australian-issue short-sleeved shirt and shorts. No way could he continue his attack, he realized, even though he still had .50-caliber ammunition left for more firing runs; the interior of the cockpit and canopy was so coated with oil that he couldn't see forward at all. But how would he be able to get back to Ngoro and land? The only way would be if one of the others could guide him home. Spotting McWherter nearby, he radioed him and asked his wingman to lead him back.[9]

Just before Kruzel's call, McWherter had been flying with Connie Reagan when he was shocked to see flames spurting out of Reagan's P-40. Excitedly, he signaled Reagan to head inland and bail out over the beach. It seemed to McWherter that Reagan understood his message when he waved back to him. As Reagan's ship began falling, McWherter followed him down, but then fire from the barges and ground batteries forced him to turn away. When he looked back, Reagan's ship was lying on the beach in what looked like a crash-landing. There was no parachute in the air that would indicate that Reagan had bailed out.[10]

Reagan had indeed crash-landed and had managed to get out of the wreck before it blew up. On his third strafing run, his ship had caught fire after being hit when he was only a few feet off the ocean, half a mile from shore. After managing to climb up, his engine had completely quit, leaving him no option but to head for shore and crash-land.[11]

Leading B flight, Jack Dale was flying so low in his first firing pass on the troops on the barges that his propeller was picking up water from the splashes his bullets were making as they hit the sea around the boats, obliging him to pull up. But just as he did, he noticed his wingman, Moe Caldwell, was also pulling up off to the right, his P-40 on fire. Caldwell had let his wheels down, apparently planning a forced landing on the beach. Suddenly, his ship flipped over and crashed into the sea, blowing up on the impact.[12]

In Ed Kiser's A flight, Frank Adkins was also hit at low altitude. He had no intention of trying a crash landing, however. Climbing to a sufficient altitude, he opened his canopy and bailed out, alighting just off the beach about three hundred yards from the Japanese. Kiser's other wingman, Spence Johnson, also almost lost his ship. In a strafing pass his P-40 touched the water, then clipped a barge with the propeller. "Something or someone beyond my power saved me," he figured. After the near-disastrous incident, he had no desire to push his luck further and turned to head back to Ngoro.[13]

Also heading back, an oil-smeared Joe Kruzel was trying to maintain formation on McWherter's wing by looking out the side from his wide-open canopy. But how was he going to be able to land once he reached the home field? He had an idea. Kruzel called McWherter on the radio and asked him to approach the field as if he were going to make a landing, but just as he neared the touch-down point, go around, and Kruzel would land instead. With the help of a handkerchief he extricated from his pocket to clean the oil around his eyes and the P-40's airspeed indicator, the oil-splattered Kruzel brought his damaged P-40 in for a normal landing at about 0740. The other two flight leaders had returned safely, too, although their ships were punctured with small holes. A check of Kruzel's bird indicated that a single round of fire had penetrated the nose and passed through the oil tank, causing the leak. Of the three other P-40s that made it back, that of Marion Fuchs—a wingman to Jack Dale—was most badly damaged, with its controls shot up.[14]

With the loss of three comrades, the pursuiters were seething that they had been ordered to fly the mission. To Spence Johnson the sacrifice of Adkins, Reagan, and Caldwell "was nothing more than murder in my estimation and could never be justified!" Fuchs felt that the mission was "senseless in all senses." He asked himself, "What were 10–12 aircraft against over 100,000 Japanese coming ashore?"[15]

Of the Dutchmen flying the five Brewster Buffalos, four—Simons, Wink, Bruggink, and Van Haarlem—managed to bring their ships back to Ngoro. De Haas went on to land at Maospati Field with hits in the engine and tail, including one through the oil tank. Four of the seven Hurricane pilots returned to Ngoro, too, including Marinus—in a shot-up ship—Hamming, Kok, and Dejalle. Their leader, Bruinier, his wooden propeller damaged in a hard encounter with a barge, went on to Maospati, as did Boonstoppel, while De Wilde crash-landed his damaged Hurricane in a rice field near Bodjonegoro.[16]

One other Dutch aircraft made it into Ngoro, too, but it was not on the strafing mission. A Lockheed L-12A was bringing in radio crystals for the Hurricanes when on its approach to the field a pair of the returning P-40s— either those of Dale and Fuchs or Kiser and Johnson—attacked the hapless Dutch twin-engine transport, believing it to be Japanese. The Americans fired a couple of shots before the flight leader realized their mistake when he recognized the red, white, and blue flag insignia on the side of the aircraft. The two crew members of the Lockheed who manned its 7.7 mm machine guns in the side windows did not return the fire.[17]

Demoralized by the experience he and his squadron mates had gone through, Jack Dale asked his friend Kurtz "when in hell will we get out of here, Frank?" Now Kurtz and Fisher gave Dale and the other pursuiters and enlisted men the long-awaited news: they had flown their last mission and were to turn their P-40s over to the Dutch pilots and prepare to leave for evacuation from Jogjakarta to Australia.[18] At least that was according to the instructions that Eubank had given orally to Fisher in the early hours of the morning. Dutch commander Lieutenant Anemaet also was now informed of the decision regarding the Americans.[19]

At about 0900, Ens. Alexander van der Vossen was seated in one of the remaining flyable P-40s, ready for takeoff. He had read the P-40 pilot's manual and received verbal instructions from one of the 17th's pilots and a crew chief. Van der Vossen had arrived earlier at Ngoro by car to join his 2-Vl.G.-IV comrades and help transfer any in-commission P-40s to Bandoeng's Andir Field.[20] Suddenly, someone yelled "Stop! Get out!" Two Zeros were over the field, strafing everything in sight. With the help of the American, a terrified Van der Vossen climbed out of the cockpit, dropped to the ground, and headed for safety.[21] Bedlam ensued as everyone on the field—Dutch and American alike—ran for the jungle. For the next twenty minutes the two Zero pilots leisurely flew up and down the field at low altitude, pouring 7.7 mm machine gun and 20 mm cannon fire into the P-40s, Hurricanes, and Brewsters they spotted in their dispersal positions. The Japanese strafers met no opposition; the field's antiaircraft guns had been withdrawn earlier.[22]

Returning to the field after the Zeros broke off their attack, the shaken Dutch and Americans surveyed the damage. All of the P-40s were either burned or riddled, as were the Brewsters. Only two of the Hurricanes had survived the blistering strafing. The Dutch Lockheed L-12A, left out in the middle of one of the runways, was a shambles, too.[23]

But how did the Japanese discover their camouflaged field? Looking at the wreck of the Lockheed, the Dutch believed they had the answer. The Dutch pilot had left it out in the open after landing, shaken after his encounter with the two P-40s minutes earlier. The patrolling Zeros must have spotted it and realized that this was the secret field of the Americans.[24] Fisher, however, believed the Japanese had discovered the field the preceding day but had been unable to attack because of heavy rain. It was for this reason that he had ensured that all the remaining planes were dispersed and hidden after returning from the strafing mission.[25]

As the 17th Provisional now prepared to evacuate Ngoro, they first set about destroying any equipment, ordnance, and supplies that could be of any use to the Japanese and ensuring that no P-40s being left were flyable.

Sgt. Julian Guerrero, for one, joined other enlisted men in setting fire to the squadron's stores of fuel and the few remaining pursuit ships. Attempting to destroy one of the aerial bombs in the ammo dump, Bob McWherter and others asked one of the ground crew how to do it. When they were told to hit it around the nose with a sledgehammer to crack the case, however, they looked at each other and exclaimed, "No way!"[26]

Before the squadron's personnel piled into their vehicles to return to Blimbing to pick up their personal possessions, Fisher and Kurtz approached Lieutenant Anemaet with an offer: Would he and the other Dutch pilots and ground crew want to join the 17th Pursuiters in the evacuation trip to Jogjakarta and fly on with them to Australia? "Airplanes can be built quicker than pilots trained and made combat-ready," he told the 2-Vl.G.-IV commander.[27]

Touched by the offer, Anemaet accepted on the spot but explained that he would need to obtain permission from NEIAF headquarters first. As Van der Vossen listened next to him, Anemaet put in a call to Col. E. T. Kengen, second in command to Major General Van Oyen. Anemaet described the situation at Ngoro to Kengen and related Fisher's offer to join the 17th Pursuit in its evacuation to Australia.[28] The reply was a resounding "No!" "There are planes at Andir Field ready to be manned by you," Kengen maintained. Any pilot who left with the Americans would be considered a deserter, he declared.[29] A disappointed Anemaet passed the message to his fellow pilots. They would have to remain. Their reaction was bitter. When Anemaet told Fisher of Kengen's rejection of his offer, the American commander's reply was in defiance of the deputy Dutch commander's order. If Anemaet and the others changed their mind and wanted to be "disobedient," the offer still stood, Fisher stated. But, reluctant to disobey an order, the Dutchmen declined.[30]

It was about 1010 when the officers and men of the 17th boarded their cars and trucks, the downcast Dutch pilots and ground crew looking on. Anemaet came forward for a formal goodbye. The tall, thin Dutch commander, so highly respected by the Americans, stuck out his hand and said simply, "Thank you for all you have done. We have tried, but we are finished." It was a sad moment for Fisher, Kurtz, and the 17th Pursuit, leaving their courageous comrades to an uncertain fate as they themselves were being given the opportunity to escape the doomed island.[31]

ONLY ONE HOUR AFTER reversing course to head north to Tjilatjap, at about 0915 on the morning of March 1, Lieutenant Nix on the *Edsall* received electrifying orders from Admiral Glassford: all American Navy vessels were to "clear the [Java] region." Nix's earlier orders to proceed to Tjilatjap were being cancelled.[32] Once again Nix changed course and now headed his destroyer south again. For Gerry Keenan and the thirty pilots and one enlisted man in his charge, the switch in orders was received like a reprieve from a death sentence.

ON BOARD THE *Pecos*, fellow *Langley* survivors Gerry Dix and Bill Ackerman—jammed in with more than seven hundred other men—were also feeling relieved this morning; the southbound oiler was now getting beyond range of the land-based bombers that had attacked Christmas Island the previous morning. Soon they would be safely in Australia, they figured. But at about 1000 their reverie was broken when the sound of a radial engine was heard high in the sky. When the *Pecos*'s lookout spotted a single-engine carrier-type aircraft far out to port and shouted the unwelcome news, the alarm was sounded and the crew ran to their battle stations. To Dix, Ackerman, and the other *Langley* survivors, history seemed to be repeating itself. Like the reconnaissance plane that had discovered the *Langley* two days earlier, this one would certainly report its finding that would lead to an attack on the *Pecos*. The oiler's captain, Cmdr. Paul Abernethy, ordered his gunners to commence firing, but the fire of the two three-inch guns and ten water-cooled machine guns proved unable to reach the intruder, now passing out of sight.[33]

Although many lookouts continuously searched the sky the next hour and a half, it came as a surprise when at 1153 a crewman looked up and suddenly shouted, "Here they come!" A Japanese dive bomber, easily identified by its fixed landing gear as an Aichi D3A Type 99 "Val," was in a steep descent over the *Pecos* and had released its 550-pound bomb. As the alarm blared, half of the oiler's guns began firing. Dix, Ackerman, and the other passengers dove for cover while crew members ran for their stations. The bomb exploded in the water off the port side.[34] But one by one, at intervals of about one minute, eight other Vals lined up behind each other to release their bombs as Commander Abernethy skillfully switched his ship's direction each time. The second bomb exploded in the water, too, off to starboard, and the next six pilots also missed. But the *Pecos*'s luck ran out when the missile of the ninth dive bomber crashed through the main deck and tore a hole fifteen feet wide, causing the *Pecos* to list. Fires started in fuel tanks, and dense smoke filled the passageways, but the list was quickly checked.[35]

Only nineteen minutes after the Vals concluded their attack and headed eastward, lookouts spotted a second group of the dive bombers. The *Pecos*'s engines were now up to speed again, and its list gradually decreasing, but there was a huge hole in the deck and fires were still burning. Like the first group, the Japanese went into their dives one by one, a minute separating each bomb release, beginning at 1224. This time the gunners of the *Pecos* were ready for them, but the oiler's maneuverability was reduced because of the effects of the first attack. Despite the *Pecos*'s attempts to evade, the first bomb struck the motor launch stored on the starboard, and the second penetrated the main deck, causing a new list to port. Although the third bomb fell into the sea, the heavy list, smoke, and fire caused by the two hits convinced many of the panic-stricken *Langley* survivors that the *Pecos* was going down. When someone yelled "abandon ship," the crew hastily lowered two whaleboats, and some one hundred men in the aft jumped overboard or into the whaleboats. Hugging the funnel on the port side, Dix, Ackerman, and others watched in horror as the screw of the *Pecos* chewed up one of the whaleboats and its occupants while the other boat drew more and more out of sight astern.[36]

As the *Pecos* listed heavily to port, its guns still firing at the dive bombers, a fourth bomb exploded in the water, as did the fifth and sixth, but the seventh detonated on the forecastle, killing the crews of two of the five-inch guns and starting fires below deck. The bomb of the eighth Val passed through a hole near a three-inch gun and exploded deep in the hull, buckling bulkheads. After the ninth Val dropped its bomb just off to port, causing a tremendous shock wave, the Japanese headed back to their carrier, leaving its victim smoking and on fire but still operating. It was 1303.[37]

During the next hour and fifteen minutes the crew managed to reduce the *Pecos*'s list to ten degrees and increase its speed southward. After the oiler's radio was repaired, its officers called for help and gave the ship's location. About seventy nautical miles northwest, the *Whipple* picked up the calls and reversed direction, planning to catch up with the *Pecos* just after dark. But at 1415 the hopes of Commander Abernethy and his surviving crew and passengers were deflated when another nine dive bombers appeared overhead. For some reason they did not attack, however, but remained at altitude until another nine Type 99s joined them ten minutes later. This time the flight leader of the newly arrived group led his pilots down closely spaced together, and the Vals released their bombs one after the other in the face of intense fire from the *Pecos*'s gunners. Thanks to quick maneuvering, the *Pecos* evaded all of them, although there were two near misses.[38]

For Dix, suffering from a broken jaw and an injured arm, even the near misses were a painful experience. Each explosion bounced him up and down on the deck from the concussive effect. At the same time, it would cause him to slide down toward the port rail across the deck, and he would have to crawl back up next to the bulkhead on the starboard side that he had chosen as the best location against the strafing attacks that he expected.[39]

Perhaps intimidated by the antiaircraft fire from the *Pecos,* the earlier-arriving group of Vals now began their dives at a higher altitude than those of the first three groups to attack. At 1425 the lead pilot tipped over into his dive, his comrades closely following behind. His bomb missed, as did those of the next five pilots following him, but the seventh and eighth "Vals," releasing at only fourteen hundred feet, caused grave damage to the oiler. The first bomb exploded in the water just off the starboard side, wiping out most of the machine gun crews on that side, and the second detonated near the bow on the port side, caving in the hull below the waterline.[40]

As tons of seawater now poured in, the *Pecos* began going down bow first. The radioman had managed to transmit SOS messages but had not received any acknowledgments, even from the *Whipple,* now heading in the direction of the *Pecos*. With water up to one foot of the main deck, the oiler listing heavily to port, Commander Abernethy gave the abandon ship order at 1530.[41]

Joining the others going over the side, Dix and Ackerman lowered themselves from the stern on a rope and landed on the screw shaft, which was well out of the water. When the shaft was about ten feet above the water, Dix jumped and called to Ackerman to do so, too. The shaft was now twenty feet out of the water, but Ackerman jumped anyway.[42] The two pursuit pilots found debris all around them and chose two long timbers nearby to provide flotation. Dix put his arms over one end of the timbers and Ackerman did the same at the other end. From their vantage point they watched transfixed as the *Pecos* twisted to port, the stern rising higher and higher. When it reached a vertical position, they witnessed "all manner of debris and bodies" falling forward from the deck into the sea. It was a sight that Dix would never forget.

During the next hours Dix and Ackerman held on to the two timbers, discomfited by the waves of oily water that splashed in their faces. Each time, they turned opposite the wind to try to keep the waves at their back instead. They were grateful that the oil and gas discharged by the *Pecos* did not catch fire. In the beginning they heard the calls of other survivors nearby, but soon they were scattered and out of sight. As darkness set in, they heard no more cries for help. But they had heard other sounds: heavy explosions in the distance to the northeast. They wondered if the *Edsall,* which they believed was steaming for Java with their pursuit pilot comrades, was under attack.[43]

As darkness descended, visibility toward the horizon was still good. Then, at 1910 one of the men in the whaleboat noticed a dark silhouette approaching them. Six minutes later another man in a raft fired a white flare that was seen at once by the crew of a destroyer about a mile away. It was the *Whipple.*[44] For the next two hours and forty-three minutes the *Whipple* maneuvered in circles to pick up widely scattered survivors.

When they heard cries of "Help!" and "Over here!" from those around them, Dix and Ackerman first realized that there was a ship nearby that was going to try to rescue them. A sailor came swimming over to them with a rope, put it around the timbers, and began pulling the two airmen toward the ship. Both were pulled aboard on another rope, the knotted line hanging from the ship's railing. Dix collapsed "like a wet dishrag" and fell heavily on the deck. Their faces and clothes covered with oil, Dix and Ackerman were carried to the wardroom, where they were cleaned of the oil and given coffee. It was then that they learned that it was the *Whipple* that had rescued them. But Sergeant Mabry was not with them; he either was killed in the attack on the *Pecos* or drowned afterwards.[45]

AT ABOUT 1030 ON THE MORNING of March 1 three sedans and two trucks carrying what was left of the 17th Pursuit Squadron (Provisional) pulled into Blimbing after the short drive from Ngoro Field. The officers and men immediately headed for their rooms in the Dutch houses that had served as their quarters and began collecting personal items, including diaries. Then they settled any outstanding bills before saying goodbye to the Dutch women who had cooked for and looked after them the past month. For many it was an emotional experience having to bid them farewell.[46]

Paul Gambonini had little to take with him and was waiting ready to reboard his truck when Capt. George F. "Doc" Adams, the 17th's medical officer, asked him if he would drive him and his medical enlisted staff in his car instead. Adams remembered that Gambonini had driven to Jogjakarta before and thus knew the way, unlike himself. Gambonini readily accepted the offer. It was a better arrangement than having to stand up in the bed of the truck all that distance. Joe Kruzel was also fortunate, riding in one of the two other sedans brought back from Ngoro. But it was a tight fit to get five other pilots into the vehicle, too. In the other car Jim Morehead was squashed in with Roger Williams, Marion Fuchs, and three others. But six-foot, four-inch Hal Lund and the remaining five pilots would have to join the squadron's enlisted men, forced to stand in the bed of the two trucks.[47]

While Gambonini knew the way to Jogjakarta, the others didn't. For that reason Anemaet had insisted that their Dutch liaison officer, Arie Geurtz, accompany them on the long, 145-mile trip to the southern Javanese city. Riding in one of the trucks, Geurtz could also do double duty as a guide and interpreter, the Dutch commander had reasoned.[48] But with only a road map to guide them, the truck drivers were told to be careful and keep together. Nevertheless, the trucks did get separated from the cars. Some Dutch troops they ran into were able to put one of them on the right track again, thanks to Pvt. Clinton Washburn's command of Dutch. But they were all worried when

Jack Dale at Magoewo Airfield, Jogjakarta, awaiting an evacuation flight to Australia following the Japanese air raid on the field, March 1, 1942. *Courtesy Joseph J. Kruzel.*

the soldiers told them the advancing Japanese were not far away. Seeing the Dutch blowing up sugar mills on the way only added to their anxiety.[49]

Kurtz was also anxious for another reason: they were running late, and he wasn't sure if Colonel Eubank knew they were on their way. The caravan stopped at a town on the route where Kurtz put in a call to Jogjakarta, but he was informed that Eubank couldn't be found, nor could a message be delivered to him. After the men finished a quick meal at the hotel, they climbed back into their vehicles and were on the road again.[50] After passing Soerakarta (Solo) they were now on the last leg of their tiring trip, Jogjakarta just thirty miles further to the southwest, according to their map. But as they approached the outskirts of the city they realized they didn't know on what side the airfield was located. Then they saw flames and smoke climbing in the sky, a sure sign of the field's position, and headed in that direction. As they drove up to the field, a disheartening sight greeted them: the hangars and five bombers—three LB-30s and two B-17Es—burning away. How were they going to get evacuated now?[51]

But then they spotted a single B-17E parked on the edge of the field, serial number 41–2507 on the tail. Its pilot, Elliott Vandevanter, told them he had managed to get off the field just before the bombers struck and had flown out to sea to wait out the attack. But he felt lucky; the bombers did not have a Zero escort. Otherwise his goose would have been cooked.[52]

Accompanied by the pilots, Kurtz and Fisher reported in to Colonel Eubank, commanding what was left of the Far East Air Force in Java. Eubank's attitude struck the pursuiters as hostile. The stern-faced colonel "made it quite clear that he was in charge." They were to comply "precisely with his orders as to who and when they would get out." To Bill Hennon it seemed that Eubank "would have left them all behind if he had had his way."[53] But with eighteen anxious pursuiters and their crew chiefs and armorers vying for places on the single B-17E available to take them out, Eubank was taking a necessarily tough stance, even given the benefit of doubt regarding his motives towards their evacuation. Seniority would be the yardstick he would use for selection. He himself topped the list, followed by his executive officer, Maj. Ed Broadhurst; his liaison officer, Captain Kurtz; and the 17th Pursuit's commander, Capt. Bill Fisher. The former 20th Pursuit's CO, 1st Lt. William Lane, was next in seniority, but Eubank wanted to hold him back to arrange for evacuation of the remaining officers and men on flights that Eubank said were expected in. Of the pilots themselves, the 17th's acting CO, Ed Kiser, and his fellow 40-H Philippine veterans, Jack Dale and Joe Kruzel, topped the list, but Ed Gilmore was not selected. Lane wanted him to remain behind with him to ensure that the enlisted men were evacuated. Rounding out the pilot selectees were Ben Irvin, Bill Hennon, Jim Morehead, Andy Reynolds, and Bob Dockstader. But Eubank, always more favorably inclined towards enlisted men than officers, offered places to nine of the 17th Pursuit's ground crewmen. But that was it. Adamant about not overloading the war-weary Flying Fortress, Eubank would not allow Vandevanter to take more than twenty-three passengers. That left two-thirds of the 17th's evacuees to hope for the arrival of additional planes to take them out.[54]

As final preparations were being made for the flight, the air raid siren went off, and all dived for the safety of a drainage ditch. It looked like a Zero was approaching—and their solitary Fortress was sitting out on the field, defenseless. Ever combative, Jim Morehead drew his .45 and along with other pilots took potshots at the Japanese as the plane swung over the field at 1410. Sgt. Clay Harper joined in with his old Springfield '03 rifle. But the feeble opposition was halted by Lane, who screamed, "Stop it! Stop it! He'll be back to strafe us!" However, the Zero made no effort to strafe them or the B-17. It was evidently on a reconnaissance flight to assess the bombing damage done earlier.[55]

As dusk began to envelop the area, Eubank signaled for the boarding to begin. Kurtz and at least six others moved forward to the pilot's compartment and sat down on the floor. Vandevanter made as many of his passengers cram forward as possible so he could get the Fortress's tail up for the take-off. But as he was about to taxi onto the runway, someone yelled to stop—there was pounding on the side of the aircraft. Jim Morehead opened the rear access door and saw little Les Johnsen excitedly begging to be taken aboard. Morehead reached down, grabbed his hand, and pulled him aboard. With no one expressing their disapproval of taking another passenger, Vandevanter turned into the cratered runway, revved his engines, and went into his takeoff roll for the eleven-hundred-mile haul south to Broome, Australia.[56]

Watching the Fortress pass out of sight, Paul Gambonini and the others left on the field wondered if Eubank was being candid with them when he told them that other bombers would be coming in later that evening. But there was nothing for them to do but wait. In the meantime they collected all the squadron's papers and records and threw them into a bonfire they had started. They didn't want them to fall into Japanese hands. Following this last official act of the 17th Pursuit, Lane led his subdued charges into Jogjakarta for a last dinner.[57] On their return to the field, two bits of good news awaited them. Two B-17s had come in from Madioen at 1850, one piloted by Lt. Harold Smelser and the other by Lt. Dick Beck. Each had been ordered to stop at Jogjakarta and pick up evacuees. Then three more B-17s and two LB-30s came in to land. It looked like the pursuiters were not going to be left behind after all.[58]

But what cheered them at the personal level was to find their buddy Frank Adkins on the field. Given up for lost, he had showed up in the company of a car full of the Dutch pilots left behind at Ngoro that morning. United with his elated comrades, the ebullient Adkins proceeded to regale them with his account of escaping the Japanese after bailing out of his P-40 over Kragan early that morning. He had grabbed a bicycle near the beach from a passing Javanese, pedaled as fast as he could away from the Japanese landing area, and was picked up and dropped off back at Ngoro. He found the field deserted except for the Dutch pilots and mechanics still there who informed him that his comrades had all left for Jogjakarta for evacuation. But Anemaet, Bruinier, and the others were getting ready to leave, too, following another Japanese attack on the field at 1430 by seven bombers at low altitude and six strafing Zeros. Ordered to Andir Field, Bandoeng, the Dutchmen took Adkins with them when they departed at 1500 and were now dropping him off at Jogjakarta, midway on their long trip.[59]

As the B-17s and LB-30s were being serviced by Gambonini and the other pilots and men of the 17th Pursuit and 7th and 19th Bomb Groups still on the field awaiting evacuation, passenger lists were being drawn up for the bomber pilots in the operations building. To Beck, "everyone was in a jangle of nervous confusion." They were expecting another raid in the full-moon night, and the Dutch were preparing to blow up the airdrome.[60]

Lieutenant Lane had been checking with the bomber pilots to see how many of his pilots and men they could take on board, but the pursuit squadron personnel were in competition for places with the 7th and 19th Group evacuees. Lane was set to ride out with Lt. Ed Teats of the 19th Group, his 39-A classmate from Kelly Field who had flown into Broome in his B-17E 41–2452. But how about places for the other nineteen or so remaining pilots and enlisted men of the 17th Pursuit? Teats told Lane he was already overloaded—a maximum safe load of twenty passengers had been set. However, he indicated he was willing to "take a gamble" and bring aboard four more of the 17th Pursuit's personnel—Ed Gilmore, Paul Gambonini, Bob McWherter, and Frank Adkins, who had just arrived on the field as Teats's B-17 was being serviced—and would send five others over to Lt. Ed Green's B-17E, which had come in from Broome with Teats. But Lane would have to send the ten extra to the other ships to try to obtain places.[61]

Lane informed fifteen others that they would likely have to remain behind with the 7th Group's Lt. David McCartney in order not to overload the ships. But on their own the men went to the other bombers and appealed to be taken aboard, and all were given places. All the 17th's remaining pilots—Spence Johnson, Roger Williams, Hal Lund, and Marion Fuchs, plus Doc Adams—and all the enlisted men had now secured places out of Jogjakarta. When Hal Lund boarded the B-17E to which he had been assigned, he found that it was "loaded to the gills." The bomb bay had been closed and planks put across it so that passengers could stand on it during the flight. His own group of nine—including the navigator—was crammed in the bombardier's compartment.[62]

Between 2200 and 2300 that night the five heavily loaded B-17Es taxied out onto the runway, which was partially lit from the burning planes and hangars, and lifted off, destination Broome. At about thirty minutes past midnight, the two 7th Group LB-30s—AL 508 piloted by Murray Crowder and AL 515 by Elbert Helton—cleared the field. As their LB-30 crews and evacuees looked down, they observed dynamite flashes as the field was being blown up.[63]

Just after witnessing the takeoff of the two LB-30s, Arie Geurtz and Toni Schoolwerth, the latter the 19th Bomb Group's Dutch liaison officer at Singosari Field, had given word to set off the charges placed earlier on the field, as authorized by Captain Lindner, the Dutch officer in charge of demolition of Jogjakarta airdrome. As explosions filled the air, Geurtz and Schoolwerth prepared to leave. With Schoolwerth in his staff car and Geurtz following right behind in the car Eubank had turned over to him on his departure that afternoon, they headed for the road to Bandoeng. They were driving with only their parking lights on, but the full moon was providing sufficient illumination.[64]

Thousands of feet overhead, heading southeast over the Indian Ocean, Hal Lund reached into his musette bag for the bottle of champagne his cousin had given him on Lund's departure from San Francisco more than three months earlier. He pulled the cork, had a swig, then passed the bottle around to the other eight in the cramped compartment of the B-17E. After emptying the bottle, all were asleep within ten minutes, their stress relieved.[65]

CHAPTER SIXTEEN

"Give Us Twenty-four Hours to Get Out of This God-damned Place"

LOOKING DOWN FROM THE high-flying B-17E, Frank Kurtz could make out the northwestern coastline of Australia in the brilliant moonlight. It was 0200 on Monday, March 2, some seven hours after Lieutenant Vandevanter had taken his ship out of Jogjakarta loaded down with evacuees. To Kurtz the coast looked like flat desert only, bathed in "a ghostly hue.¹ Continuing south, Vandevanter soon made out what he figured should be Broome. As he descended and circled the area, flares suddenly lit up the night sky, providing a path for the B-17 to come in to the field. It appeared that men in a moving auto were throwing kerosene flares out of the vehicle to indicate the perimeters of the runway for him.

After the Flying Fortress touched down for an uneventful landing, Kurtz joined Colonel Eubank and the others, including the Ngoro pursuit veterans Ed Kiser, Jack Dale, Joe Kruzel, Ben Irvin, Bill Hennon, Jim Morehead, Andy Reynolds, Bob Dockstader, and Les Johnsen, and headed for the field's long hangar. Drowsy after the long night flight, they were hoping for a few hours' sleep on terra firma. But sleeping would prove impossible; there were too many mosquitoes buzzing about, disturbing their slumber. Giving up, Kurtz arose and looked out the hangar door. The first pale light of dawn was breaking. He could make out a general store, a gas station, two horses, and the hangar shack "perched on the edge of nothing." Striking up a conversation with an old sheep rancher who approached him, Kurtz inquired if there had been "any trouble" at Broome. "No," the Australian replied, except that Japanese planes had been coming over once in a while. In fact, he added, one had flown over that very night, very high.²

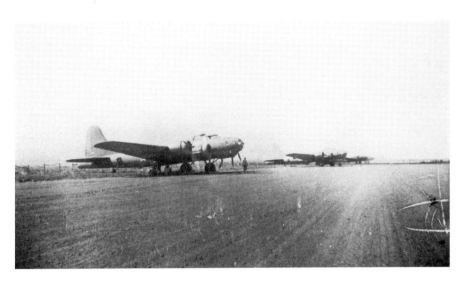

B-17Es lined up at Broome Airfield, March 2, 1942, after having flown FEAF evacuees out of Java. *Courtesy Victor Poncik.*

After the others awoke, too, Kurtz and the evacuees and B-17E crew joined Lt. Col. Dick Legg and his staff for breakfast. When Kurtz mentioned to Legg that he had heard that a Japanese reconnaissance plane was over Broome the night before, Legg—in charge of Broome's evacuation operations—did not seem to know about it. After his aircraft was refueled, Vandevanter immediately took off with the Java evacuees for Perth, another eleven hundred miles to the south, on the way to Melbourne, their ultimate destination.[3] By now, another five B-17s and two LB-30s that had left Jogjakarta with evacuees late the night before had landed. On bringing his B-17E in at about 0600, Ed Teats told Paul Gambonini, Ed Gilmore, Bob McWherter, and the other evacuees to help roll out gas drums to the ship from the fuel truck so that the Broome ground crews could get the Fortress gassed up quickly. Like Vandevanter, Teats wanted to get off for Perth as soon as possible. On takeoff after a quick breakfast for all, Gambonini was standing between Teats and the copilot in the cockpit, ready to fill in for one or the other to allow him to go back and get some sleep on the long haul south.[4]

Ed Green's and Dick Beck's B-17Es also took off for Perth after being serviced, as did the two LB-30s piloted by Elbert Helton and Murray Crowder. But after landing at 0630, Duane Skiles was not able to take his B-17E, No. 41–2454, off to Perth. It needed work on its defective brakes first. In bringing it in, Skiles had feared he would need to make a crash landing, but he managed to develop enough braking to stop in time. Harold Smelser's No. 41–2449 was being held on the ground, too. Only those ships serviced by noon were being allowed to proceed to Perth and on to Melbourne, and although Smelser had brought his B-17E in at 0710, it still had not been gassed up when the noon hour arrived. Smelser and his crew were ordered to wait overnight.[5]

Delays in servicing all the aircraft bringing evacuees in from Java were becoming a real problem for Legg and his staff. Maj. Ray Schwanbeck and his maintenance section, assisted by the aircrews of the planes landing at Broome, were working "almost twenty-four hours a day" to get all the aircraft, including those flying into Broome from Perth, refueled and serviced, but the numbers coming in were overtaxing their capabilities. Refueling was taking up to twelve hours. The gasoline, in fifty-gallon drums, had to be brought to the field from dispersed fuel dumps in two aged trucks by natives and two 19th Group enlisted men detailed as drivers, then hand-pumped into the aircraft.[6]

To mess officer John Rouse on Legg's staff, "the place looked like LaGuardia Field at its busiest." The entire small airdrome was covered with ships coming south from Java and north from Perth, now to include all the aircraft of his Air Transport Command—three B-24As and other transports—that Major General Brett in Melbourne had ordered in to help with the evacuation. Sleeping accommodations were a nightmare. Aircraft crews were "sleeping on floors, porches, or any other shelter they can find."[7]

But Rouse and his comrades were also concerned that all the activity at the small airdrome was attracting the attention of the Japanese. The Broome staff feared the Japanese might try to take the field to stop it from being used as an evacuation center. "It would be fairly easy to do," he observed, "as we have practically no defenses."[8] Their apprehension was heightened when at 1500 that afternoon a Japanese four-engine flying boat identified as a Mavis appeared over Broome at about thirteen thousand feet. It circled leisurely over the harbor before heading back north. But a late-morning reconnaissance of Broome that day by a single-engine aircraft was not detected.[9]

As darkness descended, Skiles's crew, increasingly anxious about a possible Japanese aerial attack, was still working on the brakes of their 41–2454. Smelser's 41–2449 was still on the field, too. Smelser himself had been ordered at 1600 to take another B-17E with another combat crew to Perth and leave his own unserviced ship and crew at Broome. At 2110 he took off and headed south.[10]

Although a few aircraft were not serviced by evening, Dick Legg felt that his men had put in good day's work. He estimated that they had pumped seventeen thousand gallons of gasoline—equivalent to 340 fifty-gallon barrels—into some two hundred aircraft that had landed from the north and south.[11] But Legg's duties were not over even at midnight. As he was returning from the Broome hospital at about 0200, he was surprised to see signal lights flashing out in the bay and to hear a plane flying low over the town. Suspecting someone was trying to signal the pilot of a Japanese reconnaissance plane, he picked up Rouse and with cocked pistols they set out to search the area of the signal lights, ready to shoot the fifth columnist on sight if they found him. But much to their disappointment they discovered that it was just the Broome radio station operator who had been flashing warning signals to the aircraft, thinking it was an allied plane coming in to land and was flying too close to the radio tower. However, no friendly plane came in. Legg and Rouse were convinced that the mystery plane was Japanese on yet another reconnaissance of Broome.[12]

IN A TORRENTIAL RAINSTORM, the American freighter *Sea Witch* began pulling out of Tjilatjap harbor at 0100 on March 2, its voyage to deliver twenty-seven crated P-40Es completed. The crew told Pfc. Charley Bowles that the storm was a lucky break for them, for they were sure a Japanese submarine was lying in wait for them at the end of the channel. During the night run out to the open sea, Bowles and others who were awake at that hour were suffering from acute anxiety, but when no sub attack materialized they began to relax. Evidently the rough weather had saved them.[13]

As daylight broke, the skies were clear again and the *Sea Witch* was making good speed in open sea on its return trip to Australia. During the day Bowles and the crew spotted a reconnaissance plane approaching the freighter, a cause for concern, but after making two passes at about ten thousand feet without attacking, the Japanese headed back from where it had come.[14]

AT ABOUT 1400 THAT AFTERNOON Jan Bruinier arrived at Bandoeng with his commanding officer, Ricardo Anemaet, Alex van der Vossen, and the other Dutch pilots who had left Ngoro in cars the afternoon of the day before. They were all dead tired after the all-night drive from Jogjakarta. Checking in at Dutch air force headquarters in Bandoeng, they were told by the chief of staff, Lt. Col. C. Giebel, to go to Andir Field to test the American P-40Es that had been shipped up by train from Tjilitjap. Their 2-Vl.G.-IV squadron, after having lost its Hurricanes at Ngoro, was to be reequipped with twelve P-40Es that had arrived in crates at Tjilatjap two days earlier.[15]

But when they reported in at Andir, they found no flyable P-40s waiting for them, contrary to what Colonel Kengen had told them before they departed Ngoro the day before. The aircraft were at the complex of the Technische

Captured P-40E off *Sea Witch*, with the NEIAF flag insignia overpainted on the fuselage and wing, Andir Field, Bandoeng, May–June 1942. *Author's collection.*

Dienst near a cemetery on the road from Andir, where they had arrived earlier that day and where they were being uncrated and assembly operations were being started. Bruinier and Van der Vossen were angered to find that they had been deceived; these ships were not ready to take up, as they had been led to believe. They figured it would take days for the TD to assemble them, and with the Japanese pressing south in their direction. Disgusted, Bruinier went back to Bandoeng and asked Dutch army headquarters if they had any job for him that could use his RAF experience, but he was told no. He decided with Van der Vossen and the others of Anemaet's squadron to stay with their CO and await capture by the Japanese, although other Dutch officers around them were trying to arrange for evacuation.[16]

Arie Geurtz and Toni Schoolwerth had also arrived from Jogjakarta after their own all-night drive. On reporting in to Major General Van Oyen, they were met by his adjutant instead, 1st Lt. H. Creutzberg, who was keen to know about the last days of the 17th Pursuit Squadron and 19th Bomb Group from the Dutch liaison officers of each. At the end of the detailed briefing, Creutzberg asked them if they would like to be evacuated on a B-17E that had been left at Andir Field that was scheduled to go out with evacuees at midnight the following evening. Not wishing to remain behind and become prisoners of the Japanese if they could help it, Geurtz and Schoolwerth readily accepted the offer.[17]

EARLY ON THE MORNING of Tuesday, March 3, Dick Legg and his staff at Broome decided to warn the pilots of all the flying boats in the harbor and the land aircraft on the field to get out before 1000. After the assumed reconnaissance of the flying boat the night before, they expected a Japanese raid for sure and figured it would be sometime after that hour. However, they didn't know if the attack would be by planes from Japanese carriers known to be operating in the Indian Ocean north of Broome or from land-based aircraft from newly seized bases in the Dutch East Indies.[18]

Captain Ben Funk didn't need any warning from Legg. He had brought his B-24A, with a load of evacuees from Java, into Broome at about 0400 and immediately checked with Legg's operations officer. In reply to Funk's query, Major Schwanbeck informed him that indeed a Japanese plane had flown over the previous night. That was enough for the veteran Funk. He told his crew and passengers to be ready for takeoff no later than 0600, half an hour before sunrise. After a quick refueling and breakfast, he lifted off on time, headed for Perth.[19]

In his B-17E that had overnighted on the field too, Lt. Dick Beck also headed out with his load of evacuees, taking off downhill and downwind, to the east. Checking his watch, Beck noted that it was exactly 0800. From overhead he noticed a B-24A parked at the east end of the runway, apparently waiting to take off to the west.[20] But Lt. Hal Smelser's 41–2449 was still on the ground, left there with its crew that had flown it in from Java after Smelser flew out the evening before on another B-17E. And so was Duane Skiles's 41–2454. After working into the small hours to fix *Eager Alice*'s brakes, Skiles's crew had slept fitfully in the hangar shack. To TSgt. Charley Reeves, the bombardier, the situation "didn't seem healthy." He and the others had woken up at 0500 to get an early start on the day. After a quick breakfast of hot beans, coffee, and field rations, they walked to their ship at 0600 and stood by, anxious to take off.[21]

Skiles checked in with Legg at the concrete block schoolhouse that served as Legg's office and quarters and asked him when he could take off, now that his ship was in good shape, refueled, and ready to go. But Legg reminded Skiles that he and his crew were evacuees just like the others and would have to wait until the passenger list was drawn up. They had until 1000 to get out, anyway. At once irritated and impatient, Skiles and his crew went back to their B-17 and spent the next hours whiling away the time.

Capt. Paul Davis and Maj. Edson Kester were also waiting for passenger lists to be completed for their B-24As. The two Air Transport Command pilots had been ordered to Broome the day before by General Brett to take Java evacuees south to Perth. At about 0915 Kester was handed the list of passengers for his aircraft, serial number 40-2374. The unarmed bomber, with a crew of three only, would be carrying nineteen evacuees, including Capt. Charles Stafford, the medical officer of the 7th Bomb Group with wounded under his care, as well as seven crew chiefs and armorers of the 17th Pursuit who had been waiting for transfer to Perth and Melbourne after arriving from Jogjakarta on a B-17E two nights earlier.

At about 0923 Kester and his copilot, Capt. Bill Ragsdale, went into their takeoff roll and thundered down the dusty strip, east to west. Seven minutes later, when the struggling B-24A had reached an altitude of six hundred feet, Sgt. Melvin Donoho—an armorer of the 17th Pursuit from Covington, Oklahoma—heard a "funny noise" above the sound of the four motors and looked up from his position in the bottom of the bomb bay. Donoho then saw something that looked like an electric charge for a welding arc jumping, coming in one side of the fuselage above his head. It kept hitting the wall with splattering fire. "Incendiaries," he realized. He tried to get as low as he could, then crawled forward on the B-24A's midway catwalk. Other passengers above him were trying to move back to the tail to avoid being burned. But the flames had now caught the overhead gas tank and the rear of the bomber had become an inferno. "It's all over," Donoho figured, and lay down, waiting for the inevitable.[22]

Suddenly, the blazing B-24A struck the water and cracked open, its fuselage shooting through the greenish water at high speed. Thrown free, Donoho only realized what had happened when he saw the surface above. After coming to the surface, he saw that the fuselage had been broken in two parts, separated by about fifty feet of water. Both wings were gone. The tail was sticking up but was now descending. No one was around it, but next to the nose, which was still floating, he saw about fifteen or sixteen survivors bobbing up and down and swimming about. More were being helped out of the nose into the water by what he believed were medical officers who had been aboard.[23] Donoho spotted his squadron mate, Sgt. Willard Beatty, in the water and swam over to him. They grabbed three life jackets that were floating near the tail of the B-24A, planning to give the third one to any other swimmer they could find. Although they couldn't see the shore, they guessed in what direction it was located and started swimming for it. After a few minutes, they thought of their ship and looked back; there was no trace of it.

Back at the field, Dick Legg and his old friend Capt. Jack Berry were having a breakfast of coffee and cheese that Berry had brought back from Melbourne the afternoon before on Paul Davis's B-24A. As they stood in the doorway of the schoolhouse office, looking around the field that was just two hundred yards away, they were shocked to see three Japanese Zeros suddenly coming down the runway. It looked like they were after the two B-17s parked at one end of the field.[24] Standing near the rear of one of the B-17s—Duane Skiles's 41-2454—TSgt. Charley Britt looked up and yelled, "Make a run for it, fellows—here come some Zeros!" Britt, TSgt. Charley Reeves, and the rest of Skiles's crew ran and jumped into a hole some fifty feet away. Looking up, they saw that one of the Zeros had peeled off and was heading at a height of fifty feet for their defenseless ship. Incendiary fire from its nose guns instantly set the fully fueled bomber ablaze on the first pass. Then the pilot turned his attention to the B-24A near the middle of the field before returning and firing at Skiles's crew in the hole. After several passes, the Japanese eventually caved in their hole with 20 mm rounds, covering them with dirt.[25]

Near the operations building, Capt. Paul Davis was still waiting for the passenger list for his B-24A *Arabian Knight* when he spotted the three Zeros heading towards the runway. Along with his navigator, 2nd Lt. Edward Yerington, he hurriedly got out of the bomber, parked near the operations building, and began running, looking for "something to get into or under." They settled for some low scrub brush. From their shelter they watched the three Zeros diving and rolling over the field. There were three others, too, over Roebuck Harbor, methodically shooting up the flying boats on the water. Suddenly, one of the Japanese picked out *Arabian Knight* and streaked down to within fifty feet of the bomber, right in line with where Davis and Yerington were sheltering in the bush. In one pass, the incendiaries from its 7.7 mm guns set the fully fueled B-24A ablaze, and then it exploded. Nearby, a Lockheed Hudson blew up in a blinding flash, too, and one of its motors hurtled through the air and crashed to the ground only fifty feet away.[26]

An evacuee scheduled to go out on Hal Smelser's 41-2449, Sgt. John Kunkel, stayed by the B-17E on the first pass of the three Zeros over the field that had ignited Skiles's ship, but as soon as they went by he ran and jumped into a gun pit out in the middle of the field, landing among the crews operating two of the .30-caliber machine guns set up in it. As the Zeros came in at treetop level in their strafing runs, shooting up both ends of the runway, the gunners fired at them, but without evident effect. And Kunkel's means of transport out of Broome was now burning fiercely after exploding into several pieces.[27]

Another machine gunner *was* having results in firing at the Japanese over the field, but he was not American. Flying Officer Gus Winckel had spotted the nine Zeros on their approach to Broome, had hurried over to his Lockheed Lodestar parked on the runway, and had pulled the flexible .30-caliber

Browning M1919 waist gun from its mounting. With a box of four hundred rounds of ammunition that his wireless operator, Bill Maks, had picked up from the plane, Winckel took up a position in the open near his ship, ready for the Zeros. After three of the Japanese had finished their work on the B-17Es and the B-24A, one of them headed straight for Winckel's Lodestar, so low that the Dutchman could see his face. With the twenty-three-pound machine gun against his shoulder, the barrel in his hand, and "angry as hell," Winckel gave the Zero pilot a "good blast." The recoil almost knocked him to his feet, but he had hit the Zero, which went smoking off to sea.[28]

In twenty minutes it was all over as the Japanese headed back north, leaving behind a scene of death and destruction. Dick Legg could see Dutch flying boats out in Roebuck Bay at low tide exploding and burning. He knew they were loaded with women and children refugees from Java and that there would be many dead and injured. There were reports that fourteen of the flying boats had been destroyed as they were about to take off. Legg and his staff spent the next hours mobilizing every able-bodied person to help in efforts to bring as many of the Dutch civilians as they could find on the shore back up to the airfield. There was only one Aussie medic among the rescuers, plus a few American medical officers who had been in transit, to administer to the wounded. The Broome police buried many of the twenty-one Dutch dead they found in a mass grave; to Legg they seemed to number seventy.[29]

Anxious to help the Dutch women and children, the Qantas operations manager at Broome headed for Legg's schoolhouse office. "What can I do, sir?" Capt. Lester Brain asked the highly agitated American commander. "Give us twenty-four hours to get out of this God-damned place and you can have it!" Legg barked back. Taken aback, Brain turned to leave, but, gaining his self-control, Legg then asked the Australian if he had any of his planes in the area. Worried not to have had any word on Kester and his crew and passengers, he wanted Brain to mount an aerial search for possible survivors among the Americans. But the Qantas officer argued that it was more important to evacuate the wounded to Perth. Legg demurred, but that afternoon, under the chaotic conditions that prevailed among the panic-stricken residents, he and his staff made arrangements to get all the women and children, as well any wounded, out by air.[30]

TSgt. Charley Reeves and the other Army Air Forces men who had lost their means of transport for the transfer to Perth were worried. How were they to get out? That evening they met with Legg to find out his plans for them. Legg told them that planes were expected in that night up to midnight, but he didn't know how many. He was compiling a priority list, but "if your name wasn't called by 0200, you should try to get out of Broome "quick" and "by whatever means you could"—even if it meant walking on the single road leading south.[31] Legg also informed the local representatives that the Americans would all be evacuated by planes expected in from the south but advised the residents to get out of town by morning; he believed the Japanese would be back the next morning to bomb the area. Legg's warning sparked a "general exodus" among the locals that evening. They feared not only another raid, but also a parachute landing by the Japanese.[32]

It was with relief that Reeves and the others watched a B-24A coming in to land that evening from Perth. After its crew unloaded medical supplies and doctors, they took on evacuees. But on takeoff with a full load, Captain Mathews ran his ship off the runway, damaging the undercarriage. Fortunately, no one was injured, but that would be the end of the road for the B-24A, serial number 40-2373. It could be repaired, but orders were issued to destroy it because of the fear of a Japanese landing.[33] By 0230 Reeves despaired of getting out of Broome that night when his name still had not been called for the priority list of evacuees. Along with eight others, he decided to accept the offer of a civilian contractor of a lift to Port Hedland, 275 miles southwest of Broome. The Aussie was heading there with his five Ford trucks and thirty men.[34]

But Reeves's worries that night were nothing compared to those of fellow FEAF sergeants Mel Donoho and Willard Beatty. After surviving the crash of Kester's B-24A into Roebuck Bay that morning, they had been swimming in their life jackets all day towards what they hoped was Broome's shore, as suggested by the wisp of smoke that was rising from that direction. By nightfall they could see the outline of the shore, which they figured was less than a quarter of a mile away. But Broome's thirty-foot tide was now going out, frustrating their efforts to make any headway. And Beatty was tiring fast. It was beginning to look like they would end up as the last casualties to be suffered by the 17th Pursuit Squadron (Provisional) in the Java campaign.[35]

ABOUT 2100 ON THE EVENING of March 4, 1942, a stark naked, badly sunburned man staggered up to the hangar at Broome's airfield. Entering through the door, he surprised the men congregated in the hangar, whom he saw were fellow FEAF evacuees from Java. One of the men shouted, "There's Mo!" recognizing Sgt. Melvin Donoho, reported as missing after the crash of the B-24A into Roebuck Harbor on the morning of March 3.[1] Another of the evacuee group notified Lt. Col. Dick Legg, in charge of evacuation operations at Broome, that one of the B-24A passengers had just walked in. Legg told him to bring the man to his office. Reporting in to the CO, Donoho related his thirty-six-hour ordeal in graphic terms. After escaping from the B-24A wreck, he and fellow survivor Sgt. Willard Beatty had struggled all day and night against Broome's renowned tide, then the next day flowed with it but were unable to reach shore. Beatty gave up two hundred yards short of land, but Donoho continued swimming until he finally reached the beach about 1800 that evening. Trudging along the shoreline in the direction of what he thought was Broome, he had managed to reach the town, then continued one-fourth of a mile to the airfield on the other side of Broome.[2]

Donoho not only was exhausted, he was angry. Oblivious to the fact that he was an enlisted man in the presence of an officer, Donoho wanted to know why Legg had not sent out a search mission for any survivors of the B-24A crash. "If someone had gotten off his dead ass, grabbed a boat, and gone looking for them," then maybe others besides himself would still be alive, he told Legg to his face. Maintaining his self-composure during the outburst, Legg listened quietly. He did not mention that he had tried to mount an aerial search for survivors within hours after the crash.[3]

Donoho was given something to eat and put to bed in the hospital. On the following night he was flown to Perth with the last group of Air Force evacuees to go out. Legg himself left for USAFIA headquarters in Melbourne at 0130 that night in a B-24A along with his friend Capt. Jack Berry; they were the last Air Force personnel to leave. His Java air evacuation work was now finished.[4]

AT 0900 ON MARCH 4 the Dutch freighter *Abbekerk* safely arrived at Perth's port of Fremantle with forty-six of Donoho's fellow mechanics and armorers of the 17th Pursuit Squadron (Provisional) plus four wounded pilots of the squadron and hundreds of other FEAF personnel evacuated from Tjilatjap by sea four and one-half days earlier. Except for the failed attack of the Japanese reconnaissance plane, it had been an uneventful, albeit uncomfortable, trip with over a thousand men jammed on board. Ironically, the sea evacuation had proven safer for the men of the 17th Pursuit than the preferred air evacuation, which had cost the lives of 6 of the squadron's 110 enlisted men in the B-24A crash.[5]

Evidently, because of the maintenance of radio silence, Fremantle's harbor master had no idea that the *Abbekerk* was due in. A new base section had been set up the day before at Perth, but the CO proved incompetent and had done nothing to prepare for the arrival of the *Abbekerk* and its FEAF passengers. It took all day to get a train and back up its passenger wagons opposite the Dutch ship. Finally, in early evening the evacuees were offloaded down the stairway onto the dock and boarded the train for an Australian army camp at Northam, some fifty miles east of Perth. It was not before 0200 the next morning that the *Abbekerk* evacuees reached the camp. Most were too tired to fill the straw mattresses given them and just lay down on the floor to sleep. The next morning they were rudely surprised to find that the Aussie army commander seemed to think the evacuees were there to do infantry drill. "They don't even seem to know that there is a war going on, since this is as close as they have been to it," Sgt. Cecil Ingram of the 17th Pursuit evacuee group complained in his diary. It would be over a week before Ingram and the others were sent south for their new assignments.[6]

With the arrival of Tommy Hayes, Gene Bound, Frank Neri, and Bill Stauter at Fremantle on the *Abbekerk,* all of the pilots of the 17th Pursuit had now been safely evacuated. But unknown to the others, two of their comrades, shot down and assumed lost, were still alive, trapped on Java. Bill Gallienne had survived his bailout on February 20 offshore of Java and had been dragged up on the beach by Javanese and put in a native pigpen. An American doctor tended to his wounds, including his eye that had been blinded in the fire of his P-40, but he was captured by the Japanese and would spend the rest of the war in a POW camp.[7] Connie Reagan, shot down on the 17th's last mission of March 1, had a stranger experience. After crash-landing his blazing P-40 in a rice paddy off a northern Java beach, Reagan hid in the jungle during daytime to evade the Japanese spreading out over Java and at night moved towards nearby mountains on the east coast. But when he tried to get down to shore to get a boat, pro-Japanese Javanese caught him and turned him over to the enemy. Trading on his Irish origin, Reagan protested that he was an Irish war correspondent and thus from a neutral nation, but the Japanese knew less about Ireland and its wartime status than did Reagan. He ended up in a political prison for the duration of the war.[8]

But what of the fate of the thirty-three pilots and twelve enlisted men who had been on board the *Langley* on its way to Java when sunk on February 27? Gerry Dix and Bill Ackerman, rescued by the *Pecos* and then the *Whipple*, arrived safely back at Fremantle on the destroyer on March 4. Still a mystery today, however, is what happened to the pilots and the one enlisted man who had survived the sinking of the *Langley* and had been picked up by the *Edsall* before the destroyer was sunk on March 1, one and a half hours after the *Pecos*. Japanese accounts seem to indicate that those who survived the sinking and were picked up by the cruiser *Chikuma* were taken to a POW camp at Kendari, Celebes, where they evidently were executed.[9]

The 17th Pursuit's comrades during the last days of the aerial campaign— the Dutch pursuit pilots under Lieutenant Anemaet who flew the last missions with them from Ngoro—also were taken captive on the fall of Java but survived their POW experiences. The 17th's Dutch liaison officer, Arie Geurtz, survived the campaign, too, being flown out of Bandoeng on March 2 along with his 19th Bomb Group counterpart, Toni Schoolwerth.

AS THE JAVA CAMPAIGN wound down and the morale of U.S. forces sank, the USAFIA in Melbourne became particularly sensitive about any unfavorable publicity by American troops on the performance of U.S. Army personnel in the Java campaign. On March 1, following the Japanese landings on Java, it banned all under its command from mentioning in private correspondence any references to the effect of Japanese operations, casualties suffered, or equipment destroyed in advance of any official announcements on the subject. Furthermore, personnel were to make no criticism of the "equipment, appearance, physical condition, or morale" of U.S. armed forces and their allies.[10] The ban was extended on March 9 to include all war correspondents who had been covering the Java campaign following the publication in the Australian press of an article by Harold Guard revealing the bad news of the fall of Java and "tending to cause unfavorable reaction." The U.S. government, for one, didn't want references to American military operations in the loss of the Dutch East Indies made public. On that day—as the Dutch surrendered to the Japanese—a curtain of censorship fell over the ill-starred campaign. The U.S. government had requested the Australian chief censor to prohibit all references to U.S. military operations in the Dutch East Indies (as well as in Australia) in all Australian news releases and any messages filed for transmission outside of Australia.[11]

Before the ban there had been no problem from censors in allowing the publication of articles on the course of the two-month-long campaign. This is not surprising, as the articles tended to focus on the exploits of individual American pilots in seemingly successful air operations that could serve to bolster American morale at home. Unable to assess the events themselves, the correspondents accepted at face value the accounts given them by the airmen. For example, among other FEAF accomplishments, the B-17 gunners were knocking down Zeros in considerable numbers, although in reality, no Zeros were lost to B-17 fire in the Java campaign. The tendency of many FEAF officers to glorify their feats during the Java campaign, ostensibly gained under the most heroic of circumstances, was deplored by Maj. Emmett O'Donnell, who had served at Bandoeng as operations officer of the FEAF. To O'Donnell it was "sheer hokum" to be fed to the "folks at home." "Far too many of our missions were out and out failures," he confided to his wartime diary. O'Donnell, now in India, wanted the U.S. command to be "honest with ourselves" and make an "open-minded and objective assessment" of its performance in the Java campaign instead of "living in a flimsy fool's paradise."[12]

Did the army command in Australia live up to O'Donnell's expectations in making its assessment of the record of the pursuit pilots in the Java campaign? With the arrival of Gen. Douglas MacArthur in Australia on March 21, 1942, to take over command of all Allied forces in the Southwest Pacific Area, the evaluation was turned over to his 5th Air Force, successor to the Far East Air Force. On April 3, MacArthur's headquarters released to the press the first official statement on the record of the 17th Pursuit Squadron (Provisional) in the Java campaign. In an article appearing in the *New York Times* the following day, headlining the "heavy toll" inflicted on the Japanese (and evidently cleared by the censors), correspondent Byron Darnton gave a virtually verbatim account of the 5th Air Force's assessment. Darnton referred to the numbers of Japanese aircraft shot down by the pursuiters, the exploits of individual pilots, and the difficult conditions under which the 17th fought. "American losses were comparatively light," it was reported. No reference was made to the tragic loss of thirty-one pilots and twelve enlisted men being transferred to Java on the *Langley*.[13] Not surprisingly, MacArthur was continuing his practice of releasing glowing accounts of the operations of units under his command that he had initiated in the form of "communiqués" during the months of his failed Philippine command. O'Donnell would have regarded the 5th Air Force's account as more "hokum" for the American public, desperate as it was for news of the Allies' successes at this low point in the Pacific War.

The Fifth Air Force's account and Darnton's article implied that the 17th Pursuit Squadron was successful in its Java mission, being officially credited with thirty-nine aerial victories plus twenty-six probables. The author's calculations—based on individual pilots' accounts compared with daily operations reports of the Japanese squadrons involved—reveal a different picture. The mission of the 17th Pursuit in Java was to intercept Japanese aircraft mounting attacks on the Soerabaja air base and harbor and the B-17 field at Singosari, both in eastern Java.[14] Although some B-17 pilots complained that the 17th never provided escort on their missions or otherwise protected them, such an assignment was neither possible nor feasible, in view of the long distances flown by the bombers.[15] On a few occasions the P-40 pilots did fly cover for the B-17s landing and taking off from Singosari, however. In carrying out its mission, the 17th Pursuit was credited in the 5th Air Force's assessment with shooting down fourteen "heavy bombers" plus an undisclosed number of probable victories over the bombers. Counting an "Me 110" (actually a Type 96 twin-engine Nell) also claimed as downed, the bomber total reaches fifteen. However, detailed Japanese records of the units involved indicate that only three such bombers (two Type 1 Bettys and the Type 96) were actually destroyed in aerial combat with the P-40s, plus a fourth (another Betty) so badly damaged that it crashed in the Java Sea on its return to base (see Appendix Table 15).

This was not the "heavy toll" inflicted on Japanese bomber crews of Darnton's article, considering the great number of sorties flown against East Java targets. Two factors explain the meager results. First is the ineffectiveness of the Dutch Air Defense Command at Soerabaja. A primitive operation lacking radar, it usually gave the 17th Pursuit at Ngoro inadequate warning of incoming Japanese bomber formations to allow the interceptors to reach the required altitude and position themselves for successful attacks on the bombers (in those cases in which the ADC did not send the 17th off on wild goose chases based on erroneous sightings). Second, whenever the pursuiters were in a position to engage the bombers, they were invariably met by escorting Zeros that diverted them from their mission and took a toll on the American pilots in their outmatched P-40s in swirling dogfights.

The Fifth Air Force report claimed that the 17th Pursuit shot down twenty

Zeros over the Dutch East Indies, whereas in actuality the Japanese lost only three of their fighters to the P-40s, including during strafing attacks as well as bomber escort duty. According to the records of the Tainan Kokutai and 3rd Kokutai, one Zero was shot down on February 3 over Malang (but three more that day by Dutch pilots), a second on February 19 over Soerabaja, and a third over Bali on February 20. In addition to the Zeros, the 17th was officially credited in the report with four army Type 97 "Nate" fighters that they encountered over Palembang on February 17. In actuality, only one Nate was downed in that engagement, according to the records of the unit involved. Preoccupied as they were in trying to escape the relentless attacks on them rather than observe crashes of their nemeses, the pursuiters could not be sure if they were scoring sure victories and tended to make excessive claims.

The unofficial history of the 17th Pursuit Squadron, compiled on the basis of day-to-day events, reported an even greater confirmed aerial victory total than the Fifth Air Force assessment: fifty as against thirty-nine. "Various sources" were the basis for such a total. The history mentions that the ADC in Soerabaja maintained that the 17th had shot down more than sixty-five Japanese aircraft in the campaign. However, in an apparently final accounting, the Army Air Forces scaled back the confirmed claims to twenty-five aircraft, toting up victories credited to individual 17th Pursuit pilots.[16] Not included in these totals are Japanese aircraft downed by pilots flying out of Darwin who were meant to go to Java to join the 17th Pursuit. As described in chapters 8 and 10, Bob Buel shot down a Kawanishi H6K4 "Mavis" on February 15, and Bob Oestreicher during the Darwin raid of February 19 severely damaged an Aichi D3A1 "Val" that was unable to return to its carrier and was forced to ditch in the Timor Sea.

What price did the 17th Pursuit pay for its destruction of eight Japanese aircraft during the Java campaign? The 17th Pursuit history indicates that nine of its pilots flying out of Ngoro were lost in aerial combat, including four listed as missing in action at the time the history was compiled. Since two were found after the war to have survived, the toll of the 17th Pursuit is reduced to seven, or one-sixth of the total of forty-two pilots who reached Ngoro. Of an additional fifteen who managed to fly to Timor but failed to arrive at Ngoro, one was killed in combat and another in bailing out, bringing the total of dead in the Dutch East Indies operation to nine. In addition, four were badly wounded, including one in an accident.[17]

But these figures cover only operations of the 17th Pursuit (into which the 20th and 3rd Pursuit Squadrons [Provisional] were integrated) in the Dutch East Indies. In addition, 61 other pilots had been assigned to the 33rd and 13th Pursuit Squadrons (Provisional), also ordered to Java, but never made it.

Of the 10 pilots of the 33rd Pursuit who reached Darwin on February 15, 9 were airborne during the Darwin attack of February 19 (plus one 3rd Pursuit pilot attached to the 33rd). All the 33rd Pursuiters were shot down, with 4 killed (Pell, Peres, Perry, and Hughes). Bob Buel of the 3rd Pursuit, left behind at Darwin, was shot down and killed four days earlier over the Timor Sea while downing a Mavis flying boat. When one adds the 31 pilots of the 33rd and 13th Pursuit Squadrons (Provisional) who lost their lives in the sinking of the *Langley,* the grand total of pilots of the five provisional pursuit squadrons assigned to Java who were subsequently killed reaches 45. This number represents thirty-six percent of the total of 124 pilots assigned to the five squadrons. Contrary to the impression given by the incomplete assessment of the 5th Air Force, Java campaign pursuit pilot losses were not "comparatively light."

In terms of P-40s lost through combat or accidents, the author has documentation on the loss of a total of 110 aircraft of the 129 assigned to the five squadrons. These figures include all 68 assigned to the 17th, 20th, and 3rd Pursuit Squadrons (Provisional), including the seven survivors destroyed at Ngoro by the 17th on the evacuation of the field on March 1. Combat losses (excluding the *Langley* figures) amounted to thirty-one, including twenty shot down over the Dutch East Indies, one over the Timor Sea, and nine over Darwin, plus one on the ground at Darwin.

The losses as a result of accidents are understated to the extent that P-40s wrecked at Amberley Field prior to assignment to squadrons and during Ngoro operations were not repaired and put back into commission. Particularly egregious was the record of the 3rd Pursuit Squadron: of the twenty-five P-40s assigned, because of accidents only seven made it all the way from Amberley to Darwin to Koepang and on to Ngoro. So many pilots of the provisional squadrons had crashed along the route from Amberley and passing through Charleville, Cloncurry, Alice Springs, Daly Waters, and on to Darwin—the author has identified nineteen such accidents—that the standing joke was that one could follow the two-thousand-mile route to Darwin by noting the P-40 wrecks below.

It was no laughing matter to Grant Mahony, Buzz Wagner, and Allison Strauss, tasked at Amberley with the responsibility of training these inexperienced young pilots. On February 1, fed up with the accident rate, they had radioed the War Department that it would take three months and fifteen wrecked planes to train the seventy "so-called pursuit pilots" for combat operations. In a later report covering experience gained during the Java campaign, Mahony asserted that the pilots had been sent from the United States with just two hours in a pursuit plane and almost no gunnery training. "They could neither land nor take off," he maintained. He advised the chief of the Army Air Corps in Washington to provide fresh graduates of flying school picked for pursuit squadrons with operational training in pursuit planes—including takeoffs and landings, combat tactics, gunnery, and use of the radio—*before* they were sent out to a combat zone.[18]

Mahony exaggerated the situation to make his valid points, and there were other factors accounting for the high incidence of accidents. However, pilot inexperience was clearly the root problem. Of the 124 pilots assigned to the five provisional squadrons, 92, or three-quarters, were flying school graduates of the classes of 41-E, F, G, and H, five months or less out of flying school at the time they were shipped overseas.[19] With few exceptions, mainly in the 41-E class, they had less than ten to fifteen hours of flying a P-40, though they could usually manage a takeoff and landing, Mahony's assertion notwithstanding. In addition, pilot inexperience aside, many accidents were believed to be a result of faulty assembly of the P-40s by mechanics with no previous experience in assembling pursuit ships and reportedly no technical manuals to guide them. The extreme conditions of the featureless Australian outback over the long route to Darwin were also an unfair test of the limited flying and navigational abilities of the novice pursuiters.

"What goofy brass hat was responsible for sending these inexperienced boys over for such a grim duty?" a ground officer of the 7th Bombardment Group raged in talking to the forty-eight so-called fighter pilots on board the transport *Republic* heading for Australia in November 1941. He had heard "dark remarks" that the experienced pursuit pilots back home "were able to pull enough strings to keep from having to come themselves" so that the ones sent were those "who didn't have the experience or the pull."[20] However, this explanation ignores the fact that many of the 41-G pilots on board—among the least experienced—had pressed the 35th Pursuit Group commander at Hamilton Field against his will to be included among those being sent to PLUM, eager as they were for the opportunity for possible combat operations (as noted in chapter 1). However, there were certainly more experienced pilots serving in pursuit squadrons in the United States, Hawaii, and the Canal Zone who could have been ordered to PLUM in November and December 1941. Dick Legg complained in his diary in early February 1942 that the AAF did not regard the Southwest Pacific as a priority area in assigning pursuit pilots. "What a way to do things!" he complained. "All priority groups protecting the U.S."[21]

The official history of the USAAF in World War II indicates that at the end of 1941 there were sixty-seven groups in the Army Air Forces, of which by the author's calculations twenty-two were pursuit groups.[22] The USAAF faced priority problems in allocating its combat aircraft to these groups, but the question here is allocation of pilots, not planes. Legg was concerned that too few pursuit groups were being assigned to the Southwest Pacific. Only the 35th Group and contingents of the 20th, 14th, and 51st Groups—all California-based—were shipped out to PLUM, and the pilots of their squadrons were mainly recent flying school graduates. Couldn't Arnold and the War Department have assigned more experienced pilots from the other eighteen pursuit groups serving in the United States, Hawaii, and the Canal Zone at the time?[23]

The alternative to sending experienced pilots would have been to wait until the recently graduated novices had benefited in the United States from training in the pursuit squadrons to which they had been assigned to an extent—as indicated in Mahony's memo to the Air Corps—that would warrant sending them to PLUM for combat duty. But, as Army Chief of Staff George C. Marshall had confidentially admitted to the Australian envoy to the United States in February 1942, "urgent circumstances" had obliged him to dispatch "some bomber and fighter squadrons to the SWPA since December 7, 1941, without sufficient operational training" (and resulting in "some loss of aircraft).[24] The desperate need for pursuit pilots to bolster MacArthur's defense of the Philippines (and subsequently to oppose the Japanese advance in the Dutch East Indies) was clearly on Marshall's mind, but it still does not explain why more experienced pilots were not sent.

Nine days later, Arnold radioed Brett at ABDACOM on Java in response to Brett's concerns, maintaining that "our records show that more experienced personnel is [sic] being sent to you than will be available in any other theater. It is believed that with these personnel you will be able to carry on effectively."[25] Arnold was referring to pilots to equip the newly activated 49th and 31st (redesignated 35th) Pursuit Groups. But the pilots allocated to these groups were also inexperienced, contrary to Arnold's assertions. At the end of February, 86 of the 102 pilots assigned to the 49th Group had no pursuit time at all, and nine had an average of fifteen hours only. In the 35th Group, 27 of the 29 pilots assigned at that date had no pursuit training. Dismayed by the alarming number of accidents being caused by pilot error due to lack of experience, Brett ordered his operations officer at USAFIA to give more consideration to pilot training.[26]

But the deplorable state of the two new groups would now change with the infusion of the newly arrived Java veterans to give them a cadre of battle-seasoned leaders. The 49th Group—slated for transfer in their P-40Es to Darwin for the defense of northern Australia—was bolstered with the assignment of the most experienced pilots—all eight veterans (but excluding Gilmore) of both the Philippines and Java campaigns. Walt Coss, Al Strauss, Jack Dale, Joe Kruzel, Ed Kiser, Cy Blanton, Bill Hennon, and Ben Irvin all joined the three squadrons of the 49th, along with Jim Morehead, Les John-

Spence Johnson (*left*) and Paul Gambonini as pilots assigned to the 40th Pursuit Squadron, 35th Pursuit Group, Antil Plains Aerodrome south of Townsville, Australia, April 1942. *Courtesy of Paul Gambonini.*

sen, Andy Reynolds, Bob Dockstader, Robert Oestreicher, Bob Vaught, and Ray Melikian. The composition of the 35th Group—soon to be taking their P-39s and P-400s (an export version of the P-39) into combat with Zeros over New Guinea—was completely transformed with the addition of thirty-five Java (and Darwin) veterans, including Bill Stauter, Ray Thompson, Paul Gambonini, Hubert Egenes, B. J. Oliver, Tommy Hayes, Spence Johnson, Jesse Hague, Bob McWherter, George Parker, Frank Adkins, and Bob McMahon, whose Java or Darwin experiences have been prominently featured in this book. Three others, former 33rd Pursuiters Max Wiecks, Gerry Dix, and Jim Naylor, were assigned to the newly arrived 8th Pursuit Group that would be proceeding at the end of April to New Guinea with their P-39s and P-400s. Finally, ten of the Dutch East Indies veterans—Bryan Brown, Dave Coleman, Al Dutton, John Lewis, Vern Head, Bob Kerstetter, Pete Childress, Bruce Erwin, Tom Christian, and Bob Kaiser—found themselves assigned to the 67th Pursuit Squadron and leaving for Tontouta, New Caledonia, for eventual transfer to Guadalcanal in P-400s. Of the remaining pilots who had been assigned to one of the five provisional pursuit squadrons, five did not receive combat assignments. Ed Gilmore, Parker Gies, Dwight Muckley, and

35th Pursuit Group pilots, apparently at Port Moresby, June 1942. *Left to right:* Gene Wahl (39th Pursuit Squadron), Tommy Hayes (Headquarters Squadron), George Parker (39th Pursuit Squadron). *Courtesy Hal Lund.*

Ken Glassburn were assigned to aircraft assembly or test flying at Amberley Field, while Bryce Wilhite also remained in Australia, going to the 45th Service Group based at Charleville.

For Al Strauss, Spence Johnson, Bill Stauter, Jesse Hague, Jesse Dore, Dwight Muckley, and John Lewis, the new assignments would be their last. The first to die was Strauss, appointed CO of the 49th Group's 8th Pursuit Squadron. On April 27, 1942, intercepting a Japanese bomber attack on Darwin, Strauss's P-40E was hit by escorting Zeros and plunged straight down into Darwin Harbor.[27] The next to go was Stauter, shot down on June 26 over Port Moresby in his 40th Squadron P-39, also by Zeros escorting bombers in a raid on the oft-targeted town. Squadron mate Spence Johnson died on July 2 in a Port Moresby hospital after he was unable to abort his takeoff at Seven Mile Drome and his P-400 exploded in rocks at the end of the runway.[28] On August 2, Hague and Dore were shot down over Cape Ward Hunt while flying escort with the 41st Pursuit Squadron when they were attacked by five Zeros. Hague was reported safe the following day, but not Dore.[29] There are no Japanese records confirming it, but apparently Hague was taken prisoner and executed by the Japanese. Dore is still carried on records as missing in action.

On the day before Hague and Dore were lost, 67th Pursuiter John Lewis was going to test-hop squadron mate Bryan Brown's P-400 at Tontouta Field on New Caledonia. On takeoff the Allison engine cut out, and the modified

Jesse Hague at Mount Gambier, Australia, as a member of the 41st Pursuit Squadron, 35th Pursuit Group, March–April 1942. *Courtesy Peg Hague Baum.*

P-39 crashed, killing Lewis instantly. He was the second of the Dutch East Indies veterans to die in an accident: on June 5 Dwight Muckley lost his life when the B-26 in which he was flying crashed in the Amberley-Archerfield area, killing all aboard.[30]

An eighth pursuit veteran of the Java campaign also died in World War II, but not in the Pacific. Hubert Egenes had returned home in late 1942 after completing his tour of duty with the 35th Group and was reassigned to the 362nd Fighter Squadron, 357th Fighter Group, Eighth Air Force, in Europe.

On March 16, 1944, while strafing a German airdrome, he was shot down and killed by ground fire.[31] A similar fate befell the 17th Pursuit's second commander, Grant Mahony, who had left his comrades to go to India on February 25, 1942. After serving in India and then China, Mahony had returned to the United States in May 1943 but went back to India in December that year for another tour of duty. Returned once more to the States in May 1944, the restless, ever combative Mahony—now a lieutenant colonel—volunteered seven months later for yet another combat assignment, as deputy commanding officer of the 8th Fighter Group, now supporting the recapture of the Philippines. On January 3, 1945, his luck finally ran out. Tagging along on a strafing mission to Puerto Princessa, Palawan, he went down to attack a float plane in the harbor and was hit by antiaircraft fire, and his P-38 plunged straight into the ground.[32]

POSTSCRIPT

On July 6, 1983, the author managed to fulfill a longstanding ambition: to find the location in eastern Java where the 17th Pursuit Squadron (Provisional), known to him only through the writings of George Weller, had launched its desperate aerial battles forty-one years earlier. The opportunity had been afforded following his assignment as a consultant on a World Bank mission to Indonesia that month. July 6 was a Friday, an off day for government employees, so it had proved possible to borrow a Ministry of Labor vehicle and its driver for the search.

Setting out in the morning from Surabaya, the author, accompanied by another consultant sharing his interest, headed southwest and soon reached the town of Jombang, which he knew was only some twenty miles north of the wartime Ngoro Field and nearby Blimbing village. Reaching Blimbing first, the author succeeded in communicating in his very limited Bahasa Indonesia language with the village headman, who guided them to purplish-stained ruins of concrete buildings. Excitedly, they explored the shells of the structures and realized they must have been those of the old sugar mill and its quarters where the pilots and enlisted men of the 17th had stayed in February 1942. Then they went on to Ngoro village and an adjoining area found to be planted to sugar cane. "Ya, ya, Tuan," the village chief confirmed, there *were* American pilots here during World War II. Exploring through the open areas of the high-standing cane and the connecting pathways, they came across a concrete foundation of a small building that the author speculated might be what remained of the 17th Pursuit's operations shack.

The author now had physical proof that it *was* true that a small group of

The author inspecting the remains of Dutch sugar mill buildings at Blimbing, East Java, July 6, 1983, where 17th Pursuit personnel lived in February 1942. *Author's collection.*

valiant American pursuit pilots had operated from a secret airfield cut out of a cane field in the jungle of eastern Java for a fleeting month early in World War II. With that realization, the author vowed to tell their story as completely as possible from whatever information he could obtain from surviving participants and the families of the deceased. He would be fulfilling George Weller's ardent 1944 wish that "someone must speak for them."[33]

APPENDIX

TABLE 1 Pilots of 21st Pursuit Squadron, 35th Pursuit Group embarked on USAT *Republic* for Philippines, November 21, 1941

PILOT	SERIAL NO.	FLIGHT CLASS	HOME TOWN
Hubert I. Egenes	O-398687	40-F Kelly	Story City, Iowa
Jack R. Peres	O-416707	41-F Kelly	Santa Barbara, Calif.
W. David Coleman	O-421050	41-E Stockton	Portland, Ore.
Chester E. Trout	O-421145	41-E Stockton	Clackamas County, Ore.
William P. Borden	O-424896	41-F Kelly	Snoqualmie Falls, Wash.
Robert J. Buel	O-424901	41 F Kelly	Fresno, Calif.
Bennett L. Johnson	O-424962	41-F Kelly	Omaha, Neb.
Robert A. Kaiser	O-424966	41-F Kelly	Oakland, Calif.
Ralph G. Martin	O-424979	41-F Kelly	Detroit, Mich.
Philip T. Metsker	O-425026	41-F Kelly	Chicago, Ill.
Kenneth L. Glassburn	O-425075	41-F Kelly	Kansas City, Mo.
Oscar W. A. Handy	O-425080	41-F Kelly	Long Beach, Calif.
Henry O. Null Jr.	O-425137	41-F Kelly	Los Angeles, Calif.
Robert W. Kerstetter	O-425518	41-F Kelly	Toledo, Ohio
Donald O. McIntosh	O-427451	41-G Kelly	Chicago, Ill.
Robert F. McMahon	O-427453	41-G Kelly	Mitchell, S.Dak.
Joe P. Martin	O-427457	41-G Kelly	Kalamazoo, Mich.
Walter L. Hurd Jr.	O-427544	41-G Kelly	Stanhope, Iowa
James W. Ingram	O-427547	41-G Kelly	Fieldon, Ill.
Robert G. Hazard	O-427563	41-G Kelly	Modesto, Calif.
Wallace B. MacLean	O-427601	41-G Kelly	Mitchell, S.Dak.
James Calvin Smith	O-427668	41-G Kelly	Troy, Ohio
Donovan G. Goodyear	O-427687	41-G Kelly	Marion, Iowa

Sources: Air Base Headquarters, Hamilton Field, Calif., Special Orders No. 253, October 27, 1941; Kelly Field, Texas, *Gig Sheet,* classes 41-E, 41-F, and 41-G.

TABLE 2   Pilots of 34th Pursuit Squadron, 35th Pursuit Group embarked on
USAT *Republic* for Philippines, November 21, 1941

PILOT	SERIAL NO.	FLIGHT CLASS	HOME TOWN
Dwight S. Muckley Jr.	O-398662	40-F Kelly	Johnstown, Pa.
Russell L. Callison	O-403883	41-A unknown	St. Clair County, Ill.
Bryan W. Brown Jr.	O-421035	41-E Stockton	El Paso, Tex.
Wade O. Holman	O-421092	41-E Stockton	Montague County, Tex.
George W. Hynes Jr.	O-421104	41-E Stockton	San Antonio, Tex.
William C. Stauter	O-421136	41-E Stockton	Hammond, Ind.
Ray S. Thompson	O-421139	41-E Stockton	Leona, Tex.
Lee M. Boren	O-424897	41-F Kelly	Hollywood, Calif.
John M. Lewis	O-425014	41-F Kelly	Chamberlain, S.Dak.
Harold G. Lund	O-425017	41-F Kelly	San Francisco, Calif.
Ray Melikian	O-425024	41-F Kelly	Kerman, Calif.
Elton S. Perry	O-425042	41-F Kelly	Phoenix, Ariz.
Fred M. Cooper	O-425070	41-F Kelly	Aberdeen, S.Dak.
William A. O'Neill	O-425102	41-F Kelly	Chicago, Ill.
H. Allen Graham	O-425156	41-F Kelly	Winfield, Kans.
William H. B. Erwin	O-425404	41-F Kelly	Kansas City, Mo.
Quanah P. Fields	O-425515	41-F Kelly	Grove, Okla.
Robert Spence Johnson	O-425517	41-F Kelly	Mesa, Ariz.
James L. Naylor Jr.	O-427613	41-G Kelly	El Paso, Tex.
Henry G. Newman	O-427617	41-G Kelly	Douglas, Ariz.
Melvin J. Price	O-427659	41-G Kelly	Georgetown, Tex.
Vernon H. B. Wilhite	O-427674	41-G Kelly	Cullman, Ala.
Frederic J. Rupp	O-427814	41-G unknown	Alameda County, Calif.

Sources: Air Base Headquarters, Hamilton Field, California, Special Orders No. 253, October 27, 1941; Kelly Field, Texas, *Gig Sheet,* classes 41-E and 41-F; Air Corps Advanced Flying School, Stockton Field, California, list of graduates, class 41-E.

TABLE 3 Pilots of 35th Pursuit Group embarked on USAT *President Polk* for Philippines, December 18, 1941

PILOT	SERIAL NO.	FLYING SCHOOL CLASS	HOME TOWN
William Lane Jr.	O-22547	39-A Kelly	unknown
Paul B. Gambonini	O-375422	none	Petaluma, Calif.
Thomas L. Hayes Jr.	O-403857	41-A Kelly	Brooks, Ore.
Winfred H. Gallienne	O-404048	41-A Kelly	San Francisco, Calif.
Paul C. May	O-412180	41-C Kelly	Des Moines, Iowa
James B. Morehead	O-413480	41-C Stockton	Washington, Okla.
Marion J. Fuchs	O-417953	41-D Stockton	Big Springs, Tex.
Gene L. Bound	O-418188	41-D Stockton	Dallas, Tex.
Lloyd P. Carlos	O-421039	41-E Stockton	Los Angeles, Calif.
Albert H. Dutton	O-421064	41-E Stockton	Portland, Ore.
James V. Hamilton	O-421082	41-E Stockton	Jones County, Tex.
Vernon L. Head	O-421087	41-E Stockton	Cleburne, Tex.
Kenneth L. Koebel	O-421117	41-E Stockton	Pima County, Ariz.
Roger H. Williams	O-421151	41-E Stockton	Sterling City, Tex.
William R. Perine	O-421303	41-E Brooks	Wayne County, Mich.
Donald E. Workman	O-421371	41-E Brooks	Morgan County, Ill.
John E. Bridge	O-421622	41-E Kelly	North Hollywood, Calif.
William H. Eldridge	O-421935	41-E Kelly	Oklahoma City, Okla.
Peter M. Childress	O-424911	41-F Kelly	Los Angeles, Calif.
Robert B. Dockstader	O-424926	41-F Kelly	Long Beach, Calif.
George A. Parker	O-425097	41-F Kelly	Riverside, Calif.
Jesse R. Hague	O-425516	41-F Kelly	Adel, Iowa
William O. Farrior	O-427482	41-G Kelly	Fort Deposit, Ala.
John G. Glover	O-427496	41-G Kelly	Fargo, N.Dak.
Verne P. Augustine	O-427580	41-G Kelly	Wahpeton, N.Dak.
Gerald J. Dix	O-427676	41-G Kelly	Sullivan, Ind.
John R. Vann	O-429998	41-H Mather	Gray County, Kans.

Sources: Headquarters 4th Air Force, Hamilton Field, California, Special Orders No. 180, December 17, 1941; Kelly Field, Texas, *Gig Sheet,* classes 41-E, 41-F, and 41-G; Air Corps Advanced Flying School, Stockton Field, California, lists of graduates, classes 41-C, 41-D, and 41-E; Moffett Field, California, *The Hangar,* class 41-H, August 1941 (for Mather Field 41-H advanced training class).

TABLE 4 Pilots of 14th, 20th, and 51st Pursuit Groups embarked on USAT *President Polk* for Philippines, December 18, 1941

PILOT	SERIAL NO.	GROUP	FLYING SCHOOL CLASS	HOME TOWN
Larry D. Landry	O-378814	20th	41-E Kelly	Baton Rouge, La.
Robert H. Vaught	O-382764	14th	41-H unkn.	Los Angeles, Calif.
Clarence E. Simpson Jr.	O-394515	14th	41-H Mather	Dallas, Tex.
James J. Handley	O-414955	20th	41-C?	Hunt County, Tex.
Bernard J. Oliver	O-418161	20th	41-D Stockton	Prescott, Ariz.
Jesse Dore Jr.	O-421063	51st	41-E Stockton	Glenwood Springs, Colo.
Wallace J. Hoskyn	O-421095	20th	41-E Stockton	Seattle, Wash.
Elwin H. Jackson	O-421106	20th	41-E Stockton	Glendale, Calif.
Lester J. Johnsen	O-421107	20th	41-E Stockton	South Bend, Wash.
Robert C. McWherter	O-421123	20th	41-E Stockton	Paris, Tex.
William L. Turner	O-421146	20th	41-E Stockton	Lubbock, Tex.
Robert G. Oestreicher	O-421298	51st	41-E Brooks	Columbus, Ohio
James F. Ryan	O-421325	20th	41-E Brooks	Pottawatomie, Okla.
Eugene A. Wahl	O-421361	51st	41-E Brooks	Indianapolis, Ind.
Frank E. Adkins	O-421570	51st	41-E Kelly	Clarksville, Tenn.
Rupert L. Selman	O-421651	20th	41-E Kelly	Hazlehurst, Miss.
Andrew J. Reynolds	O-421656	20th	41-E Kelly	Seminole, Okla.
Cornelius L. Reagan	O-421657	20th	41-E Kelly	Florence, Ky.
Richard E. Pingree	O-421661	14th	41-E Kelly	Ogden, Utah
Morris C. Caldwell	O-421696	51st	41-E Kelly	Nashville, Tenn.
William P. Ackerman Jr.	O-429897	51st	41-H Mather	Sydney, Neb.
Charles C. McNutt Jr.	O-429965	51st	41-H Mather	Travis County, Tex.
Harry E. Pressfield	O-429973	51st	41-H Mather	Santa Clara, Calif.
Burt H. Rice	O-429978	14th	41-H Mather	Reno, Nev.
William R. Walker	O-430001	14th	41-H Mather	Jacksonville, Tex.
Robert W. Wallace	O-430003	14th	41-H Mather	Tulare, Calif.
Max R. Wiecks	O-430006	14th	41-H Mather	Dallas, Tex.
Emmons C. Williams	O-430009	14th	41-H Mather	unknown

Sources: Headquarters, 4th Air Force, Hamilton Field, California, Special Orders No. 180, December 17, 1941; Kelly Field, Texas, *Gig Sheet,* class 41-E; Moffett Field, California, *The Hangar,* class 41-D, May 29, 1941, (for 41-D Stockton Field advanced flying class); Brooks Field, Texas, "Flying Cadet Class 41-E, 45th Reunion, Fort Worth Texas, October 3–5, 1986"; and Moffett Field, California, *The Hangar,* class 41-H, August 1941 (for Mather Field 41-H advanced training class).

TABLE 5 Philippines pursuit pilots sent to Australia, December 1941–January 1942

RANK	PILOT	SERIAL NO.	FLYING SCHOOL CLASS	HOME TOWN
Capt.	Floyd J. Pell	O-20701	38-C Kelly	Ogden, Utah
Capt.	Charles A Sprague	O-20769	38-C Kelly	Bridgeport, Conn.
1st Lt.	Boyd D. Wagner	O-21623	38-B Kelly	Johnstown, Pa.
1st. Lt	William A. Sheppard	O-364059	40-A Kelly	Pittsburgh, Pa.
1st Lt.	Gerald M. Keenan	O-388608	40-A Kelly	Chicago, Ill.
1st Lt.	Gerald McCallum	O-388622	40-A Kelly	Ruston, La.
1st Lt.	Grant Mahony	O-388626	40-A Kelly	Vallejo, Calif.
1st Lt.	Walter L. Coss	O-388651	40-A Kelly	Brighton, Pa.
1st Lt.	Allison W. Strauss	O-388826	40-A Kelly	Wadesville, Ind.
2nd Lt.	Frank V. Neri	O-396658	40-D Kelly	Rochester, N.Y.
2nd Lt.	Ben S. Irvin	O-399532	40-G Kelly	Washington, Ga.
2nd Lt.	Jack D. Dale	O-401140	40-H Kelly	Willoughby, Ohio
2nd Lt.	Edwin B. Gilmore	O-401165	40-H Kelly	Highland Park, Mich.
2nd Lt.	George E. Kiser	O-401180	40-H Kelly	Somerset, Ky.
2nd Lt.	Joseph J. Kruzel	O-401183	40-H Kelly	Wilkes-Barre, Pa.
2nd Lt.	Nathaniel H. Blanton	O-401361	40-H Kelly	Shawnee, Okla.
2nd Lt.	William J. Hennon	O-406549	41-B Kelly	Mound, Minn.
2nd Lt.	Carl Parker Gies	O-407083	41-B Kelly	Salem, Ore.
2nd Lt.	James M. Rowland	O-418435	41-D Kelly	Fort Worth, Tex.

Source: Bartsch, *Doomed at the Start,* 171, 217, 220–21.
Note: Pell and McCallum arrived in Australia on November 17, 1941 (radiogram, Air Board Darwin, 18 November 1941, in Series A1196, Symbol 60/501/76, NAA).

TABLE 6 Pilots and aircraft of 17th Pursuit Squadron (Provisional),
Amberley Field, Australia, January 16, 1942

PILOT	SERIAL NO.	FLYING SCHOOL CLASS	PLANE NUMBER	PILOT FATE IN JAVA CAMPAIGN
Capt. Charles A. Sprague (CO)	O-20769	38-C	1	KIA, Bali, Feb. 20
1st Lt. Gerald A. McCallum	O-388622	40-A	10	KIA, Java, Feb. 25
1st Lt. Walter L. Coss	O-388651	40-A	15	Evac. by air, Feb. 28
2nd Lt. Frank V. Neri	O-396658	40-D	unknown	Crashed, Java, Jan. 29; Evac. by *Abbekerk*, Feb. 27
2nd. Lt. Ben S. Irvin	O-399532	40-G	12	Evac. by air, Mar. 1
2nd Lt. Jack D. Dale	O-401140	40-H	4	Evac. by air, Mar. 1
2nd. Lt. Edwin B. Gilmore	O-401165	40-H	5	Evac. by air, Mar. 1
2nd Lt. George E. Kiser	O-401180	40-H	2	Evac. by air, Mar. 1
2nd. Lt. Joseph J. Kruzel	O-401183	40-H	16	Evac. by air, Mar. 1
2nd Lt. Nathaniel H. Blanton	O-401361	40-H	17	Evac. by air, Feb. 28
2nd Lt. William J. Hennon	O-406549	41-B	11	Evac. by air, Mar. 1
2nd Lt. Carl Parker Gies	O-407083	41-B	6	Crashed, Rockhampton, Jan. 16; remained in Australia
2nd Lt. James M. Rowland	O-418435	41-D	unknown	KIA, Java, Feb. 3
2nd Lt. Bryan W. Brown Jr.	O-421035	41-E	9	Crashed, Townsville, Jan. 16; transferred to 3rd Pursuit Squadron
2nd Lt. William C. Stauter	O-421136	41-E	8	Shot down, Java, Feb. 20; evac. by *Abbekerk*, Feb. 27
2nd Lt. Ray S. Thompson	O-421139	41-E	7 or 3	Evac. by air, Feb. 28
2nd Lt. Chester E. Trout	O-421145	41-E	13	Dengue fever, Darwin, Jan. 22; remained in Australia

Sources: As compiled from 17th Pursuit Squadron (Provisional) Roster, January 14, 1942, in "History of the 5th Air Force," Doc. 902, Appendix II, microfilm A7385, AFHRA; Walter L. Coss diary, Notebook No. 1 (1942); research of Gordon Birkett.

TABLE 7   Pilots of 20th Pursuit Squadron (Provisional), Amberley Field, Australia, January 27, 1942

PILOT	SERIAL NO.	FLYING SCHOOL CLASS	TAKEOFF DARWIN– KOEPANG	FATE IN JAVA CAMPAIGN
1st Lt. William Lane Jr. (CO)	O-22547	39-A	Feb. 4	Evac. by air, Mar. 1
2nd Lt. Paul B. Gambonini	O-375422	none	Feb. 4	Evac. by air, Mar. 1
2nd Lt. Larry D. Landry	O-378814	41-E	Feb. 4	KIA, Bali, Feb. 5
2nd Lt. Dwight S. Muckley	O-398662	40-F	Feb. 4	Evac. by air, Feb. 28
2nd Lt. Hubert I. Egenes	O-398687	40-F	Feb. 5	Evac. by air, Feb. 28
2nd Lt. Thomas L. Hayes Jr.	O-403857	41-A	Feb. 4	WIA, Feb. 20; evac. by *Abbekerk*, Feb. 27
2nd Lt. Winfred H. Gallienne	O-404048	41-A	Feb. 4	Shot down, Bali, Feb. 20; POW
2nd Lt. James B. Morehead	O-413480	41-C	Feb. 4	Evac. by air, Mar. 1
2nd Lt. Marion J. Fuchs	O-417953	41-D	Feb. 4	Evac by air, Mar. 1
2nd Lt. Bernard J. Oliver	O-418161	41-D	Feb. 5	Evac. by air, Feb. 28
2nd Lt. Gene L. Bound	O-418188	41-D	Feb. 4	Shot down, Bali, Feb. 5; evac. by *Abbekerk*, Feb. 27
2nd Lt. Wm. David Coleman	O-421050	41-E	Feb. 5	Crashed, Lombok, Feb.6; evac. Bali by air, Feb. 16
2nd Lt. Albert H. Dutton	O-421064	41-E	Feb. 5	Crashed, Lombok, Feb 6; evac. Bali by air, Feb. 16
2nd Lt. Wallace J. Hoskyn	O-421095	41-E	Feb. 5	KIA, Java, Feb. 21
2nd Lt. George W. Hynes Jr.	O-421104	41-E	Feb. 4	Shot down, Java, Feb 21; died Feb. 22
2nd Lt. Elwin H. Jackson	O-421106	41-E	Feb. 5	Evac. by air, Feb. 28
2nd Lt. Lester J. Johnsen	O-421107	41-E	Feb. 5	Evac. by air, Mar. 1
2nd Lt. Robert C. McWherter	O-421123	41-E	Feb. 4	Evac. by air, Mar. 1
2nd Lt. William L. Turner	O-421146	41-E	Feb. 4	Evac. by air, Feb. 28
2nd Lt. Roger H. Williams	O-421151	41-E	Feb. 5	Evac. by air, Mar. 1
2nd Lt. James F. Ryan	O-421325	41-E	Feb. 5	Evac. by air, Feb. 28
2nd Lt. Andrew J. Reynolds	O-421656	41-E	Feb. 5	Evac. by air, Mar. 1
2nd Lt. Cornelius L. Reagan	O-421657	41-E	Feb. 4	Shot down, Java, Mar. 1; POW
2nd Lt. George A. Parker	O-425097	41-F	Via B-24, Feb 4	Evac. by air, Feb. 28
2nd Lt. Jesse R. Hague	O-425516	41-F	Feb. 4	Evac. by air, Feb. 28

Note: 2nd Lt. James V. Hamilton assigned earlier, but killed in accident Jan. 23.

TABLE 8 Pilots and aircraft of 3rd Pursuit Squadron (Provisional), Amberley Field, Australia, February 4, 1942

PILOT	SERIAL NO.	FLYING SCHOOL CLASS	PLANE NO.	FATE IN JAVA CAMPAIGN
1st Lt. Grant Mahony (CO)	O-388626	40-A		Transf. to India by air, Feb. 25
1st Lt. Allison W. Strauss	O-388826	40-A		Crashed, Timor, Feb. 9; evac. Koepang by air, Feb. 19
2nd Lt. Ben S. Irvin	O-399532	40-G		Evac. Java by air, Mar. 1
2nd Lt. Bryan W. Brown Jr.	O-421035	41-E		Crashed, Daly Waters, Feb. 6; remained in Australia
2nd Lt. Lloyd P. Carlos	O-421039	41-E	52	As for Strauss
2nd Lt. Vernon L. Head	O-421087	41-E	27	As for Strauss
2nd Lt. Wade O. Holman	O-421092	41-E		Aborted Cloncurry flight, Feb.5; transf. to 13th Pursuit
2nd Lt. Robt. G. Oestreicher	O-421298	41-E	43	Engine trouble, Darwin, Feb. 7; remained in Australia
2nd Lt. Eugene A. Wahl	O-421361	41-E	22	Evac. Java by air, Feb. 28
2nd Lt. Frank E. Adkins	O-421570	41-E		Shot down, Java, Mar. 1; evac. Java by air, Mar. 1
2nd Lt. Morris C. Caldwell	O-421696	41-E		KIA, Java, Mar. 1
2nd Lt. Robert J. Buel	O-424901	41-E	54	Mech. trouble, Darwin, Feb. 7; KIA, Timor Sea, Feb. 15
2nd Lt. Peter M. Childress	O-424911	41-F		As for Strauss
2nd Lt. Robert B. Dockstader	O-424926	41-F		Evac. Java by air, Mar. 1
2nd Lt. Bennett L. Johnson	O-424962	41-F		Sent back, Darwin to Amberley, Feb. 8; transf. to 13th Pursuit
2nd Lt. Robert A. Kaiser	O-424966	41-F		Sent back, Darwin to Amberley, Feb. 8
2nd Lt. Ralph G. Martin	O-424979	41-F	13	Crashed, Charleville, Feb. 5; remained in Australia
2nd Lt. John M. Lewis	O-425014	41-F		As for Strauss
2nd Lt. Harold G. Lund	O-425017	41-F		Evac. Java by air, Mar. 1
2nd Lt. Ray Melikian	O-425024	41-F		As for Bryan Brown
2nd Lt. Philip T. Metsker	O-425026	41-F		Killed in crash, Timor, Feb. 9
2nd Lt. Oscar W. A. Handy	O-425080	41-F		Crashed, Darwin, Feb. 6; transf. to 13th Pursuit
2nd Lt. William H. B. Erwin	O-425404	41-F		As for Strauss
2nd Lt. Quanah P. Fields	O-425515	41-F		KIA, Java, Feb. 19
2nd Lt. R. Spence Johnson	O-425517	41-F	45	Evac. Java by air, Mar. 1

Source: Special Orders No. 20, Hq Base Section 3, Brisbane, Feb. 4, 1942.

TABLE 9 Pilots and aircraft of 33rd Pursuit Squadron (Provisional), Amberley Field, Australia, February 8, 1942

PILOT	SERIAL NO.	FLYING SCHOOL CLASS	PLANE NO.	FATE IN JAVA CAMPAIGN
Capt. Floyd J. Pell (CO)	O-20701	38-C	3	KIA, Darwin, Feb. 19
2nd Lt. Robert H. Vaught	O-382764	41-H	28	Remained in Darwin
1st Lt. Gerald M. Keenan	O-388608	40-A	181	Lost in *Langley/Edsall* sinkings Feb. 27 and Mar. 1
2nd Lt. Jack R. Peres	O-416707	41-F	189	As for Pell
2nd Lt. Jesse R. Dore	O-421063	41-E	179	Blown tire, Alice Springs, Feb. 14; remained in Australia
2nd Lt. Kenneth L. Koebel	O-421117	41-E	196	As for Keenan
2nd Lt. John E. Bridge	O-421622	41-E		As for Keenan
2nd Lt. Richard E. Pingree	O-421661	41-E	180	Killed in crash, Port Pirie, Feb. 19
2nd Lt. William H. Eldridge	O-421935	41-E	195	As for Keenan
2nd Lt. William P. Borden	O-424896	41-F		As for Keenan
2nd Lt. Lee M. Boren	O-424897	41-F	190	As for Keenan
2nd Lt. Elton S. Perry	O-425042	41-F	51	As for Pell
2nd Lt. Robert W. Kerstetter	O-425518	41-F	193	Crash-landed, Coffs Harbor, Feb. 11; remained in Australia
2nd Lt. David E. Latane	O-426399	41-G	138	As for Dore
2nd Lt. Robert F. McMahon	O-427453	41-G	22	Shot down and wounded, Darwin, Feb. 19
2nd Lt. John G. Glover	O-427496	41-G	36	As for McMahon
2nd Lt. James L. Naylor Jr.	O-427613	41-G		Aborted flight and crashed, Amberley, on return, Feb. 11
2nd Lt. V. H. Bryce Wilhite	O-427674	41-G	25	Blown tire, Port Pirie, Feb. 16; remained in Australia
2nd Lt. Gerald J. Dix	O-427676	41-G		Survived *Langley* sinking, Feb. 27; rescued by *Whipple*, Mar. 1
2nd Lt. Donovan G. Goodyear	O-427687	41-G		As for Keenan
2nd Lt. Charles W. Hughes	O-427738	41-G	94	As for Pell
2nd Lt. Richard C. Suehr	O-428531	41-H	15	Nosed over S of Darwin, Feb. 15; remained in Australia
2nd Lt. Burt H. Rice	O-429978	41-H	31	As for McMahon
2nd Lt. William R. Walker	O-430001	41-H	46	As for McMahon
2nd Lt. Max R. Wiecks	O-430006	41-H	9	As for McMahon

Sources: As compiled from "Roster of the 33rd Pursuit Squadron Provisional—Capt. Pell Commanding," February 12, 1942, file 5th AF AG 322.99, in "History of the 5th Air Force"; Pell, "Flight Assignments, 33rd Pursuit Squadron, Brisbane, February 4, 1942."

TABLE 10   Pilots of 13th Pursuit Squadron (Provisional), Amberley Field, Australia, February 13, 1942

PILOT	SERIAL NO.	FLYING SCHOOL CLASS	FATE IN JAVA CAMPAIGN
Capt. Boyd D. Wagner (CO)	O-21623	38-B Kelly	Remained in Australia
1st Lt. James R. Bruce Jr.	O-373817	39-A Kelly	As for Wagner
1st. Lt. Thomas H. Hubbard	O-380248	39-B Kelly	As for Wagner
2nd Lt. Clarence E. Simpson	O-394515	41-H Mather	Lost in *Langley/Edsall* sinkings, Feb. 27 and Mar. 1
2nd Lt. Wade O. Holman	O-421092	41-E Stockton	Crashed, Williamtown, Feb. 13; proceeded on to *Langley* and lost as for Simpson
2nd Lt. William R. Perine	O-421303	41-E Brooks	As for Simpson
2nd Lt. Donald E. Workman	O-421371	41-E Brooks	As for Simpson
2nd Lt. Bennett L. Johnson	O-424962	41-F Kelly	As for Simpson
2nd Lt. William A Kennedy Jr.	O-424972	41-F Kelly	As for Simpson
2nd Lt. Kenneth L. Glassburn	O-425075	41-F Kelly	Injured in crash, Williamtown, Feb. 13; remained in Australia
2nd Lt. Oscar W. A. Handy	O-425080	41-F Kelly	As for Simpson
2nd Lt. Donald O. McIntosh	O-427451	41-G Kelly	As for Simpson
2nd Lt. Joe P. Martin	O-427457	41-G Kelly	Crashed, Maylands, Feb. 17; boarded *Langley* anyway and lost as for Simpson
2nd Lt. Robert G. Hazard	O-427536	41-G Kelly	Returned from combat zone
2nd Lt. Verne P. Augustine	O-427580	41-G Kelly	As for Simpson
2nd Lt. Wallace B. MacLean	O-427601	41-G Kelly	As for Simpson
2nd Lt. James Calvin Smith	O-427668	41-G Kelly	As for Simpson
2nd Lt. John E. Bentley	O-427696	41-G unkn	As for Simpson
2nd Lt. Harrison A. Gorman	O-427717	41-G unkn	As for Simpson
2nd Lt. Laurence H. Green	O-427721	41-G unkn	As for Simpson
2nd Lt. Wilfred B. Jones	O-427742	41-G unkn	Enroute combat zone Feb. 23
2nd Lt. William A. Levitan	O-427754	41-G unkn	Crashed, Richmond
2nd Lt. Horace C. Atkinson	O-428463	41-H Craig	As for Simpson
2nd Lt. Arthur E. England	O-428483	41-H Craig	As for Simpson
2nd Lt. William C. Herbert	O-428495	41-H Craig	Returned to Amberley from Mascot
2nd Lt. Justin J. Hower	O-428503	41-H Craig	As for Simpson
2nd Lt. Earl R. Kingsley	O-428506	41-H Craig	Crashed, Richmond
2nd Lt. Paul J. Magre	O-428515	41-H Craig	Sick; left plane at Laverton
2nd Lt Haley W. Skinner	O-428537	41-H Craig	As for Simpson
2nd Lt. Edward C. Schmillen	O-428570	41-H Craig	As for Simpson

(cont. next page)

(*Table 10 cont.*)

2nd Lt. Aime L. Dierkens	O-428649	41-H Craig	As for Simpson
2nd Lt. William P. Ackerman Jr.	O-429897	41-H Mather	Survived *Langley* sinking Feb. 27; rescued by *Whipple* Mar. 1
2nd Lt. Charles C. McNutt	O-429965	41-H Mather	As for Simpson
2nd Lt. Harry E. Pressfield	O-429973	41-H Mather	Returned from combat zone
2nd Lt. John R. Vann	O-429998	41-H Mather	As for Simpson
2nd Lt. Robert W. Wallace	O-430003	41-H Mather	As for Simpson

Source: "Operations Java Campaign: Pilots of the 13th and 33rd Squadrons Wrecked or Aircraft Out on the Way to USS *Langley* and from Port Pirie to Darwin," Brisbane, February 24, 1942 , Doc. 946, Microfilm A7385, AFHRA; Air Corps Advanced Flying School, Craig Field, Selma, Alabama, October 31, 1941, "Roster of Graduates Class 41-H."

TABLE 11 Enlisted men of 17th Pursuit Squadron (Provisional) assigned to Ngoro Field, Java, January–February 1942

ENLISTED MAN	SERIAL NO.	DUTY	HOME TOWN	JAVA EVACUATION
S/Sgt. Anthony Jackson	02715267	crew chief	Montgomery County, Ohio	Air
S/Sgt. James G. Weidman	06138551	armorer	Ore.	Air
S/Sgt. William W. Fairbank	06274700	armorer	Sheridan, Wyo.	Air
S/Sgt. Clifton H. Piper	06564050	crew chief	Spokane, Wash.	Air
S/Sgt. Jack G. Evans	06564416	crew chief	N.J.	Air
S/Sgt. Louis A. Boise	06566048	radioman	Salt Lake City, Utah	Air
S/Sgt. John M. Rex	06581412	crew chief	Ogden, Utah	Air; killed, Broome B-24 crash, Mar. 3
S/Sgt. Harold N. Varner	06788219	crew chief	San Rafael, Calif.	Air
Sgt. Clarence H. Johnston	06250204	armorer	Anderson County, Tex.	Air
Sgt. Willard J. Beatty	06256686	armorer	Denver, Colo.	Air; died of wounds, Mar. 7, Broome B-24 crash, Mar. 3
Sgt. Lyle O. Smith	06917487	crew chief	Colfax, Ill.	Air
Sgt. Charles L. Schaffer	15012163	crew chief	Columbus, Ohio	Air
Sgt. Melvin O. Donoho	18003946	armorer	Covington, Okla.	Air; survived Broome B-24 crash, Mar. 3
Sgt. Clyde R. Brackelsberg	18018010	armorer	Grand Junction, Colo.	*Abbekerk,* Feb. 27
Cpl. Angelo Prioreschi	06255512	crew chief	E. Cleveland, Ohio	Air
Cpl. Lawrence E. Norton	06566625	armorer	Marion County, Ore.	Air
Cpl. Victor W. Cunningham	06938515	crew chief	Springfield, Mo.	Air
Cpl. Luther H. Rivers	14029007	crew chief	Atlanta, Ga.	Air
Cpl. William E. O'Rear	15062381	crew chief	South Bend, Ind.	Left behind
Cpl. Lewis R. Wilsey	19051217	crew chief	Southgate, Calif.	Air
Pfc. Lyman S. Goltry	06581911	crew chief	Glenwood, Iowa	Air
Pfc. Glenn E. Harkins	19010712	armorer	Hansen, Idaho	Air
Pfc. James I. Collett	19049032	crew chief	Hayward, Calif.	Air
Pvt. Richard G. Sheetz	13000321	armorer	Shenandoah County, Va.	As for Rex

(cont. next page)

(Table 11 cont.)

Pvt. Edgar C. Kimball	15018691	crew chief	Rosco, Ohio	*Abbekerk*, Feb. 27
Pvt. Bernard W. Badura	16028213	armorer	Genoa, Neb.	*Abbekerk*, Feb. 27
Pvt. Herbert M. Frady	17004260	armorer	Little Falls, Minn.	Air
Pvt. Benjamin L. Culpepper	17013056	armorer	Pine Bluff, Ark.	Air
Pvt. Orville F. Rickmar	17015698	armorer	St. Francis County, Mo.	Air
Pvt. Henry L. Foy	18014888	armorer	Sweetwater, Tex.	*Abbekerk*, Feb. 27
Pvt. Cecil E. Stevens	18021372	armorer	Big Springs, Tex.	Air
Pvt. R. E. Colbert	18029821	armorer	Washita County, Okla.	Air
Pvt. Woodrow W. Myers	18055961	armorer	Missouri Valley, Iowa	Air
Pvt. Richard E. Pitts	19015832	crew chief	Houlton, Ore.	Air
Pvt. Edgar M. Chumbley	19051879	crew chief	Sacramento, Calif.	Air
Pvt. Clinton W. Washburn	20924635	radioman	Utah County, Utah	Air

Source: As compiled from Fourth Air Force, Hamilton Field, Calif., Special Orders No. 180, December 17, 1941; USAFIA Melbourne, Special Orders No. 64, March 19, 1942; George Weller, "Luck to the Fighters," *Military Affairs*, Winter 1944, 262–64; "Crew Chiefs and Armorers Assigned to Pilots" (on board the USAT *President Polk*) in Gambonini papers; "Crew Chiefs and Armament Men of the 17th Pursuit (Prov.) Who Were Evacuated from Java by Air and Boat."

TABLE 12   Enlisted men of 20th Pursuit Squadron (Provisional) assigned to Ngoro Field, Java, February 1942

ENLISTED MAN	SERIAL NO.	DUTY	HOME TOWN	JAVA EVACUATION
S/Sgt. Ruben C. Compton	06193995	crew chief	West Plains, Mo.	Air
S/Sgt. Edgar M. English	06260967	crew chief	Silberton, Tex.	Air
S/Sgt. Robert H. Jung	06381827	armorer	Seattle, Wash.	*Abbekerk,* Feb. 27
S/Sgt. Reecy F. Wassan	06399037	crew chief	Ouachita County, La.	Air
S/Sgt. James E. Freeman	06735513	crew chief	San Antonio, Tex.	Air
S/Sgt. David R. Griffith Jr.	06853664	line chief	Luzerne County, Pa.	Air
S/Sgt. Leo D. Steinmetz	06914316	crew chief	Jefferson County, Kans.	Air; killed, Broome B-24 crash, Mar. 3
Sgt. Samuel F. Foster	06252463	armorer	Ark.	As for Steinmetz
Sgt. Ernest R. Austin	06281353	crew chief	Brownfield, Tex.	Air
Sgt. Thomas F. Johnstone	06563868	armorer	Renville, Minn.	*Abbekerk,* Feb. 27
Sgt. Julian P. Guerrero	06580686	crew chief	Des Moines, Iowa	*Abbekerk,* Feb. 27
Sgt. Bernard L. Merriman	06861667	armorer	Tekamah, Neb.	Air
Sgt. Clay M. Harper	06862781	crew chief	Lyons, Kans.	Air
Sgt. Phillip B. Killian	06863638	armorer	St. Paul, Neb.	Air
Sgt. William F. Hardgrove	06933946	crew chief	St. Louis, Mo.	Air (C-53)
Sgt. Delbert L. Kelly	15066274	crew chief	Cincinnati, Ohio	Air
Sgt. F. S. Little	18021424	armorer	Stephenville, Tex.	*Abbekerk,* Feb. 27
Sgt. Dale G. Holt	19051992	crew chief	Lebanon, Mo.	Air
Sgt. Michael Ewas	unknown	crew chief	unknown	Air (C-53)
Cpl. Ollie C. Hale	00055577	radioman	unknown	Air
Cpl. Robert S. Reeves	06933598	crew chief	Alvia, Iowa	*Abbekerk,* Feb. 27
Cpl. Jack T. Taylor	18034892	armorer	Gregg County, Tex.	As for Steinmetz
Cpl. Kenneth H. Perry	19006107	crew chief	Spokane, Wash.	*Abbekerk,* Feb. 27
Pfc. Jack D. Crawford	18034698	armorer	Henderson, Tex.	*Abbekerk,* Feb. 27
Pfc. Frank I. Rautio	19012607	armorer	Daly City, Calif.	*Abbekerk,* Feb. 27
Pfc. George R. Lovejoy	20910959	crew chief	Sierra Madre, Calif.	Air
Pfc. Frederick J. Deyo	37019055	armorer	St. Paul, Minn.	*Abbekerk,* Feb. 27
Pvt. Harlan R. Sanders	06285481	armorer	El Paso, Tex.	Air
Pvt. Raymond E. Wilson	06568845	armorer	Los Angeles, Calif.	*Abbekerk,* Feb. 27

(cont. next page)

(*Table 12 cont.*)

Pvt. Herman E. Langjahr	06874554	armorer	Pine Hill, N.J.	Air (with 19th BG)
Pvt. Clarence R. Flodin	06953759	armorer	Denver, Colo.	*Abbekerk,* Feb. 27
Pvt. Ashley Ewart	17010401	crew chief	Helena, Ark.	Air
Pvt. Edgar E. Fink	19013394	crew chief	Alameda County, Calif.	*Abbekerk,* Feb. 27
Pvt. James F. Walsh	19019318	radioman	unknown	Air (C-53)
Pvt. Vernon U. Bynum	19024217	armorer	Coffeeville, Kans.	*Abbekerk,* Feb. 27
Pvt. Gail D. Cox	19038610	armorer	San Bernardino, Calif.	*Abbekerk,* Feb. 27

Source: As compiled from Fourth Air Force, Hamilton Field, Calif., Special Orders No. 180, December 17, 1941; USAFIA Melbourne, Special Orders No. 64, March 19, 1942; George Weller, "Luck to the Fighters," *Military Affairs,* Winter 1944, 262–64; "Crew Chiefs and Armorers Assigned to Pilots" (on board the USAT *President Polk*) in Gambonini papers; "Crew Chiefs and Armament Men of the 17th Pursuit (Prov.) Who Were Evacuated from Java by Air and Boat."

TABLE 13 Enlisted men of 3rd Pursuit Squadron (Provisional) assigned to
Ngoro Field, Java, February 1942

ENLISTED MAN	SERIAL NO.	DUTY	HOME TOWN	JAVA EVACUATION
S/Sgt. William F. Kelly	06224897	crew chief	Everett, Wash.	*Abbekerk*, Feb. 27
S/Sgt. Leo M. Burden	06255609	crew chief	Abilene, Tex.	Air
S/Sgt. Murray D. Nichols	06256440	armorer	Lubbock, Tex.	*Abbekerk*, Feb. 27
S/Sgt. William L. Fletcher	06546145	armorer	Port Angeles, Wash.	*Abbekerk*, Feb. 27
S/Sgt. James E. Swanson	06561236	crew chief	Oakland, Calif.	Air
S/Sgt. Robert W. Ebel	06587323	armorer	Evanston, Idaho	*Abbekerk*, Feb. 27
S/Sgt. John G. Elliott	06731619	crew chief	Cook County, Ill.	Air
S/Sgt. Emerson A. Witner	06755311	armorer	Weatherly, Pa.	*Abbekerk*, Feb. 27
S/Sgt. Michale Zubritsky	06941248	unknown	Washington County, Pa.	Air
S/Sgt. Cecil B. Ingram	06951659	radioman	Longview, Tex.	*Abbekerk*, Feb. 27
Sgt. Lewis C. McNeil	06268269	armorer	Lubbock, Tex.	*Abbekerk*, Feb. 27
Sgt. Jack Strange	06372869	unknown	Habersham County, Ga.	Air
Sgt. David E. Burnside	06569627	armorer	Spokane, Wash.	*Abbekerk*, Feb. 27
Sgt. John H. Leland	06581917	crew chief	Seattle, Wash.	*Abbekerk*, Feb. 27
Sgt. Manford B. McClanahan	06912883	armorer	Cook County, Ill.	*Abbekerk*, Feb. 27
Sgt. Anton Lysczyk	06913480	crew chief	Bessemer, Mich.	*Abbekerk*, Feb. 27
Sgt. John H. Breeling	06930884	crew chief	Ross, N.Dak.	*Abbekerk*, Feb. 27
Sgt. Eugene D. Chapman	18031492	radioman	Cushing, Tex.	*Abbekerk*, Feb. 27
Cpl. Bland King	17015907	crew chief	unknown	Air
Cpl. Selby E. Cockcroft	18026116	crew chief	Sherman, Tex.	Air
Cpl. ——Martin	unknown	radioman	unknown	*Abbekerk*, Feb. 27
Pfc. James P. Sheppard	06314650	armorer	San Antonio, Tex.	*Abbekerk*, Feb. 27
Pfc. Vernon D. Root	06581870	armorer	Bellingham, Wash.	*Abbekerk*, Feb. 27
Pfc. Gerald G. Hough	06583149	crew chief	Lorain, Ohio	*Abbekerk*, Feb. 27
Pfc. James A. Schott	06912402	radioman	Benton, Mo.	*Abbekerk*, Feb. 27
Pfc. Lehman H. Klob	17015957	crew chief	Farmington, Mo.	*Abbekerk*, Feb. 27
Pfc. L. P. Bedwell	18036729	crew chief	Lamesa, Tex.	*Abbekerk*, Feb. 27
Pfc. George H. Nelson	19013221	armorer	Oakland, Calif.	Air
Pvt. Anthony J. Hanna	06997532	armorer	Shenandoah, Pa.	*Abbekerk*, Feb. 27
Pvt. Carl F. Warner	12010727	crew chief	Cape May County, N.J.	Air

(*cont. next page*)

(Table 13 cont.)

Pvt. Francis M. Tomnovec	16001814	armorer	Kankakee, Ill.	*Abbekerk,* Feb. 27
Pvt. Howard O. Phillips	17021205	armorer	Crawford County, Kans.	*Abbekerk,* Feb. 27
Pvt. Vergil L. Gumm	37030183	crew chief	Minn.	Air
Pvt. Daryl W. Touchstone	20813192	unknown	Abilene, Tex.	Air

Source: As compiled from Fourth Air Force, Hamilton Field, Calif., Special Orders No. 180, December 17, 1941; USAFIA Melbourne, Special Orders No. 64, March 19, 1942; George Weller, "Luck to the Fighters," *Military Affairs,* Winter 1944, 262–64; "Crew Chiefs and Armorers Assigned to Pilots" (on board the USAT *President Polk*) in Gambonini papers; "Crew Chiefs and Armament Men of the 17th Pursuit (Prov.) Who Were Evacuated from Java by Air and Boat."

TABLE 14 Personnel embarked on USS *Langley,* Fremantle, Australia, February 22, 1942

NAME	SERIAL NO.	FLYING SCHOOL	SQUADRON	HOME TOWN
Pilots				
1st Lt. Gerald M. Keenan	O-388608	40-A	33rd	Chicago, Ill.
2nd Lt. Clarence E. Simpson	O-394515	41-H	13th	Dallas County, Tex.
2nd Lt. Wade O. Holman	O-421092	41-E	13th	Montague County, Tex.
2nd Lt. Kenneth L. Koebel	O-421117	41-E	33rd	Pima County, Ariz.
2nd Lt. William R. Perine	O-421303	41-E	13th	Wayne County, Mich.
2nd Lt. Donald E. Workman	O-421371	41-E	13th	Morgan County, Ill.
2nd Lt. John E. Bridge	O-421622	41-E	33rd	N. Hollywood, Calif.
2nd Lt. William H. Eldridge	O-421935	41-E	33rd	Oklahoma City, Okla.
2nd Lt. William P. Borden	O-424896	41-F	33rd	Snoqualmie Falls, Wash.
2nd Lt. Lee M. Boren	O-424897	41-F	33rd	Hollywood, Calif.
2nd Lt. Bennett L. Johnson	O-424962	41-F	13th	Omaha, Neb.
2nd Lt. William A. Kennedy Jr.	O-424972	41-F	13th	Knoxville, Tenn.
2nd Lt. Oscar W.A. Handy	O-425080	41-F	13th	Long Beach, Calif.
2nd Lt. Donald O. McIntosh	O-427451	41-G	13th	Chicago, Ill.
2nd Lt. Joe P. Martin	O-427457	41-G	13th	Kalamazoo, Mich.
2nd Lt. Verne P. Augustine	O-427580	41-G	13th	Wahpeton, N.Dak.
2nd Lt. Wallace B. MacLean	O-427601	41-G	13th	Mitchell, S.Dak.
2nd Lt. James Calvin Smith	O-427668	41-G	13th	Troy, Ohio
2nd Lt. Gerald J. Dix	O-427676	41-G	33rd	Sullivan, Ind.
2nd Lt. Donovan G. Goodyear	O-427687	41-G	33rd	Marion, Iowa
2nd Lt. John E. Bentley	O-427696	41-G	13th	Norfolk County, Mass.
2nd Lt. Harrison A. Gorman	O-427717	41-G	13th	Nantucket County, Mass.
2nd Lt. Laurence H. Green	O-427721	41-G	13th	Middlesex County, Mass.
2nd Lt. Horace C. Atkinson	O-428463	41-H	13th	Bucks County, Pa.
2nd Lt. Arthur E. England	O-428483	41-H	13th	Perry County, Ala.
2nd Lt. Justin J. Hower	O-428503	41-H	13th	Northampton County, Pa.
2nd Lt. Haley W. Skinner	O-428537	41-H	13th	Nemaha County, Kans.
2nd Lt. Edward C. Schmillen	O-428570	41-H	13th	LaSalle County, Ill.
2nd Lt. Aime L. Dierkens	O-428649	41-H	13th	Passaic County, N.J.
2nd Lt. William P. Ackerman Jr.	O-429897	41-H	13th	Sydney, Neb.
2nd Lt. Charles C. McNutt	O-429965	41-H	13th	Travis County, Tex.

(*cont. next page*)

(Table 14 cont.)

2nd Lt. John R. Vann	O-429998	41-H	13th	Gray County, Kans.
2nd Lt. Robert W. Wallace	O-430003	41-H	13th	Tulare, Calif.

Enlisted Men

T/Sgt Robert T. Marshall	06563501	16th/51PG	Thayer County, Neb.
T/Sgt Leo R. Hughes	07033246	16th/51PG	Stanislaus, Calif.
S/Sgt Edward H. Steiger	06569695	Hq/35PG	Lacrosse, Wash.
S/Sgt Richard K. Smith	06582534	Hq/35PG	Sioux City, Iowa
S/Sgt John W. Murray	06914209	Hq/35PG	Boone County, Iowa
Sgt John W. Mabry	06561678	Hq/35PG	Alameda, Calif.
Sgt. Carl Boysen	06939619	Hq/35PG	Sheridan County, Neb.
Cpl. Leon W. Weaver	13003385	unknown	Ephrata, Pa.
Cpl. George H. Bunnell	16027625	Hq/35PG	Clay County, Ill.
Pfc Jose A. Aguilar	18014837	unknown	El Paso, Tex.
Pfc James W. Denny	18043547	unknown	Yavapai County, Ariz.
Pvt. Harold W. Vogel	06914485	Hq/20PG	Kings County, N.Y.

Sources: "Organizational Personnel for USS *Langley*," Feb. 19, 1942, in "History of the 5th Air Force," doc. 937, Microfilm A7385, AFHRA; memo, Hazel F. Flynn, AGD, "Report of Deaths," to OIC, Casualty Section, Personnel Actions Branch, AGO, December 10, 1947; USAAC, Hamilton Field, California, *Historical and Pictorial Review, 10th Pursuit Wing and 45th Air Base;* www.wwiimemorial .com.

TABLE 15   Japanese aircraft shot down or badly damaged by pursuit pilots in
the Dutch East Indies campaign, January–March 1942

DATE	LOCATION	PLANE TYPE	UNIT	PILOT	RESULT	CREDIT
Feb. 3	Soerabaja	A6M2 Zero	3rd Kokutai	PO2c Hatsumasa Yamaya	Shot down	Probably Dutch pilot
Feb. 3	Soerabaja	A6M2 Zero	3rd Kokutai	PO3c Masami Morita	Shot down	Probably Dutch pilot
Feb. 3	Soerabaja	A6M2 Zero	3rd Kokutai	PO3c Sho-ichi Shoji	Shot down	Probably Dutch pilot
Feb. 3	Malang	A6M2 Zero	Tainan Kokutai	S1c Kyoji Kobayashi	Shot down	Walt Coss
Feb. 6	Savu Sea	G3M2 Nell	1st Kokutai	WO Seiai Iwamoto	Shot down	McWherter/ Reynolds/ Egenes
Feb. 15	Timor Sea	H6K4 Mavis	Toko Kokutai	Kinichi Furukawa	Shot down	Robert Buel
Feb. 17	Palembang	Ki-27 Nate	11th Sentai	unknown	Shot down	Uncertain
Feb. 18	Soerabaja	G4M1 Betty	Takao Kokutai	PO1c Kinichi Shimada	Shot down	Uncertain
Feb. 18	Soerabaja	G4M1 Betty	Takao Kokutai	Ensign Hisao Yamada	Shot down	Uncertain
Feb. 18	Java Sea	G4M1 Betty	Takao Kokutai	FPO2c Seiji Miyamoto	Damaged and ditched	Probably Ben Irvin
Feb. 18	Soerabaja	G4M1 Betty	Takao Kokutai	FPO2c Masatomi Ota	Heavily damaged but returned	Uncertain
Feb. 19	Soerabaja	A6M2 Zero	Tainan Kokutai	Lt. Masao Asai	Shot down	Probably Cy Blanton
Feb. 19	Timor Sea	D3A1 Val	Soryu Air Group	PO1c Takeshi Yamada	Heavily damaged, ditched in sea	Robert Oestreicher
Feb. 20	Bali	A6M2 Zero	3rd Kokutai	S1c Tomekichi Otsuki	Shot down	Joe Kruzel
Feb. 23	Malang	G4M1 Betty	Takao Kokutai	unknown	Heavily damaged	Jim Morehead
Feb. 23	Malang	G4M1 Betty	Takao Kokutai	unknown	Damaged	Jim Morehead

Sources: Tagaya, *Mitsubishi Type 1 Rikko "Betty" Units of World War II;* Izawa, "Rikko and Gingga:
Japanese Navy Twin [Engine] Bomber Units"; Christopher Shores and Brian Cull with Yasuho Izawa,
Bloody Shambles, vol. 2; Hata and Izawa, *Japanese Naval Aces and Fighter Units in World War II.*

NOTES

PROLOGUE

1. Bix, *Hirohito and the Making of Modern Japan*, 327, 329; "National Policies Set at Liaison Conference," *Japan Times and Mail*, July 29, 1940; Butow, *Tojo and the Coming of War*, 170.

2. Butow, *Tojo*, 151–53; "National Policies"; Hattori, *Dai Toa Senso Zenshi* [The complete history of the Greater East Asia War], 1:33–37.

3. "National Policies"; Bix, *Hirohito*, 368, 375, 376; Hattori, *Dai Toa Senso Zenshi* 1:39; Tsunoda, "The Navy's Role in the Southern Strategy," in *The Fateful Choice*, 241, 243–46, 252, 253, 255, 258, 259; Hata, "The Army's Move into Northern Indochina," in *Fateful Choice*, 159, 160, 162, 175, 176, 177, 178–79.

4. Hata, "Army's Move," 192, 203; Kluckhohn, "Hull Deplores Attack on Indochina as Blow to Pacific Status Quo," *New York Times*, September 24, 1940; Kluckhohn, "U.S. Embargoes Scrap Iron, Hitting Japan," *New York Times*, September 27, 1940; Matloff and Snell, *Strategic Planning for Coalition Warfare, 1941–1942*, 64; Willmott, *Empires in the Balance*, 120–21.

5. Willmott, *Empires*, 121.

6. As quoted in Tsunoda, "Navy's Role," 281.

7. Hattori, *Dai Toa Senso Zenshi*, 1:93; Tsunoda, "Navy's Role," 295; Tolischus, "Japanese Report U.S. Is in a Secret Accord to Defend Southeast Asia Against Drive," *New York Times*, April 21, 1941.

8. Bix, *Hirohito*, 395, 397–99, 400–402; Hattori, *Dai Toa Senso Zenshi*, 1:125, 128, 129; Layton, with Pineau and Costello, *And I Was There*, 121.

9. Matloff and Snell, *Strategic Planning*, 64, 65; Layton, *And I Was There*, 121.

10. Willmott, *Empires*, 66, 68; Bix, *Hirohito*, 403, 405; Hattori, *Dai Toa Senso Zenshi*, 1:166.

11. Hattori, *Dai Toa Senso Zenshi*, 1:173; Bix, *Hirohito*, 409, 413–14.

12. George C. Marshall to H. H. Arnold, July 16, 1941, memo, in *The Papers of George*

Catlett Marshall, 2:567–68; Stimson diary, September 12, 1941, in Henry Lewis Stimson Papers, microfilm, Library of Congress.

13. "Memorandum of Conference between Secretary Hull and Secretary Stimson," October 6, 1941, and diary entry, October 28, 1941, both in Stimson diary; Sherry, *The Rise of American Air Power*, 107.

PART ONE

1. Bix, *Hirohito*, 417–19; Hattori, *Dai Toa Senso Zenshi*, 1:195.

2. Prange, *At Dawn We Slept*, 285, 297, 299, 325; Boeicho Boeikenshusho Senshi-shitsu, *Senshi sosho*, vol. 24, *Hito malay homen kaigun shinko sakusen*, 48, 53.

3. Bix, *Hirohito*, 424, 425–26, 427; Department of the Army, *Reports of General MacArthur*, 2:70; Agawa, *The Reluctant Admiral*, 237.

4. Willmott, *Empires*, 74; Bix, *Hirohito*, 421–22; Hattori, *Dai Toa Senso Zenshi* 1:223, 278, and 2:4.

5. Pogue, *George C. Marshall*, 2:194–95; Marshall and Stark, "Memorandum for the President—Estimate Concerning Far Eastern Situation," November 5, 1941, WPD 4389–29, War Plans Department, General Correspondence 1939–42, RG 165, NARA.

6. Stimson diary, November 25, 1941, Stimson Papers; "Conference in the Office of Chief of Staff, 10:40 A.M., November 26, 1941," WDCSA/381 Philippines (12–4–41), Top Secret Correspondence 1941–42, RG 165, NARA.

7. Pogue, *George C. Marshall*, 206; Stimson diary, November 27, 1941, Stimson Papers.

8. Bix, *Hirohito*, 433–35; Hattori, *Dai Toa Senso Zenshi*, 1:260, and 2:6, 25; Ugaki, *Fading Victory*, 34; *Senshi sosho*, 24:170; Prange, *At Dawn*, 445; Toland, *The Rising Sun*, 187.

9. "Report of Conference," Manila, December 6, 1941, Ser. I, Subject Files, Item 12, Hart Papers, Navy Historical Center; Leutze, *A Different Kind of Victory*, 224–25, 226; Middlebrook and Mahoney, *Battleship*, 90–91.

10. U.S. Army, Army Forces Far East, *Philippines Air Operations Record: Phase One*, Japanese Monograph No. 11, 9; *Senshi sosho*, vol. 34, *Nampo shinko rikugun koku sakusen*, 200, 294; Shores and Cull with Izawa, *Bloody Shambles*, 1:73.

11. Interrogation of Capt. Masamichi Fujita, October 20, 1945, in U.S. Strategic Bombing Survey (Pacific), *Interrogations of Japanese Officials*, 1:71.

12. Toland, *Rising Sun*, 223.

13. Willmott, *Empires*, 163, 166.

14. Totals as compiled by author in Bartsch, *December 8, 1941*, 409.

15. Cablegram 736, December 7, 1941, 3:22 pm, Gerow for Adjutant General for MacArthur, WPD 4544–20, War Plans Department, General Correspondence 1939–42, RG 165, NARA, reproduced in Bartsch, *December 8, 1941*, 259.

16. Radiogram, MacArthur to Marshall, December 14, 1941, in MacArthur Memorial Archives.

17. Matloff and Snell, *Strategic Planning*, 85–87.

18. Ibid., 85.

19. Ind, *Bataan: The Judgment Seat*, 70; USAFFE, Special Orders No. 52, October 24,

1941, in Record Group 2, MacArthur Memorial Archives; Brereton, *The Brereton Diaries*, 24–25.

20. Radiogram, evidently to AGWAR, undated, in MacArthur Memorial Archives.

21. Connaughton, *MacArthur and Defeat in the Philippines*, 193.

22. Brereton, *Diaries*, 62.

23. Radiogram, Marshall to MacArthur, December 24, 1941, in MacArthur Memorial Archives.

24. Radiograms, MacArthur to AGWAR, December 27, 1941 and January 7, 1942, in MacArthur Memorial Archives.

25. Far East Air Force, "General Brereton's Headquarters Diary: Summary of the Activities for the Period 8th Dec. 1941–24 Feb. 1942," December 27 and 28, 1941, entries.

26. Willmott, *Empires*, 88; USAFIA, "Report of Organization and Activities United States Army Forces in Australia from December 7, 1941 to June 30, 1942" (hereafter cited as USAFIA Report), in RG 407, USAFIA, NARA; radiograms, Marshall to Brett, December 23, 1941, and to Merle-Smith, December 22, 1941, both in box T1601, RG 338, NARA.

27. Willmott, *Empires*, 258–70; Matloff and Snell, *Strategic Planning*, 122.

28. Matloff and Snell, *Strategic Planning*, 122; Willmott, *Empires*, 261–62, 267.

29. Matloff and Snell, *Strategic Planning*, 123–24.

30. Ibid., 124–25; Willmott, *Empires*, 260.

31. Bland, ed., *The Papers of George Catlett Marshall*, 3:41.

32. Willmott, *Empires*, 269.

33. Ibid., 281–83.

34. U.S. Army, Army Forces Far East, *Naval Operations in the Invasion of the Netherlands East Indies, Dec. 1941–Mar. 1942*, Japanese Monograph No. 101, 16.

35. Willmott, *Empires*, 265; Womack, *The Dutch Naval Air Force against Japan*, 157–58, 164.

36. Willmott, *Empires*, 265–66.

37. Shores and Cull with Izawa, *Bloody Shambles*, 1:60.

38. Matloff and Snell, *Strategic Planning*, 95.

39. "Australian-American Cooperation: Notes of Conference Held on January 4, 1942," in RG 407, USAFIA, NARA; "General Brereton's Headquarters Diary," January 4, 1942.

40. Brereton, *Diaries*, 75.

CHAPTER 1

1. Brown, "Attack to Defend," *Daedalus Flyer,* Winter 2001, 23; Pehl, "Fighters to Plum," undated manuscript, 1.

2. Pehl, "Fighters to Plum," 1.

3. Coleman interview.

4. Morehead, *In My Sights,* 32–33, and Morehead, *In My Sights Completed,* 89; J. Baugher P-40C serials, http://www.jbaugher.com; Morehead interview, January 7, 1995.

5. Lund interview.

6. 35th Pursuit Group, Hamilton Field, Special Orders No. 10, October 3, 1941; Wilhite memoir, 107.

7. McMahon memoir.

8. Radiogram, Air Board to Darwin, November 18, 1941, and radiogram to Darwin, November 17, 1941, Series A1196, Symbol 60/501/76, National Archives of Australia (NAA).

9. Radiogram, Department of Air to Department of External Affairs, October 24, 1941, Series A1196, Symbol 60/501/76, NAA; radiogram, Van Merle-Smith to Douglas MacArthur, October 31, 1941, and USAFFE, Special Orders No. 52, October 24, 1941, both in MacArthur Memorial Archives.

10. Grant Mahony to mother, November 1, 1941; The Grouper, "Headquarters and Headquarters Squadron," *Nichols News* 3, no. 3 (August 1941).

11. Memo, Department of Navy to Department of Air, November 15, 1941, and Airintel to Darwin, November 17, 1941, both in A1196, 60/501/76, NAA.

12. Darwin to Air Board, November 18, 1941, A1196, 60/501/76, NAA.

13. McMahon memoir; Fourth Air Force, Riverside, California, Special Orders No. 253, October 27, 1941; Smith diary, November 21, 1941; Wilhite memoir, 117, 121, 123; USAFIA Report, 1.

14. McMahon memoir.

15. Wilhite to parents, November 24, 1941; McMahon memoir.

16. Smith diary, November 21, 1941; Wilhite memoir, 126.

17. Egenes to Larson, November 22, 1941; Wilhite memoir, 141.

18. McMahon memoir.

19. McMahon memoir; Wilhite memoir, 123. Unknown to the pilots, the forty-nine-year-old Galwey had been designated transport administrative officer under the senior troop commander, Brig. Gen. Julian F. Barnes (USAFIA Report, 1).

20. Wilhite memoir, 136–37; McMahon memoir; Gladman telephone interview; Borckardt telephone interview.

21. Wilhite memoir, 136–37; Egenes to parents, November 30, 1941.

22. Egenes to parents, November 30, 1941; Smith diary, November 29, 1941.

23. Parker diary, December 6, 1941.

24. Ibid., December 7, 1941.

25. Ibid., December 7, 8, 9, 1941; Koval to author, October 28, 2002; Burnside to author, October 26, 2002; Bynum memoir, "World War II Journal" ; Charles, *Troopships of World War II*, 235; Zander, "Synopsis of My Foreign Service Tour," unpublished manuscript, ca. 1943.

26. Parker diary, December 8 and 9, 1941; Nichols to author, February 17, 1997; Zander, "Synopsis."

27. Dix memoir; Hayes to author, November 17, 1993; Gambonini memoir; Farrior to Marks, February 28, 1993.

28. Wilhite memoir, 147.

29. Ibid., 148.

30. Ibid., 148; Egenes to parents, December 18, 1941.

31. Wilhite memoir, 158–60; USAFIA Report, 4.

32. USAFIA Report, 4; Egenes to parents, December 18, 1941.

33. Wahl interview; Wahl telephone interviews, July 18 and 19, 2005.

34. Wahl telephone interview, July 19, 2005; Oestreicher to father, December 23, 1941.

35. Fourth Interceptor Command, Riverside, California, Special Orders No. 133, December 15, 1941.

36. Holt interview.

37. Wahl telephone interview, July 18, 2005; Holt interview.

38. Katz telephone interview; Wahl telephone interview, February 22, 1994; Oestreicher, "The First of the Many," unpublished manuscript.

39. Fourth Interceptor Command, Special Orders No. 133; Fourth Air Force, Hamilton Field, California, Special Orders No. 180, December 17, 1941; Max Wiecks to author, September 4 and 20, 2003; telephone interview with Reid Wiecks, October 31, 2004.

40. Fourth Interceptor Command, Special Orders No. 133; Parker diary, December 12 and 17, 1941; Hague diary, December 18, 1941; Gambonini memoir; Wahl telephone interview, July 19, 2005.

41. Hague diary, December 18, 1941; Baum to author, December 7, 1993 and January 12, 1994.

42. Fourth Air Force, Hamilton Field, Special Orders No. 180; Landry to parents, December 7, 1941; Hansen to author, March 15, 1994.

43. Landry to parents, December 23, 1941.

44. Eleanor Johnsen to author, September 3, 1993; Lester J. Johnsen diary.

45. Parker diary, December 18, 1941; Head diary, December 18, 1941; Gambonini memoir.

46. Hague and Head diaries, December 18, 1941; Gambonini memoir; Bernard J. Oliver, "An Autobiography."

47. Gambonini memoir; Hayes diary, December 18, 1941.

48. Hague and Head diaries, December 18, 1941.

49. Oestreicher retrospective diary; Les Johnsen diary; Landry to parents, December 18, 1941; McWherter memoir, "Diary of a Fighter Pilot," 10.

50. Nichols to author, January 15 and February 17, 1997; Fourth Air Force, Hamilton Field, Special Orders No. 180.

51. Head, Hague, and Hayes diaries, December 18, 1941; Gambonini memoir; Gambonini interview, March 5, 1994.

52. Parker and Head diaries, December 18, 1941.

53. Parker diary, December 19, 1941.

54. Parker, Head, and Hague diaries, December 19, 1941; Hayes diary, December 20, 1941.

55. Head, Hayes, and Parker diaries, December 19, 1941; Landry to parents, December 19, 1941.

56. Later it was found out that the Japanese submarine I-23 had fired eight to nine shells at the oil tanker *Agwiworld* twenty miles off of Monterey Bay but had missed, and by zigzagging the tanker had escaped. Twenty-five miles off Cape Mendocino,

the submarine I-17 had shelled and fired two torpedoes at another oil tanker, the SS *Emidio;* hit in the stern, she managed to beach herself off Crescent City (http://www .militarymuseum.org/Agwiworld.htmc and Emidio/htmc).

57. Hague diary, December 23, 1941.

58. Maj. Elliott Thorpe, Bandoeng, cablegrams to Col. Van Merle-Smith, December 18 and 19, 1941, T1596, RG 338, NARA; Boer to author, July 15 and August 5 and 8, 2005.

59. Thorpe cablegrams.

60. "History of the 5th Air Force (and Its Precedents)," Part I (hereafter cited as "History of the 5th Air Force"), microfilm A7385, AFHRA, 33; Capt. Floyd J. Pell, Headquarters, Townsville, to Chief of Air Corps, December 11, 1941, in AIR AG 320.2, NAA.

61. Robert Spence Johnson diary, December 23, 1941; Smith diary, December 22, 1941; Wilhite memoir, 173.

62. Wilhite memoir, 175.

63. Ibid., 176; McMahon memoir.

64. Wilhite memoir, 175; Smith diary, December 23, 1941.

65. Wilhite memoir, 176–77.

66. McMahon memoir.

67. Wilhite memoir, 176.

68. Mahony flight log; Bartsch, *Doomed at the Start,* 171; Peter Dunn, Australia at War, http://www.ozatwar.com; Mangan diary, December 17–24, 1941; radiogram, Darwin to Far East Air Force, repeated to Air Board Melbourne, December 21, 1941, in Series A1196, 60/501/76, NAA.

69. Mangan diary, December 24, 1941.

70. Bartsch, *Doomed at the Start,* 171.

71. Rorrison, *Nor the Years Contemn,* 35, 73; Birkett, "Early USAAF P-40E Operations," Part 3; Mangan diary, December 31, 1941.

CHAPTER 2

1. Wilhite memoir, 178–79.

2. McMahon memoir.

3. Smith diary, December 25, 1941.

4. Wilhite memoir, 179–80.

5. McMahon memoir.

6. "Conference Notes, December 28, 1941," in "History of the 5th Air Force," App. II, doc. 64.

7. "Conference Notes"; Launder, *College Campus in the Sky,* 16; Rogers to author, August 22, 2005.

8. "Conference December 29 [1941]," in McAfee, "The 27th Reports, or How to Get Scrogged, Buggar All."

9. Ibid.

10. Lt. Col. John H. Davies to Commanding Officer, No. 3 FTS, "Syllabus of A-24 and P-40 Pilots," December 30, 1941, in McAfee, "The 27th Reports."

11. "Conference December 29."

12. Memo, Davies to Clagett, January 1, 1942, in McAfee, "The 27th Reports."

13. McMahon memoir.

14. Wilhite memoir, 183.

15. McMahon memoir.

16. Wilhite memoir, 184.

17. Bartsch, *Doomed at the Start,* 217; Gies diary, December 31, 1941.

18. Bartsch, *Doomed at the Start,* 435–38.

19. Gies diary, December 31, 1941.

20. Gies diary, January 1, 1942; Blanton taped narrative, 1993.

21. Bartsch, *Doomed at the Start,* 221.

22. Ibid.; Hennon diary, January 1, 1942.

23. USAFIA Report, 12; "General Brereton's Headquarters Diary," January 2, 1942, 0845.

24. Rorrison, *Nor the Years Contemn,* 34.

25. "General Brereton's Headquarters Diary," January 2, 1942, 0845; Davies to Clagett, January 1, 1942, in McAfee, "The 27th Reports."

26. Davies to Clagett, January 1, 1942.

27. Ibid.

28. "General Brereton's Headquarters Diary," January 2, 1942, 1015; Brereton, *Diaries,* 74.

29. Clagett to U.S. Military Observer, Bandoeng, December 25, 1941, in "History of the 5th Air Force," App. II.

30. Shores and Cull with Izawa, *Bloody Shambles,* 2:205; "History of the 5th Air Force"; Hata and Izawa, *Japanese Naval Aces and Fighter Units in World War II,* 133.

31. McMahon memoir.

32. Wilhite diary, January 7, 1942.

33. Wilhite memoir, 185.

34. William A. Sheppard and Edwin C. Gilmore, "Statement," no date (ca. 1945), Walter D. Edmonds materials, AFHRA; Erickson S. Nichols to Chief of Air Section, USAFIA, "Report on Trip to Brisbane, January 15, 1942," in "History of the 5th Air Force," App. II, Doc. 197.

35. Rorrison, *Nor the Years Contemn,* 70; Nichols, "Report on Trip to Brisbane" ; Glassburn telephone interview; Sheppard and Gilmore, "Statement."

36. McMahon memoir.

37. Wilhite memoir, 190; McMahon memoir.

38. Davies to Brereton, January 4, 1942, in McAfee, "The 27th Reports"; Assembly Records for P-40Es off the USAT *Republic* at Brisbane, January 1942, in RG 407, USAFIA, NARA.

39. Hague diary, January 5, 1942; Head diary, December 26 and 30, 1941.

40. Hague, Head, and Parker diaries, January 6, 1942.

41. Ibid.

42. Hague diary, January 7, 1942.

43. Head diary, January 7, 1942.

44. Head and Parker diaries, January 7, 1942.

45. Hague diary, January 7, 1942.

46. Ibid., January 11, 1942.

47. Head diary, January 7, 1942; Hayes, Hague, and Parker diaries, January 8, 1942.

48. Hague and Head diaries, January 8, 1942.

49. Parker, Head, and Hague diaries, January 9, 1942.

50. Hayes diary, January 9, 1942.

51. Gies diary, January 6, 1942.

52. Ibid., January 2, 3, 4, and 5, 1942; Sheppard and Gilmore, "Statement"; Blanton, "Statement of Activities during the Early Days of the War," February 20, 1945; Blanton taped narrative, 1993.

53. Gies diary, January 6, 7, 8, 1942; Blanton taped narrative, 1993.

54. Gies diary, January 7, 1942; Sheppard and Gilmore, "Statement." Colonel Johnson had been appointed CO of Base Section 3, responsible for U.S. Air Forces in the Brisbane area, on January 5 (USAFIA, Melbourne, General Order No. 1, January 5, 1942).

55. Gies diary, January 7, 1942; Kruzel memoir.

56. Gies diary, January 7, 1942; Sheppard and Gilmore, "Statement."

57. Gies diary, January 8, 1942; Blanton taped narrative, 1994. Capt. Earl E. Hicks was a ground officer of the 11th Bomb Squadron, 7th Bomb Group, who had arrived in Brisbane on the *Republic* on December 22, 1941.

58. Gies diary, January 8, 1942; Blanton taped narrative, 1993.

59. Gies diary, January 8, 1942.

60. Ibid., January 9, 1942.

61. Ibid., January 10, 1942; Hennon diary, January 7–10, 1942; Sheppard and Gilmore, "Statement."

62. "History of the 5th Air Force," App. I, docs. 903 and 958; Julian Barnes, USAFIA, to CO, Headquarters USA, Brisbane, January 12, 1942, in "History of the 5th Air Force." Barnes indicated that Sprague was to pick the pilots for his outfit.

63. Gies and Hennon diaries, January 10, 1942. Sprague had met with Brereton's chief of staff, Col. Francis Brady, in his cottage at Darwin. Evidently Brady had requested him to form the group (Gowen log).

64. Hennon diary, January 10, 1942.

65. Gies diary, January 10, 1942; Blanton taped narratives, 1993 and 1994.

66. Gies diary, January 11, 1942; Hennon diary, January 10, 1942.

PART TWO

1. "General Brereton's Headquarters Diary," January 8 and 10, 1942; Brereton, *Diaries,* 76; Allied Forces, ABDA Command, *Despatch by the Supreme Commander of the ABDA Area to the Combined Chiefs of Staff on the Operations in the South-West Pacific, 15th January to 25th February 1942.*

2. Brereton, *Diaries,* 77.

3. Ibid.

4. Gerard Casius, "Batavia's Big Sticks," *Air Enthusiast,* August–November 2003, 12.

5. Ibid., 13; Dull, *A Battle History of the Imperial Japanese Navy, 1941–1945,* 61–62.

6. Willmott, *Empires in the Balance,* 287; Dull, *Battle History,* 61–62.

7. Willmott, *Empires,* 287, 289; Dull, *Battle History,* 51; Womack, *Dutch Naval Air Force,* 51.

8. Salecker, *Fortress Against the Sun,* 99–100; Casius, "Batavia's Big Sticks," 13–14.

9. Radiogram, Marshall to MacArthur, January 31, 1942, in MacArthur Memorial Archives; Headquarters ABDACOM, Lembang, telephone listings, in NAA.

10. "General Brereton's Headquarters Diary," January 15, 1942, 2000; USAFIA, Melbourne, General Orders No. 4, January 17, 1942; Cline, *Washington Command Post,* 379.

11. "General Brereton's Headquarters Diary," January 15, 1942, 2100.

12. Brereton, *Diaries,* 79.

13. "General Brereton's Headquarters Diary," January 18 and 19, 1942; Brereton, *Diaries,* 79.

14. Brereton, *Diaries,* 81.

15. 5th Bomber Command, Journal, January 17, 1942.

16. Mitchell, *On Wings We Conquer,* 174–75.

17. Salecker, *Fortress,* 106, 111; 5th Bomber Command, Journal, January 15, 16, and 19, 1942; Mitchell, *On Wings,* 174.

18. Casius, "Batavia's Big Sticks," 14; Dull, *Battle History,* 62–63; Willmott, *Empires,* 291.

19. Dull, *Battle History,* 63; Womack, *Dutch Naval Air Force,* 85–86.

20. 5th Bomber Command, Journal, January 24, 25, 27, 1942; Casius, "Batavia's Big Sticks," 14–15; Willmott, *Empires,* 290–91.

21. Womack, *Dutch Naval Air Force,* 88–89; Dull, *Battle History,* 52; Willmott, *Empires,* 289–90; Casius, "Batavia's Big Sticks," 16.

22. Womack, *Dutch Naval Air Force,* 88–89.

23. "General Brereton's Headquarters Diary," January 22–26, 1942; Wigmore, *The Japanese Thrust,* 259; radiogram, Brereton, Hq USAFIA, to CO, RAAF Station Amberley, January 24, 1942, in box T1610, RG 338, NARA; radiogram, Brett, ABDACOM, to Hq USAFIA, January 27, 1942, in box T1597, RG 338, NARA. Brereton in his *Diaries* (p. 81) maintained that he *opposed* diverting the 17th Pursuit (*sic*) to Port Moresby, but the documentary evidence indicates he left it to ABDACOM to decide.

24. Matloff and Snell, Strategic Planning, 132.

25. USAFIA, Melbourne, General Order No. 7, January 27, 1942; Allied Forces, ABDA, *Despatch by the Supreme Commander,* 10–11; Brereton, *Diaries,* 83; "General Brereton's Headquarters Diary," January 27 and 28, 1942; Edmonds, *They Fought with What They Had,* 312; Weller, "Luck to the Fighters," *Military Affairs,* Winter 1944, 295. On TDY for FEAF headquarters, Maj. Dick Legg had inspected the air warning system on January 25 and gave a (most likely) unfavorable report to Maj. Rosie O'Donnell, FEAF headquarters' operations officer, the following day (Legg diary, January 25 and 26, 1942).

26. "General Brereton's Headquarters Diary," January 28, 1942; Mitchell, *On Wings,* 174–76.

27. "General Brereton's Headquarters Diary," January 30 and 31, 1942; Burnett, Air Board, cables to Brett, ABDACOM, January 28 and 31, 1942, in A 1196, 60/501/88, NAA.

28. Willmott, *Empires*, 292–93, 294; Womack, *Dutch Naval Air Force*, 95; Army Forces, Far East, *Naval Operations*, 25.

29. Ferrell, ed., *The Eisenhower Diaries*, 46.

CHAPTER 3

1. Gies diary, January 12, 1942; Birkett to author, October 24, 2003. The message from General Barnes ordering the formation of the squadron specified that Sprague could select any pilot available at Brisbane for the squadron except Al Strauss, Buzz Wagner, Grant Mahony, and Gerry Keenan, who were being reserved to lead squadrons to be formed later (radiogram No. 30, Barnes, USAFIA, to CO, Hq USA Brisbane, January 12, 1942, in "History of the 5th Air Force," App. II).

2. Gies and Hennon diaries, January 12, 1942.

3. Assembly Records for P-40Es; Gies diary, January 12, 1942.

4. Coss diary, Notebook No. 1; radiogram, 3 SFTS to Air Board, January 13, 1942, in James McAfee collection.

5. Coss, Notebook No. 1; Gies diary, January 13, 1942; list of pilots, January 15, 1942, in "History of the 5th Air Force," App. II.

6. Gies diary, January 14, 1942.

7. Gies and Hennon diaries, January 14, 1942; USA, Base Section 3, Brisbane, Special Orders No. 2, January 14, 1942.

8. Wagner statement in interview by Roosevelt der Tatevision, no date, in Edmonds materials, AFHRA; Weller, "Luck," Winter 1944, 268.

9. Gies diary, January 15, 1942.

10. Blanton taped narrative, 1993; Coss, Notebook No. 1.

11. Blanton taped narrative, 1993.

12. Hennon diary, January 15, 1942; radiogram, USAFIA to Brisbane, January 17, 1942, in T1609, RG 338, NARA.

13. Boise to author, June 15, 1994.

14. Head, Hayes, and Hague diaries, January 12, 1942.

15. Head and Hayes diaries, January 13, 1942.

16. Head, Hague, and Gambonini diaries, January 12, 1942; Dutton diary, January 10 and 11 (*sic*), 1942.

17. Head and Hague diaries, January 13, 1942.

18. Hague diary, January 13, 1942. USAFIA headquarters had moved to Melbourne from Brisbane on January 5, 1942, ostensibly to coordinate better with the chiefs of the Australian army, navy, and air staffs based there (USAFIA Report, 12; Edmonds, *They Fought with What They Had*, 267).

19. Head and Hague diaries, January 14, 1942. The colonel was evidently Lt. Col. Geoffrey Galwey of *Republic* fame.

20. Parker diary, January 14, 1942. Parker and the others hadn't been informed that their Pursuit Combat Team was officially ordered attached to the 7th Bomb Group (off

the *Pensacola* convoy) the day before by oral orders of the group's commanding officer (USA, Air Corps Troops, Camp Ascot, Special Orders No. 3, January 13, 1942; "History of the 5th Air Force," App. II, doc. 901).

21. Head diary, January 14, 1942.

22. Head diary, January 16, 1942.

23. Parker and Hague diaries, January 16, 1942.

24. Hayes diary, January 17, 1942; Oliver diary, January 16, 1942; USA, Air Corps Troops, Amberley Field, List of Pilots at Amberley Field, January 21, 1942.

25. Weller, "Luck," Winter 1944, 271; Holt to author, September 10, 1994; Wilhite diary, January 16, 1942; Wilhite memoir, 194; Rorrison, *Nor the Years Contemn,* 70–71. The ground echelons of the 7th Group's 11th and 22nd Bomb Squadrons sailed from Brisbane on the *Polk* on January 16 for Java on detached service (McPherson, *Four Decades of Courage,* 277).

26. Guerrero to author, November 29, 2002.

27. Perry diary, as excerpted in Weller, "Luck," Winter 1944, 271.

28. Holt to author, September 10, 1994; radiogram, U.S. to Australian Naval Attaché to Naval Officer [on USAT *Polk*], December 26, 1941, in "History of the 5th Air Force," App. II.

29. "Crew Chiefs and Armorers Assigned to Pilots" (on board the USAT *President Polk),* 1942, in Gambonini collection; list of thirty-five enlisted men departing Amberley for Blimbing, in USAFIA, Melbourne, Special Orders No. 64, March 19, 1942.

30. Spence Johnson diary, January 10, 1942; Wilhite diary, January 13, 1942; McMahon memoir.

31. Wilhite diary, January 13, 1942.

32. Nichols to Chief of Air Section, USAFIA, "Report on Trip to Brisbane, January 15, 1942," in "History of the 5th Air Force."

33. Hague diary, January 13, 1942; McMahon memoir.

34. McMahon memoir; Wilhite diary, January 9, 1942.

35. USAFIA, Office of Air Operations, "Ferry Flight Instructions" to Capt. Charles Sprague, 17th Pursuit Squadron (Provisional), no date.

36. Ibid. stipulates only one Fairey Battle would escort the second echelon.

37. Blanton memoir.

38. Gies and Hennon diaries, January 16, 1942.

39. Gies diary, January 16, 1942; U.S. Army, Air Forces in Australia, A-4, Aircraft Movements Status and Statistics Section, "Location and Status of Damaged Aircraft in Australia," no date (ca. 1942).

40. Gies diary, January 16, 1942.

41. Hennon diary, January 16, 1942; USAFIA, Melbourne, Special Orders No. 106, April 30, 1942.

42. Coss, Notebook No. 1; Blanton taped narrative, 1993.

43. Brown, "Attack to Defend," *Daedalus Flyer,* Winter 2001, 24.

44. Gies diary, January 16, 1942.

45. Blanton memoir.

46. Gies diary, January 16 and 17, 1942.

47. Rorrison, *Nor the Years Contemn*, 65.

48. Hennon diary, January 17, 1942.

49. Ibid.; Sheppard and Gilmore, "Statement."

50. Hennon diary, January 17, 1942.

51. Coss to author, June 22, 1994; Blanton taped narrative, 1993.

52. Coss, June 22, 1994; Kruzel memoir.

53. Blanton memoir.

54. Ibid.; Coss, Notebook No. 1.

55. Blanton memoir.

56. Coss, Notebook No. 1.

57. Blanton memoir.

58. McMahon memoir.

59. Parker diary, January 16, 1942; Wilhite diary, January 13, 1942.

60. Head and Hague diaries, January 16, 1942; Parker diary, January 17, 1942.

61. Head diary, January 17, 1942. Head obviously had not heard of Wagner's exploits in the Philippines.

62. Dutton diary, January 16, 1942; Head diary, January 17, 1942.

63. Les Johnsen diary, January 9 (*sic*), 1942; Selman to author, November 8, 1994.

64. Hague, Parker, and Head diaries, January 17, 1942.

65. Parker diary, January 19, 1942; Head diary, January 18 and 19, 1942.

66. Head was referring to Bryan Brown's P-40 at Townsville, assembled by the *Republic* pilots. Head diary, January 18, 1942. The mechanics were reported by the U.S. War Department to be bringing with them "all the tools" they needed for assembling P-40s (radiogram, U.S. to Australian Naval Attaché to Naval Officer [on USAT *Polk*], December 26, 1941, in "History of the 5th Air Force," App. II).

67. List of enlisted men leaving Amberley January 17 and 19, 1942, in USAFIA, Special Orders No. 64; Hennon diary, January 19, 1942; Boise interview; Rorrison, *Nor the Years Contemn*, 65; Coss, Notebook No. 1.

68. The B-17C apparently did not leave until the following morning (USAFIA, Special Orders No. 64). Head diary, January 19, 1942; RAAF, Operations Record Book, A-50 Form for Maryborough, January 19, 1942, NAA; Badura diary, January 19, 1942.

69. Parker and Oliver diaries, January 19, 1942.

70. Hague diary, January 18, 1942.

71. "General Brereton's Headquarters Diary," January 19, 1942. Frank Neri had come in after Gilmore the day before (Hennon diary, January 18, 1942).

72. Blanton memoir; "Reminiscences of Pilots Who Knew Bud [Sprague]," no date.

73. Hennon diary, January 19, 1942; Coss to author, January 18, 1994; Sheppard and Gilmore, "Statement"; Blanton memoir. ABDACOM headquarters on January 15 had ordered the P-40 group to operate from Amboina, Kendari, and Samarinda as soon as nonaromatic 100-octane fuel could be provided at the locations and nine camouflaged pens constructed at each site (radiogram, ABDACOM to CLG, January 15, 1942, in "History of the 5th Air Force," App. II).

74. Weller, "Luck," Winter 1944, 273; Coss to author, January 18, 1994; Sheppard and Gilmore, "Statement"; Blanton memoir.

75. "General Brereton's Headquarters Diary," January 19, 1942, 0840; Weller, "Luck," Winter 1944, 273.

76. Hennon diary, January 19, 1942.

77. Ibid., January 20, 1942; "Seventeenth Pursuit Squadron (Provisional) History" Microfilm A0723, AFHRA (hereafter cited as "Seventeenth Pursuit History"), doc. 1922.

78. Badura diary, January 21, 1942; Rorrison, *Nor the Years Contemn*, 84; Boise to author, September 11, 1994. Hennon in his diary entry of January 19 and Blanton's memoir have the enlisted men arriving on January 19 instead, but this would appear to be two days too early, given that the DC-2s left on that date from Amberley.

79. Boise to author, September 11, 1994; Hennon diary, January 21, 1942.

80. Hennon diary, January 21, 1942; Blanton to author, March 30 and May 27, 1994; Blanton memoir; Coss, Notebook No. 1. It is not clear if the B-17C had now arrived with the remaining ten crew chiefs and armorers of the squadron.

81. "Reminiscences of Pilots Who Knew Bud"; Blanton memoir.

82. Rorrison, *Nor the Years Contemn*, 85; radiogram, Hq USA Darwin to Hq USAFIA Melbourne, for Brereton, January 22, 1942, in "History of the 5th Air Force," Doc. 973.

83. Hennon diary, January 22, 1942; "Seventeenth Pursuit History," doc. 1922; Weller, "Luck," Winter 1944, 273.

84. Radiogram, ABDACOM Batavia to Air Board Melbourne, January 21, 1942, in T1594, RG 338, NARA; radiogram, Hq USA Darwin to Hq USAFIA Melbourne, January 22, 1942; Army Forces Far East, *Naval Operations*, 23. ABDACOM's indecision on its choice of base in the Indies was apparently the reason for the delay in issuing movement orders. On January 20 Brett had proposed one squadron each for Kendari, Soerabaja, and Batavia (Brett radiogram to Barnes, January 20, 1942, in "History of the 5th Air Force," App. II, docs.). Brereton in his *Diaries* (p. 81) indicated he was under pressure by the Australians to move the 17th Pursuit to Townsville and Port Moresby, but he apparently was referring to the movement of the next provisional squadron, the 20th (see below, chapter 4).

85. Hennon diary, January 23, 1942.

86. Radiogram, Brett, USAFIA to Operations Officer, Amberley, January 13, 1942; radiogram, Brett to Brereton (in Brisbane), January 21, 1942, in T1610, RG 338, NARA; radiogram, Hq USA Darwin to Hq USAFIA Melbourne, January 22, 1942; Sheppard and Gilmore, "Statement"; Kiser, "Historical Information"; USAFIA, "Ferry Flight Instructions."

87. Blanton memoir; Sheppard and Gilmore, "Statement"; Kruzel memoir. Brett had told U.S. Army headquarters at Darwin ten days earlier that it would be "desirable to have a PBY flying boat held in readiness to act as a rescue plane should an aircraft be forced into the Timor Sea (radiogram, Brett, USAFIA Melbourne to Hq USA Darwin, January 13, 1942, in "History of the 5th Air Force," App. II, docs.), but this proposal never materialized.

88. Blanton memoir; radiogram, Hq USA Darwin to Hq USAFIA Melbourne, January 22, 1942 (for Brereton, giving 2230 January 22 GMT as the takeoff time, corresponding to 0800 January 23 local Northern Territory Australia time). The 17th Pur-

suit history gives January 22 as the date of departure for Koepang, as do Rorrison (*Nor the Years Contemn,* 85), and Weller ("Luck," Winter 1944, 275), but I have used Hennon's diary as a contemporary firsthand source that also matches the Headquarters U.S. Army, Darwin, documentation.

CHAPTER 4

1. Parker diary, January 20, 1942.

2. Head and Wilhite diaries, January 20, 1942; Hague diary, January 23, 1942.

3. Oliver diary, January 21, 1942; Head diary, January 20, 1942.

4. Suehr to author, March 21, 1994; radiogram, Wavell to Brett (Bandoeng), no date (ca. January 18, 1942), in Gordon Birkett collection; Head and Oliver diaries, January 21, 1942.

5. Latane flight log; Latane to author, November 28, 1997; Suehr to author, March 21, 1994; Suehr telephone interview, September 19, 2008.

6. Wilhite memoir, January 21, 1942.

7. Parker diary, January 21, 1942.

8. Hague diary, January 21 and 22, 1942; Parker diary, January 22, 1942; Dutton diary, January 20 (*sic*), 1942.

9. Hague diary, January 21, 1942; Gies diary, January 23, 1942.

10. Parker diary, January 22, 1942.

11. Hague diary, January 23, 1942.

12. Ibid.

13. Parker diary, January 22, 1942; Head diary, January 23, 1942. Hamilton's ship was P-40E serial number 41–5592 (Birkett to author, January 2, 2005).

14. Parker diary, January 22, 1942.

15. Parker diary, January 23, 1942.

16. Gambonini and Parker diaries, January 23, 1942.

17. Hague diary, January 24, 1942; Fuchs to author, March 24, 1994; Morehead, *In My Sights,* 44.

18. Hague diary, January 24, 1942; Wilhite and Parker diaries, January 23, 1942.

19. Morehead, *In My Sights,* 45.

20. Head diary, January 23, 1942; Wilhite diary, January 27, 1942. Hamilton's P-40E was No. 95, serial number 41–5398, and that of Morehead was No. 98, serial number 41–5415 (Birkett to author, March 14, 2005).

21. Hague diary, January 24, 1942.

22. Ibid; Fuchs to author, March 24, 1994.

23. Hague diary, January 24, 1942.

24. Head diary, January 23, 1942; Head interview.

25. Parker diary, January 24, 1942; Dutton diary, January 23 (*sic*), 1942; Birkett to author, January 5, 2005. Peres's P-40E was No. 85, serial number 41–5368.

26. Parker and Head diaries, January 24, 1942; Hague diary, January 26, 1942.

27. Wilhite diary, January 27, 1942.

28. Blanton memoir, May 1999.

29. Ibid; Kruzel memoir.

30. Weller, "Luck," Winter 1944, 275; Hennon diary, January 23, 1942; "Seventeenth Pursuit History."

31. Hennon diary, January 23, 1942; Sheppard and Gilmore, "Statement"; Blanton memoir.

32. Hennon diary, January 23, 1942; Sheppard and Gilmore, "Statement."

33. Hennon diary, January 24, 1942; Sheppard and Gilmore, "Statement."

34. Sheppard and Gilmore, "Statement."

35. Ibid; Blanton memoir.

36. Blanton memoir; Hennon diary, January 24, 1942.

37. Blanton memoir; Hennon diary, January 24, 1942.

38. Blanton memoir; Hennon diary, January 24, 1942; Legg diary, January 23 and 24, 1942.

39. Legg diary, January 19 and 23, 1942; Legg memoir.

40. Harvard University, *Fiftieth Anniversary Report, Class of 1930*, s.v. "Willard Reed."

41. Parker diary, January 25, 1942.

42. Parker, Head, McWherter, and Oliver diaries January 25, 1942; McWherter memoir.

43. Radiogram, Brereton, Hq USAFIA Melbourne to CO, RAAF station Amberley, January 24, 1942; draft radiogram, Brereton to Base Section 3, Amberley, January 24, 1942, both in box T1610, RG 338, NARA.

44. Radiogram, Brereton to CO, RAAF station Amberley, January 24, 1942. In a meeting with Brereton on January 21 in Lennon's Hotel, the RAAF deputy chief of air staff had asked him if a squadron of P-40s couldn't be based temporarily at Port Moresby in view of its extreme vulnerability to Japanese attack and threat to Townsville following the likely fall of Rabaul. Brereton concurred and the following day recommended to Wavell—the ABDACOM commander—that the request be approved. In the meantime, Brereton was proceeding on the assumption that it would gain Wavell's approval, and a joint conference was held at RAAF headquarters on January 23 to make practical arrangements for the move. When no reply to Brereton's request had been received, Chief of Air Staff Burnett followed up on January 25 with a personal request to Wavell (Radiogram No. 341, Brereton to Wavell, January 22, 1942, in box T1610, RG 338, NARA; see also radiogram, Brisbane W/T to Airboard Melbourne, January 21, 1942; "Minutes of Conference, January 23, 1942"; radiogram, CAS to Wavell, No. 657, January 25, 1942, all in RAAF files, 60/501/88, NAA).

45. No documentation lists the twenty-five selected, but the author has constructed the composition of the squadron based on various sources. See Appendix 7 for the names of the squadron members.

46. Gies diary, January 23, 24, 25, 1942.

47. Radiogram, Brereton, Hq USAFIA Melbourne, to Hq USA Brisbane, January 26, 1942, in box T1610, RG 338, NARA. Unknown to Lane, Brereton was awaiting approval from his superior at ABDACOM for the shift of Lane's twenty-five P-40Es from Java to Australian defense. This day Brereton fired off another radiogram to ABDACOM, this

one to Brett, regarding the lack of response to his request of January 22. If he were not instructed to the contrary, he would order Lane's squadron to proceed to Port Moresby from Townsville on January 28, he informed Brett (radiogram, Brereton to Brett, January 26, 1942, in T1610, RG 338, NARA). But Brereton also ordered the commander of Base Section 2 at Townsville to hold the P-40s and pilots there until further orders (radiogram, Brereton to CO, Base 2, Townsville, January 26, 1942, in, "History of the Fifth Air Force," doc. 980).

48. Oliver diary, January 25, 1942; Parker and Gies diaries, January 26, 1942; www .surfcity.kund.dalnet.se/commonwealth_turnbull.htm.

49. Oliver, Dutton, McWherter, and Parker diaries, January 26, 1942; Oliver flight log, January 26, 1942; McWherter memoir.

50. Parker and Head diaries, January 27, 1942; Hague diary, January 28, 1942.

51. Parker diary, January 27, 1942.

52. Ibid.; Hague diary, January 28, 1942.

53. Head and Gies diaries, January 27, 1942; Gambonini flight log, January 27, 1942.

54. Parker and Head diaries, January 27, 1942. A message came into Headquarters USAFIA in Melbourne this day after Brereton left for Darwin on his way back to Java. Brett had turned down his (and Burnett's) request for Lane's squadron to go to Port Moresby; there was an "urgent requirement for it for defense purposes in Java" (radiogram, Brett, ABDACOM, to Hq USAFIA Melbourne, January 27, 1942, in box T1597, RG 338, NARA).

55. Parker diary, January 28, 1942.

56. Head and Gies diaries, January 28, 1942; Gambonini diary, January 29, 1942.

57. Radiograms, Barnes, USAFIA Melbourne, to Hq USA Townsville, January 28, 1942, and to Brett, ABDACOM, January 28, 1942, both in box T1610, RG 338, NARA; USAFIA, Special Orders No. 64, paragraph 26.

58. Weller, "Luck," Winter 1944, 275.

59. Ibid., 275–76; "3rd Kokutai hikotai sento kodo chosho" ("3rd Kokutai aircraft echelon combat log," hereafter cited by number or name of kokutai or aircraft carrier and "Kodocho"), January 26, 1942, via Tagaya to author, April 27, 2005. The strafers were six Zeros of the 3rd Kokutai flying from newly occupied Kendari Field. They also shot down a KNILM Grumman Goose amphibian, PK-AFS, piloted by Capt. Cornelis ten Katen, as he tried to escape by diving into a ravine, killing all five on board, and burned a KNILM DeHaviland Dragon Rapide on the ground, killing the female pilot and all five passengers (Gillison, Royal Australian Air Force, 417; Mayborn et al., Grumman Guidebook, 39; Boer to author, November 7, 2005).

60. Badura diary, January 24, 25, 26; Badura to author, January 19, 1994; Boise interview.

61. Coss, Notebook No. 1.

62. White, Queens, 171.

63. Geurtz memoir, no date, 23; Geurtz to Casius, February 19, 1978; Boer to author, October 4, 2007.

64. Coss to author, February 23 and September 14, 1994; Schep to author, March 23, 1994; Boer to author, October 13 and 16, 2006, citing flying instructor L. van der Heide.

Coss himself recalled that the plane was a Beech Staggerwing, like the one he had seen in the Philippines, but there was only one Staggerwing in the Dutch East Indies at the time, a float plane version operated by the American Christian Missionary Alliance.

65. Coss to author, September 14, 1994.

66. Coss, "Notes," 1943. Ngoro Field was in existence as an auxiliary field as far back as 1939, but it was nothing more than a simple emergency field until Lt. Willem Boxman, the camouflage officer of 1-Vl.G.-IV, made arrangements before the war for developing it as a secret field through the elaborate deceptive construction work that Coss viewed at first hand (Schep to author, September 14, 1993, and March 23, 1994).

67. Coss, "Notes," 1943; Coss to author, June 22, 1994.

68. Coss to author, September 14, 1994.

69. Geurtz memoir, 23–24; Geurtz to author, January 8 and 10, 1994; Geurtz to Casius, March 4, 1978.

70. Weller, "Luck," Winter 1944, 279; "Seventeenth Pursuit History," January 26, 1942; Hennon diary, January 27, 1942; Blanton memoir.

71. White, *Queens,* 180–81; Shores and Cull with Izawa, *Bloody Shambles,* 1:228; radiogram 00381, ABDACOM to Immediate Army Melbourne, January 27, 1942, Serial SD.4852, NAA.

72. Weller, "Luck," Winter 1944, 280; White, *Queens,* 181; Shores and Cull with Izawa, *Bloody Shambles,* 1:228; Hennon diary, January 27, 1942.

73. Blanton memoir; Blanton, "Statement of Activities"; Sheppard and Gilmore, "Statement"; Blanton taped narrative, 1993; Hennon diary, January 28, 1942; "Seventeenth Pursuit History," doc. 1922; Weller, "Luck," Winter 1944, 279.

74. Legg diary, January 25, 1942; Kiser, "Historical Information"; Fisher interview with Walter D. Edmonds and USAAF personnel, May 27, 1942; USAFFE, "Report of a Trip by B.G. H. B. Clagett, Lt. Col. Lester Maitland, and Captain Allison Ind, July 27–August 20, 1941," October 1, 1941, 11; William Fisher, "Summary of Interceptor Activity," Melbourne, August 1942; Schep to author, February 22 and March 10, 1995; Bruinier to author, August 14, 1995; Boer to author, October 25, 2007. The ADC was part of the antiaircraft artillery of the Dutch army. Since its cooperation with the Dutch Army Air Force was experiencing problems following the outbreak of war, an air force liaison officer was posted to the command in December 1941 (Boer to author, October 18, 2007).

75. Sheppard and Gilmore, "Statement."

76. Ibid.; Schep to author, January 4, 1995.

77. Blanton memoir; Blanton taped narrative, 1993; Hennon diary, January 28, 1942.

78. Weller, "Luck," Summer 1945, 137; Kruzel to Groves, September 15, 1975; Anemaet to Bosch to Groves, February 29, 1976.

79. Kent diary, January 28, 1942; Dalley to author, March 17, 2008; Blanton telephone interview, November 30, 2004; White, *Queens,* 171. With a 9,200-pound takeoff weight, compared to 4,462 pounds, the P-40E was twice as heavy as the CW-21B, which could climb to 13,120 feet in four minutes compared to the (understated) 7.6 minutes it took the P-40E to reach 15,000 feet (Angelucci with Bowers, *The American Fighter,* 75, 174).

80. Badura diary, January 28 and 29, 1942.

81. Blanton memoir; Blanton taped narrative, 1993; Weller, "Luck," Winter 1944, 281; Sheppard and Gilmore, "Statement"; Hennon diary, January 29, 1942.

82. Blanton memoir; Blanton taped narrative, 1993.

83. Blanton memoir; Blanton taped narrative, 1993; Blanton to author, August 13, 2003. Weller gives a different account of the fate of the ear (Weller, "Luck," Winter 1944, 281), but the account of Blanton as a direct participant is the version accepted here. Later, Neri was treated in Bandoeng by the Far East Air Force flight surgeon Capt. James E. Crane (Weller, "Luck," Winter 1944, 281) but would remain hospitalized during the whole period the 17th Pursuit was based at Ngoro.

84. Hennon diary, January 29, 1942.

85. Hennon diary, January 27 and 31, 1942; "Seventeenth Pursuit History," doc. 1922.

86. Badura diary, January 31, 1942; USAFIA, Special Orders No. 64.

87. In addition to Kruzel's, they had lost Neri's, Irvin's, Kruzel's at Darwin, Brown's, and Gies's. The 17th Pursuit history incorrectly records twelve of the P-40Es as transferred to Ngoro.

PART THREE

1. Ferrell, *Eisenhower Diaries*, 47 (February 5, 1942); Allied Forces, ABDA, *Despatch by the Supreme Commander*, 9.

2. Dull, *Battle History*, 53; Allied Forces, ABDA, *Despatch by the Supreme Commander*, 7–9, 10.

3. Two of the victims of the Japanese aerial attack of February 3 were Signal Corps Lt. Col. William H. Murphy and Maj. Joseph A. Burch, a former civilian radio installations expert. They were proceeding to Soerabaja from FEAF headquarters in Bandoeng to inspect radio equipment (radar sets?) located by the U.S. Navy for possible use by the Dutch Air Defense Command in Soerabaja. Their B-18 was shot down by Zeros, and both died in the hospital the following day (Batchelder, "Appendix B: Col. William Herbert Murphy," 4–6; Boer to author, April 14, 2009).

4. Brereton, *Diaries*, 85–87; "General Brereton's Headquarters Diary," February 7, 1942; Carter and Mueller, comps., *The Army Air Forces in World War II: Combat Chronology, 1941–1945*, February 5, 1942.

5. Allied Forces, ABDA, *Despatch by the Supreme Commander*, 2, 10; Ferrell, *Eisenhower Diaries*, 47 (February 4, 1942); most secret cablegrams, Curtin to Wavell, February 6, 1942; Dept. of External Affairs to Australian Minister, Washington, February 6, 1942; and Wavell to Curtin, February 9, 1942, all in NAA; Combined Chiefs of Staff, Washington, to Wavell, in radiogram, Barnes to Brett, February 6, 1942, in box T1610, RG 338, NARA; Birkett to author, May 20, 2005.

6. Radiogram, Barnes to Brett, February 6, 1942, in box T1610, RG 338, NARA.

7. Radiogram, War Department No. 252 to Barnes, February 5, 1942, copied to Brett, February 8, 1942, in ibid. .

8. Radiogram, Brett to Barnes, February 2, 1942, in ibid.

9. Radiogram, Brett to Barnes, February 7, 1942, in ibid.

10. Radiogram, Brett to Arnold, Washington, February 9, 1942, in "History of the 5th Air Force," App. II, doc. 1009.

11. USAFIA, Base Section 3, Brisbane, Special Orders No. 22, February 6, 1942.

12. Radiogram, Barnes to Darwin, February 10, 1942, in box T1610, RG 338, NARA.

13. Radiograms, ABDACOM Nos. 311 and 330, Brett to Barnes, February 12 and 14, 1942, in box T1597, RG 338, NARA.

14. Boer, *Het Verlies van Java*, 20–21, 23; Boer to author, July 13 and 16, 2009.

15. Radiograms, Brett to Barnes, February 11 and 12, 1942, in box T1597, RG 338, NARA.

16. Radiogram, Barnes to Brett, February 13, 1942, in box T1610, RG 338, NARA.

17. Radiograms, Barnes to Brett, February 7, 9, and 13, 1942, and radiogram, Barnes to Hq Brisbane, February 4, 1942, box T1610; and radiograms, Brett to Barnes, February 7 and 12, 1942, in box T1597, all in RG 338, NARA.

18. Brereton, *Diaries,* 88. Brett himself a day earlier in a radiogram to the War Department had proposed a new defense strategy for the Malay Barrier based on "working from the flanks of Burma" while still maintaining "a strong defense force in Java" (radiogram, Brett to AGWAR, February 7, 1942, in "History of the 5th Air Force," App. II, doc. 1250.

19. Radiogram, Brett to Barnes, February 13, 1942, in box T1597, RG 338, NARA.

20. Johnsen, "You Men on Java Are Not Forgotten," *Air Force Magazine,* September 1980, 112; Willmott, *Empires,* 299; Dull, *Battle History,* 66. Johnsen, one of the 20th Pursuit (Provisional) pilots on Java, recalled thirty-eight years later that he had heard the message on a broadcast by President Roosevelt, whereas it was obviously through receipt of a copy of Arnold's message instead. Roosevelt did not use these words in his fireside chat of February 23, 1942.

CHAPTER 5

1. Parker and Hague diaries, January 29, 1942; Morehead in Hammel, *Aces Against Japan,* 12. Capt. Paul Davis in his B-24A (serial number 40–2370) had been ordered to guide the 20th Pursuit pilots to Darwin (radiogram, Barnes to Brett, ABDACOM, January 28, 1942, in box T1610, RG 338, NARA).

2. Parker and Gambonini diaries, January 29, 1942.

3. Morehead in Hammel, *Aces,* 12–13; Les Johnsen diary, January 29, 1942.

4. Morehead, *In My Sights,* 148; Hague diary, January 29, 1942.

5. Oliver to author, August 7, 1993; Oliver flight log, January 29, 1942; Gambonini diary, January 29, 1942; Jackson telephone interview.

6. Gambonini, Parker, Hague, and Les Johnsen diaries, January 29, 1942; Coleman interview.

7. Hague dairy, January 29, 1942; Salecker, *Fortress Against the Sun,* 84, 87; Raleigh, *Pacific Blackout,* 167–68.

8. Hague and Gambonini diaries, January 29, 1942; Oliver to author, August 7, 1993; McWherter memoir.

9. Gambonini and Parker diaries, January 30, 1942; Oliver to author, August 7, 1993; Oliver flight log, January 30, 1942.

10. Parker, Gambonini, Les Johnsen, and Hague diaries, January 30, 1942.

11. Gambonini, Oliver, and McWherter diaries, January 30, 1942; Oliver to author, August 7, 1993.

12. Parker, Hague, Gambonini, and Legg diaries, January 30, 1942; Raleigh, *Pacific Blackout*, 168; radiogram, USAFIA Melbourne to Hq, USA, Brisbane, February 1, 1942, in box T1610, RG 338, NARA.

13. Parker and Hague diaries, January 31, 1942.

14. Les Johnsen and Hague diaries, January 31, 1942.

15. Gambonini and Hague diaries, January 31, 1942; Morehead, *In My Sights*, 48–49.

16. Gambonini diary, January 31, 1942; Morehead, *In My Sights*, 49.

17. Hague and Gambonini diaries, January 31, 1942.

18. Morehead, *In My Sights*, 49; Hague, Parker, and Gambonini diaries, January 31, 1942.

19. Radiogram No. 278, Hq USAFIA Brisbane to Hq USAFIA Melbourne, January 30, 1942, and memo, USA, Base Section 3, January 29, 1942, both in "History of the 5th Air Force," App. II, documents.

20. "History of the 5th Air Force," Appendix II, documents; radiograms, Barnes, USAFIA Hq to Brett, January 31, 1942, and to Hq USA Brisbane for Air Officer, January 31, 1942, both in box T1610, RG 338, NARA.

21. Radiogram, Wagner, Mahony, and Strauss [to USAFIA Hq Melbourne?], February 1, 1942, "History of the 5th Air Force," App. II, doc. 65.

22. Radiogram, Ross G. Hoyt for USAFIA Hq Melbourne to Brett, NEI, January 31, 1942, in box T1610, RG 338, NARA.

23. Radiogram No. 10, ABDACOM to Hq USAFIA Melbourne, February 1, 1942, in box T1597, RG 338, NARA.

24. Radiogram, Hq USAFIA Melbourne to Hq USA Brisbane, January 27, 1942, in box T1610, RG 338, NARA.

25. Head diary, January 29, 30, 31 and February 1, 1942.

26. Legg diary, February 1, 1942; radiogram, Barnes to Hq Brisbane, February 1, 1942, in box T1610, RG 338, NARA.

27. Radiogram, Hq USAFIA Melbourne to Hq USA Brisbane, January 27, 1942, and radiogram No. 530, Barnes to Hq USA Brisbane, February 1, 1942, in box T1610, RG 338, NARA; Head diary, February 1, 1942.

28. Head diary, February 1, 1942.

29. Ibid., February 2, 1942.

30. Radiogram, Hq USAFIA Melbourne to Hq USA Brisbane, February 1, 1942.

31. Badura diary, February 1, 1942; "Seventeenth Pursuit History"; Sheppard and Gilmore, "Statement." The CW-21B pilot has not been identified but may have been the commanding officer of 2-Vl.G-IV squadron, 1st Lt. Ricardo Anemaet, who had arrived back at the squadron on January 28 and recalled once leading the 17th Pursuit to Ngoro (Anemaet to Bosch to Groves, February 29, 1976).

32. Hennon diary, January 31 and February 1, 1942. The "Seventeenth Pursuit His-

tory" indicates that twelve aircraft were flown into Ngoro on this date but has missed the loss of Kruzel's ship and the fact that Hennon was at Madioen with Sprague's plane. The arriving pilots were Sprague, Jack Dale, Cy Blanton, Ed Gilmore, Bo McCallum, Ray Thompson, Walt Coss, Jim Rowland, Ed Kiser, and Bill Stauter. One pilot arrived without his plane: either Kruzel—whose ship had been lost—or one of the two junior pilots (Thompson or Stauter) if Kruzel had taken his ship for the movement to Ngoro.

33. Coss, "Notes," 1943; Burnside to author, October 26, 2002; Dockstader, "Statement," November 10, 1944; Blanton taped narrative, 1993; Blanton to author, October 4, 2003; Weller, "Luck," Winter 1944, 284.

34. Coss, "Notes," 1943; Weller, "Luck," Winter 1944, 284; Blanton taped narrative, 1993; Anemaet to Bosch to Groves, February 29, 1976; Ingram diary, February 10, 1942.

35. Coss to author, February 23, 1994; Dockstader, "Statement"; Sheppard and Gilmore, "Statement"; Blanton taped narrative, 1993; Boise to author, September 11, 1994.

36. Weller, "Luck," Winter 1944, 284; Blanton, "Statement of Activities"; Coss to author, March 16, 1994; Burnside to author, October 26, 2002.

37. [Mahony], USAF Detachment, Bangalore, India, "Obstacles to Pursuit Effectiveness in Past Operations," February 28, 1942.

38. Blanton, "Statement of Activities"; Coss, "Notes," 1943; Blanton taped narrative, 1993; Geurtz to Casius, February 19, 1978; Weller, "Luck," Winter 1944, 283.

39. Blanton, "Statement of Activities"; Coss interview, April 17, 1994; Kruzel memoir.

40. Hennon diary, February 1 and 2, 1942.

41. Coss, "Notes," 1943; "Seventeenth Pursuit History."

42. Weller, "Luck," Winter 1944, 281; Badura diary, February 1, 1942.

43. Dean diary, February 2, 1942. The message Legg received must have been the radiogram Marshall sent to Hq USAFIA, received on February 2, warning that a Japanese carrier might be operating off the northeast coast of Australia and ordering Barnes to take "every precaution" that the planes were not caught on the ground (radiogram No. 235, Adams and Marshall to Commanding General, USAFIA, February 1, 1942, in box T1601, RG 338, NARA).

44. Wilhite diary and memoir, January 29 (sic), 1942; McMahon memoir.

45. McMahon memoir.

46. Ibid.; Wilhite diary and memoir, January 29, 1942.

47. Head diary, February 3, 1942; Wilhite diary and memoir, January 29, 1942.

48. McMahon memoir; Wilhite diary and memoir, January 29, 1942; Head diary, February 3, 1942.

49. Wilhite diary, January 29, 1942. Two RAAF Lockheed Hudsons from Townsville had also been sent out to look for an enemy carrier but had sighted only one large and two small unidentified ships (radiogram, Merle-Smith to MILID, Washington, February 3, 1942, in box T1610, RG 338, NARA). At 0630 on this day, USAFIA headquarters informed Townsville that a squadron of P-40s was enroute to Townsville and other fields for dispersal and could be used for defense in the event of a Japanese attack (radiogram, Hq USAFIA Melbourne to Hq USA Townsville, February 3, 1942, in box T1610, RG 338, NARA).

50. Gies diary, February 3 and 4, 1942; McMahon memoir.

51. Alexander L. P. Johnson, "Report" re inspection of Amberley Field, February 3, 1942, in "History of the 5th Air Force," Appendix II; Legg diary, February 3, 1942.

52. Coss to author, January 6, 1995; Blanton memoir.

53. Sheppard and Gilmore, "Statement"; "Seventeenth Pursuit History"; Kiser, "Historical Information."

54. Coss, "Statement"; Sheppard and Gilmore, "Statement"; "General Brereton's Headquarters Diary," February 3, 1942.

55. Coss, "Statement."

56. Hennon diary, February 3, 1942; "Seventeenth Pursuit History"; "Takao Kokutai Kodocho," February 3, 1942 (via Tagaya to author, July 6, 2006). Time reported by the Japanese has been converted to local Soerabaja time, one and one-half hours earlier in 1942.

57. Weller, "Luck," Winter 1944, 286; "Seventeenth Pursuit History."

58. Hennon diary, February 3, 1942; Weller, "Luck," Winter 1944, 286; "Seventeenth Pursuit History"; "Takao Kokutai Kodocho," February 3, 1942. The bombers they were chasing were seventeen Mitsubishi Type 1 "Bettys" in two *chutai* (air divisions) minus one aircraft of the Takao Kokutai. The third *chutai* of nine ships had not been spotted, perhaps being far ahead as they were returning to their Kendari base. The twenty-six *Rikko* bombers had bombed Perak Field and Soerabaja harbor at 1050. Their Zero escort fighters did not show up until 1100, when they immediately engaged in combat with Dutch and American fighters below them until 1115 and then linked up with the Bettys for the return trip. The bomber Hennon hit did not go down and returned safely; none of the Bettys were lost, but two Zeros and a C5M "Babs" reconnaissance plane were shot down by the Dutch pilots and another Zero by a PBY (Tagaya, *Mitsubishi Type 1 Rikko "Betty" Units of World War II*, 32; Izawa, "Rikko and Gingga," no date, 68; "Takao Kokutai Kodocho" and "3rd Kokutai Kodocho," February 3, 1942, via Tagaya to author, July 6, 2006; Boer to author, January 12, 2007).

59. Sheppard and Gilmore, "Statement"; Coss, "Statement." The old-model G3M "Nell" bombers of the 1st Kokutai were heading north after having bombed Singosari Field at 1040. ("1st Kokutai Kodocho," February 3, 1942, via Tagaya to author, July 6, 2006).

60. Sheppard and Gilmore, "Statement"; Coss, "Statement."

61. Coss, "Statement." Coss's flight had apparently run into Zeros of the 3rd Kokutai that had arrived over the Soerabaja area at 1100 and immediately entered into combat with Dutch Hawks and CW-21Bs in addition to the three Americans. They were not escorting the Nells, which apparently crossed over their area at the time Coss's flight tried to intercept the bombers ("3rd Kokutai Kodocho," February 3, 1942, via Tagaya to author, July 6, 2006).

62. Sheppard and Gilmore, "Statement"; Coss, "Statement." Coss destroyed the Zero of S1c Kyoji Kobayashi, who was flying in the last position of a seven-ship Tainan Kokutai formation that, with another *chutai* of seven Zeros, was heading north after having strafed Singosari Field and shot down a B 17C ("Tainan Kokutai Kodocho," February 3, 1942, via Tagaya to author, July 6, 2006).

63. White, *Queens*, 173.

64. Ibid., 174–75; "Takao Kokutai Kodocho," February 3, 1942.

65. Perry diary, in Weller, "Luck," Winter 1944, 279, 288. Two C-53 transports had left Koepang at 2000 for Soerabaja, evidently carrying twenty enlisted men (radiogram A 446, Koepang to ACH Darwin, February 1, 1942, in box T1596, RG 338, NARA).

66. The pilot was Sgt. R. Ch. Halberstadt in Lieutenant Anemaet's flight; he was killed instantly (Shores and Cull with Izawa, *Bloody Shambles,* 2:153).

67. Perry diary, in Weller, "Luck," Winter 1944, 289.

68. Boxman account of March 23, 1994, Schep to author, February 22 and March 10, 1995. Of the eight Curtiss Hawks of 1-Vl.G-IV that had taken off from Maospati as twenty-seven Betty bombers of the Kanoya Kokutai were bombing their field, three were shot down and two others landed back at Maospati, badly damaged. One of the three pilots killed was Hennon's friend Capt. Max van der Poel, the CO of the squadron, who drowned after bailing out and landing in a river. The pilot of the seventh ship landed at Maospati undamaged (Shores and Cull with Izawa, *Bloody Shambles,* 2:151–53; Boer to Stanaway, July 26, 2005; "Kanoya Kokutai Kodocho," February 3, 1942, via Tagaya to author, July 6, 2006).

69. Haye to Schep, February 2, 1984. Twelve CW-21Bs had taken off from Perak Airdrome in three flights of four each and attacked the Zeros of the 3rd Kokutai in violent combat. In Lieutenant Kingma's section, three were shot down in an encounter with sixteen of the Zeros, with two killed and Kingma badly burned in bailing out; only Haye, who landed at Ngoro, was unscathed. In Lieutenant Bedet's section, one crashlanded, Bedet was wounded and was barely able to land back at Perak, a third landed damaged at Maospati, and Beerling landed at Ngoro. In Anemaet's section, attacked by Zeros over the field as they tried to land for refueling, one was shot down and the pilot (Halberstadt) killed, two managed to get down safely, and Anemaet himself landed but ran into a bomb crater (Shores and Cull with Izawa, *Bloody Shambles,* 2:153).

70. Radiogram, Barnes, Hq USAFIA Melbourne, to Hq USA Darwin, January 31, 1942, in box T1610, RG 338, NARA; Gambonini diary, February 1, 1942.

71. Parker, Hague, and Gambonini diaries, February 1, 1942.

72. Hague diary, February 1, 1942.

73. Jackson telephone interview; Gambonini and Hague diaries, February 1, 1942.

74. Gambonini, Parker, Hague, McWherter, Dutton, and Oliver diaries, February 1, 1942; Gambonini, Hoskyn, and Oliver flight logs; Morehead, *In My Sights,* 52.

75. Gambonini, Oliver, and Parker diaries, February 2, 1942.

76. Parker and Hague diaries, February 3, 1942.

77. Hague and Gambonini diaries, February 3, 1942.

78. Gambonini and Dutton diaries, February 3, 1942. This was evidently the same report the Amberley pilots had received the same day.

79. Parker diary, February 4, 1942; radiogram, Barnes, Hq USAFIA Melbourne, to Hq USA Darwin, February 3, 1942, in box T1610, RG 338, NARA.

80. Parker diary, February 4, 1942.

81. Parker, Gambonini, Hague, and McWherter diaries, February 4, 1942; Les John-

sen diary, February 3 (*sic*), 1942. See Appendix Table 7 for list of pilots taking off and remaining behind.

82. Parker, Hague, and Gambonini diaries, February 4, 1942; Morehead, *In My Sights*, 51.

83. Morehead, *In My Sights*, 51–52; Parker and Gambonini diaries, February 4, 1942.

84. Hague and Gambonini diaries, February 4, 1942; Parker diary, February 5, 1942.

85. Gambonini, Hayes, and Hague diaries, February 4, 1942; Parker diary, February 5, 1942; Morehead, *In My Sights*, 52. Unknown to Lane, Bud Sprague had wanted to send a guide aircraft to Bali to meet Lane's squadron and escort the pilots directly to Ngoro instead, overflying Soerabaja (O'Donnell diary, February 4, 1942), but Ente Van Gils made the decision without consulting the 17th Pursuit commander.

CHAPTER 6

1. Parker and Gambonini diaries, February 5, 1942; Morehead, *In My Sights*, 52.

2. Hague and Gambonini diaries, February 5, 1942; McWherter memoir.

3. Morehead, *In My Sights*, 53.

4. Gambonini and Hague diaries, February 5, 1942.

5. Parker diary, February 5, 1942.

6. Hayes and Gambonini diaries, February 5, 1942; Morehead, *In My Sights*, 53; Bound, Report on combat February 5, 1942.

7. Morehead, *In My Sights*, 53; Hayes to author, November 17, 1993.

8. Hague diary, February 5, 1942.

9. Ibid.; Morehead, *In My Sights*, 53; Weller, "Luck," Winter 1944, 294; "3rd Kokutai Kodocho," February 5, 1942, via Tagaya to author, July 6, 2006.

10. Lane to Mrs. Ada May Landry, February 19, 1943; Bound, Report on combat; Gambonini, Hayes, and Hague diaries, February 5, 1942; Gambonini Distinguished Service Cross citation; Fuchs to author, March 24, 1994; Morehead, *In My Sights*, 53. There is no documentation that Gallienne was in third position or Reagan in eighth position, but it is more logical that the more senior Gallienne was Hague's element leader.

11. Lane to Mrs. Landry; Gambonini DSC citation; Bound, Report on combat. Japanese records indicate that the 3rd Kokutai had attacked with nine Zeros only, formed up in three *shotai* of three planes each. Three were descending to strafe the field when they spotted Lane and Bound and were joined by the three of the second *shotai*. The first *shotai* remained above to provide cover, but at its altitude it engaged the P-40s, too. A terrified Lane had estimated the six of the second and third *shotai* as twenty-four. ("3rd Kokutai Kodocho," February 5, 1942; Lane to Mrs. Landry).

12. Bound, Report on combat. Bound's impression was faulty. Not one of the Zeros was lost in this attack (Hata and Izawa, *Japanese Naval Aces*, 427; "3rd Kokutai Kodocho," February 5, 1942).

13. Bound, Report on combat; Bound Silver Star citation; "Jesse Hague Is Honored for Bravery against Japanese," *Guthrie County Vedette* [Panora, Iowa], April 16, 1942. The condition of Bound's shoulder was described in his Silver Star citation.

14. "Jesse Hague Is Honored," *Guthrie County Vedette;* Hague diary, February 5, 1942.

15. Hague probably had flown over seven-thousand-foot Mount Bromo, a very noticeable landmark in East Java.

16. Muckley Distinguished Service Cross citation; Gambonini diary, February 5, 1942; Lane to Mrs. Landry; Weller, "Luck," Winter 1944, 293.

17. Lane to Mrs. Landry; Gambonini and Hague diaries, February 5, 1942; Reagan interview with Jonathan Juarez. The 3rd Kokutai claimed eleven P-40s shot down after landing at their Balikpapan base at 1340, although they indicated they had engaged only eight P-40s, an example of double-counting. In actuality, they shot down only the P-40s of Bound and Landry in the thirty-five-minute engagement ("3rd Kokutai Kodocho," February 5, 1942).

18. Hayes interview, April 16 and 17, 1994.

19. Ibid. There were actually thirty-one of the Bettys, eight of the Takao Kokutai and twenty-three of the Kanoya Kokutai (Shores and Cull with Izawa, *Bloody Shambles,* 2:163).

20. Gambonini diary, February 5, 1942; Gambonini Distinguished Service Cross citation; Gambonini flight log.

21. Gambonini diary, February 5, 1942.

22. Hayes diary, February 5, 1942; Morehead, *In My Sights,* 55; Morehead to author, May 1, 1993.

23. Morehead, *In My Sights,* 55.

24. Gambonini, Lund, and Morehead interview; Morehead, *In My Sights,* 55–56.

25. Les Johnsen diary, February 5 (*sic*), 1942; Guttman, "American Ace from Java to Germany," *World War II,* February 2001, 37.

26. Gambonini diary, February 5, 1942; Guttman, "American Ace," 37.

27. Hayes interview; Hayes to author, November 17, 1993.

28. Morehead, *In My Sights,* 56.

29. Guttman, "American Ace," 37; Gambonini, Lund, Morehead interview.

30. Perry diary, excerpted in Weller, "Luck," Winter 1944, 292.

31. Parker diary, February 5, 1942.

32. Hague and Parker diaries, February 5, 1942.

33. Parker diary, February 5, 1942. Lane was actually at the 5th Bomber Command base at Singosari (5th Bomber Command, Journal, February 5, 1942; Sheppard and Gilmore, "Statement").

34. Hague and Hennon diaries, February 5, 1942; "Seventeenth Pursuit History." It is not documented that Muckley flew to Ngoro in Gallienne's ship, but Gallienne is reported as arriving by transport and Bill Hennon talked with Muckley this day at Ngoro.

35. Blanton taped narratives, 1993 and 1994; Blanton telephone interview, January 12, 2004.

36. Blanton taped narrative, 1994; Fuchs, October 8, 1994; Guerrero, November 29, 2002.

37. Hayes and Gambonini diaries, February 5, 1942; Fuchs to author, March 24, 1994.

38. Hennon diary, February 4, 1942; "Seventeenth Pursuit History," doc. 1922; Shores and Cull with Izawa, *Bloody Shambles,* 2:156, 158, 160; Weller, "Luck," Winter

1944, 290–91; radiogram, ABDACOM No. 377 to AGWAR (re Sprague promotion), in box T1597, RG 338, NARA.

39. Hennon diary, February 5, 1942.

40. Ibid.; "Seventeenth Pursuit History," doc. 1922.

41. "Seventeenth Pursuit History," doc. 1922. Six B-17Es at Singosari had taken off at 0930 for a raid on the Japanese base at Balikpapan, Borneo. The ADC apparently warned the base of incoming Japanese bombers, too, for the base sounded the air raid alarm at 0950. Missed by the ADC was the force of twenty-seven Zeros of the Tainan Kokutai, followed fifty-five minutes later by eleven Zeros of the 3rd Kokutai that had left Balikpapan that morning for a strafing mission of Soerabaja area targets. The Dutch could only muster their four remaining CW-21Bs and two Hawk 75s to intercept; two of the CW-21Bs and both Hawks were lost in the ensuing combat. At twenty-two thousand feet over Soerabaja, Sprague's flight did not see the action below them. The Dutch losses of February 3 and 5 spelled the end of their capability to defend East Java from Japanese aerial attacks (Shores and Cull with Izawa, *Bloody Shambles*, 2:160–61; 5th Bomber Command, Journal; Army Forces Far East, *Naval Operations*, 25).

42. "Seventeenth Pursuit History," doc. 1922; Hennon diary, February 5, 1942; White, *Queens*, 177; Sheppard and Gilmore, "Statement"; Schep to author, February 22 and March 10, 1995. Subsequent to Dale's discussions with the ADC, its liaison position was expanded to become a liaison team, staffed by American officers, who would handle operational contacts with the 17th Pursuit at Ngoro (Boer to author, October 18 and 29, 2007). Although they had no language problem, the Dutch pilots were also angry over the ADC's incompetence, which put them at perilous disadvantage against the Japanese. It was sending them directly to the targeted Japanese position rather than to a safe location in which to gain altitude first in preparation for an interception. The unsatisfactory situation reflected the ADC's lack of training and experience in interception operations matched by the inability of its schoolboy spotters to recognize aircraft as friend or foe. It did not help matters that the ADC's commander, Colonel Ente Van Gils, an old artillery officer, was "unreasonable" and had an "inflammable" personality, giving rise to conflicts with Lieutenant Anemaet, among others (Schep to author, January 4, 1995; Van der Vossen to author, September 25, 1995).

43. Watson, *Army Air Action in the Philippines and Netherlands East Indies, 1941–1942*, USAF Historical Study No. 111.

44. Hague diary, February 5, 1942.

45. Holt interview.

46. Guerrero to author, November 29, 2002.

47. Les Johnsen diary, February 4 (*sic*), 1942; McWherter diary, February 5, 1942; Hoskyn flight log, February 5, 1942.

48. Les Johnsen diary, February 4 (*sic*), 1942.

49. Ibid.; Johnsen, "You Men," 107.

50. Johnsen, "You Men," 107; McWherter memoir.

51. McWherter and Dutton diaries, February 6, 1942; Boyd D. Wagner interview

with Roosevelt der Tatevision; McWherter memoir; Coleman interview; Shores and Cull with Izawa, *Bloody Shambles,* 2:165. The Japanese aircraft was a Mitsubishi Type 96 "Nell" of the 1st Kokutai, one of three patrolling in search of the Allied fleet in the area. The Americans had never seen one before.

52. Dutton, Gambonini, and McWherter diaries, February 6, 1942; Egenes to Larson, March 14, 1942; Les Johnsen diary, February 5 (*sic*), 1942; Coleman interview; McWherter memoir; Wagner interview; Shores and Cull with Izawa, *Bloody Shambles,* 2:165; White, *Queens,* 178.

53. McWherter memoir.

54. Coleman interview.

55. Ibid. Coleman had made his forced landing at Korleko on the east coast of Lombok. Allied Forces, ABDA, *Despatch by the Supreme Commander,* 61.

56. Coleman interview; Dutton diary, February 6, 1942.

57. McWherter memoir; Hague diary, February 6, 1942.

58. McWherter memoir; White, *Queens,* 179.

59. Les Johnsen diary, February 5 (*sic*), 1942; Oliver and Hoskyn flight logs, February 6, 1942.

60. Gambonini, Lund, and Morehead interview; Morehead, *In My Sights,* 56; Gambonini diary, February 6, 1942.

61. Gambonini diary, February 6, 1942; Les Johnsen diary, February 5 (*sic*), 1942; Oliver to author, August 7, 1993; Gambonini flight log, February 6, 1942; Gambonini, Lund, and Morehead interview; Morehead, *In My Sights,* 56.

62. Johnsen, "You Men," 108; Les Johnsen diary, February 5 (*sic*), 1942; Oliver flight log, February 6, 1942; Hague diary, February 6, 1942.

63. Dutton diary, February 6, 1942; Coleman interview.

64. Gambonini diary, February 6 and 7, 1942; "Seventeenth Pursuit History"; Coss, Notebook No. 1; Gambonini, Lund, and Morehead interview; Morehead, *In My Sights,* 56, 59.

65. Oliver and Hoskyn flight logs, February 7, 1942; "Seventeenth Pursuit History"; Les Johnsen diary, February 6 (*sic*), 1942.

66. Weller, "Luck," Winter 1944, 286, 295–96.

67. Hennon, Hague, and Parker diaries, February 6, 1942; Blanton taped narrative, 1993; Weller, "Luck," Winter 1944, 295–96.

68. Hennon diary, February 6, 1942; Blanton taped narratives, 1993 and 1994; Boise interview; Weller, "Luck," Winter 1944, 296. Weller was told, and Blanton recalled, that it was Walt Coss with him rather than Hennon, but Hennon in his diary recorded that he was with Blanton during the operation.

69. "Seventeenth Pursuit History," doc. 1922; Parker diary, February 7, 1942.

70. "Seventeenth Pursuit History."

71. Ibid.; Hague diary, February 7, 1942.

72. Gambonini and Oliver diaries, February 7, 1942; Morehead, *In My Sights,* 59; Shores and Cull with Izawa, *Bloody Shambles,* 2:166. Nine Zeros from the Tainan Kokutai had strafed the flying boat base.

73. "Seventeenth Pursuit History," doc. 1922; Hennon, Hague, and Parker diaries, February 7, 1942.

74. "Seventeenth Pursuit History"; Parker diary, February 7, 1942.

75. "Seventeenth Pursuit History"; 5th Bomber Command, Journal, February 7, 1942; Morehead, *In My Sights*, 59. Eight B-17Es had taken off from Singosari at 0520 for a reconnaissance bombing mission, its objective a carrier reported southeast of Makassar. Two of the bombers aborted the mission because of mechanical problems. After a fruitless forty-five-minute search, the remaining six returned to Singosari (5th Bomber Command, Journal, February 7, 1942).

76. Hague diary, February 7, 1942.

77. Morehead, *In My Sights*, 59.

78. "Seventeenth Pursuit History"; Hennon diary, February 7, 1942.

79. Hennon diary, February 7, 1942.

80. McWherter memoir.

81. "Seventeenth Pursuit History" has Gilmore as Sprague's wingman, but it was Parker, according to Parker's diary, February 8, 1942.

82. "Seventeenth Pursuit History"; Parker, McWherter, and Hague diaries, February 8, 1942.

83. "Seventeenth Pursuit History"; Oliver flight log, February 8, 1942. The B-17Es were the five remaining of a flight of nine that had taken off at 0735 on a mission to bomb Kendari. At 1040, nine Zeros of the Tainan Kokutai flying from Balikpapan and diverted to Soerabaja because of bad weather over their target of Denpasar had by chance encountered the American bombers at fourteen thousand feet and shot down two and damaged three before breaking off to return to Balikpapan (Shores and Cull with Izawa, *Bloody Shambles*, 2:167; 5th Bomber Command, Journal, February 8, 1942). The 17th Pursuit pilots must have spotted the B-17Es just after the combat as the Zeros were returning to their Borneo base.

84. "Seventeenth Pursuit History"; Parker diary, February 8, 1942.

85. "Seventeenth Pursuit History"; McWherter diary, February 8, 1942; McWherter memoir.

86. "Seventeenth Pursuit History"; Hennon and McWherter diaries, February 8, 1942; McWherter memoir.

87. Hennon and McWherter diaries, February 8, 1942; "Lifetime Pals Swap Stories on the War in the Air," *Des Moines Register*, November 12, 1942.

88. "Seventeenth Pursuit History"; Hennon diary, February 8 and 9, 1942; "Lifetime Pals."

89. "Lifetime Pals."

90. Coleman interview.

91. Coleman interview; "Seventeenth Pursuit History"; February 12, 1942.

92. Gambonini, Hennon, Oliver, and Parker diaries, February 8, 1942; Hayes diary, February 5, 1942; Guttman, "American Ace." "Seventeenth Pursuit History" erroneously indicates that Hayes and Reagan arrived at Soerabaja in P-40s.

93. Gambonini diary, February 8 and 9, 1942; "Seventeenth Pursuit History."

CHAPTER 7

1. USA, Base Section 3, Brisbane, Special Orders No. 20, February 4, 1942; Head and Legg diaries, February 4, 1942.

2. Lt. Col. John H. Davies memo to Commanding Officer, 91st Bomb Squadron, Archerfield, February 3, 1942, in McAfee collection.

3. Radiograms No. 557 and No. 558, Hq, USAFIA Melbourne to Hq USA, Brisbane, February 3, 1942, in box T1610, RG 338, NARA.

4. Head diary, February 4, 1942.

5. Gies diary, February 3 and 4, 1942.

6. Radiograms, Barnes to Brett, ABDACOM, February 2 and 3, 1942, in box T1610, RG 338, NARA.

7. Ingram diary, February 4, 1942; USA, Base Section 3, Brisbane, Special Orders No. 21, February 4, 1942.

8. Head and Ingram diaries, February 5, 1942; Gies diary, February 5–12, 1942; "91st Squadron," in McAfee, "The 27th Reports."

9. Ralph Martin taped narrative to author, January 1999; Martin interview, September 29, 2005; Head and Legg diaries, February 5, 1942.

10. Martin interview; Head diary, February 5, 1942; Robert Oestreicher retrospective diary, n.d.

11. Head diary, February 5, 1942; Oestreicher retrospective diary.

12. Ingram diary, February 5, 1942; "91st Squadron," in McAfee, "The 27th Reports."

13. Ingram and Head diaries, February 5, 1942.

14. Ibid., February 6, 1942.

15. Head and Johnson diaries, February 6, 1942; Oestreicher retrospective diary.

16. Brown, *Suez to Singapore*, 486.

17. Ibid., 486–87; Brown to author, September 30, 1994; Melikian telephone interview; Head and Johnson diaries, February 6, 1942; Oestreicher retrospective diary. Johnson and Oestreicher recorded that three of the pilots hit the fence, with Oestreicher identifying Gene Wahl as the third person, but Wahl denies it (Wahl telephone interview, December 3, 2005). The third pilot may have been the second pilot that Cecil Brown indicated had bounced in the landing.

18. Brown, *Suez to Singapore*, 486–87.

19. Ibid., 487. The author has not been able to identify the pilot.

20. Oestreicher retrospective diary; Spence Johnson diary, February 6, 1942; Gies diary, February 5–12, 1942.

21. Oestreicher retrospective diary; Head diary, February 6, 1942.

22. Head and Anderson diaries, February 6, 1942; radiogram, Barnes to Darwin, February 8, 1942, in box T1610, RG 338, NARA.

23. Radiogram, Darwin to ABDACOM and USAFIA, AIR 235038, British National Archives; "91st Squadron," in McAfee, "The 27th Reports"; Ingram diary, February 6, 1942.

24. Head and Ingram diaries, February 6, 1942.

25. Head and Anderson diaries, February 6, 1942.

26. Head diary, February 7, 1942; Oestreicher retrospective diary.

27. Ingram diary, February 7, 1942.

28. Radiogram, Wheless, Darwin, to Amberley, February 7, 1942, in McAfee collection; "91st Squadron," in McAfee, "The 27th Reports."

29. Head diary, February 8, 1942; 5th Bomber Command, Journal, February 7, 1942; Edmonds, *They Fought with What They Had*, 324; Wade to author, April 29, 1989; Oestreicher retrospective diary; Dockstader, "Statement," November 10, 1944. Based on information of Horace Wade, it is assumed that Bruce, Hubbard, and Christian were among the 19th Group evacuees in the LB-30s, most of whom did not remain at Darwin but went to the 5th Bomber Command base at Singosari.

30. Head diary, February 8, 1942. Johnson and Kaiser, along with Oscar Handy, arrived back at Amberley on February 17 (Dean diary, February 17, 1942).

31. Head and Ingram diaries, February 8, 1942; Mahony flight log, February 8, 1942.

32. Ingram diary, February 8, 1942.

33. Radiogram, ACH Darwin to ABDACOM, February 8, 1942, in "History of the 5th Air Force," App. II.

34. McMahon to author, March 2, 1994; Wilhite diary, February 5 (*sic*), 1942; Radiogram No. 530, Hq USAFIA to Hq USA Brisbane, February 1, 1942, in box T1610, RG 338, NARA.

35. USAFIA, General Orders No. 6, January 26, 1942, in box T788, and radiogram, Barnes to Brisbane, January 31, 1942, in box T1610, both in RG 338, NARA; Hurd telephone interview. Larry Selman (41-E), Oscar Handy (41-F), Ken Glassburn (41-F), and Wallace MacLean (41-G) had been assigned to the assembly depot on January 31, while Walter Hurd (41-G) and his buddies Jim Ingram (41-G) and H. Allen "Red" Graham (41-F) had decided not to continue as pursuit pilots and had signed up with the Air Transport Command following its establishment at Amberley on January 26.

36. McMahon memoir.

37. Gies diary, February 5, 1942.

38. "Pell's Bells," August 5, 1942; Latane flight log, February 4, 1942.

39. McMahon to author, March 2, 1994; Pell, "Flight Assignments, 33rd Pursuit Squadron Provisional, Brisbane, February 4, 1942."

40. Wilhite memoir, 199; Wilhite diary, February 6, 1942; Pell, "Flight Assignments."

41. McMahon to author, March 2, 1994; Wilhite memoir, 199; radiograms, Barnes to Hq USA Brisbane, January 31 and February 7, 1942, in box T1610, RG 338, NARA.

42. Wilhite memoir, 199.

43. Ibid., 200; USAFIA, A-4,"Location and Status," February 8, 1942, entry for P-40E serial number 41-5436; RAAF, Operations Record Book, A-50 Form, Hq, 3 SFTS, Amberley Field, February 9, 1942, NAA.

44. Wilhite memoir, 201; Operations Record Book, A-50 Form, Amberley, entry for February 9, 1942.

45. Wilhite diary, February 8 (*sic*), 1942; Wilhite memoir, 201.

46. Latane flight log, February 10, 1942; Wilhite diary, February 10, 1942; Wilhite

memoir, 205; USA, Base Section 3, Brisbane, Special Order No. 22, February 6, 1942; radiogram, Barnes to USA Brisbane, February 1, 1942, in box T1610, RG 338, NA.

47. Wilhite memoir, 205.

48. Latane flight log, February 10, 1942; Wilhite memoir, 201.

49. Kelsay to author, May 4, 1994; 5th Bomber Command, Journal, February 8, 1942; Head interview.

50. Ingram diary, February 9, 1942; "91st Squadron," in McAfee, "The 27th Reports." The Liberator was evidently a B-24A of the Air Transport Command, flown by Capt. Paul Davis from Singosari to Darwin at 0035 on February 8 (5th Bomber Command, Journal, February 8, 1942).

51. Fisher interview with Edmonds; Combined Operational Intelligence Centre (COIC), Situation Report No. 45, February 11, 1942, NAA; Head diary, February 9, 1942; radiogram, Merle Smith to MILID, February 10, 1942, in box T1610, RG 338, NARA. Situation Report No. 45 gives takeoff time as 1340 and Fisher's return at 1430, but Merle Smith's times (adjusted from Greenwich Mean Time) appear more accurate.

52. "91st Squadron," in McAfee, "The 27th Reports."

53. Childress to mother, March 9, 1942; Head diary, February 9, 1942; Head interview; Kelsay to author, May 4, 1994.

54. Childress to mother; Head interview; Kelsay to author, May 4, 1994.

55. Childress to mother; Head diary, February 9, 1942; Head interview.

56. Kelsay to author, May 4, 1994. The LB-30 arrived back at Darwin at 2230, seven hours after taking off (COIC, Situation Report No. 45).

57. Radiogram, Merle Smith to MILID, February 10, 1942, in box T1610, RG 338, NARA; COIC, Situation Report No. 45. According to the situation report, the crash site was reported by the RAAF Hudsons, on a patrol mission, as near the river Pono, southwest of the coastal village of Atapocpue, about twenty miles west of the town of Atambua.

58. Head diary, February 9, 1942; Head interview; COIC, Situation Report No. 45.

59. Head interview; Childress to mother.

60. Childress to mother; Head diary, February 10, 1942; Lewis to wife, March 11, 1942.

61. Northwest area to Bandoeng, message from Koepang, February 15, 1942, in box T1596, RG 338, NARA; Head diary, February 15, 1942; "History of the 5th Air Force," App. II, doc. 1021; COIC, Situation Report No. 45.

62. "91st Squadron," in McAfee, "The 27th Reports"; Gillison, *Royal Australian Air Force*, 419.

63. Radiogram, Merle Smith to MILID, February 10, 1942, in box T1610; Ingram diary, February 9, 1942.

64. Ingram diary, February 9 and 10, 1942.

65. "Seventeenth Pursuit History."

66. Ibid., doc. 1924.

67. Ibid.; Oliver to author, August 7, 1993; Hague diary, February 9, 1942.

68. "Diary of the 19th Bomb Group in Java, 1942," entry for February 9, 1942.

69. "Seventeenth Pursuit History"; Weller, "Luck," Spring 1945, 36.

70. Hague diary, February 9, 1942.

71. Ibid.; "Jesse Hague Is Honored," *Guthrie County Vedette.*

72. Hague diary, February 9, 1942; "Jesse Hague Is Honored," *Guthrie County Vedette;* Weller, "Luck," Summer 1945, 148.

73. McWherter memoir; McWherter diary, February 9, 1942.

74. McWherter memoir; McWherter and Hague diaries, February 9, 1942; "Seventeenth Pursuit History."

75. "Seventeenth Pursuit History"; Parker diary, February 9, 1942; Oliver flight log, February 9, 1942.

76. Coss, "Notes," 1943; Hague and Parker diaries, February 9, 1942; "Seventeenth Pursuit History." None of the seventeen Betty bombers were lost on this mission, according to operations records of their Takao Kokutai.

77. Spence Johnson diary, February 10, 1942.

78. Wahl telephone interview, December 3, 2005.

79. Spence Johnson diary, February 9 and 10, 1942.

80. Ibid., February 10, 1942; Mahony flight log, February 9 (*sic*), 1942; Lund interview.

81. Spence Johnson diary, February 10, 1942; Wahl interview.

82. "Seventeenth Pursuit History"; Spence Johnson and Hennon diaries, February 11, 1942; Lund and Wahl interviews; Dockstader, "Statement."

83. "Seventeenth Pursuit History"; Johnson, Parker, Hennon, and Gambonini diaries, February 11, 1942; Dockstader, "Statement."

84. Ingram diary, February 10 and 11, 1942; Gambonini diary, February 9, 1942.

85. Gambonini memoir and diary, February 9, 1942.

86. Ibid., February 10 and 11, 1942.

87. McWherter memoir; Fujita, *Foo,* 58. The men of the 131st Field Artillery Battalion at Singosari were also offered "mak mak" at a nearby settlement they called Monkey Village. "Beer and sex could be had for next to nothing." "'Mak mak' was the most plentiful commodity known to us," one enlisted man recalled (Fujita, *Foo,* 58).

88. Spence Johnson diary, addendum. The pilot was actually a first lieutenant at the time.

89. Johnsen, "You Men," 108.

90. Perry diary, excerpted in Weller, "Luck," Summer 1945, 149.

91. Hennon diary, February 10 and 11, 1942.

92. "Seventeenth Pursuit History"; Gambonini memoir and diary, February 11, 1942. The squadron history erroneously recorded that McCallum led B flight.

93. "Seventeenth Pursuit History"; Parker, Gambonini, and Oliver diaries, February 11, 1942; Oliver and Gambonini flight logs, February 11, 1942. As an alternative to the ADC warning system, natives throughout East Java would beat on hollow logs, passing the warnings on every two miles or so until they reached Ngoro. In the view of the pilots, it was a more effective system than that of the ADC, because the drum warnings reaching the pursuiters about five minutes ahead of the ADC calls (Kiser, "Historical Information"). This time, however, the natives also erred in their warning.

94. "Seventeenth Pursuit History"; Parker diary, February 10, 1942.

95. Head diary, February 10, 1942; Head interview; Childress to mother.

96. Head diary, February 10, 1942.

97. Ibid., February 11, 1942; Childress to mother. Koepang had informed Darwin by radio this day that seven pilots of the flight had been located and were proceeding to Koepang (radiogram, Koepang to ACH Darwin, February 11, 1942, in box T1610, RG 338, NARA).

CHAPTER 8

1. McMahon memoir; McMahon to author, March 2, 1994.

2. RAAF, Operations Record Book, A-50 form, Amberley Field, entry for February 11, 1942; McMahon memoir. Evidently Gerry Dix in Pell's A flight remained behind to fly in Keenan's flight, while McMahon's flight comprised only Bob Vaught, David Latane, and himself.

3. McMahon memoir; McMahon to author, March 2, 1994; Wilhite diary, February 11, 1942; Wilhite memoir, 205.

4. McMahon memoir; Wilhite memoir, 205. This was the first time Pell had ever commanded a pursuit squadron.

5. Naylor to author, May 14, 1994.

6. Wilhite memoir, 206; Wilhite diary, February 11, 1942; McMahon to author, March 2, 1994; "Operations Java Campaign: Pilots of the 13th and 33rd Squadrons Wrecked or Aircraft Out on the Way to USS *Langley* and from Port Pirie to Darwin," (Brisbane), February 24, 1942.

7. Wilhite memoir, 206.

8. McMahon to author, March 2, 1994, Wilhite memoir, 206.

9. Wilhite memoir, 206–207; Wilhite diary, February 12, 1942; McMahon to author, March 2, 1994.

10. Wilhite memoir, 207; Wilhite diary, February 12, 1942. The RAAF Operations Record Book, A-50 Form, for RAAF Station Canberra does not indicate a stopover by Pell's group this day, February 12, 1942.

11. McMahon memoir; McMahon to author, March 2, 1994.

12. McMahon to author, March 2, 1994; Wilhite memoir, 207. Keenan had lost Bill Borden from his flight of fourteen at Mascot when he was unable to take off because of engine trouble. After Keenan sent his message from Sydney, he found he was now down to twelve ships when Gerry Dix was forced to drop out and return to Sydney after his Allison engine started cutting out on takeoff (Dix memoir, March 24, 1994). The RAAF A-50 Form record for Amberley reports fifteen P-40s departing at 0810 on February 12 for the south, obviously Keenan's group. However, fourteen would seem to be the correct figure, giving twenty-five as the total for the two groups leaving in the 33rd Pursuit (Provisional).

13. Latane flight log, February 11 (*sic*), 1942; McMahon memoir; Wilhite diary, February 13, 1942.

14. McMahon to author, March 2, 1994.

15. RAAF, Operations Record Book, A-50 Form, Hq, RAAF Station Point Cook, February 12, 1942, entries.

16. Ibid., February 13, 1942; radiogram, Barnes to Hq AAF Mascot, February 13, 1942, in box T1610, RG 338, NARA; Dix memoir. When Brett at ABDACOM was notified that there were only two P-40s at Darwin despite earlier having been informed that there were fifteen there that he wanted, he became furious. He needed those P-40s to escort an important convoy from Darwin to Koepang and to remain there to provide cover for the unloading of the ships, scheduled to arrive at Koepang on February 18. Barnes immediately responded that he was diverting Pell with fifteen P-40s to meet his requirements and would arrange for replacements for the fifteen to proceed to Perth to board the *Langley* (radiograms, ABDACOM to Army Melbourne for CGS, Darwin, February 10, 1942, and to USAFIA, February 12, 1942, both in box T1597, and radiogram, Barnes to ABDACOM , February 13, 1942, in box T1610, all in RG 338, NARA). The RAAF in Koepang expected the P-40s would be remaining in Koepang as part of the defensive reinforcements of the base being brought in by the convoy (RAAF Operations Record Book, Form A-50, No. 2 G.R. Squadron, entry for February 1–16, 1942).

17. McMahon to author, March 2, 1994; McMahon memoir.

18. Wilhite memoir, 207.

19. Latane flight log, February 12 (*sic*), 1942.

20. McMahon memoir; Wilhite memoir, 209; author's calculations.

21. McMahon, March 2, 1994.

22. Radiogram, Barnes to Darwin, February 10, 1942, in box T1610, RG 338, NARA.

23. The nine were Horace Atkinson, Aime Dierkens, Arthur England, William Herbert, Justin Hower, Earl Kingsley, Paul Magre, Edward Schmillen, and Haley Skinner. The tenth 41-H Craig Field pilot on the *Mormacsun,* Richard Suehr, had been assigned earlier to the 33rd Pursuit (Richard Suehr telephone interview, September 18, 2008; Ferguson and Pascalis, *Protect and Avenge,* 21).

24. Gies diary, February 13, 1942; RAAF, Operations Record Book, A-50 Form, Amberley Field, entry for February 13, 1942. Evidently the first flight had originally been ordered to land at Richmond Field, too, which had refueling facilities, unlike Mascot Field (radiogram, Barnes to CO, Base Section 3, February 13, 1942, in box T1610, RG 338, NARA). It is believed that Jim Bruce led this flight, as Thomas "Speed" Hubbard was the leader of the second flight (his P-40E No. 7 is shown in a photograph at Richmond Field), and they were the two flight leaders.

25. Glassburn to author, May 31, 1994; Glassburn flight log, February 13, 1942. Bruce's flight evidently flew on to Mascot from Williamtown later in the day, as indicated in Barnes's irate radiogram to Base Section 3 cited above.

26. Sanders diary, February 2, 12, 16, 23, 1942; Sanders to Dwight Messimer, March 8, 1993; radiogram, Barnes to Brett, ABDACOM, February 8, 1942, in box T1610, RG 338, NARA. The 51st Group had arrived at Melbourne on the *Coolidge* on February 1, 1942. On February 8 it was ordered (less one squadron) shipped to Java by vessel with fifty-one crated P-40Es (radiogram, Barnes to Brett, ABDACOM, February 8, 1942).

27. "Seventeenth Pursuit History," doc. 1927; Broadhurst to mother, January 24, 1942; "Diary of the 19th Bomb Group," entry for February 12, 1942; Hague diary, February 12, 1942.

28. "Seventeenth Pursuit History," doc. 1927; Gambonini diary, February 12, 1942.

29. Hoskyn and Mahony flight logs, February 12, 1942; Robert C. McWherter memoir; Parker, Gambonini, and Hennon diaries, February 12, 1942. Unknown to the pursuiters, the Japanese had suspended attacks since February 10 because of "continuous inclement weather" over the target route (Hq, Army Forces Far East, Military History Section, *Naval Operations in the Invasion of the Netherlands East Indies,* Japanese Monograph No. 101, 28).

30. "Seventeenth Pursuit History"; Ferguson, "Activities of the 91st Bomb Squadron since Beginning of War," no date, 2.

31. "Seventeenth Pursuit History," doc. 1926, February 7 and 12, 1942.

32. "Seventeenth Pursuit History"; Hennon diary, February 12, 1942; Weller, "Luck," Spring 1945, 40.

33. 5th Bomber Command, Journal, February 12, 1942; Burnside to author, October 26, 2002; Murray Nichols memoir.

34. Burnside to author, October 26, 2002; Nichols memoir; Nichols to author, February 17, 1997.

35. McAfee diary, February 9, 10, 11, 1942; McAfee, "The 27th Reports"; Bender diary; Bender memoir.

36. "Seventeenth Pursuit History"; Oliver flight log, February 13, 1942.

37. "Seventeenth Pursuit History," doc. 1926; Hague and Gambonini diaries, February 13, 1942; Mahony, Gambonini, and Hoskyn flight logs, February 13, 1942.

38. Oliver diary, February 13, 1942.

39. Gambonini diary, February 14 and 15, 1942; Hennon diary, February 13 and 14, 1942; Gambonini interview.

40. Oliver and Parker diaries, February 14, 1942; Oliver flight log, February 14, 1942; Blanton taped narrative, 1994.

41. "Seventeenth Pursuit History," doc. 1927; Hague diary, February 13, 1942; Coss to author, February 23, 1994.

42. Head diary, February 12, 1942.

43. Childress to mother, March 9, 1942; Head diary, February 13, 1942; Head interview.

44. McMahon to author, March 2, 1994; McMahon memoir.

45. McMahon to author, March 2, 1994; McMahon memoir; Wilhite memoir, 209; Wilhite diary, February 15, 1942.

46. McMahon memoir; McMahon to author, March 2, 1994; Latane flight log, February 13 (*sic*), 1942.

47. McMahon described this situation as happening at Alice Springs, but he obviously meant it at Oodnadatta, which he had forgotten to mention in his memoir as their refueling stop.

48. McMahon memoir; Latane flight log, February 13 (*sic*), 1942.

49. Latane flight log, February 13 (*sic*), 1942; "Operations Java Campaign: Pilots of the 13th and 33rd Squadrons Wrecked or Aircraft Out on the Way to USS *Langley* and from Port Pirie to Darwin," February 24, 1942.

50. Radiogram, S-3 [Housel], USAFIA Hq, Melbourne, to CO, US Hq, Alice Springs, February 14, 1942, in box T1611, RG 338, NARA; McMahon to author, March 2, 1994.

51. McMahon memoir; McMahon to author, March 2, 1994.

52. McMahon memoir.

53. Ibid.

54. Ibid.; McMahon to author, March 2, 1994.

55. McMahon memoir; "Operations Java Campaign."

56. McMahon memoir. USAFIA headquarters, Melbourne, was erroneously informed later that McMahon had run into a tractor "at Alice Springs" and damaged the wing (radiogram, Barnes to Hq, USA, Alice Springs, February 23, 1942, in box T1611, RG 338, NARA.

57. McMahon memoir. Pell had informed Brett at ABDACOM on reaching Darwin that he had arrived with ten P-40s but that eight were out of commission (radiogram, Pell to ABDACOM, February 15, 1942, "forward to Brett," in "History of the Fifth Air Force," Appendix II).

58. McMahon memoir; McMahon to author, March 2, 1994; "Roster of Officers and Enlisted Men on Duty at the Station, Hq, FEAF Detachment, RAAF Field, Darwin, February 20, 1942."

59. McMahon memoir. The P-40 that McMahon selected was probably the one that Oscar Handy had cracked up on landing at Darwin on February 6 as part of Mahony's 3rd Pursuit (Provisional) flight from Amberley.

60. Gordon, *Voyage from Shame*, 26; Alford, letter to the Editor, *Air International*, October 1986; Rorrison, *Nor the Years Contemn*, 131; Edmonds, *They Fought with What They Had*, 349. Pell's detachment of P-40s had not yet arrived at Darwin to escort the convoy to Koepang, as ABDACOM had ordered on February 10. At any rate, most of Pell's aircraft would require maintenance work on their arrival.

61. Gordon, *Voyage from Shame*, 26–28; Edmonds, *They Fought*, 349; Piper, *The Hidden Chapters*, 69. Primary documentation that could confirm this account has not been located by the author.

62. Gordon, *Voyage from Shame*, 26–28.

63. Ens. C. D. Smith, quoted in Schultz, *The Last Battle Station*, 122–23.

64. Gordon, *Voyage from Shame*, 28–29. Buel had attacked the flying boat as it was on its homeward course northwards back to its base at Amboina after having stalked the convoy for three hours and dropped 60 kg bombs on it. Tail gunner Marekumi Takahara survived the crash and was taken prisoner of war in Australia. He vividly described the last moments of each of the combatant aircraft to his captors (Gordon, *Voyage from Shame*, 28–29).

65. Oestreicher retrospective diary.

66. Radiogram No. 866, Pell, Hq USAFIA Darwin, to Brett, ABDACOM, February 16, 1942, in AIR 23/5038, No. 121540, British National Archives.

67. McMahon memoir.

68. McMahon memoir; radiogram No. 866, Pell to Brett, February 16, 1942.

69. McMahon memoir. McMahon in 1944 reported that Oestreicher had told him that Buel and he had taken off and headed out for the convoy together, but he had returned and reported that he had lost sight of Buel when they headed on separate courses (confidential memo, Robert F. McMahon to Commanding Officer, AAF Field, Santa Rosa, California, July 19, 1944). In line with this statement, and contrary to his retrospective diary entry, Oestreicher's flight log for February 15, 1942, does not indicate he flew two missions that day, only a "combat mission patrol" of three hours, fifteen minutes, evidently the earlier one of the two he mentioned in his diary (Oestreicher flight log, entry for February 15, 1942). On the other hand, Wheless in a postwar interview indicated he sent Buel out alone when he was unable to contact Oestreicher by radio as he was patrolling (Edmonds, *They Fought,* 349).

70. McMahon memoir.

71. Wilhite diary, February 14, 1942; Wilhite memoir, 208.

72. Wilhite diary, February 15, 1942; Wilhite memoir, 208. The P-40s may have been from the *Mormacsun,* which had arrived at Brisbane on January 25, 1942, with sixty-seven crated P-40Es.

73. Wilhite memoir, 208–209.

74. Wilhite diary, February 15, 1942; Wilhite memoir, 209. USAFIA headquarters in Melbourne radioed Brett at ABDACOM at 1900 that evening of February 15 that there were now sixteen P-40s at Port Pirie enroute to Fremantle, plus nine at Laverton Field, Melbourne, also enroute, with fifteen others at Brisbane scheduled to join them but "held up by weather." All were being transferred to Fremantle to ensure there would be thirty-two—with pilots—to load onto the *Langley* (radiogram, Barnes to Brett, February 15, 1942, in box T1611, RG 338, NARA).

75. Wilhite diary, February 15, 1942; Wilhite memoir, 209.

76. Wilhite diary, February 16, 1942; Wilhite memoir, 209.

PART FOUR

1. Willmott, *Empires in the Balance,* 302–303; Womack, *Dutch Naval Air Force,* 106–107.

2. Willmott, *Empires,* 302–303; Womack, *Dutch Naval Air Force,* 116; Shores and Cull with Izawa, *Bloody Shambles,* 2:175.

3. Willmott, *Empires,* 303–306.

4. Willmott, *Empires,* 307–308.

5. Alford, *Darwin's Air War, 1942–1945,* 14–20; Powell, *The Shadow's Edge,* 57, 75; Lockwood, *Australia's Pearl Harbor,* dust cover; Willmott, *Empires,* 304; "*Kaga* Kodocho," February 19, 1942, via Jim Sawruk.

6. Womack, *Dutch Naval Air Force,* 116; Tagaya, *Mitsubishi Type 1 Rikko,* 34; Izawa, "Rikko and Gingga," 72; Shores and Cull with Izawa, *Bloody Shambles,* 2:180; Alford, *Darwin's Air War,* 19–20.

7. Lockwood, *Australia's Pearl Harbor,* dust jacket.

8. Willmott, *Empires,* 305–307.

9. Cable No. 5292, Secretary, Prime Minister's Department to Australian Minister in Washington, February 21, 1942, repeated to Wavell as No. 5293, and cable No. 327, Australian Legation, Washington, to Prime Minister, received February 21, 1942, both in NAA.

10. Radiogram No. 395, ABDACOM to AGWAR, February 17, 1942, and radiogram No. 509A, ABDACOM to AGWAR, February 21, 1942, both in AFHRA microfilm A 7118, United States Army Forces in Australia, AFHRA.

11. Secret letter, Wavell to Curtin, February 21, 1942, in NAA.

12. Matloff and Snell, Strategic Planning, 135, footnote; Morton, *Strategy and Command*, 177; Weller, "Luck," Spring 1945, 49.

13. Radiogram No. 402, Arnold, AGWAR, to Barnes, USAFIA, February 23, 1942, in box T1601, RG 338, NARA.

14. USS *Phoenix*, "War Diary," February 22, 1942, in RG 38, NARA; Cavaye, "Report of Proceedings by Commodore of Convoy which Sailed from Fremantle, Australia, on February 22, 1942, at 1400 for Colombo."

15. USS *Phoenix*, "War Diary," February 23, 1942; Cavaye, "Report of Proceedings"; radiogram No. 196, Barnes to Brett, February 23, 1942, in RG 338, box T1611, RG 338, NARA; radiogram No. 1996, Wavell ABDACOM to CCS, Washington, February 22, 1942, in AIR 23/5044, British National Archives. Helfrich's plan, as approved by Wavell on February 22, was for the *Langley* to be detached on February 23 and the *Sea Witch* on February 25 (Boer to author, July 23, 2009).

16. USS *Phoenix*, "War Diary," February 25, 1942; Cavaye, "Report of Proceedings"; radiogram No. 208, Brett USAFIA to ABDACOM for Governor General NEI, February 25, 1942, in box T1611, RG 338, NARA.

17. Boer, *Het Verlies*, 20–24; Boer to author, July 13, 2009.

18. Radiogram, Brereton ABDACOM to Brett, USAFIA, February 24, 1942, in "History of the 5th Air Force (and Its Precedents)," Appendix II, Doc. 741, in microfilm A 7385, AFHRA. The decision was Brereton's last as deputy commander, ABDAIR, which was formally dissolved on February 23 and reconstituted as Java Air Command under Dutch direction.

19. Glassford, "Narrative of Events in the Southwest Pacific from 14 February to 5 April 1942," May 18, 1942.

20. Brereton, *Diaries*, 95–99.

21. Cablegram DBA No. 22, CCS Washington to ABDACOM, February 22, 1942, in AIR 23/5044, British National Archives; Brereton, *Diaries*, 98.

22. Boer, "Joint Actions by Allied Air and Naval Forces at Java on 26–27 February 1942," *World War II Quarterly* 5, no. 4 (2008): 6.

23. Glassford, "Narrative of Events"; cablegram, Wavell to CCS, February 22, 1942, in AIR 23/5044, British National Archives; radiogram, Marshall, Washington, to Brett, February 22, 1942, "History of the Fifth Air Force," App. II, doc.; FEAF, Bandoeng, General Order No. 18, February 24, 1942, in author's collection; "S-3 Diary for 7th Bombardment Group, AFCC (Dec. 1, 1941–Feb. 27, 1942)," entry for February 24, 1942; Cox, *Air Power Leadership on the Front Line*, 35.

24. Cablegram No. 350, Casey, Washington, to Prime Minister Curtin, February 24, 1942, in NAA.

25. Cablegram, Wavell, ABDACOM, to Prime Minister Curtin, February 25, 1942, and most secret cablegram, Page, London, to Prime Minister Curtin, February 27, 1942, both in NAA.

26. Cablegram, Page to Curtin, February 27, 1942.

27. "S-3 Diary for 7th Bombardment Group," entry for February 25, 1942.

28. Most secret telegram, Wavell to British Joint Staff Mission, Washington, February 25, 1942, in NAA.

29. Radiogram No. 424, Marshall to Brett, February 25, 1942, in box T1601, RG 338, NARA.

30. Cablegram, Wavell to Curtin, February 25, 1942.

31. Radiogram No. 424, Marshall to Brett, February 25, 1942.

32. President Franklin D. Roosevelt to Queen of Netherlands, February 26, 1942.

33. Durdin, "Van Mook Appeals for Aid to Java," *New York Times,* February 24, 1942.

34. Gowen log, February 24, 1942.

35. Radiogram No. 214, Brett, USAFIA, to Naiden, ABDACOM, Bombay, February 26, 1942, in box T1611, RG 338, NARA.

CHAPTER 9

1. McMahon to author, March 2, 1994; 105 Fighter Control Unit Hq, Encl. 1A, "Activities of 33rd Pursuit Squadron Provisional from February 15 to 19, 1942," undated, Series A 9695, Item 1242, NAA (reproduced in Oestreicher to Paul Wurtsmith, CO, 49th Fighter Group, memo, "Activities of the 33rd Pursuit Squadron Provisional, February 15–19, 1942," July 21, 1942 (hereafter cited as Oestreicher memo to Wurtsmith), in "History of the 5th Air Force," App. II.

2. Oestreicher retrospective diary; Oestreicher flight log, February 16, 1942; McMahon to author, March 2, 1994; McMahon memoir. Conflicting accounts by McMahon and Oestreicher make it difficult to reconstruct the outcome of this patrol.

3. McMahon to author, March 2, 1994; Rorrison, *Nor the Years Contemn,* 131, 133.

4. McMahon to author, March 2, 1994; McMahon memoir; radiogram No. 815, Connelly, Hq USA Darwin to Amberley, February 16, 1942, in McAfee collection. McMahon recalled the accident as occurring at the RAAF field, but documentation indicates otherwise.

5. Oestreicher memo to Wurtsmith; McMahon to author, March 2, 1994; McMahon memoir.

6. Oestreicher Memo; McMahon memoir.

7. McMahon memoir.

8. Ibid. In his July 1942 memo on the 33rd Pursuit's activities, Oestreicher mentions this afternoon mission "to patrol above a two-ship [sic] convoy that was returning to Darwin," but indicates that he led it and was with Elton Perry, Bill Walker, and John Glover. He did not provide an account of what transpired during the mission. His ret-

rospective diary does not mention this patrol, although his flight log cites a mission of three and one-half hours on that date.

9. McMahon to author, March 2, 1994; Shane Johnston e-mail to author, October 13, 2002.

10. McMahon to author, March 2, 1994. The convoy returned to Darwin in the morning, so it is assumed that at the time of the early morning patrol takeoff, it would have been about fifty miles out (Birkett to author, May 20, 2005).

11. McMahon to author, March 2, 1994.

12. Ibid. Wing Commander Griffith was thirty-six years old, an engineer in civilian life, and had been appointed to the command of RAAF Station Darwin on February 1, 1942 (Gillison, *Royal Australian Air Force*, 420, 424; Rorrison, *Nor the Years Contemn*, 119).

13. Penciled note, February 17, 1942, to radiogram, Pell to USAFIA for forwarding to Brett, February 15, 1942, "History of the 5th Air Force," App. II, doc. 1007; radiogram, Barnes to Brett, February 18, 1942, in box T1611, RG 338, NARA; Oestreicher Memo; Rorrison, *Nor the Years Contemn*, 156. It is inexplicable why Pell's detachment was still being ordered to Koepang when, expecting an imminent Japanese landing on Timor, the Australian command at Darwin the day before had ordered the evacuation of all RAAF personnel at Koepang to Darwin except for a small group to operate the radio station. That afternoon it had dispatched six Hudson bombers from Darwin to transport the personnel at Koepang back to Darwin (RAAF Operations Record Book, Form A-50, RAAF No. 2 G.R. Squadron, Koepang, February 18, 1942).

14. Oestreicher Memo; Oestreicher retrospective diary; Wiecks interview with Edmonds; Rorrison, *Nor the Years Contemn*, 154, 157.

15. Walking slowly northward, Suehr ran across no human beings, only "wild cattle and insects," and slept in trees at night. While crossing a lake he lost the supplies the A-24 had dropped, and he subsisted thereafter on berries and a wild frog he caught bare-handed After eventually reaching a railroad track, he was picked up by a train heading to Darwin. After arriving there he entered a hospital "for a long stay," then he was transferred in April 1942 to the 39th Pursuit Squadron, 35th Pursuit Group. (Cutler diary, May 18, 1942; Suehr to author, February 26, 2005).

16. "Seventeenth Pursuit History"; Coss to author, March 24, 1995.

17. Coss, Notebook No. 2; Coss to author, March 24, 1995.

18. Coss to author, March 24, 1995; Parker diary, February 15, 1942.

19. Coss to author, March 24, 1995; Weller, "Luck," Spring 1945, 43.

20. Coss to author, March 24, 1995; Hennon diary, February 15, 1942.

21. Coss to author, June 22, 1994, and March 24, 1995; Hennon diary, February 15, 1942.

22. "Seventeenth Pursuit History"; Hennon diary, February 15, 1942; Coss to author, March 24, 1995.

23. Coss to author, March 24, 1995; Hennon diary, February 15, 1942; Weller, "Luck," Spring 1945, 43.

24. Weller, "Luck," Spring 1945, 42, 43. Weller had just arrived in Batavia from Singapore with other evacuees.

25. Ibid., 43–44; Hennon diary, February 15, 1942.

26. Weller, "Luck," Spring 1945, 44–46.

27. Boer to author, April 4 and 6, 2006; Crane memoir.

28. Crane memoir.

29. FEAF headquarters, along with ABDAIR, had shifted from Lembang to Bandoeng on February 7. The building was previously occupied by the Royal Netherlands Military Academy, whose cadets had moved out the previous month ("General Brereton's Headquarters Diary," February 7, 1942; Boer to author, April 4 and 6, 2006; O'Donnell diary, February 7, 1942).

30. Weller, "Luck," Spring 1945, 42.

31. "General Brereton's Headquarters Diary," February 15, 1942; "91st Squadron," in McAfee, "The 27th Reports"; 5th Bomber Command, Journal, February 14 and 15, 1942. There is no documentation confirming that the purpose of summoning Backus was to have the 91st participate in the attack, but there could have been no other reason for bringing Backus's squadron all the way across Java to Batavia.

32. Weller, "Luck," Spring 1945, 46–47; "General Brereton's Headquarters Diary," February 16, 1942. The B-17s and LB-30s flew the mission, but under "almost complete instrument flying conditions," as the Headquarters Diary noted.

33. Hennon diary, February 16, 1942; Coss to author, March 24, 1995. This plane may have been the Hurricane of 258 Squadron evacuated from Palembang's P-2 field to Kemayoran, then ferried to Tjililitan for operational duties (Terence Kelly, *Hurricane over the Jungle,* 162).

34. Cull, *Hurricanes over Singapore,* 151; Launder, *College Campus in the Sky,* 36; Launder to author, February 6, 2006; "91st Squadron," in McAfee, "The 27th Reports."

35. Coss to author, March 24, 1995.

36. Ibid.; "Seventeenth Pursuit History," doc. 1927; Hennon diary, February 17, 1942; "Youngsters Get Distinguished Service Award," INS, April 7, 1942; "General Brereton's Headquarters Diary," February 17, 1942. The 17th Pursuit history gives take-off at 0630, but Hennon's diary states it was "at about 09:00 or 10:00," which relates better with the 1020 attack time of Brereton's headquarters diary. The Type 97 "Nate" fighters were from the Japanese army's 11th Sentai, which had advanced to Palembang to protect the Moesi River anchorage and oil refineries (Army Forces Far East, *Java-Sumatra Air Operations Record [December 1941–March 1942],* Japanese Monograph No. 69, 51).

37. Shores and Cull with Izawa, *Bloody Shambles,* 2:197–98; "Seventeenth Pursuit History"; Hennon diary, February 17, 1942; "General Brereton's Headquarters Diary," February 17, 1942.

38. Shores and Cull with Izawa, *Bloody Shambles,* 2:197; Coss to author, March 24, 1995; "Seventeenth Pursuit History"; Hennon diary, February 17, 1942; "Youngsters"; "General Brereton's Headquarters Diary," February 17, 1942; Weller, "Luck," Spring 1945, 47.

39. Coss to author, March 24, 1995; Coss, "Notes," 1943; "Youngsters."

40. Hennon diary, February 17, 1942; "General Brereton's Headquarters Diary," February 17, 1942; "Youngsters."

41. Weller, "Luck," Spring 1945, 47; Shores and Cull with Izawa, *Bloody Shambles,* 2:198.

42. Coss to author, March 24, 1995; Hennon diary, February 17, 1942.

43. Coss to author, March 24, 1995; Mahony flight log, February 17, 1942.

46. Hennon diary, February 17, 1942.

45. "Seventeenth Pursuit History"; Hennon diary, February 17, 1942; Weller, "Luck," Spring 1945, 47; "General Brereton's Headquarters Diary," February 17, 1942; "Youngsters." The INS story ("Youngsters") gives five Type 97s shot down, but "Seventeenth Pursuit History" and "General Brereton's Headquarters Diary" list four only. Hennon (in the INS story) credits himself with a Type 97, too, but not Kiser or Egenes, although the Fifth Air Force Fighter Command later credited Kiser with a "Zero" this day. In actuality, only one of the six Nates was lost, and its pilot bailed out safely. The Japanese pilots claimed three P-40s shot down (Shores and Cull with Izawa, *Bloody Shambles,* 2:198; Army Forces Far East, *Java-Sumatra Air Operations,* 52; Boer, *De Luchtstrijd om Indie,* 109).

46. Coss to author, March 24, 1995; Hennon diary, February 17, 1942; Mahony flight log, February 17, 1942; "Seventeenth Pursuit History." The 91st Bomb Squadron did not fly the mission, evidently because of their inability to install bomb adaptors on the A-24s. They stopped briefly this day at Andir on their way to Singosari Field (Launder to author, February 6, 2006; "91st Squadron," in McAfee, "The 27th Reports).

47. Coss to author, March 24, 1995; Mahony flight log, February 18, 1942; "General Brereton's Headquarters Diary," February 18, 1942; "Seventeenth Pursuit History."

48. Hennon diary, February 17 and 18, 1942.

49. Hague diary, February 16, 1942.

50. Oliver diary, February 15, 1942; Spence Johnson diary, February 16, 1942.

51. Badura and Gambonini diaries, February 16, 1942.

52. "Seventeenth Pursuit History"; Geurtz to Casius, March 26, 1978; Fisher interview with Edmonds, May 27, 1942; Fisher, talk to G-4 officers, WDGDS, Washington, D.C., March 20, 1942, in FDR Presidential Library; Fisher, "Summary of Interceptor Activity," Melbourne, August 1942; Weller, "Luck," Spring 1945, 48; Boer to author, October 18, 25, 27, and 29, 2007. Officially, Fisher was a staff member of Ente Van Gils, but the ADC commander had been instructed by the Dutch divisional commander not to interfere with fighter operations and to leave fighter control to Fisher (Boer to author, October 25, 2007).

53. Coss, "Notes," 1943.

54. Oliver, Parker, and Gambonini diaries, February 17, 1942; Gambonini flight log, February 17, 1942.

55. Parker diary, February 18, 1942; Brereton, *Diaries,* 94.

56. Hague and Parker diaries, February 18, 1942.

57. Hague diary, February 18, 1942.

58. Gambonini diary, February 18, 1942; Gambonini unpublished foreword to Morehead, *In My Sights.*

59. Blanton taped narrative, 1993; Gambonini unpublished foreword; "Seventeenth Pursuit History," doc. 1927. The 17th Pursuit history gives "approximately 1150" as the

time of the interception, vs. 1158 (1328 Tokyo time) in Japanese records (Izawa, "Rikko and Gingga, 71).

60. The time of interception is that of Japanese records converted to Soerabaja time (Izawa, "Rikko and Gingga," 72).

61. Gambonini diary, February 18, 1942; Gambonini unpublished foreword.

62. Weller, "Luck," Spring 1945, 51–52; Blanton taped narrative, 1993.

63. Gambonini diary and flight log, February 18, 1942; Gambonini unpublished foreword.

64. Ben Irvin Silver Star Citation; Gambonini, Parker, and Oliver diaries, February 18, 1942; "Seventeenth Pursuit History"; list of Fifth Air Force confirmed victories for February 18, 1942, in "All 5th Ftr. Comd. Confirmed Victories, 7 Dec. 1941–14 August 1945," decimal file 731.375, AFHRA. In the first Japanese attack since February 9, twenty-one Betty bombers of the Takao Kokutai had set out from Kendari on a mission to bomb Soerabaja harbor. The first *chutai* of nine missed the rendezvous with the eight escorting Zeros of the Tainan Kokutai, proceeding from Borneo, and arrived over the target alone. In the attack by the P-40s beginning at 1158 (1328 Tokyo time), the tail-end plane was shot down at 1202, while the lead plane of the second *shotai* (three planes) of one of the other two *chutai* (evidently of six planes each only) was also downed (at 1212) by the P-40s. A third Betty was so badly damaged by a P-40 that it crashed in the sea on the return flight. A fourth bomber was destroyed by a direct hit from an antiaircraft battery after dropping its bombs. Nine others sustained damage in the attacks, including one that made it back with 150 bullet holes and two dead and two wounded crew. In their bombing of Soerabaja harbor the Bettys sank the old Dutch cruiser *Soerabaja,* a submarine, and a few small vessels. The Zeros—none of which were lost—had gone on and strafed Maospati Field at Madioen after completing their escort duty (Izawa, "Rikko and Gingga," 71–72; Shores and Cull with Izawa, *Bloody Shambles,* 2:201; Tagaya, *Mitsubishi Type 1 Rikko,* 33–34).

65. Spence Johnson diary, February 18, 1942; Blanton taped narrative, 1993.

66. Eckley, memoir, "A Pilot's Story"; Kent diary, February 18, 1942; "Diary of the 19th Bomb Group," February 18, 1942; Eckley memoir; caption for Eckley's "Singosari Savior" painting. The "railroad track" turned out to be white crushed coral lined with black oil to simulate a railroad bed, an effort to mislead the Japanese attackers.

67. Birkett to author, September 6, 2004; www.home.st.net.au/~dunn/ozcrashes/wa26.htm; radiogram, Housel, S-3, USAFIA, to RAAF Pearce and Perth, February 17, 1942, in box T1611, RG 338, NARA.

68. Radiogram, USAFIA Hq to Operations Officer, Port Pirie, February 15, 1942; radiogram, Barnes to CO, Perth, February 16, 1942, both in box T1611, RG 338, NARA. It is assumed Keenan left Port Pirie on February 14 for the two-day flight.

69. Wilhite memoir, 210.

70. Radiogram, Barnes to CO, Base Section 5, Perth, February 18, 1942, and radiogram, Barnes to Brett, February 19, 1942, both in box T1611, RG 338, NARA.

71. "Operations Java Campaign: Pilots of the 13th and 33rd Squadrons Wrecked or Aircraft Out on the Way to USS *Langley* and from Port Pirie to Darwin," Brisbane, February 24, 1942.; Ferguson and Pascalis, *Protect and Avenge,* 21; radiogram, Housel

to CO, RAAF Station Richmond, February 18, 1942, in box T1611, RG 338, NARA. The eight pilots of the 13th Pursuit (Provisional) who would not be boarding the *Langley* because of accidents were Ken Glassburn, Wilfred Jones, Robert Hazard, William Levitan, Earl Kingsley, William Herbert, Paul Magre, and Harry Pressfield.

72. McDowell, *49th Fighter Group*, 4. It was evidently Col. Ross Hoyt, air officer of USAFIA in Melbourne, who had ordered Morrissey detached for this assignment. Hoyt himself had flown to Perth earlier to make the arrangements (Hoyt, "MacArthur—Manila to Melbourne," in draft memoir, IRIS 34472, AFHRA).

73. Head diary, February 16, 1942.

74. Ibid., February 17, 1942. At 1152 thirty-three Mitsubishi Type 96 "Nell" bombers attacked the Koepang area and also dropped propaganda leaflets warning the natives not to aid the Dutch and threatening anyone who assisted in demolition work (radiogram, Merle-Smith to MILID, February 18, 1942, in box T1611, RG 338, NARA).

75. Head diary, February 18, 1942; Gillison, *Royal Australian Air Force*, 421.

76. Head diary, February 18, 1942; Head interview; Childress to mother, March 9, 1942; Gillison, *Royal Australian Air Force*, 421; Powell, *The Shadow's Edge*, 64; RAAF Operations Record Book, A-50 Form, RAAF No. 2 G.R. Squadron, Koepang, February 19, 1942.

77. Coleman interview; Dutton diary, February 16, 1942; Boer to author, July 24, 2006.

CHAPTER 10

1. RAAF Operations Record Book, Form A-50, No. 2 G.R. Squadron, Koepang, entry for February 19, 1942; Childress to mother, March 9, 1942; Head diary, February 19, 1942.

2. McMahon memoir; Oestreicher memo to Wurtsmith.

3. McMahon memoir.

4. Ibid., Rorrison, *Nor the Years Contemn*, 159.

5. McMahon memoir. The crew chief had spotted Zeros from the carrier *Akagi* engaging Oestreicher's flight from 1000 ("*Akagi* Kodocho," February 19, 1942, via Jim Sawruk).

6. Rorrison, *Nor the Years Contemn*, 159.

7. McMahon memoir.

8. McMahon recalled the Zeros attacking him as six in number. Japanese records indicate two *shotai* of six Zeros from the carrier *Kaga* had descended to attack Pell's flight on the ground at 1005 ("*Kaga* Kodocho," February 19, 1942, via Jim Sawruk).

9. McMahon to author, March 2, 1994.

10. Oestreicher memo to Wurtsmith. Oestreicher in his report to Wurtsmith, reproducing RAAF information, and Wiecks in his 1944 interview with Walter D. Edmonds maintain that Peres was still with the others as the first element leader, with Perry on his wing at this time, but McMahon distinctly recalls that Peres had come in to land before the Zeros' attack on the field (Cranston, "Ten Men Alone," *Canberra Times*, February 19, 1992). In his interview with Douglas Lockwood in Australia in the early

1960s, McMahon gave the same account regarding Peres's alerting him from the vehicle, but Lockwood evidently didn't believe McMahon's assertion that it was Peres and in his book only identified him as "an airman" (Lockwood, *Australia's Pearl Harbor*, 36). If Peres had left the patrol at about 0940–0950, he could have been on the ground at the time McMahon mentions he saw him. The discovery of Peres's crashed plane (see chapter 11) near those of Pell's flight members would seem to confirm that Peres had indeed taken off with Pell's group during the attack on the field.

11. Bill Walker account related to McMahon, in McMahon to author, June 12, 1994. Oestreicher in his 1942 memo to Wurtsmith maintained as his own experience that he spotted a single Zero, diving on the formation from two thousand feet higher, which broke up the formation and forced the Americans to dive. Oestreicher yelled "Zeros, Zeros, Zeros" before going into his dive. Climbing back into the sun, he was able to get a short burst into one of the Zeros, which rolled in its climb and fired at Oestreicher. He spun out, regaining control at about four thousand feet. Spotting eighteen more Japanese at about twenty-thousand feet, he radioed his B flight and advised the pilots to head for the clouds south of Darwin. This account does not jibe with those of the two surviving pilots of B flight: Wiecks, who does not mention Oestreicher at all in his interview, and Walker, who provided McMahon with a different account.

12. Walker account related to McMahon, in McMahon to author, June 12, 1994. Walker had been attacked by a nine-plane *chutai* of Zeros from the *Akagi* that claimed it encountered and shot down four P-40s between 1000 and 1010 ("*Akagi* Kodocho," February 19, 1942, via Jim Sawruk).

13. Wiecks interview with Edmonds; Wiecks account related to McMahon in McMahon to author, March 2, 1994. An Australian East Point artillery spotter situated in a thirty-foot watchtower saw Wiecks hit the water about ten miles out to sea, according to his range finding equipment (Johnston to author, January 31, 2007).

14. Wiecks interview with Edmonds. According to the "*Akagi* Kodocho," he would have been shot down some ten to fifteen minutes later. However, if his time of 0955 is correct, then he would have been downed by Zeros of the *Kaga* instead, which reported "controlling the air over Darwin" from 1015 but not engaging in combat ("*Kaga* Kodocho," February 19, 1942, via Jim Sawruk).

15. Wiecks account related to McMahon, in McMahon to author, March 2, 1994. Perry crashed into the sea about one mile offshore of Casuarina Beach (Johnston to author, January 31, 2007).

16. Recollection of the event as witnessed by Bert Oakes, 2/4 Pioneer Battalion, via Johnston to author, January 31, 2007. Hughes's body was never officially recovered. He is still listed as missing in action.

17. McMahon to author, March 2, 1994; Freake to Johnston, March 20, 2003; Ruwoldt interview, at www.australiansatwarfilmarchive.gov.au/aafwa/interviews/1596.aspx. Freake and Ruwoldt witnessed the combat from their nearby machine gun positions.

18. Rice account related to McMahon, in McMahon memoir; Johnston to author, May 27, 2005; Oestreicher memo to Wurtsmith.

19. John Glover account related to McMahon, in McMahon memoir. Only one Zero was lost in the attack, hit by machine gun fire and down on Melville Island.

20. Ibid.; McMahon to author, June 12, 1994.

21. Glover account related to McMahon, in McMahon memoir; Oestreicher memo to Wurtsmith.

22. McMahon memoir.

23. McMahon recalled the strafers of the PBY as two-seat aircraft, but the PBY crew recognized them as Zeros (Messimer, *In the Hands of Fate*, 248–49).

24. McMahon memoir; McMahon telephone interview.

25. McMahon memoir; see Map 7.

26. Oestreicher retrospective diary.

27. Ibid.; Oestreicher memo to Wurtsmith.

28. Oestreicher retrospective diary and Oestreicher memo to Wurtsmith. Oestreicher evidently attacked two D3A "Vals" from the carrier *Soryu*. Japanese records indicate that a *shotai* of three *Soryu* Vals was attacked by a single enemy aircraft that scored six hits on the first and third ships in the formation (Sawruk to author, January 28, 2005, citing the *kodo chosho* [combat log] reports for the four carriers of the Darwin attack). The heavily damaged Val of P.O.1c Takeshi Yamada ditched in the Timor Sea on its return, and Yamada and his crewman were rescued by a destroyer (http://www.J-aircraft.org posting by Bernard Baeza, May 15, 2009, citing *kodo chosho* for the carrier *Soryu*). The only Val shot down during the raid was that of W.O. Katsuyoshi Tsuru of the *Kaga*, which was hit by antiaircraft fire over Darwin Harbor and crashed into the sea (Smith, *Fist from the Sky*, 184–85).

29. Oestreicher retrospective diary and Oestreicher memo to Wurtsmith.

30. Oestreicher retrospective diary.

31. Freake to Johnston, March 20, 2003; Johnston to author, January 31, 2007.

32. Bushby to Johnston, undated.

33. George to Johnston, March 2002.

34. Undated letter in Pell family memorabilia.

35. Lockwood, *Australia's Pearl Harbor*, 133–34.

36. Lockwood: 134, 136.

37. Bujold to author, February 25, 1997; Lockwood, *Australia's Pearl Harbor*, 133; Shores and Cull with Izawa, *Bloody Shambles*, 2:180–81.

38. Head diary, February 19, 1942; Childress to mother, March 9, 1942. The attackers were twenty-seven Bettys of the Kanoya Kokutai and twenty-seven Nells of the 1st Kokutai, flying from Kendari. They concentrated their attack on the runways and installations at the RAAF field (Tagaya, *Mitsubishi Type 1 Rikko*, 34; Izawa, "Rikko and Gingga," 72; Shores and Cull with Izawa, *Bloody Shambles*, 2:180).

39. Bujold to author, February 25, 1997; Rorrison, *Nor the Years Contemn*, 181.

40. Wilhite memoir, 212.

41. Ibid., 213.

42. Ibid.; Pingree to author, August 14, 2004. Two days later a new tire arrived for Wilhite's ship, and the following day orders were received from USAFIA in Melbourne for Wilhite to fly to Laverton, where he was to pick up some B-17 parts and transport them to Archerfield, outside Brisbane. He would not be going to Java after all (radiogram 3-33, Barnes, USAFIA, to CO, Port Pirie, February 22, 1942, in T1611, RG 338, NARA).

43. Hague diary, February 19, 1942; Dull, *Battle History,* 56.

44. Dull, *Battle History,* 56; "Diary of the 19th Bomb Group," February 19, 1942; "General Brereton's Headquarters Diary," February 19, 1942; Hague diary, February 19, 1942; McAfee, "The 27th Reports."

45. Fifth Air Force, "Report of the 17th Pursuit Squadron (Provisional) in Java," n.d. (ca. 1942), in "History of the 5th Air Force" (hereafter cited as "Report of the 17th Pursuit"); "Diary of the 19th Bomb Group," February 19, 1942. Paul Gambonini, who was not at the field, indicated in his diary that the takeoff was "about 11:00," but the Soerabaja air raid alarm didn't go off until 1205, according to "Diary of the 19th Bomb Group," February 19, 1942.

46. "Report of the 17th Pursuit"; Hennon diary, February 19, 1942; Shores and Cull with Izawa, *Bloody Shambles,* 2:210. Japanese records indicate that the eighteen Rikko turned back because of "adverse weather" (Shores and Cull with Izawa, *Bloody Shambles,* 2:210; Izawa, "Rikko and Gingga," 72).

47. Hague diary, February 23, 1942.

48. Blanton taped narrative, 1993. Blanton believed there may have been another nine Zeros above the group that attacked. Japanese records do indicate that two *chutai* of nine Zeros each had attacked the P-40s (Shores and Cull with Izawa, *Bloody Shambles,* 2:210–11).

49. Blanton taped narrative, 1993. Blanton may have shot down the leader of the nine-plane formation, Lt. Masao Asai, the only Japanese pilot lost in the engagement (Shores and Cull with Izawa, *Bloody Shambles,* 2:210).

50. Blanton taped narrative, 1993; White, *Queens,* 191; Geurtz to author, March 28, 1994. Blanton had crash-landed offshore near the village of Paciran, about twenty-five miles to the northwest of Soerabaja.

51. Blanton taped narrative, 1993.

52. Mahony and Oliver flight logs; "Report of the 17th Pursuit"; Spence Johnson diary, February 19, 1942. Days later, Dwight Muckley identified Fields's body after it had been taken to Soerabaja for burial (Hague diary, February 23, 1942). One account indicated that bullet holes were found in his parachute shroud and one in his head (Weller, "Luck," Spring 1945, 61).

53. Oliver diary, February 19, 1942; Oliver to author, August 7, 1993; Hague diary, February 23, 1942.

54. Mahony flight log, February 19, 1942; "General Brereton's Headquarters Diary," February 19, 1942; Hennon diary, February 19, 1942. Only one Zero was lost, that of Asai, who failed to return, according to Japanese records. The eighteen Japanese pilots claimed fourteen shot down and three probables, with pilots in each of the two *chutai* putting in for seven victories, a clear case of double counting (Shores and Cull with Izawa, *Bloody Shambles,* 2:210).

55. Blanton taped narrative, 1993; Hennon diary, February 19, 1942.

56. McMahon to author, June 12, 1994; McMahon memoir; Oestreicher memo to Wurtsmith.

57. McMahon to author, June 12, 1994; McMahon memoir; Oestreicher memo to Wurtsmith; Alford to author, April 12, 2008. Walker's ship was evidently shot up by a

shotai of three Zeros off the *Kaga* that reported attacking five (*sic*) P-40s on the ground at 1027 ("*Kaga* Kodocho," February 19, 1942, via Jim Sawruk).

58. Childress to mother, March 9, 1942; Head diary, February 19, 1942; Head interview.

59. Oestreicher retrospective diary.

CHAPTER 11

1. McDowell, *49th Fighter Group,* 4; Robert E. Phillips chronology, February 19 and 20, 1942; Dix memoir, March 24, 1994; Messimer, *In the Hands of Fate,* 34.

2. McDowell, *49th Fighter Group,* 4; USS *Phoenix,* "War Diary," February 19, 1942, in RG 338, NARA; Radiogram, Brett to ABDACOM for Naiden, February 27, 1942, in box T1611, RG 338, NARA.

3. Messimer, *In the Hands of Fate,* 16, 34; Gerald Dix, "Twenty Three Years of Military Service as a Fighter Pilot," memoir, no date (ca. 1995).

4. Messimer, *In the Hands of Fate,* 35; Wahl and Lamb, "A Report on the Fate of the *Edsall* and the 42 USAAC *Langley* Survivors," 1988; Radiogram, Brett to ABDACOM for Naiden, February 27, 1942, in box T1611, RG 338, NARA. Only seven of the twelve replacements have been identified as Headquarters, 35th Group, men, while another was from Headquarters, 20th Pursuit Group and two others from the 16th Pursuit Squadron, 51st Group, who may not have been replacements at all. The units of two of the men are unknown. See Appendix Table 14 for names.

5. McDowell, *49th Fighter Group,* 4. USAFIA headquarters on February 18 had ordered Wagner to report back immediately to Laverton Field, Melbourne, but evidently Wagner did not receive the message until the morning of the twentieth (radiogram, Barnes to CO, Base Section 5, Perth, February 18, 1942, in box T1611, RG 338, NARA).

6. Coss to author, February 11, 1996; Radiogram, Brett to AGWAR, February 23, 1942, in box T1597, RG 338, NARA.

7. Coss to author, February 11, 1996.

8. Ibid.

9. 5th Bomber Command, Journal, February 20, 1942. The A-24s had taken off from Singosari at 0645 after their Dutch bombs had—with difficulty—been loaded on their racks.

10. Coss to author, February 11, 1996; Hayes diary, February 20, 1942; Weller, "Luck," Summer 1945, 125; "Seventeenth Pursuit History," doc. 1927.

11. Coss to author, February 11, 1996. The attacking Zeros were from one of two groups of seven 3rd Kokutai A6M2s that had taken off from Makassar, Celebes (Shores and Cull with Izawa, *Bloody Shambles,* 2:212).

12. Hayes interview, April 16 and 17, 1994; Guttman, "American Ace," 37; 5th Bomber Command, Journal, February 20, 1942.

13. Joseph Kruzel, Purple Heart citation. Kruzel's victim was apparently S1c Tomikichi Ohtsuki, who had left the other two in his *shotai* to reconnoiter over the Japanese cruiser *Nagara* and a destroyer in the Bali invasion force (Shores and Cull with Izawa, *Bloody Shambles,* 2:212).

14. Oliver to author, August 7, 1993. None of the Japanese ships was damaged or sunk by either the A-24s or LB-30s, according to Japanese records.

15. Oliver to author, August 7, 1993.

16. Spence Johnson diary, February 20, 1942.

17. George E. Kiser to Adjutant Generals Department, memo, February 12, 1943, Kiser collection.

18. Gallienne account related to fellow POW Walter Haines, in Haines to author, January 18, 2007.

19. Coss to author, February 11, 1996.

20. Ibid.; Hoskyn and Oliver flight logs (for estimated time of return to Ngoro).

21. Hague and Hayes diaries, February 20, 1942; Hayes interview, April 16 and 17, 1994; Coss to author, April 17, 1994.

22. Gambonini and Parker diaries, February 20, 1942; "Report of the 17th Pursuit"; Kiser to Adjutant Generals Department, memo, February 12, 1943.

23. Hennon diary, February 20, 1942, and February 5–March 31, 1942 summary; "Report of the 17th Pursuit"; Hoskyn flight log, February 20, 1942. Japanese records indicate only one Zero was shot down, the pilot killed (Hata and Izawa, *Japanese Naval Aces*, 376).

24. Coss to author, February 11, 1996; Hennon diary, February 20, 1942.

25. Kemp Tolley, *Cruise of the* Lanikai; USS *Lanikai* log, February 20, 1942.

26. Spence Johnson diary, February 20, 1942; Tolley, *Cruise*, 199–200; *Lanikai* log, February 20, 1942.

27. Hague diary, February 17 (*sic*), 1942; Tolley to author, December 2, 1995.

28. Tolley, *Cruise*, 200; *Lanikai* log, February 20, 1942.

29. McMahon to author, March 2, 1994; Max Wiecks, "Award of Purple Heart," to Air Force Reference Branch, July 29, 1997.

30. Wiecks interview with Edmonds.

31. Witney to Johnston, August 8, 2001; Oestreicher memo to Wurtsmith; McMahon memoir; Johnston to author, August 31, 2007.

32. The skeletal remains of Peres were not found until September 7, 1942, still in his P-40E No. 189. Aborigines had found the wreck of the plane and Peres's body in an inaccessible part of their sacred area north of Shoal Bay Coastal Reserve, sixteen miles northeast of the RAAF airdrome. Peres could only be identified by engravings on the Bulova watch he still wore (Rorrison, *Nor the Years Contemn,* 160; diary of cattle owners Oscar and Evan Herbert, September 5–7, 1942, via Shane Johnston). Hughes is also still listed as missing in action by the Adjutant General's Department. A P-40E believed to have been piloted by Perry was seen hitting the water about one mile off the Casuarina Beach area by Australian army personnel stationed in the nearby Nightcliff area (Johnston to author, June 3, 2009).

33. McMahon to author, June 12, 1994.

34. Ibid.; Lockwood, *Australia's Pearl Harbor,* 134–35.

35. McMahon to author, June 12, 1994.

36. Weller, "Luck," Summer 1945, 127; "Seventeenth Pursuit History," doc. 1927; Oliver diary, February 20, 1942. "Seventeenth Pursuit History" notes that Johnson had

called in February 20, but if so, it must have been in the evening, as he was on the beach at Rajeg Wesi all day. Only years later, on Gallienne's release as a POW after the war, was it learned that he had bailed out after being shot down. After landing in the water he was dragged up on the beach by natives and put in a pigsty. Some days later he was found by an American doctor, who administered to his facial burns and eye lost in the fire of his P-40. He was eventually captured by the Japanese (Gallienne account to Walter Haines, in Haines to author, January 18, 2007).

37. Parker diary, February 20, 1942; "Seventeenth Pursuit History," doc. 1927; "Diary of the 19th Bomb Group," entry for February 20, 1942. At 1552, nine Zeros of the Tainan Kokutai flying from newly occupied Denpasar Field attacked Singosari Field without warning. As four remained overhead as cover, the other five strafed the base for about five minutes, setting five of the B-17Es on fire, of which three were completely destroyed (5th Bomber Command, Journal, and "Diary of the 19th Bomb Group," entry for February 20, 1942; "Tainan Kokutai Kodocho," February 20, 1942, via Tagaya to author, March 6, 2005; Shores and Cull with Izawa, *Bloody Shambles*, 2:213).

38. Gambonini diary, February 20, 1942; Gambonini flight log, February 20, 1942.

39. "Arizona Flier's Close Call, Other Thrills Told by Vet," Associated Press, April 10, 1943; Weller, "Luck," Spring 1945, 57–58.

40. Hennon and Parker diaries, February 20, 1942; Les Johnsen diary, no date.

41. Tolley, *Cruise*, 200; *Lanikai* log, February 20, 1942. Johnson would not arrive back at Ngoro until February 23, "after having been running several days," as he recorded in his diary that day.

42. Translation of letter of C. D. van der Herst, Departement van Opsporingsdienst van Overleden, Batavia, July 4, 1947, and E. N. Rundle, RAAF, "Report on Death of Unknown Marking by Sgt. Christian Bram, Royal Dutch Navy," October 8, 1945, both in Series A705, Control Symbol 166/1/105, NAA, via Birkett to author, February 11, 2006. Bram did not indicate whether the pilot's body was found in his parachute or was removed from his crashed plane. In a memorandum of June 7, 1948, the RAAF reported that the body, identified as that of USAAF Capt. Charles A. Sprague, was disinterred from the (Nusa Penida) grave by a Captain McNamar and was transported to Calcutta for burial ([Unidentified] Missing U.S. Aircraft, Series A9845, Control Symbol 307, Item Barcode 6950647, NAA via Birkett to author, February 11, 2006). There is nothing in U.S. records indicating the circumstances of death of Sprague or of recovery of his remains or of his final burial site, although George Weller in a letter to Walter D. Edmonds, March 14, 1947, seems to have correct information (Edmonds, *They Fought*, 396). According to the *West Point Assembly*, March 1992 (p. 158), Sprague's body was disinterred from its Calcutta grave and returned "home" to its final resting place at West Point.

CHAPTER 12

1. Parker diary, February 21, 1942; "Seventeenth Pursuit History." Mahony had been promoted to captain on February 4.

2. Parker diary, February 21, 1942; Weller, "Luck," Summer 1945, 130; "Seventeenth Pursuit History"; Pehl to author, February 10, 1994. Parker is not cited in the "Seven-

teenth Pursuit History" as a member of B flight, with Spence Johnson—not at Ngoro this day—erroneously included instead. The Betty bombers sighted were part of the force of twenty-one from the Takao Kokutai on the Soerabaja mission. Since they are recorded in Japanese records as having bombed Soerabaja harbor, damaging a cruiser and a merchant ship, it would appear that they were on their return home rather than seeking to avoid interception by the P-40s on the flight to the target, as Parker had assumed (Izawa, "Rikko and Gingga," 73).

3. Oliver to author, August 7, 1993.

4. Ibid.; Oliver diary, February 21, 1942; McWherter to Mr. and Mrs. Hoskyn, February 19, 1943. The "Seventeenth Pursuit History" erroneously cites Andy Reynolds and Bill Turner as forming the second element of Coss's flight, whereas it was actually made up of Gene Wahl and Wally Hoskyn, according to Oliver's diary.

5. Oliver to author, August 7, 1993; McWherter to Mr. and Mrs. Hoskyn, February 19, 1943.

6. "Diary of the 19th Bomb Group," entry for February 21, 1942. Failure to fly the mission did not make any difference anyway, as the B-17s returned unmolested by Zeros. However, after landing, three Zeros did show up over the field in a strafing attack but inflicted no damage. Japanese records report that the second *chutai* of the 3rd Kokutai flew to Singosari after its attack on the P-40s, claiming one B-17 flamed and two others damaged in its strafing passes. Six Zeros of the 3rd Kokutai and six from the Tainan Kokutai, all flying from the newly seized Bali field, had escorted twenty-one Betty bombers of the Takao Kokutai from Balikpapan on the Soerabaja mission. Apparently one group of the Zeros had attacked A and B flights and the other C and D flights. The Zero pilots claimed six P-40s shot down, with another lost to fire from a Betty. The Japanese suffered only one loss: a Betty that had been hit and made a forced landing on the return trip—evidently the lone Betty attacked by Oliver, Wahl, and Hoskyn (Shores and Cull with Izawa, *Bloody Shambles*, 2:217).

7. Egenes to Larson, March 14, 1942.

8. Parker diary, February 21, 1942; Weller, "Luck," Summer 1945, 131; "Seventeenth Pursuit History."

9. McAfee diary, February 21, 1942.

10. Sanders diary, February 21 and 22, 1942. The *Holbrook* and other ships in the MS-5 convoy were delayed in departing because of a meeting in Melbourne between the USAFIA headquarters and the Royal Australian Navy on February 21 that resulted in new instructions on the destination of the convoy (USS *Phoenix*, "War Diary," entry for February 21, 1942).

11. USS *Phoenix*, "War Diary," February 22, 1942; Wahl and Lamb, "Report," 1988.

12. Sanders diary, February 22, 1942. Sanders need not have worried. Unknown to all except the captain of the escorting light cruiser USS *Phoenix*, the *Holbrook*, the *Duntroon*, and the other Australian MS-5 troopship, *Katoomba*, had received new orders the day before. With the *Phoenix* they were to sail to the "Burma area" instead of to Java (radiogram, Barnes to Brett, February 20, 1942, and radiogram, Barnes to USA Hq, Perth, February 21, 1942, both in box T1611, RG 338, NARA; USS *Phoenix*, "War Diary," February 21, 1942).

13. Bowles to Messimer, January 2, 1984, and August 21, 1989.

14. "Seventeenth Pursuit History"; "Diary of the 19th Bomb Group," entry for February 22, 1942. The "Seventeenth Pursuit History" indicates A flight was just "to cover the field," but it must have been referring to Singosari Field.

15. Parker and Gambonini diaries, February 22, 1942.

16. Parker diary, February 22 and 23, 1942; Gambonini diary, February 22, 1942; Hennon diary, February 21 and 22, 1942.

17. Weller, "Luck," Summer 1945, 130; Pehl, "Fighters to Plum," 11–19; McAfee diary, February 21, 1942.

18. Hennon diary, February 22, 1942; Shores and Cull with Izawa, *Bloody Shambles,* 2:219–20; 5th Bomber Command, Journal, February 22, 1942; "General Brereton's Headquarters Diary," February 22, 1942; "Seventeenth Pursuit History."

19. McWherter to Mr. and Mrs. Hoskyn.

20. Weller, "Luck," Summer 1945, 130–31.

21. Ibid., 131; Hennon diary, February 22, 1942; Military Personnel Records Center, Air Force Branch, "Statement of Military Service of Grant Mahony."

22. "Seventeenth Pursuit History."

23. Ibid.; Oliver diary and Oliver flight log, February 23, 1942; "Diary of the 19th Bomb Group," entry for February 23, 1942; "Takao Kokutai Kodocho," and "Tainan Kokutai Kodocho," February 23, 1942, via Tagaya to author, February 27, 2005. The nine Betty bombers of Takao Kokutai, escorted by nine Zeros of Tainan Kokutai, had taken off from newly occupied Denpasar Airfield on Bali on an attack mission against the 17th Pursuit's Ngoro Field, which apparently had been discovered a day or two earlier by Zeros flying over it. When the bombers were unexpectedly jumped by P-40s before reaching Ngoro, they changed their target to Singosari Field (Tainan and Takao Kokutai *kodochos,* February 23, 1942; Weller, "Luck," Winter 1944, 284). The "Seventeenth Pursuit History" is in error in recording that Hague, Kruzel, and Adkins were flying with McCallum in A flight: Hague did not fly this day, while Oliver's diary places Thompson and himself in McCallum's flight.

24. "Seventeenth Pursuit History"; Morehead, *In My Sights,* 73; Morehead to author, May 29, 1995; "Takao Kokutai Kodocho," February 23, 1942.

25. Morehead, *In My Sights,* 73–74; Morehead to author, May 29, 1995; Hague diary, February 23, 1942.

26. Kezar interview with Walter D. Edmonds and USAAF personnel; Morehead, *In My Sights,* 74.

27. Morehead, *In My Sights,* 74–75; "Diary of the 19th Bomb Group," entry for February 23, 1942.

28. Morehead, *In My Sights,* 75; Gambonini, Lund, and Morehead interview.

29. Kezar interview with Edmonds; "Diary of the 19th Bomb Group," entry for February 23, 1942.

30. Weller, "Luck," Summer 1945, 147; Ingram diary, February 22 (*sic*), 1942.

31. "Seventeenth Pursuit History"; Morehead to author, May 29, 1995.

32. Morehead to author, May 5, 1995. Records of the Takao Kokutai indicate that none of the nine G4M1s on the raid was shot down, although the lead aircraft in the

second three-plane *shotai* took eighty hits and had its left engine knocked out, while the *shotai*'s number two aircraft took nine hits and two others a couple of hits each during the twenty-minute combat with the P-40s. Concerned that the leader of the *shotai* had been badly wounded, the attack commander decided to dump the formation's bombs on Singosari Field and immediately led the nine ships back to their Bali field. All returned safely, including the Betty with the wounded officer that managed to limp back on one engine ("Takai Kokutai Kodocho," February 23, 1942, via Tagaya to author, January 1, 2002, and February 27, 2005).

33. Hague diary, February 23, 1942.

34. Sanders diary, February 23, 1942.

35. The *Langley* had left the convoy at 2315 on February 22, destination unknown, as directed by the captain of the *Phoenix* (Cavaye, "Report of Proceedings"). Evidently unknown to the convoy commander (and to Major Sanders), the *Phoenix* captain had received a dispatch at 2124 ordering him to direct the *Langley* to proceed to Tjilatjap, Java, "with all dispatch." At 2155, he signaled the *Langley* to comply with the directive (USS *Phoenix*, "War Diary," February 22, 1942).

36. Dix memoir, March 24, 1994.

37. Ibid.,; Dix, "Twenty Three Years," 4.

38. "Seventeenth Pursuit History"; Oliver, Gambonini, Parker, Hague, and Ingram diaries, February 23, 1942; Fisher, talk to G-4 Officers; Weller, "Luck," Summer 1945, 132. Coss had been promoted to captain on February 19 (U.S. Army, Adjutant General's Department, *Official Army Register, 1 January 1947*). The "Seventeenth Pursuit History" is erroneous in indicating that twenty officers were selected.

39. Weller, "Luck," Summer 1945, 132; Hague diary, February 23, 1942.

40. Weller, "Luck," Summer 1945, 132, 142–43; Coss to author, March 16, 1994; Blanton taped narrative, 1993; Ingram diary, February 23, 1942.

41. Parker and Hague diaries, February 23, 1942; Blanton taped narrative, 1993.

42. Hague diary, February 23, 1942; Parker diary, February 23 and 24, 1942; Blanton taped narratives, 1993 and 1994.

43. Ingram and Hague diaries, February 24, 1942.

44. Ingram, Parker, and Oliver diaries, February 24, 1942; Coss to author, January 18, 1994; "S-3 Diary for 7th Bombardment Group," February 24, 1942.

45. Hague and Hayes diaries, February 24, 1942; Hayes interview, April 16 and 17, 1994; Guerrero to author, November 29, 2002. The Malang–Jogjakarta train covered 240 miles, taking them south first, then west to Blitar before heading north to skirt Mount Liman and on to Kediri and Kertosono, where they picked up the route followed by the others.

46. Hayes diary, February 24, 1942; Hayes interview; Hague diary, February 25, 1942.

CHAPTER 13

1. Gambonini diary, February 24, 1942; "Seventeenth Pursuit History."

2. "Seventeenth Pursuit History," doc. 1927; Gambonini diary, February 24, 1942; Tagaya to author, January 1, 2002. The 17th Pursuit history includes B. J. Oliver and

George Parker in A and D flights, respectively, but the two had left Ngoro the day before. The history also indicates the P-40s approached Soerabaja at twenty-one thousand feet, but Gambonini as a participant records the altitude as twenty-seven thousand feet. According to Japanese records, the twenty-four Takao Kokutai G4M1s attacked shipping in Soerabaja harbor in two waves. The first *chutai* reported combat with four P-40s, which are assumed here to have been those of Kiser's B flight. The nine escorting Zeros—six from the 3rd Kokutai and three from Tainan Kokutai—intercepted the P-40s but did not succeed in downing any (Tagaya to author, January 1, 2002; Shores and Cull with Izawa, *Bloody Shambles*, 2:226).

3. Mahony flight log, February 23 (*sic*), 1942; Gambonini flight log, February 24, 1942; Shores and Cull with Izawa, *Bloody Shambles*, 2:226; "Seventeenth Pursuit History" (for P-40 status figures). None of the twenty-four G4M1s were lost, although one returned with a crewman who was slightly wounded in the combat with the P-40s (Tagaya to author, January 1, 2002).

4. Weller, "Luck," Spring 1945, 57, and Summer 1945, 133.

5. Gambonini and Hennon diaries, February 24, 1942; "Seventeenth Pursuit History"; Parker diary, February 25, 1942; Weller, "Luck," Summer 1945, 134. "Seventeenth Pursuit History" failed to mention the evacuation of two of the pilots and erroneously reported sixteen enlisted men ordered out instead of the twenty-five recorded by Parker.

6. Radiogram, Brett to AGWAR, February 23, 1942, in box T1597, RG 338, NARA; Burnside to author, October 26, 2002; Weller, "Luck," Summer 1945, 134; "Seventeenth Pursuit History."

7. "Seventeenth Pursuit History," docs. 1932–33; Nichols memoir; Nichols to author, February 17, 1997.

8. Gambonini diary, February 24, 1942; "Reminiscences of Pilots Who Knew Bud"; Weller, "Luck," Winter 1944, 284. Saburo Sakai of the Tainan Kokutai claimed he had discovered the field on February 19 after diverting to nearby Djombang before his return to base following an escort mission to Soerabaja (Sakai, with Caidin and Saito, *Samurai*, 93; Shores and Cull with Izawa, *Bloody Shambles*, 2:210). Four days later, nine G4M1s of the Takao Kokutai were ordered to bomb Ngoro Field, but they didn't reach their destination after being attacked by P-40s over Malang (Tagaya to author, February 27, 2005).

9. McAfee diary, February 25, 1942. After an aborted takeoff the night before, because of an engine failure McAfee, Bender, and Stafford, as well as Arie Geurtz's wife and infant daughter plus a pregnant friend, finally managed to leave at 0120 on the night of February 27–28 in the repaired C-53 piloted by Lieutenants Moore and Crandell, and they reached Darwin safely (McAfee diary, February 27 and 28, 1942; Bender memoir; Geurtz to Casius, March 4, 1978; Geurtz memoir, 25–28).

10. "Seventeenth Pursuit History"; Gambonini and Hennon diaries, February 25, 1942.

11. Ibid.; Weller, "Luck," Summer 1945, 135; Gerald McCallum, Distinguished Service Cross citation; Shores and Cull with Izawa, *Bloody Shambles*, 2:231; Hennon diary, February 25, 1942.

12. "Seventeenth Pursuit History"; Gambonini diary, February 25, 1942; Weller, "Luck," Summer 1945, 135.

13. Weller, "Luck," Summer 1945, 135; "Seventeenth Pursuit History." None of the Zeros were lost in the combat with the P-40s. On the contrary, their Tainan Kokutai pilots claimed eight of the thirteen (sic) P-40s shot down, of which four were uncertain. One of the G4M1s of the Takao Kokutai was hit by antiaircraft fire in their attack on shipping in Soerabaja harbor but returned to base on one engine (Tagaya to author, January 1, 2002).

14. "Seventeenth Pursuit History"; Hennon diary, February 25, 1942.

15. Boer to author, October 16, 2006; "Seventeenth Pursuit History." The 17th Pursuit history and the diaries of Hennon, Gambonini, and Les Johnsen mention the arrival of the Brewsters on the following day, not on the twenty-fifth, and all in one group. The Dutch account used here is accepted as correct. The Dutch pilots were being assigned to provide additional fighter protection for the warships of the Allied Combined Striking Force in Soerabaja port to oppose the Japanese invasion force believed heading for East Java (Boer, "Joint Actions," 7).

16. McWherter diary, February 25, 1942.

17. Weller, "Luck," Summer 1945, 135; "Seventeenth Pursuit History"; Hennon diary, February 25, 1942.

18. Parker, Hague, and Oliver diaries, February 25, 1942; Weller, "Luck," Summer 1945, 134.

19. Parker diary, February 25, 1942; "S-3 Diary for 7th Bombardment Group," entries for February 24 and 25, 1942.

20. Poncik to author, February 28, 1994.

21. Wade to Lewellyn, December 16, 1990; Mrs. H. G. Mahony to Miss Smith, December 22, 1942.

22. "S-3 Diary for 7th Bombardment Group," February 25, 1942; Anderson diary, February 25 and 26, 1942; Dorr, *The 7th Bombardment Group/Wing, 1918–1995*, 96; Morris, "To Tokyo, Dammit," *Colliers*, June 6, 1942, 13; Laurie telephone interview.

23. Hague diary, February 25, 1942; Parker and Badura diaries, February 26, 1942; Hayes interview, April 16 and 17, 1994; James Schott movement record (1941–42), Schott collection; Ingram diary, March 1, 1942; Burnside to author, October 26, 2002. The sea evacuation rumors were true. On February 24 Colonel Eubank had detailed Maj. C. B. Cosgrove and 2nd Lt. William H. Ambrosius of his Fifth Bomber Command to drive to Tjilatjap from Malang and arrange for water transportation of FEAF personnel to Australia. After arriving in Tjilatjap the following day, Cosgrove and Ambrosius arranged for the Dutch freighter *Abbekerk* to make the trip (Fifth Bomber Command, Malang, Special Orders No. 22, February 25, 1942, in "Fifth Air Force History," Appendix II, doc. 1144; Ambrosius diary, February 24, 25, 26, 1942).

24. Hayes interview; Hayes diary, February 26, 1942; Hague diary, February 25, 1942; Parker diary, February 25 and 26, 1942; Burnside to author, October 26, 2002.

25. Hennon diary, February 26, 1942; "Seventeenth Pursuit History"; Kiser to Commanding Officer, 50th Fighter Group, memo, "History of Time in Combat Zone," April 19, 1943.

26. "Report of the 17th Pursuit"; Hennon and Gambonini diaries, February 26, 1942; Boer, "Joint Actions," 2; Shores and Cull with Izawa, *Bloody Shambles,* 2:234; Weller, "Luck," Summer 1945, 136. The "Report of the 17th Pursuit" indicates all twelve pilots were 17th Pursuiters, while Boer maintains three were Dutch, which is accepted here. The Bettys were from the Kanoya Kokutai, flying from Makassar, according to Boer.

27. "Report of the 17th Pursuit"; Hennon and Gambonini diaries, February 26, 1942. According to Japanese records, none of the eight Zeros was actually shot down (Shores and Cull with Izawa, *Bloody Shambles,* 2:234).

28. Gambonini diary, February 26, 1942.

29. Spence Johnson diary, February 26, 1942; Sheppard and Gilmore, "Statement"; "Seventeenth Pursuit History"; Weller, "Luck," Summer 1945, 136.

30. White, *Queens,* 219–20; Kreps and Broadhurst telephone call to Bleasdale, February 25, 1942, 1345, in telephone log, "S-3 Diary for Seventh Bombardment Group," January 14–February 9, 1942, IRIS 77576, Reel 1145, AFHRA.

31. White, *Queens,* 219–20. After returning to Singosari to arrange for his command's move to Jogjakarta, Eubank proceeded to the Malang train station and left in the early evening of February 26 for Jogjakarta, where he arrived at 0110 the following morning ("S-3 Diary for 7th Bombardment Group," February 27, 1942).

32. "Report of the 17th Pursuit"; Hennon, Gambonini, and Les Johnsen diaries, February 26, 1942; G. J. de Haas memo, April 15, 1946, via Schep to author, January 7, 1996; Weller, "Luck," Summer 1945, 136; Boer to author, October 16 and 17, 2006; Boer, "Joint Actions," 7. The seven Brewsters were from 1-Vl.G.-V and 2-Vl.G.-V.

33. Hennon diary, February 26, 1942; "Seventeenth Pursuit History"; Morehead, *In My Sights,* 76; Dockstader telephone interview.

34. Boer to author, October 20, 2006; Boer, "Joint Actions," 7; Anemaet to Bosch to Groves, February 29, 1976; Les Johnsen diary, February 26, 1942.

35. C. a. m. Koopmans interview with Max Schep, March 16, 1985, via Schep to author, January 5, 1998. The Dutch flag replaced the orange insignia according to regulations issued on February 23 (Boer, *Het Verlies,* 35).

36. Boonstoppel memoir, September 3, 1968, via Schep to author, January 4, 1995.

37. Boer to author, October 20 and 23, 2006; "Seventeenth Pursuit History."

38. Crane memoir; Crane to author, October 31, 2006.

39. Eckley diary addendum, January 1, 2000; Crane memoir; Edmonds, *They Fought,* 408.

40. Kik memoir, May 5, 2000, at http://abbekerk.wordpress.com.

41. Edmonds, *They Fought,* 408; Crane memoir; Taggart, *My Fighting Congregation,* 126–27. The 7th Group's chaplain, William Taggart, had managed to have the senior U.S. Army officer on board accept a number of *Marblehead* and *Houston* crew for the trip.

42. Hayes interview.

43. Crane memoir; Hayes interview; Eckley diary, February 26, 1942; Shores and Cull with Izawa, *Bloody Shambles,* 2:192, 219.

44. Nichols to author, February 17, 1997; Crane memoir. Nichols and forty-five other enlisted men of the 17th Pursuit had boarded the *Abbekerk.* Since of the forty-five who

had left Ngoro on February 23 and 24 twelve were held back at Jogjakarta for air evacuation, it would appear that thirteen other enlisted men had left Ngoro for Jogjakarta and Tjilatjap for evacuation, too, after those dates ("Crew Chiefs and Armament Men of the 17th Pursuit [Prov.] Who Were Evacuated from Java by Boat" 1942).

45. Boer to author, July 16 and August 3, 2009, as based on interviews with Benschop.

46. Boer, *Het Verlies*, 148, 160; Boer to author, July 15, 16, and 17, 2009.

47. Boer to author, July 14, 15, 16, and 17, 2009.

48. Hennon diary, February 26, 1942; Morehead, *In My Sights*, 76–77.

49. Geurtz memoir, 28; Spence Johnson diary, February 26, 1942.

PART FIVE

1. Messimer, *In the Hands of Fate*, 51–52, 64, 116–17; Kehn, *A Blue Sea of Blood*, 116; Tagaya, "Technical Development and Operational History of the Type 1 Rikko," manuscript, 66–67; Shores and Cull with Izawa, *Bloody Shambles*, 2:241.

2. USAFIA radiogram No. 391, Brett to AGWAR, February 28, 1942, in T1611, RG 338, NARA; USAFIA radiogram No. 505, Brett to Adjutant General, March 5, 1942, in Executive Group Files, WPD, 1939–42, Entry 422, Executive 4, RG 165, NARA. While Helfrich had proven unhelpful in providing protection for the *Langley*, the Dutch head of the Java Air Command had tried to provide assistance. When Major General Van Oyen and his staff at JAC in Bandoeng learned around 0600 on the morning of February 27 that the *Langley* would not be arriving in Tjilatjap that morning as planned because of problems that had arisen, Van Oyen tried to reach Helfrich to ask if the *Langley* required protective cover for its last, most dangerous, part of its trip to Java; he was prepared to send his fighters at Andir Field outside Bandoeng to provide such cover. Unable to reach Helfrich, Van Oyen then phoned army commander—and now commander-in-chief, ABDA Area—Lieutenant General Ter Poorten with the offer of fighter protection but was told that all fighters of JAC were to remain available for air cover for the Combined Striking Force as it operated along the north coast of Java. Van Oyen protested, arguing that the *Langley* was more vulnerable than the JSF but was overruled There were not enough fighters for both missions, and protection of the JSF remained the top priority, Ter Poorten maintained (Boer, "Joint Actions," 14–15).

3. Radiogram No. 478, Marshall to Brett, February 28, 1942, in box T1601, RG 338, NARA.

4. Radiogram, Brett, USAFIA, to ABDACOM, Bandoeng, for Gen. Naiden, USAAF, February 26, 1942, in box T1611, RG 338, NARA.

5. Helfrich is believed to have instigated the order, envisioning that the pilots would fly the P-40s on the *Sea Witch* that had arrived at Tjilatjap earlier that day (Kehn, *Blue Sea*, 119; Kehn to author, July 27 and 28, 2009). His air command counterpart, Major General Van Oyen, was not informed of Helfrich's decision despite Van Oyen's obvious responsibility for use of the American pilots. Helfrich had a record of failing to coordinate with Van Oyen and not returning his calls (Boer to author, July 29 and 30, 2009).

6. Dull, *Battle History*, 82–87.

7. Ibid., 90, 92.

8. Boer, *Het Verlies*, 213; Boer to author, July 17 and 27, 2009; Eubank statement in USAFIA radiogram No. 505, Brett to Adjutant General, March 5, 1942, in Executive Group Files, WPD, 1939–42, Entry 422, Executive 4, RG 165, NARA.

9. Kehn, *Blue Sea*, 122, 139–58; http://www.combinedfleet.com/tone_t.htm.

10. Eubank statement in USAFIA radiogram No. 505; Boer to author, July 17 and 27, 2009.

11. USAFIA radiogram No. 227, Brett to ABDACOM, March 2, 1942, in box T1612, RG 338, NARA.

12. "Third Kokutai Kodocho" for March 3, 1942, via Tagaya to author, August 4, 2007.

13. Memo, Commander-in-Chief, ABDA Area, March 3, 1942, forwarded to Marshall in Marshall's memo for Adjutant General, March 3, 1942, both in Executive Group Files, WPD, 1939–42, Entry 422, Executive 4, RG 165, NARA. Van Oyen had been informed of the evacuation from the message Eubank's liaison officers brought with them to Bandoeng on March 2 (Boer to author, August 3, 2009).

14. Ibid. When Van Oyen learned on March 2 of Eubank's departure and the manner of his leaving from Eubank's liaison officers, he became furious and decided to file the complaint to Marshall with Ter Poorten's backing (Boer to author, July 17 and August 3, 2009, based on Creutzberg (Van Oyen's adjutant) interview with Boer).

15. Radiogram, Marshall to Brett, March 3, 1942, in Executive Group Files, WPD, 1939–42, Entry 422, Executive 4, RG 165, NARA.

16. Cablegram No. 505, Brett to Adjutant General for Marshall, March 5, 1942, in Executive Group Files, WPD, 1939–42, Entry 422, Executive 4, RG 165, NARA.

17. Cablegram No. 551, Brett to Marshall, March 8, 1942, in Executive Group Files, WPD, 1939–42, Entry 422, Executive 4, RG 165, NARA. Creutzberg, Van Oyen's adjutant, in a 1995 interview indicated that the field at Tasikmalaja, fifty miles southeast of Bandoeng, had been readied for B-17 and B-24 operations as a forward field if operations from Singosari and Jogjakarta proved impossible (Boer to author, June 17, 2008). It is not known if Van Oyen passed this information to Eubank.

18. Radiogram No. 192, Brett to Naiden, February 26, 1942, in box T1611, RG 338, NARA. The CCS on February 22 had radioed Wavell that "air forces that can more usefully operate in battle from bases outside Java and all air personnel for whom there are no aircraft ... should be withdrawn" (radiogram DBA 22, Combined Chiefs of Staff, Washington, to ABDA Commander, February 22, 1942, in AIR/23/5044, British National Archives).

19. CCS, radiogram DBA 22. I am grateful to NEI campaign authority Peter Boer for clarifying the command situation at this time (Boer to author, July 27, 2009).

20. It would appear that Eubank himself had authorized the evacuation of the Ngoro pilots (as indicated in chapter 14). "Dutch Headquarters in Bandoeng" could not have given permission, or Van Oyen would not have included mention of the Ngoro pilots' evacuation in his complaint to Marshall.

21. Boer to author, July 22 and 29, 2009.

22. As noted by Boer (to author, July 28, 2009).

23. Boer, *Het Verlies*, 391, 405. Japanese photos of captured *Sea Witch* P-40s would indicate that at least some of the half-assembled ships were not destroyed. For a detailed account of the last weeks of Dutch land and air resistance on Java, Boer's book is the authoritative source. It is forthcoming in an English-language translation.

24. Willmott, *Empires*, 361.

25. Ibid.

CHAPTER 14

1. INS newscast, May 20, 1942, Dix collection; Dix memoir; Messimer, *In the Hands of Fate*, 51.

2. INS newscast; McConnell, "Operations, Actions, and Sinking of USS *Langley*, 22 February–5 March 1942," in Naval Historical Center; Messimer, *In the Hands of Fate*, 43, 51; Kehn, *Blue Sea of Blood*, 116.

3. Messimer, *In the Hands of Fate*, 51–52. The Japanese bombers were sixteen Bettys from the Takao Kokutai that had taken off from Denpasar, Bali, following the reconnaissance plane's report. With neither torpedoes nor armor-piercing bombs available at their new base, they carried a mixture of high explosive 250 kg and 60 kg bombs (Tagaya, "Technical Development," 66).

4. Tagaya, "Technical Development," 66; Messimer, *In the Hands of Fate*, 57.

5. Messimer, *In the Hands of Fate*, 64; INS newscast; Tagaya, "Technical Development," 67; McConnell, "Operations."

6. INS newscast; Shores and Cull with Izawa, *Bloody Shambles*, 2:241; Dix memoir; McConnell, "Operations." The strafing Zeros were six from the 3rd Kokutai and nine from the Tainan Kokutai, all of which had escorted the G4M1s to the target (Shores and Cull with Izawa, *Bloody Shambles*, 2:241).

7. McConnell, "Operations"; Messimer, *In the Hands of Fate*, 79, 95, 97; Kehn, *Blue Sea*, 117.

8. INS newscast; Messimer, *In the Hands of Fate*, 113.

9. Messimer, *In the Hands of Fate*, 116–17; McConnell, "Operations."

10. Boer, "Joint Actions," 10, 16.

11. "Seventeenth Pursuit History"; Boer, "Joint Actions," 20.

12. Boer, "Joint Actions," 20.

13. "Seventeenth Pursuit History"; Boer, "Joint Actions," 22; Boer to author, October 17, 2006; De Haas memo, April 15, 1946, via Schep to author, January 7, 1996; Galusha, "Synopsis of Last Flight of 91st Bomb Squadron in Java," 22 November 1943; 5th Bomber Command, Journal, February 27, 1942. Dutch participants give the time of takeoff as 1515, not 1615, as indicated in "Seventeenth Pursuit History," which also incorrectly states the composition of the two flights. Morehead (A flight) and Dockstader (B flight) had left for Tjilatjap, while Gambonini (B flight) and Les Johnsen (A flight) were mistakenly left out of the listing (Gambonini and Les Johnsen diaries, February 27, 1942).

14. Spence Johnson diary, February 27, 1942; "91st Squadron," in McAfee, "The 27th Reports"; Galusha, "Synopsis."

15. "91st Squadron," in McAfee, "The 27th Reports"; Galusha, "Synopsis"; Boer, "Joint Actions," 13.

16. Spence Johnson and Gambonini diaries, February 27, 1942; Johnsen, "You Men," 112.

17. Galusha, "Synopsis"; 5th Bomber Command, Journal, February 27, 1942.

18. Galusha, "Synopsis"; "91st Squadron," in McAfee, "The 27th Reports"; Boer, "Joint Actions," 14.

19. Boer, "Joint Actions," 23; Boer to author, June 17, 2008.

20. "Seventeenth Pursuit History"; Johnsen, "You Men," 112; Gambonini diary, February 27, 1942. Gambonini's assessment was closer to reality. Japanese records show no transports either damaged or sunk in this early stage of the Battle of the Java Sea. However, because of the Allied attack on the invasion force, the transports were briefly withdrawn to the north, delaying the invasion by twenty-four hours (Army Forces Far East, *The Imperial Japanese Navy in World War II*, Japanese Monograph No. 116; Shores and Cull with Izawa, *Bloody Shambles*, 2:240).

21. Hennon diary, February 27 and February 3–March 31, 1942; Hayes interview; Morehead, *In My Sights*, 77.

22. Morehead to author, August 5, 2009. Morehead and the others never met up with Dutch 2nd Lieutenant Benschop, their assigned contact. In his postwar interview with Peter Boer, Benschop didn't refer to meeting the Ngoro pilots, although he did note that there were some American personnel of the 17th Pursuit at Tjilatjap Harbor (Boer to author, August 3, 2009). Perhaps when the *Langley*, expected in earlier, did not arrive, Benschop did not feel the need to seek out and discuss with the Ngoro pilots the now seemingly aborted plan to ferry the *Langley* P-40s to Andir.

23. Hennon diary, February 27, 1942; Morehead, *In My Sights*, 77. The reporter could not have been George Weller, as he was not at Tjilatjap on February 27, not arriving until March 2 (Weller, "6 Hours by Flying Fortress, but 11 Days When You Crawl Away under Jap Bombs," *New York Post*, March 16, 1942).

24. Crane memoir; Hayes interview.

25. Hayes to author, November 30, 1993; Hayes interview.

26. Crane and Nichols memoirs; Eckley and Ambrosius diaries, February 27, 1942. The gunboats were the *Asheville* and *Tulsa*, which were leaving port to look for the survivors of the *Langley* (Miles, "South from Cilacap," *South China Yangtze Patrol Asiatic Fleet*, December 1995, 4).

27. Kik memoir (www.abbekerk.wordpress.com) and Crane memoir; Burnside to author, October 26, 2002.

28. Parker and Oliver diaries, February 27, 1942. The six pilots were obviously those in Irvin's group sent to Tjilatjap to meet the *Langley*.

29. Legg diary, February 14, 17, 25, 27, 1942; Legg memoir.

30. Gowen log, February 24, 1942; District Officer, Broome, to Commissioner of Police, February 22, 1942; Vance to Edmonds, "Notes on the Java Story," no date (ca. 1947).

31. Womack, *Dutch Naval Air Force*, 136; Vance to Edmonds.

32. Vance to Edmonds; District Officer, Broome, to Commissioner of Police.

33. Vance to Edmonds.

34. Messimer, *In the Hands of Fate,* 122–25; Kehn, *Blue Sea,* 118; Wahl and Lamb, "Report," 1988.

35. Messimer, *In the Hands of Fate,* 129; Wahl and Lamb, "Report"; Kehn, *Blue Sea,* 118–19.

36. Messimer, *In the Hands of Fate,* 127–28; McConnell, "Operations," 5–6; Dix memoir.

37. Hennon diary, February 28, 1942.

38. Parker diary, February 28, 1942; Coss to author, January 18, February 23, and March 16, 1994; Blanton telephone interview, January 12, 1994; Holt interview.

39. Bowles to Messimer, January 2, 1984; Major Johnson to CO, Ordnance Section, 64th Bomb Squadron, January 29, 1943, Dwight Messimer collection.

40. Bowles to Messimer, January 2, 1984; Bowles telephone interview with Dwight Messimer.

41. "Seventeenth Pursuit History"; Shores and Cull with Izawa, *Bloody Shambles,* 2:242; Gambonini diary, February 28, 1942; radiogram, Eubank to Hq USAFIA, February 28, 1942, in box T1594, RG 338, NARA.

42. Boer to author, October 17, 2006; Shores and Cull with Izawa, *Bloody Shambles,* 2:242; Gambonini diary, February 28, 1942; "Seventeenth Pursuit History."

43. Boer to author, October 17, 2006; Gambonini diary, February 28, 1942. Unknown to the pursuiters, the field had been discovered earlier, as noted in chapter 12.

44. Eckley and Hayes diaries, February 28, 1942; Ingram diary, March 1, 1942.

45. Taggart, *My Fighting Congregation,* 128; Eckley and Hayes diaries, February 28, 1942; Ingram diary, March 1, 1942; Crane memoir.

46. Kik memoir.

47. Taggart, *My Fighting Congregation,* 129; Perry diary, excerpted in Weller "Luck," Summer 1945, 143–44.

48. Perry diary, in Weller, "Luck," Summer 1945, 144; Eckley and Hayes diaries, February 28, 1942; Paul W. Eckley to author, November 25 and December 1, 2006; Crane memoir.

49. Crane memoir; Perry diary, in Weller, "Luck," Summer 1945, 144; Eckley and Hayes diaries, February 28, 1942; Kik memoir. According to Japanese records, the plane was a Nakajima B5N2 "Kate" on a search and attack mission from the carrier *Hiryu* that was patrolling in the waters south of Tjilatjap between 1513 and 1743 for Allied vessels fleeing Java. It dropped a 60 kg bomb but missed (Sawruk to author, November 24, 2006; Tagaya to author, November 23, 2006).

50. Kehn, *Blue Sea,* 119; Kehn to author, July 29, 2009. Glassford had apparently been informed by Crouch that the P-40 pilots had been rescued after the sinking of the *Langley* (Kehn to author, July 27, 2009).

51. Messimer, *In the Hands of Fate,* 126–30; Kehn, *Blue Sea,* 119, 121.

52. Coss to author, March 16, 1994.

53. Parker and Oliver diaries, February 28, 1942; Holt interview; Jackson to author, August 31, 1994; Coss to author, March 16, 1994; Blanton, "Statement of Activities"; List

of air evacuees, Broome, March 2, 1942, microfilm B0086, AFHRA. Oliver is not shown with Coss and Blanton on the Broome list but went out on one of the two B-17Es (according to his diary), not that of Al Key.

54. Oliver and Parker diaries, February 28, 1942; Oliver memoir; Holt interview.

55. List of air evacuees, Broome; Hague diary, February 28, 1942; Knudson diary, March 1, 1942.

56. White, *Queens*, 226. At 0030 on March 1, some forty transports carrying the 48th Division and the 56th Regiment hove to off Kragan, where the troops went ashore in moonlight and calm weather (Gillison, *Royal Australian Air Force*, 440).

57. Fisher, "Notes," March 13, 1942. Kurtz in White's book maintained that "after a final desperate call to Dutch general van Oeyen [*sic*]," he agreed to allow the evacuation of the Ngoro pilots provided they first strafe the Japanese landing barges (White, *Queens*, 226). Fisher in his "Notes" did not mention any such call to Van Oyen (by Kurtz or himself) or evacuation conditions from him. Neither Major Fisher nor Captain Kurtz would have called Van Oyen, lacking the authority to do so. Curiously, Fisher in his "Notes" indicates that the order to attack the Japanese force came to him directly from the Dutch—skipping over Eubank, his commander—and was only reconfirmed by Eubank to him. However, Van Oyen, a stickler for regulations, never worked outside of the chain of command and thus would never have given such an order directly to him (Boer to author, July 17, 2009).

58. Fisher in his "Notes" stated that it was "a telephone call from Air Defense Command Headquarters" (in Soerabaja) received by him while the strafing mission was underway that authorized him to discontinue further operations by the Ngoro pilots and report to Eubank. Eubank days before Fisher prepared his March 13, 1942, "Notes" stated (in providing additional detail on the call) that Fisher had been informed by the ADC's commander, Col. Ente van Gils, "that instructions had been received from Bandoeng for American personnel to report to Jogjakarta for evacuation"—meaning the Americans at Ngoro (Cablegram No. 551, Brett to Marshall, March 8, 1942, in Executive Group Files WPD 1939–42, Entry 422, Executive 4, RG 165, NARA. There is no Dutch or American documentation that cites any such message from Bandoeng. Considering that Van Oyen was adamantly opposed to the evacuation of the Ngoro pilots (as noted in Part Five of this book), it would appear that the permission to evacuate came from Eubank, their commander, instead.

59. Hennon diary, March 1, 1942. It is assumed that Fisher did call Kiser with the news of the landing and the mission order, although Hennon does not mention the circumstances of his being sent to Soerabaja.

60. White, *Queens*, 226–27; Fisher, "Notes"; Hennon diary, March 1, 1942; Boer to author, July 27, 2009.

CHAPTER 15

1. Boer to author, October 27, 2006; Bruinier to author, August 14, 1995.

2. The Brewsters would be flown by De Haas, Simons, Wink, Van Haarlem, and

Bruggink, while Bruinier, Boonstoppel, De Wilde, Marinus, Hamming, Kok, and Dejalle were scheduled to fly the Hurricanes (Boer to author, October 27, 2006).

3. Gambonini diary, March 1, 1942.

4. White, *Queens,* 226–27; "Report of the 17th Pursuit"; Kiser to CO, 50th Fighter Group, memo; Hennon diary, March 1, 1942.

5. A tenth P-40, pilot unidentified, is reported as participating too (Hennon diary, March 1, 1942; Kiser to CO, 50th Fighter Group, memo), but evidently aborted after takeoff. "Report of the 17th Pursuit" has McWherter in Dale's flight and Fuchs in Kruzel's, but McWherter recalls flying as Kruzel's wingman (McWherter to author, February 14, 1995).

6. Boer to author, October 27 and November 2, 2006; De Haas memo, April 15, 1946, in Schep to author, January 7, 2006, Max Schep collection; A. Kok interview with Max Schep.

7. De Haas memo; Kruzel memoir; "Report of the 17th Pursuit"; Weller, "Luck," Summer 1945, 139. In actuality, there were forty-one transports in the invasion force (Dull, *Battle History,* 74, 93).

8. White, *Queens,* 227; McWherter, "Diary of a Fighter Pilot." The Tainan Kokutai flew five shifts of four Zeros each over the invasion convoy but did not mention in its after-action reports having seen any of the strafers below them (Tagaya to author, February 19, 2005).

9. McWherter, "Diary of a Fighter Pilot"; Kruzel memoir; Kruzel to Groves, September 15, 1975. There were nine destroyers supporting the landing at Kragan (Dull, *Battle History,* 74, 92–93).

10. Weller, "Luck," Summer 1945, 140; Les Johnsen, McWherter, and Hennon diaries, March 1, 1942.

11. Reagan interview with Suarez.

12. White, *Queens,* 227; Weller, "Luck," Summer 1945, 139; Les Johnsen diary, March 1, 1942.

13. Hennon, Les Johnsen, Spence Johnson, and Gambonini diaries, March 1, 1942; "Report of the 17th Pursuit"; Weller, "Luck," Summer 1945, 140–41.

14. Kruzel memoir; "Report of the 17th Pursuit"; Gambonini diary, March 1, 1942.

15. Spence Johnson diary, March 1, 1942; Fuchs to author, March 24, 1994.

16. Boer to author, October 27, 2006, February 2 and 20, 2007; Bruggink to author, July 10, 1995; De Haas memo.

17. Boer to author, March 1 and 2, 2005. Not surprisingly, this embarrassing incident is not mentioned in the 17th Pursuit history, nor by the pilots concerned.

18. White, *Queens,* 228.

19. Anemaet was informed that Fisher had been instructed "by Eubank's staff" to have the American personnel at Ngoro report to Jogjakarta after the March 1 morning mission had been flown, a recollection he repeated twice in a postwar interview (Boer to author, July 16, 2009). It would appear he was referring to the instructions Eubank gave Fisher (directly) at the time Fisher called Eubank in the small hours of March 1 (chapter 14).

20. Van der Vossen to author, September 25, 1995; Anemaet interview with Schep, via Schep to author, January 4, 1995; Boer to author, July 16, 2009.

21. Bosch to Groves, October 11, 1975; Van der Vossen to author, September 25, 1995; Van der Vossen interview with Max Schep, January 6, 1994; Fisher, "Notes."

22. Fisher, "Notes"; Fisher talk to G-4 Officers; Filon to Schep, August 23, 1988; Hennon diary, March 1, 1942. The strafers were a two-plane *shotai* of the Tainan Kokutai flying out of Denpasar. Two others of the second *shotai* remained over the field to provide top cover. According to the mission report, they had discovered Ngoro Field during the course of their patrol providing cover for the Kragan landing force (Tagaya to author, February 19 and 21, 2005).

23. "Seventeenth Pursuit History"; Bosch to Groves, October 11, 1975; Boer to author, August 3, 2009.

24. Boer to author, March 1, 2005; Van der Vossen to author, September 25, 1995; Bruinier to author, July 26, 1995; Kok 1968 via Schep, January 5, 1998; Bosch to Groves, October 11, 1975.

25. Fisher, "Notes." Indeed, the Japanese had found the field earlier, as noted in chapter 12.

26. Guerrero to author, November 29, 2002; McWherter to author, February 14, 1995.

27. Van der Vossen to author, September 25, 1995; Van der Vossen interview with Schep, January 6, 1994; Bruinier to author, July 26, 1995; White, *Queens,* 229.

28. Van der Vossen interview with Schep, January 6, 1994; Van der Vossen to author, September 25, 1995; Bruggink to author, June 27, 1995; Anemaet interview with Schep, via Schep to author, January 4, 1995; Boer to author, August 3, 2009.

29. Van der Vossen to author, September 25, 1995; Bruinier to author, July 26, 1995; Bruggink to author, June 27, 1995; Van der Vossen interview with Schep, June 4, 1994. Kengen was referring to the crated P-40s of the *Sea Witch* that were being transported to Andir from Tjilatjap. Contrary to the recollections of Van der Vossen and Bruinier, Anemaet indicated in postwar interviews that he was not told by Kengen that there were aircraft waiting for them at Andir and did not know about that until arriving at Bandoeng the following day (Boer to author, August 3, 2009).

30. Van der Vossen, September 25, 1995. In his 1943 narrative for *Queens Die Proudly,* apparently in deference to wartime sensitivities, Kurtz states that Anemaet on his own declined the offer when first made, not that he checked with headquarters afterwards and was turned down in his request (White, *Queens,* 229).

31. White, *Queens,* 229; Anemaet to Bosch to Groves, February 29, 1976.

32. Kehn, *Blue Sea,* 122; Kehn to author, July 27 and 29, 2009. Glassford's order followed a final meeting with Vice Admiral Helfrich, who announced he was disbanding his ABDAFLOAT command, evacuating Java, and releasing Glassford from his command to send his ships to Australia (Boer to author, July 24, 2009).

33. Messimer, *In the Hands of Fate,* 124, 130–32. The reconnaissance plane was evidently a Nakajima B5N2 "Kate" patrolling from one of the four fleet carriers only eighty miles to the east of the *Pecos* (Sawruk to author, March 16, 2007).

34. Sawruk to author, March 10, 2007; Messimer, *In the Hands of Fate,* 134–35.

35. Messimer, *In the Hands of Fate,* 136–37, 140–44; account of Naval Aviation Pilot 1st Class Shinsaku Yamakawa, http://www.geocities.com/dutcheastindies/pecos.html. The nine Vals were a *chutai* from the carrier *Kaga* that attacked the *Pecos* from 1153 to 1305, according to Japanese records (Sawruk to author, March 10, 2007).

36. Messimer, *In the Hands of Fate,* 146–49; Dix, "Twenty Three Years."

37. Messimer, *In the Hands of Fate,* 146–55; Sawruk to author, March 10, 2007. Messimer, based on recollections of survivors, gives the time of attack as 1300 to 1335, but the Japanese record of the attack by the nine Type 99s of the *Soryu* gives the time as 1254 to 1303 when converted from Tokyo IJN time (Sawruk to author, March 10, 2007; Boer to author, November 2, 2007, for the time conversion).

38. Messimer, *In the Hands of Fate,* 155–59; Sawruk to author, March 10, 2007; Boer to author, November 2, 2007. The first group of nine Type 99s was from the *Akagi.* Because of miscalculation they had arrived ahead of the nine of the *Hiryu,* which were slated to bomb the *Pecos* before the *Akagi* group (Messimer, *In the Hands of Fate,* 159).

39. Dix memoir.

40. Messimer, *In the Hands of Fate,* 159–60; Sawruk to author, March 10, 2007. The attack of the *Akagi* is recorded by the carrier as occurring between 1415 and 1455, evidently including waiting time overhead and time spent observing the results of the efforts of the pilots, while that of the *Hiryu* is listed as from 1425 to 1450 by the carrier (Sawruk to author, March 10, 2007; Boer to author, November 2, 2007). Messimer (p. 159) indicates 1450 and 1500 as the starting times of the two attacks.

41. Messimer, *In the Hands of Fate,* 160–61.

42. Dix memoir, and Dix, "Twenty Three Years."

43. Dix memoir, and Dix, "Twenty Three Years"; Messimer, *In the Hands of Fate,* 175, 177. Indeed, they might have heard the sounds of the *Edsall* being shelled and bombed in its final location after the Tjilatjap order was canceled (as described in Part Five). Between 1625 and 1715, and again between 1730 and 1740, three waves of Type 99 dive bombers from the *Hiryu, Kaga,* and *Soryu* struck the destroyer with 550-pound bombs. Cruisers and battleships also joined in, the combined attacks sending the cruelly mismatched destroyer to the bottom with almost all its crew and thirty-one pilots and one enlisted man of Keenan's group apparently lost. To this day the exact fate of the survivors is not definitively known (Sawruk to author, March 10, 2007; Messimer, *In the Hands of Fate,* 177; Kehn to author, May 26 and 30, 2006; Smith, *Fist,* 186–87.

44. Messimer, *In the Hands of Fate,* 178–79.

45. Dix memoir; Dowd, "Last of the *Pecos,*" *China Gunboatman,* June 1997, 4; Wahl and Lamb, "Report." During its three-hour rescue operation, the *Whipple* picked up 233 men, or about one-third of the number of crew and passengers aboard the *Pecos* at the time it was first attacked by the dive bombers (Messimer, *In the Hands of Fate,* 187).

46. Weller, "Luck," Summer 1945, 141; Sheppard and Gilmore, "Statement," no date (ca. 1945), Edmonds materials, AFHRA.

47. Gambonini diary, March 1, 1942; Paul Gambonini to author, March 5, 1994; Gambonini, Lund, and Morehead interview; Holt interview; Kruzel to Groves, September 15, 1975.

48. Geurtz to Casius, March 26, 1978; Geurtz memoir, 28–29; Geurtz telephone interview.

49. White, *Queens,* 230; Weller, "Luck," Summer 1945, 142.

50. White, *Queens,* 231; Lund interview.

51. Sheppard and Gilmore, "Statement"; Hennon diary, March 1, 1942; White, *Queens,* 231–32; 5th Bomber Command, Journal, March 1, 1942. Seven Takao Kokutai G4M1s had bombed the airfield at 1400 just before the evacuees' arrival (Izawa, "Rikko and Gingga, 74).

52. White, *Queens,* 232.

53. Kruzel to Groves, September 15, 1975; Hennon diary, March 1, 1942. Jack Dale in a 1944 interview maintained that he and the others had been ordered by Eubank to report back to Ngoro but that they had disobeyed the command (Dale interview with Walter D. Edmonds and USAAF personnel). Dale apparently exaggerated the situation. It was most unlikely that Eubank issued such an order after having agreed to their evacuation from Ngoro.

54. List of air evacuees, Broome; White, *Queens,* 232; Sheppard and Gilmore, "Statement."

55. White, *Queens,* 232–33; Gambonini diary, March 1, 1942, addendum; Weller, "Luck," Summer 1945, 142; Morehead, *In My Sights,* 82; Holt "round robin" letter, no date. Kruzel recalled that the Japanese was a single-engine aircraft that flew a straight and steady course over the field at ten thousand to fifteen thousand feet (Kruzel to Groves, September 15, 1975). In fact, five Zeros of the Tainan Kokutai arrived over Jogjakarta at 1350, and while three evidently flew top cover, the other two strafed the field at low altitude but expended only 350 rounds of ammunition ("Tainan Kokutai Kodocho," March 1, 1942, via Tagaya to author, August 4, 2007).

56. White, *Queens,* 235; Morehead, *In My Sights,* 82; Gambonini, Lund, and Morehead interview; "Seventeenth Pursuit History"; Gambonini diary, March 1, 1942, addendum.

57 Gambonini diary, March 1, 1942, addendum; Weller, "Luck," Summer 1945, 143; Boise interview.

58. Beck, "Early Exploits," *Yearbook of Class of 40-A Flying School,* Kelly Field; Smelser interview with Walter D. Edmonds and USAAF personnel.

59. Spence Johnson and Gambonini diaries, March 1, 1942; Weller, "Luck," Summer 1945, 141; Fuchs to author, March 24, 1994; Tagaya to author, February 19, 2005; Bruinier to author, January 26, 1995; Boer to author, February 2, 2007; Van der Vossen to author, September 25, 1995; Bruggink to author, June 27, 1995; Bosch to Groves, April 28, 1976. Seven Takao Kokutai G4M1s from Denpasar arrived over Ngoro at 1335 but didn't bomb until 1421, while six escorting Zeros of the 3rd Kokutai strafed the field afterwards (Tagaya to author, February 19, 2005).

60. Gambonini diary, March 1, 1942, addendum; Weller, "Luck," Summer 1945, 143; Boise interview.

61. Teats as told to McCullough, "Turn of the Tide," Installment 10, *Philadelphia Inquirer,* January 11, 1943; Sheppard and Gilmore, "Statement"; Gambonini diary, March 1, 1942; Seamon diary, undated entry; McWherter, "Diary of a Fighter Pilot."

62. Weller, "Luck," Summer 1945, 143; List of air evacuees, Broome; Lund interview.

63. Smelser interview with Edmonds; Smelser flight log, March 1, 1942; Smelser diary, March 12, 1942; Sheppard and Gilmore, "Statement"; Gambonini diary, March 1, 1942, addendum; Teats, "Turn of the Tide"; Hoffman to "Little Bum," May 26, 1942; Poncik to author, February 28, 1994.

64. Geurtz memoir; Geurtz to Casius, March 4 and April 2, 1978; Geurtz telephone interview.

65. Lund interview.

CHAPTER 16

1. White, *Queens,* 235.

2. Ibid., 236.

3. Ibid., 237; Morehead, *In My Sights,* 84; RAAF, Operations Record Book, A-50 Form, Station Hq Pearce, entry for March 2, 1942, NAA.

4. Gambonini diary, March 2, 1942 and addendum; A-50 Form, Pearce, entry for March 2, 1942.

5. Heyman diary, April 23, 1942; A-50 Form, Pearce, entry for March 2, 1942; Rorrison, *Nor the Years Contemn,* 258; White, *Queens,* 237; Smelser diary, March 12, 1942.

6. Womack, *Dutch Naval Air Force,* 136; Rouse diary, February 28 and March 2, 1942.

7. Rouse diary, March 2, 1942; radiogram, Brett to Legg, March 2, 1942, in box T1612, RG 338, NARA; Rorrison, *Nor the Years Contemn,* 242, 258–59.

8. Rouse diary, March 1, 1942.

9. Womack, *Dutch Naval Air Force,* 137; "3rd Kokutai Kodocho," March 2, 1942, via Tagaya to author, August 4, 2007. Japanese records for the only unit operating H6K "Mavises" in the area do not cite any reconnaissance of Broome this day ("Toko Kokutai Kodocho," March 2, 1942, via Justin Taylan to author, September 11, 2007).

10. White, *Queens,* 237; Smelser diary, March 12, 1942; Smelser flight log, March 2, 1942.

11. Legg diary, March 2, 1942.

12. Rouse diary, March 3, 1942; Womack, *Dutch Naval Air Force,* 137; Knudson diary, March 3, 1942. According to Japanese records, no reconnaissance of Broome was carried out this evening. The mystery plane may have been a Dutch Dornier flying boat, X-36, that had missed its Broome destination that evening and landed on the sea ninety miles south of Broome (Prime, *Broome's One Day War,* 13).

13. Bowles to Messimer, January 2, 1984.

14. Ibid.

15. Anemaet interview with Schep, via Schep to author, January 4, 1995; Bruinier to author, July 26, 1995; Boer to author, July 27 and August 3, 2009; Creutzberg interview with Boer, in Boer to author, June 17, 2008. Under an ABDAIR plan of February 22— taken over by JAC the following day—of the twenty-seven *Sea Witch* P-40Es expected to arrive at Tjilatjap, twelve were to go to 1-Vl.G.-IV (which became 2-Vl.G.-IV) for assembly at Andir, twelve to the RAF's 605 Squadron for assembly at Tasikmalaja, and

three to Madioen for assembly and shipment to the 17th Pursuit at Ngoro (Boer, *Het Verlies,* 23; Boer to author, July 23 and 30, 2009).

16. Anemaet interview with Schep; Van der Vossen to author, September 25, 1995; Bruinier to author, August 14, 1995; Grunewald to Schep, August 8, 1984; Boer, *De Luchstrijd,* 247; Boer, *Het Verlies,* 198. Indeed, it would take considerable time to assemble them. By the afternoon of March 6 they were still being assembled, with a few more days needed to complete the work, but by now Dutch General Headquarters concluded that Java was lost (Boer, *Het Verlies,* 373).

17. Geurtz memoir, 29–31.

18. Rouse diary, March 3, 1942.

19. Funk e-mail to Murdock, March 20, 2000.

20. Beck to author, March 26, 1994.

21. White, *Queens,* 237; McPherson, *Four Decades of Courage,* 340.

22. Weller, "Heroes Stay Where Going Is Toughest," *Syracuse Herald Tribune,* February 28, 1943. Kester's B-24A had been attacked by three of nine Zeros of the 3rd Kokutai that had flown from Koepang, Timor, 540 miles to the north, their range extended by 87-gallon drop tanks. They shot the bomber down on the first pass, six miles offshore (Womack, *Dutch Naval Air Force,* 137–38; Rorrison, *Nor the Years Contemn,* 260; "3rd Kokutai Kodocho," March 3, 1942, via Tagaya to author, August 4, 2007).

23. Weller, "Heroes"; "Sgt M. Donoho Made 32-Hour Swim to Safety," *Enid (Oklahoma) Morning News,* May 19, 1944; Van Apeldoorn, *Departure Delayed,* 213–14.

24. Legg memoir; Knudson diary, March 2, 1942.

25. White, *Queens,* 238.

26. Yerington, "The Evacuation of Java," memoir, no date; Gowen log, March 5, 1942; Legg memoir.

27. Rorrison, *Nor the Years Contemn,* 260; Gowen log, March 4, 1942; Legg memoir.

28. Womack, *Dutch Naval Air Force,* 138; "Life of a War Hero," *Broome Times,* date not indicated, ca. 2002; Sean Cowan, "Survivor Recalls Broome Attack" (unidentified newspaper, Broome, ca. 2002); http://www.kmike.com/BrowningMG/T1205S1.HTM. The Zero crashed in the sea off Broome, its pilot, W.O. Osamu Kudo dead. Kudo had been responsible for shooting down Kester's B-24A. A second Zero, piloted by S1c Yasuo Matsumoto, crashed near Roti Island on the return trip to Koepang when he ran out of fuel because of hits in his gas tank from ground fire (Womack, *Dutch Naval Air Force,* 137–38; Prime, *Broome's One Day War,* 40). Winckel's heroics are contradicted by the diary of Lt. Cecil Knudson, who was flying as copilot to Davis. After first heading for *Arabian Knight,* Knudson had caught a ride to the field's hangar as the Zeros were strafing the harbor. He recorded that he got in a trench with a Dutchman with an aerial .30-caliber machine gun and fired a few rounds from a borrowed .45 pistol at the first Zeros over them. When the Dutchman was ducking instead of firing back, Knudson took over the machine gun and emptied a box and a half of ammunition before giving it back. He saw a Zero going down to the west that he believed he had hit (Knudson diary, March 3, 1942).

29. Legg memoir; Inspector, District Office, Broome, to Commissioner of Police, March 5, 1942, Arvon Staats collection; Womack, *Dutch Naval Air Force,* 138.

30. Rorrison, *Nor the Years Contemn*, 263; Legg and Rouse diaries, March 3, 1942; 31. White, *Queens*, 239.

32. Inspector, District Office Broome, to Commissioner.

33. Rouse diary, March 5, 1942; Kelly, *Allied Air Transport Operations Southwest Pacific Area in World War II*, 1, 313.

34. White, *Queens*, 240.

35. Weller, "Heroes"; "Sgt M. Donoho." Already presumed dead were five other fellow squadron men who had boarded the B-24A that morning. They included SSgts. John M. Rex and Leo D. Steinmetz, Sgt. Samuel L. Foster, Cpl. Jack Taylor, and Pvt. Richard G. Sheetz. In addition to Kester and Ragsdale, the navigator, 1st Lt. Poad Keats, and radio operator, SSgt. Howard C. Cliff, were lost, as were FEAF evacuees Capt. Charles A. Stafford (the 7th Bomb Group's medical officer), Capt. Harry W. Markey, 2nd Lts. Howard K. Petschel and Richard L. Taylor, SSgt. Elvin P. Westcott, Cpl. Hubert McDonald, and Pvts. Nicholas D. Bunardzya, Joseph H. Gordon, and Clarence B. Johnson (note prepared by Arvon Staats, to author, September 29, 1999).

EPILOGUE

1. Weller, "Flyer Pulls Ripcord at 150 Feet," *Chicago Daily News*, February 24, 1943, and as related by Melvin Donoho to Ted Hanks, in Hanks to Dannacher, January 18, 1997.

2. Hanks to Dannacher; "Sgt M. Donoho."

3. Hanks to Dannacher. The outburst may have cost Donoho a decoration. When the 40th Fighter Squadron submitted the recommendation to Legg—now 35th Group CO—it was turned down.

4. "Sgt M. Donoho"; Legg diary, March 6, 1942; Legg memoir. That morning, Sergeant Beatty was found on the beach, completely delirious. He was flown to Perth, where he died in the hospital twenty-four hours later without regaining consciousness (Weller, "Flyer Pulls Ripcord").

5. Coss list of sea and air evacuees of the 17th Pursuit Squadron, in Coss collection.

6. Vance to Edmonds, "Notes on Java Story"; Eckley diary, March 4, 1942; Ambrosius diary, March 4 and 5, 1942; Ingram diary, March 4, 5, 7, 1942.

7. As related to fellow POW Walter Haines, in Haines to author, January 18, 2007.

8. Reagan interview with Juarez.

9. Kehn to author, October 22, 2006. Kehn analyzes the fate of the *Edsall* in his *A Blue Sea of Blood*.

10. Memo, 27th Bomb Group, USAFIA, Batchelor Field, March 1, 1942, in McAfee collection.

11. Radiogram, Brett to Chief Censor, Canberra, March 9, 1942, in box T1612, and radiogram, AGWAR to USAFIA, March 7, 1942, in box T1601, RG 338, NARA.

12. O'Donnell diary, March 2, 1942, in Special Collections, U.S. Air Force Academy Library.

13. "Report of the 17th Pursuit"; Darnton, "U.S. Forces Reveal Heavy Toll in Java," *New York Times*, April 4, 1942.

14. Weller, "Luck," Winter 1944, 282.

15. See, for example, Smelser interview with Edmonds.

16. "Report of the 17th Pursuit"; "Roster of the 17th Pursuit Squadron during the Java campaign," microfilm, Air Force Historical Research Agency.

17. Killed were Bud Sprague, Jim Rowland, Larry Landry, Phil Metsker, Wally Hoskyn, Quanah Fields, George Hynes, Gerald McCallum, and Morris Caldwell. Frank Neri, Tommy Hayes, Bill Stauter, and Gene Bound were the injured pilots.

18. "History of the 5th Air Force," App. II, doc. 65; Grant Mahony, 10th Air Force, Delhi, India, memo to Chief of the Air Corps, March 17, 1942, in Mahony collection.

19. Twenty had graduated in October 1941 in the 41-H class, nineteen in September 1941 in 41-G, twenty-two in August 1941 in 41-F, and thirty-one in July 1941 in 41-E (see Appendix Tables).

20. Tull interview with Walter D. Edmonds and USAAF personnel, February 1944, in Edmonds materials, AFHRA.

21. Legg diary, February 9 and 10, 1942.

22. Craven and Cate, *The Army Air Forces in World War II*, 6:413; Maurer, *Air Force Combat Units of World War II*.

23. One of the Java veterans has maintained that the 35th Group commanding officer had held back more qualified pilots to activate new groups (Hayes interview).

24. Most secret cablegram, Australian Legation Washington No. 263, to Department of External Affairs, February 12, 1942, in NAA. In response to MacArthur's cablegram of December 15, 1941, from the Philippines in which he asked about the level of experience of the P-40 pilots being sent him, Lieutenant General Gerow, Marshall's War Plans Chief, informed him (based on information Gerow had obtained from Arnold's staff) that they were "qualified P-40 pilots with varying degrees of gunnery and combat training" (WPD 4622–44 memo, December 1941, in OPD Executive Board No. 8–4, 1941, RG 165, NARA). However, during a visit to Darwin on June 26, 1942 as members of an inspection team under Maj. Gen. Robert C. Richardson sent out to the SWPA by Marshall, two Air Force colonels, "just over from Washington," admitted to 49th Fighter Group officers that "it was a great mistake" in December 1941 to have sent over "green pilots just out of school into combat" (Preddy diary, June 26 and 27, 1942; Bland, *Papers of George C. Marshall*, 3:199–200; Ferguson and Pascalis, *Protect and Avenge*, 64).

25. Radiogram, Arnold to ABDACOM (Brett), February 21, 1942, in box T1596, RG 338, NARA.

26. Radiogram No. 503, Brett to A-3, March 15, 1942, in Doug Cox collection.

27. Ferguson and Pascalis, *Protect and Avenge*, 47.

28. Rogers to author, November 16 and 17, 2006, citing squadron records.

29. History of the 41st Fighter Squadron, microfilm, AFHRA.

30. http://www.ozatwar.com/ozcrashes/qld218.htm.

31. "These Iowa Aces Made the Air Too Hot for 35 Enemy Planes," *Des Moines Sunday Register*, August 6, 1944.

32. Military Personnel Records Center, Air Force Branch, "Statement of Military Service of Grant Mahony"; Stanaway and Hickey, *Attack and Conquer*, 316.

33. Weller, "Luck," Winter 1944, 260.

SOURCES

This story about the pilots and enlisted men of the five provisional pursuit squadrons assigned to the Java campaign of early 1942 covers their experiences from the time of their arrival in Australia in December 1941–January 1942 through the end of the ill-fated operation in the initial days of March 1942. It has been pieced together mainly from the diaries that many of the participants kept, supplemented by their flight log books, memoirs they wrote for their families and for the author, interviews with them conducted by Walter D. Edmonds and Army Air Forces intelligence officers (1942–45) and by the author (1994–2008), and their correspondence with their families in wartime and with the author since 1993. In addition, several USAAF prewar Special Orders provided by the participants (or their families) also helped document their movements.

No official history was ever prepared on the operations of the provisional pursuit squadrons, nor a formal record maintained of such operations, unlike the case for the bomber groups in the Java campaign. A brief semiofficial history in a diary format issued by the Fifth Air Force headquarters in Australia appears in many slightly varying versions, but it was limited to Java operations only and written retrospectively (probably in late 1942) by an unidentified participant and apparently based on pilot recollections, as suggested by its numerous factual errors (ascertained by the author) on the composition of flights flown on combat missions.

Official records in the form of radiograms, cablegrams, and Special Orders provided supplementary information, particularly on the formation and experiences of the provisional pursuit squadrons in Australia before their transfer to the Dutch East Indies. Messages to and from USAFIA, AGWAR, and ABDACOM in the January–March 1942 period as found in National Archives Record Group 338 for the USAFIA command were particularly valuable. (These records have since been transferred to Record Group 495.2.) In addition, generally untapped records of the National Archives of Australia—located and provided to the author by Gordon Birkett—were useful regarding movements of the provisional pursuit squadrons in Australia and the high-level decisions of ABDACOM, as revealed in Australian government cable traffic to and from Washington and London. Radiograms between ABDACOM and the Combined Chiefs of Staff maintained in the Public Records Office (now British National Archives), London, supplemented such background information on the Dutch East Indies campaign.

While the focus of this book is on the experiences of the Americans, I also wanted to include those of the valiant Dutch in those cases in which they flew and fought along with their allies on Java. Furthermore, on the dissolution of ABDACOM in late February 1942, American pursuit and bomber crews still on Java at the time fell under Dutch command until the end of the campaign. The information provided me—mainly via e-mail—by the authority on the Netherlands East Indies Air Force, Peter Boer, as based on his meticulous research of records and interviews of survivors, proved invaluable in relating the intertwined experiences of the Dutch at all levels of command. Additional source material on NEIAF experiences was sent me from the Netherlands by Max Schep, as gleaned from his postwar interviews of survivors, and by three of the Dutch pilots who flew in the campaign (Bruggink, Bruinier, and Van der Vossen).

I have not included the personal experiences of the Japanese in this story but have used the operational records of their flying units to match against those of the Americans and Dutch in all significant combat events. Translations of these *kodo chosho* were provided me by Osamu Tagaya and Jim Sawruk from their copies of the Japanese originals. The invaluable detail provided is included in the notes.

The story of American pursuit pilots in the Java campaign appears here for the first time in book form. An (acknowledged) incomplete account by the war correspondent George Weller, covering Java operations alone, published as a three-part article in 1944–45, represents the starting point of this project. In more recent years Chris Shores and Brian Cull, in their two-volume *Bloody Shambles,* have briefly included the operations of the 17th Pursuit Squadron, among others, during its Java period, and with the assistance of Yasuho Izawa viewed the Japanese side.

As in my previous books I have attempted to provide a broader context for the tactical-level air operations I describe. In the Prologue and the introductions to the five parts of the book I have summarized the relevant political and strategic decisions of the Americans, Dutch, Australians, and Japanese and their campaign-level ground-sea-air operations. In this effort, among other published sources, I have relied on Maurice Matloff's and Edwin Snell's *Strategic Planning for Coalition Warfare, 1941–1942* and H. P Willmott's *Empires in the Balance* for coverage on the Allied side, while Herbert Bix's *Hirohito and the Making of Modern Japan* and Takushiro Hattori's *Dai Toa Senso Zenshi* (The complete history of the Greater East Asia War) were particularly useful accounts providing the Japanese perspective.

PUBLISHED WORKS

Books

Agawa, Hiroyuki. *The Reluctant Admiral: Yamamoto and the Imperial Navy.* Trans. John Bester. New York: Kodansha International, 1979.

Alford, Bob. *Darwin's Air War, 1942–1945: An Illustrated History.* Darwin: The Aviation Historical Society of the Northern Territory, 1991.

[Allied Forces, ABDA Command]. *Despatch by the Supreme Commander of the ABDA Area to the Combined Chiefs of Staff on the Operations in the South-West Pacific, 15th January 1942 to 25th February 1942.* London: HMSO, 1948.

Angelucci, Enzo, with Peter Bowers. *The American Fighter.* New York: Orion Books, 1987.

Bartsch, William H. *December 8, 1941: MacArthur's Pearl Harbor.* College Station: Texas A&M University Press, 2003.

———. *Doomed at the Start: American Pursuit Pilots in the Philippines, 1941–1942.* College Station: Texas A&M University Press, 1992.

Bix, Herbert P. *Hirohito and the Making of Modern Japan.* New York: HarperCollins, 2000.

Bland, Larry I., ed. *The Papers of George Catlett Marshall,* vol. 2, *"We Cannot Delay,"* July 1, 1939–December 6, 1941. Baltimore: Johns Hopkins University Press, 1986.

———, ed. *The Papers of George Catlett Marshall,* vol. 3, *"The Right Man for the Job,"* December 7, 1941–May 31, 1943. Baltimore: Johns Hopkins University Press, 1991.

Boeicho Boeikenshusho Senshishitsu [Japanese Defense Agency, War History Section]. *Senshi sosho* [Official war history], Vol. 24, *Hito Malay homen kaigun shinko sakusen* [Philippines and Malaya area navy offensive operations]. Tokyo: Asagumo Shimbunsha, 1969.

Boeicho Boeikenshusho Senshishitsu [Japanese Defense Agency, War History Section]. *Senshi sosho* [Official war history], Vol. 34, *Nampo Shinko rikugun koku sakusen* [Southern Offensive army air operations]. Tokyo: Asagumo Shimbunsha, 1970.

Boer, Peter C. *De Luchtstrijd om Indie: Operaties van de Militaire Luchtvaart KNIL in de periode December 1941 tot Maart 1942*. Houten: Van Holkema and Warendorf, 1990.

————. *Het Verlies van Java: Een Kwestie van Air Power*. Amsterdam: Bataafsche Leeuw, 2006.

Brereton, Lewis H. *The Brereton Diaries*. New York: William Morrow & Co., 1946.

Brown, Cecil. *Suez to Singapore*. New York: Random House, 1942.

Butow, Robert J. C. *Tojo and the Coming of War*. Princeton: Princeton University Press, 1961.

Carter, Kit C., and Robert Mueller, comps. *The Army Air Forces in World War II: Combat Chronology, 1941-1945*. Maxwell AFB: Albert F. Simpson Historical Research Center, Air University, 1973.

Charles, Roland W. *Troopships of World War II*. Washington, D.C.: Army Transportation Association, 1947.

Cline, Ray S. *Washington Command Post: The Operations Division*. Washington, D.C.: Chief of Military History, U.S. Army, 1951.

Connaughton, Richard. *MacArthur and Defeat in the Philippines*. New York: Overlook Press, 2001.

Cox, Douglas A. *Air Power Leadership on the Front Line: Lt. Gen. George H. Brett and Combat Command*. Maxwell AFB: Air University Press, 2006.

Craven, Wesley F., and James L. Cate. *The Army Air Forces in World War II*. Vol. 6. Chicago: University of Chicago Press, 1955.

Cull, Brian. *Hurricanes over Singapore: RAF, RNZAF, and NEI fighters in Action against the Japanese over the Island and the Netherlands East Indies, 1942*. London: Grub Street, 2004.

Dorr, Robert. *7th Bombardment Group/Wing, 1918-1995*. Paducah, Ky.: Turner Publishing Co., 1996.

Dull, Paul S. *A Battle History of the Imperial Japanese Navy, 1941-1945*. Annapolis: Naval Institute Press, 1978.

Edmonds, Walter D. *They Fought with What They Had: The Story of the Army Air Forces in the Southwest Pacific*. Boston: Little Brown & Co., 1951.

Ferguson, S. W. and William K. Pascalis. *Protect and Avenge: The 49th Fighter Group in World War II*. Atglen: Schiffer, 1996.

Ferrell, Robert H., ed. *The Eisenhower Diaries*. New York: W. W. Norton and Co., 1981.

Fujita, Frank. *Foo: A Japanese-American Prisoner of the Rising Sun*. Denton: University of North Texas Press, 2001.

Gillison, Douglas. *Royal Australian Air Force, 1939-1942*. Canberra: Australian War Memorial, 1962.

Gordon, Harry. *Voyage from Shame: The Cowra Breakout and Afterwards*. Lucia: University of Queensland Press, 1994.

Hammel, Eric M. *Aces Against Japan*. New York: Pocketbooks, 1995.

Harvard University. *Fiftieth Anniversary Report, Class of 1930*.

Hata, Ikuhiko. "The Army's Move into Northern Indochina." In *The Fateful Choice: Japan's Advance into Southeast Asia, 1939-1941*, ed. James W. Morley. New York: Columbia University Press, 1980.

————, and Yasuho Izawa. *Japanese Naval Aces and Fighter Units in World War II*. Annapolis: Naval Institute Press, 1989.

Hattori, Takushiro. *Dai Toa Senso Zenshi* [The complete history of the Greater East Asia War]. 2 vols. Tokyo: Masu Shobo, 1953. English translation, microfilm, Library of Congress.

Ind, Allison. *Bataan: The Judgment Seat*. New York: Macmillan, 1944.

Kehn, Donald M., Jr. *A Blue Sea of Blood: Deciphering the Mysterious Fate of the USS Edsall*. Minneapolis: Zenith Press, 2008.

Kelly, Robert H. *Allied Air Transport Operations Southwest Pacific Area in World War II*. Brisbane: 2003.

Kelly, Terence. *Hurricane over the Jungle*. London: William Kimber, 1977.

Kelly Field [AFB], Texas. *Gig Sheet*. Vols. for classes 41-E, 41-F, and 41-G. N.d.

Launder, Richard. *College Campus in the Sky*. Lincoln: Writers Club Press, 2001.

Layton, Edwin T., with Roger Pineau and John Costello. *And I Was There: Pearl Harbor and Midway—Breaking the Secrets*. New York: William Morrow, 1985.

Leutze, James A. *A Different Kind of Victory: A Biography of Admiral Thomas C. Hart*. Annapolis: Naval Institute Press, 1981.

Lockwood, Douglas. *Australia's Pearl Harbor: Darwin 1942*. Melbourne: Cassell, 1966.

McDowell, Ernest R. *49th Fighter Group*. Carrollton, Tex.: Squadron/Signal Publications, 1989.

McPherson, Irene W. *Four Decades of Courage: Development of United States Air Power and the 7th Bombardment Group*. Bloomington, Ind.: AuthorHouse, 2006.

Matloff, Maurice, and Edwin M. Snell. *Strategic Planning for Coalition Warfare, 1941–1942*. Washington, D.C.: Chief of Military History, U.S. Army, 1953.

Maurer, Maurer. *Air Force Combat Units of World War II*. Washington, D.C.: Zenger Publishing Co., 1980.

Mayborn, Mitch, et al. *Grumman Guidebook*. Dallas: Flying Enterprise Publications, 1976.

Messimer, Dwight R. *In the Hands of Fate: The Story of Patrol Wing Ten*. Annapolis: Naval Institute Press, 1985.

Messimer, Dwight R. *Pawns of War: The Loss of the USS* Langley *and the USS* Pecos. Annapolis: Naval Institute Press, 1983.

Middlebrook, Martin, and Patrick Mahoney. *Battleship: The Loss of the Prince of Wales and the Repulse*. London: Allen Lane, 1977.

Mitchell, John H. *On Wings We Conquer: The 19th and 7th Bomb Groups of the United States Air Force in the Southwest Pacific in the First Year of World War II*. Springfield, Mo.: GEM Publishers, 1990.

Morehead, James B. *In My Sights Completed: The Memoir of a P-40 Ace*. Petaluma, Calif.: Morehead Enterprises, 2003.

————. *In My Sights: The Memoir of a P-40 Ace*. Novato: Presidio Press, 1998.

Morton, Louis. *Strategy and Command: The First Two Years*. Washington, D.C.: Office of Military History, U.S. Army, 1961.

Piper, Robert K. *The Hidden Chapters: Untold Stories of Australians at War in the Pacific*. Carlton, Vic., Australia: Pagemaster Party Ltd., 1995.

Pogue, Forrest C. *George C. Marshall,* vol. 2, *Ordeal and Hope, 1939–1942.* New York: Viking Press, 1967.

Powell, Alan. *The Shadow's Edge: Australia's Northern War.* Carlton, Australia: Melbourne University Press, 1988.

Prange, Gordon W. *At Dawn We Slept: The Untold Story of Pearl Harbor.* New York: McGraw-Hill, 1981.

Prime, Mervyn W. *Broome's One Day War.* Broome, Australia: Broome Historical Society, 1992.

Raleigh, John M. *Pacific Blackout.* New York: Dodd, Mead & Co., 1943.

Rorrison, James D. *Nor the Years Contemn: Air War on the Australian Front, 1941–42.* Brisbane: 1992.

Sakai, Saburo, with Martin Caidin and Fred Saito. *Samurai!* New York: E. P. Dutton, 1957.

Salecker, Gene E. *Fortress Against the Sun: The B-17 Flying Fortress in the Pacific.* Coshohocken, Pa.: Combined Publishing, 2001.

Schultz, Duane. *The Last Battle Station: The Story of the U.S.S.* Houston. New York: St. Martins Press, 1985.

Sherry, Michael S. *The Rise of American Air Power: The Creation of Armageddon.* New Haven: Yale University Press, 1987.

Shores, Christopher, and Brian Cull with Yasuho Izawa. *Bloody Shambles,* vol. 1, *The Drift to War to the Fall of Singapore.* London: Grub Street, 1992.

———. *Bloody Shambles,* vol. 2, *The Defence of Sumatra to the Fall of Burma, 1942.* London: Grub Street, 1993.

Smith, Peter C. *Fist from the Sky: Japan's Dive-Bomber Ace of World War II.* Mechanicsburg: Stackpole Books, 2006.

Stanaway, John C., and Lawrence J. Hickey. *Attack and Conquer: The Eighth Fighter Group in World War II.* Atglen, Pa.: Schiffer Publishing Co., 1995.

Tagaya, Osamu. *Mitsubishi Type 1 Rikko "Betty" Units of World War II.* Oxford: Osprey, 2001.

Taggart, William C. *My Fighting Congregation.* New York: Doubleday Doran and Co., 1943.

Toland, John. *The Rising Sun: The Decline and Fall of the Japanese Empire, 1936–1945.* New York: Random House, 1970; reprint New York: Modern Library, 2003.

Tolley, Kemp. *Cruise of the Lanikai.* Annapolis: Naval Institute Press, 1973.

Tsunoda, Jun. "The Navy's Role in the Southern Strategy." In *The Fateful Choice: Japan's Advance into Southeast Asia, 1939–1941,* ed. James W. Morley. New York: Columbia University Press, 1980.

U.S., Department of the Army. *Reports of General MacArthur: Japanese Operations in the Southwest Pacific Area.* Vol. 2, pt. 1. Washington, D.C.: Government Printing Office, 1966.

U.S. Army, Adjutant General's Office. *Official Army Register, January 1, 1942.* Washington, D.C.: Government Printing Office, 1942.

———. *Official Army Register, January 1, 1947.* Washington, D.C.: Government Printing Office, 1947.

U.S. Army, Army Forces Far East, Military History Section. *The Imperial Japanese Navy in World War II.* Japanese Monograph No. 116. Tokyo: 1962. Microfilm, Library of Congress.

———. *Java–Sumatra Air Operations Record (December 1941–March 1942).* Japanese Monograph No. 69. Tokyo: 1962. Microfilm, Library of Congress.

———. *Naval Operations in the Invasion of the Netherlands East Indies, Dec. 1941–Mar. 1942.* Japanese Monograph No. 101. Tokyo: 1962. Microfilm, Library of Congress.

———. *Philippines Air Operations Record: Phase One.* Japanese Monograph No. 11. Tokyo: February 1952. Microfilm, Library of Congress.

U.S. Army Air Corps, Hamilton Field, California. *Historical and Pictorial Review, 10th Pursuit Wing and 45th Air Base.* Baton Rouge: Army and Navy Publishing Company, 1941.

U.S. Strategic Bombing Survey (Pacific), Naval Analysis Division. "Interrogation of Captain Fujita, Masamichi, IJN." In *Interrogations of Japanese Officials.* OPNAV-P-03-100, Vol. 1, no. 67. Tokyo: n.p., 1945.

Ugaki, Matome. *Fading Victory: The Diary of Admiral Matome Ugaki, 1941–1945.* Pittsburgh: The University of Pittsburgh Press, 1991; reprint Annapolis: Naval Institute Press, 2008.

Van Apeldoorn, Jan. *Departure Delayed.* Melbourne: Robertson and Mullens, 1943.

Watson, Richard L., Jr. *Army Air Action in the Philippines and Netherlands East Indies, 1941–1942.* USAF Historical Study No. 111. Washington, D.C.: Asst. Chief of Air Staff, Historical Division, March 1945.

White, W. L. *Queens Die Proudly.* New York: Harcourt Brace and Co., 1943.

Wigmore, Lionel. *The Japanese Thrust.* Canberra: Australian War Memorial, 1957.

Willmott, H. P. *Empires in the Balance: Japanese and Allied Pacific Strategies to April 1942.* Annapolis: Naval Institute Press, 1982.

Womack, Tom. *The Dutch Naval Air Force against Japan: The Defense of the Netherlands East Indies, 1941–1942.* Jefferson, N.C.: McFarland & Co., 2006.

Articles

Alford, Robert. Letter to the Editor. *Air International,* October 1986.

"Arizona Flyer's Close Call, Other Thrills Told by Vet." Associated Press, April 10, 1943.

Bartsch, William H. "The Other Pearl Harbor." *Historically Speaking,* November 2003, 32–33.

Beck, Richard. "Early Exploits." *Yearbook of Class of 40-A Flying School,* Kelly Field.

Boer, Peter C. "Joint Actions by Allied Air and Naval Forces at Java on 26–27 February 1942." *World War II Quarterly* 5, no. 4 (2008): 5–35.

———. "Small Unit Cohesion: The Case of Fighter Squadron 3-VL.G.IV." *Armed Forces and Society,* Fall 2001, 33–54.

Brown, Bryan W., Jr. "Attack to Defend." *Daedalus Flyer,* Winter 2001, 22–25.

Casius, Gerard. "Batavia's Big Sticks." *Air Enthusiast,* August–November 2003, 1–20.

Cowan, Sean. "Survivor Recalls Broome Attack." Unidentified newspaper, Broome, ca. 2002.

Cranston, Frank. "Ten Men Alone." *Canberra Times,* February 19, 1992.

Darnton, Byron. "U.S. Fliers Reveal Heavy Toll in Java." *New York Times,* April 4, 1942.

Dowd, Melvin J. "Last of the *Pecos.*" *China Gunboatman,* June 1997.

Durdin, F. Tillman. "Van Mook Appeals for Aid to Java." *New York Times,* February 24, 1942.

The Grouper, "Headquarters and Headquarters Squadron," *Nichols News* [Nichols Field, Rizal, Philippine Islands] 3, no. 3 (August 1941).

Guttman, Jon. "American Ace from Java to Germany." *World War II,* February 2001, 34–40, 76.

International News Service (INS) newscast, May 20, 1942. Copy in private collection of Gerald Dix.

"Jesse Hague Is Honored for Bravery against Japanese," *Guthrie County Vedette* [Panora, Iowa], April 16, 1942.

Johnsen, Lester J. "You Men on Java Are Not Forgotten." *Air Force Magazine,* September 1980, 106–12.

Kluckhohn, Frank L. "Hull Deplores Attack on Indochina as Blow to Pacific Status Quo." *New York Times,* September 24, 1940.

———. "U.S. Embargoes Scrap Iron, Hitting Japan." *New York Times,* September 27, 1940.

"Life of a War Hero." *Broome Times,* ca. 2002.

"Lifetime Pals Swap Stories on the War in the Air." *Des Moines Register,* November 12, 1942.

Miles, Lion G. "South from Cilacap." *South China Yangtze Patrol Asiatic Fleet Newsletter,* December 1995.

Morris, John R. "To Tokyo, Dammit!" *Colliers,* June 6, 1942, 12–13, 61.

"National Policies Set at Liaison Conference," *Japan Times and Mail,* July 29, 1940.

Obituary of Floyd J. Pell. *West Point Assembly,* March 1992.

"Sgt. M. Donoho Made 32-Hour Swim to Safety." *Enid (Okla.) Morning News,* May 19, 1944.

Teats, Edward C., as told to John M. McCullough. "Turn of the Tide." Installment 10, *Philadelphia Inquirer,* January 11, 1943.

"These Iowa Aces Made the Air Too Hot for 35 Enemy Planes," *Des Moines Sunday Register,* August 6, 1944.

Tolischus, Otto D. "Japanese Report U.S. Is in a Secret Accord to Defend Southeast Asia Against Drive." *New York Times,* April 21, 1941.

Weller, George. " Flyer Pulls Ripcord at 150 Feet." *Chicago Daily News,* February 24, 1943.

———. "6 Hours by Flying Fortress, but 11 Days When You Crawl Away under Jap Bombs." *New York Post,* March 16, 1942.

———. "Heroes Stay Where Going Is Toughest." *Syracuse Herald Tribune,* February 28, 1943.

———. "Luck to the Fighters." *Military Affairs,* Winter 1944, 259–96; Spring 1945, 33–62; Summer 1945, 125–50.

"Youngsters Get Distinguished Service Award." International News Service, April 7, 1942.

Air Corps Advanced Flying School, Craig Field, Alabama. "Roster of Graduates, Class 41-H, October 3, 1941." Author's collection.

Air Corps Advanced Flying School, Stockton Field, California. "Graduation Exercises, Class 41-E, July 11, 1941." Author's collection.

"All 5th Ftr. Cmd. Confirmed Victories, 7 Dec. 1941–14 August 1945." Decimal file 731–375, AFHRA.

Assembly Records for P-40Es off the USAT *Republic* at Brisbane, January 1942. RG 407, USAFIA, NARA.

"Australian-American Cooperation: Notes of Conference Held on January 4, 1942." RG 407, NARA.

Batchelder, Alf. "Appendix B: Col. William Herbert Murphy," no date. In private collection of Bruce Yoran.

Birkett, Gordon. "Early USAAF P-40E Operations." Ca. 2002. In private collection of Gordon Birkett.

Blanton, N. H. "Statement of Activities during the Early Days of the War," February 20, 1945. Edmonds materials, Air Force Historical Research Agency.

Boer, Peter. "De Slag om de Tjater Pas," no date. Author's collection.

Bound, Gene. Report on combat, February 5, 1942. In private collection of Boyd Wagner.

Cavaye, Cdre. P. L. "Report of Proceedings by Commodore of Convoy which Sailed from Fremantle, Australia, on February 22, 1942, at 1400 for Colombo." Colombo: March 6, 1942. In private collection of Gordon Birkett.

Combined Operational Intelligence Centre, Situation Report No. 45, February 11, 1942. National Archives of Australia. In private collection of Gordon Birkett.

"Conference December 29 [1941]," in McAfee, "The 27th Reports."

"Conference Notes, December 28, 1941," "History of the 5th Air Force," Appendix II, doc. 64.

"Conference in the Office of Chief of Staff, 10:40 A.M., November 26, 1941," WDCSA/381 Philippines (12-4-41), Top Secret Correspondence, 1941–42, RG 165, NARA.

Coss, Walter B. "Notes," 1943. In private collection of Walter B. Coss.

———. "Statement," July 7, 1942 [re February 3, 1942, combat]. In private collection of Walter B. Coss.

"Crew Chiefs and Armament Men of the 17th Pursuit (Prov.) Who Were Evacuated from Java by Boat," 1942. In private collection of Walter Coss.

"Crew Chiefs and Armorers Assigned to Pilots" (on board the USAT *President Polk*), 1942. In private collection of Paul Gambonini.

De Haas, G. J., April 15, 1946, memorandum. In private collection of Max Schep.

———. Statement to the Historical Section, Royal Netherlands Air Force, April 15, 1946. In private collection of Max Schep.

District Officer, Broome, to Commissioner of Police, February 22, 1942. In private collection of Arvin Staats.

Dockstader, Robert B. "Statement," November 10, 1944. Edmonds materials, Air Force Historical Research Agency.

Ferguson, Omar N. " Activities of the 91st Bomb Squadron since Beginning of War," no date. In private collection of Harry Galusha.

Fisher, William P. "Notes," March 13, 1942. Edmonds materials, Air Force Historical Research Agency.

———. "Summary of Interceptor Activity," Melbourne, August 1942. Edmonds materials, Air Force Historical Research Agency.

———. Talk to G-4 Officers, WDGDS, Washington, D.C., March 20, 1942. In Franklin Delano Roosevelt Presidential Library, Hyde Park, New York.

Galusha, Harry. "Synopsis of Last Flight of 91st Bomb Squadron in Java," 22 November 1943. In private collection of Harry Galusha.

Gambonini, Paul. Unpublished foreword to Morehead, *In My Sights*. In private collection of James B. Morehead.

Glassford, Rear Adm. W. A. "Narrative of Events in the Southwest Pacific from 14 February to 5 April 1942," May 18, 1942. Microfilm NRS 1970–7, Naval Historical Center.

"History of the 5th Air Force (and Its Precedents)," Part I, December 1941–August 1942. Microfilm A7385, Air Force Historical Research Agency.

Imperial Japanese Navy. "*Akagi* hikotai sento kodo chosho" February 1942 entries. In private collection of James Sawruk.

———. "1st Kokutai hikotai sento kodo chosho" February 1942 entries. In private collection of Osamu Tagaya.

———, "*Kaga* hikotai sento kodo chosho," February 1942 entries. In private collection of James Sawruk.

———. "Kanoya Kokutai hikotai sento kodo chosho," February 1942 entries. In private collection of Osamu Tagaya.

———. "Tainan Kokutai hikotai sento kodo chosho," February 1942 entries. In private collection of Osamu Tagaya.

———. "Takao Kokutai hikotai sento kodo chosho," February 1942 entries. In private collection of Osamu Tagaya.

———. "3rd Kokutai hikotai sento kodo chosho," February 1942 entries. In private collection of Osamu Tagaya.

Izawa, Yasuho. "Rikko and Gingga: Japanese Navy Twin [Engine] Bomber Units," no date. Author's collection.

Johnson. Col. Alexander L. P. "Report," (re inspection of Amberley Field, February 3, 1942). In "History of the 5th Air Force," Appendix II.

Kiser, George E. "Historical Information," no date. In private collection of George E. Kiser.

List of air evacuees, Broome, March 2, 1942, Microfilm B0086, Air Force Historical Research Agency.

List of pilots qualified to fly the P-40E, Amberley Field, January 15, 1942. "History of the 5th Air Force," Appendix II.

Mahony, Grant. USAF Detachment, Bangalore, India, "Obstacles to Pursuit Effectiveness in Past Operations," February 28, 1942. In private collection of Grant Mahony.

Marshall, George C., and Harold R. Stark. "Memorandum for the President—Estimate Concerning Far Eastern Situation." November 5, 1941, WPD 4389–29, War Plans Department, General Correspondence, 1939–42, RG 165, NARA.

McAfee, James B., ed. "The 27th Reports, or How to Get Scrogged, Bugger All," no date. In private collection of James McAfee.

McConnell, Robert P. "Operations, Actions, and Sinking of USS *Langley*, 22 February–5 March 1942," March 9, 1942. In Naval Historical Center, Washington, D.C.

Military Personnel Records Center, Air Force Branch. "Statement of Military Service of Grant Mahony." In private collection of Grant Mahony.

"Minutes of Conference, January 23, 1942," RAAF files, 60/501/88, National Archives of Australia.

Moffett Field, California. "The Hangar," Class 41-D, May 29, 1941, and Class 41-H, August 1941. In collection of the author.

Nichols, Erickson S., to Chief of Air Section, USAFIA. "Report on Trip to Brisbane, January 15, 1942." In "History of the 5th Air Force," App. II, doc. 197.

"91st Squadron," in McAfee, "The 27th Reports."

Oestreicher, Robert G. "The First of the Many," no date. In private collection of Trudi Oestreicher Katz.

105 Fighter Control Unit Headquarters. Encl. 1A, "Activities of 33rd Pursuit Squadron Provisional from February 15 to 19, 1942," undated. Series A1242, National Archives of Australia.

"Operations Java Campaign: Pilots of the 13th and 33rd Squadrons Wrecked or Aircraft Out on the Way to USS *Langley* and from Port Pirie to Darwin," Brisbane, February 24, 1942. Doc. 946, Microfilm A7385, AFHRA.

Pehl, Charles. "Fighters to Plum," no date. In private collection of Charles Pehl.

Pell, Floyd. "Flight Assignments, 33rd Pursuit Squadron Provisional, Brisbane, February 4, 1942." In private collection of Trudi Oestreicher Katz.

"Pell's Bells," August 5, 1942. In private collection of Richard Suehr.

Phillips, Robert E. Chronology, February 19 and 20, 1942. In private collection of Dwight Messimer.

"Reminiscences of Pilots Who Knew Bud [Sprague], no date. In private collection of Charles Sprague.

"Report of Conference," Manila, December 6, 1941, Ser. I, Subject Files, Item 12, Thomas C. Hart Papers, Naval Historical Center, Washington, D.C.

"Roster of Officers and Enlisted Men on Duty at the Station, Headquarters, FEAF Detachment, RAAF Field, Darwin, February 20, 1942. In private collection of James McAfee.

"Report of the 17th Pursuit Squadron (Provisional) Activity in Java" (typescript), in private collections of William J. Hennon and William A. Sheppard.

"Roster of the 33rd Pursuit Squadron Provisional—Capt. Pell Commanding," February 12, 1942, File 5th AF, AG 322.91, in "History of the 5th Air Force."

Royal Australian Air Force. Operations Record Books, A-50 Form, for Headquarters, RAAF Station Point Cook; Headquarters Station Pearce; No. 3 Service Flying Training School, Amberley; Canberra, Maryborough, and Amberley Field; and RAAF No. 2 G.R. Squadron, Koepang, January, February, and March 1942 entries. In National Archives of Australia and private collection of Gordon Birkett.

Rundle, E. N., RAAF. "Report on Death of Unknown Marking by Sgt. Christian Bram, Royal Dutch Navy, October 8, 1945, Series 705, 166/1/05, National Archives of Australia.

Schott, James. Movement record (1941–42), In private collection of James Schott.

"Seventeenth Pursuit Squadron (Provisional) History." Microfilm A0723, docs. 1922–27, 1932–33. Air Force Historical Research Agency.

Sheppard, William A., and Edwin B. Gilmore. "Statement." No date (ca. 1945). Edmonds materials, Air Force Historical Research Agency.

Tagaya, Osamu. "Technical Development and Operational History of the Type 1 Rikko," 2000. Author's collection.

"Translation of Letter of C. D. van der Herst, Departement van Opsporingsdienst van Overleden," Batavia, July 4, 1947. Series 705, 166/1/05, National Archives of Australia.

U.S. Army, Air Corps Troops, Amberley Field. List of pilots at Amberley Field. January 21, 1942. Author's collection.

U.S. Army Air Forces, Fifth Air Force. "Report of the 17th Pursuit Squadron (Provisional) in Java," n.d. (ca. 1942). In "History of the 5th Air Force," Appendix II, doc. 930A.

U.S. Army Air Forces in Australia, A-4, Aircraft Movements Status and Statistics Section. "Location and Status of Damaged Aircraft in Australia," no date (ca. 1942. In private collection of Gordon Birkett.

U.S. Army Forces in Australia. "Report of Organization and Activities United States Army Forces in Australia from December 7, 1941, to June 30, 1942," Melbourne, no date. RG 407, NARA.

———, Office of Air Operations, "Ferry Flight Instructions" to Capt. Charles Sprague, 17th Pursuit Squadron (Provisional), no date (January 1942). In private collection of George E. Kiser.

U.S. Army Forces Far East. "Report of a Trip by B.G. H. B. Clagett, Lt. Col. Lester Maitland, and Capt. Allison Ind, July 27–August 20, 1941" to Commanding General, Philippine Department, October 1, 1941. In Bartsch collection, MacArthur Memorial Archives, Norfolk, Virginia.

Wahl, Eugene, and Charles Lamb. "A Report on the Fate of the *Edsall* and the 42 USAAC *Langley* Survivors," 1988. In private collection of Eugene Wahl.

Wiecks, Max. "Award of Purple Heart," to Air Force Reference Branch, July 29, 1997. In private collection of Reid Wiecks.

Zander, Peter J. "Synopsis of My Foreign Service Tour," ca. 1943. In private collection of Peter J. Zander.

Official Diaries and Journals

"Diary of the 19th Bomb Group in Java, 1942," comp. 1st Lt. John H. M. Smith, Second Bomber Command, Fort George Wright, Wash., October 19, 1943. In private collection of Henry Godman.

5th Bomber Command, Journal, January 13–March 19, 1942. In archives, 7th Bombardment Group (H) Historical Foundation, Cushman, Arkansas.

"S-3 Diary for 7th Bombardment Group, AFCC (Dec. 1, 1941–Feb. 27, 1942)," handwritten. In private collection of Robert F. Dorr.

"S-3 Diary for Seventh Bombardment Group, AFCC" (with telephone log), January 14–February 9, 1942, handwritten. IRIS 77576, Reel 1145, Air Force Historical Research Agency.

U.S. Army, Far East Air Force. "General Brereton's Headquarters Diary: Summary of the Activities for the Period 8th Dec. 1941–24 Feb. 1942." In Lewis Brereton collection, Dwight D. Eisenhower Presidential Library, Abilene, Kansas.

USS *Lanikai*. Log, February 1942. In private collection of Kemp Tolley.

USS *Phoenix*. "War Diary." February 1, 1942, to February 28, 1942. RG 38, NARA.

General and Special Orders

Air Base Headquarters, Hamilton Field, Calif. Special Orders No. 253, October 27, 1941. In private collection of Kenneth Glassburn.

Fifth Bomber Command, Malang. Special Orders No. 22, February 26, 1942. In "History of the 5th Air Force," Appendix II, doc. 1144.

Fourth Air Force, Hamilton Field, Calif. Special Orders No. 180, December 17, 1941. In private collection of B. J. Oliver.

Fourth Interceptor Command, Riverside, Calif. Special Orders No. 133, December 15, 1941. In private collection of Trudi Oestreicher Katz.

35th Pursuit Group, Hamilton Field. Special Orders No. 10, October 3, 1941. In private collection of Kenneth Glassburn.

U.S. Army Forces in Australia, Camp Ascot. Special Orders No. 3, January 13, 1942. In "History of the 5th Air Force," Appendix II, doc. 901.

U.S. Army Forces in Australia, Base Section 3, Brisbane. Special Orders No. 2, January 14, 1942. In private collection of Vernon L. Head.

———. Special Orders No. 20, February 4, 1942. In private collection of Vernon L. Head.

———. Special Orders No. 21, February 4, 1942. In box T789, RG 338, NARA.

———. Special Orders No. 22, February 6, 1942. In private collection of Trudi Oestreicher Katz.

U.S. Army Forces in Australia, Melbourne. General Orders No. 1, January 5, 1942; No. 4, January 17, 1942; No. 6, January 26, 1942; and No. 7, January 27, 1942. In box T788, RG 338, NARA.

———. Special Orders No. 21, February 4, 1942; No. 64, March 19, 1942; and No. 106, April 30, 1942. In box T789, RG 338, NARA.

U.S. Army Forces Far East. Special Orders No. 52, October 24, 1941. In Record Group 2, MacArthur Memorial Archives, Norfolk, Virginia.

Official Communications

ABDACOM to AGWAR, No. 395A, February 17, 1942. Microfilm A7118, Air Force Historical Research Agency.

———, No. 509A, February 21, 1942. Microfilm A7118, Air Force Historical Research Agency.

ABDACOM to CLG, January 15, 1942. In "History of the 5th Air Force," Appendix II.

ABDACOM to USAFIA (Darwin), radiograms, January 10–February 25, 1942. Box T1597, RG 338, NARA.

AGWAR to ABDACOM, radiograms, February 7–March 7, 1942. Box T1596, RG 338, NARA.

AGWAR to USAFIA, radiograms, December 27, 1941–March 8, 1942. Box T1601, RG 338, NARA.

Australia, Air Board, to Darwin, radiogram, November 18, 1941. Series A1196, NAA.

Australia, Department of Navy, to AIR, memo, November 19, 1941. Series A1196, NAA.

Australian Legation, Washington, to Prime Minister, cablegram No. 327, February 21, 1942. In private collection of Gordon Birkett.

Barnes, Julian, Headquarters, USAFIA, to CO, Headquarters USA, Brisbane, January 12, 1942. In "History of the 5th Air Force," Appendix II.

Base Section 3 to Air Board, Melbourne, January 13, 1942. In private collection of James McAfee.

Brereton to Base Section No. 2, Townsville, January 26, 1942. In "History of the 5th Air Force," Appendix II, Doc. 980.

Brereton, ABDACOM, to Brett, USAFIA, February 24, 1942. In "History of the 5th Air Force," Appendix II, Doc.741.

Brett to Arnold, February 9, 1942. In "History of the 5th Air Force," Appendix II, Doc. 1009.

Brisbane W/T to Airboard Melbourne, radiogram, January 21, 1942. In private collection of Gordon Birkett.

British Naval Headquarters, Batavia, to Melbourne, January 26, 1942, enclosing provisional list of telephone numbers, General Headquarters, Southwest Pacific Command. In National Archives of Australia and private collection of Gordon Birkett.

CAS to Wavell, radiogram No. 657, January 25, 1942. In National Archives of Australia and private collection of Gordon Birkett.

Casey, Washington, to Curtin, cablegram No. 350, February 24, 1942. In National Archives of Australia and private collection of Gordon Birkett.

Clagett, Brig. Gen., to U.S. Military Observer, Bandoeng, December 25, 1941. In "History of the 5th Air Force," Appendix II.

Combined Chiefs of Staff, Washington, to ABDACOM, DBA No. 22, February 22, 1942. AIR 23/5044, British National Archives.

Commander-in-Chief, ABDA Area, March 3, 1942. Executive Group Files, WPD, 1939–42, Entry 422, Executive 4, RG 165, NARA.

Curtin to Wavell, cablegram, February 6, 1942. In National Archives of Australia and private collection of Gordon Birkett.

Daly Waters to USAFIA, radiograms, February 25–March 12, 1942. Box T1593, RG 338, NARA.

Davies, Lt. Col. John H., to Brig. Gen. Clagett, January 1, 1942, in McAfee, "The 27th Reports."

———, to Commanding Officer, 91st Bomb Squadron, Archerfield, February 3, 1942. In private collection of James McAfee.

———, to Commanding Officer, No. 3 FTS, "Syllabus of A-24 and P-40 Pilots," December 30, 1941. In McAfee, "The 27th Reports."

———, to Maj. Gen. Brereton, January 4, 1942. In private collection of James McAfee.

Dept. of External Affairs to Assistant Minister, Washington, cablegram, February 6, 1942. In National Archives of Australia and private collection of Gordon Birkett.

Far East Air Force (Java) to USAFIA, radiograms, January 3–March 2, 1942, box T1594, RG 338, NARA.

Inspector, District Office, Broome, to Commissioner of Police, March 5, 1942. In private collection of Arvon Staats.

Java [miscellaneous] to USAFIA, radiograms, January 5–March 7, 1942, box T1595, RG 338, NARA.

Johnson, Maj., to CO, Ordnance Section, 64th Bomb Squadron, January 29, 1943. In private collection of Dwight Messimer.

Kiser, George E., to Adjutant Generals Department, memo, February 12, 1943. In private collection of George E. Kiser.

———, to Commanding Officer, 50th Fighter Group, memo, "History of Time in Combat Zone," April 19, 1943. In private collection of George E. Kiser.

MacArthur, Douglas, to George C. Marshall, December 14 and December 27, 1941, and January 7, 1942. In MacArthur Memorial Archives, Norfolk, Virginia.

Marshall to Brett, February 22, 1942. In "History of the 5th Air Force," Appendix II, Doc. 1126.

Marshall, George C., to Adjutant General, March 3, 1942. Executive Group Files, WPD, 1939–42, Entry 422, Executive 4, RG 165, NARA.

Marshall, George C., to Douglas MacArthur, December 24, 1941, and January 31, 1942. In MacArthur Memorial Archives, Norfolk, Virginia.

McMahon, Robert F., to Commanding Officer, AAF Field, Santa Rosa, California, July 19, 1944. In private collection of Robert McMahon.

Merle-Smith, Van, to Douglas MacArthur, October 31, 1941. In MacArthur Memorial Archives, Norfolk, Virginia.

Oestreicher, Robert G., to Paul Wurtsmith, CO, 49th Fighter Group, "Activities of the 33rd Pursuit Squadron Provisional, February 15–19, 1942," July 21, 1942. In "History of the 5th Air Force," Appendix II.

Page, London, to Curtin, cablegram, February 27, 1942, NAA and private collection of
    Gordon Birkett.
Pell, Capt. Floyd J., Headquarters, Townsville, to Chief of Air Corps, December 11,
    1941. In AIR AG 320.2, National Archives of Australia.
Roosevelt, President Franklin D., to Queen of Netherlands, February 26, 1942. In
    Franklin Delano Roosevelt Presidential Library, Hyde Park, New York.
Secretary, Prime Minister's Office, to Australian Minister, Washington, cablegram No.
    5292, February 21, 1942. In National Archives of Australia and private collec-
    tion of Gordon Birkett.
U.S. to Australian Naval Attaché to Naval Officer [on USAT *Polk*], December 26, 1941. In
    "History of the 5th Air Force," Appendix II.
USAFIA, outgoing radiograms, December 30, 1941–January 19, 1942. Box T1609, RG
    338, NARA.
————, outgoing radiograms, January 20–February 13, 1942. Box T1610, RG 338, NARA.
————, outgoing radiograms, February 14–28, 1942. Box T1611, RG 338, NARA.
————, outgoing radiograms, March 1–13, 1942. Box T1612, RG 338, NARA.
USAFIA to AGWAR, radiograms, January 1, 1942–March 8, 1942. Box T1602, RG 338,
    NARA.
USAFIA No. 505, Brett to Adjutant General for Marshall, March 5, 1942. Executive
    Group Files, WPD, 1939–42, Entry 422, Executive 4, RG 165, NARA.
USAFIA No. 551, Brett to Marshall, March 8, 1942. Executive Group Files, WPD, 1939–
    42, Entry 422, Executive 4, RG 165, NARA.
Wavell, Field Marshal Archibald, to Prime Minister Curtin, February 21, 1942. In Na-
    tional Archives of Australia and private collection of Gordon Birkett.
Wavell to British Joint Staff Mission, Washington, cablegram, February 25, 1942. In Na-
    tional Archives of Australia and private collection of Gordon Birkett.
Wavell to Combined Chiefs of Staff, Washington, ABDACOM No. 1996, February 22,
    1942. AIR 23/5044, British National Archives.
Wavell to Combined Chiefs of Staff, Washington, February 22, 1942. AIR 23/5044, Brit-
    ish National Archives.
Wavell to Curtin, cablegram, February 25, 1942. In National Archives of Australia and
    private collection of Gordon Birkett.
Wavell to Curtin, cablegram, February 9, 1942. In National Archives of Australia and
    private collection of Gordon Birkett.
Wavell radiograms in AIR 23/5038, British National Archives.

PERSONAL MATERIALS

Diaries, Memoirs, Notebooks, and Flight Logs

(All in the private collection of the writer except where indicated.)
Ambrosius, William H. Diary.
Anderson, J. Allen. Diary.
Badura, Bernard W. Diary.
Bender, Frank. Diary; memoir, ca. 1942.

Blanton, Nathaniel H. Memoir to Betty Ann, May 1999.

Boonstoppel, P. Memoir, September 3, 1968.

Bynum, Vernon. Memoir, "World War II Journal," no date.

Coss, Walter L. Notebooks No. 1 and No. 2.

Crane, James E. Memoir, ca. 1943 or 1944.

Cutler, Samuel. Diary.

Dean, Claude L. Diary, in private collection of Anthony Weller.

Dix, Gerald. Memoir, March 24, 1994, and memoir, "Twenty Three Years of Military Service as a Fighter Pilot," no date (ca. 1995).

Doan, Oliver. Diary.

Dutton, Albert H. Diary.

Eckley, Paul W. Diary, and memoir, "A Pilot's Story," no date.

Gambonini, Paul B. Diary; memoirs, no date; and flight log, 1941–42.

Geurtz, Arie. Memoir, no date.

Gies, C. Parker. Diary.

Glassburn, Kenneth. Flight log, 1941–42.

Gowen, John K. Log, in Edmonds materials, Air Force Historical Research Agency.

Hague, Jesse R. Diary.

Hayes, Thomas L., 20th Pursuit Squadron (Provisional). Diary.

Head, Vernon L. Diary.

Hennon, William J. Diary.

Herbert, Evan and Oscar, Australian civilians. Diary, in private collection of Shane Johnston.

Heyman, Alfred A. Diary.

Hoskyn, Wallace. Flight log, 1941–42.

Hoyt, Ross. "MacArthur—Manila to Melbourne," chapter in draft memoir, IRIS 34472, microfilm, Air Force Historical Research Agency.

Ingram, Cecil. Diary.

Johnsen, Lester J. Diary.

Johnson, Robert Spence. Diary.

Kent, James A. Diary, in private collection of Edward Rogers.

Kik, Adriaan. Memoir, May 5, 2000. At http://Abbekerk.worldpress.com.

Knudson, Cecil E. Diary, in Air Force Historical Research Agency.

Kruzel, Joseph J. Memoir, March 2001.

Latane, David. Flight log, 1941–42.

Legg, Richard A. Diary, in private collection of Carlos Dannacher; memoir, January 1989.

Mahony, Grant. Flight log, 1941–42.

Mangan, J. Harrison. Diary.

McAfee, James. Diary.

McMahon, Robert F. Memoir, 2001–2004.

McWherter, Robert C. Diary, and memoir, "Diary of a Fighter Pilot," no date.

Nichols, Murray. Memoir, 1997.

O'Donnell, Emmett. Diary, in Special Collections, U.S. Air Force Academy Library, Colorado Springs, Colo.

Oestreicher, Robert G. Retrospective diary.

Oliver, Bernard J. Diary; memoir, "An Autobiography," 2003; and flight log, 1941–42.

Parker, George A. Diary.

Perry, Kenneth H. Diary, as excerpted in Weller, "Luck to the Fighters."

Preddy, George. Diary, in private collection of Trudi Oestreicher Katz.

Rouse, John. Diary, in Air Force Historical Research Agency.

Sanders, Homer. Diary, in private collection of Dwight Messimer.

Seamon, Walter E. Diary, in Edmonds materials, Air Force Historical Research Agency, as "anonymous.")

Smelser, Harold. Diary, and flight log, 1941–42.

Smith, James Calvin. Diary.

Stimson, Henry L. Diary, in Henry L. Stimson Papers, Library of Congress.

Wilhite, V. H. Bryce. Diary, and memoir, no date.

Yerington, Edward O. Memoir, "The Evacuation of Java," no date.

Correspondence

Alford, Bob, to author, e-mail, April 12, 2008.

Anemaet, R. a. d., to J. W. T. Bosch to Patty Groves, February 29, 1976.

Badura, Bernard, to author, January 19, 1994.

Baum, Peg Hague, to author, December 7, 1993 and January 12, 1994.

Beck, Richard, to author, March 26, 1994.

Birkett, Gordon, to author, e-mails, October 24, 2003; September 6, 2004; January 2, March 14, and May 20, 2005; February 11, 2006.

Blanton, Nathaniel, to author, August 13 and October 4, 2003, and March 27 and 30 and May 27, 1994.

———, taped narrative to author, July 1993 and March 30–April 1, 1994.

Boer, Peter, to author, e-mails, March 1 and 2, July 15, August 5 and 8, and November 7, 2005; April 4 and 6, July 24, October 13, 16, 17, 20, 23, and 27, 2006; January 12, February 2 and 20, October 4, 18, 25, 27, and 29, and November 2, 2007; June 17, 2008; April 14, July 13–17, 23–25, 27–30, and August 3–4, 6, 2009.

———, to John Stanaway, e-mail, July 26, 2005.

Boise, Louis, to author, June 15 and October 24, 1994.

Bosch, J. W. T., to Patty Groves, October 11, 1975 and April 28, 1976.

Bowles, Charles W., to Dwight Messimer, January 2, 1984 and August 21, 1989.

Broadhurst, Edwin, to mother, January 24, 1942.

Brown, Bryan, to author, September 30, 1994,.

Bruggink, Gerard, to author, June 27 and July 10, 1995.

Bruinier, Jan B. H., to author, January 26, July 26, and August 14, 1995.

Bujold, Real, to author, February 25, 1997.

Burnside, David, to author, October 26, 2002.

Bushby, Les, to Shane Johnston, no date.

Childress, Peter, to mother, March 9, 1942.

Coss, Walter, to author, January 18, February 23, March 16, April 17, June 22, and September 14, 1994; January 6 and March 24, 1995; February 11, 1996.

Crane, James E., Jr., to author, e-mails, January 2 and 8 and October 31, 2006.

Dalley, Joseph W., to author, e-mail, March 17, 2008.

Dutton, Albert, to Millie Lewis, September 30, 1942.

Eckley, Paul, to author, November 25 and December 1, 2006.

Egenes, Hubert, to Harold Larson, November 22, 1941 and March 14, 1942.

———, to parents, November 24 and 30 and December 18, 1941.

Farrior, William, to Roger Marks, February 28, 1993.

Filon, R. A., to Max Schep, August 23, 1988.

Freake, Clyde, to Shane Johnston, March 20, 2003.

Fuchs, Marion, to author, March 24, 1994.

Funk, Ben, to Harry Murdock, March 20, 2000.

———, to Harry Murdock, e-mail, March 20, 2000.

George, Max, to Shane Johnston, May 2002.

Geurtz, Arie, to author, January 8 and 10 and March 28, 1994.

———, to Gerry Casius, February 19, March 4, and April 2, 1978.

Glassburn, Kenneth, to author, May 31, 1994.

Grunewald, G. G., to Max Schep, August 8, 1984.

Guerrero, Julian, to author, November 29, 2002.

Haines, Walter, to author, January 18, 2007.

Hanks, Ted, to Carlos Dannacher, September 19, 1994 and January 18, 1997.

Hansen, Katherine Landry, to author, March 15, 1994.

Haye, H. M. to Max Schep, February 2, 1984.

Hayes, Thomas, to author, November 17 and 30, 1993.

Hoffman, Arthur, to "Little Bum," May 26, 1942.

Holt, Dale, "round robin" letter, n.d.

———, to author, September 10, 1994.

Jackson, Elwin, to author, August 31, 1994.

Johnsen, Eleanor, to author, September 3, 1993.

Johnston, Shane, to author, e-mails, May 27, 2005, January 31, 2007, and June 3, 2009.

Kehn, Don, to author, e-mails, May 26 and 30 and November 24, 2006; July 27–29, 2009.

Kelsay, Clyde B., to author, May 4, 1994.

Koval, Albert, to author, October 28, 2002.

Kruzel, Joseph, to Patty Groves, September 15, 1975.

Landry, Larry, to parents, December 7, 19, 22, and 23, 1941.

Lane, William, to Mrs. Ada May Landry, February 19, 1943.

Latane, David, to author, e-mail, November 28, 1997.

Launder, Richard, to author, e-mail, February 6, 2006.

Lewis, John, to wife, March 11, 1942.

Mahony, Grant, to mother, November 1, 1942.

Mahony, Mrs. H. G., to Miss Smith, December 22, 1942.

Martin, Ralph, to author, taped narrative, January 1999.

McMahon, Robert, to author, March 2 and June 12, 1994.

McWherter, Robert, to author, February 14, 1995.

———, to Mr. and Mrs. Hoskyn, February 19, 1943.

Morehead, James B., to author, May 1, 1993; May 5 and 29, 1995; and August 5, 2009.

Naylor, James, to author, May 14, 1994.

Nichols, Murray, to author, January 15 and February 17, 1997.

Oestreicher, Robert, to father, December 23, 1941.

Oliver, Bernard J., to author, August 7, 1993.

Pehl, Charles, to author, February 10, 1994.

Perry, Ausman, to author, May 24 and September 26, 1994.

Pingree, Jane, to author, August 14, 2004.

Poncik, Victor, to author, February 28, 1994.

Rogers, Edward, to author, e-mail, August 22, 2005.

Sanders, Homer, to Dwight Messimer, March 8, 1983.

Sawruk, James, to author, e-mails, January 28, 2005, ; November 24, 2006, ; and March 10, 2007.

Schep, Max, to author, September 14, 1993 ; March 23, 1994 ; January 4, February 22, and March 10, 1995; and January 5, 1998.

Selman, Larry, to author, November 8, 1994.

Staats, Arvon, to author, September 29, 1999.

Suehr, Richard, to author, March 21, 1994 and February 26, 2005.

Tagaya, Osamu, to author, e-mails, January 2, 2002; February 19 and 27, 2005; March 6 and April 27, 2005; July 6 and November 23, 2006; February 21 and August 4, 2007.

Taylan, Justin, to author, e-mail, September 11, 2007.

Tolley, Kemp, to author, December 2, 1995.

Van der Vossen, Alex, to author, September 25, 1995.

Vance, Reginald, "Notes on Java Story," to Walter D. Edmonds, no date (ca. 1947).

Wade, Horace, to author, April 29, 1989.

———, to Robert Lewellyn, December 16, 1990.

Wiecks, Max, to author, September 4 and 20, 1993.

Wilhite, V. H. Bryce to parents, November 24, 1941.

Witney, R. W., to Shane Johnston, August 8, 2001.

INTERVIEWS

Anemaet, R. a. d., with Max Schep, June 2, 1971.

Blanton, Nathaniel, with author, telephone, January 12 and November 30, 2004.

Boise, Louis, with author, Chico, Calif., September 11, 1994.

Borckardt, Margaret Smith, with author, telephone, August 16, 1994.

Bowles, Charles, with Dwight Messimer, August 1989.

Coleman, W. David, with author, Orinda, Calif., November 17, 1993.

Coss, Walter, with author, Somerset, Va., April 17, 1994.

Creutzberg, H., with Peter Boer, February 1975.

Dale, Jack, Orlando, Fla., with Walter D. Edmonds and USAAF Personnel, November 14, 1944.

Dockstader, Robert, with author, telephone, December 31, 1996.

Fisher, William P., with Walter D. Edmonds and USAAF Personnel, May 27, 1942.

Gambonini, Paul, with author, Novato, Calif., March 5, 1994.

———, Hal Lund, and James Morehead, with author, Novato, Calif., July 6, 1994.

Geurtz, Arie, with author, telephone, March 9, 2007.

Gladman, Robert, with author, telephone, August 7, 1994.

Glassburn, Kenneth, with author, telephone, January 20, 1994.

Hayes, Thomas, with author, Spottsylvania, Va., April 16 and 17, 1994.

Head, Vernon L., with author, Carmel, Calif., January 15, 1994.

Holt, Dale, with author, Auburn, Calif., September 10, 1994.

Hurd, Walter, with author, telephone, September 19, 1994.

Jackson, Elwin, with author, telephone, September 3, 1994.

Katz, Trudi Oestreicher, with author, telephone, February 25, 1994.

Kezar, Dalys C., with Walter D. Edmonds and USAAF Personnel, Colorado Springs, March 20, 1944; April 10, 1945.

Kok, A., with Max Schep, 1968 and September 17, 1983.

Koopmans, C. a. m., with Max Schep, March 16, 1985.

Laurie, John, with author, telephone, October 22, 2006.

Lund, Harold, with author, San Rafael, Calif., December 4, 1993.

McMahon, Robert, with author, telephone, July 22, 2008.

Martin, Ralph, with author, Dulles, Va., September 29, 2005.

Melikian, Ray, with author, telephone, February 16, 1994.

Morehead, James B., with author, Novato, Calif., May 1 and July 14, 1993; January 7, 1995.

Reagan, Cornelius, with Jonathan Juarez, Spring 2005, DVD, Library of Congress

Ruwoldt, Rex, at www.australiansatwarfilmarchive.gov.au/aafwa/interviews.1596.aspx.

Smelser, Harold, with Walter D. Edmonds and USAAF Personnel, April 6, 8, and 9, 1942.

Suehr, Richard, with author, telephone, September 18 and 19, 2008.

Tull, James E., with Walter D. Edmonds and USAAF Personnel, February 1944.

Van der Vossen, Alex, with Max Schep, January 6 and June 4, 1994.

Wagner, Boyd D., with Roosevelt der Tatevision, no date, Edmonds materials, Air Force Historical Research Agency.

Wahl, Eugene, with author, Pacific Grove, Calif., March 19, 1994.

———, with author, telephone, February 22 and July 28, 1994; July 18 and 19 and December 3, 2005; December 13, 2006.

Wiecks, Max, with Walter D. Edmonds and USAAF Personnel, Noemfoor, New Guinea, October 11, 1944.

Wiecks, Reid, with author, telephone, October 31, 2004.

WEB SITES

www.jbaugher.com

www.militarymuseum.org/Agwiworld.htmc

www.militarymuseum.org/Emidio.htmc

www.ozatwar.com

www.surfcity.kund.dalnet.se/commonwealth_turnbull.htm

www.home.st.net.au-dunn/ozcrashes/wa26.htm

www.combinedfleet.com/tone_t.htm.

www.geocities.com/dutcheastindies/pecos.html

www.kmike.com/BrowningMG/T1205S1.htm

www.abbekerk.wordpress.com (Memoir of Adriaan Kik)

www.j-aircraft.org/smf/index.php

INDEX

Page numbers with illustrations appear in *italics*.

tion, 244; Pell's body at, 236, Walker at, 244, 252

Berry, Jack, 328–29, 333

B-18: arrives Darwin with Pell, 21, carries supplies for 20th Pursuit Squadron (Provisional), 89; piloted by Henry Rose, 148; shot down near Soerabaja, 384n.3

Blanton, Nathaniel "Cy," 70, 242, 243, 262, arrives Ngoro, 386–87n.32; at Ascot, 49; at Blimbing, 112; belly-lands P-40E, 241–42, 243 413n.50; brake problem of at Amberley, 70; in combat with Zeros, 241–42, 413n.49; at Darwin, 75, 76, 379n.78; evacuation of to Australia, 305; extricates Reed from P-40, 139–40, 393n.68; on ferry flight north, 63, 70; and Fields, 181; on flight to Australia, 40; on flight to Soerabaja, 78, 83, 85; to 49th Pursuit Group, 340; on interception missions from Ngoro, 140, 141, 218–20, 413n.49; leads 20th Pursuit (Provisional) pilots to Ngoro Field, 132, 144, 178–79; at Lennon's Hotel, 49, 52; at Ngoro, 113, 116, 120, 180, and recon missions, 218–20, 238–40; at Soerabaja, 94, 96, 243, 244, 267; and severed ear of Neri, 96, 98, 384n.83; victory claim of, 220

Blenheim bombers, 10

Blimbing, 96, 179; characteristics of, 112; evening meals at, 165–66; houses at for P-40 pilots, 91, 96, 112, 133, 165, 179; Java evacuees leave, 266, 316; living arrangements for 17th Pursuit Squadron (Provisional), 91–92, 93, 112; pilots bored at, 216; sugar mill remains at, 344, 345; 17th Pursuit Squadron (Provisional) arrives at, 98, 112

Blitar, 419n.45

Bodjonegoro, 310

Boise, Louis A. "Bud," 63, 74, 76

Bombay, 198, 203

Bonnington, John, 74, 76, 89

Boonstoppel, P, 277, 310, 428–29n.2

Bopp, Roy, 226

Borden, Bill: aborts flight at Sydney, 173, 174, 399n.12; decides to proceed to Fremantle, 192; lands at Maylands, 220; left behind at Port Pirie, 183, 192; on Port Pirie-Perth flight, 220; rejoins Amberley-Perth flight, 174; selected for Port Pirie-Darwin flight, 175

Borneo, 16

Bound, Gene, 86, 275; arrives Fremantle, 333; in Bali combat, 126–27, 390n.11, 390n.12, 391n.17; on board *Abbekerk*, 280, 298; evacuated to Jogjakarta, 268, 274; in Malang hospital, 268; and Malang-Jogjakarta-Tjilatjap rail trip, 274, 275; on *Polk*, 48; shot down over Bali, 127, 390n.13, 436n.17; visits Poncik, 274–75

Bowles, Charles W., on board *Sea Witch*, 261; departs Tjilatjap, 325; and Fremantle-Tjilatjap voyage, 261, 301–02; and unloading of crated P-40Es, 302

Boxman, Willem, 120, 383n.66

Brady, Francis, 48, 374n.63

Brain, Lester, 330

Bram, Christian, 256–57, 416n.42

Bren gun carrier, 225

Brenner, Francis E, 26

Brereton, Lewis H., 11, 12, 13, 55, 57, 58, 86, 150, as ABDAIR deputy commander, 53–54, 99, 200, 404n.18; at ABDACOM headquarters, 59; acts as ABDAIR commander, 54; arrives ABDACOM headquarters, 55; announces ferry route to Philippines broken, 56; announces P-40 pilots to defend NEI, 56, 378n.73; appoints Mahony as commander of 17th Pursuit Squadron (Provisional), 262; arrives Australia to take over USAFIA, 41, 55; arrives Colombo, *201*; and assembly

Brereton, Lewis H. (*cont.*)
and training situation in Australia, 41, 42; assigned to India, 270; authority of to end allied air operations on Java, 289; concerned about Java air situation, 99, 103, 104; departs Java, 200–01, 276; and diversion of *Sea Witch* to Java, 200, 404n.18; and FEAF for Burma, 104, 200; meets 17th Pursuit Squadron (Provisional) pilots at Darwin, 56, 75; orders Mahony to India, 270; orders 20th Pursuit Squadron (Provisional) to Port Moresby, 58, 375n.23, 379n.84, 381n.47, 382n.54; and Peirse request for Sprague, 217–18; and prewar mission to Australia, 12, 22; and pressure from Australians for P-40s, 17, 57–58, 379n.84, 381n.44; relieved of USAFIA command, 58; transfers Darwin FEAF staff to ABDACOM, 55; visits Ngoro Field, 217–18; and Wavell, 53, 55, 58, 104; withdraws FEAF from Java, 200

Brett, George H., 12, 110, 145, 198, 200, 212, 379n.87; appointed deputy commander ABDACOM, 53; arrives Australia, 13; assumes command USAFIA, 12, 13, 201, 203, 283; and Broome, 299, 324, 328; and Burnett request for P-40Es, 58, 59, 381–82n.47, 382n.54; and defense of Java, 203, 283, 385n.18; departs Java for Australia, 201; and evacuation FEAF from Java, 200, 203, 284, 288, 289; and routing of *Langley* and MS-5 convoy, 102–03, 198, 199, 203; and Helfrich, 283; meets Wavell on arrival Batavia, 53, *54;* orders pursuit squadrons to Darwin, 103, 400n.16; and pilot training, 109, 340; and P-40 reinforcements for Java, 58, 101, 102, 203, 283, 379n.84; and P-40 squadrons for Tjisaoek, 103; responds to Dutch complaint to Marshall, 287–90; and *Sea Witch* routing, 283, 286;

supports Eubank's defense against accusations, 288, 289; suspends air ferry flights to Koepang, 101; and 20th Pursuit Squadron (Provisional) to Java, 89, 122; and his transfer to India, 196, 201; and "unreasonable requests" of Dutch, 289, 290; and winding up of ABDACOM, 200

Brewster Buffalo fighters: at Andir Field, 212; arrive at Ngoro Field, 273, 277, 421n.15, 422n.32; escort A-24s, 295, 296; interception mission from Ngoro Field, 276; and Java invasion force attack, 296; on Kragan strafing mission, 306, 307, 308, 310, 428–29n.2; in Malaya and Singapore, 10; in NEIAF, 16; range of, 294; strafed at Ngoro Field, 311

Brisbane, 34–35, 374n.54; aircraft of *Pensacola* convoy arrive at, 12; Koepang evacuation flights to, 223; *Pensacola* convoy ordered diverted to, 11; *Polk* arrives at, 63–64; *Republic* arrives at 32, 189

Brisbane assembly depot, 152, 154

BRITAIR, and Java invasion forces, 285; RAF and RAAF squadrons of, 285; remains on Java, 285; squadron personnel of become POWs, 290

British Far Eastern Fleet, 9

British North Borneo, 8, 11, 16

Britt, Charley, 329

Broadhurst, Edwin, 178, 318

Broome, 223, 300, 324, 327, 433n.12; air defenses of, 324; air evacuations to, 305, 319, 320, 322–25; aircraft servicing problems at, 287, 300, 324; civilian evacuations from, 299; Dutch flying boats destroyed at, 330; evacuation of, 330–31; Japanese reconnaissance over, 322, 323, 324, 325, 327, 433n.9, 433n.12; and Java evacuees to south, 287; Legg arrives at, 299; panic at, 287; rescue efforts at, 330, 332;

as U.S. bomber base in Java defense, 287, 288; and Winckel return fire, 434n.28; Zero attack on, 287, 328–30, 434n.28

Brown, Bryan: accidents of at Townsville and Daly Waters, 70, 148, 378n.66; on ferry flight north, 70; selected for PLUM, 19; selected for 17th Pursuit Squadron (Provisional), 62, 65; to 67th Pursuit Squadron, 341

Brown, Cecil, 148

Bruce, Jim, 151, 192; arrives Darwin, 150, 396n.29; assigned to 13th Pursuit Squadron (Provisional), 175, 400n.24; lands at Mascot Field, 400n.24, 400n.25; lands at Maylands, 220; leads 13th Pursuit Squadron (Provisional) to Newcastle, 177, to Laverton Field, 191, to Melbourne, 192, to Port Pirie, 192, to Perth, 220; on P-40 familiarization flight, 150; ordered back to Amberley from Perth, 221

Bruggink, Gerard, 277, 310, 428–29n.2

Bruinier, Jan: and Anemaet, 307, 430n.29; awaits capture, 326; on Kragan strafing mission, 307, 308, 310, 428–29n.2; leaves Ngoro for Andir, 319, 325; reports in at NEIAF headquarters, 325

B-17C: as guide for 3rd Pursuit Squadron (Provisional) to Daly Waters and Darwin, 147, 149; shot down over Java, 388n.62; as transport for 17th Pursuit Squadron (Provisional), 74, 378n.68, 379n.80; as transport for 20th Pursuit Squadron (Provisional), 105, 106–07, 108

B-17Ds, 5, 10, 13; aborted missions of, 56; arrive in Philippines, 4, 8; bases for in Australia and NEI, 12; for defense of Australian, British, and Dutch territories, 8; destroyed at Clark Field, 11; as deterrent to Japanese southern movement, 4; at Pasirian, 262;

transfer of to Australia from Philippines, 12

B-17Es, 317, 326–27, 335, 336; arrivals of at Singosari, 56, 58; attack Bali invasion force, 240, 258–59; attack Kragan invasion vessels, 288; attack Palembang, 212, 407n.32; at Broome, 285, 287, 329, *323*, destroyed at Singosari, 100, 256, 288, 416n.37, 417n.66, evacuate FEAF personnel to Australia, 285, 299, 301, 305, 317, 318–19, 320, 321, 322–24, 327; guide pursuit squadrons to Koepang, 209, 224, 225; losses of, 58; missions of from Singosari, 56, 133, 392n.42, 394n.75, 394n.83; operations of at Singosari, 141, 142, 178 424n.17; , and Project X, 13; proposed operations of from Tasikmalaja, 424n.17; transferred to Jogjakarta from Malang, 276;

B-24s: as deterrent to Japanese southern movement, 4; and air bases for in Australia and NEI, 12; and operations from Tasikmalaja, Singosari and Jogjakarta, 424n.17; sent to Far East under Project X, 13

B-24As, 126, 131, 299, 331, 333; assigned Legg for Java evacuation, 299; attacked at Broome, 287; destroyed on ground at Broome, 329; for escort of 20th Pursuit Squadron (Provisional) to Darwin, Koepang and Bali, 89, 105, *106*, 107, 121, 123, 125, 126, 385n.1; and evacuations to Australia, 301, 305, 327, 328; shot down on takeoff at Broome, 328, 332, 434n.22, 434n.28, 435n.35; transports 3rd Pursuit Squadron (Provisional) enlisted men to Java, 159, 160

B-26, 342

Buel, Robert "Blackie": arrives on *Republic,* 189, at Ascot Race Track, *189;* on convoy search patrol, 403n.69; Darwin P-40 mechanical problems of,

Chungking, 11
Churchill, Winston, 14
Clagett, Henry B., 38
Clark Field, 10
Cleveland, Mr. and Mrs., 36, 37, 39
Cliff, Howard C., 435n.35
Cloncurry: accommodations at, 71–72; as
    ferry stop, 42; heat of, 71, 72; refueling
    aircraft at, 147; 17th Pursuit Squadron
    (Provisional) arrives at, 71; 3rd Pursuit
    Squadron (Provisional) at, 146, 147;
    20th Pursuit Squadron (Provisional)
    at, 107
Cockcroft, Selby, 305
Cocos Islands, 304
Coffs Harbor, 171
Coleman, William D. "Dave," at Bali
    Hotel, 144, 223; and boat trip to Den-
    pasar, 138; as candidate for PLUM,
    20; at Charleville, 106; crash lands
    on Lombok, 135–36, 393n.55; evacu-
    ated by Dutch to Australia, 223; on
    Koepang-Bali flight, 135; on Lom-
    bok, 137–38; selected for 17th Pursuit
    Squadron (Provisional), 62; selected
    for 20th Pursuit Squadron (Provi-
    sional), 87; to 67th Pursuit Squadron,
    341
Colleen, 250
Collett, Jim, 96
Colombo, 199, 200–01, 202
Combined Chiefs of Staff (CCS): agrees
    to diversion of P-40s to Australia,
    100; composition of, 14; establish-
    ment of, 14; introduces and revises
    P-40 allocation schedule, 101, 102;
    returns Wavell to India, 201; turns
    over ABDACOM to Dutch, 201; and
    winding up of ABDACOM, 200, 202;
    and withdrawal of air forces from
    Java, 200, 288, 289, 424n.18
Combined Fleet, ABDAFLOAT, 99
Combined Fleet, Japanese Navy, 7
Combined Striking Force: losses of in

Battle of Java Sea, 285; planned attack
    of on invasion transports, 295; pro-
    tective patrols above, 294, 295, 297,
    421n.15
Connelly, Louis J., 84, 136, 245: evades
    "Messerschmitt 110," 135; guides
    20th Pursuit Squadron (Provisional),
    Darwin-Koepang-Bali, 134, 134–35;
    flies Philippine veterans to Australia,
    39, 40, 48; and 33rd Pursuit Squad-
    ron (Provisional) flight to Koepang,
    209, 225
Corregidor, 16
Cosgrove, C.B., 421n.23
Coss, Walt, 62, 63, 84, 113, 210, 249–50;
    298, 417n.4; accommodations for at
    Blimbing, 112; and air evacuation
    to Australia, 305; at Amberley, 62;
    arrives Del Monte, 40; arrives Ngoro,
    111, 386–87n.32; arrives Soerabaja,
    85; at Ascot Race Track, 57; on Bali
    attack mission, 247, 248, 249, 251; at
    Batavia, 211; on B-17 protection mis-
    sions, 178, 180; in combat with Zeros
    and Bettys, 116–119, 161–62, 240, 249;
    as executive officer to Sprague, 90; in
    February 3rd combat, 116–119, 388n.61,
    388n.62; to 49th Pursuit Group, 340;
    guided by Dutch to Ngoro Field, 90–
    91, 382–83n.64; inspects Ngoro Field,
    91; on Koepang-Soerabaja flight, 78,
    85; leads 17th Pursuit Squadron (Pro-
    visional) evacuees to Jogjakarta, 266–
    68; on interceptions from Ngoro, 115,
    140, 160, 167, 258; at Jogjakarta, 268,
    298, 301; leads 17th Pursuit Squad-
    ron (Provisional) flight north to Dar-
    win, 68, 70, 71, 72; leads 20th Pursuit
    Squadron (Provisional) to Ngoro,
    138–39; on Palembang attack mission,
    209–10, 213–14, 215; promoted to cap-
    tain, 419.38; shoots down Zero, 118,
    388n.62
Craig Field, 80, 176

Crandell, John, 133–34, 150, 420n.9

Crane, James E., on *Abbekerk,* 279–80, 281, 298, 303–04; assigned at Lembang, 212; and evacuation of wounded to Tjilatjap, 278–79; and Neri as patient, 212; and Sprague, 212

Crawford, Jack, 181

Crescent City, 371–72n.56

Creutzberg, H., 326, 326–27, 424n.17

Criswell, J.R., 156

Crouch, Edwin, 301, 304, 427n.50

Crowder, Murray, 320, 323

C-39, 35

Culpepper, Ben, 66, 96

Cunningham, Vic, 66

Curtin, John, 100, 198

Curtiss Hawk 75s: in combat with Zeros, 120, 388n.61, 389n.68, 392n.41; disadvantages of against Zeros, 121; losses of, 388n.68, 392n.41

CW-21s, 94, 277; in Tandjoeng Perak aerial show, 96; compared with P-40E, 383n.79; disadvantages of against Zero, 121; in February 3rd interception, 119, 388n.61, 389n.69; lead 17th Pursuit Squadron (Provisional) to Ngoro, 111, 386n.31; losses of, 392n.41; in NEIAF, 16; pilots of shot down, 119, 389n.69; of 2-Vl.G-IV at Maospati, *97*

Dale, Jack, 94, 278; and air evacuation to Australia, 308, 311, 318, 322, 432, n.53; on alert at Ngoro, 180, 258, 272, 275; at Amberley, 52; and Anemaet, 277; arrives Brisbane, 49; arrives Del Monte, 40; arrives Ngoro, 386–87n.32; at Ascot, 49; in attack on Java invasion force, 295; on B-17E protective mission, 178; in combat with Zeros, 272; confers with ADC, 133, 392.42; on ferry flight to Darwin, 70; to 49th Pursuit Group, 340; on interception missions from Ngoro, 116, 140, 141, 142, 160, 167, 258, 269, 272,

275–76; at Jogjakarta, 317; in Kragan strafing mission, 308, 309, 310, 311, 429n.5; and Kurtz, 308, 311; leads pursuit pilots to Ngoro, 138–39, 164–65; at Lennon's Hotel, 49, 52; at Magoewo airfield, *317*

Daly Waters, 245; accidents at, 148–49; characteristics of airfield, 148, 185, 186; 17th Pursuit Squadron (Provisional) arrives at, 71; 33rd Pursuit Squadron (Provisional) arrives at, 185; 20th Pursuit Squadron (Provisional) arrives at, 108

Darnton, Byron, 335

Darwin, 101, 206, 209, 342, 420n.9, 436n.24; attack on, 195, 196, 198, 226–238; evacuation of, 196; convoy returns to, 206, 208; Japanese losses in attack on, 196, 198; and Koepang evacuees, 223, 224; *Langley* at, *102, 221*; in 1942, *197*; and Pell flight to Koepang, 224–25; P-40 squadron to protect, 103; and 20th Pursuit Squadron (Provisional) flight to Koepang delayed, 121–22; 33rd Pursuit Squadron (Provisional) flight ordered to, 174; weaknesses of defenses of, 100, 196;

Darwin convoy to Koepang, 190, 195, 205; Buel search for, 188; flying boat attack on, 188, 190, 205, 402n.64; heads for Koepang, 188; ordered back to Darwin, 206, 406n.10; pursuit squadron to protect, 103, 206, 400n.16; P-40 search patrols for, 190, 205, 206–07

Darwin harbor, 342; Aichi Val shot down over, 412n.28; McMahon over, 231, 232–33, *233*, 234; ships sunk in, 196; as target for Japanese, 196

Darwin hospital, 232

Darwin RAAF field, 103, 149, 151, 156, 186, 224, 406n.13; and arrival of Pell, 21; attacked by Japanese, 196, 235, 412n.38; A-24s land at, 149; Handy cracks up at, 149; as jumping off point for NEI ferry flights, 42; and meeting of Brereton with 17th Pursuit Squadron (Provisional), 75; P-40E remains at, *239, 243;* 17th Pursuit Squadron (Provisional) arrives at, 71, 72, 379n.80; 3rd Pursuit Squadron (Provisional) arrives at, 149, *151;* 33rd Pursuit Squadron (Provisional) at, 187, 205, 224

Davao, 11, 13

Davies, John "Big Jim": and assembly of P-40s, 45; designated in charge of training *Pensacola* convoy pilots, 38; and 91st Bomb Squadron to Darwin, 145; ordered send A-24s to Darwin, 145; presents training program, 38; reviews training program, 41–42, 45

Davis, Paul, 305; arrives Broome, 329, 434n.28; attacked by Zeros on Darwin-Java flight, 159; awaits take off for Perth, 327–28; B-24A of destroyed at Broome, 329; and escort of 20th Pursuit Squadron to Darwin, 89, 385n.1, to Koepang, 121, 122–23, to Bali, 125; transports 3rd Pursuit Squadron (Provisional) men to Java, 159, 160, 397n.50

DC-2s, arrive Soerabaja, 89; provided by RAAF, 63; transports 17th Pursuit Squadron (Provisional) men to Darwin, 74, 76, 89, 379n.78, to Koepang, 89

Dean, Claude, 113

De Haas, G.J.,295; arrives Ngoro, 277; briefed on Japanese invasion force, 295; flies CSF protective patrol, 294; on interception mission, 302; on Kragan strafing mission, 307, 308, 310, 428–29n.2; leads Brewster attack on Java invasion force, 295

DeHaviland Dragon Rapide, 382n.59

DeHaviland Tiger Moth, 90

Dejalle, N., 310, 428–29n.2

Del Monte, as advanced FEAF base, 56; on ferry route to Philippines, 12, 42; Philippine ferry pilots at, 39

Denpasar airfield, 223, 249–50; and Bali strike mission, 248, 249; damaged P-40Es at, *138,* 144; Japanese aerial attack on, 126–30; Japanese attack missions from, 418n.23, 432n.55; loss of to Japanese, 196, 249; and 20th Pursuit Squadron (Provisional), 124, 126, 132, 136; strafed by Coss and Mahony, 249, 251; Zeros and Bettys based at, 276, 283, 416n.37, 430n.22, 432n.55; and Zero-P-40 combat over, 126–129

Deterrent strategy, 4, 5, 8, 10

De Wilde, F.J., 277, 310, 428–29n.2

Deyo, Fred, 120, 262

Dierkens, Aime, 400n.23

Dix, Gerald "Gerry," 174, 246, 266, 291; abandons ship, 293; aborts flight at Sydney, 173, 174, 399n.12; arrives Fremantle, 334; to 8th Pursuit Group, 341; on *Langley,* 266, 291; on *Pecos,* 304, 313–15; on *Polk, 293;* rescued by *Edsall, 293, 300;* rescued by *Whipple,* 315–16, 334; selected for 33rd Pursuit Squadron (Provisional), 154; in water, 315; wounded during attack on *Langley,* 292–93

Djember, 143, 166–67

Djombang, 90, 420n.8

Dockstader, Robert: and air evacuation to Australia, 318, 322; in combat with Bettys, 269; on Darwin-Koepang flight, 163; to 49th Pursuit Group, 341; on mission to meet *Langley,* 277, 425n.13; at Ngoro, 165

Donalson, I.B. Jack, 20

Donoho, Melvin, 76; in attack on Kester's B-24A, 328; award for turned down, 435n.3; flown to Perth, 333; reports in to Legg, 332; survives B-24A crash, 331; swims to shore, 328, 331, 332

Doorman, Karel, 99, 285, 295

5th Bomber Command, 298–99, 391n.33:
aborted missions of, 56; and coordination of with Air Defense Command, 217; evacuation of to Australia,
285; Java operations of, 13; moves to
Jogjakarta, 276, 277; operational obstacles experienced, 100; Philippines
FEAF evacuees to, 396n.29; proposed
operations from Broome of, 285; P-40
protection for, 178, 180; striking force
of expanded, 58; and weather problems, 56
5th Interceptor Command, 94
55th Pursuit Squadron, 28
51st Pursuit Group: allocated to Java, 198;
arrives Fremantle, 246; arrives Melbourne, 101, 400n.26; crew chiefs and
armorers for PLUM, 27; departs Fremantle, 260; departs Melbourne, 177;
diverted to India/Burma, 199, 200,
265; ground crews of to board *Langley,* 246, 247; ordered to NEI, 101, 177,
178, 400n.26; P-40Es assigned to, 27;
P-40Es of shipped by sea to Java, 101,
400n.26; and pilots assigned PLUM,
26–27, 28; and pilots for Pursuit Combat Team, 28, 30; sails for NEI, 103
56th Regiment, 428n.56
1st Air Fleet, 196, 285, 286
1st kokutai, 388n.59, 392–93n.51, 412n.38
Fisher, William P., 216, 217, 240, 273,
288, 295, 311, 428n.57; aborts flight
to Koepang, 157, 216, 397n.51; and Air
Defense Command operations, 216,
217, 218, 408n.52; and Anemaet, 312;
arrives Darwin, 150; and Eubank,
318; and evacuation of Ngoro pilots,
266, 270, 305–06, 307, 311, 428n.57,
428n.58, 429n.19; as interceptor control officer, 216; and Kragan strafing
mission, 295, 306, 307, 311, 428n.59;
ordered to Air Defense Command,
150, 156; orders pilots to Tjilatjap to
meet *Langley,* 277; selected for air

evacuation to Australia, 318; takes
P-40 to Java, 150, 156; visits Ngoro
Field, 216, 217
Flinders Range, 184
Flores, 135
Flores Sea, 240
Flying Fish Cove, 300
Formosa, 10
Forrest, 192, *193*
48th Division, 428n.56
40th Fighter Squadron, 435n.3
40th Pursuit Squadron, 341, 342
41st Pursuit Squadron, 342, 343
45th Service Group, 342
41-C flying school graduates, 20, 28
41-E flying school graduates, 339;
assigned to Hamilton Field, 19, 20;
assigned to PLUM, 28; assigned
to provisional pursuit squadrons,
436n.19; candidates for PLUM, 19, 20,
21; selected for 3rd Pursuit Squadron
(Provisional), 111; selected for 33rd
Pursuit Squadron (Provisional), 152
41-F flying school graduates, 339;
assigned to provisional pursuit
squadrons, 436n.19; assigned to 35th
Pursuit Group, 20; as candidates for
PLUM, 20, 21; selected for 3rd Pursuit
Squadron (Provisional), 111; selected
for 33rd Pursuit Squadron (Provisional), 152, 154
41-G flying school graduates, 339; at
Amberley Field, 67, 111; arrive on
Mormacsun, 80; assigned to provisional pursuit squadrons, 436n.19;
assigned to 35th Pursuit Group, 20;
as candidates for PLUM, 20, 21, 339;
selected for 33rd Pursuit Squadron
(Provisional), 152, 154
41-H flying school graduates, 339;
assigned to provisional pursuit
squadrons, 436n.19; of *Holbrook,* 50,
80; of *Mormacsun,* 80; in 91st Bomb
Squadron, 156; selected for 13th Pur-

suit Squadron (Provisional), 176, 400n.23; selected for 33rd Pursuit Squadron (Provisional), 152, 154

49th Fighter Group, 436n.24

49th Pursuit Group: arrives Melbourne, 101, 221; and defense of northern Australia, 340; designated to serve under RAAF, 100–01; inexperience of pilots assigned to, 340–41; influx of Java veterans to, 340; squadrons of, 340

14th Army, 12

14th Pursuit Group, 27, 28

4th Antitank Regiment, 235

4th Interceptor Command, 28

Foster, Samuel L., 435n.35

Freake, Clyde, 235, 411n.17

Freeman, Jim, 305

Fremantle, 198; and *Abbekerk, 284, 333;* and loading of P-40Es on *Langley,* 102, 221–22, 246; *Holbrook* departs from, 260; *Langley* arrives at from Darwin, 221; *Whipple* arrives at from Java, 334

French Indochina, 2, 3

Fuchs, Marion, 136, 137, 278; and air evacuation to Australia, 320; in Japanese aerial attack on Bali, 126, 128, 129–30; arrives Ngoro, 144, 165; on B-17 protection mission, 180; on Kragan strafing mission, 308, 310, 429n.5; in New Zealand, 47; in Ngoro-Jogjakarta evacuation, 316; picked for 20th Pursuit Squadron (Provisional), 86; on *Polk,* 30; at Soerabaja, 140, 144; victory claims of, 220; visits Jogjakarta, 181, 216;

Funk, Ben, 327

Gallienne, Winfred "Bill," 88, 179; in Bali combat, 126, 390n.10; in C-53 to Ngoro, 131, 133, 391n.34; in combat with Bettys, 219; in combat with Zeros, 126, 219, 249, 390n.10; crash lands on Java beach, 140–41, 179;

on interceptions from Ngoro, 140; lands Soerabaja, 131, 160; missing, 254; picked for 20th Pursuit Squadron (Provisional), 86; as POW, 334, 415–16n.36; shot down into sea, 249, 250, 333, 415–16n.36; wounds of, 333, 415–16n.36

Galusha, Harry: on Amberley-Charleville flight, 146; arrives Darwin, 150; arrives Pasirian, 178; in attack on Java invasion force, 295–97; and A-24s, 150; ordered to fly to Jogjakarta, 297

Galwey, Geoffrey: in command of 35th Pursuit Group pilots on *Republic,* 24; criticizes Wagner dress, 67; designated transport administrative officer, 370n.19; and "spy" lecture, 376n.19

Gambonini, Paul, 88, 122, 136, 137, 167, 217, 256 431n.45; aborts Bali attack mission, 250, 256; and air evacuation to Australia, 320, 323; at Amberley, 81; at Antil Plains Aerodrome, *341;* arrives Ngoro, 144, 165; on B-17 protection mission, 180; and combat missions from Ngoro, 218, 269, 272, 302–03, 419–20n.2; on Darwin-Koepang flight, 123; evacuates Ngoro, 316; in Japanese attack on Bali, 126, 128–29, 130; on Java invasion force mission, 296, 297, 425n.13; at Jogjakarta, 181, 216, 319; and Kragan strafing mission, 307; in New Zealand, 47; at Ngoro, 165, 271, 272, 278, 307; picked for 20th Pursuit Squadron (Provisional), 86; on *Polk,* 29, 30, 31; at Soerabaja, 137, 140, 144, 261; to 35th Pursuit Group, 341

Garbutt Field, 70

Gaskell, Charlie, 19

General Staff, Japanese Army, 7

George, Harold: left behind in Philippines, 12; request to bring to Australia, 109; sends Philippine ferry pilots to Australia, 39, 40

Hayes, Tommy: on *Abbekerk,* 280, 298, 304; arrives Fremantle, 341; arrives Ngoro, 144; arrives Soerabaja, 144, 394n.92; and Bali P-40E of, 136, 144; on B-17 protection mission, 178; boards *Polk,* 29; in combat with Zeros, 248; crashes on landing at Ngoro, 250, 436n.17; evacuated to Jogjakarta, 268, 419n.45; in Japanese aerial attack on Bali, 126, 128, 129, 130; on Jogjakarta-Tjilatjap rail trip, 275; in Malang hospital, 268; picked for 20th Pursuit Squadron (Provisional), 86; at Port Moresby, *342;* selected for sea evacuation, 275; stays behind at Denpasar, 132, 137; and stopover in New Zealand, 47; to 35th Pursuit Group, 341; visits Jogjakarta, 181, 216

Hazard, Robert, 409–10n.71

Head, Vernon, 66, 245; at Amberley Field, 65, 73, 79, 82, 83, 110, 378n.61; on Amberley-Charleville-Cloncurry-Daly Waters-Darwin flight, 145–46, 147, 148, 149; arrives Brisbane, 63–64; arrives Darwin from Timor, 224; arrives Penfui, 222; assembles P-40Es, 73, 74; assigned P-40E, 111; assigned to Ascot, 64–65; crash lands on Timor, 158; at Darwin, 149, 151; in Darwin attack, 238; and Darwin-Koepang flight, 156, 157–58; departs Koepang for Darwin, 222–23; explores Brisbane, 64, 65; and Lane, 88; and Lowood, 110, 114; in New Zealand, 46–47, 48; on *Polk,* 30, 46; selected for 3rd Pursuit Squadron (Provisional), 111; to 67th Pursuit Squadron, 341; on Timor, 158–59, 167–69, 182–83, 222–23;

Headlam, Frank, 223

Headquarters Squadron, 35th Pursuit Group, 28, 30

Heide, L. van der, 382n.64

Helfrich, C.E.L.: as ABDAFLOAT commander, 199, 283, 284; and Brett, 283; and coordination of with van Oyen, 423n.5; disbands ABDAFLOAT, 430n.32; evacuates Java, 430n.32; and *Langley* pilots to fly *Sea Witch* P-40Es, 423n.5; orders *Edsall* to Java, 423n.5; 430n.32; orders *Langley* to Java, 199, 404n.15; orders *Sea Witch* to Java, 200, 404n.15; and protection of *Langley,* 283, 423n.2; releases Glassford from command, 430n.32

Helton, Elbert, 320, 323

Hennon, William, 98, 132, 166, 244, 263, 273; and air evacuation to Australia, 318, 322; at Amberley, 50, 59, 62; on Amberley-Darwin flight, 68, 70; on Bali attack mission, 249, 250, 261; on B-17 protection missions, 178; in combat with Zeros, 272, 273, 276; at Darwin, 75, 76, 78, 379n.78; at Djember, 143, 166; extricates Reed from P-40E, 139–40, 393n.68; on familiarization flight for newcomers, 143; to 49th Pursuit Group, 340; flown to Australia from Philippines, 41, 50; heads back to Ngoro from Tjilatjap, 301, 306; on interceptions from Ngoro, 116, 132–33, 140, 142, 167, 272, 276, 388n.58; and Kragan strafing mission order, 306, 428n.59; at Lennon's hotel, 52; at Madioen, 113, 386–87n.32; at Maospati, 98, 111; at Ngoro, 132, 391n.34; on Palembang mission, 209, 213, 214, 215, 216, 408n.45; and P-40E mechanics, 141, 179; picks up Kurtz and Fisher, 306; rejects evacuation offer, 270; sent to Tjilatjap to meet *Langley,* 277, 282, 301, 306; victory claims of, 250, 276, 388n.58, 408n.45; visit to Soerabaja, 180–81, 261, 262

Herbert, William, 400n.23; 409–10, n.71

Hicks, Earl E., 49, 374n.57

Hiei, 286

Hirohito, Emperor: approves decision

India, 198, 199, 270
Indian Ocean, 285
Indonesia, 344
Ingram, Cecil, 165; on *Abbekerk,* 333;
    assigned 3rd Pursuit Squadron (Pro-
    visional), 146; at Cloncurry, 147; at
    Darwin, 149, 150; and Darwin air raid
    warning, 151; on Darwin-Java flight,
    159; on evacuation trip to Soerabaja,
    267; at Jogjakarta, 268; at Ngoro, 165;
    at Soerabaja, 160, 267; transported to
    Perth from Fremantle, 333
Ingram, Jim, 396n.35
Ipswich, 79
Ireland, 334
Irvin, Ben, 84; and air evacuation to Aus-
    tralia, 318, 322; arrives Amberley, 50;
    at Amberley, 62; on B-17 protection
    missions, 178, 180; in combat with
    Zeros, 272; at Darwin, 75; on Darwin-
    Koepang flight, 163; dengue fever at
    Koepang, 84, 89; on ferry flight to Dar-
    win, 70; flown to Australia from Phil-
    ippines, 41, 50; to 49th Pursuit Group,
    340; on interceptions from Ngoro, 272;
    Koepang P-40E of destroyed, 89, 123,
    163; on mission to meet *Langley,* 277,
    278, 297; at Ngoro, *265;* radios Sprague
    from Koepang, 89–90; selected for 3rd
    Pursuit Squadron (Provisional), 110;
    victory claims of 220

Jackson, Elwin, 141; and air evacua-
    tion to Australia, 305; on Amberley-
    Charleville flight, 106; attacks G4M1s,
    162; on B-17 protection mission, 178;
    at Denpasar, 136; during stopover in
    New Zealand, 47; evacuates Ngoro,
    266; flies Soerabaja-Ngoro, 138–
    39, 141; and mechanical problem of
    P-40E, 121; on *Polk,* 30
Jacobs, J.W.: cracks up A-24, 206, 405n.4;
    on supply drop to Suehr, 187–88,
    205–06

Jansen, J., 223
Japanese-American negotiations, 5, 7, 8,
    9, 10
Japanese Navy: in Battle of Java
    Sea, 285–86; carriers of reported
    approaching Australia, 100, 113, 114; in
    Java landings, 285; operations plan of
    approved, 7
Japanese Navy carriers: in attack on Dar-
    win, 195, 196, 198, 410n.5, 411n.12,
    412n.14, 412n.28, 413–14n.57; in attack
    on *Pecos,* 431n.35; false report on
    location of, 100, 122, 387n.43; near
    Makassar, 394n.75; patrol south of
    Tjilatjap, 427n.49, 430n.33
Japanese Navy submarines, 371–72n.56
Japanese paratroops, 195
Japanese time conversion, 388n.56,
    409n.60, 431n.37
Java, 148, 273, 285; aerial defense of,
    200, 202, 203, 289; allied support
    for defense of, 202; deemed lost by
    Dutch, 434n.16; as destination for
    Langley P-40Es, 102, 198; Dutch in
    command of defense of, 202; Dutch
    interceptor force on destroyed, 100;
    evacuation of allied forces from, 178,
    202; evacuation of allied forces to,
    195; hiatus in Japanese aerial attacks
    on, 178, 180, 216; Japanese plans for
    seizure of, 16, 195, 198; in Malay Bar-
    rier, 14; reinforcements for defense of,
    199, 200, 202; routing of *Langley* and
    MS-5 convoy to, 198, 417n.12; transfer
    of aircraft to, 199, 203
Java Air Command: ABDAIR command
    transferred to, 289; and air protec-
    tion cover for *Langley,* 433n.2; and
    air protection for Combined Strik-
    ing Force, 423n.2; and EASGROUP,
    200; established, 200; and Java inva-
    sion force landings, 285, 295; and plan
    for distribution of *Sea Witch* P-40Es,
    433–34n.15; and transfer of *Langley*

P-40Es to Andir, 281, 282; van Oyen
as commander of, 202

Java Sea, 213, 296

Jogjakarta: airdrome at ordered
destroyed, 286, 288, 320; Brereton departs from for Colombo, 201;
and Eubank evacuation orders, 276–
77, 286, 301; Eubank shifts to from
Malang, 422n.31; evacuation trains
to, 267, 268, 270; and FEAF personnel
evacuation to Broome, 284, 286, 301,
308; LB-30s at, 248; 91st Bomb Squadron ordered to, 297; Ngoro pilots
evacuate to, 286, 422–23n.44; Ngoro
pilots waiting evacuation from, 273,
298, 301; visits of pilots to, 181, 216

Johns, Keith, 235

Johnsen, Les, 256; aborts Darwin-
Koepang take-off, 123; arrives
Koepang, 134; at Charleville, 106; on
B-17 protection mission, 180; at Cloncurry, 107; and contact with Javanese,
166; and Darwin-Koepang flight,
134; at Denpasar, 136; on Denpasar-
Soerabaja flight, 137; and evacuation flight to Australia, 319, 322; first
combat mission of, 142; flying time
of in P-40s, 29; flies to Ngoro from
Soerabaja, 138; to 49th Pursuirt Group,
340–41; and Java invasion force mission, 296, 425n.13; on Koepang-
Denpasar flight, 134; and missions at
Ngoro, 278; at Penfui airdrome, 134;
on Polk, 30;

Johnson. Alexander L.P.: appointed commander of Base Section 3, 374n.54;
chastises pilots at Amberley, 115; confines pilots to Amberley, 115; inspects
Amberley Field, 115; interferes with
Legg's operations, 115; orders formation of new pursuit group, 50; orders
Philippine veterans to Ascot, 49; puts
Brisbane off limits to pilots, 67–68;
reprimands Philippine veterans, 49;
and state of pilots' dress, 67; in verbal
exchange with Wilhite, 83

Johnson, Bennett "Benny," 151, 175,
396n.30

Johnson, Clarence B., 435n.35

Johnson, G.S., 261

Johnson, Robert S. "Spence," 148, 163,
164, 416–17n.2; and air evacuation to
Australia, 320; allows destruction of
P-40E on beach, 256; at Antil Plains
Aerodrome, 341; on Bali attack mission, 249, 251–52; at Blimbing, 216;
arrives Brisbane, 32; on B-17 protection mission, 178; in combat with
Zero, 249; composes ode re "mak
mak," 166; at Darwin, 163; on Darwin-
Koepang flight, 163; and death of
Fields, 243; dispirited with Java situation, 276, 282; and forced landing on
Java, 250–51, 254; on Java invasion
force mission, 295, 296; killed in takeoff accident, 342; on Kragan strafing
mission, 308, 309–10; at Ngoro, 180,
278; on Ngoro interception mission,
272; on Republic voyage, 33; selected
for 17th Pursuit Squadron (Provisional), 62; to 35th Pursuit Group, 341;
walks back to Ngoro, 256, 272, 415–
16n.36, 416n.41,

Johore/Singapore, 99

Joint Army-Navy Board, 3

Jolo Island, 42

Jombang, 344

Jones, Wilfred, 409–10n.71

Kaga: and Val dive bomber attacks on
Edsall, 431n.43, on Pecos, 431n.35;
launches Darwin aerial attack, 196;
and Val dive bomber losses in Darwin attack, 412n.28; and Zeros attack
P-40Es at RAAF Darwin, 410n.8,
411n.14, 413–14n.57

Kaiser, Robert, 151, 341, 396n.30

Kalgoorlie, 192

Kanoya kokutai: in attack on Bali, 391n.19; in attack on Darwin RAAF field, 412n.38; in attacks on Java, 117, 389n.68; in attack on Soerabaja, 422n.26

Katen, Cornelius ten, 382n.59

Katoomba, 103, 265, 417n.12

Kawanishi H6K4 "Mavis" : bombs Darwin convoy, 188, 402n.64; and Pell patrol, 190; and reconnaissance of Broome, 324, 433n.9; shot down by Buel, 189, 337, 402n.64; shoots down Buel, 189, 402n.64

Keats, Poad, 435n.35

Kediri, 419n.45

Keenan, Gerald "Gerry," 153, 174, 376n.1; arrives Brisbane from Philippines, 35; in charge of pilot training, 38; leads 33rd Pursuit Squadron (Provisional) from Amberley to Sydney, 170, 173, 399n.12; lands at Point Cook, 174; on *Langley,* 266; leads pilots from Port Pirie to Perth for *Langley,* 175, 192, 221, 409n.68; and loading of *Langley,* 212, 221–22; meets Philippines pilots, 49; on Melbourne-Port Pirie flight, 174; and new order for *Langley* to head south again, 313; and order for *Langley* to return to Tjilatjap, 304–05; runs Lowood training, 80–81; selected for 33rd Pursuit Squadron (Provisional), 152

Kelsay, Clyde: on Darwin-Koepang flights, 156, 157, 179; returns to Darwin from Koepang, 158; selected to guide 3rd Pursuit Squadron (Provisional) to Koepang, 156

Kendari: as American refueling stop, 56; as base for 21st koku sentai, 57, 113; airfield of, 57; A6M2 Zeros at, *118,* 382n.59; B-17 missions against, 394n.83; dropped as American Java base, 78; G4M1 Bettys at, 388n.58, 409n.64; Japanese aerial attacks

from, 100, 196, 412n.38; Japanese carrier force arrives at, 195; Japanese seize, 57; *Langley* survivors executed at, 334

Kengen, E.T., 285, 312, 312, 430n.29

Kerstetter, Robert, 154, 171–72, 341

Kertosono, 268, 419n.45

Kester, Edson: B-24A of attacked and shot down by Zero, 328, 434n.22, 434n.28; and evacuees from Broome to Perth, 327–28; fate of, 330; killed, 435n.35

Key, Al, 305, 427–28n.53

Key, Fred, 305

Kik, Adriaan, 279, 303

King, Bland, 305

King Creek, 235

Kingma, J., 389n.69

Kingsley, Earl, 221, 400n.23, 409–10n.71

Kirishima, 286

Kiser, George E., "Ed," "Kay," 63, 132, 141; as acting squadron commander, 275; and air evacuation to Australia, 318, 322; at Amberley Field, 51; arrives Amberley Field, 50; and Anemaet, 277; arrives Ngoro, 386–87n.32; on Bali attack mission, 249, 261; on B-17 protective missions, 178, 262; in combat with Bettys, 263, 264–65, 269, 419–20n.2; and CSF support, 295; damages P-40E at Townsville, 70; on ferry flight north, 68; flown from Philippines to Australia, 41, 50; to 49th Pursuit Group, 340; on interception missions from Ngoro, 116, 132, 140, 142, 160, 162, 167, 258, 269, 276, 419–20n.2; on Java invasion fleet reconnaissance, 273; and Kragan strafing mission, 306, 308, 310; at Lennon's hotel, 52; leads P-40s over Java invasion force, 295, 297; on Palembang mission, 209, 214, 215, 408n.45; remains at Ngoro, 278; and 2-Vl.G-IV pilots at Blimbing, 278; victory claims of, 269, 408n.45; on visits to Soerabaja, 180–81, 261, 262;

Lane, William, Jr.: aborts Amberley-Charleville flight, 105; aborts Amberley-Townsville flights, 88, 89; aborts Darwin-Koepang flight, 121–22; and air evacuations from Jogjakarta, 320; and air raid on Magoewo field, 318; at Amberley, 82; and Bali combat with Zeros, 126–27, 132, 390n.11; and B-17 protection mission, 180; at Charleville, 107; as commander of Pursuit Combat Team, 30; at Denpasar, 126; evacuation flight of to Australia, 320; as executive officer to Sprague, 133, 218; guided to Ngoro, 132, 167, 390n.85; held back at Jogjakarta, 318, 319; on interception missions from Ngoro, 140, 167; leads Amberley-Charleville-Cloncurry-Daly Waters-Darwin flight, 105, 107, 108; leads Darwin-Koepang flight, 123; leads Koepang-Denpasar flight, 124; lands at Singosari, 131, 391n.33; at Lowood, 81, 82; in New Zealand, 47; and Nichols, 30; ordered to form 20th Pursuit Squadron (Provisional), 86; ordered to Java, 89; ordered to Port Moresby, 86–87; ordered to Soerabaja, 121, 122; and Palembng mission, 218; on *Polk*, 48; remains at Ngoro, 278; selects pilots for 20th Pursuit Squadron (Provisional), 86, 87

Langjahr, Herman, 119–20

Lanzing, Col., *54*

Larrakeyah Barracks, 231

Latane, David: on Amberley-Perth flight, 399n.2; arrives Brisbane, 80; blows tire at Alice Springs, 184–85; and impression of Pell, 153; left behind at Alice Springs, 185; picked for Port Pirie-Darwin flight, 175

Laurie, John, 275

Laverton Field, 414n.5; P-40Es at for *Langley*, 403n.74; and RAAF personnel climbing on P-40Es, 174; as 33rd Pursuit Squadron (Provisional) stop, 172, 174; Wilhite at, 174, 191, 412n.42

LB-30s: arrive Singosari, 56, 58; assigned Legg, 299; attack Bali invasion force, 240, 247–48, 415n.14; attack Java invasion force, 288; and attacks on Palembang, 212, 407n.32; bring Philippine evacuees to Darwin, 150, 396n.29; Broome operations of, 285; burning at Magoewo airfield, 317; destroyed at Darwin, 196; and evacuations to Australia, 285, 317, 319, 323; fly Wavell to Colombo, 202, 275; guide 3rd Pursuit (Provisional) to Koepang, 156–57, 158, 179; losses of, 58; and Seventh Bomb Group, 56; to transport 33rd Pursuit Squadron (Provisional) mechanics to Koepang, 209

Lee Point, 228

Legaspi, 11

Legg, Dick, 86, 113, 145, 327, 339–40; and aerial search for Broome survivors, 330, 332; and aircraft servicing problems at Broome, 324, 324–25; appointed Air Officer Base Section 3, 110, 299; arrives Broome, 299; arrives Java, 85; arrives Soerabaja, 85; and attack on Broome, 328–29; and Broome aborigine problems, 300; and Donoho, 332, 435n.3; and Dutch flying boats at Broome, 330; inspects Air Defense Command headquarters, 93–94, 375n.25; and interference of Col. Johnson, 115; and Japanese carrier warning, 113, 387n.43; and Japanese reconnaissance flights over Broome, 323, 325; leaves Broome, 333; meets 20th Pursuit Squadron (Provisional) pilots at Cloncurry, 107–08; ordered to Broome for FEAF evacuation, 299, 333; ordered to form additional pursuit squadrons, 111; ordered to start

rent to Japanese expansion, 4; limits Wavell's authority, 14; and messages from and to NEI governor general, 287; and oil embargo, 4; plans USAAF groups for NEI defense, 16; and P-40 reinforcements for Java, 203, 283; proposes establishment of Far East unified command, 14; and *Sea Witch* to Java, 283; sends inspection team to SWPA, 340; sends Japanese carrier warning, 387n.43; and strategy to delay war with Japan, 8; and van Mook, 199; and withdrawal of FEAF from Java, 200, 287

Martin, Joe, 220–21, 246

Martin, Ralph, 65, 146–47, 154

Martin B-10 bombers: attack Japanese forces off Balikpapan, 56, 57, off Tarakan, 54, 55; based at Andir, 212; export version of in NEIAF, 16

Maryborough Airport, 74

Mascot Field, 172, 176, 177, 399n.12, 400n.24

Mataram, 138

Mather Field, 27

Mathews, Captain, 331

Matsumoto, Yasuo, 434n.28

May, Paul, 73, 82

Maylands civil airdrome, 220, 221, 246

McAfee, Jim: air evacuation of from Ngoro, 420n.9; arrives Blimbing, 179; arrives Soerabaja, 179, 180; assigned duties at Ngoro, 180, 260; evacuation order for, 272; and fate of Java, 260; identifies body of Fields, 262; visits Soerabaja, 261–62

McCallum, Gerald "Bo," 142, 178, 272; on alert at Ngoro, 116, 120, 180; arrives Darwin from Philippines, 21–22; arrives Ngoro, 386–87n.32; bails out, 272; at Blimbing, 112; body of found, 273, 275, 436n.17; on B-17 protection missions, 178, 262; in charge of 17th Pursuit Squadron (Provisional), 270;

in combat with Bettys, 263; in combat with Zeros, 272; on ferry route flight to NEI, 70; on interception missions from Ngoro, 140, 141, 160, 162, 167, 272, 398n.92, 418n.23; leads 3rd Pursuit Squadron (Provisional) to Ngoro, 164–65; at Ngoro Field, *271;* on Palembang mission, 209, 214, 215; and Pell mission to Australia, 22; promoted to captain, 270; with 17th Pursuit Squadron (Provisional) at Amberley, 62;

McCartney, David, 320

McConnell, Robert P., 247, 266; and attack on *Langley*, 291–93; orders abandon ship, 293; orders area cleared, 294

McCown, Johnny, 20

McDonald, Hubert, 435n.35

McFarland, Cecil S., 41

McMahon, Robert F., 111, 190, 209; and accident at Darwin, 207; and air raid alarm at Darwin, 208; at Amberley Field, 42, 67–68, 111, 114; on Amberley-Sydney-Canberra-Melbourne flight, 171–74; and Amberley tent, *43;* arranges New Year's Eve party, 38–39; assembles P-40Es, 44; and *Bahootee the Cootee,* 188, 207; bails out during Darwin attack, 233–34; at Berrimah hospital, 249, 252, 254; in combat with Darwin Zeros, 226–27, 230–34, 410n.8; damages P-40E at Daly Waters, 186; 402n.56; over Darwin harbor, 231, 232–33, *233;* as flight leader, 153; at Honolulu, 24; lands at Darwin, 187; at Lennon's Hotel, 34, 38–39; and location of downed Darwin P-40E, *255;* at Melbourne, 173, 174; and patrols from Darwin, 206–07, 405n.2; and Pell query about Buell and Oestreicher, 191; and Peres during attack, 225–26, 410–11n.10; and P-40E repairs at Darwin, 191, 205, 206; and PLUM assignment, 21; at Port Pirie,

McMahon, Robert F. (*cont.*)
  183; on Port Pirie-Alice Springs-Daly
  Waters-Darwin flight, 183–186; and
  replacement P-40E at Darwin, 188,
  207, 208, 402n.59; on *Republic* voyage, 23; and response to Japanese carrier scare, 114, 115; and run-in with
  Griffith, 208; selected for Port Pirie-
  Darwin flight, 173, 175; as squadron
  adjutant, 173; and Suehr forced landing, 186–87; and supply drop to Suehr,
  187–88, 191, 205–06; and take-off for
  Koepang during Darwin attack, 224–
  27, 410n.5; to 35th Pursuit Group, 341;
  training program of, 45–46
McNamar, Captain, 416n.42
McNeil, Lewis, 274
McNutt, Charles, 30
McWherter, Robert, 88, 273; and air
  evacuation to Australia, 320, 323;
  arrives Denpasar, 136; attacks G3M
  Nell, 135; at Blimbing, 141–42; on B-17
  protection mission, 178; at Cloncurry,
  107; in combat with Zeros and Bettys,
  161–62, 163; and evacuation of Ngoro
  Field, 312; on familiarization flight,
  143–44; first combat mission of, 142;
  flies Soerabaja to Ngoro, 138–39; on
  Koepang-Bali flight, 135, 136; on Kragan strafing mission, 308, 309, 429n.5;
  leads Kruzel back to Ngoro, 310; left
  behind at Koepang, 125, 134; on *Polk,*
  30; remains at Ngoro, 278; to 35th Pursuit Group, 341; in 20th Pursuit Squadron (Provisional), 88; visits Ngoro
  town, 142, 166
Meigs, 35
Melbourne, 200, 299; airfield at, 172;
  Coolidge arrives at, 400n.26; 51st Pursuit Group arrives at, 400n.26; and
  Java evacuees to, 287, 299, 328; *Mariposa* arrives at, 101; and MS-5 convoy,
  103, 246, 417n.10; USAFIA shifted
  to, 57

Melikian, Ray, 148, 341
Melville Island, 196, 205, 206, 411n.19
Merle-Smith, Van S., 21, 32
Menzies Hotel, 173
Merak, 285
Messel, Gerson "Fiets" van, 31, 32
Messerschmitt Bf 109, 232
Messerschmitt 110, 135, 336
Messimer, Dwight, 436n.40
Metsker, Phil: on Darwin-Koepang flight,
  158; departs Darwin for Koepang, 156;
  killed in bail out over Timor, 159, 163,
  183, 436n.17; selected for 17th Pur-
  suit Squadron (Provisional), 62; visits
  Ascot, 65
Militaire Luchtvaart, 281
military strategy, Japan, 7–8
military strategy, U.S.: and Arcadia Con-
  ference, 13; and coordination of allied
  operations, 11; and delaying war with
  Japan, 8; and diplomatic negotiations
  with Japan, 5; and Europe first priority, 13; and heavy bombers as deterrent to Japanese expansion, 4, 5, 8;
  and planning for cooperation with
  Great Britain and Netherlands East
  Indies, 5, 9; and remaining on defen-
  sive in the Pacific, 8, 13; and role of
  Malay Barrier, 13–14; and support of
  Australia as a base, 14; and support
  for air defense of Australia, Neth-
  erlands East Indies, Singapore, and
  Philippines, 5
Mindanao, 13, 150
Mines Field, 27
Minnie from Trinidad, 275
Miss Nadine, 150
Mitsubishi A6M2 Zeros, 159, 271, 336,
  342; in allied attack on Kragan, 308;
  arrive Kendari, 57; attack Broome,
  287, 329–30, 434n.22, 434n.28; attack
  Clark and Iba fields, 10, 11; attack
  Koepang, 382n.59; attack Soerabaja,
  388n.58, 388n.61, 388n.62; in Bali

combat, 126–29, 390n.11; in combat with 17th Pursuit Squadron (Provisional) P-40Es, 117–19, 126–29, 161–62, 218–20, 240–41, 242, 248–51, 258–60, 272–73, 276, 336, 388n.58, 388n.61, 413n.48, 413n.49, 413n.54, 414n.11, 414n.13, 415n.23, 417n.6, 419–20n.2, 421n.13, 422n.27; in combat with Dutch fighters, 16, 388n.58; in Darwin attack, 196, 226–34, 244, 410n.5, 410n.8, 411n.11, 411n.12, 411n.14, 411n.19; discover Ngoro Field, 311, 418n.23; in dogfighting, 154; losses of in Darwin attack, 196; losses of to Dutch, 388n.58; losses of to 17th Pursuit Squadron (Provisional), 336–37, 413n.49, 421n.13; in Malaya attack, 10; outmatch P-40Es, 336; shoot down B-18, 384n.3; strafe B-17Ds at Pasirian, 262; strafe B-17Es at Singosari, 256. 261, 416n.37, 417n.6; strafe *Langley,* 283, 292; strafe Magoewo Field, 318, 432n.55; strafe Maospati Field, 409n.64; strafe Ngoro Field, 311; strafe Perak Field, 119, 389n.69; threat of to ferry route, 42; of 3rd kokutai, *118*

Mitsubishi C5M "Babs," 388n.58

Mitsubishi G3M Type 96 "Nell" bombers: in attacks on Koepang, 410n.74, on Malang, 116–17, 388n.59, 388n.61, on NEI, 16; bomb Christmas Island, 300–01; bomb Darwin RAAF field, 196, 412n.38; losses of in NEI campaign, 336, 392–93n.51

Mitsubishi G4M1 "Betty" bombers, 240, 294; arrive Kendari, 57; attacked by P-40Es, 161–63, 262–65, 269, 272, 418n.23, 420n.3, 420n.8; in attacks on NEI, 16, 391n.19; in attacks on Soerabaja, 116–17, 218–20, 258–59, 388n.58, 398n.76, 416–17n.2, 418n.23, 418–19n.32, 419–20n.2, 419–20n.3; of Kanoya kokutai, *117;* bomb Darwin RAAF field, 196, 412n.38; bomb *Langley,* 283, 291–93, 425n.3, 425n.6; bomb Magoewo airfield, 432n.51; bomb Maospati Field, 369n.68; bomb Ngoro Field, 432n.59; bomb ships in Soerabaja harbor, 276, 409n.64, 421n.13; bomb Singosari Field, 160–61, 262, 264, 276, 418n.23; losses of, 162, 198, 336, 409n.64, 418–19n.32; mission to bomb Ngoro, 418n.23, 420n.8; speed of, 162;

Modjokerto, 212, 213, 268

Moesi River, 195, 212, 214, 407n.36

Monkey Village, 398n.87

Monterey Bay, 371n.56

Mook, Hubertus van, 199, 203

Moore, A. Douglas, 133–34, 150, 420n.9

Morehead, Jim: and air evacuation to Australia, 318, 319, 322; attacks Bettys, 263–64, 265; as candidate for PLUM, 20; on Amberley-Charleville-Daly Waters-Darwin flight, 105, 108; in combat with Zeros, 263; on Darwin-Koepang flight, 123; at Denpasar, 126; flies escort to Connelly, 136 37; guided to Ngoro, 141; in Hamilton fatal accident, 82–83, 380n.20; on interception missions from Ngoro, 218; in Japanese aerial attack on Bali, 126, 129–30; to 49th Pursuit Group, 340; on Koepang-Bali flight, 125; at Magoewo field, 318; on mission to meet *Langley,* 277, 282, 297, 425n.13, 425n.22; on Ngoro evacuation, 316; at Ngoro Field, *265;* nicknamed "Wild Man Morehead," 265; and Palembang mission, 218; and P-40E of repaired, 136; in prewar midair collision, 20; refuels at Singosari, 263–64; in Soerabaja air raid, 140; victory claims of, 265; victory roll over Ngoro, 264

Mormacsun: arrives Brisbane, 56, 80, 176, 403n.72; and combat teams assigned to Amberley, 79; and crew chiefs and

against, 418n.23; 420n.8; aircraft maintenance work at, 112, 179; alert duty at, 142, 160, *265;* anti-aircraft guns at, 311; bombed, 319, 432n59; camouflage of, 91, 111, 139, 383n.66; Coss inspects, 90–91; Davis unable locate, 159–60; developed by Boxman as secret field, 383n.66; discovered by Japanese, 271, 303, 311, 418n.23, 427n.43, 430n.22, 430n.25; Dutch pilots at, 120, 277–78; features of, 112, 160; initial evacuations from, 266–68; lunches at, 113; P-40E lands at, *259;* P-40Es on alert at, *181;* P-40Es lost at evacuation of, 338; as prewar emergency field, 383n.66; readiness huts at, 112–13; Reed killed at, 139; remains of in 1983, 344–45; *Sea Witch* P-40s slated for, 200; selected for 17th Pursuit Squadron (Provisional), 85; 17th Pursuit Squadron (Provisional) pilots arrive at, 111; strafed by Zeros, 311, 319, 430n.22, 432n.59

Ngoro town, 142.

Nichols, Erickson S., 50, 67

Nichols, Murray: on *Abbekerk,* 281, 298, 422–23n.44; appointed as 1st Sgt, 270; on Darwin-Singosari flight, 179; and evacuees from Ngoro, 270; and Kurtz, 270; on *Polk,* 30;

91st Bomb Squadron: on Amberley-Charleville-Daly Waters-Darwin flight, 146, 148, 149, 150; arrives Pasirian, 178; attacks Bali invasion force, 240; attacks Java invasion force, 295–97; at Darwin, 149, 150, 151–52; on Darwin-Koepang flight, 156, 157; ordered to Darwin and Java, 145; ordered to Jogjakarta, 297; and Palembang mission, 212, 213, 407n.31, 408n.46; shot at on landing at Penfui, 159; stops at Andir Field, 408n.46

19th Bomb Group, 178, 220; attacks Java invasion force, 286; attacks Palem-

bang, 212; and Bali attack mission, 248; and B-17Es of arrive Java, 56; and B-17Es of attack Jolo, 56; and dispersion of B-17Es, 178; flight crews of evacuate Java, 286, 320; ground echelon of arrives Jogjakarta from Malang, 274; mission of against Balikpapan, 57; personnel of at Tjilatjap to board *Abbekerk,* 279; Philippine evacuees of flown to Darwin, 150, 396n.29

19th Light Machine Gun Regiment, 235, 253

Nix, Joshua J., 304, 312

Northam, 333

Nusa Penida, 256, 257

Oakes, Bert, 411n.16

O'Donnell, Emmett "Rosie": and air warning system at Soerabaja, 375n.25; as commander of 14th Bomb Squadron, 212; deplores glorification of FEAF operations, 335, 336; as FEAF operations officer, 209; orders Legg to Soerabaja, 86; and Palembang mission, 209, 212, 213, summons Sprague to Bandoeng, 209, 212

Oestreicher, Robert: on aborted Darwin-Koepang flight, 209, 224; on Amberley-Cloncurry-Daly Waters-Darwin flight, 147, 148, 149; attached to 33rd Pursuit Squadron (Provisional), 205; attacks Val dive bombers, 234–35, 337, 412n.28; and hours in P-40s, 27; lands after Darwin attack, 235; left behind at Darwin, 163; in Darwin attack, 227, 234, 235, 254, 410n.4, 411n.11; to 49th Pursuit Group, 341; and mechanical problems of P-40E, 148, 150, 151, ordered to Daly Waters, 245; on patrols from Darwin, 206–07, 405n.2, 405–06n.8; on *Polk,* 30; and repair work on P-40E, 150, 245; reports to Pell, 190, 191; and search for Buell and convoy, 190, 205,

Percival, Arthur, 99

Peres, Jack: and aborted Darwin-Koepang flight, 209; and air raid alarm at Darwin, 208; on Amberley-Sydney flight, 170; in Darwin attack, 254, 410–11n.10; on Darwin RAAF field, 225–26, 228; as flight leader for 33rd Pursuit Squadron (Provisional), 153; and forced landing at Fort Lytton, 83, 380n.25; and location of downed P-40E, *255*, 410–11n.10, 415n.32; at Melbourne, 173; on patrols from Darwin, 2–6-07; picked for Port Pirie-Darwin flight, 175; on Port Pirie-Alice Springs-Daly Waters-Darwin flight, 183–84, 185; remains of found, 415n.32; returns to Darwin RAAF field, 227, 228, 410–11n.10; and run-in with Griffith, 208

Perrin, Edward S., 299, 300

Perry, Elton: and aborted Darwin-Koepang flight, 209; in Darwin attack, 227, 228, 254, 410–11n.10; on Darwin patrol, 405–06n.8; location of downed P-40E of, *255*, 411n.15, 415n.32; picked for Port Pirie-Darwin flight, 175

Perry, Ken: on *Abbekerk,* 303–04; in attack on Soerabaja, 119–20; at Blimbing, 133, and Japanese discovery of Ngoro field, 271; and Javanese natives, 166; paints name on Hoskyn's P-40E, 262; at Soerabaja, 130–31

Perth, 220; base section at, 333; and Java evacuees, 287, 289, 323, 324, 327, 328; and loading of P-40Es on Langley, 101, 102, 221–22, 410n.72

Pescadores, 10

Petschel, Howard K., 435n.35

P-400s, 341, 342, 343

P-40Es, 121, 221, 257; of *Admiral Halstead,* 35; allocation of to ABDACOM and Australia, 57–58, 100, 101, 198;

arrive Manila, 8; assigned Pursuit Combat Team, 28, 30; assembly of, 37, 41, 43–45; *45,* 66, 73, 74, 339; assigned to 17th Pursuit Squadron (Provisional), 61,63, to 3rd Pursuit Squadron (Provisional), 110, 111, *151,* to 13th Pursuit Squadron (Provisional), *177,* 192, to 33rd Pursuit Squadron (Provisional), 101, 102, *193,* to 20th Pursuit Squadron (Provisional), 86; in attack on Darwin, 226–38; in attack on Java invasion force, 296–97; on Bali attack mission, 247–50; and Burnett request for, 57, 58, 59; compared to CW-21Bs, 383n.79; on *Coolidge,* 101, 103; crashes of at Pasirian, 164; damaged at Daly Waters, 149, at Denpasar, *138;* over Darwin harbor, *233;* for defense of NEI, 16–17, 203; destroyed at Clark and Iba fields, 11; diverted to India/Burma, 198–99; as escort for A-24s, 295; and ferry to Java, 101, 400n.26; as fighter-bombers, 210; "hangar queens" at Darwin repaired, 188, 206; on Kragan strafing mission, 306, 307; and Kruzel decoration, 182, *182;* and *Langley,* 102, 156, 200, 212, 221, 246, 281, 283, 292, 403n.74; at Laverton, 174; lost in Darwin attack, 196, *255;* at Lowood, 81; maintenance of at Ngoro, 112, 166, 181–82, 272; on *Mariposa,* 101, 103, on *Mormacsun,* 80, 403n.72; in MS-5 convoy, 103; at Ngoro, 111, 113, 181, *181,259,* 272; ordered transferred to Dutch, 288–89, 311; and Palembang mission, 209, 210, 212, 213; in *Pensacola* convoy, 12; performance of, 160, 162, 276, 272; and Philippine ferry pilots, 34–35; and Pingree, 238; on *Polk,* 12, 30, 66; as protection for CSF, 294, 295, 297; range of, 164; reinforcements of for van Oyen, 290; remains of Pell's no. 3 at Darwin, *239;*

of *Sea Witch,* 199–200, 286–87, 302, 325, *326;* strafed at Ngoro by Zeros, 311; total number of assigned provisional pursuit squadrons, 338; total number lost of provisional pursuit squadrons, 338; and training of pilots, 38, 73; Vaught's no. 28 at Darwin, 224, 235, *236;* at Waingapoe, *164;* worn out, 302, 306, 307

Philippines: airpower build-up of, 8; air reinforcements to, 11, 12, 13, 340; American air power in, 10; B-17s arrive at, 4; and Australia, 14; defense of, 12, 290; and Japanese aerial attacks on, 11; Japanese invasion of, 10, 12; Japanese operational strategy for capture of, 8; and MacArthur defense plan, 8; and Mahony/Coss experiences, 211–12; as offensive base against Japan, 4; recapture of, 344; and War Department policy towards reinforcements, 3

Phillips, Tom, 9

Piet Hein, 257

Pingree, Dick: body of extricated, 239; engine trouble of at Port Pirie, 192, 221; killed in crash of P-40E, 238; left behind at Port Pirie, 183, 192, 221; selected for Port Pirie-Darwin flight, 175

Plan Dog, 3

Playfair, Ian, 53

PLUM: as apparent destination of USAT *Garfield,* 25; assignment of P-40 pilots to, 19, 339, 340; as destination of 51st Pursuit Group pilots, 26–27; as Philippines, 19; Pursuit Combat Team assigned to, 28

Poel, Max van der, 113, 389n.68

Point Cook, 174

Polk pilots: at Amberley, 65, 111; arrive Amberley, 73; assigned to 24th Pursuit Group, 65; attached to 7th Bomb Group, 65, 376–77n.20; and meetings on *Polk,* 48; and move north from Amberley, 73, 74; and P-40E assembly, 73, 79; ordered to Lowood, 79; picked for 3rd Pursuit Squadron (Provisional), 111; and stopover in New Zealand, 46–47

Poncik, Vic 274, 275

Pono River, 397n.57

Poorten, Hein ter, 202; accuses Eubank of desertion, 287; appointed commander-in-chief, ABDA area, 201; meets Wavell on arrival Batavia, 53; message of complaint to Marshall, 287, 424n.14; rejects van Oyen request for air protection of *Langley,* 423n.2; surrenders to Japanese, 290

Port Hedland, 331

Port Moresby, 58; Stauter killed at, 342; 35th Pursuit Group at, *342;* 20th Pursuit Squadron (Provisional) ordered to, 86–87, 375n.23, 381n.44, 381–82n.47, 382n.54

Port Pirie: crash of Pingree at, 238–39; and flight to Darwin, 174; *Langley* P-40Es at, 403n.74; search for maps at, 175; and 33rd Pursuit Squadron (Provisional), 103, 170, 173, 174, 409n.68

Portuguese Dili, 195, 198

Pownall, Sir Henry, 53

Pressfield, Harry, 30, 409–10n.71

Price, Melvin: and Amberley tent of, *43,* 43; assigned to Base Section 3, 156; Christmas of in Brisbane, 30, and Australian date, 37; at Lennon's Hotel, 32–33, 36; and Pell's will, 156

Prince of Wales, 11

Prioreschi, Angelo, 84, 89, 305

Project X, 13

provisional pursuit squadrons, 338–339

P-38, 344

P-39s, 341, 342

Puerto Princessa, 344

Purnell, William R., 53

Pursuit Combat Team: arrives Brisbane, 63; and armorers and crew chiefs of, 65, 66, 74, 76, 86, 146; assigned to Ascot Race Track, 64–65; attached to 7th Bomb Group, 65, 376–77n.20; boards *Polk*, 29; flying school class composition of, 28; formed, 28; Lane as commander of, 30; lectured on spy situation, 64, 376n.18; and pilots' lack of P-40 flying time, 28–29

Qantas, 330

Ragsdale, Bill, 328, 435n.35

Rainbow 5 War Plan, 5

Rajeg Wesi Bay, 251, 252, 256, 415–16n.36

Rangoon, 268

Reagan, Cornelius "Connie": arrives Ngoro, 144; arrives Soerabaja, 144, 394n.92; in Bali combat with Zeros, 126, 128, 390n.10; on B-17 protection missions, 178, 180; crash-lands at Kragan, 309, 334; and damaged P-40E, 136, 144; at Denpasar, 137; evades capture, 334; on Kragan strafing mission, 308, 309; leaves Bali for Soerabaja, 144; at Ngoro, 278; on *Polk*, 30; as POW, 334; selected for 20th Pursuit Squadron (Provisional), 86; victory claims of 220

Reed, Willard "Jess": burial of, 140; detached to 17th Pursuit Squadron (Provisional), 85, 86; killed in Ngoro accident, 139–40; and Ngoro operations, 132; surveys possible fields for 17th Pursuit Squadron (Provisional), 85; trains Dutch STM pilots, 86, 139; visits Blimbing, 96

Reeves, Charlie, 327, 329, 330–31

Reeves, Robert, 181

Republic pilots: at Amberley Field, 66–67; assemble P-40Es, 43, 44; assigned to 17th Pursuit Squadron (Provisional), 62; and flight training for, 41–42, 45, 67; and 41-G pilots of, 111; ordered to Amberley Field, 39; and P-40 flying qualifications, 62; picked for 3rd Pursuit Squadron (Provisional), 111, for 20th Pursuit Squadron (Provisional), 87

Repulse, 11,

Rex, John, 76, 435n.35

Reyers, A., 223

Reynolds, Andy, 417n.4; arrives Denpasar, 136; at Denpasar, 136, attacks G3M Nell, 135; on B-17 protective missions, 178, 180; in combat with Zero, 273; flies Soerabaja to Ngoro, 138–39; to 49th Pursuit Group, 341; on interception missions from Ngoro, 272; on Koepang-Bali flight, 135, 136; on mission to meet *Langley*, 277; on *Polk*, 30; in 20th Pursuit Squadron (Provisional) at Amberley, 88; visits Jogjakarta, 181, 216

Rice, Burt: in combat with Zeros, 228, 231; evacuated on *Manunda*, 254; found by Australians, 253; in take-off from Darwin, 226; location of downed P-40E, *255;* and return to Darwin field, 225; scheduled for Darwin-Koepang flight, 209; selected for Port Pirie-Darwin flight, 175; shot down in Darwin attack, 228, 253

Richardson, Robert C., 436n.24

Richmond Field: P-40Es out of commission at, 221; P-40Es wrecked at, 221; 13th Pursuit Squadron (Provisional) ordered to, 176, 400n.24; refuels at, *177,* 400n.24

Ridley, H., 235

Roebuck Bay, 287, 330, 331, 332

Rongotai, 47

Rockhampton, 68–69, 70

Roosevelt, Franklin D.: and aid to Britain if Japan attacks, 10; and Australia as a base, 14; declines military pact with Britain and NEI, 2; and defensive stance in Pacific and Far East, 3,8; and Dutch queen, 203; fears Japanese attack, 8–9, 10; freezes Japanese assets in U.S., 3; and Germany as priority, 3; and help for NEI, 203; and message to men on Java, 385n.20; orders scrap iron and steel embargo, 2

Rose, Henry J., 148

Roti Island, 434n.28

Rouse, John, 324, 325

Rowland, James: at Amberley Field, 51, 62; arrives Amberley, 50; arrives Ngoro, 386–87n.32; body of found, 132; on ferry flight north to Darwin, 68; flown to Australia from Philippines, 41, 50; at Lennon's Hotel, 52; with 17th Pursuit Squadron (Provisional) at Amberley, 62; shot down and killed, 115–18, 120, 132, 436n.17

Royal Australian Air Force, 192; and BRITAIR, 285, 290; and Koepang personnel evacuated to Darwin, 406n.13; and prewar cooperation with FEAF, 12; provides DC-2s as transports, 63; squadrons of, 433–34n. 15

Royal Australian Navy, 417n.10

Royal Netherlands Military Academy, 407n.29

Ruegg, Robert, 79

Ruwoldt, Rex, 411n.17

Ryan, Jim: and air evacuation to Australia, 305; on B-17 protective mission, 178; at Denpasar, 136; evacuates Ngoro, 266; flies Soerabaja-Ngoro, 138–39; on Polk, 30

Sakai, Saburo, 420n.8

Samarinda, 378n.73

Sampalan, 256

Sanders, Homer, 419n.35; and Calcutta as destination, 265; departs Fremantle,

260, 265; and destination of 51st Pursuit Group, 265, 417n.12; and orders to Java, 177–78, 260, 417n.12

Sanuki Maru, 57

Sanur, 248

Savu Sea, 84, 135, 164

Schaffer, Charles, 305

Scherger, Frederick, 76

Schmillen, Edward, 400n.23

Schoolwerth, Toni: arrives Bandoeng, 326; and blowing up of Magoewo airfield, 320; flown to Australia, 334; on Jogjakarta-Andir trip, 320–21; as 19th Bomb Group Dutch liaison officer, 320; offer of evacuation to, 326

Schwanbeck, Ray, 324, 327

SCR 270-B, 94

Sea Witch: and ABDAIR/JAC plan for distributing P-40Es of, 433–34n.15; aborting voyage of to Java, 283; and assembly of P-40Es onboard, 200, 286–87, 434n.16; arrives Tjilatjap, 286, 302, 423n.15; assignment of assembled P-40Es to Dutch and RAAF squadrons, 200; in August 1941, 199; and Brett, 283; captured P-40Es of, 326, 425n.23; crated P-40Es on board, 103, 203, 261; departs Fremantle, 199, 261, Melbourne, 103, Tjilatjap, 325; diversion of to India, 203; diverted to Java, 199–200, 404n.15; half assembled P-40Es of destroyed by Dutch, 290; and Langley pilots to fly P-40Es of, 423n.5; and Marshall, 283; and MS-5 convoy, 265–66; ordered to Bombay, 286; P-40 ammunition on board, 200; return trip of to Australia, 325; routing of, 199, 200; and 692nd Ordnance Company, 261; and transportation of crated P-40Es to Bandoeng and Tasikmalaja, 200, 283, 286; and unloading of crated P-40Es, 200, 302

Selman, Larry, 30, 73, 396n.35

17th Pursuit Squadron (Provisional),
93, 94, 96, 101, 133, 141, 180–81, 200,
244, 256, 271, 311; armorers and crew
chiefs assigned to, 63; on Bali attack
mission, 247–51; at Blimbing, 98, 112,
216, 316; on B-17 protection missions,
141, 178, 259–60, 261, 262, 417n.6;
and Brewster Buffalo reinforcements
for, 273; in combat with Zeros, 161–
62, 218–20, 240–41, 242, 243, 259,
260, 269–70, 272–73, 276, 302–03,
413n.48, 413n.54, 417n.6, 419–20n.3,
421n.13; and contact with Javanese,
166; at Darwin, 75, 76–78, 379n.84,
479–80n.88; enlisted men of board
Abbekerk, 422–23n.44; enlisted men
of to Darwin, 63, 379n.18, 379n.80;
enlisted men evacuees killed at
Broome, 328, 333, 435n.35; escort
A-24s in Bali attack, 240, 247; evacuations of, 75, 256, 266–68, 270, 273,
275, 276–77, 285, 286, 288, 303, 305,
306,311–12, 316–21, 328, 333, , 419n.38,
420n.5, 422–23n.44, 428n.57, 429n.19,
432n.51; on ferry flight north, 68, 70–
71, 72; formed, 61; and interception
missions of, 100, 115–19, 120, 132–33,
140, 142, 160–62, 218–20, 254, 258,
272, 302, 392n.41; 409n.64, 419–20n.2,
420n.13, 422n.26; and Java mission
of, 336–37; on Koepang-Soerabaja
flight, 78, 83–84, 85; and Kragan strafing mission, 286, 288, 308–10, 311,
429n.5; and *Langley*, 277, 426n.28; and
Mahony as commanding officer, 262;
at Ngoro, 111, 384n.87; NEI base for,
75, 379n.84; and number of P-40Es
of, 98, 101, 102, 113, 275, 302, 384n.87,
386–87n.32; and official report on
record of, 335; on Palembang mission, 209–15, 217, 407n.36, 408n.45;
and patrol flights, 140, 217; and
P-40E conditions, 270; and protection mission for CSF, 294–97, 425n.13,
426n.20; and P-40 replacements for,
256, 270; pilots of dispirited, 260, 271,
273, 276, 282, 303; and pilots killed
or wounded in Java campaign, 337,
436n.17; at readiness huts, 112, 113,
160; and *Sea Witch* P-40Es for, 200,
433–34n.15; selection of pilots for,
62; at Soerabaja, 89–90, 93, 94; and
Sprague loss, 256; unofficial history
of, 337; victory claims of, 162–63, 220,
243, 250, 337; work of enlisted men
at Ngoro, 66, 112, 181, 247, 262, 270,
272, 302;

7th Bomb Group, 156, 286; and *Abbekerk*,
279, 303; air evacuees of, 320; and
attacks on Balikpapan, 57, on Java
invasion force, 286, on Jolo, 56, on
Manado, 56, on Palembang, 212;
B-17Es of arrive Java, 56; enlisted
men of on *Polk* for Soerabaja voyage, 66, 94, 377n.25; at Jogjakarta,
274; mechanics of assemble P-40Es,
44, 56, 66; *Polk* P-40 pilots attached
to, 65; 17th Pursuit Squadron (Provisional) evacuees attached to, 268

Seven Mile Drome, 342

7th Pursuit Squadron, 221

70th Pursuit Squadron, 21, 24, 25, 28

77th Pursuit Squadron, 28

79th Pursuit Squadron, 28, 30

Sheetz, Dick, 76, 435n.35

Sheppard, William "Red," 41, 50

Shoal Bay Coastal Reserve, 415n.32

Shoal Bay Peninsula, 235

Simons, H.H.J.: arrives Ngoro, 273; flies
CSF protective patrol, 294; on interception mission from Ngoro, 302–03;
on Kragan strafing mission, 310, 428–
29n.2

Simpson, Clarence, 154

Singapore: allied conference at, 11, 12;
Commonwealth troops retreat to,
59, 99; falls to Japanese, 213; Phillips
returns to from Manila, 9; refugees

2-Vl.G.-IV: and Anemaet as commanding officer, 386n.31; arrives Ngoro, 277; in combat with Zeros, 119, 120; CW-21Bs of at Maospati, *97;* and experience with Hawk 75s, 289; on Kragan strafing mission, 307; at Ngoro, 311; personal relations of with 17th Pursuit Squadron (Provisional), 94; problems of with Air Defense Command, 94; provides familiarization aerial tour of East Java, 94; re-equipment of with P-40Es, 325; stages aerial show, 94, 96; at Tandjoeng Perak, 90; and transition to P-40Es, 289

"Unholy Ten," 133
USAAF, 339, 340, 436n.24
USAAF pilot training in Australia, 38, 41–42
USAAF-RAAF conferences, 37, 38
USAFIA, 175, 247; air staff of, 50; and Alice Springs accidents, 185; Brett assumes command of, 13, 201; and defense strategy for Southeast Asia, 13; established, 13; and Japanese carrier warning, 387n.49; Lennon's Hotel headquarters of, 51; mission of, 13; moves to Melbourne, 57, 64, 376n.18; and MS-5 convoy, 417n.10; orders A-24s and P-40s to Java, 145; orders 51st Pursuit Group to NEI, 177; orders formation of 33rd Pursuit Squadron (Provisional), 152; orders 33rd Pursuit Squadron (Provisional) to Darwin, 174; and P-40 pilot training, 109; and pressure on to speed up dispatch of pursuit squadrons to Java, 58; and publicity about Java campaign, 334–35; and supply line to Philippines, 12
U.S. Army Forces in the Far East (USAFFE), 4, 12
USAT *Garfield,* 24, 25, 28
USAT *President Coolidge:* arrives Melbourne, 101, 110, 176, 221; crew chiefs

and armorers on assigned to 3rd Pursuit Squadron (Provisional), 110, 146; and departure for PLUM, 19; and ferrying P-40s to Tjilatjap, 101; and pilots for *Langley,* 221
USAT *President Johnson,* 25, 28
USAT *President Polk,* 63; arrives Brisbane, 56, 63–64; crew chiefs and armorers on assigned 3rd Pursuit Squadron (Provisional), 110; escort for, 31; munitions carried by, 29; New Zealand stopover of, 46–47; and Pursuit Combat Team boards, 29; transports 7th Bomb Group men to Soerabaja, 66, 94, 377n.25; and unloading of P-40Es on, 56; and voyage to Australia, 30–31, 46
USAT *Republic,* 187; arrives Brisbane, 32, 189; departs San Francisco, 22; docks in Honolulu, 24; docks in Suva, 25; joins *Pensacola* convoy, 24; pilots of assemble P-40Es, 43, 44; pilots of ordered to Amberley, 39; and pursuit pilots on board, 22–23, 339; on voyage to Australia, 23–24
USAT *Tasker H. Bliss,* 25
USAT *Willard Holbrook,* 261; arrives Fremantle, 246; delayed departure from Fremantle, 417n.10; departs Fremantle, 260, 265; departs Melbourne, 177; destination of changed, 417n.12; 51st Pursuit Group on board, 103; 41-H pilots on board, 80; in MS-5 convoy, 265, 417n.10; and pilots of at Ascot Race Track, 50; and unassigned pilots on board, 37
U.S. Navy, 13
USS *Edsall:* attacked by dive bombers, 431n.43; attacked by surface vessels, 431n.43; comes to assistance of *Pecos,* 286; as escort for *Langley,* 291; Java return order of rescinded, 285, 312, 431n.43; ordered to Java with *Langley* survivors, 284, 304, 312, 423n.5;

estimate, 104; and Burnett request for P-40Es, 381n.44; and Combined Chiefs of Staff, 14, 59; detaches *Sea Witch* to Java, 200, 404n.15; distressed over withdrawal into Singapore, 99; diverts *Langley* to India/Burma, 198–99; faces deteriorating situation, 16; and failed defense of NEI, 198; fears loss of Koepang, 99, 100; lack of concern for Australia defense, 100, 198; leaves India to take up ABDACOM command, 16; leaves Java for Colombo, 202, 275; limitations on authority of, 14; and lines of Japanese attack, 99; and operations in Burma, 201–02; and orders to Eubank regarding his departure, 288; and P-40 deliveries, 58; regrets failure to hold ABDA area, 202; returned as C-in-C India, 201; and routes of *Langley* and MS-5 convoy, 198, 199; strategy assigned to, 14; transfers Java air forces to van Oyen, 201; and winding up of ABDACOM, 200, 202; and withdrawal of FEAF, 424n.18

Webster, Noel, 74, 76, 89

Weidman, James, 74

Weller, George: in Bandoeng, 202; and recovery of Sprague remains, 416n.42; and reporter at Tjilatjap, 426n.23; and 17th Pursuit Squadron (Provisional) pilots at Batavia, 211–12; at Tjilatjap, 426n.23; with van Oyen, *202;* writings of, 344, 345

Wellington, 46–47

West Java: end of Dutch air and land campaign on, 290; Japanese invasion forces on, 287, 290; lies open to Japanese invasion, 195, 282; P-40Es for defense of, 200, 282

Westcott, Elvin P., 435n.35

West Point, 416n.42

Wheless, Hewitt "Shorty": drives McMahon to Batchelor hospital, 254; orders

Buel on flying boat search, 188, 403n.69; and 33rd Pursuit Squadron (Provisional) flight to Koepang, 209, 225; as USAAF operations officer at Darwin, 188

Wiecks, Max: at Berrimah Hospital, 252, 253; in Darwin attack, 227, 228, 254, 411n.11; and Darwin-Koepang flight, 209; to 8th Pursuit Group, 341; evacuated on *Manunda,* 254; and location of downed P-40E, *255;* picked for Port Pirie-Darwin flight, 175; rescued by Australians, 253; selected for PLUM, 27; shot down into Timor Sea, 252–53, 411n.13, 411n.14

Wilhite, V.H. Bryce: aborts take-off at Laverton, 174, 191; at Amberley Field, 67, 68, 73, 79, 80, 82, 111; on Amberley-Sydney flight, 172; and Amberley tent, *43,* 43; arrives Brisbane, 32; assembles P-40Es, 44–45; assigned 45th Service Group, 342; assigned to 34th Pursuit Squadron, 20; on A-24 flights, 79, 80; berated by Wagner, 155; and Borden, 192, as candidate for PLUM, 20–21; and Christmas in Brisbane, 36; decides to continue to Fremantle, 192; forced landing of, 154–55; ignores Japanese carrier scare, 113–14, 115; joins 13th Pursuit Squadron (Provisional) Squadron flight to Port Pirie, 192; and Kerstetter crash-landing, 172; and *Langley* boarding rumor, 192; at Laverton, 174, 191, 192, 412n.42; at Lennon's Hotel, 32, 33, 36; misses boarding *Langley,* 221; and New Year's Eve party, 38–39; ordered to Amberley Field, 39; and Pell will, 156; P-40Es assigned to, 154, 155; and Pingree, 192; and Pingree accident and death, 238, 239; at Port Pirie, 192, 192–93, 221, 412n.42; practices dogfighting, 154; and RAAF at Laverton, 174; on *Republic,* 23, 24, 25,

ISBN-13: 978-1-60344-176-6
ISBN-10: 1-60344-176-X

54000